Scale 1:250,000
or 3.95 miles to 1 inch
(2.5km to 1cm)

5th edition July 2006

© Automobile Association
Developments Limited 2006

Now fully updated, the 1st edition
of this atlas won the 2003 British
Cartographic Society - Ordnance
Survey Award for innovation in the
design and presentation of spatial
information.

The British Cartographic Society Promoting the Art and Science of Map Making

Ordnance Survey® This product includes mapping
data licensed from Ordnance
Survey® with the permission of the Controller of
Her Majesty's Stationery Office.
© Crown copyright 2006. All rights reserved.
Licence number 399221.

Published by AA Publishing (a trading name of
Automobile Association Developments Limited,
whose registered office is Fanum House, Basing
View, Basingstoke, Hampshire RG21 4EA, UK.
Registered number 1878835).

Mapping produced by the Cartography
Department
of The Automobile Association.
This atlas has been compiled and produced from
the Automaps database utilising electronic and
computer technology (A02873).

ISBN-10: 0 7495 4875 4 (flexibound)
ISBN-13: 978 0 7495 4875 9

A CIP Catalogue record for this book is available
from the British Library.

Printed in Spain by Graficas Estella, Estella.

A&E hospitals derived from data supplied by
Johnsons.

Information on National Parks in England provided
by The Countryside Agency.

Atlas contents

Map pages	II–VII
Mileage chart	VIII
Atlas symbols	1
Road maps 1:250,000 scale	2–237
Western Isles 1:700,000 scale	232–233
Orkney Islands 1:636,000 scale	234
Shetland Islands 1:636,000 scale	235
Channel Islands 1:150,000 scale	236
Isle of Man 1:317,000 scale	237
Index to place names	238–320
County, administrative area map	238–239

Information on National Nature Reserves in
England provided by English Nature.

Information on National Parks, National Scenic
Areas and National Nature Reserves in Scotland
provided by Scottish Natural Heritage.

Information on National Parks and National Nature
Reserves in Wales provided by The Countryside
Council for Wales.

Information on Forest Parks provided by the
Forestry Commission.

The RSPB sites shown are a selection chosen by
the Royal Society for the Protection of Birds.

National Trust properties shown are a selection
of those open to the public as indicated in the
handbooks of the National Trust and the National
Trust for Scotland.

RoadPilot® Information on fixed speed
camera locations provided
by RoadPilot © Copyright RoadPilot® Driving
Technology.

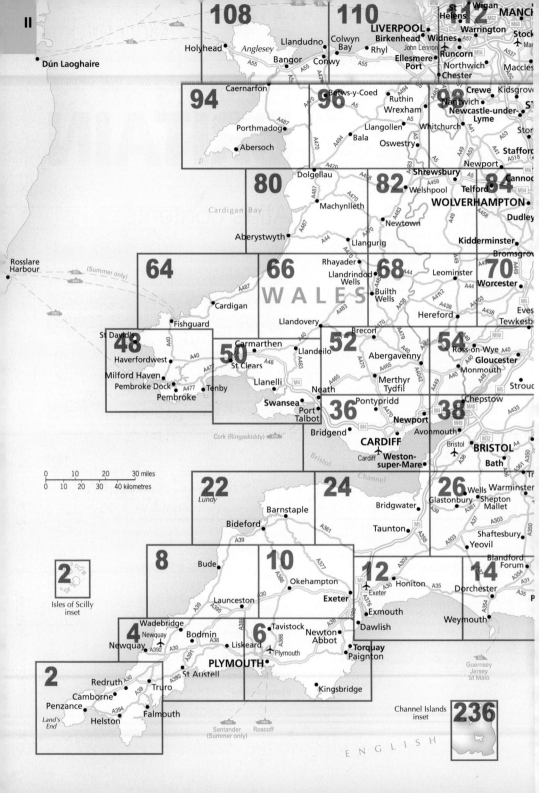

II

108 110 112 MANCH
LIVERPOOL
Holyhead *Anglesey* Llandudno Colwyn Birkenhead Widnes Warrington Stock
Bay Rhyl John Lennon Runcorn Maccles
Dún Laoghaire Bangor Conwy Ellesmere Northwich
Port Chester

94 Caernarfon 96 Betws-y-Coed Crewe Kidsgrove
Ruthin Nantwich 98 Newcastle-under- St
Wrexham Lyme
Porthmadog Llangollen Whitchurch Stor
Abersoch Bala Stafford
Oswestry Newport

80 Dolgellau 82 Shrewsbury 84 Cannon
Welshpool Telford
Cardigan Bay Machynlleth WOLVERHAMPTON
Newtown Dudley
Aberystwyth Llangurig Kidderminster
Llandovery Bromsgrov

Rosslare 64 66 Rhayader 68 Leominster 70
Harbour Llandrindod Worcester
(Summer only) Wells
Builth Hereford Eve
W A L E S Wells Tewkesbu
Cardigan
Fishguard Llandovery Brecon 52 54 Ross-on-Wye
St David's 48 Carmarthen Llandeilo Abergavenny Gloucester
Haverfordwest St Clears Monmouth
Milford Haven 50 Llanelli Merthyr Stroud
Pembroke Dock Tenby Neath Tydfil Chepstow
Pembroke Swansea 36 Pontypridd 38
Cork (Ringaskiddy) Port Newport Avonmouth Bristol BRISTOL
Talbot CARDIFF Bath
Bridgend Cardiff Weston-
Bristol super-Mare

22 24 Wells Warminster
Lundy Glastonbury Shepton
Barnstaple Bridgwater Mallet
Bideford *Channel* Taunton Shaftesbury
Yeovil
Blandford
8 Bude 10 Okehampton 12 Honiton 14 Forum
Launceston Exeter Dorchester
Exeter Exmouth Weymouth
4 Wadebridge 6 Tavistock Dawlish
Newquay Bodmin Newton Torquay Guernsey
Liskeard Abbot Paignton Jersey
PLYMOUTH Plymouth St Malo
2 Redruth St Austell Kingsbridge
Camborne Truro
Penzance Falmouth Channel Islands
Land's Helston inset 236
End Santander Roscoff
(Summer only) E N G L I S H

0 10 20 30 miles
0 10 20 30 40 kilometres

2 Isles of Scilly inset

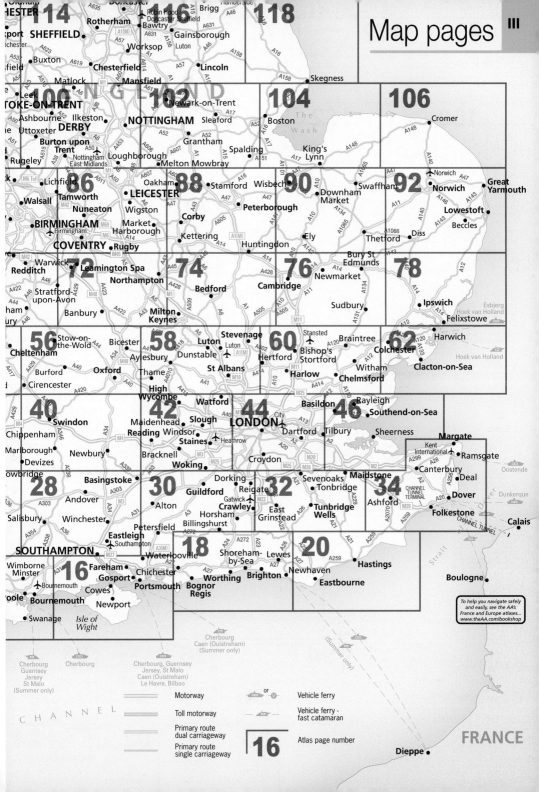

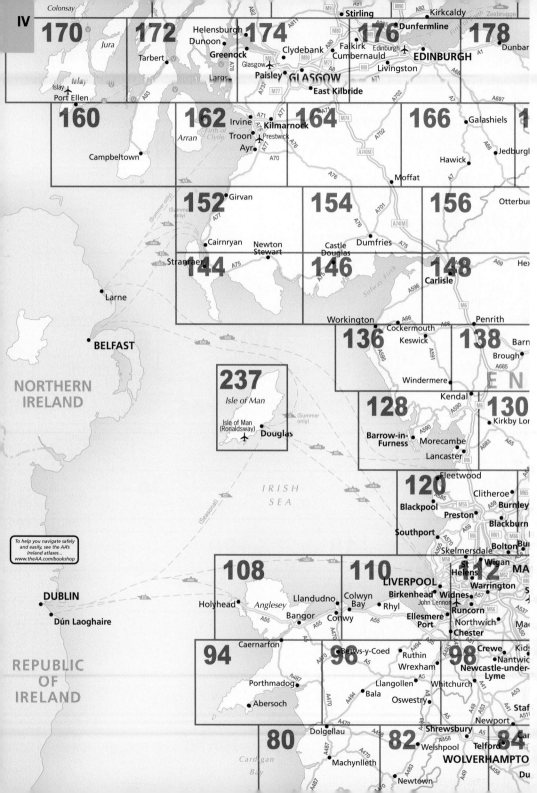

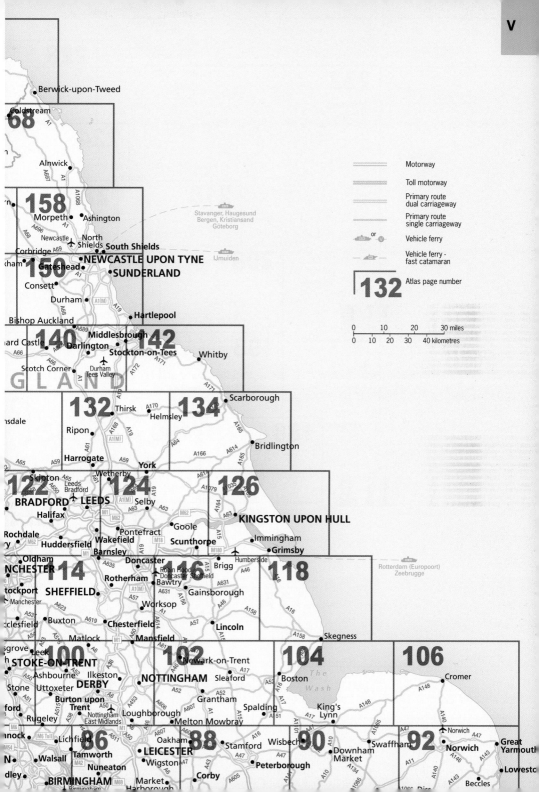

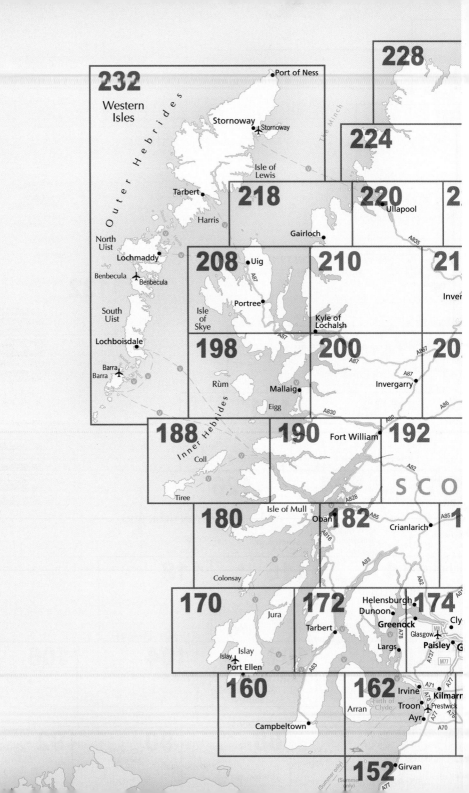

232 Western Isles

Port of Ness

Stornoway
Stornoway

Isle of Lewis

228

224

The Minch

Outer Hebrides

Tarbert

Harris

218

Gairloch

220 Ullapool

A835

North Uist

Lochmaddy

Benbecula
Benbecula

208 Uig

A87

Portree

210

Kyle of Lochalsh

21

Inver

South Uist

Lochboisdale

Isle of Skye

198

200

A87

20

A87

Invergarry

Barra
Barra

Rùm

Mallaig

Eigg

Inner Hebrides

A830

A82

A86

188

Coll

190 Fort William

192

A82

S C O

Tiree

Isle of Mull

Oban

180

182 A85

A85

Crianlarich

1

A816

A83

A82

Colonsay

170

Jura

172 Tarbert

Helensburgh
Dunoon

Greenock

Largs

174

Cly

Glasgow

Paisley G

M8

M77

Islay
Islay
Port Ellen

A83

160

162

Irvine

Kilmarr

Arran

Troon

Prestwick

Ayr

A71

A77

A77

A70

Firth of Clyde

Campbeltown

152 Girvan

A77

(Summer only)

(Summer only)

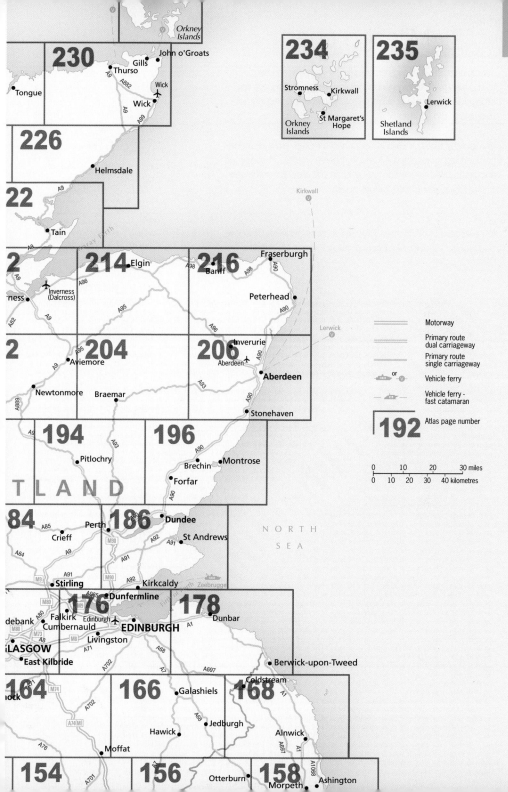

230

Tongue

Orkney Islands

John o'Groats

Gills
Thurso

A9

A882

Wick ✈

Wick

A9

A99

226

Helmsdale

22

A9

Murray Firth

Tain

2

Inverness (Dalcross) ✈

A96

A92

A9

ness

A95

214 Elgin

A96

A95

A98

216

Fraserburgh

Banff ✈

A98

A90

Peterhead

A90

Lerwick Ⓥ

2

A95

204

Aviemore

A9

Newtonmore

A889

Braemar

Inverurie

206

Aberdeen ✈

A93

A90

Aberdeen

A90

Stonehaven

A9

194

A93

Pitlochry

196

Brechin

Forfar

Montrose

A90

S T L A N D

A90

84 A85

Crieff

A84

A9

A91

186

Perth

A90

A92

A91

Dundee

St Andrews

N O R T H

S E A

M9

M90

Stirling

M80

A91

A985

M90

A92

Kirkcaldy

Firth of Forth

Zeebrugge

176

Dunfermline

debank

Falkirk

A80

Edinburgh ✈

Cumbernauld

M73

M8

EDINBURGH

Livingston

A8

178

A1

Dunbar

iLASGOW

A71

A68

East Kilbride

A702

A1

A697

Berwick-upon-Tweed

164

M74

A702

Coldstream

166

Galashiels

168

A74(M)

A68

Jedburgh

Hawick

Alnwick

A697

A1

Moffat

154

A701

A7

156

Otterburn

158

A1068

Morpeth

Ashington

234

Stromness

Kirkwall

St Margaret's Hope

Orkney Islands

235

Lerwick

Shetland Islands

Kirkwall Ⓥ

	Motorway
	Primary route dual carriageway
	Primary route single carriageway
or Ⓥ	Vehicle ferry
	Vehicle ferry - fast catamaran
192	Atlas page number

0   10   20   30 miles
0 10 20 30 40 kilometres

Mileage chart

The mileage chart shows distances in miles between two towns along AA-recommended routes. Using motorways and other main roads this is normally the fastest route, though not necessarily the shortest.

The journey times, shown in hours and minutes, are average off-peak driving times along AA-recommended routes. These times should be used as a guide only and do not allow for unforeseen traffic delays, rest breaks or fuel stops.

For example, the 378 miles (608 km) journey between Glasgow and Norwich should take approximately 7 hours 28 minutes.

journey times

distances in miles (one mile equals 1.6093 km)

Atlas symbols

Motorway with number	B road single/dual carriageway	Speed camera site (fixed location)
Toll motorway with toll station	Minor road, more than 4 metres wide, less than 4 metres wide	Section of road with two or more fixed speed cameras
Motorway junction with and without number	Roundabout	Vehicle ferry
Restricted motorway junctions	Interchange/junction	Vehicle ferry - fast catamaran
Motorway service area	Narrow primary/other A/B road with passing places (Scotland)	Airport, heliport, international freight terminal
Motorway and junction under construction	Road under construction	24-hour Accident & Emergency hospital
Primary route single/dual carriageway	Road tunnel	Park and Ride (at least 6 days per week)
Primary route junction with and without number	Steep gradient (arrows point downhill)	City, town, village or other built-up area
Restricted primary route junctions	Road toll	Spot height in metres
Primary route service area	Distance in miles between symbols	National boundary
Primary route destination	Railway station and level crossing	County, administrative boundary
Other A road single/dual carriageway	Tourist railway	Page continuation number

Tourist Information Centre (all year/seasonal)	Country park	Viewpoint	Rugby Union national stadium
Visitor or heritage centre	Agricultural showground	Picnic site	International athletics stadium
Abbey, cathedral or priory	Theme park	Hill-fort	Horse racing/Show jumping
Ruined abbey, cathedral or priory	Farm or animal centre	Roman antiquity	Motor-racing circuit
Castle	Zoological or wildlife collection	Prehistoric monument	Air show venue
Historic house or building	Bird collection	Battle site with year	Ski slope (natural/artificial)
Museum or art gallery	Aquarium	Steam centre (railway)	National Trust property (England & Wales/ Scotland)
Industrial interest	RSPB site	Cave	Other place of interest
Aqueduct or viaduct	National Nature Reserve (England, Scotland, Wales)	Windmill	Attraction within urban area
Garden	Local nature reserve	Monument	Forest Park
Arboretum	Forest drive	Golf course	National Park and National Scenic Areas
Vineyard	National trail	County cricket ground	Heritage coast

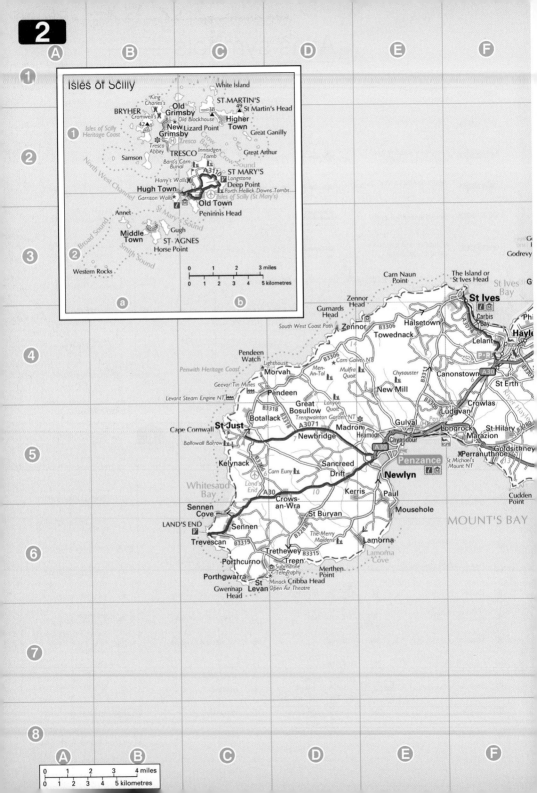

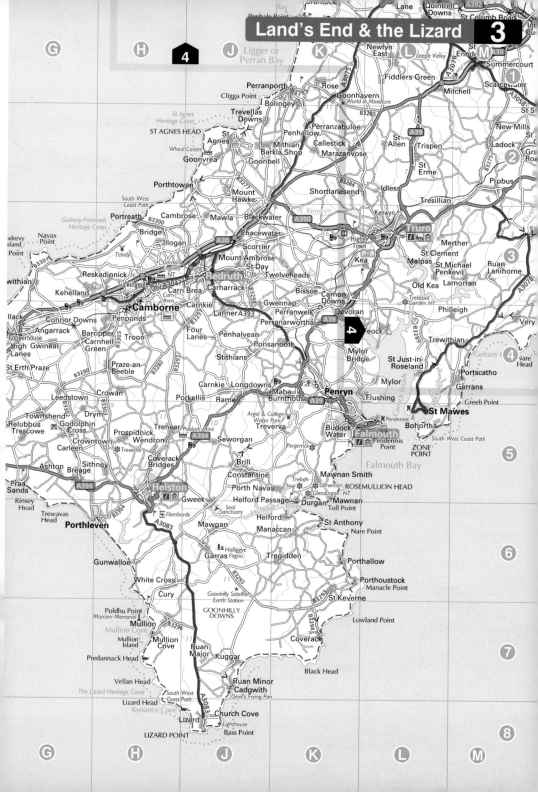

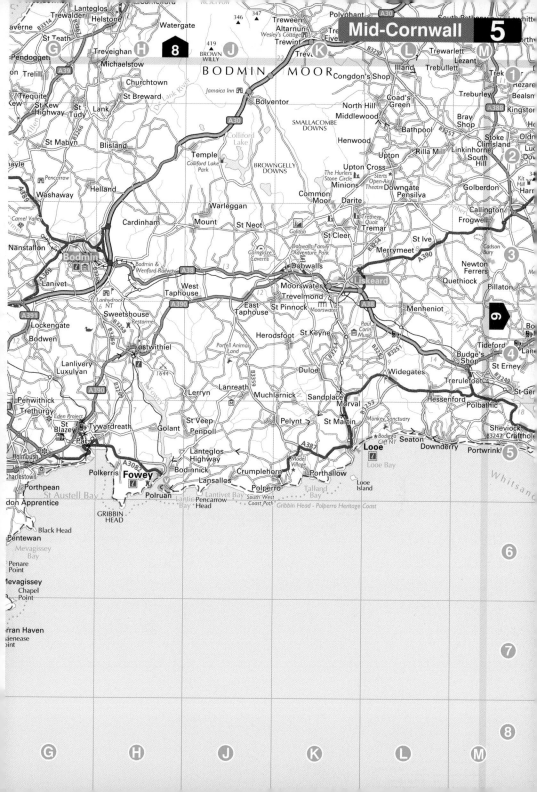

A   B   C   D   E   F

1

2

M

Higher Sharpno

Lower Sharpno

Ste

3

4

Bude
Bay

Wic

Dizzard Point   P
St   T
Gennys   Coxford
Crackington Haven   T
Cambeak   T
Sweets   Wainho
Corne

I 5   B3263
A39

Witchcroft   Marshgate

5

Pentire Point Widemouth   Tresparrett   Otte
Heritage Coast   Boscastle
Trevalga   Lesnewth

6

TINTAGEL HEAD   Tintagel   Trethevey   B3266
Tintagel   Bossiney   Davidstow
Old Post Office NT   Penhallic Point   Trewarmett   Tremail
British Cycling
Treknow   Gaia   B3314   Trefrew
Trebarwith   Energy   B3266   Crowdy
Centre   Reservoir
Delabole   Pengelly   Camelford

7

South West Coast Path   Westdowns
Port Isaac   Lanteglos   Watergate
Rumps   Bay   Trewalder
Point   Kelland   Varley   Helstone
Pentire Point   Port Quin   Head   Head   Port Gaverne   B3314   419
Padstow Bay   Bay   Port   Port   St Teath   BROWN
Quin   Isaac   Long   Treveighan   WILLY
Hayle Bay   Bee Centre   Cross   Michaelstow   BOD

8

Trevose   Stepper Point   Polzeath   Trelights   Pendoggett   Churchtown   Jamaica Inn
Head   4   St Endelli   relill   A39   St Breward
TREVO   St Minver   St Kew   St   Lank
Rock   Trequite   St Kew
St

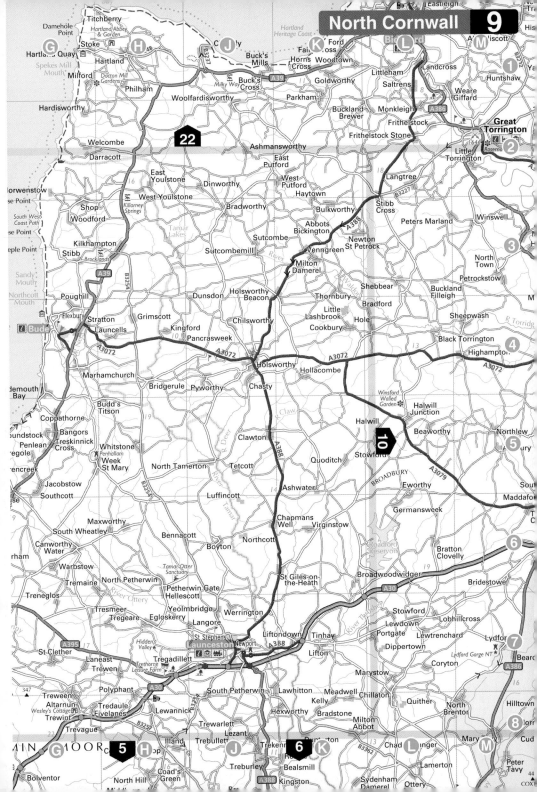

Titchberry
Damehole
Point
Hartland Abbey
& Garden
G Stoke **H** Clovelly **C** **J** **K** Ford
Hartland Quay
Stoke **H** Buck's Mills Fairy **K** Ford Cross Woodtown **L** Landcross
Milford Hartland Buck's Cross Horns Cross Woodtown Littleham Saltrens **M**
G Hartland Quay Philham Woolfardisworthy Parkham Goldworthy Littleham Saltrens Huntshaw **1**
Spekes Mill Docton Mill
Mouth Gardens Goldworthy Monkleigh Weare Giffard
Hardisworthy Woolfardisworthy Parkham Buckland Monkleigh Frithelstock **Great Torrington** **2**
Brewer Frithelstock
22 Ashmansworthy Frithelstock Stone Little Rosemoor
Welcombe East West Torrington
Darracott Youlstone Putford Langtree
orwenstow East West B3227 Winswell
se Point Shop Youlstone Dinworthy Putford Haytown Langtree Peters Marland **3**
Woodford Bradworthy Bulkworthy Stibb North
se Point Killarney Abbots Cross Town
teple Point Kilkhampton Springs Sutcombe Bickington Newton Petrockstow
Stibb Brocklands Sutcombemill Venngreen St Petrock Buckland
Poughill Milton Filleigh
Northcott B3254 Dunsdon Holsworthy Damerel Sheepwash R Torridge
Mouth Flexbury Grimscott Beacon Thornbury Shebbear
i **Bude** Stratton Kingford Chilsworthy Little Bradford Black Torrington
Launcells Pancrasweek Lashbrook Hole Highampton **4**
A3072 A3072 Holsworthy Cookbury A3072 A3072
demouth Marhamchurch Holsworthy Hollacombe
Bay Bridgerule Pyworthy Chasty Winsford Halwill
Coppathorne Budd's Walled Junction Northlew
Titson Garden Halwill Beaworthy **5**
undstock Bangors Whitstone Clawton Quoditch Stowford **10** BROADBURY A3079 bury
Penlean Treskinnick Penhallam Week Stowford Maddafo
regole Cross St Mary North Tamerton Tetcott Ashwater Eworthy
ncreek Jacobstow Luffincott Germansweek **6**
se Southcott Bratton
Maxworthy Chapmans Clovelly
South Wheatley Bennacott Well Virginstow Broadwoodwidger Bridestowe
ham Canworthy Boyton Northcott A30
Water Tamar Otter St Giles-on- Stowford
Warbstow Sanctuary the-Heath Lewdown Lobhillcross
Tremaine North Petherwin Liftondown Portgate Lewtrenchard
Treneglos River Ottery Petherwin Gate Tinhay Dipperton Lydford **7**
Tresmeer Hellescott Werrington Lifton Lydford Gorge NT Beard
Tregeare Egloskerry Yeolmbridge Langore Coryton
St Clether Tregadillett Langore **Launceston** Newport A388 Marystow
A395 Laneast Trewen St Stephens Lifton Coryton
Polyphant Trethorne Newport Meadwell Quither Hilltown
Treween Leisure Farm South Petherwin Lawhitton Kelly North
Altarnun Tredaule Lewannick Chillaton Brentor **8**
Wesley's Cottage Fivelanes A30 Hexworthy Bradstone Milton
Trewint Trewarlett Lezant Abbot Chad Mary
G **MOOR** **G** **5** **H** Illand Trebullett **J** **6** **K** **L** **M** Cud
Trevague North Hill Coad's Treburley Bealsmill Lamerton Peter
Bolventor Green Kingston Sydenham Tavy
Damerel

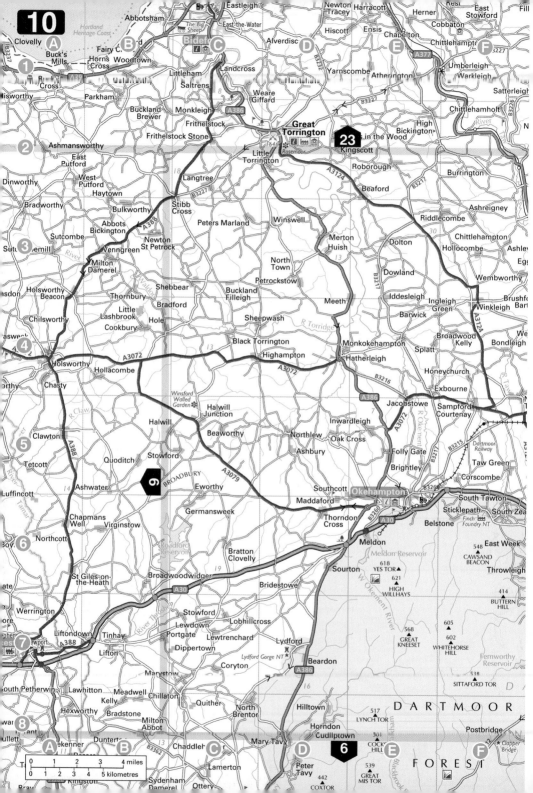

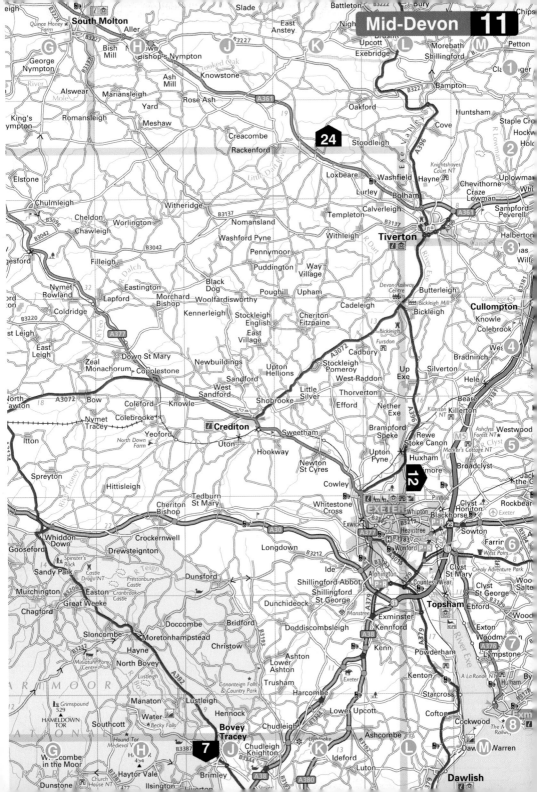

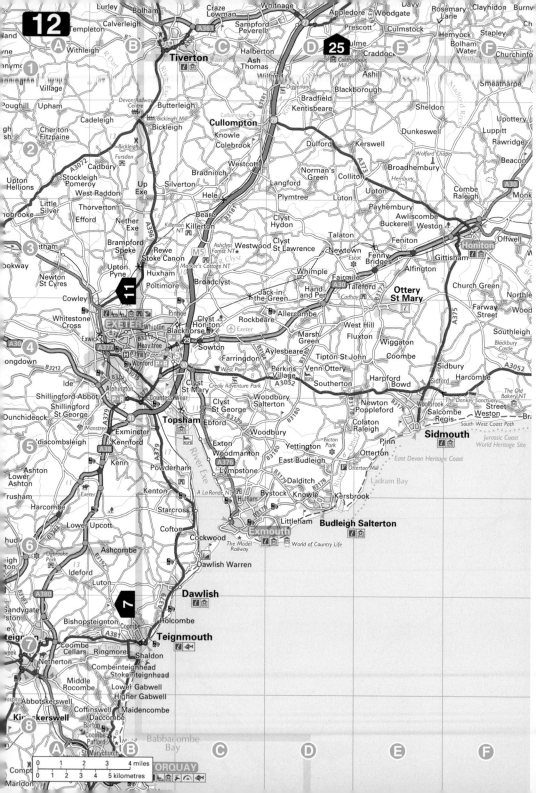

LYME BAY

Jurassic Coast
World Heritage Site

Jurassic Coast
World Heritage Site

Waldron
Iwerne
Minster
Farnham
New Town
Gussage
St Andrew
Chettle
Boveridge
Bellow
Cross
Cranborne
Alderholt
Stuckton

G
27
H
Pentridge
Gussage
St Michael
J
Wimbo
St Giles
28
K
Edmondsham
L
Dorset Heavy
Horse Centre
North Gorley
M
1
Iwerne
or S
Tarrant Hinton
Long
Crichel
Gussage
All Saints
Moor
Crichel
Romford
Verwood
Ibsley
South Gorley
Ibsley Common NT
Rockford Common N
2

Stourpaine
Pimperne
Tarrant
Launceston
Tarrant
Monkton
Manswood
Woodlands
Horton
Mannington
Three
Legged
Cross
Moors
Valley
Ringwood
Poulner
Burley
Street
Liberty Raptor
& Reptile Centre
Kingston
Great
Common
A31
Bu

d Forum
Tarrant
Rawston
Witchampton
Hinton
Martell
St
Leonards
Avon Heath
Sandford
Bisterne
ford St Mary
Charlton
Marshall
Tarrant
Rushton
Holt
West Moors
Foxbury
Hill
A338
Ripley
Thor
Hill
3
ombe
Charlton
on the Hill
Tarrant
Keyneston
Badbury Rings
Honeybrook
Colehill
Ferndown
Bournemouth
Avon
Hurn
Branksore
Spetisbury
Tarrant
Crawford
Shapwick
Abbott
Street
Hillbutts
Leigh
Park
Hampreston
Longham
Dudsbury
West
Parley
Alice in
Wonderland
Red Hill
Sopley
Burton
Walk
borne Whitechurch
Sturminster
Marshall
Pamphill
Wimborne Minster
Canford
Magna
Bearwood
Cudnell
Ensbury
Throop
Somerford
Christchu
4
Winterborne
Zelston
Corfe
Mullen
West Howe
East Howe
Moordown
A3060
Iford
Tuckton
Wick
Christchu
Bay
West
Morden
Morden
Broadstone
A3049
Wallisdown
Winton
Pokesdown
Southbourne
HENGISTBURY
Bloxworth
East
Morden
Lytchett
Matravers
Canford
Heath
Newtown
Branksome
A3049
Boscombe
uddle
Organford
Upton
Parkstone
Branksome
Park
BOURNEMOUTH
Lytchett
Minster
Hamworthy
Lake
Lower Hamworthy
Lilliput
Westbourne
POOLE
Canford
Cliffs
POOLE BAY
5
Sandford
Arne
Poole
Harbour
Brownsea
Island
Sandbanks
Toll
Purbeck Heritage Coast
Northport
Binnegar
East
Stoke
West
Holme
Stoborough
Ridge
East
Holme
Stoborough
Heath
Hartland
Moor
Studland
Bay
THE
FORELAND
Cherbourg
6
Wareham
Blue Pool
ISLE
Studland
Ballard Point
Swanage
Bay
Cherbourg
Guernsey
Jersey
St-Malo
East
Lulworth
East
Creech
Corfe
Castle NT
OF PURBECK
Ulwell
Purbeck Hills
Church
Knowle
Corfe
Castle
Swanage Railway
Harman's
Cross
Swanage
Tyneham Village
Kingston
B3069
Langton
Matravers
Durlston
DURLSTON
HEAD
Kimmeridge
Bay
Kimmeridge
South West
Coast Path
Worth
Matravers
Anvil
Point
7
Jurassic Coast
World Heritage Site
Chapman's
Pool
ST ALDHELM'S OR
ST ALBAN'S HEAD
8

G
H
J
K
L
M

22

A B C D E F

1

2

North West
Point

*Lundy
Heritage Coast* LUNDY

▲142
Marisco
Shutter Point Surf Point

3

Baggy
Point

Croyde Bay

4

*North
Heritage*

BARNSTAPLE

OR

BIDEFORD BAY **Westward Ho**

5

HARTLAND POINT Shipload
Bay

Titchberry Abbotsham

Damehole
Point Hartland Abbey
& Garden Clovelly Ford
Stoke Buck's Fairy Cross
Hartland Quay B3248 Mills Horns Woodtown
Hartland Cross
Speke's Mill Buck's A39 Goldworthy
Mouth Milford Docton Mill Milky Way Cross
Gardens Philham Woolfardisworthy Parkham

6

Buckland
Brewer

Hardisworthy

Frithel

Welcombe Ashmansworthy

7 Darracott East East
9 Putford
East West
Youlstone Dinworthy Putford
Morwenstow Haytown
Higher Sharpnose Point 16 West Youlstone
Killarney Bradworthy Bulkworthy
*South West
Coast Path* Shop Springs
Woodford Abbots Newton
Lower Sharpnose Point Kilkhampton Tamar Sutcombe Bickington St Petro
Lakes A388
Steeple Point bb Sutcom' 'ill 'Ven'
8 Brocklands Milton
Damerel
Sandy A39 B3254 River
Mouth
Poughill Dunsdon Holsworthy Thornbury
Northcott Beacon

A B C D E F

0 1 2 3 4 miles

0 1 2 3 4 5 kilometres

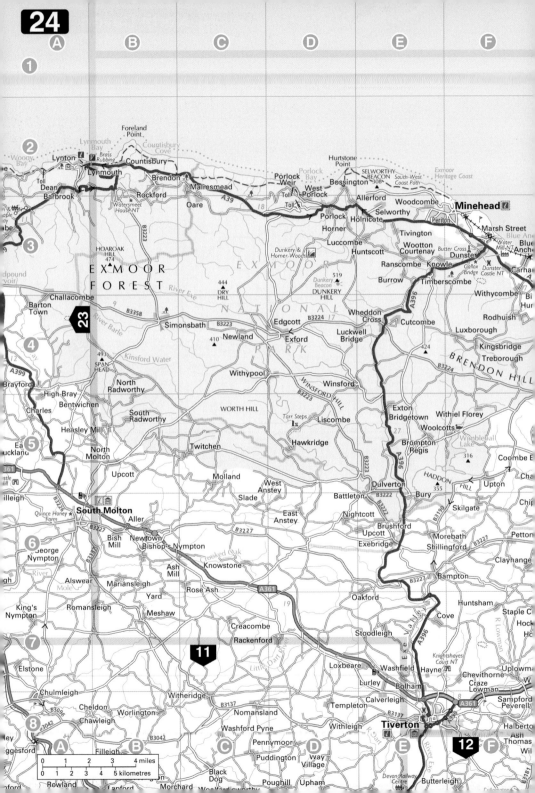

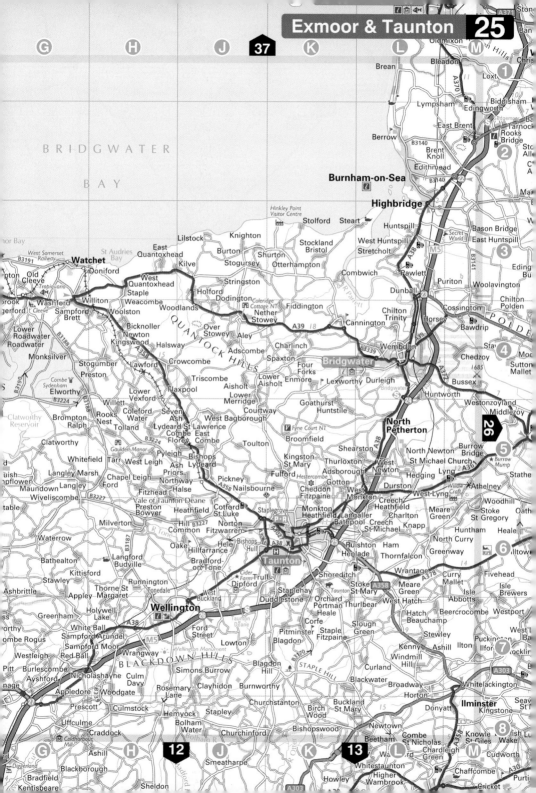

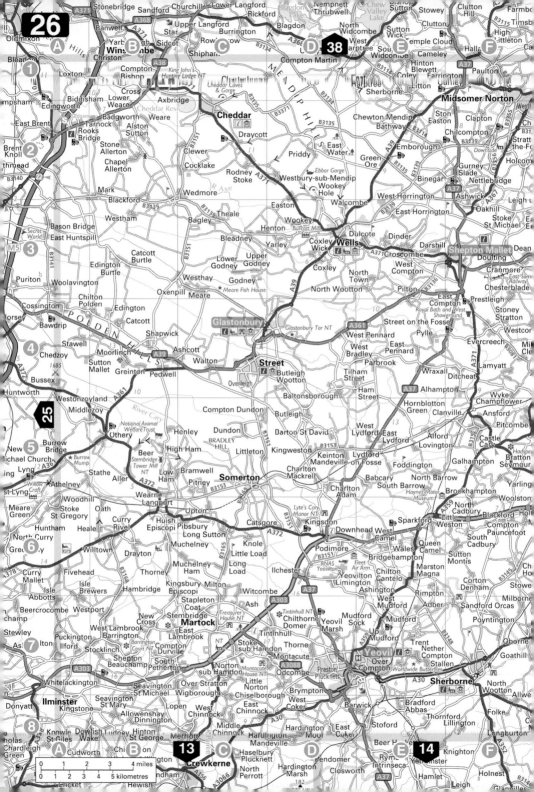

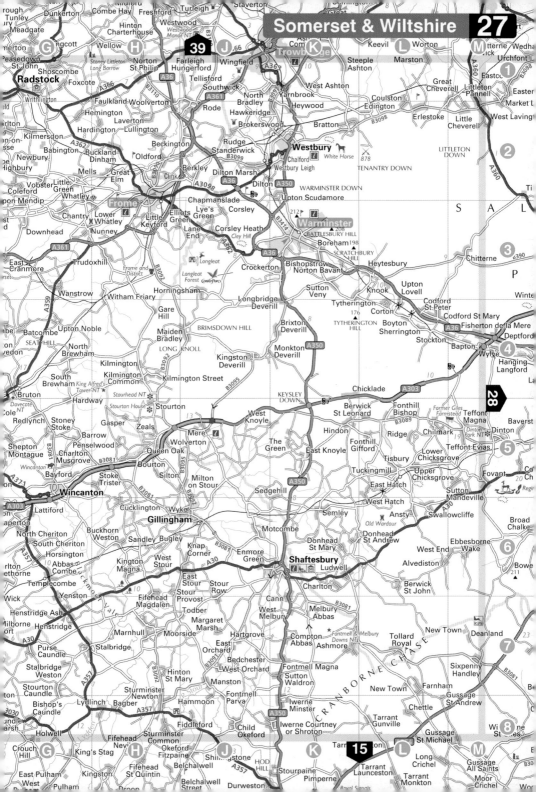

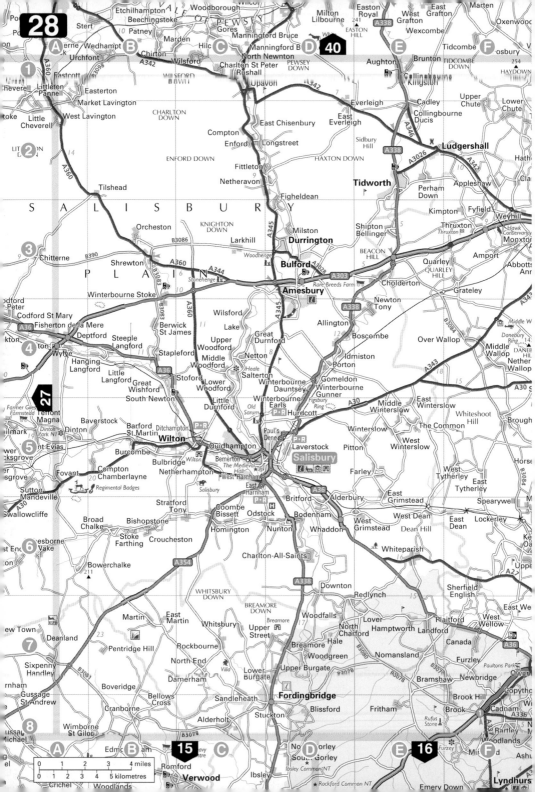

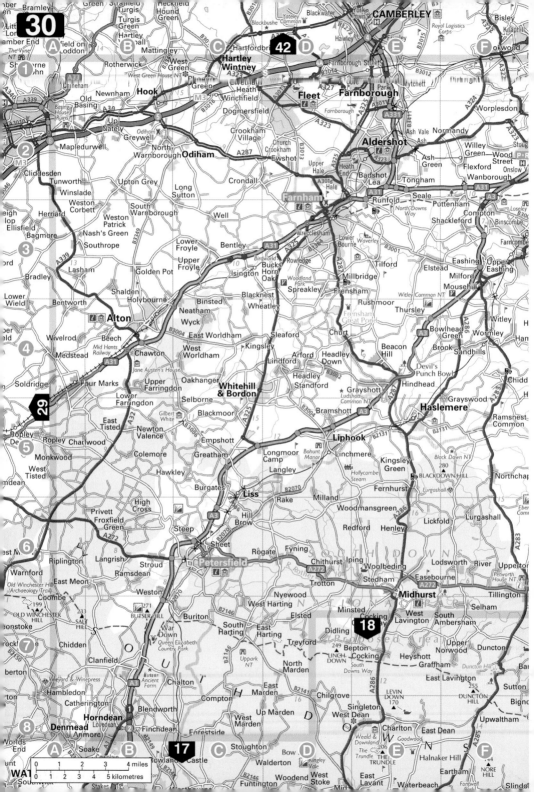

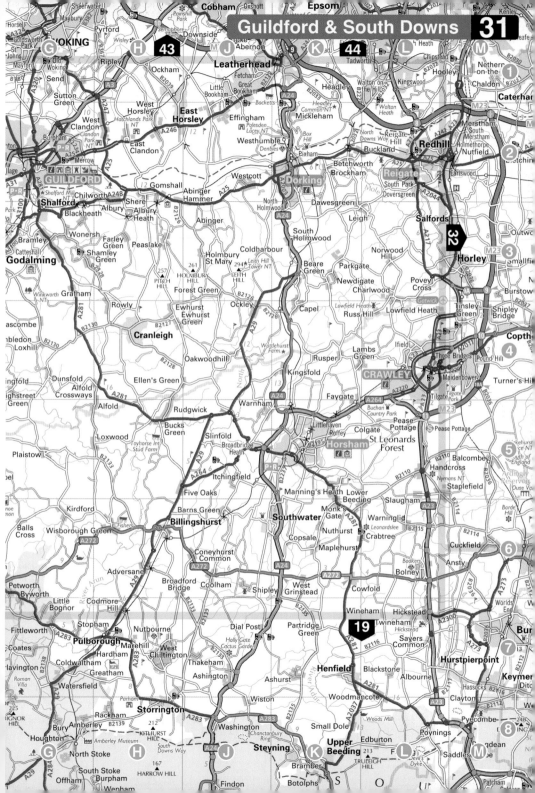

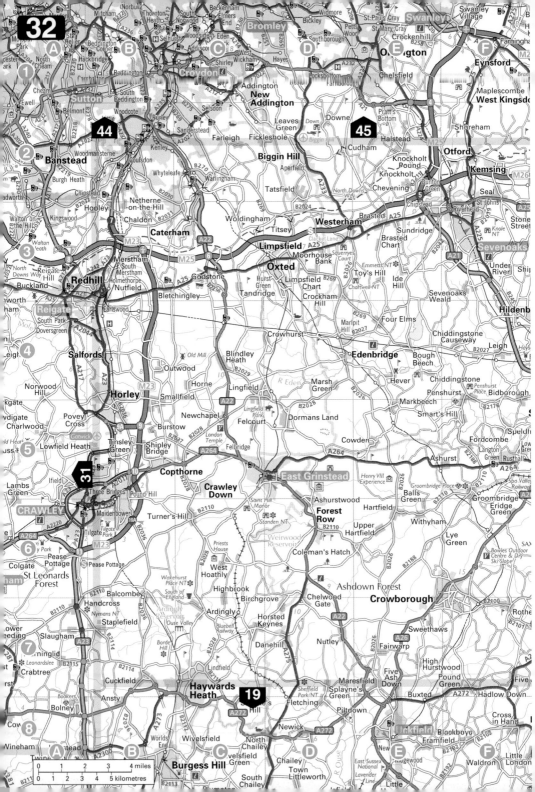

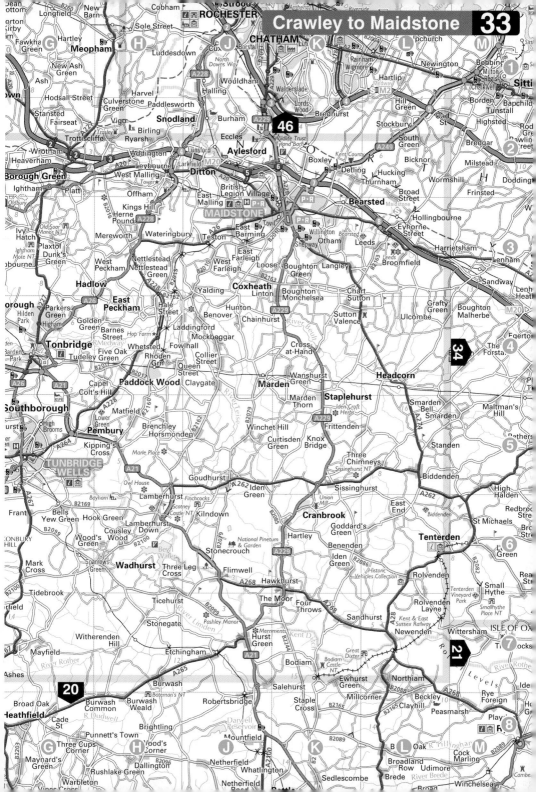

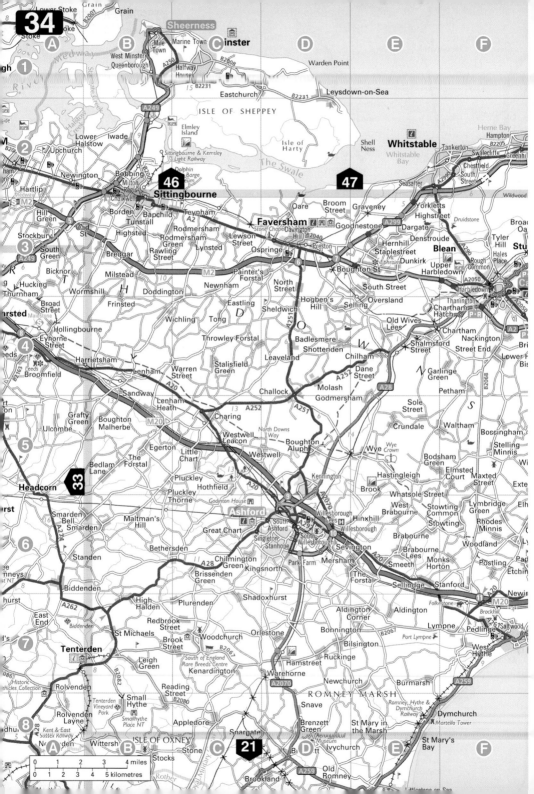

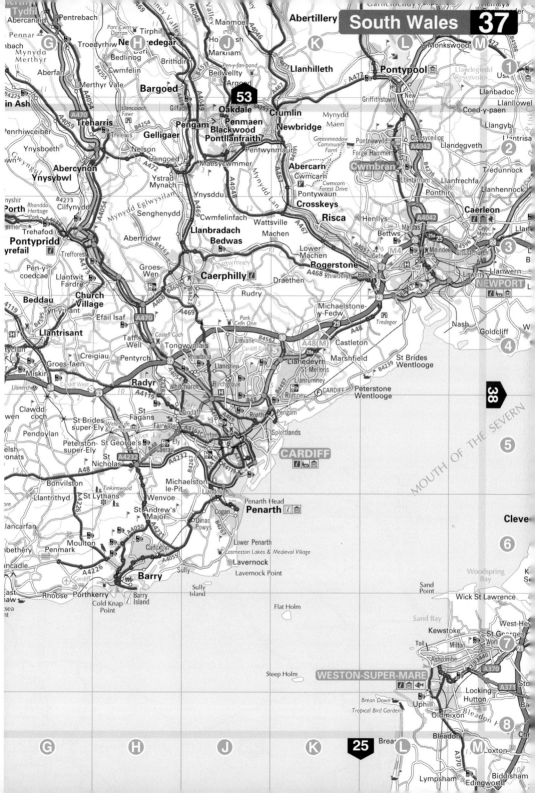

Abercanaid · Pentrebach · Pennar · Mynydd Merthyr · Aberfan · Merthyr Vale · Troedyrhiw · Nebo · Bedlinog · Cwmfelin · Parc Cwm Darran · Tirphil · Deri · Brithdir · Pen-y-fan-pond · Manmoel · Hollybush · Markham · Bedwellty · Argoed · Pentwynmawr · Abertillery · Llanhilleth · Griffithstown · New Inn · Monkswood · Usk · Llandegfedd Reservoir · Llanbadoc · Coed-y-paen · Llanllowel · Llangybi · Llantrisant

53 · Oakdale · Penmaen · Blackwood · Pontllanfraith · Crumlin · Newbridge · Mynydd Maen · Greenmeadow Community Farm · Pontnewydd · Forge Hammer · Croesyceiliog · Llandegveth

Treharris · Pengam · Gelligaer · Hengoed · Maesycwmmer · Llancaiach Fawr · Gilfach · Ystrad Mynach · Ynysddu · Abercarn · Cwmcarn · Cwmcarn Forest Drive · Pontywaun · Crosskeys · Cwmbran · Llantarnam · Llanfrechfa · Ponthir · Llanhennock · Tredunnock

Penrhiwceiber · Abercynon · Ynysybwl · Nelson · Senghenydd · Cwmfelinfach · Wattsville · Machen · Risca · Henllys · Bettws · Malpas · Caerleon · Celtic Manor · Christchurch · Llanwern

Porth · Rhondda Heritage Park · Cilfynydd · Abertridwr · Llanbradach · Bedwas · Lower Machen · Rogerstone · Mandeville · NEWPORT · Lliswerry · Llanwern

Pontypridd · Glyntaff · Trehafod · Treforest · Groes-Wen · Caerphilly · Draethen · Rudry · Michaelstone-y-Fedw · A468 Rhiwderyn · Bassaleg · Tredegar · Nash · Goldcliff

Beddau · Tyn-y-nant · Church Village · Efail Isaf · Taff's Well · Tongwynlais · Rhiwbina · Park Cefn Onn · Lisvane · Castleton · Michaelstone-y-Fedw · A48 · A48(M) · Cardiff Gate · Castleton · St Brides Wentlooge

Pen-y-coedcae · Llantwit Fardre · Creigiau · Pentyrch · Llanishen · Llanedeyrn · St Mellols · Marshfield · Peterstone Wentlooge · MOUTH OF THE SEVERN · **38**

Miskin · Groes-faen · Radyr · Whitchurch · Birchgrove · Llanrumney · Cardiff West · CARDIFF · Roath · Rumney · Pengam

Clawdd-coch · Fairwater · Canton · Splottlands · **CARDIFF** · Cleve

St Brides super-Ely · St Lythans · St George's · St Nicholas · Caerau · Llandaff · Ely · Llandough · Cosmeston Lakes & Medieval Village

Pendoylan · Bonvilston · Tinkinswood · Wenvoe · Michaelston-le-Pit · Penarth Head · **Penarth** · Woodspring Bay

Llantrithyd · St Andrew's Major · Dinas Powys · Cogan · Lower Penarth · Lavernock · Wick St Lawrence

Moulton · Penmark · Cadoxton · Sully · Lavernock Point · Sand Point · Kewstoke · West He... · St Georges

Barry · Sully Island · Flat Holm · Sand Bay · Milton · Worle · Toll · Ashcombe

Rhoose · Porthkerry · Barry Island · Cold Knap Point · Ashcombe · **7** · B3440

Steep Holm · **WESTON-SUPER-MARE** · Locking · Hutton

Brean Down · Tropical Bird Gardens · Uphill · Oldmixon · Bleadon

25 · Brean · Bleadon · Loxton · Lympsham · Biddisham · Edingworth

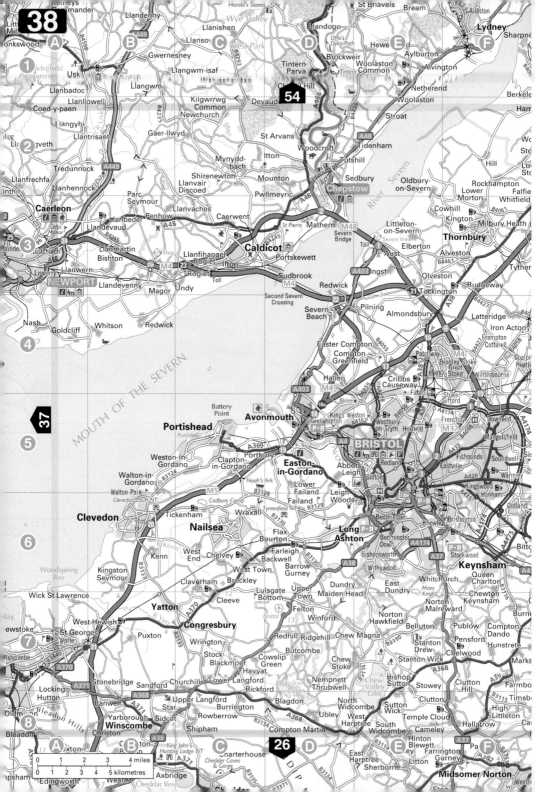

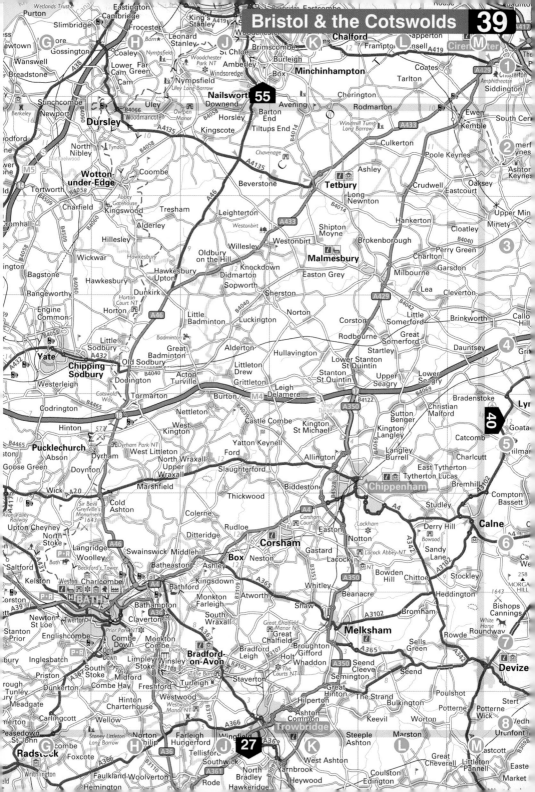

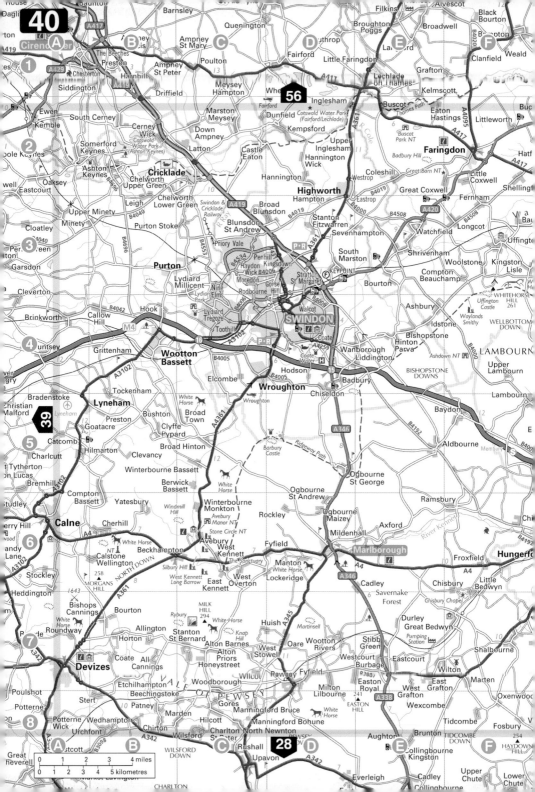

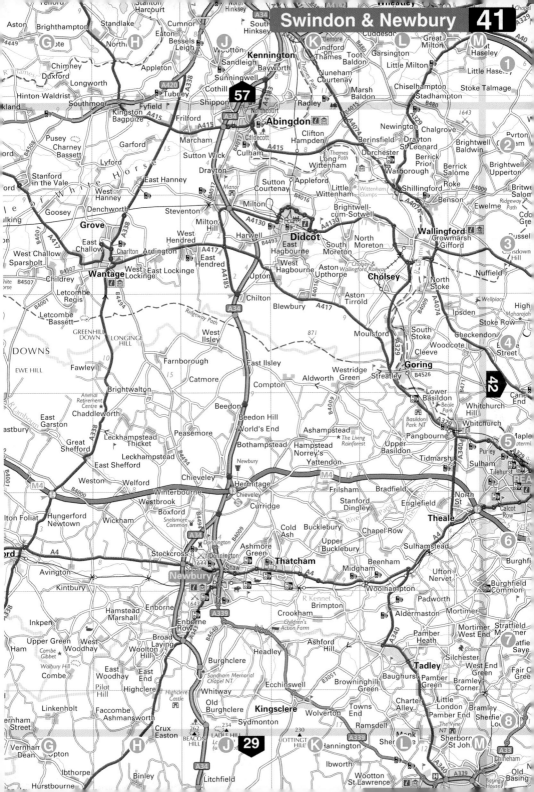

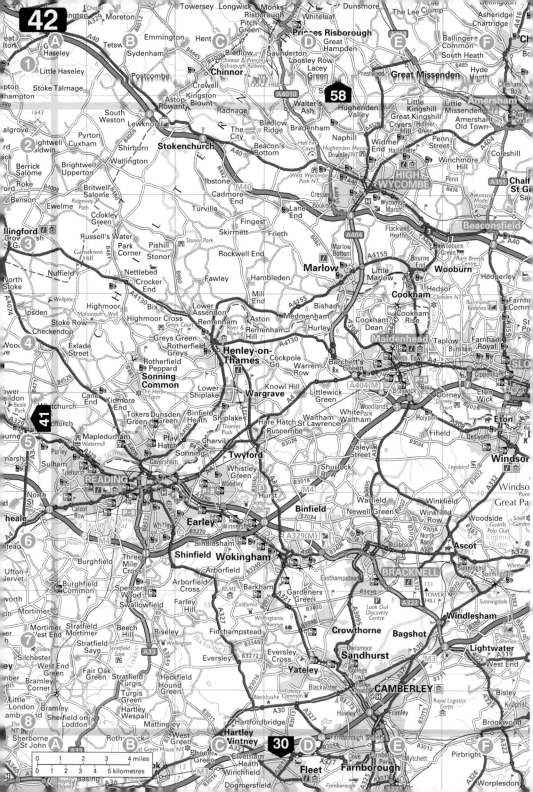

G **H** **J** **K** **L** **M**

1

62

Holliwell Point

Foulness Point

on-Crouch

Courtsend

Churchend

FOULNESS
ISLAND

2

3

4

Warden Point

5

35

MA

Leysdown-on-Sea

Westgate
on Sea West

HEPPEY

Isle of
Harty

Shell
Ness

Whitstable

Whitstable
Bay

Tankerton
Swalecliffe
Greenhill

Chestfield
South
Street

Seasalter

Herne Bay
Hampton

Herne Bay

Bishopstone Reculver

Beltinge

Broomfield

Herne

Minnis
Bay

Birchington

Acol

Monkton
Durlock

THANET

OF

6

St Nicholas
at Wade

Boyden
Gate

Sarre

Chislet

West
Upstreet

West
Stourmouth

Minster

35

Oare

Broom
Street

ey

34

Yorkletts

Highstreet

Dargate

Druidstone

Wildwood

Hoath

Hersden

Westbere

Stodmarsh

East Stourmouth

Preston

Elmstone

Westmarsh

Cop
Street
Hoaden

7

Faversham

Stone Chapel Davington
Hill

Goodnestone

Hernhill

Denstroude

A2040

Preston

Ospringe

Boughton St

Dunkirk

Staplestreet

Mt
Ephraim

Blean

Upper
Harbledown

Broad
Oak

Tyler
Hill

Rough
Common

Hales
Place

Sturry

Fordwich

Wickhambreaux

Old Town Hall

Ickham

Seaton

Durlock

Ash

Wingham Marshborough

Stone
Cross

Woodnest

8

North
Street

South Street

Overland

Harbledown

Thanington

Canterbury

Howletts

Bramling

Bekesbourne

Staple

Goodnestone

Eastry

Sheldwich

Hogben's
Hill

Selling

Old Wives
Lees

Chartham
Hatch

Chartham

ckington
et End

Bridge

Patrixbourne

Adisham

Ra

Chillenden

Betteshanger

G **H** **J** **K** **L** **M**

Leaveland

Badlesmere

Shottenden

Chilham

Dane
Street

Shalmsford
Street

Garlinge
Green

Bishopsbourne

Lower Hardres

Aylesham

Nonington

Great Mong

Tilmanstone

48

Pen Brush
Pwllderi
Llanw
Trefasser
Goodwick
Pembrokeshire
Coast Path
St Nicholas
Manorowen

64

Ynys
Daullyn
Granston
Carreg Sampson
Aber
Angloffan
Jordanston
Porthgain
Trefin
Mathry
A40
Abereiddy
Llanrhian
A487
B4331
Berea
Croes-goch
Letterston
Treglemais
B4330
Treffga
ST DAVID'S HEAD
Treleddyd-fawr
River Solva
Llandeloy
Wol
Rhodiad-
y-brenin
Caer
Farchell
Cas
Whitesand
Bay
Treffgarne
Owen
Hayscastle
Hayscastle
Cross
Bishops
Palace
Whitchurch
178
Treffga
St David's
DUDWELL
MT
Leweston
RAMSEY,
ISLAND
Solva
A487
Pen-y-cwn
RSPB
St David's Peninsula
Heritage Coast
Newgale
Roch
Wolfsdale
16
PEMBROKESHIRE
COAST
NATIONAL PARK
Simpson
Cross
Camrose
Rickets Head
Keeston
Pembrokeshire
County
Nolton Haven
Nolton
A487
St Brides Bay
St Brides Bay
Heritage Coast
Druidston
H
Haroldston
West
Portfield
Gate
B4341
Broad Haven
Broadway
B4327
Dreen-
Hill
Little Haven
Walton
West
A4076
Pembrokeshire
Coast Path
Freys
Talbenny
14
Tiers
Cross
Johns
SKOMER
ISLAND
Wooltrack Point
Walwyn's
Castle
Marloes
B4327
A477
St Ishmael's
Herbrandston
Steynton
Broad Sound
Marloes and Dale Heritage Coast
Dale
Hubberston
Waterston
B432
Westdale
Bay
Great Castle
Head
Hakin
Llanstadwell
SKOKHOLM
ISLAND
Dale
Point
Milford Haven
Milford
Haven
St Anns Head
Popton
Point
Pembro
Dock
Angle
Angle
Bay
P
Rosscrowther
Rosslare Harbour
B4320
Hundl
Freshwater
West
Castlemartin Brook
10
B4320
Linney Head
Castlemartin
B4319
S
Warren
Twyn
Merrion
PEMBROKESHIRE COAST
NATIONAL PARK
Pembrokeshire
Coast Path
Boshe

0 1 2 3 4 miles
0 1 2 3 4 5 kilometres

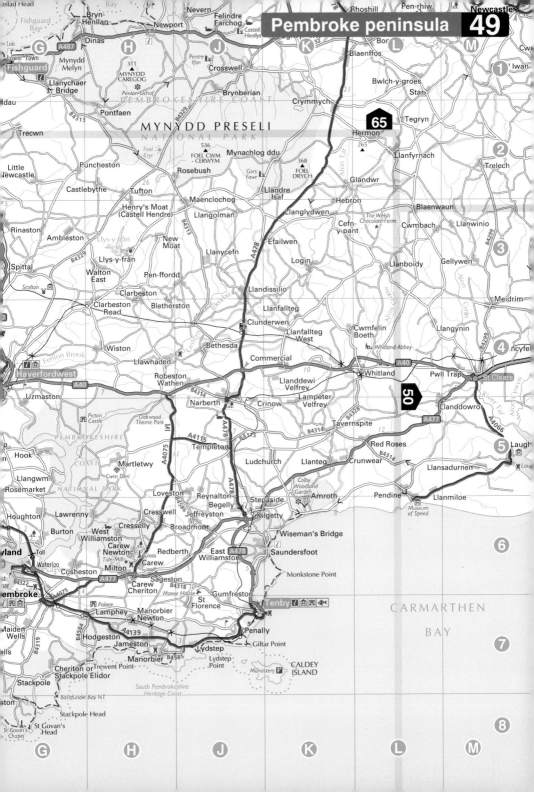

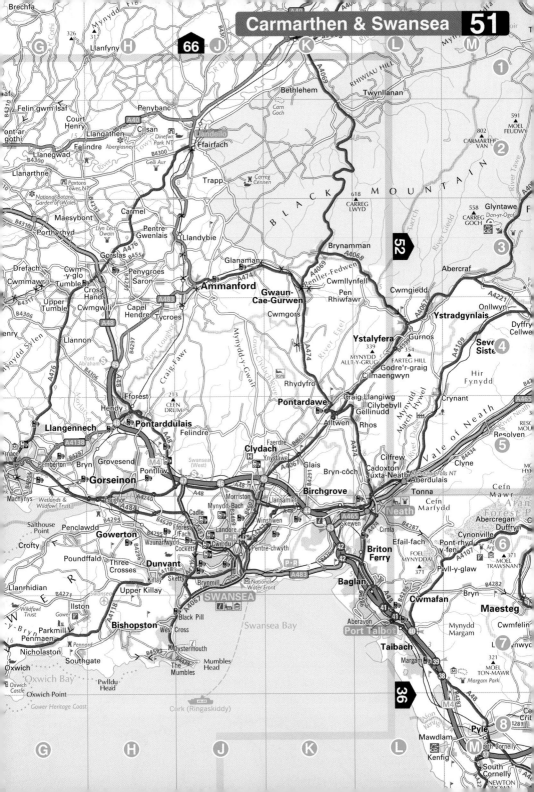

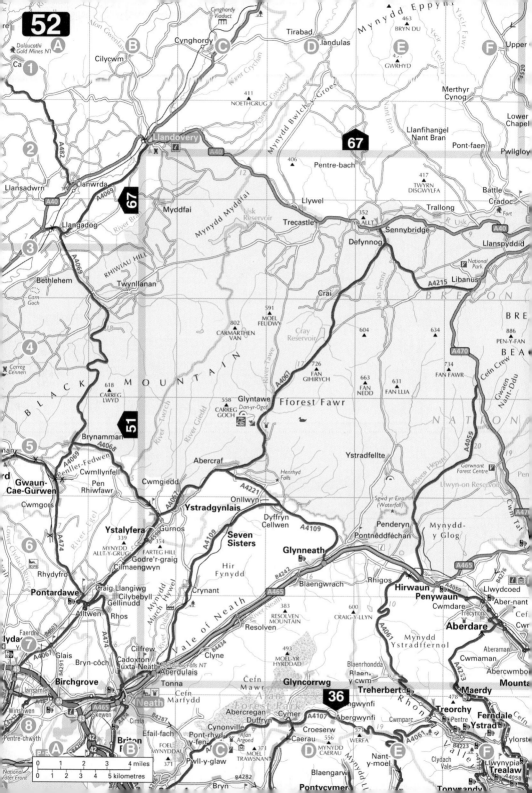

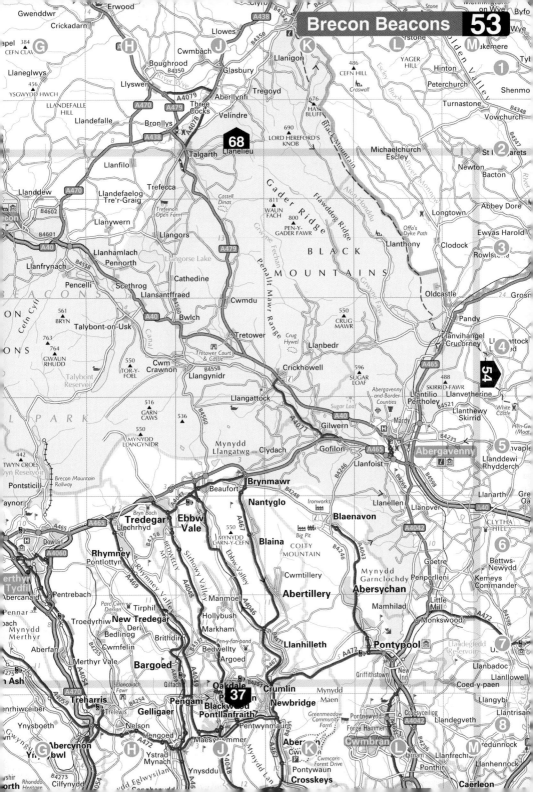

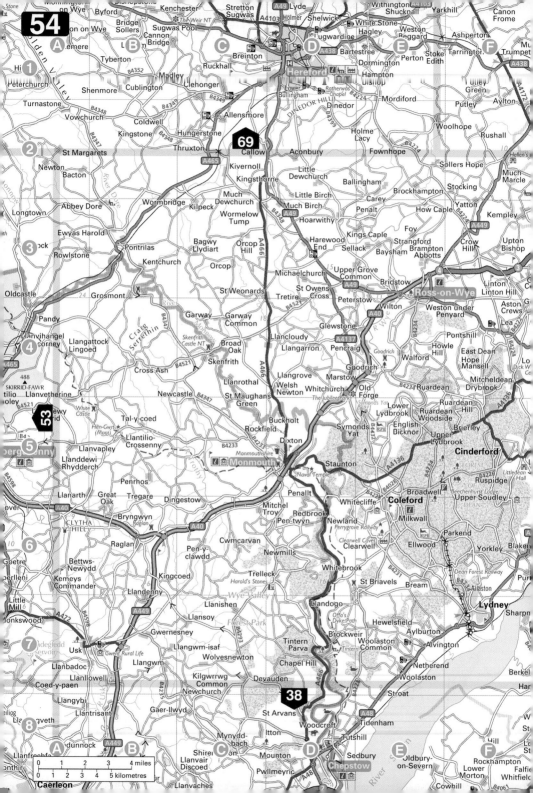

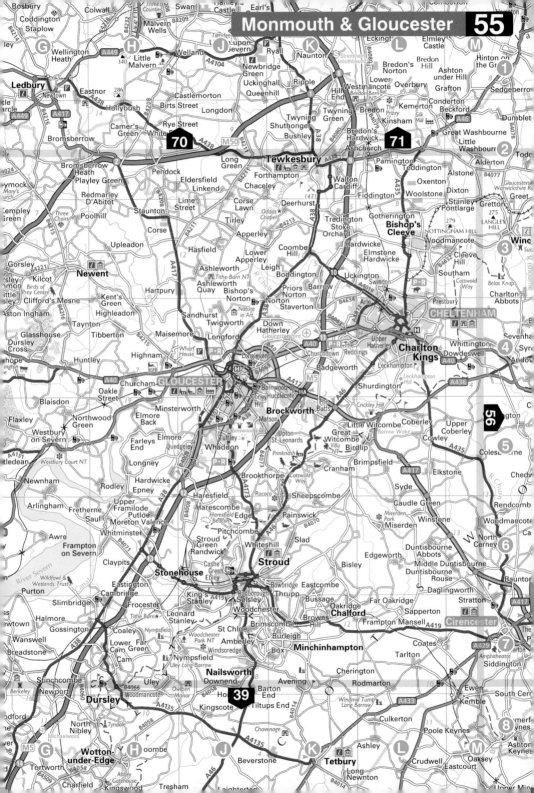

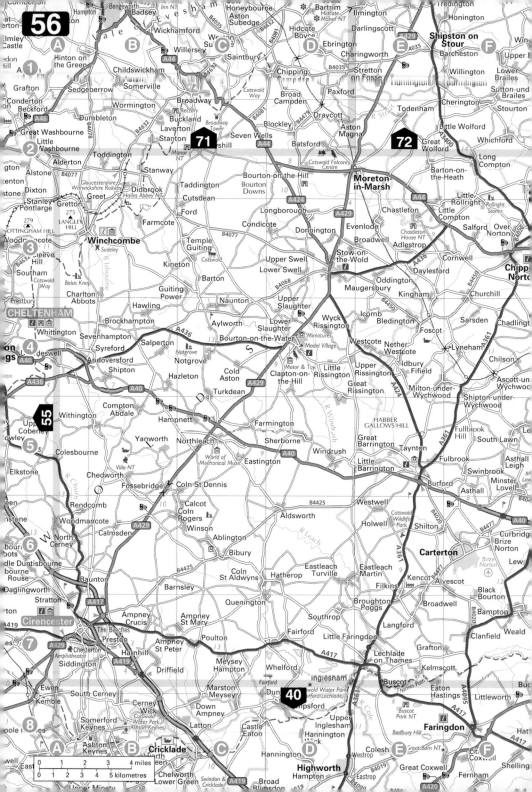

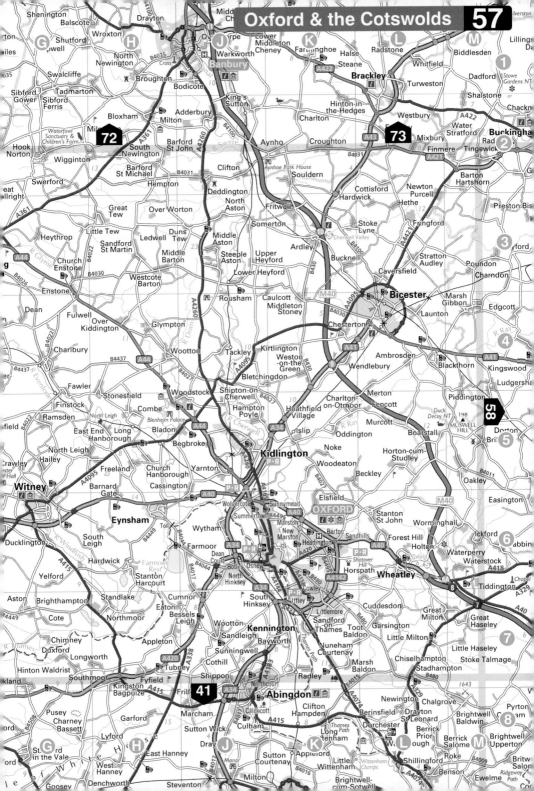

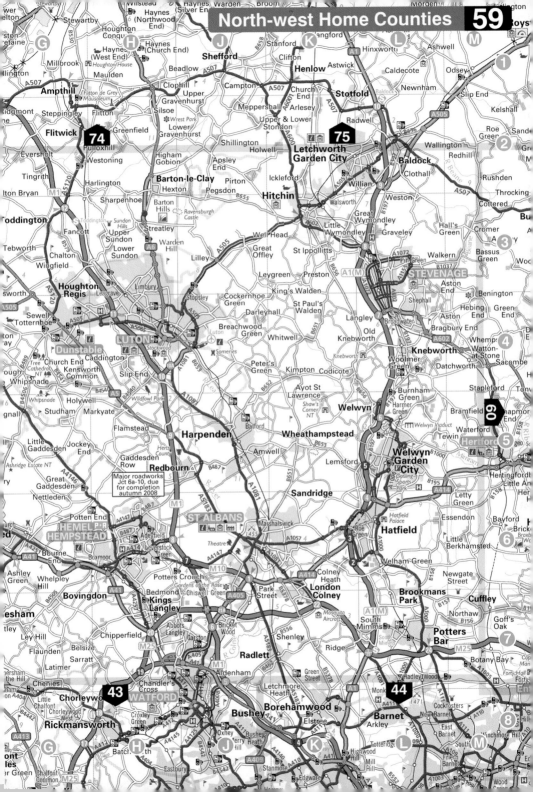

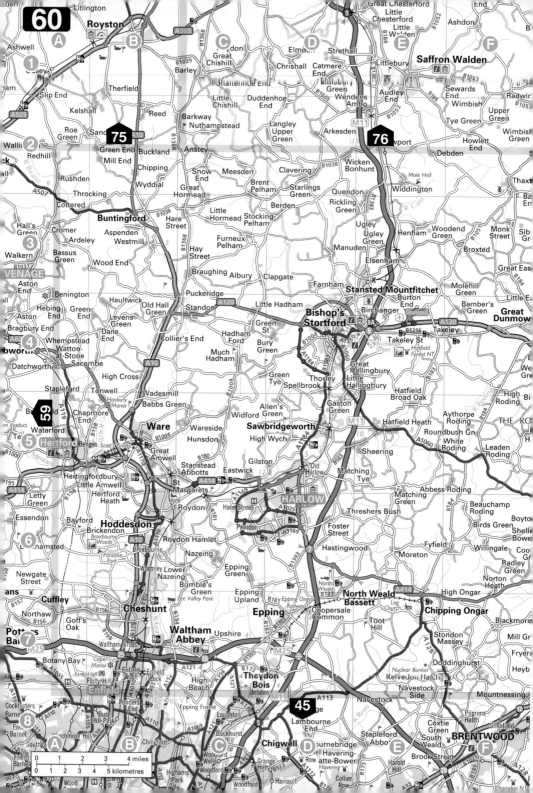

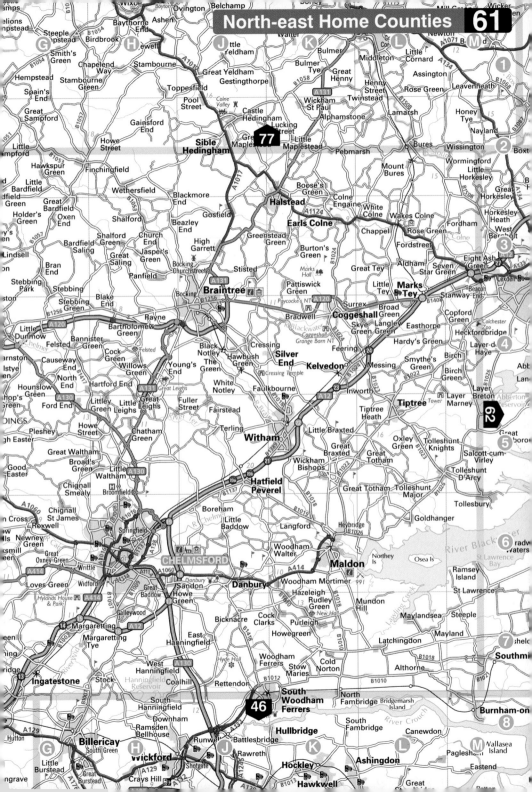

ewbourne
Hemley

River D.

Kirton

Falkenham

G

Alderton

Bawdsey

H

Hollesley
Bay

J

K

L

M

1

Walton
Old
Felixstowe

Felixstowe

79

2

Landguard Fort
Landguard
Point

3

Hoek van Holland

Hoek van Holland
Esbjerg

Naze

n on
aze

Sea

4

5

6

7

8

G   H   J   K   L   M

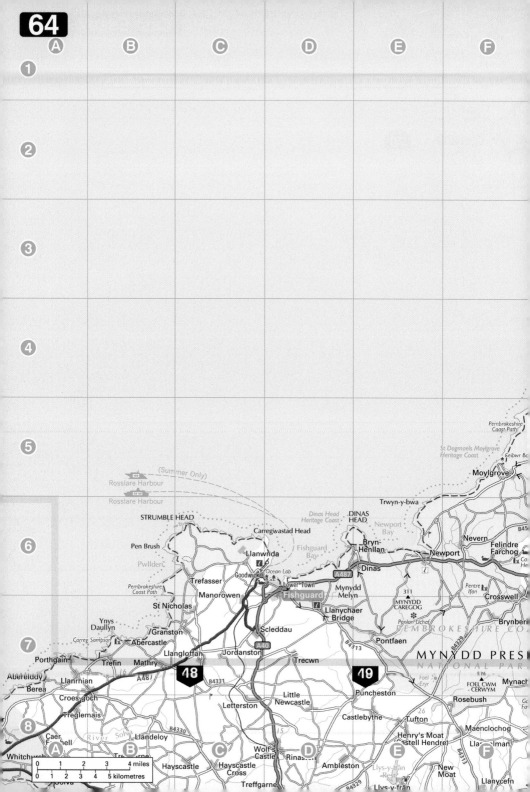

A   B   C   D   E   F

1

2

3

4

5

Pembrokeshire Coast Path

St Dogmaels Moylgrove Heritage Coast

Geibwr Bc

Moylgrove

B45

(Summer Only)

Rosslare Harbour

Rosslare Harbour

Trwyn-y-bwa

STRUMBLE HEAD

Carregwastad Head

Dinas Head Heritage Coast

DINAS HEAD

Newport Bay

Nevern

Felindre Farchog

6

Pen Brush

Llanwnda

Fishguard Bay

Bryn-Henllan

Newport

Ca He

Pwllderi

Ocean Lab

A487

Dinas

Crosswell

Pembrokeshire Coast Path

Trefasser

Goodwick

Lower Town

Mynydd Melyn

311

MYNYDD CAREGOG

Pentre Ifan

Manorowen

Fishguard

Llanychaer Bridge

Penlan Uchaf

Brynberi

St Nicholas

PEMBROKESHIRE CO

Ynys Daullyn

Scleddau

Pontfaen

7

Carreg Sampson

Abercastle

MYNYDD PRES

Porthgain

Granston

Llangloffan

Jordanston

Trecwn

B4313

NATIONAL PAR

Trefin

Mathry

18

19

Foel Eryr

526

FOEL CWM - CERWYM

Mynach

Abereiddy

Llanrhian

A487

B4331

Puncheston

Rosebush

Berea

Croes-goch

Little Newcastle

Castlebythe

26

Tufton

Maenclochog

Treglemais

Letterston

Henry's Moat (Castell Hendre)

Llan man

8

B4330

Caer F ell

River Solv

Llandeloy

15

Wolf's Castle

Rinas

Ambleston

Llys-y-frân Resr

New Moat

Whitchurch

A   B   C   D   E   F

Hayscastle

Hayscastle Cross

Treffgarne

B4329

Llanycefn

Solva

0 1 2 3 4 miles

0 1 2 3 4 5 kilometres

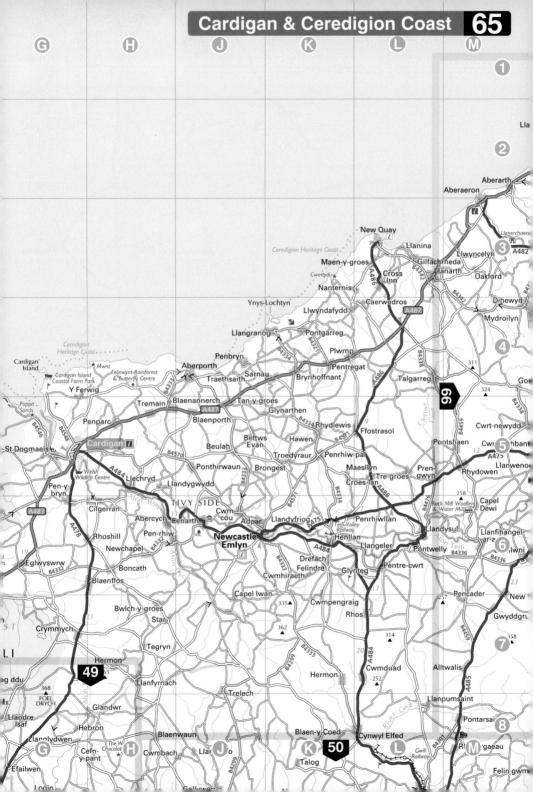

G   H   J   K   L   M

1

2

Lla

Aberarth

Aberaeron

3   A482

Llanerchaeron

New Quay

Llanina   Llwyncelyn

Maen-y-groes   Gilfachrheda   Oakford

Cross   Llanarth

Nanternis   Inn

Caerwedros   A487   Dihewyd

Cwmtydu   Mydroilyn

Ynys-Lochtyn

Llwyndafydd   Pontgarreg   4

Llangranog   Plwmp

Penbryn   Pentregat   Talgarreg   311

Aberporth   Sarnau   Brynhoffnant   324

Traethsaith   Ffostrasol   Cwrt-newydd

Tremain   Tan-y-groes   Pontshaen   99   Cwrt   hbant

Blaenannerch   Glynarthen   5   A475

Penparc   Blaenporth   Rhydlewis   Prenp-   Llanweno

Y Ferwig   Hawen   Penrhiw-pal   gwyn   Rhydowen

St Dogmaels   Beulah   Bettws   Maesllyn   Capel

Cardigan   Evan   Troedyraur   Croes-lan   Tre-groes   Rock Mill Woollen   Dewi
                                                              & Water Mill

Welsh   Ponthirwaun   Brongest   258

Wildlife Centre   Llandygwydd   Penrhiwllan   Llandysul   Llanfihangel-

Pen-y-   Llechryd   TIVY SIDE   Cwm-   6   ar-a

bryn   cou   Llandyfriog   Henllan   Pontwelly   wni

Cilgerran   Cenarth   Adpar   Teifi Valley   B4336   B4336

Abercych   Newcastle   Llangeler   Railway   Pentre-cwrt   23

Rhoshill   Pen-rhiw   Emlyn   Drefach   Glynteg   Pencader   New

Newchapel   Felindre   257   Gwyddgru

Blaenffos   Boncath   Cwmhiraeth   Rhos   314

Eglwyswrw   Capel Iwan   Cwmpengraig   Alltwalis   358

Crymmych   Bwlch-y-groes   335   362   252   7

Star   Cwmduad   Llanpumsaint

Tegryn   20   A484   Hermon   Pontarsai

Hermon   49   Trelech   Blaen-y-Coed   Cynwyl Elfed   8

FOEL   368   Glandwr   Cwmbach   50   Gwili   Rl   gaeae

DRYCH   Hebron   Blaenwaun   Talog   Railway   Felin gwm

Llanglydwen   Cefn-   The W   Llar   o   G   H   J   K   L   M

Efailwen   y-pant   Chocolate

Login

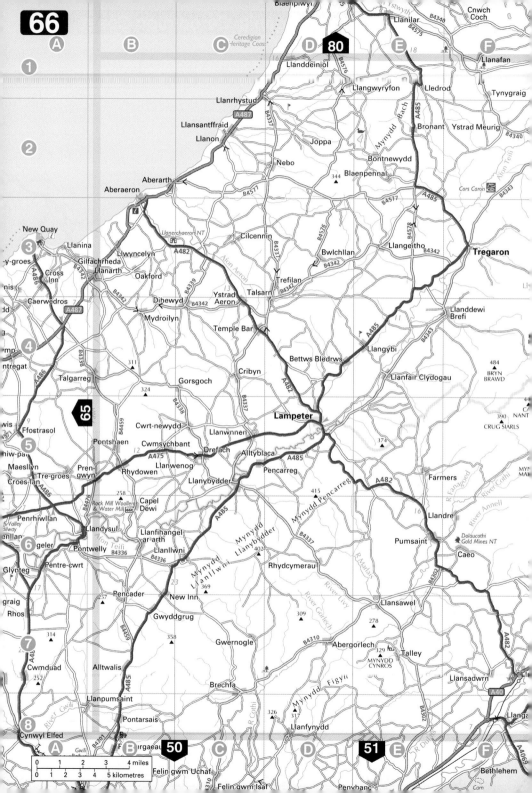

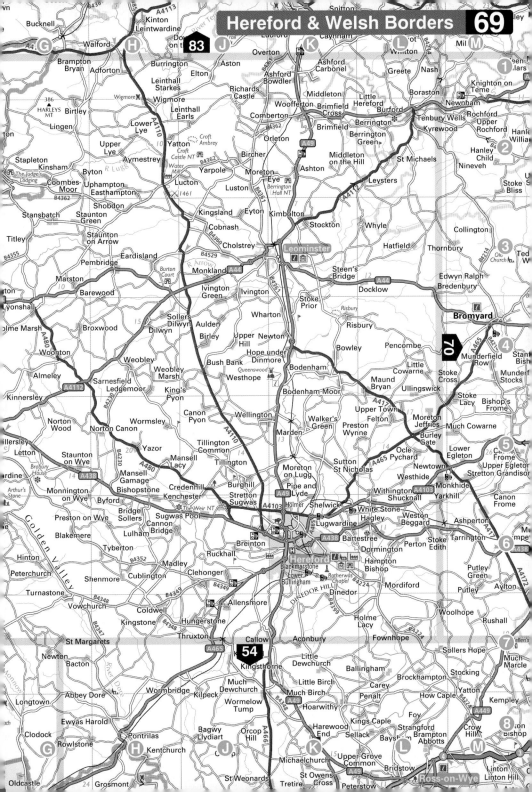

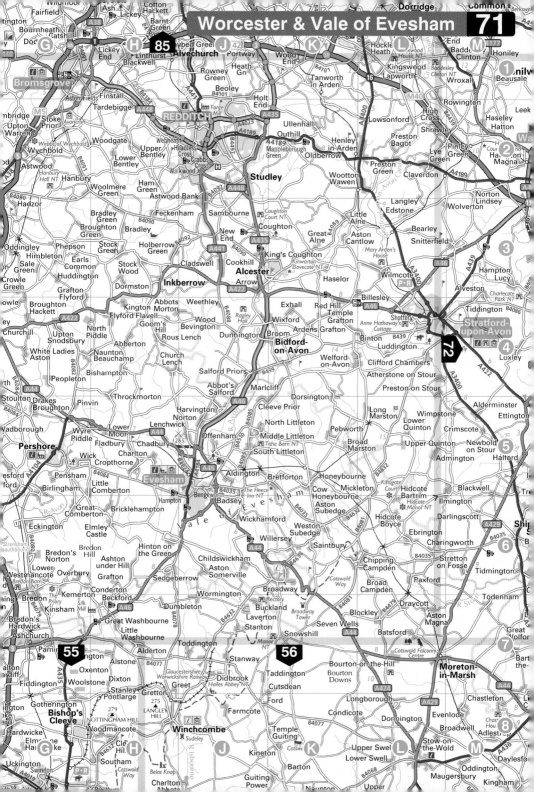

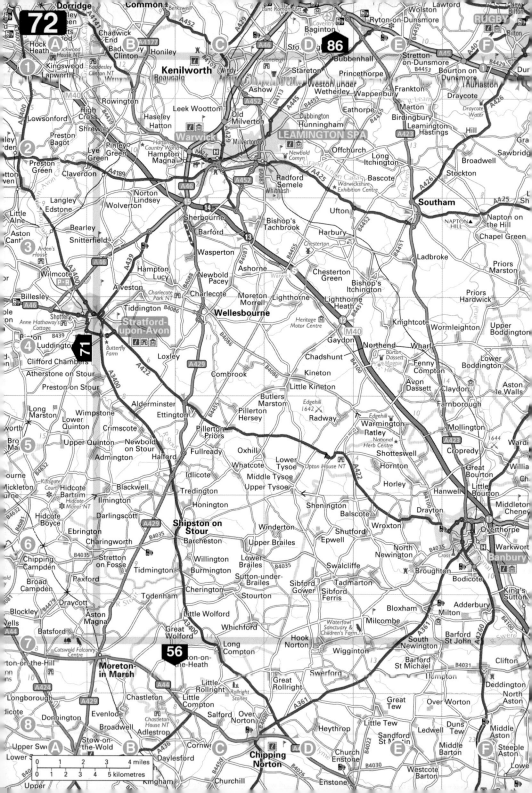

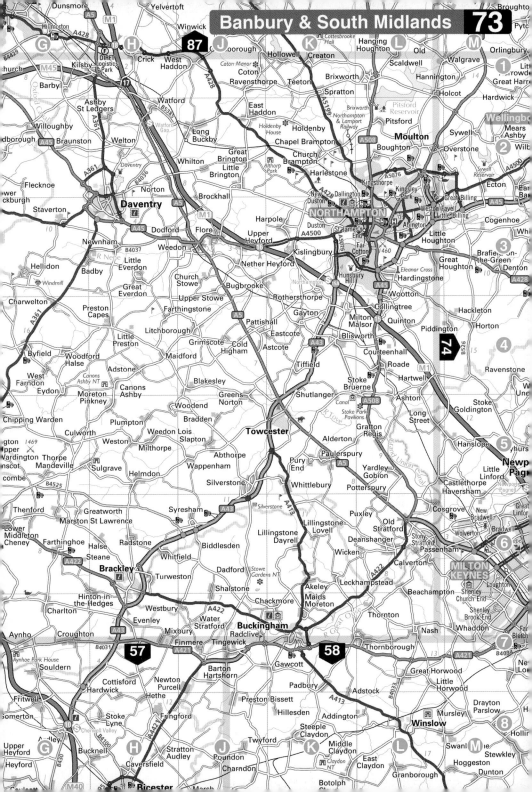

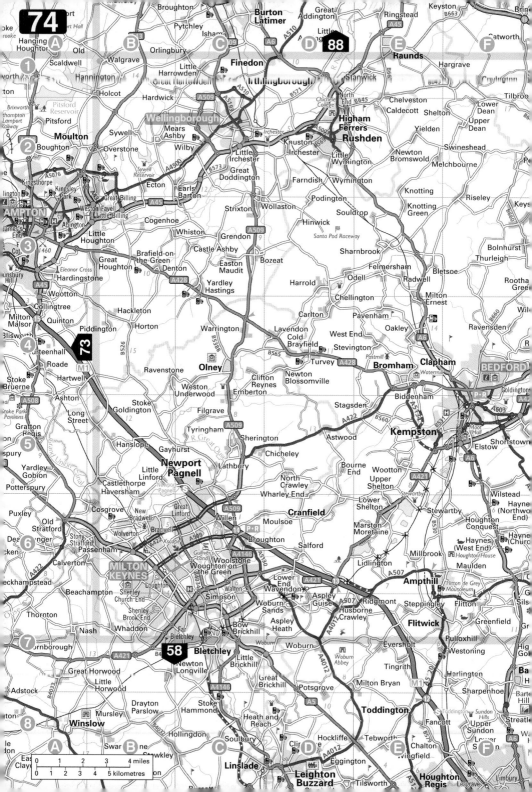

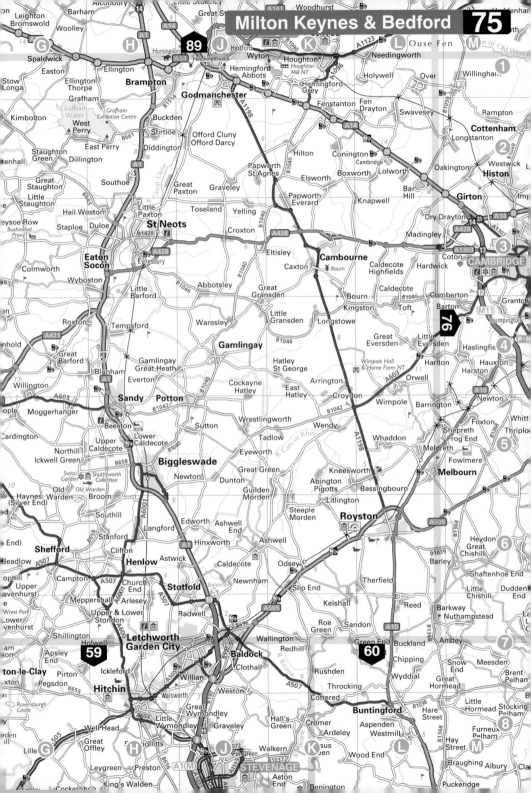

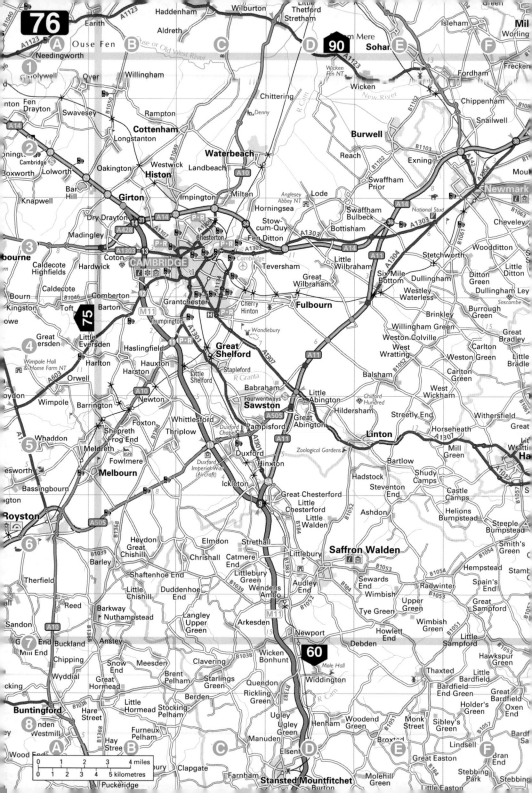

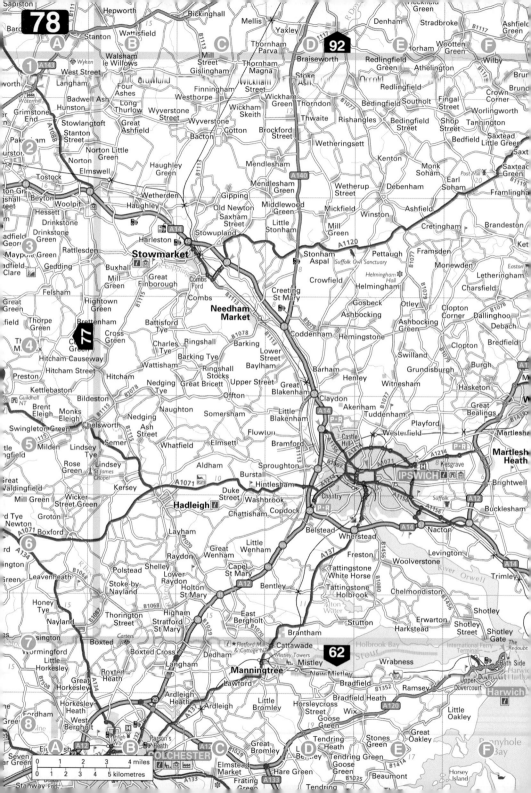

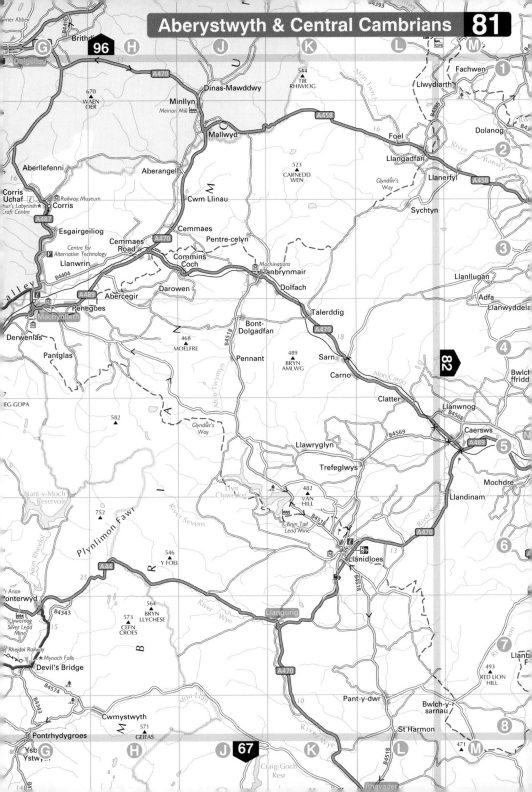

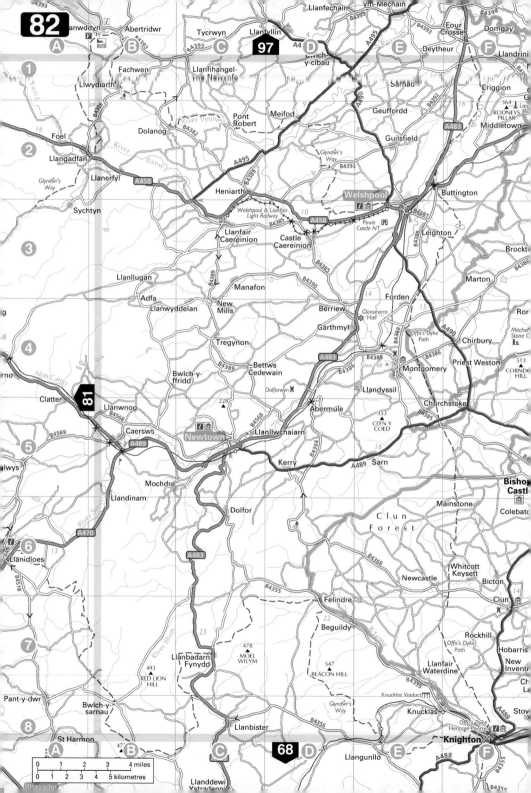

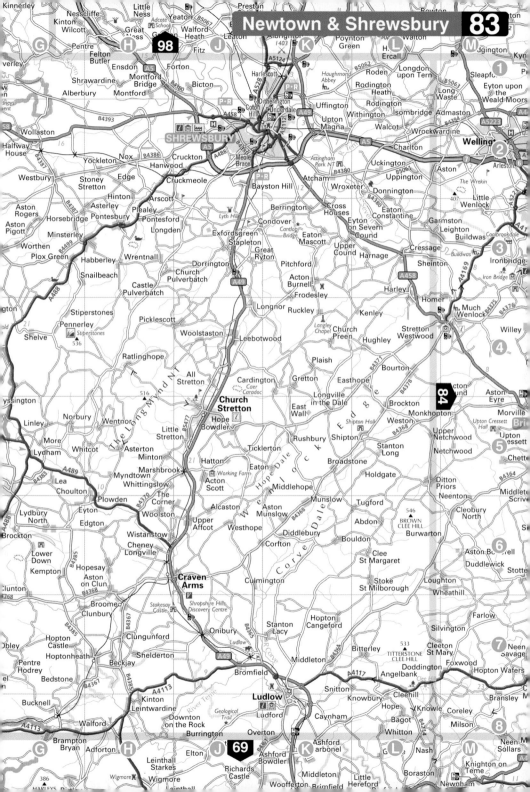

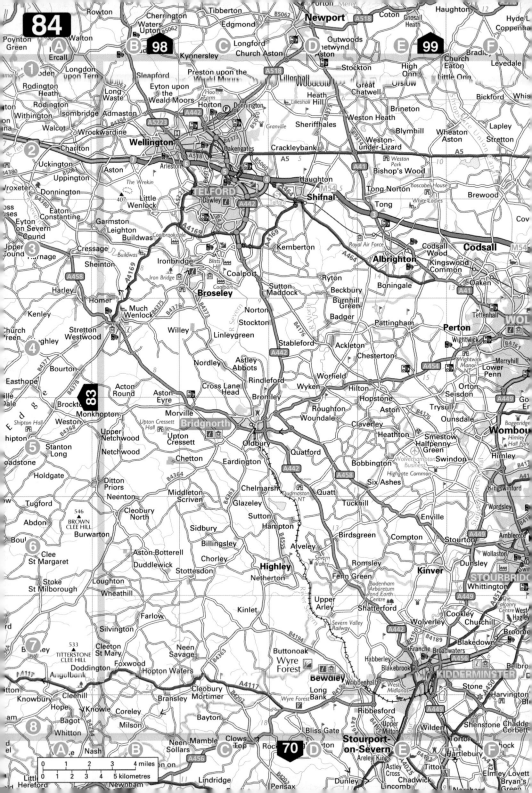

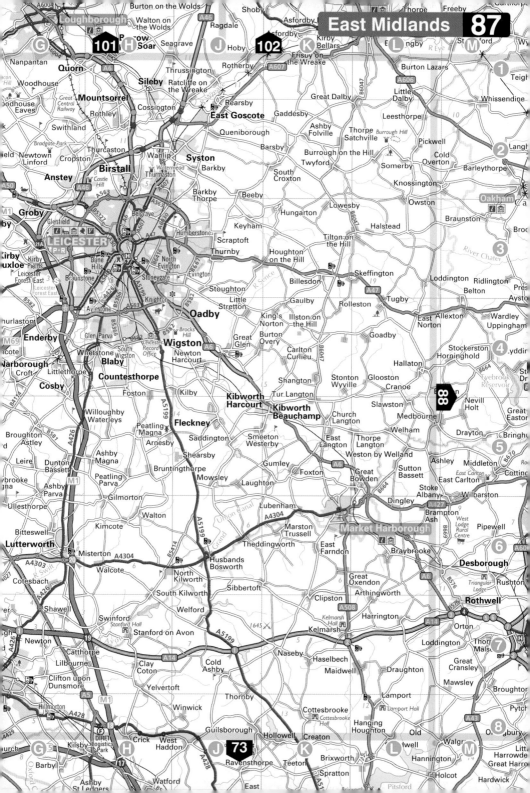

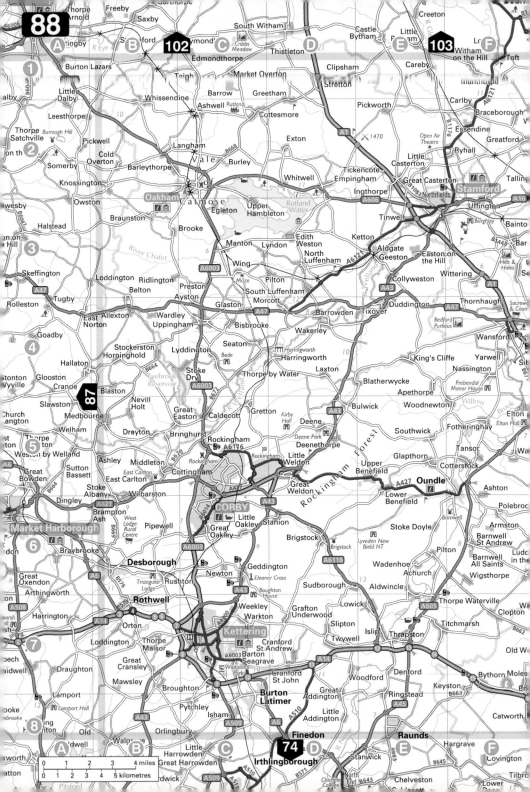

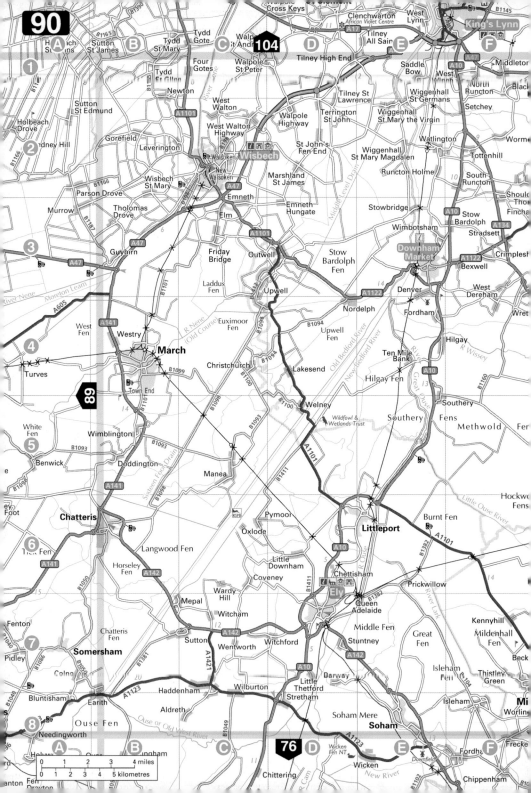

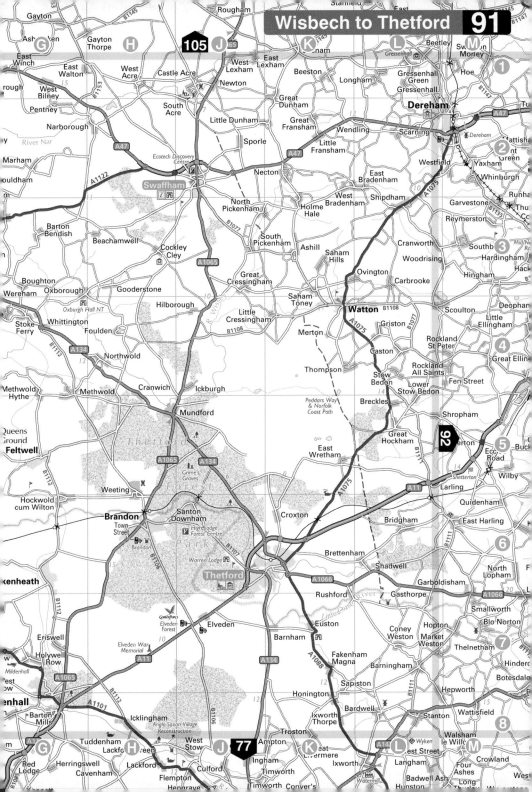

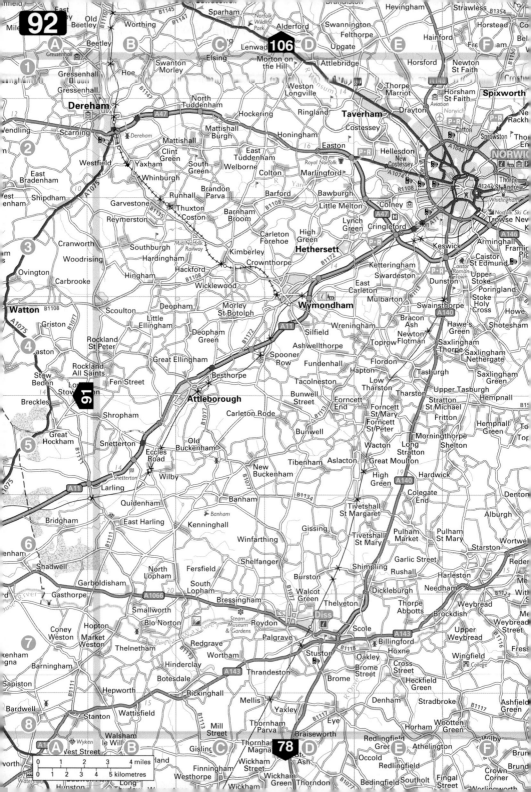

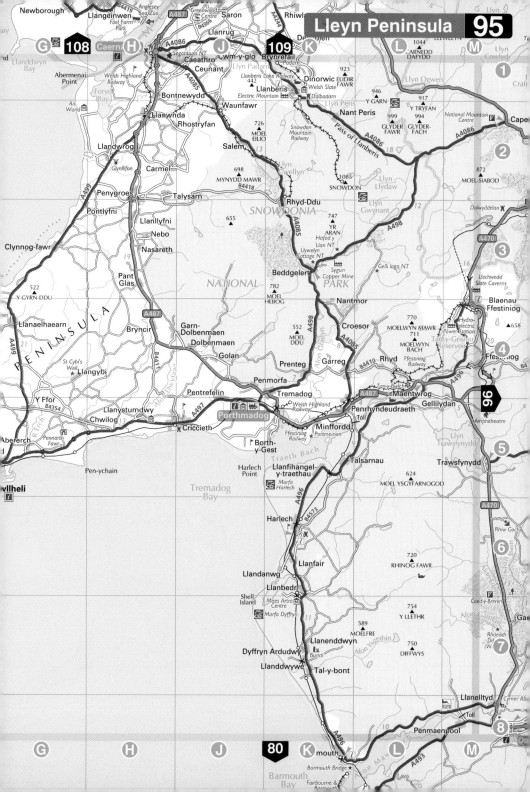

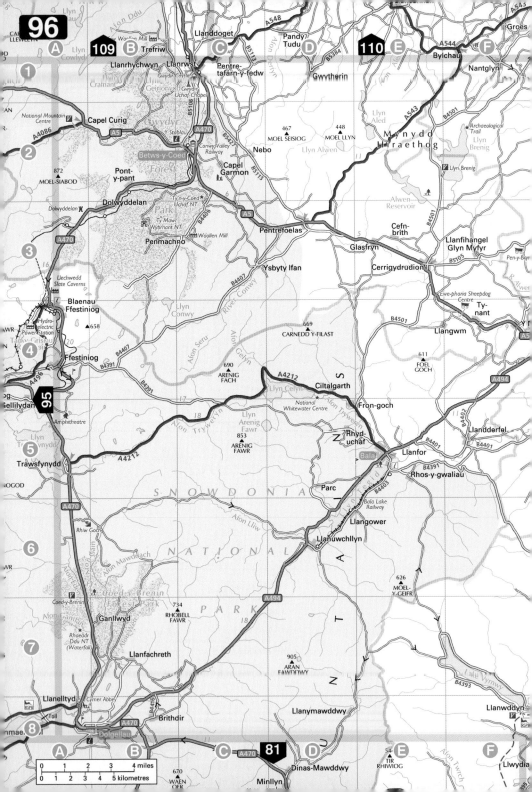

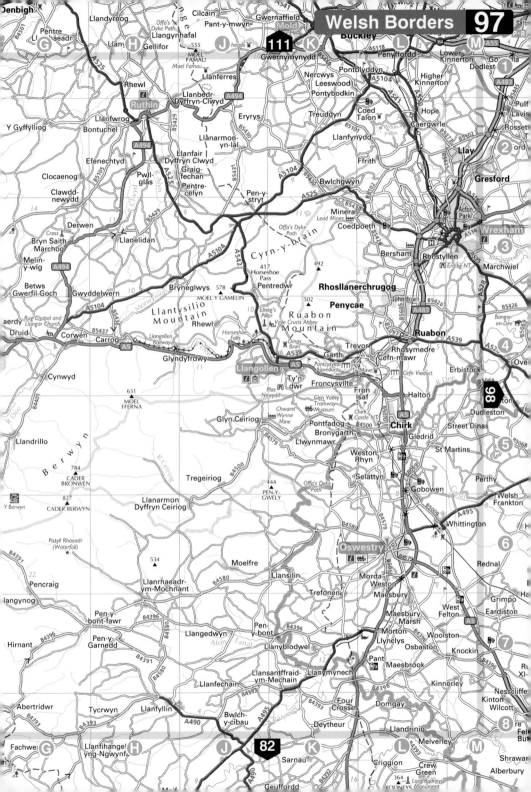

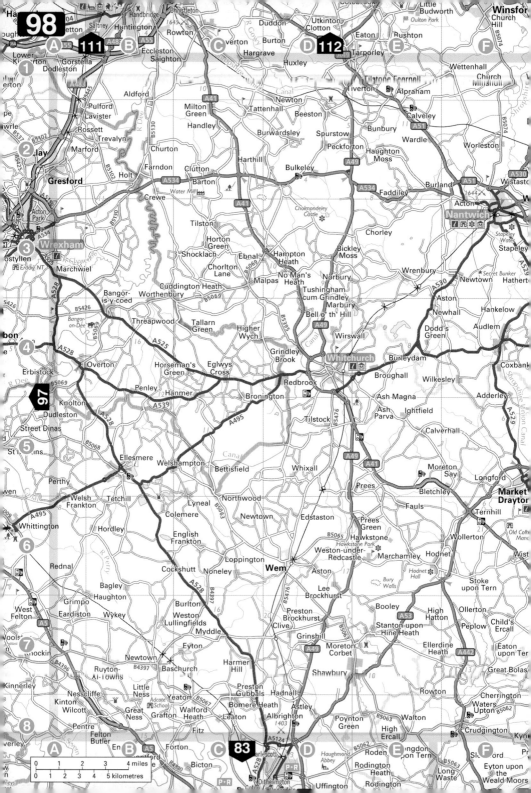

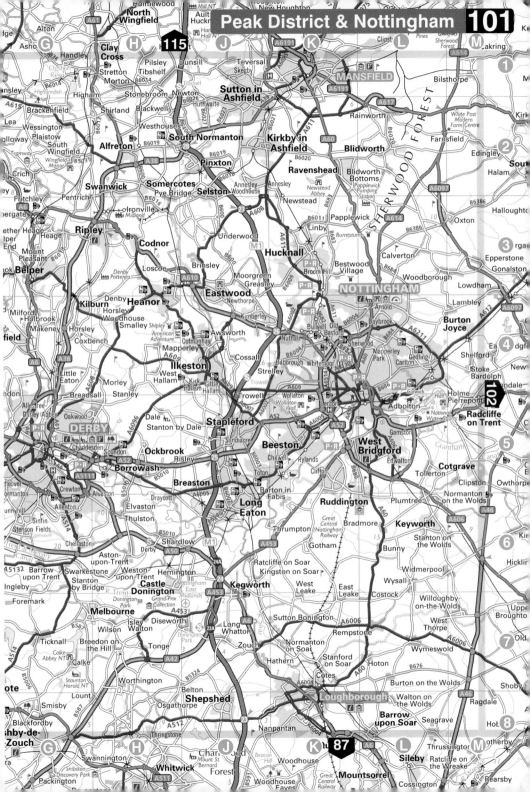

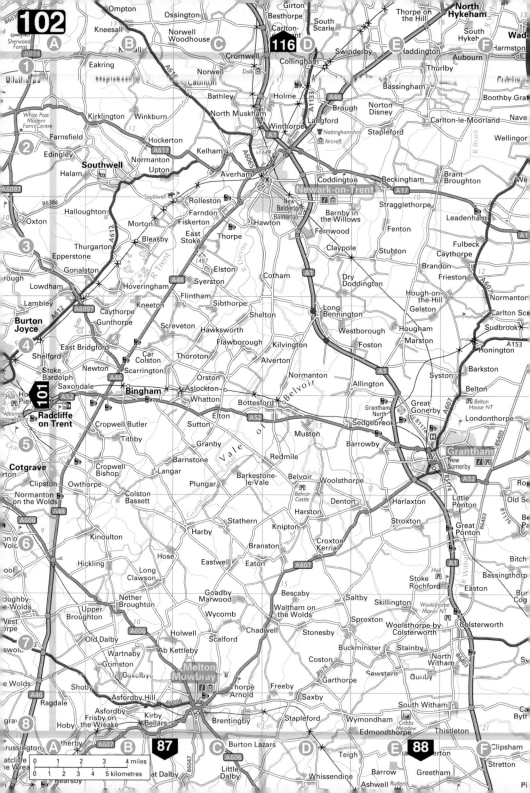

G H J K L M

① ② ③

④ Stiff

⑤

⑥

⑦

⑧ Beet

Brancaster Bay

Scolt Head Island

Holkham Bay

Peddars Way & Norfolk Coast Path

North Norfolk Heritage Coast

Blakeney Poin

Holme next the Sea
Brancaster
Brancaster Staithe
Burnham Norton
Burnham Overy Staithe
Holkham
Wells-next-the-sea
A149

Old Hunstanton
Thornham
Titchwell
Branodunum NT
Burnham Deepdale
Burnham Market
Burnham Overy
Warham St Mary
Warham All Saints
B1155
Holkham Hall

Hunstanton
Ringstead
Burnham Thorpe
Wighton

Heacham
Norfolk Lavender
Summerfield
Peddars Way & Norfolk Coast Path
North Creake
Creake
Wells & Walsingham Light Railway
The Shrine of Our Lady
Little Walsingham
Great Walsingham
A149

106

Docking
Stanhoe
South Creake
North Barsham
Hind.
Houghton St Giles
Thursfo

Sedgeford
B1454
B1155
West Barsham
East Barsham
Great Snoring
Thursford

Snettisham
Fring
Bircham Newton
B1155
Syderstone
B1454
Little Snoring
A148
Croxto

Ingoldisthorpe
Park Farm
Shernborne
Great Bircham
Bircham Tofts
Sculthorpe
Kettlestone
Dersingham
B1440
Anmer
B1153
Houghton Hall
Dunton Coxford
Shereford
Fakenham
⑥

Wolferton
Sandringham
West Newton
New Houghton
West Rudham
Tattersett
Hempton
Tatterford
Little Ryburgh
Great Ryburgh
A1067
River Wensu

Babingley River
A149
B1439
Flitcham
A148
East Rudham
Helhoughton
Toftrees
Colkirk
Great Ryburgh

Castle Rising
Hillington
Little Massingham
Harpley
East Raynham
West Raynham
Horningtoft
Gateley

Congham
Roydon
Grimston
Great Massingham
South Raynham
Whissonsett
Brisley
North Elmham

A148
A149
B1145
Gayton
Weasenham St Peter
Weasenham All Saints
Wellingham
Tittleshall
Stanfield
East Bilney
Old Beetley

King's Lynn
Ashwicken
Gayton Thorpe
B1145
Rougham
Mileham
Gressenhall
⑧

A10
iddleton
East Winch
East Walton
91
West xham
East Lexham
Bee
Longham
Gressenhall Green
Gressenhall

G H J K L M

aywood
B1145

North Runcton
Blackborough End
West Bilney
B1153
A1065
Newton
Great Dunham
South
Derehar

G H J K L M

① ② ③ ④ ⑤ ⑥ ⑦ ⑧

d

Trimingham

ham

Mundesley

Stow Mill

Knapton Paston
B1159

Edingthorpe Bacton

Walcott

d

Edingthorpe Ridlington Happisburgh
Green Witton

Whimpwell Green

Meeting Happisburgh Hempstead
House Hill Common

Honing Lessingham Ingham Sea Palling
Corner

Briggate East Ingham Waxham
Ruston

Worstead Stalham Calthorpe
Street

Dilham Hickling

Smallburgh Hickling Green Horsey

Barton Sutton
Turf Wood *Horsey Windpump NT*
Street

Tunstead

Neatishead Catfield

*Barton
Broad*

Irstead *Hickling
Broad*

Potter
Heigham

Hoveton Ludham Martham Winterton-on-Sea

oxham Bastwick

Upper Thurne **Hemsby** *Hemsby
Street Hole*

G Horning H er Street Repps J esby K `93` L M

Woodbastwick *Broadland* Thurne Clippesby Orr Scratby
Conservation Centre St Margaret

ckheath Salhouse Ranworth Pilson Burgh St California
Green Margaret Ormesby
St Michael

B1140 Billockby **Caister-on-**

A149

A1151

A1150

B1150

A1062

A1152

B1151

B1152

A1159

A B C D E F

1

2

3

4

109

Little Ormes Head

Penrhyn Bay

Rhos-on-Sea

Llandrillo-yn-Rhos

Colwyn Bay

Kinmel Bay

Kinmel Bay

Abergele Roads

Prestatyn

Rhyl

Gronant

Gwaenysgor

Llanasa

Gwesp

Trelogan

Meliden

Trelawnyd

Dyserth

Cwm

Wh

Llandudno Junction

Llanelian-yn-Rhos

Llysfaen

Rhyd-y-foel

Llanddulas

Pensarn

Towyn

Abergele

Rhuddlan

Llansanffraid Glan Conwy

Bryn-y-Maen

Dolwen

St George

Bodelwyddan

Bodelwyddan

Rhuallt

St Asaph

Tremeirchion

Caerwys

Afon-wen

Betws-yn-Rhos

Dawn

Graig

Tal-y-Cafn

Eglwysbach

Bodnant NT

Llanfair Talhaiarn

Trefnant

Bodfari

CLWYD

Llannefydd

River Elwy

Llangernyw

Henllan

Liansannan

Bylchau

Llanddoget

Pandy Tudur

Denbigh

Groes

Pentre Llanrhaeadr

Llandyrnog

Llanynys

Llanrwst

Gwydir Castle

rionyuddo

Uch

Pentre-farn-y-fedw

Gwythe

ntglyn

Ruth

Rhewl

0 1 2 3 4 miles
0 1 2 3 4 5 kilometres

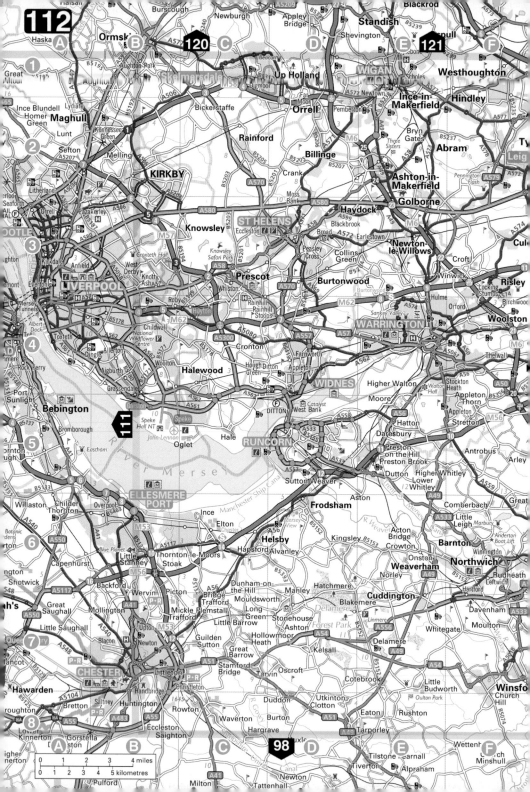

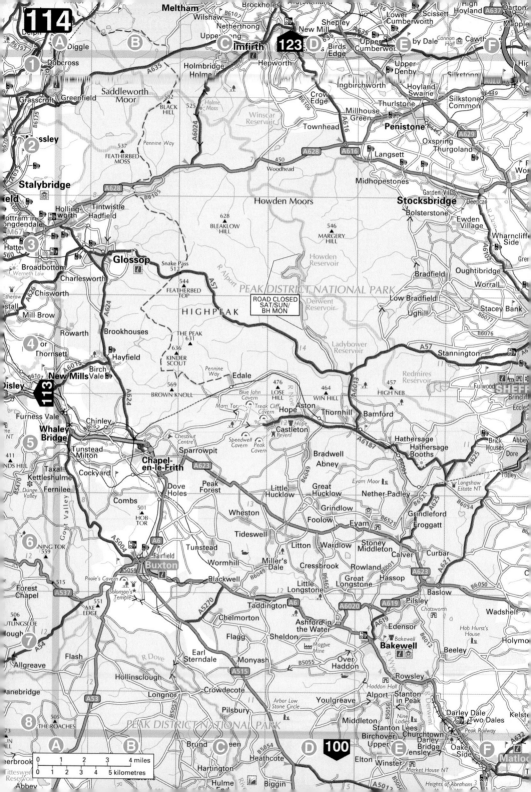

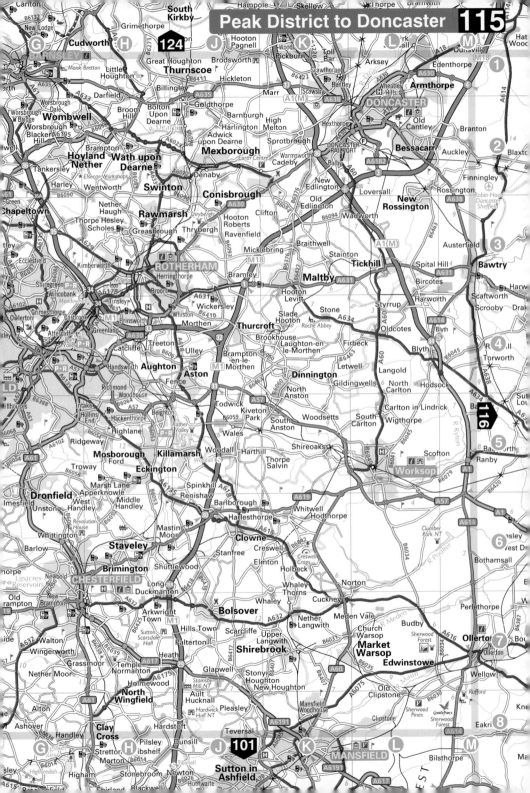

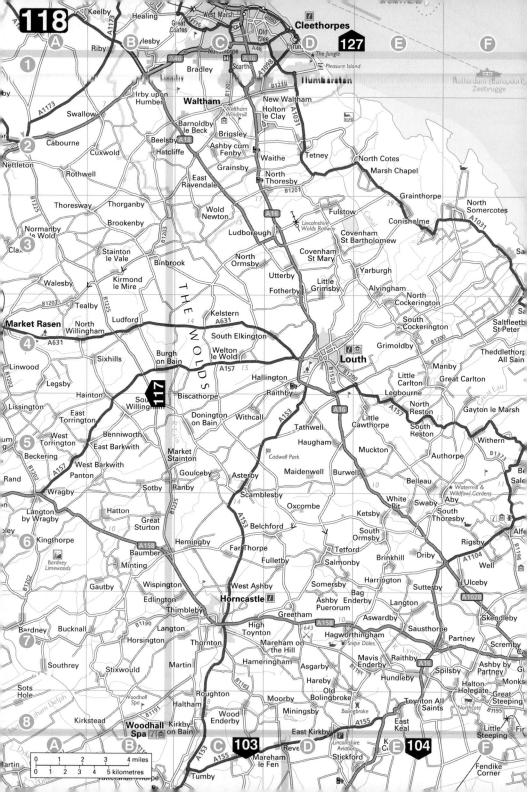

G H J K L M

① ② ③ ④ ⑤ ⑥ ⑦ ⑧

...et

...eetby St Clement
...eetby All Saints
Theddlethorpe
St Helen

A1031

Mablethorpe

A1104

Trusthorpe
A52
Sutton on Sea
...Maltby
e Marsh
Sandilands
A1111
...y
A52
Markby
Huttoft
Bilsby
Thurlby
B1449
Anderby Creek
Anderby
...Farlesthorpe
Mumby
...umberworth
Chapel Point
Hogsthorpe
Chapel St Leonards
Willoughby
Sloothby
Fantasy Island
Habertoft
Addlethorpe
Ingoldmells
Velton le Marsh
A52
Ingoldmells
...esby
Point
...y
Orby
...rpe
Burgh le Marsh
A158
Bratoft
Skegness
...Irby in the Marsh

G **104** H J K L M

Croft
Thorpe St Peter
Wainfleet Haven
...Wainfleet

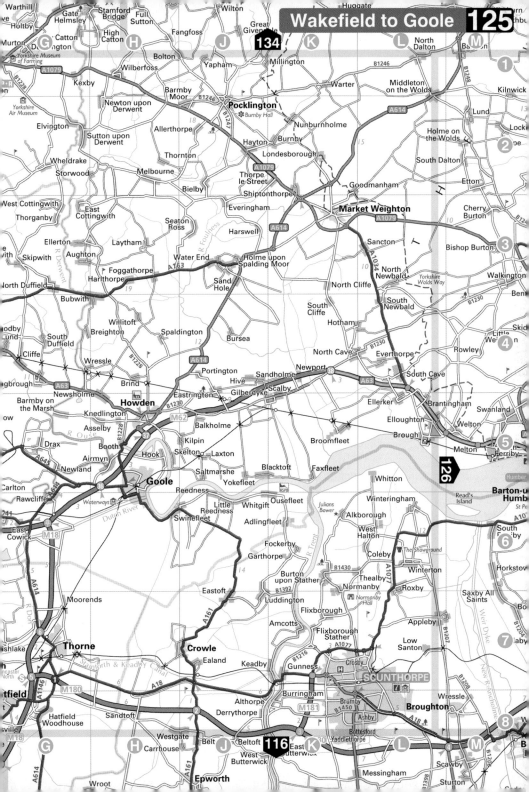

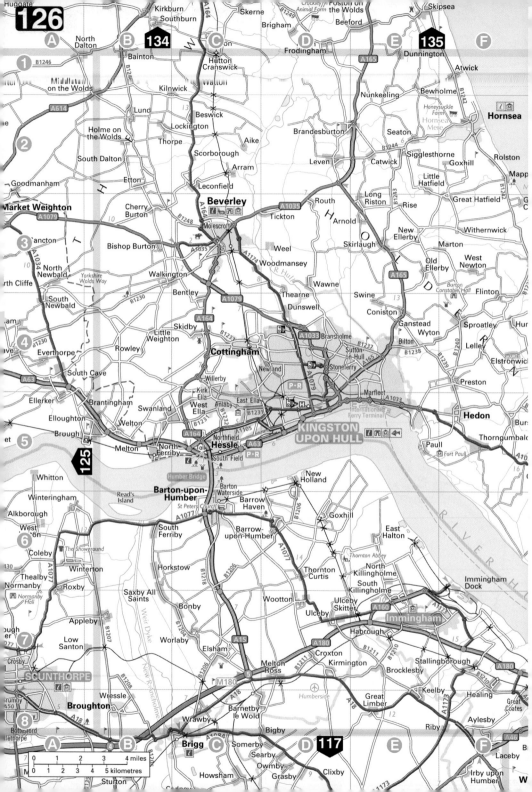

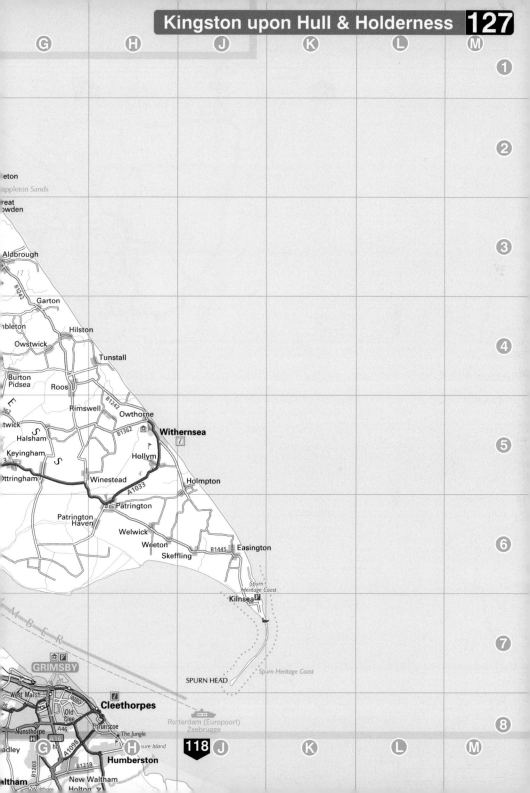

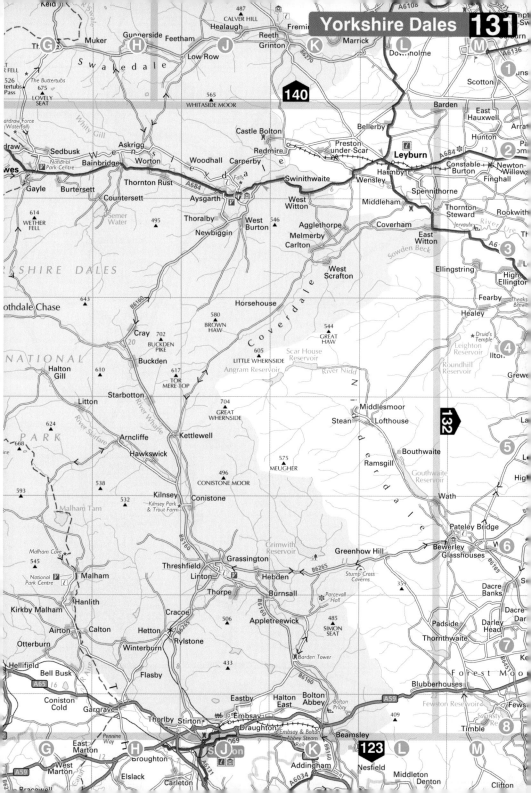

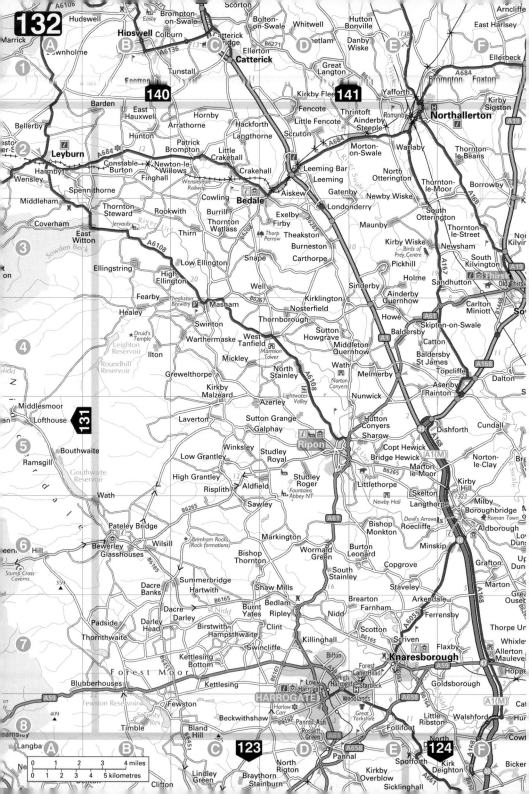

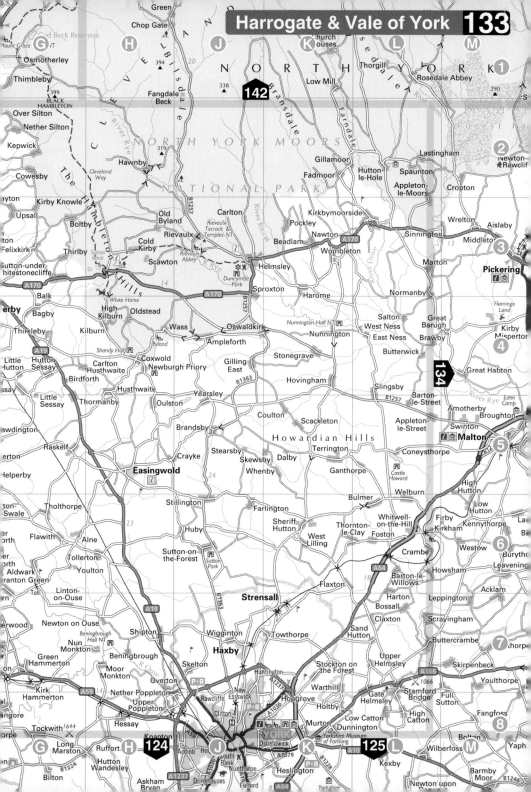

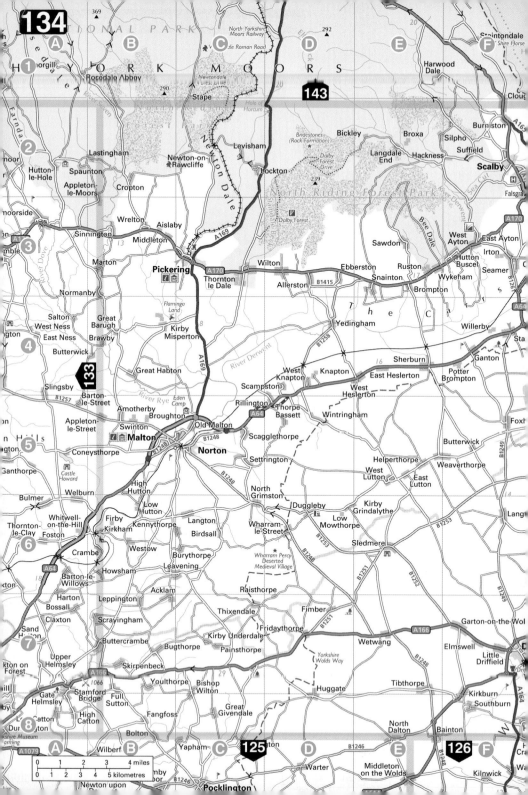

G   H   J   K   L   M

1

Cloughton
Wyke

Cromer Point

Cleveland Way

Scarborough
★ Hatherleigh
Deep Sea
Trawler
P·R
Oliver's Mount

A165
Eastfield
Osgodby
B1261
sgates
Cayton
Lebberston
Gristhorpe
R-Hertford
Folkton
Muston
A1039
Flixton
Hunmanby
Fordon
Reighton
Wold
Newton
Burton
Fleming
Grindale
Thwing
Yorkshire
Wolds Way

Cayton
Bay
The
Wyke
Filey Brigg
A1039
Filey

Filey Bay

Speeton
B1229
Buckton
Bempton
A165
B1229
Sewerby
B1253
Rudston
★ Monolith
Boynton
Bessingby
Carnaby
Haisthorpe
Thornholme
Kilham
Burton Agnes
★ Norman
Manor House
Harpham
Ruston Parva
Lowthorpe
A614
Nafferton
field
Great Kelk
Lissett
Gransmoor
Fraisthorpe
Barmston
Wansford
Gembling
Cruckley
Animal Farm
Foston on
the Wolds
Skerne
B1249
Brigham
Beeford
North
Frodingham
A165
126
Dunnington
Atwick
Nunkeeling
Bewholme

Flamborough Head Heritage Coast
Thornwick
Bay
RSPB
North Landing
Selwicks
Bay
B1259
FLAMBOROUGH
HEAD
Lighthouse
B1255
Flamborough
★ Bondville
Miniature Village
Bridlington
BRIDLINGTON
BAY
Hilderthorpe

Ulrome
Skipsea
B1242

R Hull

2

3

4

5

6

7

8

G   H   J   K   L   M

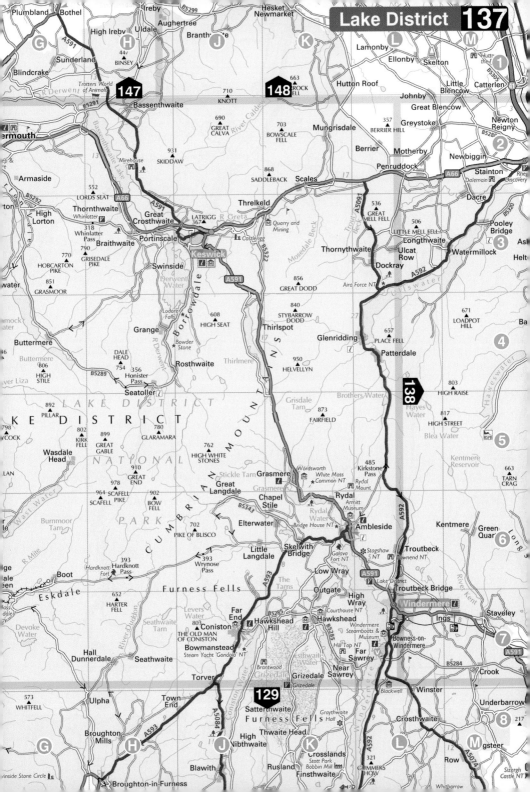

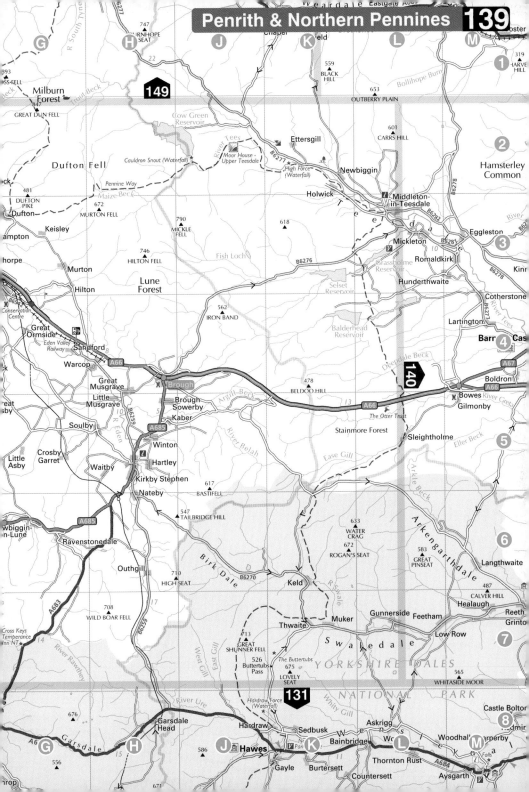

Weardale · Eastgate
Chapel · Keld

G H J K L M

747 · BURNHOPE SEAT
393 · CROSS FELL
22

1 · 319 · HARVE HILL

149

559 · BLACK HILL

653 · OUTBERRY PLAIN

Bollihope Burn

Milburn Forest
847

GREAT DUN FELL

Cow Green Reservoir

River Tees

Moor House - Upper Teesdale

Cauldron Snout (Waterfall)

Ettersgill

601 · CARRS HILL

2 · Hamsterley Common

Dufton Fell

B6277

High Force (Waterfall)

Newbiggin

Holwick

Pennine Way

Teesdale

481 · DUFTON PIKE
Dufton

672 · MURTON FELL

Maize Beck

790 · MICKLE FELL

Middleton-in-Teesdale

B6282

3 · Eggleston

Keisley
thorpe

746 · HILTON FELL

Mickleton

B6281

Romaldkirk

Murton

618

Fish Loch

Lune Forest

B6276

Grassholme Reservoir

Hunderthwaite

Hilton

Selset Reservoir

Cotherstone

B6277

562 · IRON BAND

Balderhead Reservoir

Lartington

River Tees

Conservation Centre

Great Ormside

Eden Valley Railway

Sandford

Warcop

A66

Great Musgrave

Brough

478 · BELDOO HILL

Barr **4** · Cas

140

Deepdale Beck

A67

Boldron
A66

Little Musgrave

Brough Sowerby

Argill Beck

13 · A66

Bowes · River Greta

Gilmonby

Soulby

Kaber

A685

Crosby Garret

Winton

Hartley

River Belah

The Otter Trust

Stainmore Forest

Sleightholme

Ease Gill

Eller Beck

5

Little Asby

Waitby

Kirkby Stephen

617 · BASTIFELL

Arkle Beck

wbiggin-n-Lune
A685

Nateby

547 · TAILBRIDGE HILL

633 · WATER CRAG

Arkengarthdale

583 · GREAT PINSEAT

6 · Langthwaite

Ravenstonedale

Birk Dale

672 · ROGAN'S SEAT

A683

Outhgill

710 · HIGH SEAT

B6270

487 · CALVER HILL

Healaugh

Reeth
Grinto

708 · WILD BOAR FELL

B6259

Keld

R Swale

Gunnerside · Feetham

Low Row

7

Cross Keys Temperance Inn NT

River Rawthey

Thwaite

Muker

Swaledale

713 · GREAT SHUNNER FELL

YORKSHIRE DALES

565 · WHITASIDE MOOR

526 · Buttertubs Pass

The Buttertubs

675 · LOVELY SEAT

West Gill

East Gill

NATIONAL PARK

676

131

Hardraw Force (Waterfall)

Castle Boltor
8

Garsdale Head

Garsdale

Hardraw

Sedbusk

Askrigg

Woodhall · arperby

G H · 586 · J · Hawes K · Bainbridge L M · Falls

556

Gayle · Burtersett

Thornton Rust

A684

Aysgarth

Countersett

671

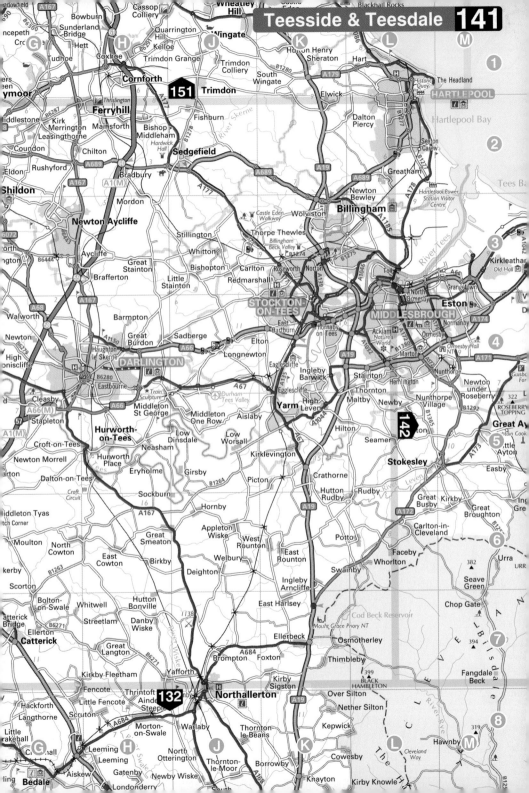

G H J K L M

1

2

3

Staithes
Heritage Centre

4

Runswick
Bay
North Yorkshire and
Cleveland Heritage Coast

derwell

Runswick
Goldsborough
Overdale
Wyke
Ellerby
B1266
A174
Lythe
Mickleby
East
Barnby
Sandsend
Sandsend
Wyke
West
Barnby
Dunsley
Whitby
Saltwick
Bay
Ugthorpe
Newholm

5

The
Green
Egton
A171
Aislaby
Sleights
Ugglebarnby
Sneaton
High Hawsker
B1447
Ness Point or North Cheek

ton Bridge
Grosmont
A169
Iburndale
Robin Hood's Bay

OORS
Fylingthorpe
Robin
Hood's Bay

Goathland
A171
Old Peak or South Cheek
Ravenscar

B1416

Buswarp
Briggswath
Stainsacre

6

North Yorkshire
Moors Railway
292
Eller Beck

A R K
Wheeldale Roman Road
Staintondale
Shire Horse Centre
Hayburn
Wyke

7

K M O O R S
20
Harwood
Dale
Cloughton
Wyke

Newtondale
Forest Drive
290
Stape
Hole of
Horcum
Cloughton

134

Bridestones
(Rock Formation)
Bickley
Broxa
Silpho
Burniston
A165
Cromer Point
Cleveland Way

Levisham
Langdale
End
Suffield
Scalby

8

Newton
Ra
Dalby
Forest
Drive
Hackness
L
Scarborough
M

G
lock
H
239
J
K
Falsgrave
Hatherleigh
Deep Sea
Trowler

North Riding Forest Park
River Derw
Sea Cut
P·R

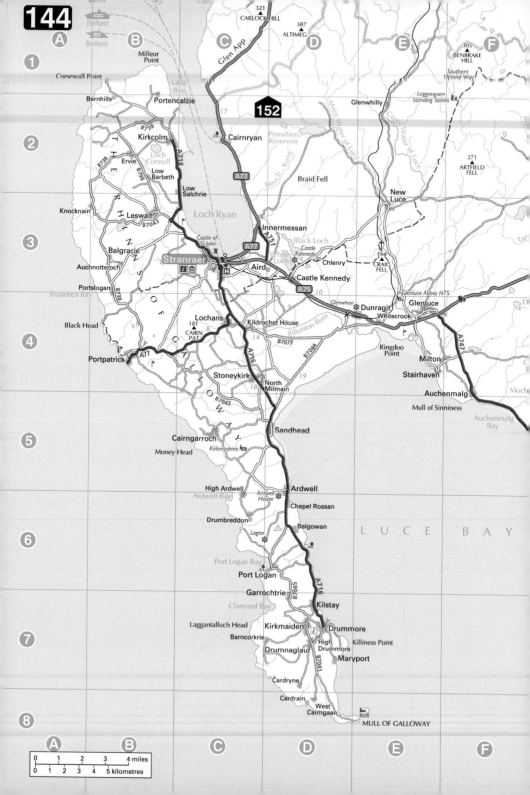

Belfast
Belfast

1

Corsewall Point

Milleur
Point

Barnhills   Portencalzie

321
CARLOCK HILL

387
ALTIMEG

Glen App

305
BENBRAKE
HILL

Southern
Upland Way

E   **F**

2

Kirkcolm

Ervie

Low
Barbeth

Low
Salchrie

Cairnryan

152

A77

Beoch Burn

Main Water of Luce

Penwhirn
Reservoir

Glenwhilly

Laggangairn
Standing Stones

271
ARTFIELD
FELL

Knocknain

Leswalt

B7043

Braid Fell

New
Luce

Cross Water of Luce

3

Balgracie

Auchnotteroch

Portslogan

Broadsea Bay

Castle of
St John

Loch Ryan

Stranraer

Innermessan

A751

A77

Aird

Black Loch

White
Loch

Castle
Kennedy

Chlenry

Castle Kennedy

A75

Glenwhan

CRAIG
FELL

Glenluce Abbey NTS

Dunragit

Whitecrook

Glenluce

4

Black Head

Lochans

Portpatrick

A77

181
CAIRN
PAT

8

A716

Kildrochet House

B7077

Piltanton Burn

B7084

14

19

Ringdoo
Point

Milton

Stairhaven

A747

Auchenmalg

Mull of Sinniness

Auchenmalg
Bay

Stoneykirk

North
Milmain

18

B7042

5

Cairngarroch

Money Head

Kirkmadrine

Sandhead

L U C E   B A Y

6

High Ardwell

Ardwell Bay

Ardwell
House

Drumbreddon

Logan

Ardwell

Chapel Rossan

Balgowan

Port Logan Bay

Port Logan

Garrochtrie

Clanyard Bay

B7065

A716

Kilstay

7

Laggantalluch Head

Barncorkrie

Drumnaglaur

Kirkmaiden

High
Drummore

B7041

Drummore

Killiness Point

Maryport

Cardryne

Cardrain

West
Cairngaan

RSPB

8

MULL OF GALLOWAY

0   1   2   3   4 miles
0 1 2 3 4 5 kilometres

A   B   C   D   E   F

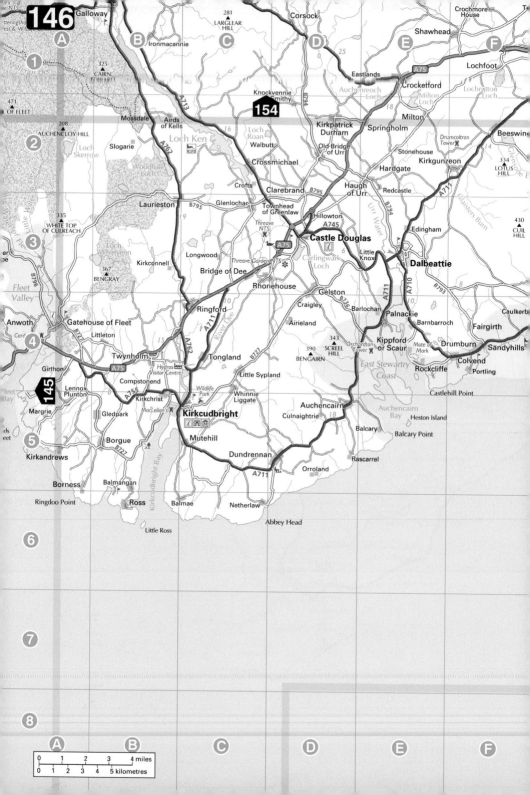

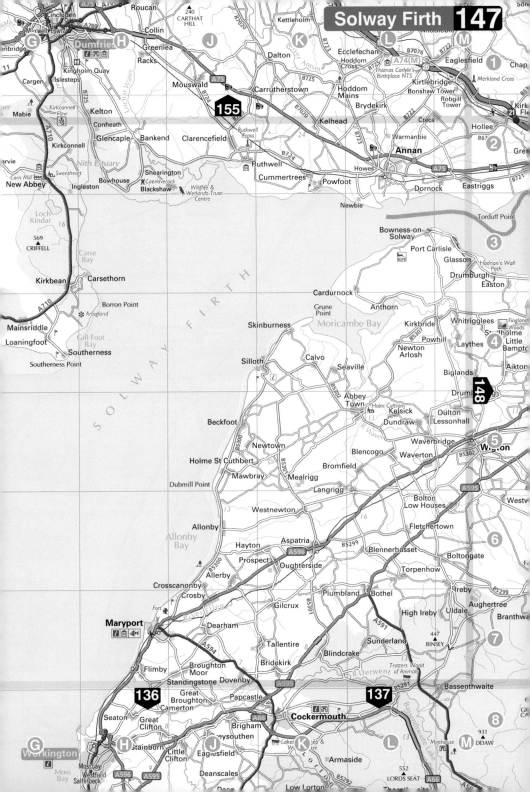

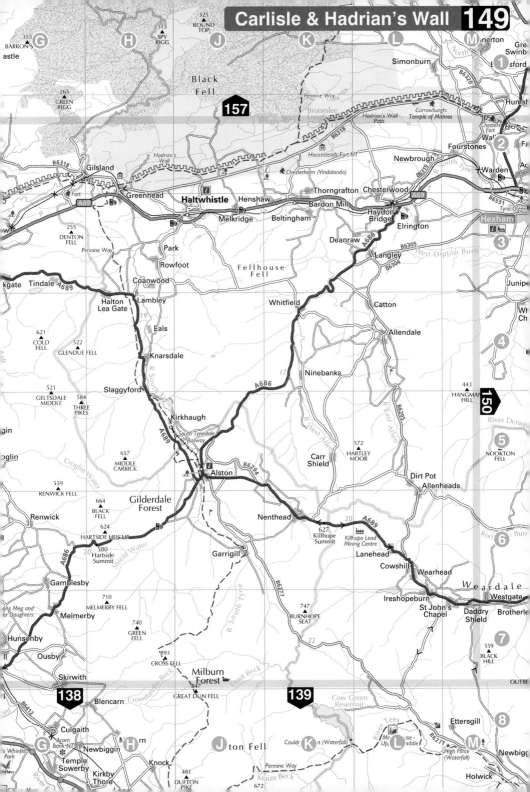

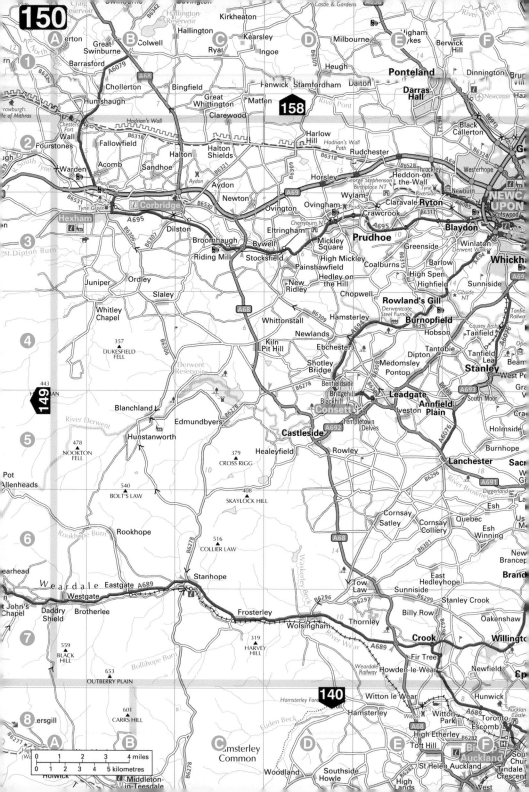

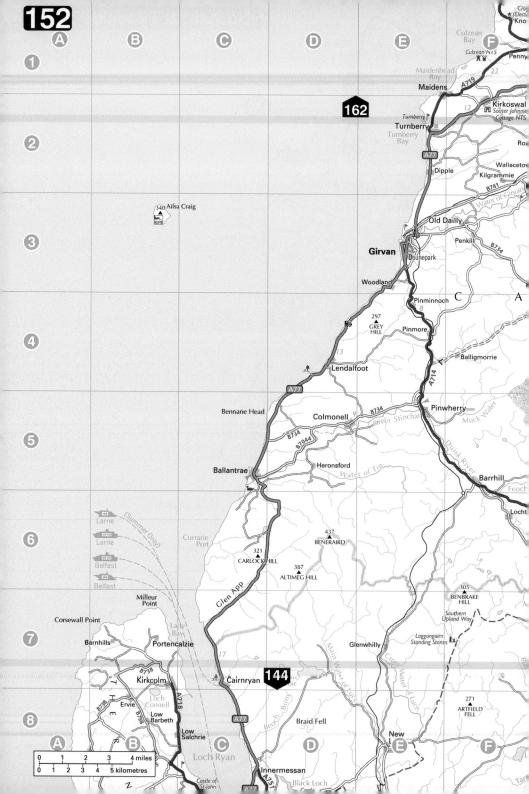

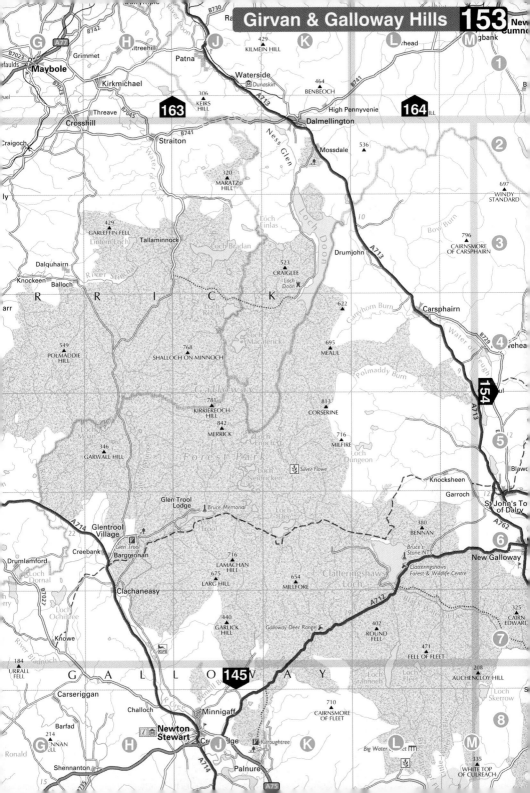

New Cumnock

Maybole

Grimmet

Kirkmichael

Threave

Crosshill

Craigoch

Straiton

Patna

Waterside

Dunaskin

306 KEIRS HILL

163

429 KILMEIN HILL

464 BENBEOCH

High Pennyvenie

Dalmellington

164

Ness Glen

Mossdale

536

697 WINDY STANDARD

320 MARATZ HILL

Loch Finlas

Loch Doon

Drumjohn

796 CAIRNSMORE OF CARSPHAIRN

3

429 GARLEFFIN FELL

Lintern Loch

Tallaminnock

Loch Bradan

523 CRAIGLEE

Loch Doon

Carsphairn

Dalquhairn

Knockeen

Balloch

R   R   I   C   K

Loch Recar

Loch Macaterick

622

695 MEAUL

Carnyhorn Burn

549 POLMADDIE HILL

768 SHALLOCH ON MINNOCH

Polmaddy Burn

154

Galloway

781 KIRRIEREOCH HILL

842 MERRICK

813 CORSERINE

346 GARWALL HILL

Loch Moan

Loch Enoch

Forest Park

716 MILFIRE

Loch Dungeon

Loch Neldricken

Silver Flowe

Knocksheen

Garroch

Glen Trool Lodge

Bruce Memorial

Loch Dee

380 BENNAN

St John's Town of Dalry

Glentrool Village

Glen Trool

Bruce's Stone NTS

A762

New Galloway

Creebank

Bargrennan

716 LAMACHAN HILL

Clatteringshaws Loch

Clatteringshaws Forest & Wildlife Centre

6

Drumlamford

Loch Dornal

Clachaneasy

675 LARG HILL

654 MILLFORE

325 CAIRN EDWARD

Loch Ochiltree

Knowe

440 GARLICK HILL

Galloway Deer Range

402 ROUND FELL

7

184 URRALL FELL

G   A   L   L   O   W   A   Y

471 FELL OF FLEET

208 AUCHENCLOY HILL

Carseriggan

145

Loch Grannoch

Loch Fleet

Loch Skerrow

214 GENNAN FELL

Challoch

Minnigaff

Barfad

Ronald

Shennanton

Newton Stewart

Kirroughtree

710 CAIRNSMORE OF FLEET

Big Water of Fleet

Cree Bridge

335 WHITE TOP OF CULREACH

Palnure

A75

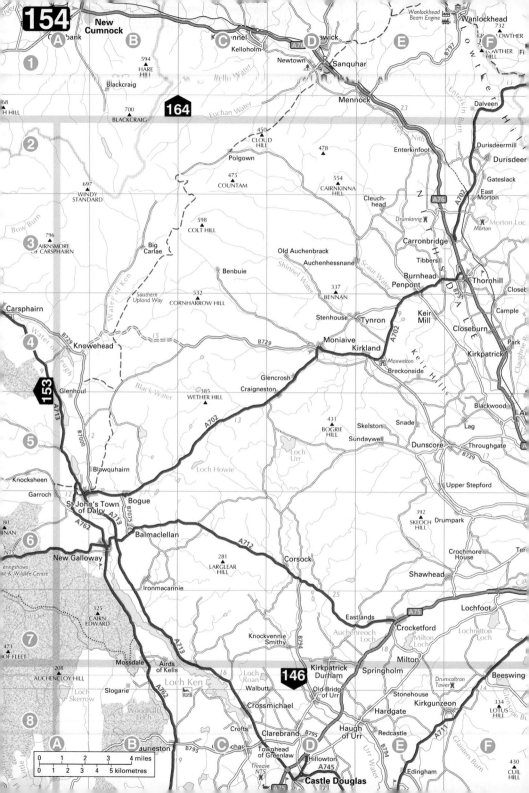

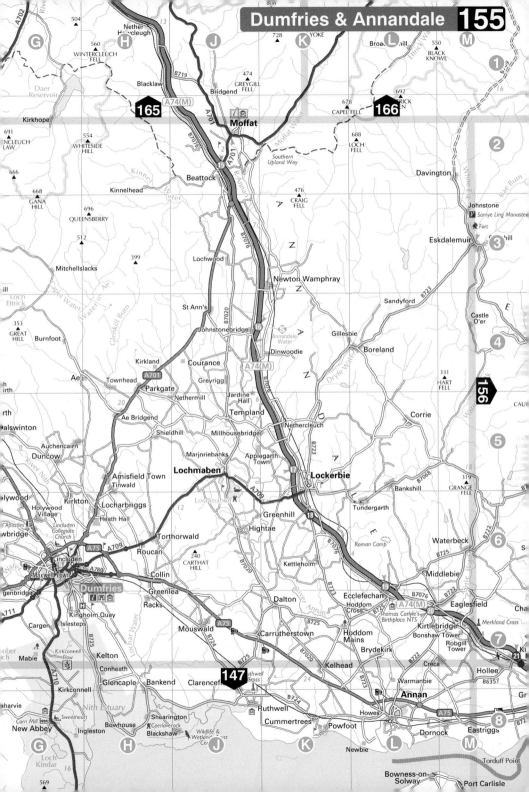

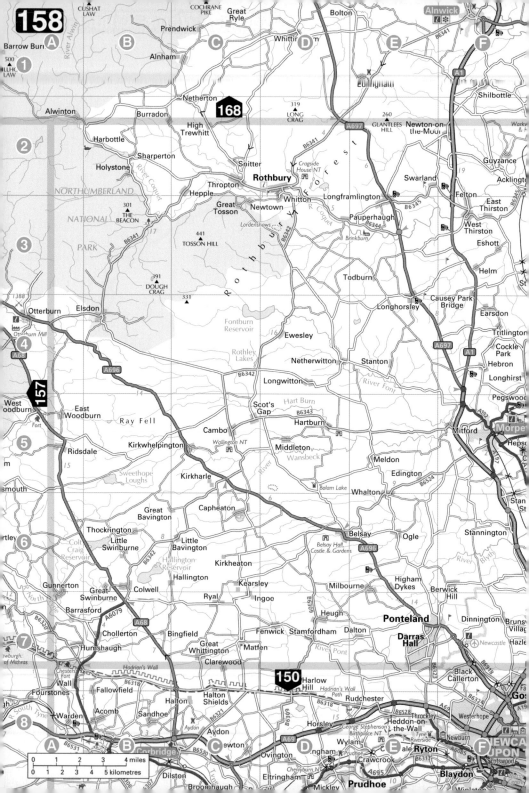

G H J K L M

1
2
3
4
5
6
7
8

Seaton Point
Lesbury
Alnmouth
A1068
Alnmouth Bay

169

Warkworth
Castle
Heritage
Amble
Coquet Island
Gloster Hill
High
Hauxley
Radcliffe
Togston
Broomhill
South
Broomhill
Red Row
Druridge Bay
West
Chevington
Druridge Bay
North Northumberland
Heritage Coast
bswood
Widdrington
Widdrington
Station
Cresswell
Ulgham
A1068
Ellington
Beacon Point
Woodhorn
A189
Ashington
A197
Hirst
Bothal
Wansbeck
Riverside
Newbiggin-by-the-Sea
A196
Guide Post
Stakeford
oppington
Bedlington
B1331
B1331
A193
Cowpen
Blyth
ngton
168
Newsham
tion
A189
A192
oods
A192
A1061
New
Hartley
Seaton
Sluice
Cramlington
B1326
A193
Seaton
**Seaton
Delaval**
St Mary's Lighthouse
A19
Dudley
Wide
Open
Earsdon
Monkseaton
**Whitley
Bay**
A1056
Killingworth
Shiremoor
Cullercoats
Tynemouth
Forest Hall
Rising
Sun
151
Bergen
Göteborg
Haugesund
IJmuiden
Kristiansand
Stavanger
forth
South
Gosforth
Longbenton
Willington
**North
Shields**
**SOUTH
SHIELDS**
Jesmond
Wallsend
Heaton
Walker
Quay
Ferry
Terminal
Tyne Tunnel
Westoe
A183
STLE
YNE
Byker
Jarrow
A194
Marsden
Bay
Elswick
Heburn
Monkton
Marsden
Souter Lighthouse NT
L M
Felling
Wardley
West
Boldon
Souter Point
Cleadon
Whitburn

G H J K

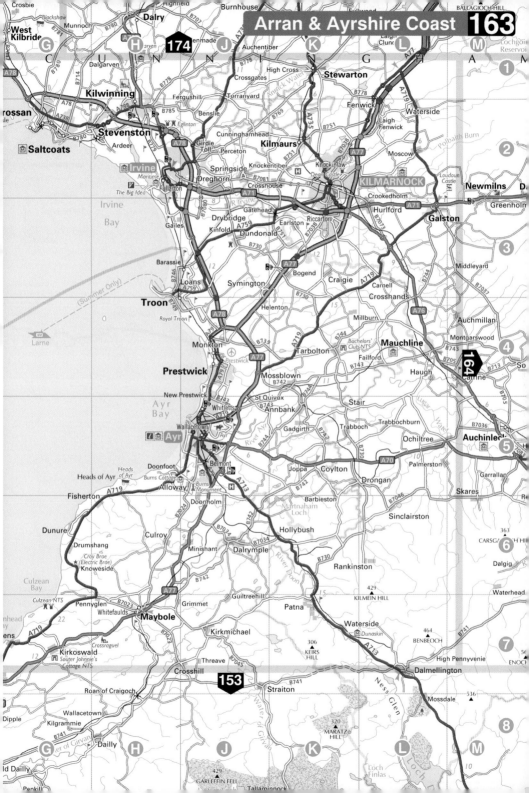

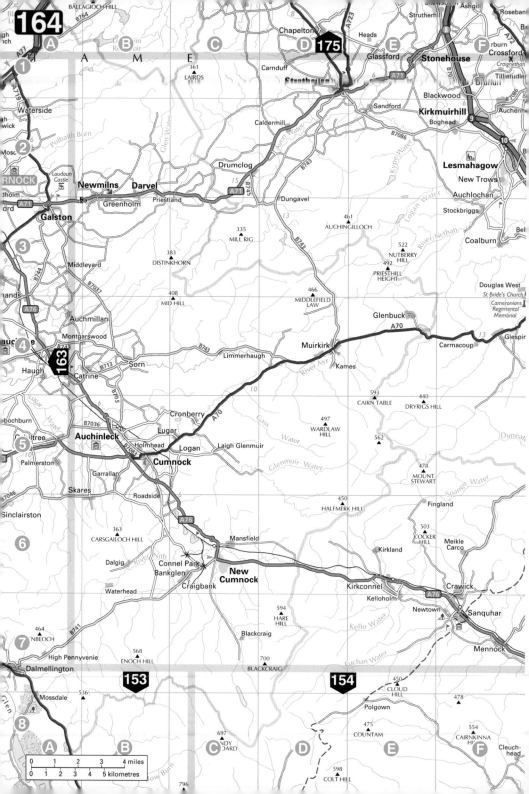

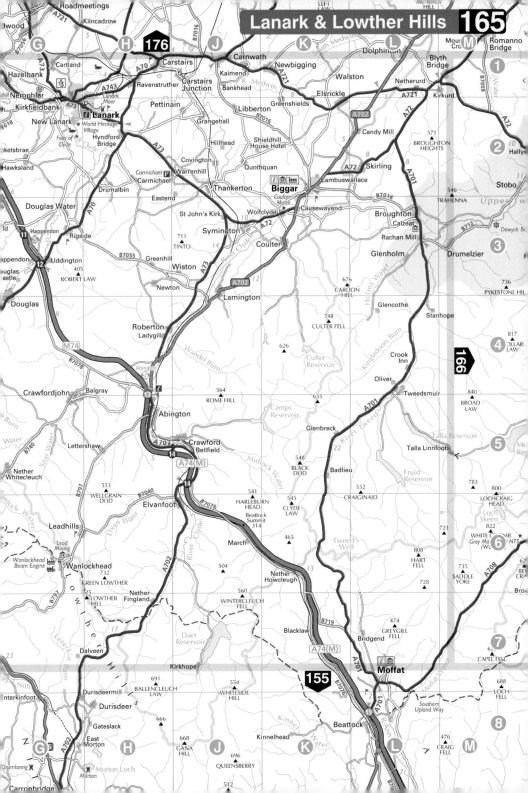

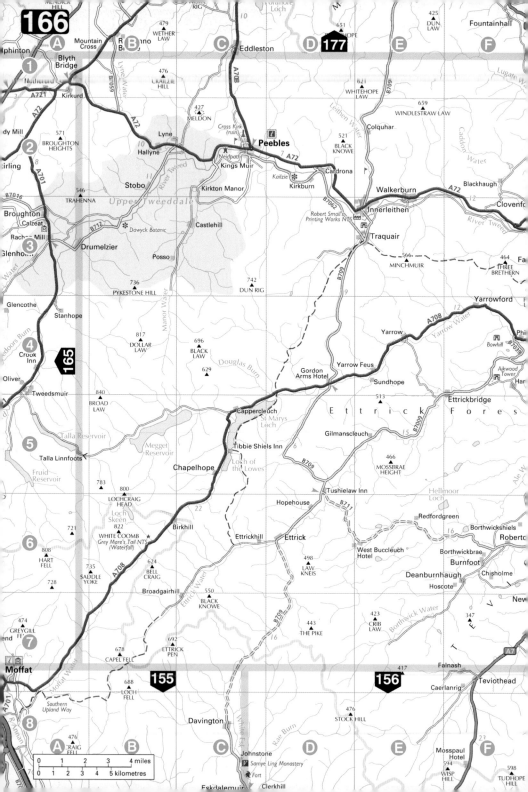

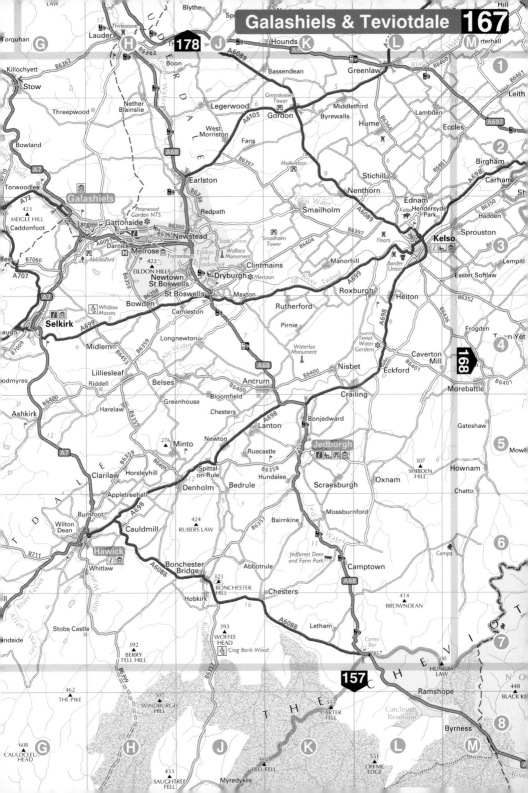

CAUSEWAY
FLOODED
AT HIGH TIDE

HOLY ISLAND

Holy
Island
Lindisfarne NT
Lindisfarne
Priory
Castle Point
Guile Point

Beal

enwick

ckton

Longstone
Lighthouse

FARNE
ISLANDS
NT
Staple
Sound
Inner
Sound
North Northumberland
Heritage Coast

Budle
Bay
Bamburgh
B1342
Bamburgh
B1340

Belford
B6349

B6348

B1341
Lucker

Warenford

Seahouses

North Sunderland

Beadnell

A1
Newstead
Chathill
Tughall
Ellingham
Preston
Swinhoe
B1340
Beadnell
Bay

Preston
Pele Tower
Brunton
Newton-by-the-Sea
Christon
Bank
Embleton
Embleton
Bay

267
CATERAN
HILL

North
Charlton
Falloden
B6341
Dunstanburgh
NT

Old Bewick
B6346

Ditchburn
South
Charlton
B1341
Rock
Dunstan
Craster

New
ewick

Eglingham
Rennington
Stamford
B1339
Howick
Hall
Howick

Beanley
B6346
Cullernose Point

owburn

Longhoughton

River Aln
Denwick
Boulmer

Bolton
Alnwick
Seaton Point

ngham
B6341
7
Lesbury

Alnmouth

Alnmouth
Bay

Edlingham
A1
Shilbottle
A1068
8

9
NG
AG
A697
GLANTLEES
HILL
Newton-on-
the-Moor
Warkworth Castle
& Hermitage
Warkworth
159

B6344
Cragside
House NT

Amble
Coquet Island

Gloster Hill
Swarland
Guyzance
Togston
High
Hauxley
Radcliffe

ramlington
B634
Felton
Acklington
Broomhill

Pauperhaugh
East
Thirston
South
Broomhill
Red Row
Druridge Bay

Brinkburn
West
Thirston
Eshott

ISLAY

Dubh Eilean
ORON

Nave Island
Ardnave Point
Gortantao Point

Ton Mhòr
Kilnave
Eilean Mòr
Sanaigmore
Loch Gorr
Rudha Lamanais
Lecht Gruinart
RSPB
B8018
B8017
Saligo Bay
Gruinart
Gleann Mòr
Loch Gorm
Coul Point
Machir Bay
Sunderland
Kilchoman
B8018
A847
Loch Indaal
Bruichladdich
Kilchiaran Bay
Bowmore
15
R H I N N S   O F   I S L A Y
Port Charlotte
231
BEINN TART A'MHILL
River Lagga
Lossit Bay
Nereabolls
Duich R
A846
Rudha na Faing
A847
Portnahaven
Port Wemyss
Orsay
Islay
RHINNS POINT
Laggan Bay
Rudha Mòr

165
MAOL BU
THE OA
Lower Killeyan
Risabus

0 1 2 3 4 miles
0 1 2 3 4 5 kilometres

Scalasaig
B8086
Garvard
Oronsay
Eilean
Ghurdmail
Rudha
Bàn

G **H** **180** **J** **181** **K** **L** **M**

Corpach Bay
Lussa River
466 ▲ BEINN BHREAC
Glen Grundale
1

Shian Bay
453 ▲ RAINBERG MÒR
Ardlussa
Lussa Point
A846
2

J U R A
Loch Righ Mòr
Rudh' ant-Sàilein
Rudha' a' Mhàil

Loch Tarbert

Keills Cho

Rudha Bholsa
363 ▲ SGARBH BREAC
506 ▲ SCRINADLE
398 ▲ BEINN TARSUINN
St Cormacs Chapel
Danr Islan
3

J u r a   F o r e s t
Bunnahabhain
316 ▲ GUIR-BHEINN
Loch a' Chnuic Bhric
784 ▲ BEINN AN OIR
734 ▲
Kilmory Knap Chapel
Kilmory Bay

Port Askaig
Kiells
Feolin Ferry
P a p s   o f   J u r a
J u r a
24
A846
Poin Knap
4

Ballygrant
Loch Finlagan
Finlaggan
Loch Ballygrant
Loch Lossit
560 ▲ GLASS BHEINN
529 ▲ DUBHA BHEINN
Keils
Craighouse
342 ▲ BRAT BHEINN
Small Isles
A846
172
Kilberry Sculptured St
Kilberry Hea
Keppoch Po
T
5

A846
Bridgend
Gartachossan
266 ▲ BEINNE DUBH
Cabrach
Rudha na Gaillich
172

Am Fraoch Eilean
Brosdale Island
Rudha na Tràille
Kilennan Burn
429 ▲ SGÒRR NAM FAOILEANN
471 ▲
McArthur's Head
Port Askaig - Kennacraig
6

454 ▲ BEINN URARAIDH
Loch Uraraidh
490 ▲ BEINN BHEIGEIR
Rudha Liath
Ardtalla
Claggain Bay
Kinerar
Tarbert
GIGHA
7

negedale
B8016
Kintour
Ardmore Point
Kildalton Cross
346 ▲ BEINN SHOLUM
Eilean a' Chuirn
Ardminish
Achamore
Rhunahaorine Point
8

G **H** **160** **J** **K** **L** **M**

Port en
A846
Ardbeg
Laphroaig
Texa
Lagavulin
Rudha na Gainn
Tayinloan
Cara
Kilnaughton Bay

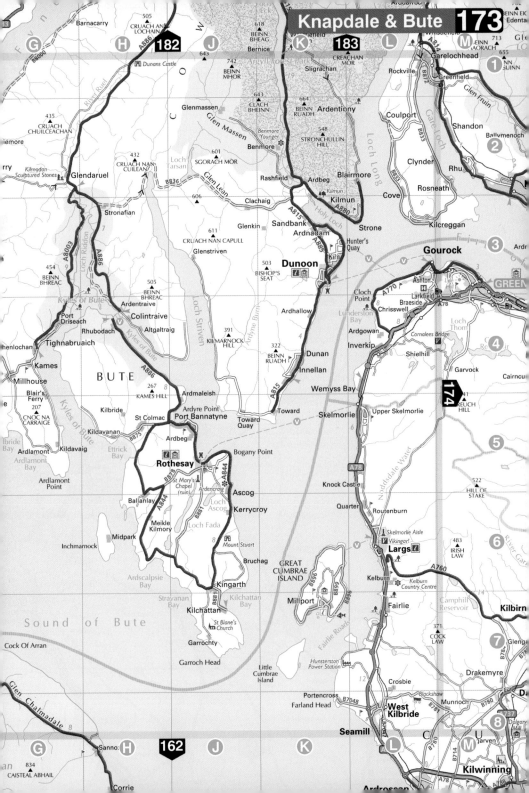

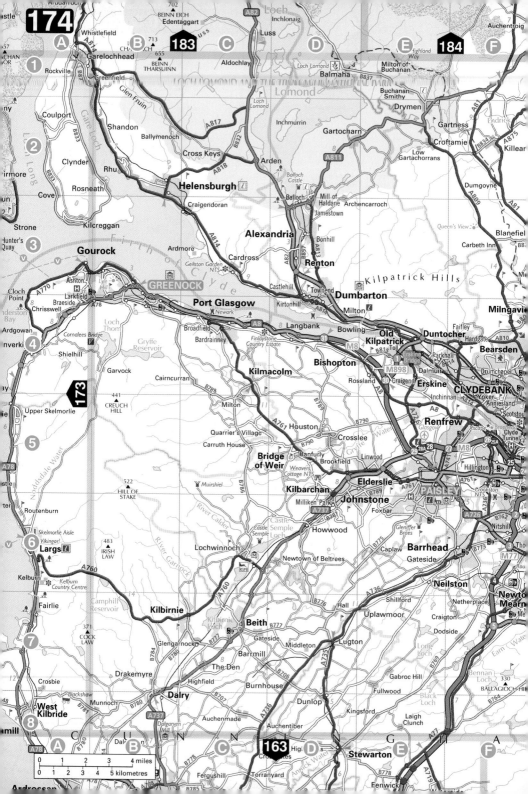

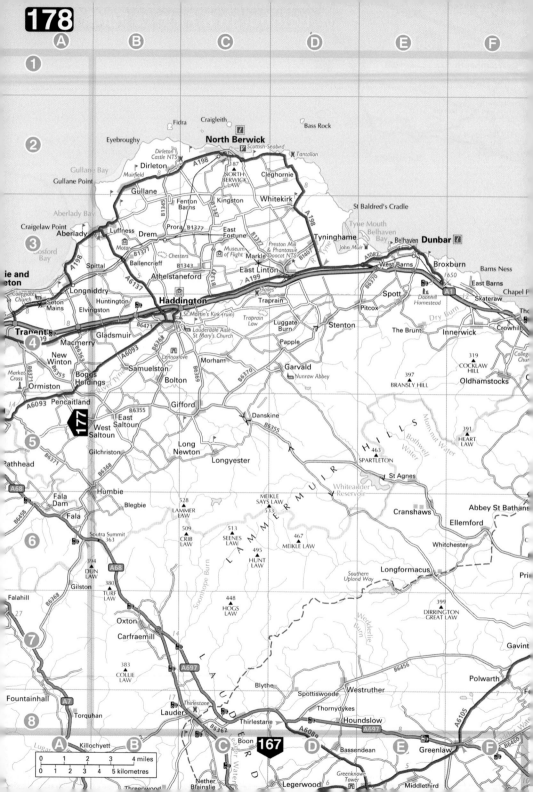

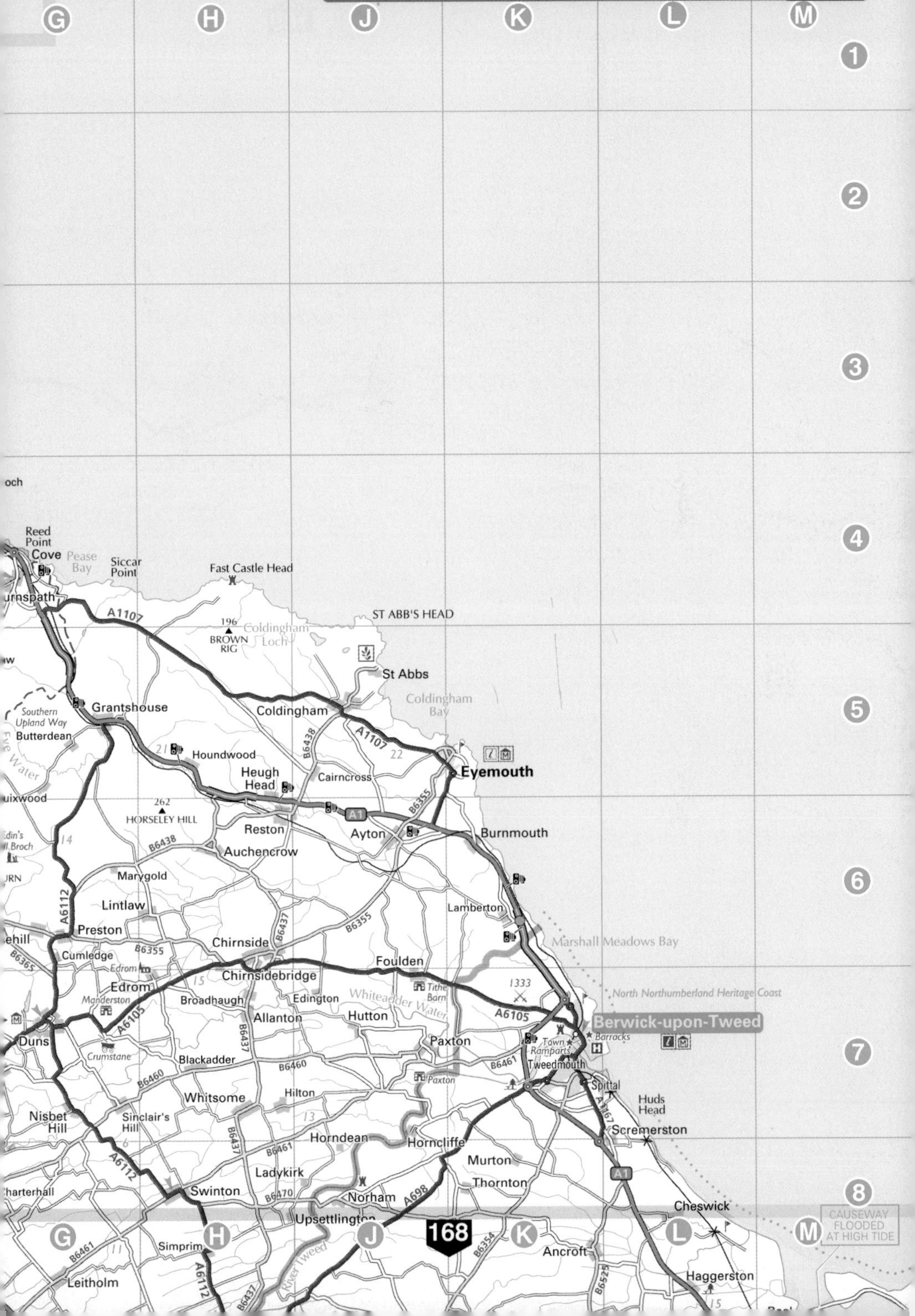

G H J K L M

1

2

3

4

Reed Point
Cove
Pease Bay
Siccar Point
Fast Castle Head
urnspath
A1107
196
BROWN RIG
Coldingham Loch
ST ABB'S HEAD
Southern Upland Way
Grantshouse
Butterdean
St Abbs
Coldingham
Coldingham Bay
Eye Water
Houndwood
A1107
22
5
Heugh Head
Cairncross
Eyemouth
uixwood
262
HORSELEY HILL
B6438
Reston
Ayton
B6355
A1
Burnmouth
din's
l.Broch
14
B6112
Auchencrow
Marygold
B6438
Lamberton
6
JRN
Lintlaw
B6437
B6355
Preston
ehill
Cumledge
B6355
Chirnside
Marshall Meadows Bay
Edrom
15
Chirnsidebridge
Foulden
North Northumberland Heritage Coast
Monderston
Broadhaugh
Edington
Tithe Barn
1333
Berwick-upon-Tweed
Duns
A6105
Allanton
Hutton
Whiteadder Water
A6105
Barracks
7
Crumstane
B6437
Paxton
Town Ramparts
Tweedmouth
Blackadder
B6460
Hilton
Paxton
B6461
Spittal
Whitsome
13
Huds Head
Nisbet Hill
Sinclair's Hill
Horndean
Horncliffe
Murton
Scremerston
6
B6437
B6461
Ladykirk
Thornton
A1
8
harterhall
A6112
Swinton
B6470
Norham
A698
Cheswick
CAUSEWAY FLOODED AT HIGH TIDE

G H J **168** K L M

Simprim
Leitholm
B6461
Upsettlington
A6112
B6437
River Tweed
Ancroft
Haggerston
B6525

A B C D **189** E F

1

Bac Mòr or Dutchmans Cap

eag

Little Colonsay

Staffa

Inch Kenneth
Inchkenneth Chapel
(ruin)

Fingal's Cave

Loch na Keal
Isle of Mull

2

491
CREACH BHEINN

Fossil Tree

3

IONA

Rudha nan Cearc

Loch

Abbey
Baile Mòr

Kintra

Loch na
Lathaich

Macleans Cross

Fionnphort

Aridhglas

A849

Sound of Iona

St Columba
Exhibition
Centre

Bunessan

376
CRUAC
MIN

Loch Assapol

ROSS OF MULL

4

Soa Island

Erraid

Uisken

Ardchiavaig

Rudha
Braithre

Rudha
Ardalanish

Torran Rocks

5

6

Eilean
Dubh

Balnahard

Rudh' a' C

Kiloran Bay

7

COLONSAY

Kiloran

Kilchattan

B8085

Scalasaig

B8086

B8085

8

Machrins

Garvard

A B C D **171** E F

0   1   2   3   4 miles
0   1   2   3   4   5 kilometres

Dubh Eilean

Oronsay

Rudha
Bàn

Colo

ISLE
OF
MULL

190

Eorsa

G

BEINN A' GHRAIG

H

Loch na Keal

B8035 17

Inahard

Macquarie Mausoleum

NAN LUS

J

BEINN MHEADHO

K

766
DUN DA
GHAOITHE

Craignure

Mull & West Highland
Narrow Gauge Railway

Ridire

Kilch

M

Mull West Duart
Bay Point

Duart

Duart

Torosay Castle

Lochdonhead

Lochdon

Gorten

Loch Don

Grass Point

KERRE

1

2

966
BEN
MORE

704
CRUACHAN
DEARG

Aird of
Kinloch

A849

Pennycross

Pennyghael

cridain

14

717
BEN
BUIE

698
BEN CREACH

A849

Loch-Fuaran

503
BEINN NA
CROISE

Leidle Water

247
CARN
BAN

Strathcoil

Croggan

Rudha Seanach

Barrnacarry Bay

3

376
BEINN
CHREAGACH

Carsaig

Malcolm's
Point

Lochbuie

Rudha
Dubh

Loch Buie

377
DRUIM
FADA

Loch
Uisg

337
MAOL
BAN

FIRTH

OF

LORNE

Insh
Island

Clachan

Clachan-Seil

Ellanbeich

Easdale

SEIL
Easdale

Balvicar

B844

B8003

4

Colonsay Oban

Cuan Ferry Village

Garbh Eileach

Cullipool
House

Torsay
Island

Degnish

Loch Mel

LUING

Arduai

Arduaine
Garden NTS

5

GARVELLACHS
Monastery & Beehive Cells

Eileach
an Naoimh

Eilean
Dubh Mòr

LUNGA

Toberonochy

SHUNA

Sound of Luing

Shuna Sound

Shuna
Point

Craobh
Haven

Craigd

182

Ardfe

6

Scarba, Lunga
and the
Garvellachs

SCARBA

448
CRUACH SCARBA

En M

En

Gulf of Corryvreckan

Aird

Loch Craignish

B8002

dha

Glengarrisdale
Bay

295
CRUACH NA
SEILCHEIG

Craignish Point

Island
Macaskin

Clockav

Wood
Circle

Ri Cru

7

Glendebadel Bay

JURA

Lealt Burn

364
BEN
GARRISDALE

Loch Crinan

Crinan

Kilmahumaig

Bellanoch

Poltal

B8025

8

Corpach Bay

G

H

171

460
BEINN
BHREAC

J

len Grundale

Lossa River

K

L

172

M

Barnluasgan

Carsaig Bay

G H **192** J K L M

1

Glen Kinglass
Glen Lochay

794

988
BEINN EUNAICH

648
BEINN DONACHAN

771
BEINN UDLAIDH

Glen Orchy
River Orchy
B8074

River Lochy

818
BEINN CHAORACH

937
BEINN CHEATHAICH

Tyndrum
A82
Strath Fillan

2

Ben Lui

Loch Lubhair
A85
Do

Kilchurn
B8077
awe
A819
Stronmilchan
Inverlochy
A85
Glen Lochy
Upper Kinchrackine
Dalmally

1130
BEN LUI

1028
BEN OSS
977
BEINN DUBHCHRAIG

Inverherive Hotel

Glen Fallloch

Crianlarich
Glen

1171
BEN MORE

3

636

739

LOCH LOMOND AND THE TROSSACHS
NATIONAL PARK

West Highland Way

1164
STOBINIAN

★ Falls of Falloch

947
BEINN BHUIDHE

Glenfyne Lodge

645
MAOL BREAC

Inverarnan
A82

946
BEINN A' CHROIN

LOCH LOMOND AND THE TROSSACHS

4

Glen Shira
Lochan Shira

658
CLACHAN HILL

Glen Fyne

Ardlui

NATIONAL PARK

865
STOB A' CHOIN

747
MEALL MÒR

184

5

Cairndow
Glen Kinglas

Ardkinglas Woodland Garden

942
BEN VORLICH

Loch Sloy

Inveruglas

Stronachlachar

Loch Katrine

Loch Fyne
Ardno

St Catherines
A815

B839

1011
BEN IME

912
BEINN AN LOCHAIN
Rest and be thankful
B828

Glen Croe
A83

881
THE COBBLER

925
BEINN NARNAIN

Succoth

416
CRUACH TAIRBEIRT

Tarbet

Inversnaid Hotel
Loch Arklet

Queen Elizabeth
Forest Park

633
CRUINN A' BHEINN

700
BEINN BHREAC

6

565
CRUACH NAN CAPULL

845
BEN DONICH

Ardgartan

Arrochar

Loch Long

973
BEN LOMOND

Loch Chon

Kinlochard
Loch

Argyll Forest Park

661
BEN REACH

Corrow
Lochgoilhead

Douglas Pier

Glen Douglas

Rowardennan Lodge

Queen Elizabeth
Forest Park

7

779
BEINN BHEULA

Invernoaden

Loch Goil

734
DOUNE HILL

Inverbeg

Rowardennan Hotel

596
BEINN UIRD

586
BEN VRACKIE

River Cur
A815

Carrick Castle

Arddarroch

Portincaple

702
BEINN EICH
Edentaggart

Glen Luss

Inchlonaig

Luss
A82

Loch

618
BEINN BHEAG
Bernice

Whistlefield Inn

657
CREACHAN

Whistlefield

BEINN CHAORACH

713

655

Loch Lomond

LOCH LOMOND AND THE TROSSACHS NATIONAL PARK

8

643
CLACH BHEINN

664
BEINN

G **173** H
Sligr
Rockville
B872

Garelochhead
Greenfield
Glen Fruin

BEINN THARSUINN

K **174** L
Aldoch
Balmaha

M
Milton of Buchanan
Buchanan Smithy
Drym

Ardentinny

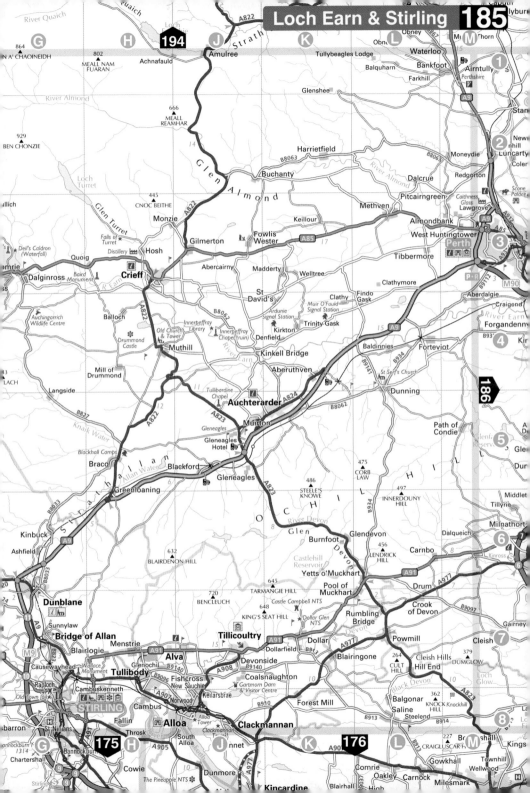

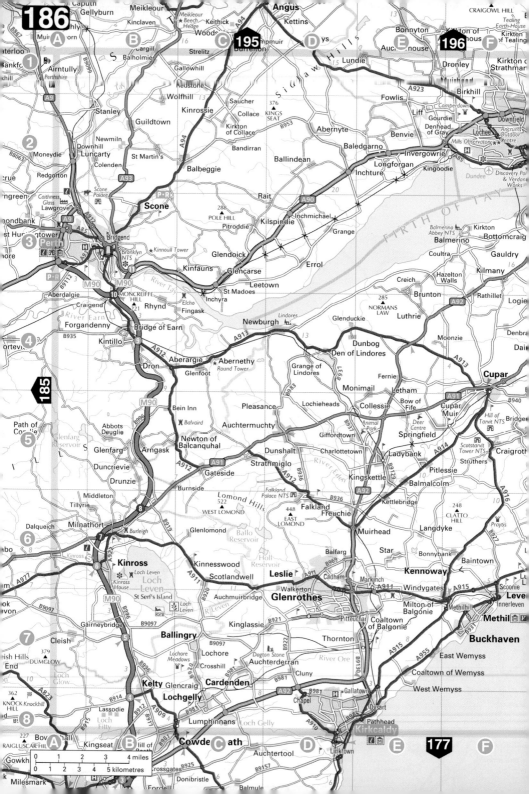

Arnabost

Grishipoll
Clabhach

Loch
Cliad

Hogh Bay   Ballyhaugh   Arin

Totronald

Feall
Bay   Arileod   Acha

Uig

Friesland
Bay

RSPB

Calgary Point   Crossapol
Bay   Rudha
Fàsachd

Gunna

Loch Breacacha

Rudha Port   Clachan   Caoles   Rudha Dubh
Bhiosd   Mor   Balephetrish   B8069
                        Bay
Loch   B8068   Ruaig
Bhasapoll
Haugh   Gott
Bay   Ballevullin   Cornoigmore   Kenovay   Bay

Kilkenneth   Tiree

                Moss   Heylipoll   B8065   Scarinish
Middleton
                    B8065   TIREE
Barrapoll   Crossapoll
        Loch a   Hynish Bay
        Phuill   B8067   Balemartine

                    Mannel
Rinn
Thorbhais
        Hynish

Balephuill
Bay

0   1   2   3   4 miles
0   1   2   3   4   5 kilometres

1

Eilean nan Each

MUCK

Port Mor

2

Ockle Point

Sanna Point

Sanna Bay

Sanna Bay

Kilmory

Branault

Ockle

3

Portuairk

Achnaha

436
MEALL NAN CON

ARDNAMU

Ardnamurchan Point

Achosnich

B8007

Loch
Mudle

Eilean Mòr

Bagh a Chaistell
(Castlebay)
Loch-Baghasdail
(Lochboisdale)

342
BEINN
NA SEILG

Kilchoan

527
BEN
HIANT

4

Rudha
Mòr

Rudha
Sgor-innis

Ormsaigmore

Mingary

Ardslignish

B8072

Bousd

Sorisdale

Coll – Oban

Ardmore Point

Sorne Point

190

Auliston Point

5

COLL

Quinish Point

Glengorm Castle

Tobermory

Calve Island

Drin

Eilean
Ornsay

Caliach Point

Dervaig

292
'S AIRDE
BEINN

Achnadrish Lodge

A848

6

Calgary

B8073

444
SPEINNE MÒR

Sou

10

Calgary Bay

Ensay

342
CARN MÒR

Loch Frisa

Treshnish Point

Burg

Glen Aros

Are

Rudh' a' Chaoil

Fanmore
CNOC AN DÀ CHINN

390

Glenaros House

7

Fladda

Ballygown

Eas Fors (Waterfall)

333
BEINN
NAN CÀRN

Killiechronan

B8035

Lunga

Gometra

19

Oskamull

B8073

Gruline

Macquari
Mausoleum

TRESHNISH
ISLES

ULVA

Loch Tuath

Loch na Keal,
Isle of Mull

Eorsa

Loch na Keal

591
BEINN A' GH.

8

Bac Mòr or Dutchmans Cap

Bac Beag

Little Colonsay

Inch Kenneth

Balnahard

966

71

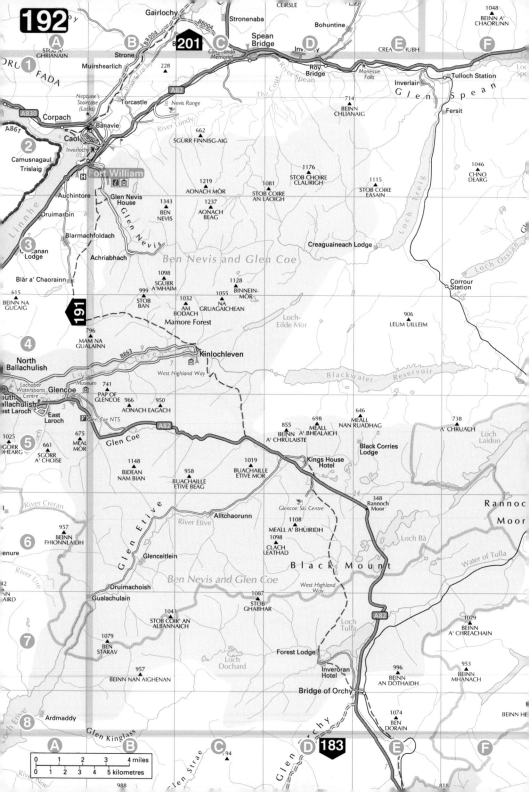

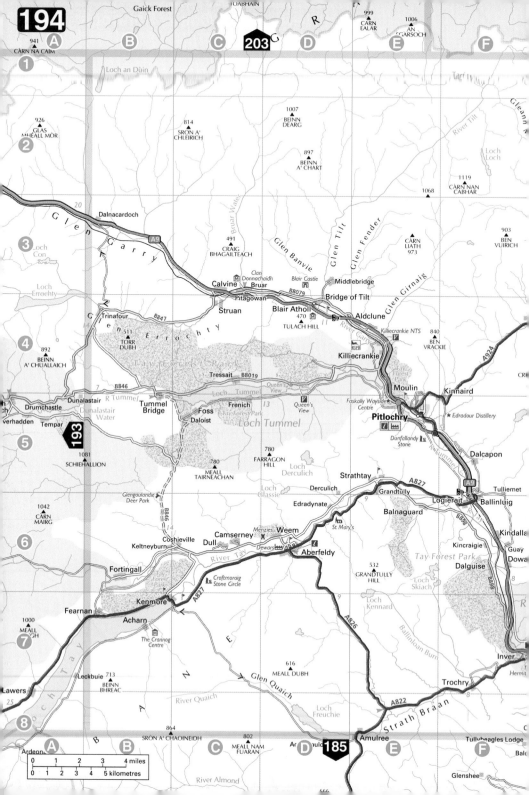

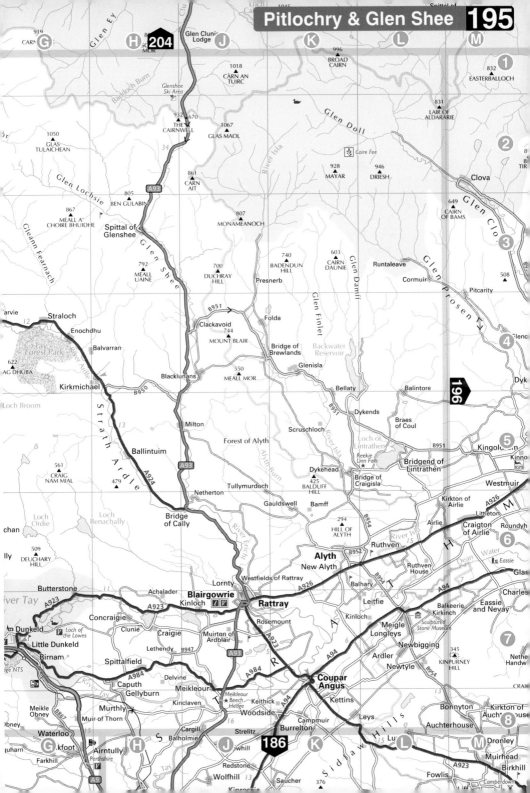

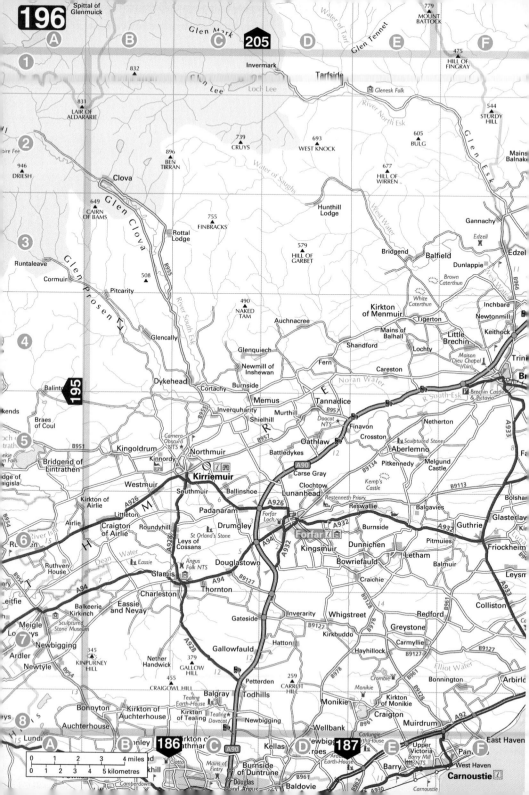

G H 206 J K L M

ter of Dye
Tannachie
Goosecruives
v Mill
465
GOYLE
HILL
Bervie Water
Crawton
454
Cairn
O'Mount
Drumlithie
Glenbervie
Mondynes
Temple
of Fiddes
Trelong
Bay
Catterline
414
FINELLA
HILL
Auchenblae
Kinneff
Fasque
Fordoun
Arbuthnott
Todhead Point
Pittarrow
Redmyre
B967
le
Fettercairn
B9120
Mains of
Haulkerton
Inverbervie
Bervie
Bay
Bogmuir
B974
Laurencekirk
Gourdon
Sauchieburn
B9120
Redford
Edzell
Woods
Luthermuir
Dykelands
Benholm
A90
B97A
A937
North
Esk
13
Johnshaven
tracathro Hospital
Marykirk
Bush
Logie Pert
Craigo
Lochside
Milton Ness
Logie
Morphie
St Cyrus
Hillside
A92
y
echin
Dun
A935
House of
Dun NTS
9
Montrose
Caledonian
Railway
Montrose
Basin
Scurdie Ness
Kinnaird
Castle
Barnhead
Ferryden
Maryton
Usan
rnell
A934
Craig
11
Westerton
132
WUDDY
LAW
Braehead
Boddin Point
nell
Lunan
Boysack
Lunan Bay
Inverkeilor
Red Head
Water
13
Chapelton
Cauldcots
Letham
Grange
A92
Marywell
Auchmithie
St Vigeans
Carlingheugh
Bay
t
Arbroath
The Deil's
Head

A **B** **C** **D** **E** **F**

1

2

3

4

5

6

7

8

Táisker

Eynort

BEINN
BHREAC

447

Loch Eynort

434
AN CRUACHIN
Glenbrittle House

Bualintur

Loch Brittle

CEANN M

Rudh' an Dùnain

So

CUIL

CANNA

210
CÀRN A' GHAILL

Garrisdale Point

A'Chill

Canna
Harbour

Sanday

Rudha
Shamhnan Insir

Sound of Canna

302
MULLACH
MÓR

R

A Bhrideanach

570
ORVAL

Kinloch

L
So

Oigh-sgeir

RÙM

810
ASKIVAL

763
SGÙRR NAN
GILLEAN

The Small Isles

Rudha nam
Meirleach

Sound o

Rudha an Fhas

So

Eilean
nan Each

189

MUCK

Por

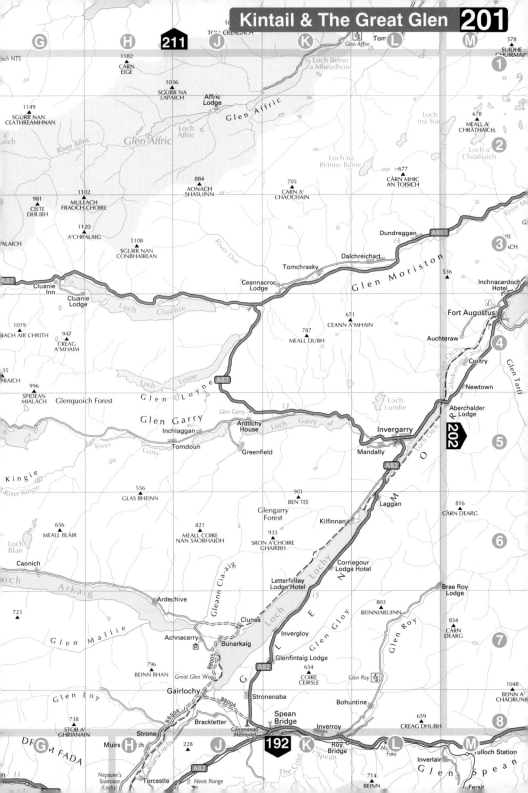

G **H** **211** **J** **K** **L** **M**

TOLL CREAGACH
Loch Affric
Tom

578
SUIDHE CHUIRMAIL **1**

1182
CARN EIGE

1149
SGURR NAN CEATHREAMHNAN

1036
SGURR NA LAPAICH

Affric Lodge

Glen Affric

Loch Beinn a Mheadhoin

Loch ma Stac

678
MEALL A' CHRÀTHAICH **2**

981
CISTE DHUBH

1102
MULLACH FRAOCH-CHOIRE

884
AONACH SHASUINN

Loch na Beinne Baine

Loch a' Chràthaich

a'aich

Loch Affric

705
CARN A' CHAOCHAIN

677
CARN MHIC AN TOISICH

River Affric

1120
A'CHRALAIG

1108
SGURR NAN CONBHAIREAN

River Doe

Dundreggan **A887** 16

Glen Moriston

505 **3**

ALAICH

Tomchrasky

Dalchreichart

536
Inchnacardoch Hotel

A87 Cluanie Inn

Ceannacroc Lodge

i

Cluanie Lodge

Loch Cluanie

671
CEANN A'MHAIN

Fort Augustus

1019
RACH AIR CHRITH

787
MEALL DUBH

Auchteraw **4**
Coiltry

947
CREAG A'MHAIM

Caledonian Canal

35
RAICH

Glen Loyne

River Oich

Newtown

Glen Tarff

996
SPIDEAN MIALACH

Loch Loyne

A87 13

Loch Lundie

Aberchalder Lodge

Glenquoich Forest

Glen Garry

Glen Garry

Invergarry

202 **5**

Inchlaggan

Ardochy House

Loch Garry

Mandally

K i n g i e

Tomdoun

Greenfield

A82

Laggan

816
CARN DEARG

River

Garry

556
GLAS BHEINN

901
BEN TEE

Kilfinnan

6

656
MEALL BLAIR

Loch Blair

821
MEALL COIRE NAN SAOBHAIDH

Glengarry Forest

935
SRON A'CHOIRE GHAIRBH

Corriegour Lodge Hotel

803
BEINN IARUINN

Brae Roy Lodge

834
CARN DEARG

Caonich

Letterfinlay Lodge Hotel

15

723

Arkaig

Ardechive

Gleann Cia-aig

Clunes

Loch Lochy

Invergloy

Glen Gloy

Glen Roy **7**

Achnacarry

Glen Mallie

Bunarkaig

Glenfintaig Lodge

654
COIRE CEIRSLE

Glen Roy

659
CREAG DHUBH

1048
BEINN A' CHAORUINN

796
BEINN BHAN

Great Glen Way

Gairlochy

B8004

Stronenaba

Bohuntine

8

738
STOB A' GHRIANAIN

Glen Loy

Brackletter

Commando Memorial

Spean Bridge

Inverroy

Inverlair

Mulloch Station

G **DF FADA** Muirs **H** Strone 228 **J** **192** **K** Roy Bridge **L** **M** Glen Spean

A82

Torcastle

Neptune's Staircase (Locks)

Nevis Range

714
BEINN

Fersit

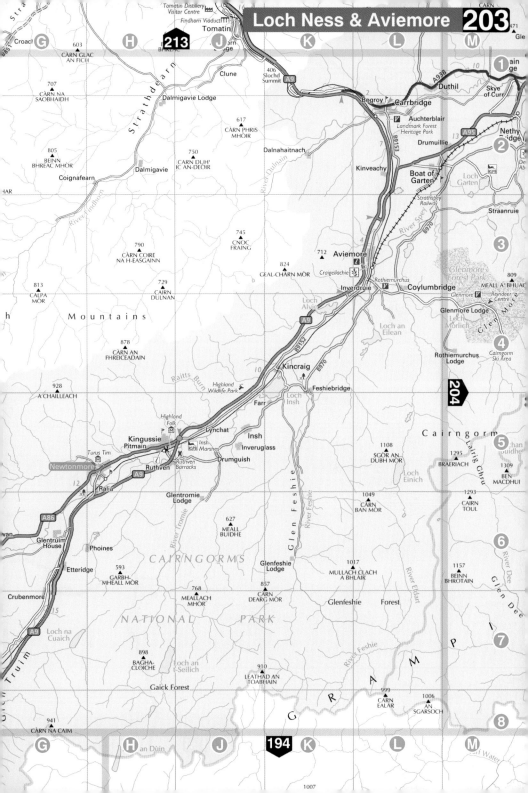

213

204

194

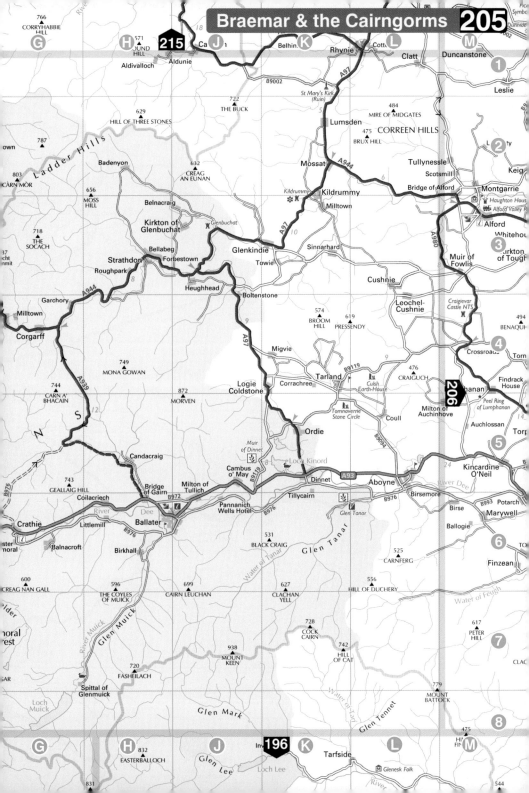

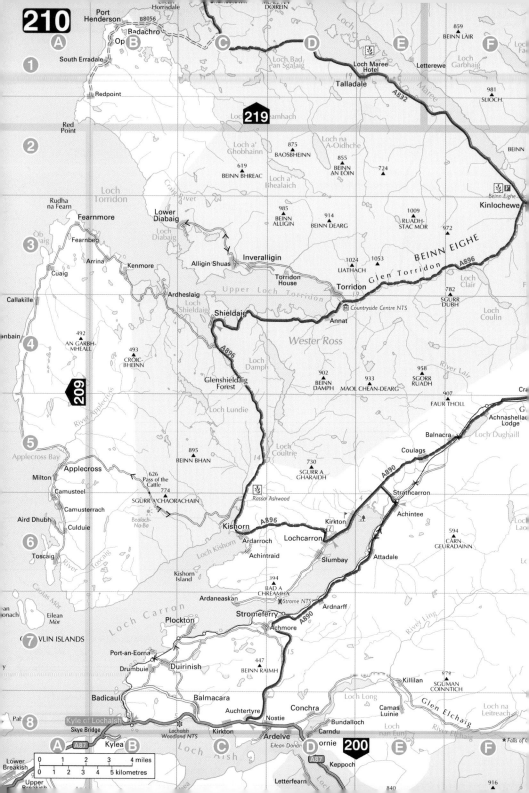

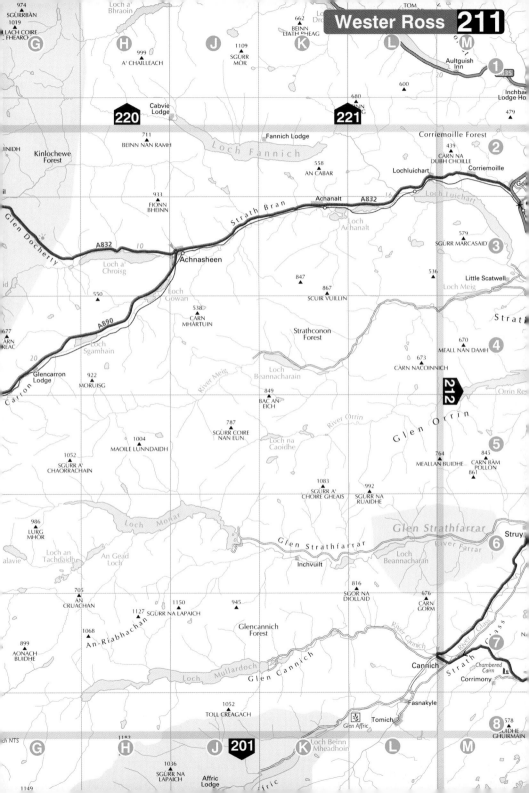

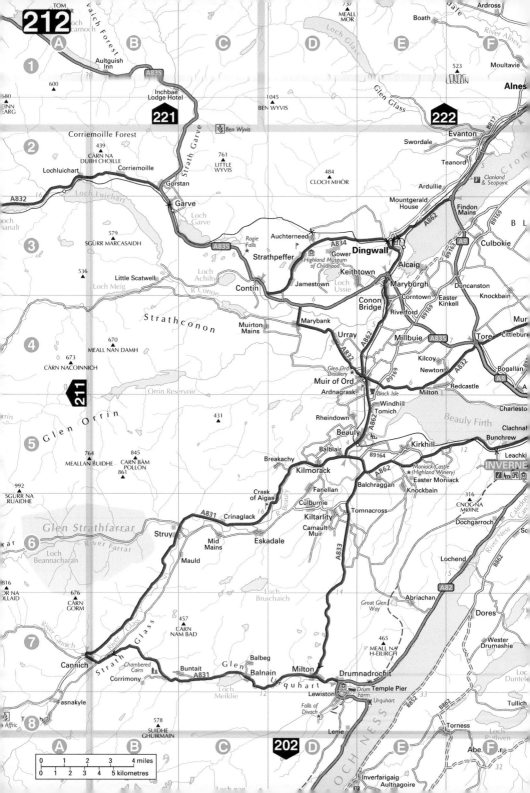

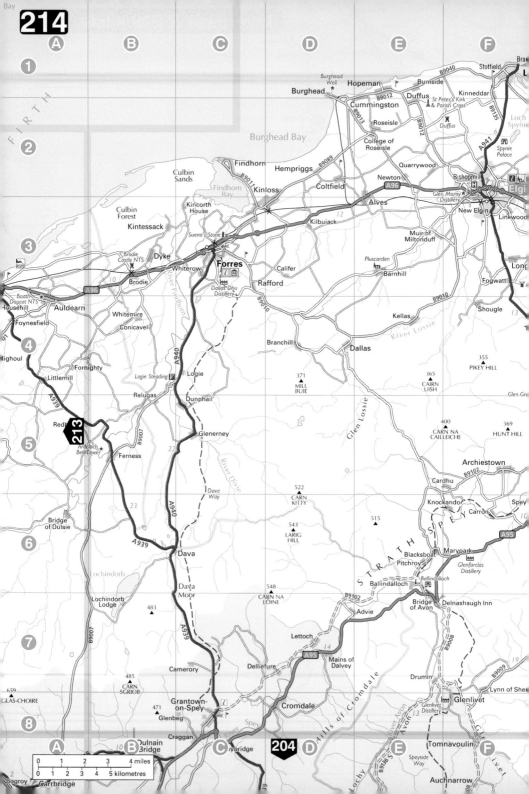

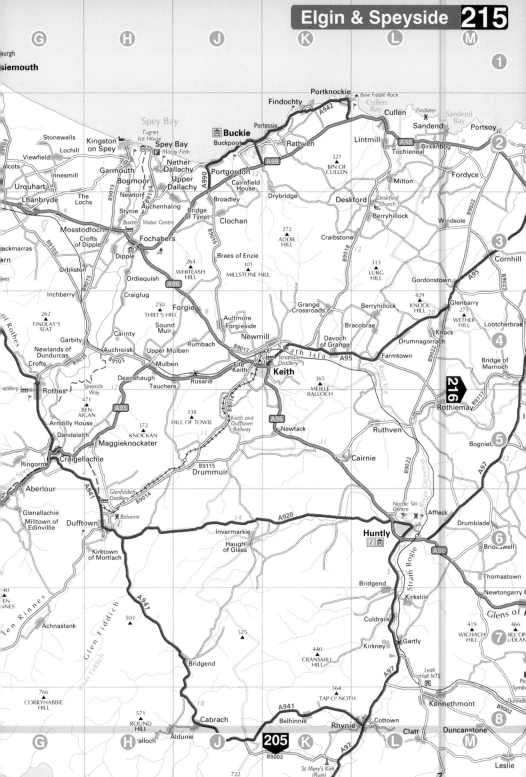

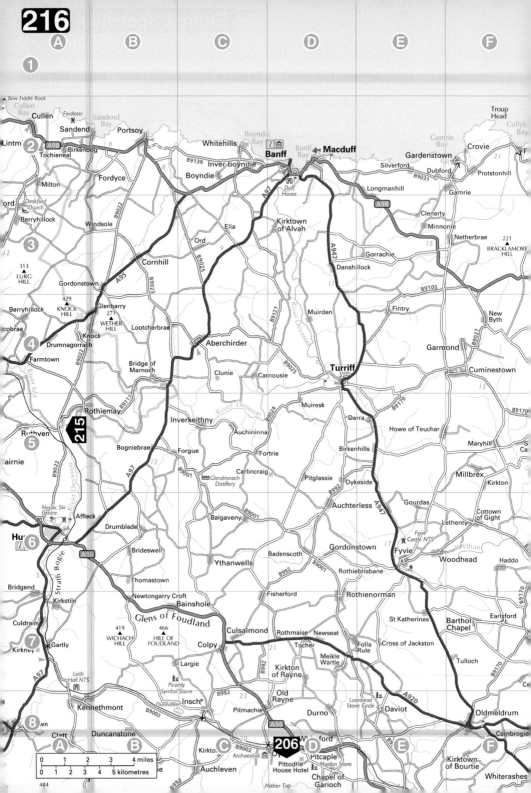

G H J K L M

① ② ③ ④ ⑤ ⑥ ⑦ ⑧

Rosehearty
Pittulie
Sandhaven
Lighthouse
Kinnaird Head
Fraserburgh
Craigiefold
Peathill
Percyhorner
Kirktown
Coburby
Pitblae
Mid Ardlaw
New Aberdour
Boyndlie
Memsie
Aberdour Bay
B9031
B9032
A90
A98
Cairnbulg
Inverallochy
Maggie's Hoosie
Whitelinks Bay
St Combs
B9033
Memsie Cairn
Rathen
Newburgh
Crofts of Savoch
Lonmay
234 WAUGHTON HILL
A981
Strichen
New Pitsligo
Bonnykelly
B9093
New Leeds
Leys
Crimond
Blackhill
Loch of Strathbeg
Rattray Head
A952
18
Denhead
Backfolds
Kirktown
St Fergus
A90
Fetterangus
Rora
New Deer
Maud
Deer Abbey
Dunshillock
Aden
Old Deer
Mintlaw
Longside
Inverugie
Buchanhaven
Peterhead
River Ugie
B9106
B9029
B9028
Blackhill of Clackriach
Bulwark
Stuartfield
Inverquhomery
A950
Peterhead Bay
Drymuir
Nethermuir
Knaven
Kinnadie
Millbreck
Clola
Nether Kinmundy
Little Dens
Hillhead of Cocklaw
Blackhill
Stirling
Buchan Ness
Boddam
Burnhaven
B9030
Cairnorrie
Brownhill
Auchnagatt
Inkhorn
Kinknockie
Lendrum Terrace
B9170
B9005
Methlick
Coldwells
Arthrath
Muirtack
Hatton
Longhaven
Bullers of Buchan
North Haven
A90
Auchiries
Slains
Cruden Bay
Ythanbank
Birness
Bogbrae
Chapel Hill
Bay of Cruden
Auchedly
Artrochie
Whinnyfold
The Skares
A948
A952
A975
Kinharrachie
Ythsie
Ellon
P R
Esslemont
Kirkton of Logie Buchan
Kirktown of Slains
Collieston
Altar Tomb of William Forbes
Pitmedden
Logierieve
A920
A90
Housieside
Forvie
B90
Udny Station
Woodland
Pettymuk
Cultercullen
Foveran
Newburgh
B9000

207

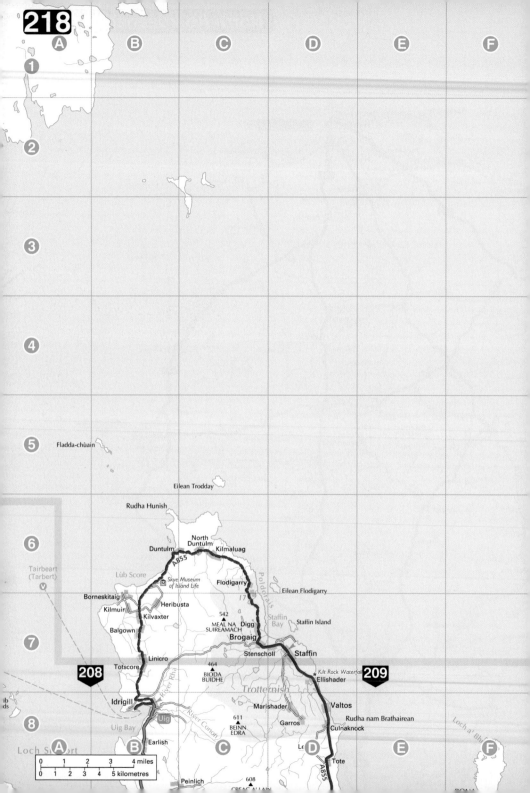

A   B   C   D   E   F

1

2

3

4

5

Fladda-chùain

6

7

8

Eilean Trodday

Rudha Hunish

North
Duntulm   Kilmaluag
Duntulm

A855

Skye Museum
of Island Life   Flodigarry

Lùb Score

Borneskitaig
Kilmuir   Heribusta
Kilvaxter
Balgown

Linicro
Totscore

Idrigill

Earlish

Tairbeart
(Tarbert)

542
MEAL NA   Digg
SUIREAMACH
Brogaig

Stenscholl   Staffin

464
BIODA
BUIDHE

Trotternish

611
BEINN
EDRA

Marishader

Garros

608

Eilean Flodigarry

Staffin
Bay   Staffin Island

Poldorais

Kilt Rock Waterfall
Ellishader

Valtos
Rudha nam Brathairean

Culnaknock

Le

Tote

A855

Loch a' Bhi

208

209

0   1   2   3   4 miles
0   1   2   3   4   5 kilometres

Loch S   ort

A   B   C   D   E   F

Peinlich

CREAC A'LAIN

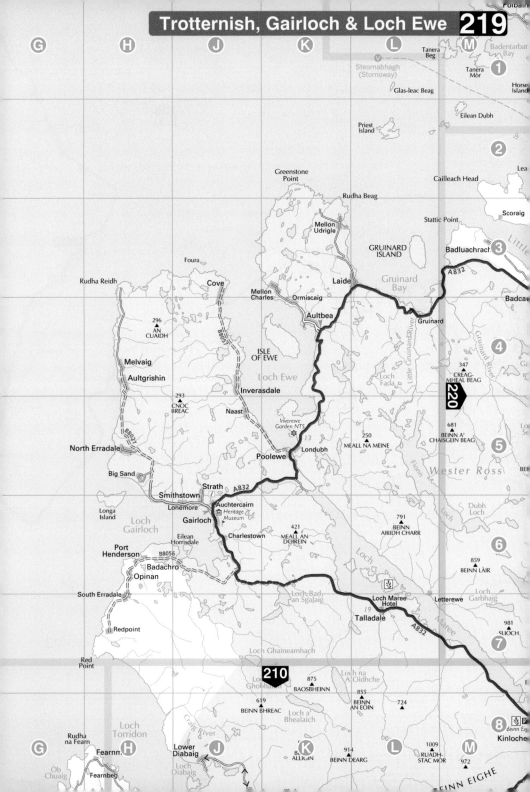

Polbain

G   H   J   K   L   M

Steornabhagh (Stornoway)

Tanera Beg
Tanera Mòr
Badentarbat Bay
1
Horse Island

Glas-leac Beag

Eilean Dubh
2
Lea

Priest Island

Cailleach Head
Scoraig

Greenstone Point

Rudha Beag

Stattic Point
Badluachrach **3**
Badca

Mellon Udrigle

GRUINARD ISLAND

A832

Foura

Cove

Laide

Gruinard Bay

Rudha Reidh

Mellon Charles
Ormiscaig

Gruinard

Little Gruinard River

Aultbea

4

296
AN CUAIDH

ISLE OF EWE

Loch Ewe

347
CREAG MHEAL BEAG

Gruinard River

Melvaig
Aultgrishin

220

Inverasdale

Loch Fada

250
MEALL NA MEINE

681
BEINN A' CHAISGEIN BEAG
5

293
CNOC BREAC

Naast

Inverewe Garden NTS

Wester Ross

B8021

North Erradale

Poolewe

Londubh

Fionn Loch

BE

Big Sand

Strath

A832

Dubh Loch
6

Longa Island

Loch Gairloch

Lonemore

Gairloch

Auchtercairn
Heritage Museum

791
BEINN AIRIDH CHARR

Smithstown

Charlestown

421
MEALL AN DOIREIN

859
BEINN LÀIR

Port Henderson

Eilean Horrisdale

B8056

Badachro

Opinan

Loch Bad an Sgalaig

Loch Maree Hotel

Letterewe
Garbhaig

7

981
SLIOCH

South Erradale

Talladale

A832

Loch Maree

Redpoint

Loch Ghaineamhach

Red Point

210

875
BAOSBHEINN

Loch na A'Oidhche

855
BEINN AN EOIN

724

8

Kinloche

Craig River

619
BEINN BHREAC

Loch a' Bhealaich

1009
RUADH-STAC MÒR

972

Rudha na Fearn

Fearnn.

Loch Torridon

Lower Diabaig

B
ALLIGIN

914
BEINN DEARG

BEINN EIGHE

Òb Chuaigh

Fearnbeg

Loch Diabaig

G   H   J   K   L   M

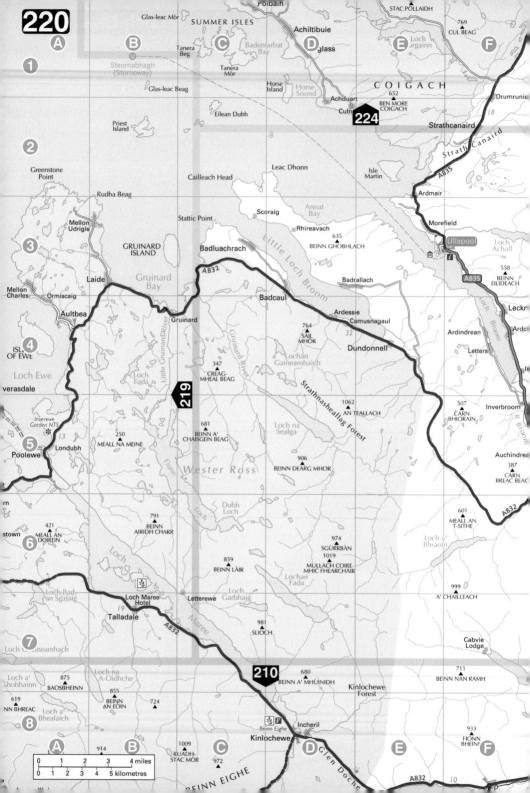

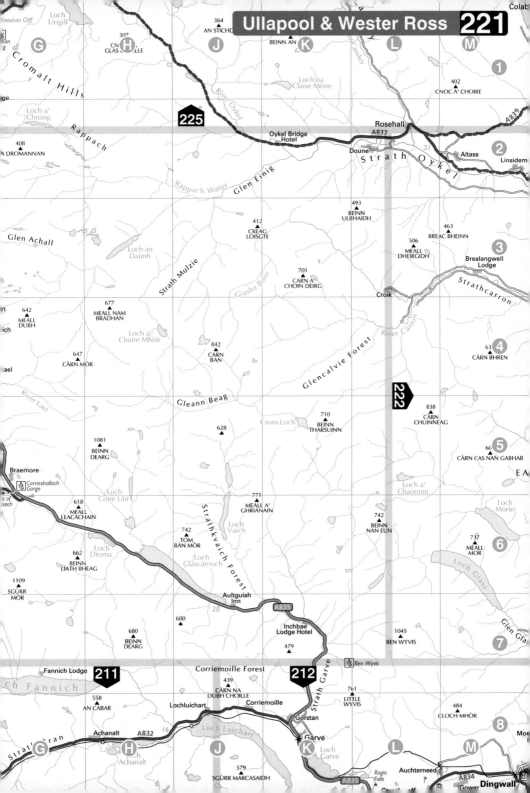

G H J K L M

1

2

3

4

5

6

7

8

Colab

Loch Urigill
Knockan Cliff

364
AN STICHD

BEINN AN

402
CNOC A' CHOIRE

A839

CN
GLAS MEALLE
307

Loch na Claise Mòire

River Oykel

225

Oykel Bridge Hotel

Rosehall
A837

Doune

Strath Oykel

Altass

Linsidem

A DROMANNAN
408

Rappach

Glen Einig

Rappach Water

493
BEINN ULBHAIDH

506
MEALL DHEIRGIDH

463
BREAC BHEINN

Brealangwell Lodge

Loch a' Chroisg

Glen Achall

Loch an Daimh

Strath Mulzie

412
CREAG LOISGTE

Giasha Burn

701
CARN A' CHOIN DEIRG

Croik

Strathcarron

642
MEALL DUBH

677
MEALL NAM BRADHAN

Loch a' Choire Mhòir

842
CARN BAN

Glencalvie Forest

River Carron

63
CÀRN BHREN

647
CÀRN MÒR

River Lael

Gleann Beag

Crom Loch

628

710
BEINN THARSUINN

222

838
CARN CHUINNEAG

66
CÀRN CAS NAN GABHAR

EA

1081
BEINN DEARG

Braemore

Corrieshalloch Gorge

s of sach

618
MEALL LEACACHAIN

Loch Coire Làir

771
MEALL A' GHRIANAIN

Loch Vaich

Strathvaich Forest

Loch a' Chaorunn

742
BEINN NAN EUN

Loch Moriel

737
MEALL MÒR

742
TOM BÀN MÒR

Loch Droma

Loch Glascarnoch

Loch Glas

662
BEINN LIATH BHEAG

1109
SGÙRR MÒR

Aultguish Inn

20

A835

Inchbae Lodge Hotel

1045
BEN WYVIS

Glen Glas

680
BEINN DEARG

600

479

Ben Wyvis

Fannich Lodge

211

Corriemoille Forest

212

Strath Garve

761
LITTLE WYVIS

484
CLOCH MHÒR

ch Fannich

558
AN CABAR

439
CÀRN NA DUBH CHOILLE

Lochluichart

Corriemoille

Gorstan

Garve

Loch Garve

L

M

Mo

Strath ran

Achanalt

A832

16

Loch Luichart

Rogie Falls

Auchterneed

A834
Gower

h Achanalt

579
SGÙRR MARCASAIDH

A835

Dingwall

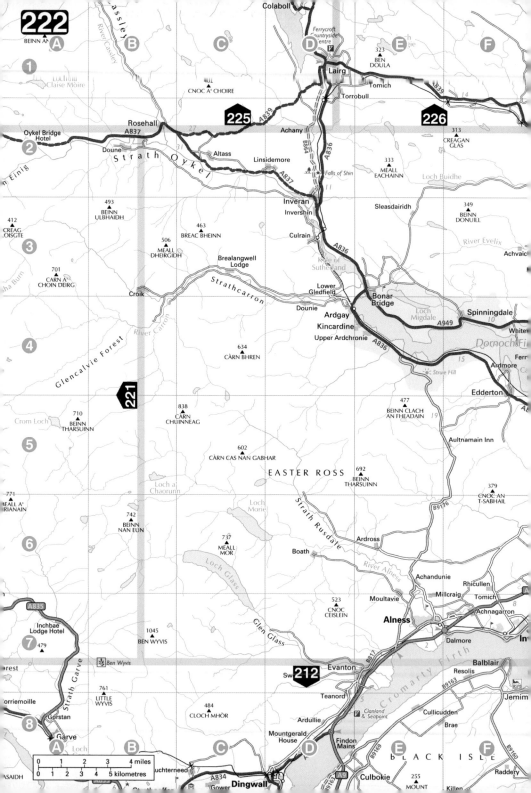

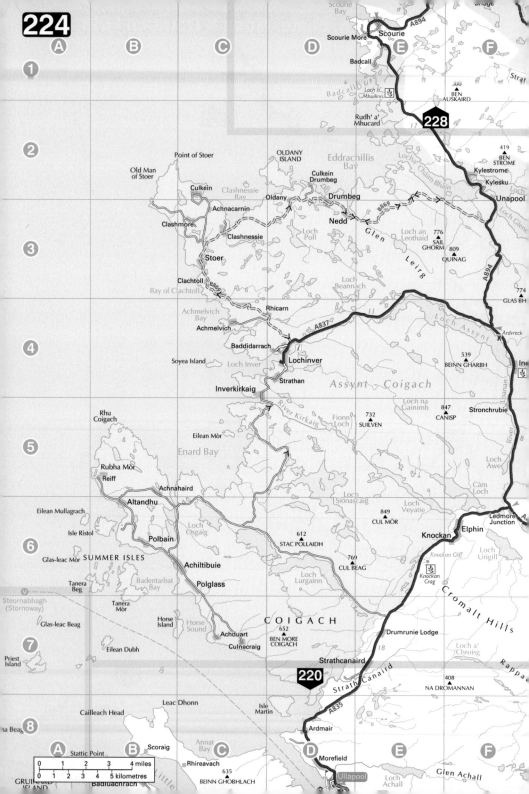

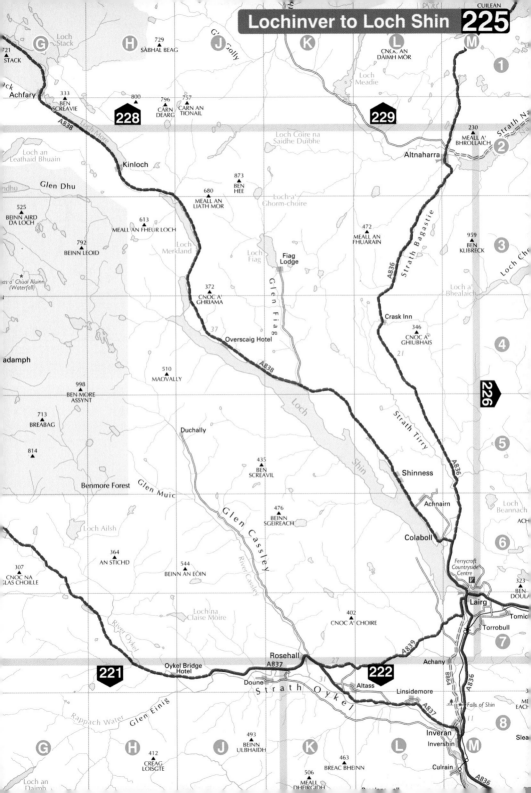

CUILEAN

G Loch
Stack
STACK

H 729
SÀBHAL BEAG

J G' Golly

K

L CNOC AN
DÀIMH MÒR

M

1

Strath Na

Achfary
333
BEN
SCREAVIE
A838

228

800

796
CÀRN
DEARG

757
CÀRN AN
TIONAIL

Loch More

Loch Meadie

Loch Coire na
Saidhe Duibhe

229

230
MEALL A'
BHROLLAICH

Altnaharra

2

Loch an
Leathaid Bhuain

Glen Dhu

ndhu

Kinloch

680
MEALL AN
LIATH MÒR

873
BEN
HEE

Loch-a'
Ghorm-choire

472
MEALL AN
FHUARAIN

959
BEN
KLIBRECK

3

Loch Che

525
BEINN AIRD
DA LOCH

792
BEINN LEOID

613
MEALL AN FHEUR LOCH

Loch
Merkland

Loch
Fiag

Fiag
Lodge

Strath Bagastie

A836

Loch a'
Bhealaich

s a' Chùal Aluinn
(Waterfall)

372
CNOC A'
GHRIAMA

Glen Fiag

Crask Inn

346
CNOC A'
GHIUBHAIS

adamph

37

Overscaig Hotel

A838

21

4

510
MAOVALLY

226

998
BEN MORE
ASSYNT

Loch

Strath Tirry

5

713
BREABAG

Duchally

Shin

Shinness

814

435
BEN
SCREAVIL

A836

Benmore Forest

Glen Muic

476
BEINN
SGEIREACH

Achnairn

Loch
Beannach

ACH

6

Loch Ailsh

Glen Cassley

Colaboll

364
AN STICHD

544
BEINN AN EÒIN

River Cassley

Ferrycroft
Countryside
Centre

307
CNOC NA
GLAS CHOILLE

323
BEN
DOUL

M

Loch'na
Claise Mòire

402
CNOC A' CHOIRE

Lairg

Tomic

River Oykel

221

Oykel Bridge
Hotel

Rosehall
A837

222

Torrobull

A839

7

Doune

Strath Oykel

31

27

Altass

Achany

Linsidemore

A837

B864

A836

Rappach Water

Glen Einig

G

H 412
CREAG
LOISGTE

J 493
BEINN
ULBHAIDH

K 463
BREAC BHEINN

L Inveran

Invershin

Falls of Shin

Culrain

ME
EACH

8

Slea

A836

Loch an
Daimh

506
MEALL
DHEIRGIDH

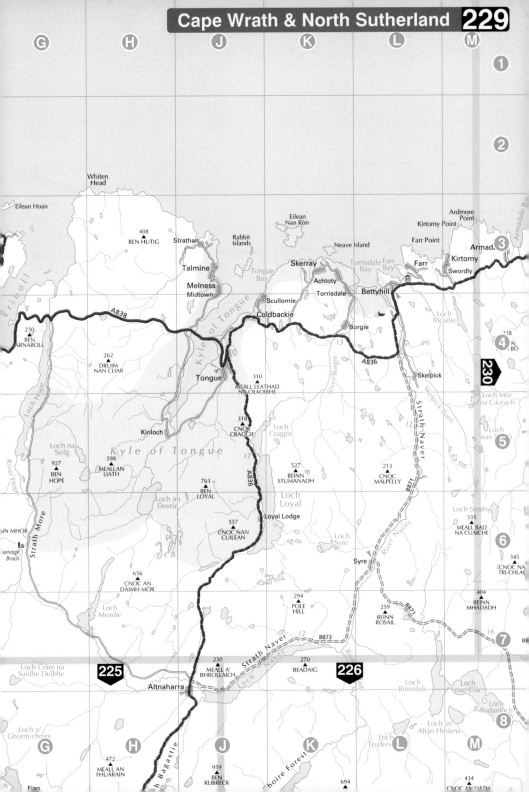

G   H   J   K   L   M

1
2
3

Whiten Head

Eilean Hoan

408 BEN HUTIG
Strathan
Talmine
Melness
Midtown

Rabbit Islands

Eilean Nan Ròn

Neave Island

Ardmore Point
Kirtomy Point
Farr Point
Armadale
Kirtomy
Swordly

Skerray
Achtoty
Torrisdale
Scullomie
Coldbackie

Tongue Bay

Torrisdale Bay
Farr Bay

Farr
Bettyhill

Loch Eriboll

A838

230 BEN ARNABOLL

262 DRUIM NAN CLIAR

Tongue

310 MEALL LEATHAD NA CRAOIBHE

318 CNOC CRAGGIE

Kinloch

Loch na Seilg

598 MEALLAN LIATH

Kyle of Tongue

927 BEN HOPE

763 BEN LOYAL

Loch an Deerie

A836

Loch Craggie

527 BEINN STUMANADH

Loch Loyal

557 CNOC NAN CUILEAN

Loyal Lodge

Loch Syre

Borgie

River Borgie

13

A836

Skelpick

Skelpick Burn

Strath Naver

Loch Meadie

228 N BO

230

Loch Mòr na Caorach

Loch nan

213 CNOC MALPELLY

B871

Loch Strathy

335 MEALL BAD NA CUAICHE

345 CNOC NA TRI-CHLAC

Strath More

656 CNOC AN DÀIMH MÓR

Loch Meadie

River Naver

Syre

259 BEINN ROSAIL

404 BEINN MHADADH

294 POLE HILL

B871

B873

12

Strath Naver

Loch Naver

River Naver

16

225

230 MEALL A' BHROLLAICH

Altnaharra

270 BEADAIG

226

Loch Rimsdale

Loch nan Clàr

Loch Còire na Saidhe Duibhe

Loch an Altàn Fhèarna

Loch Badanloch

Loch Truders

Loch an

G   H   J   K   L   M

Loch a' Ghorm-choire

472 MEALL AN FHUARAIN

959 BEN KLIBRECK

694

434 CNOC AN LIATH

4
5
6
7
8

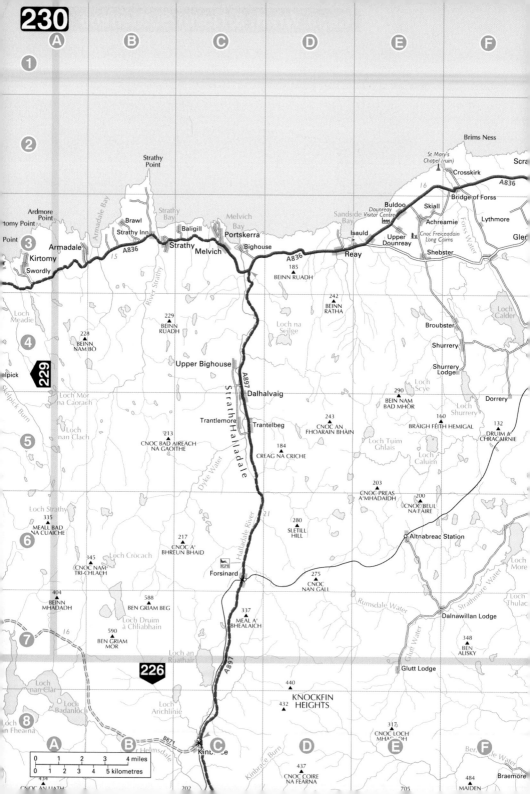

PENTLAND FIRTH

ISLAND OF STROMA

Netherton
Mell Head
Uppertown

St Margaret's Hope

DUNNET HEAD
Briga Head
DUNNET HILL
Brough
St John's Loch
Rattar
West Dunnet
Dunnet
Dunnet Bay

Scarfskerry
Castle of Mey
Mey
Gills
Gills Bay
Kirkstyle
Huna
Canisbay

DUNCANSBY HEAD
Muckle Stack
John o' Groats
Stacks of Duncansby

Stromness
Holborn Head
Thurso Bay
Thurso

Murkle
Castlehill
Castletown
Greenland
Barrock
Inkstack
Brabstermire
Slickly
Freswick
Ness Head
Freswick Bay

Olrig House
Weydale
Hilliclay
Sordale
Tain
Bowermadden
Lyth
Howe
Auckengill
Nybster
Brough Head

Roadside
Knockdee
Halcro
Kirk
Keiss

Halkirk
Clayock
Gillock
Loch Scarmclate
Loch Watten
Loch of Wester
Sinclair Bay

Scotscalder Station
Harpsdale
Spittal Hill
Spittal
Watten
Backlass
Mybster
Loch of Toftingall
Westerdale
Bilbster
Wick River
Winless
Sibster
Reiss
Castle Girnigoe & Sinclair
Noss Head
Ackergill
Staxigoe
Papigoe
Wick
Haster
Milton
Janets-town
Newton Row
Old Wick
South Head
Castle of Old Wick
Whiterow

BEINN CHAITEAG
Loch Ruard
Achavanich
BALLHARN HILL
Grey Cairns of Camster
HILL OF YARROWS
Loch of Yarrows
Cairn o' Get
Badlipster
Tannach
Loch Hempriggs
Thrumster
Sarclet

CNOCAN CONACHREAG
CORIE NA BEINN
Loch Rangag
STEMSTER HILL
Loch Stemster

227

BEN-A-CHIELT
Forse House
Swiney
Upper Lybster
Roster
Hill o'Many Stanes
Mid Clyth
Halberry Head
Clyth Ness
Occumster
Inveshore
Lybster
Lybster Bay
Houstry
Smerral
Land-hallow
Latheron
Forse
Latheronwheel
Janetstown
Dunbeath Water
Laidhay Croft
Dunbeath
Knockally

Whaligoe
Whaligoe Steps
Bruan
Ulbster

River Thurso
Strath Beg

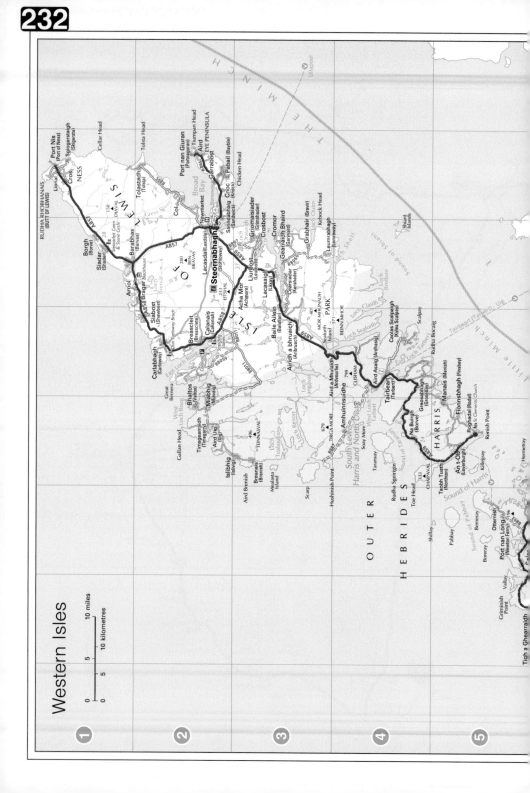

Western Isles

10 miles

10 kilometres

THE MINCH

Ullapool

RUDHA RHOBHANAIS (BUT OF LEWIS)
Port Nis (Port of Ness)
Lional
Sgiogarstaigh (Skigersta)
Cros
NESS
Cellar Head

Tolsta Head

Tumpan Head
Aird
Port nan Giuran (Portnaguran)
EYE PENINSULA
Pabail (Bayble)
Garrabost
Chicken Head

Broad Bay

Tolastadh (Tolsta)
DUNAL
158

Newmarket
STORNOWAY

Cnoc (Knock)
Sanndabhaig (Sandwick)
Griomaisiadar (Grimshader)
Crosbost
Cromor
Grabhair (Grewar)
Kebock Head

LEWIS

SIMM

Borgh (Borve)
Siadar (Shader)
Barabhas (Barvas)
A857
A857
Steornabhagh Stornoway

Arnol
Bragar
Siabost (Shawbost)
Breascleit (Breasclete)
Blackhouse

ISLE OF LEWIS

Lacasdail (Laxdale)
Lacasdale (Stornoway)
Acha Mòr (Achmore)
Liurbost (Leurbost)
Lacasaigh (Laxay)
Cearsiadar (Kershader)
Gearraidh Bhaird (Garyvard)
Leumrabhagh (Lemreway)

Shiant Islands

Carlabhagh (Carloway)
Calanais (Callanish)
Baile Ailein (Balallan)
Airidh a bhruaich (Airbruach)
PARK
BENN MHOR
Seaforth Island

Sound of Shiant

Little Minch

Bhaltos (Valtos)
Miabhig (Miavig)
Great Bernera
West Loch Roag
East Loch Roag

CLISHAM
Aird a Mhulaidh (Ardvourlie)

Gallan Head
Timsgearraidh (Timsgarry)
Aird Uig (Uig)
Islibhig (Islivig)
Breanais (Brenish)

OUTER HEBRIDES

Aird Bhrenish
Mealasta Island
Scarp

South Lewis, Harris and North Uist

Scaladale Beag
TIRGA MORE
Scaladale
Amhuinnsuidhe
Scavy Mor

Aird Asaig (Ardhasig)
Tairbeart (Tarbert)
Caolas Scalpaigh (Kyles Scalpay)
Scalpay
East Loch Tarbert
Rudha Biscaig

West Loch Tarbert

HARRIS

Greosabhagh (Grosebay)
Na Buirgh (Borve)
Manais (Manish)
Fionnsbhagh (Finsbay)
Rudha Manish

Hushinish Point
Rudha Sgeirigin
Taransay

Rodel Point

Roghadal (Rodel)
No. St. Clement's Church
An t-Ob (Leverburgh)
Renish Point

Toe Head
Taobh Tuath (Northton)
CHAIPAVAL
Killegray
Ensay
Sound of Harris

OUTER HEBRIDES

Shillay
Pabbay
Berneray
Otternish
Port nan Long (Newton Ferry)

Grimnish Point
Vallay

Tigh a Ghearraidh

ISLE OF SKYE

RONA

RAASAY

SCALPAY

EIGG

MUCK

RÙM

CANNA

Uig

The

T H E   H E R B I D E S

S E A   O F

Weaver's Point

Loch nam Madadh
(Lochmaddy)

UIBHIST A TUATH
(NORTH UIST)

BEINN NA FAOGHLA
(BENBECULA)

UIBHIST A DEAS
(SOUTH UIST)

Loch Baghasdail
(Lochboisdale)

Oban

Oban

BARRAIGH
(BARRA)

Bagh a Chaisteil
(Castlebay)

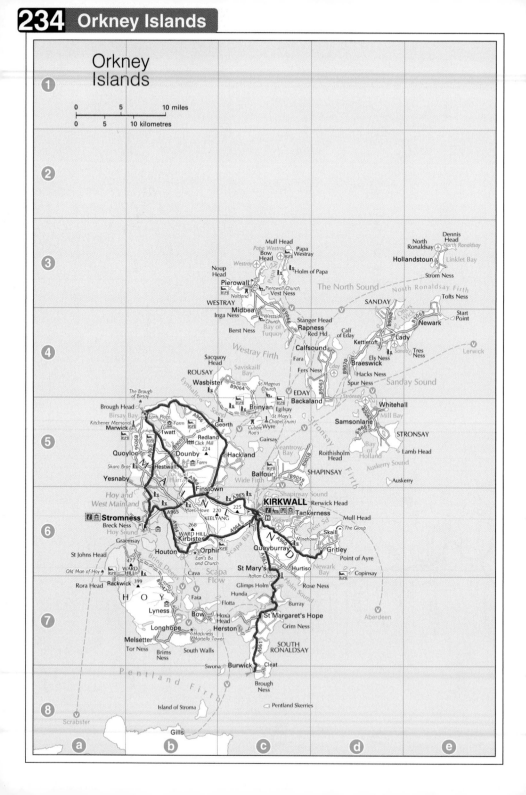

Orkney Islands

0   5   10 miles
0   5   10 kilometres

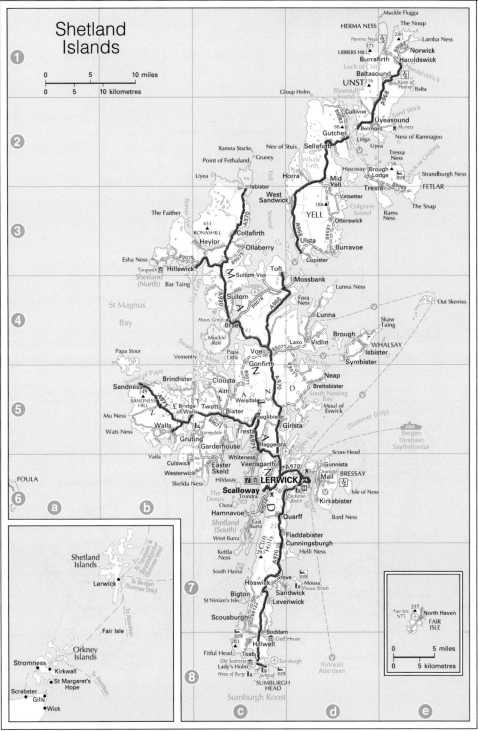

Shetland Islands

0   5   10 miles
0   5   10 kilometres

Muckle Flugga
The Noup
HERMA NESS
Herma Ness   280   Lamba Ness
171
LIBBERS HILL   Norwick
Burrafirth   Haroldswick
Baltasound   Harold's Wick
Loch of Cliff
216
UNST   Keen of
Hamar   Balta
Gloup Holm
Bluemull
Sound   Sand Wick
Cullivoe
98   Uyeasound
Gutcher   Belmont
Ramna Stacks   Nev of Stuis   Linga   Muness
Point of Fethaland   Gruney   Uyea   Ness of Ramnageo
Uyea   Whale   Sellafirth   Hascosay   Brough   Tressa
Firth   Horra   Lodge   Ness   Strandburgh Ness
Isbister   Mid   159   FETLAR
The Faither   West   Yell   Tresta
453   Sandwick   Vatsetter   The Snap
RONASHILL   188   Colgrave
Collafirth   YELL   Sound   Rams
Heylor   Ollaberry   Otterswick   Ness
Esha Ness   Toft   Ulsta   Burravoe   Out Skerries
Hillswick   Sullom Voe   Mossbank   Copister
Shetland   Bar Taing   Lunna Ness   Skaw
(North)   Sullom   Fora   Lunna   Taing
St Magnus   Mavis Grind   Braes   Ness   Brough   WHALSAY
Bay   Muckle   Laxo   Vidlin   Isbister
Roe   Papa   Voe   Symbister
Papa Stour   Little   Gonfirth   Neap
Vementry   Brettabister
Brindister   Clousta   South Nesting   Moul of
Sandness   249   Aith   Weisdale   Bay   Eswick
SANDNESS   E Bridge   Twatt   Heglibister   Bergen
HILL   of Walls   Bixter   Girlsta   Törshavn
Mu Ness   Walls   Tresta   Haggersta   Seydisfjordur
Wats Ness   Gruting   Staneydale   Score Head
Garderhouse   Whiteness   Gunnista
Vaila   Culswick   Veensgarth   BRESSAY
Easter   Tingwall   Fort   Isle of Noss
Skeld   Charlotte
Westerwick   Hildasay   LERWICK   Mail
Skelda Ness   Scalloway   Kirkabister
FOULA   The   Oxna   Trondra   Clickimin   Bard Ness
Deeps   Broch
Hamnavoe   East   Quarff
Shetland   Burra   Fladdabister
(South)   Cunningsburgh
West Burra   Helli Ness
Kettla   Cliff   293   Hills
Ness   Hoswick   Stove
South Havra   Sandwick   Mousa
Bigton   Levenwick   Mousa Broch
St Ninian's Isle   Boddam   Kirkwall
Scousburgh   Croft House   Aberdeen
Old Scatness   Hillwell   Sumburgh
Fitful Head   283   Toab
Lady's Holm   Jarlshof
Ness of Burgi   217   North Haven
SUMBURGH   Fair Isle   FAIR
HEAD   NTS   ISLE
Sumburgh Roost   0   5 miles
0   5 kilometres

Shetland
Islands
Lerwick
To Bergen &
Seydisfjordur
(Summer Only)
To Bergen
(Summer Only)
Fair Isle
To Aberdeen
Orkney
Islands
Stromness
Kirkwall
Scrabster   St Margaret's
Hope
Gills
Wick

a   b   c   d   e

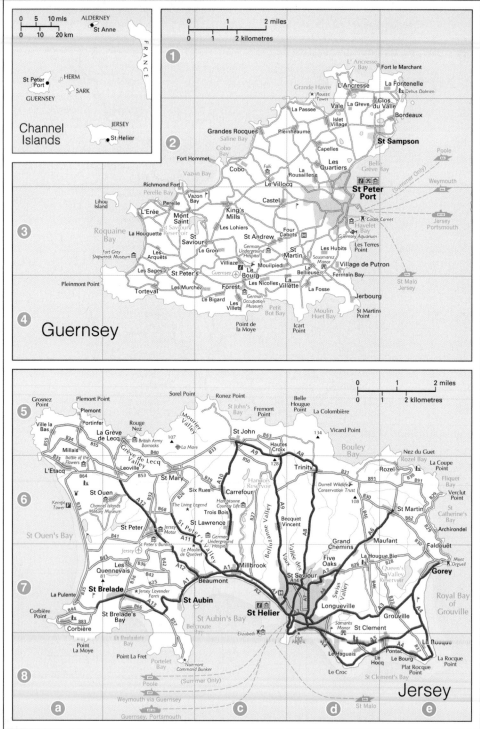

Channel Islands

ALDERNEY
St Anne

FRANCE

St Peter Port
HERM
GUERNSEY
SARK

JERSEY
St Helier

Guernsey

L' Ancresse Bay
Fort le Marchant
La Fontenelle
Dehus Dolmen
Grande Havre
L'Ancresse
Rousse Tower
Vale
La Greve
Clos du Valle
Bordeaux
La Passee
Saline Bay
Islet Village
St Sampson
Grandes Rocques
Pleinheaume
Capelles
Cobo Bay
Les Quartiers
Belle Greve Bay
Fort Hommet
Cobo
Folk
La Rousaillerie
Le Villocq
St Peter Port
Vazon Bay
Richmond Fort
Perelle Bay
Castel
Castle Cornet
Guernsey Aquarium
Havelet Bay
Lihou Island
Vazon Bay
King's Mills
Roquaine Bay
L'Erée
Mont Saint
Les Lohiers
Four Cabots
Les Terres Point
St Saviour's Reservoir
St Andrew
Les Hubits
La Houguette
St Saviour
Le Gron
German Underground Hospital
St Martin
Sausmarez Manor
Village de Putron
Fort Grey Shipwreck Museum
Les Arquêts
Villiaze
Mouilpied
Bellieuse
Fermain Bay
Les Sages
St Peter's
Guernsey
Le Bourg
La Villette
Pleinmont Point
Les Murchez
Forest
Les Nicolles
La Fosse
Jerbourg
Torteval
Le Bigard
German Occupation Museum
Les Villets
St Martins Point
Point de la Moye
Petit Bot Bay
Moulin Huet Bay
Icart Point

Jersey

Grosnez Point
Plemont Point
Sorel Point
Ronez Point
Belle Hougue Point
La Colombière
Plemont
St John's Bay
Fremont Point
Ville la Bas
Portinfer
Rouge Nez
Mourier Valley
St John
Vicard Point
La Grève de Lecq
British Army Barracks
La Mare
Hautes Croix
Bouley Bay
Millais
Battle of the Flowers
Leoville
St Mary
Six Rues
Carrefour
Trinity
Nez du Guet
Rozel Bay
La Coupe Point
L'Etacq
St Ouen
Trois Bois
Durrell Wildlife Conservation Trust
Rozel
Fliquet Bay
Kempt Tower
Channel Islands Military Museum
Hamptonne Country Life
St Martin
Verclut Point
The Living Legend
Becquet Vincent
St Catherine's Bay
St Peter
St Lawrence
German Underground Hospital
Grand Chemins
Maufant
Archirondel
St Ouen's Bay
Jersey Motor
St Peter's Bunker
Le Moulin de Quetivel
La Hougue Bie
Faldouët
Les Quennevais
Millbrook
Five Oaks
Queen's Valley Reservoir
Mont Orgueil
St Brelade
Beaumont
St Saviour
Gorey
La Pulente
Jersey Lavender Farm
St Aubin
Longueville
Royal Bay of Grouville
Corbière Point
St Brelade's Bay
St Helier
Grouville
Corbière
St Aubin's Bay
Samarès Manor
St Clement
La Rocque
Point La Moye
Elizabeth
Fort Regent
Le Haguais
Pontac
La Rocque Point
Point La Fret
Portelet Bay
Noirmont Command Bunker
Le Hocq
Le Bourg
Plat Rocque Point
Poole
Le Croc
St Clement's Bay
Weymouth via Guernsey
Guernsey, Portsmouth
St Malo

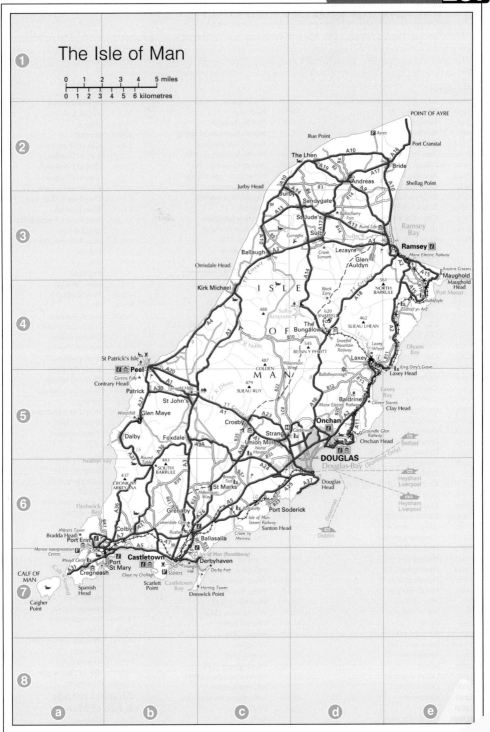

The Isle of Man

```
0   1   2   3   4   5 miles
0 1 2 3 4 5 6 kilometres
```

POINT OF AYRE

Rue Point
Ayres
Port Cranstal

The Lhen
A10
A16
Bride
A19 B9 A17 Shellag Point
Jurby Head
Jurby A17 Andreas A9
A13 Sandygate
A10 St Jude's A13 Rural Life
Curraghs Sulby Sulby R. Ramsey Bay
Ballaugh A3 Lezayre Ramsey
Orrisdale Head Cronk Sumark Glen Auldyn Manx Electric Railway
Ancient Crosses
Kirk Michael ISLE Block Eary 561 Maughold
NORTH BARRULE Maughold Head
488 620 SNAEFELL 462 Port Mooar
OF The Bungalow SLIEAU LHEAN Ballafayle
A4 A3 B10 545 Snaefell Mountain Railway Laxey Wheel Dhoon Bay
R. Neb BEINN Y PHOTT Laxey King Orry's Grave
St Patrick's Isle 487 MAN Laxey Head
Peel COLDEN Millennium Way Laxey Bay
Corrins Folly 479 Cloven Stones
Contrary Head A20 SLIEAU RUY Baldrine Clay Head
Patrick A30 Tynwald Hills Manx Electric Railway
St John's Onchan Groudle Glen Railway
Waterfall Glen Maye Crosby Onchan Head Belfast
Dalby Foxdale Strang Heysham Liverpool
A24 Union Mills DOUGLAS
Niarbyl Bay A3 A26 Norse House Douglas Bay (Summer Only)
483 B32 Heysham Liverpool
Round Table SOUTH BARRULE Broogh Fort A37 Douglas Head
437 St Marks
CRONK NY ARREY LAA B39 Millennium Way Dublin
Fleshwick Bay Grenaby A5 Ballakelly Port Soderick
A36 Silverdale Glen Isle of Man Steam Railway Santon Head
Milners Tower Colby Rushen Cronk ny Merriu
Bradda Head A7 Ballasalla
Port Erin A5 Isle of Man (Ronaldsway)
Marine Interpretation Centre Port St Mary Castletown Derbyhaven
Meayll Circle Close ny Chollagh Derby Fort
CALF OF MAN Cregneash Scarlett Hango Hill
Spanish Head Scarlett Point Castletown Bay Herring Tower
Caigher Point Dreswick Point

a   b   c   d   e
1 2 3 4 5 6 7 8

Index to place names

This index lists places appearing in the main-map section of the atlas in alphabetical order. The reference before each name gives the atlas page number and grid reference of the square in which the place appears. The map shows counties, and administrative areas, together with a list of the abbreviated name forms used in the index. The top 100 places of tourist interest are indexed in red, airports in blue.

England

BaNES	**Bath & N E Somerset (18)**
Barns	**Barnsley (19)**
Beds	**Bedfordshire**
Birm	**Birmingham**
Bl w D	**Blackburn with Darwen (20)**
Bmouth	**Bournemouth**
Bolton	**Bolton (21)**
Bpool	**Blackpool**
Brad	**Bradford (22)**
Br & H	**Brighton and Hove (23)**
Br For	**Bracknell Forest (24)**
Bristl	**City of Bristol**
Bucks	**Buckinghamshire**
Bury	**Bury (25)**
C Derb	**City of Derby**
C KuH	**City of Kingston upon Hull**
C Leic	**City of Leicester**
C Nott	**City of Nottingham**
C Pete	**City of Peterborough**
C Plym	**City of Plymouth**
C Port	**City of Portsmouth**
C Sotn	**City of Southampton**
C Stke	**City of Stoke**
Calder	**Calderdale (26)**
Cambs	**Cambridgeshire**
Ches	**Cheshire**
Cnwll	**Cornwall**
Covtry	**Coventry**
Cumb	**Cumbria**
Darltn	**Darlington (27)**
Derbys	**Derbyshire**
Devon	**Devon**
Donc	**Doncaster (28)**
Dorset	**Dorset**
Dudley	**Dudley (29)**
Dur	**Durham**
E R Yk	**East Riding of Yorkshire**
E Susx	**East Sussex**
Essex	**Essex**
Gatesd	**Gateshead (30)**
Gloucs	**Gloucestershire**
Gt Lon	**Greater London**
Halton	**Halton (31)**
Hants	**Hampshire**
Hartpl	**Hartlepool (32)**
Herefs	**Herefordshire**
Herts	**Hertfordshire**
IoS	**Isles of Scilly**
IoW	**Isle of Wight**
Kent	**Kent**
Kirk	**Kirklees (33)**
Knows	**Knowsley (34)**
Lancs	**Lancashire**
Leeds	**Leeds**
Leics	**Leicestershire**
	Lincolnshire
	Liverpool
	Luton
	Milton Keynes

Manch	**Manchester**
Medway	**Medway**
Middsb	**Middlesbrough**
NE Lin	**North East Lincolnshire**
N Linc	**North Lincolnshire**
N Som	**North Somerset (35)**
N Tyne	**North Tyneside (36)**
N u Ty	**Newcastle upon Tyne**
N York	**North Yorkshire**
Nhants	**Northamptonshire**
Norfk	**Norfolk**
Notts	**Nottinghamshire**
Nthumb	**Northumberland**
Oldham	**Oldham (37)**
Oxon	**Oxfordshire**
Poole	**Poole**
R & Cl	**Redcar and Cleveland**
Readg	**Reading**
Rochdl	**Rochdale (38)**
Rothm	**Rotherham (39)**
Rutlnd	**Rutland**
S Glos	**South Gloucestershire (40)**
S on T	**Stockton-on-Tees (41)**
S Tyne	**South Tyneside (42)**
Salfd	**Salford (43)**
Sandw	**Sandwell (44)**
Sefton	**Sefton (45)**
Sheff	**Sheffield**
Shrops	**Shropshire**
Slough	**Slough (46)**
Solhll	**Solihull (47)**
Somset	**Somerset**
St Hel	**St Helens (48)**
Staffs	**Staffordshire**
Sthend	**Southend-on-Sea**
Stockp	**Stockport (49)**
Suffk	**Suffolk**
Sundld	**Sunderland**
Surrey	**Surrey**
Swindn	**Swindon**
Tamesd	**Tameside (50)**
Thurr	**Thurrock (51)**
Torbay	**Torbay**
Traffd	**Trafford (52)**
W & M	**Windsor & Maidenhead (53)**
W Berk	**West Berkshire**
W Susx	**West Sussex**
Wakefd	**Wakefield (54)**
Warrtn	**Warrington (55)**
Warwks	**Warwickshire**
Wigan	**Wigan (56)**
Wilts	**Wiltshire**
Wirral	**Wirral (57)**
Wokham	**Wokingham (58)**
Wolves	**Wolverhampton (59)**
Worcs	**Worcestershire**
Wrekin	**Telford and Wrekin (60)**
Wsall	**Walsall (61)**
York	**York**

Scotland

Abers	**Aberdeenshire**
Ag & B	**Argyll & Bute**
Angus	**Angus**
Border	**Borders**
C Aber	**City of Aberdeen**
C Dund	**City of Dundee**
C Edin	**City of Edinburgh**
C Glas	**City of Glasgow**
Clacks	**Clackmannanshire (1)**
D & G	**Dumfries & Galloway**
E Ayrs	**East Ayrshire**
E Duns	**East Dunbartonshire (2)**
E Loth	**East Lothian**
E Rens	**East Renfrewshire (3)**
Falk	**Falkirk**
Fife	**Fife**
Highld	**Highland**
Inver	**Inverclyde (4)**
Mdloth	**Midlothian (5)**
Moray	**Moray**
N Ayrs	**North Ayrshire**
N Lans	**North Lanarkshire (6)**
Ork	**Orkney Islands**
P & K	**Perth & Kinross**
Rens	**Renfrewshire (7)**
S Ayrs	**South Ayrshire**
Shet	**Shetland Islands**
S Lans	**South Lanarkshire**
Stirlg	**Stirling**
W Duns	**West Dunbartonshire (8)**
W Isls	**Western Isles**
W Loth	**West Lothian**

Wales

Blae G	**Blaenau Gwent (9)**
Brdgnd	**Bridgend (10)**
Caerph	**Caerphilly (11)**
Cardif	**Cardiff**
Carmth	**Carmarthenshire**
Cerdgn	**Ceredigion**
Conwy	**Conwy**
Denbgs	**Denbighshire**
Flints	**Flintshire**
Gwynd	**Gwynedd**
IoA	**Isle of Anglesey**
Mons	**Monmouthshire**
Myr Td	**Merthyr Tydfil (12)**
Neath	**Neath Port Talbot (13)**
Newpt	**Newport (14)**
Pembks	**Pembrokeshire**
Powys	**Powys**
Rhondd	**Rhondda Cynon Taff (15)**
Swans	**Swansea**
Torfn	**Torfaen (16)**
V Glam	**Vale of Glamorgan (17)**
Wrexhm	**Wrexham**

Channel Islands & Isle of Man

Guern	**Guernsey**
Jersey	**Jersey**
IoM	**Isle of Man**

ORKNEY ISLANDS

SHETLAND ISLANDS

WESTERN

ISLES

HIGHLAND

MORAY

Aberdeen

SCOTLAND

ABERDEENSHIRE

ANGUS

PERTH & KINROSS

Dundee

ARGYLL & BUTE

STIRLING

FIFE

1

8 2 FALK W LOTH

Edinburgh

E LOTH

4 Glasgow 6

5

3

NORTH AYRSHIRE

S LANS

E AYRS

BORDERS

S AYRS

DUMFRIES & GALLOWAY

NORTHUMBERLAND

Newcastle upon Tyne 36

30 42 Sunderland

CUMBRIA

DURHAM

32

27 41 R & CL Middlesbrough

IoM

NORTH YORKSHIRE

Blackpool

LANCASHIRE

22

York

EAST RIDING OF YORKSHIRE

Kingston upon Hull

20

26

Leeds

54

45 56 38 37 33 19 N LINCS N E LINCS

21 25 43 50

48 55 52 49

34 31 57 Manchester 39 28

Liverpool Sheffield

IoA

CONWY FLINTS CHESHIRE DERBYS NOTTS LINCOLNSHIRE

DENBGS Stoke-on-Trent

GWYNEDD WREXHAM Derby Nottingham

60 STAFFS LEICS RUTLAND NORFOLK

SHROPSHIRE 59 61 Leicester Peterborough

29 44 Birmingham

POWYS 47 Coventry NHANTS CAMBS SUFFOLK

CERDGN WORCS WARWKS Milton Keynes BEDS

HEREFS Luton

PEMBKS CARMTH WALES ENGLAND HERTS ESSEX

MONS GLOUCS OXON BUCKS GREATER LONDON Southend-on-Sea

13 12 9 16 Swindon 53 46 51

15 11 14 W BERKS Reading MEDWAY

10 Cardiff Bristol 40 58 24

Swansea 17 35 18 SURREY KENT

WILTSHIRE

W SUSX E SUSX

HAMPSHIRE

SOMERSET Southampton 23

W SUSX

DEVON DORSET Bournemouth Portsmouth

Poole IoW

CORNWALL Torbay

Plymouth CHANNEL ISLANDS Guernsey

IoS Jersey

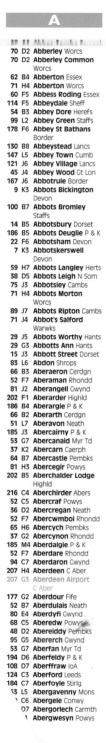

A

70 D2 **Abberley** Worcs
70 D2 **Abberley Common** Worcs
62 E4 **Abberton** Essex
71 H4 **Abberton** Worcs
60 F5 **Abbess Roding** Essex
114 F5 **Abbeydale** Sheff
54 B3 **Abbey Dore** Herefs
99 L2 **Abbey Green** Staffs
178 F6 **Abbey St Bathans** Border
130 B8 **Abbeystead** Lancs
147 L5 **Abbey Town** Cumb
121 J6 **Abbey Village** Lancs
45 J4 **Abbey Wood** Gt Lon
167 J6 **Abbotrule** Border
9 K3 **Abbots Bickington** Devon
100 B7 **Abbots Bromley** Staffs
14 B5 **Abbotsbury** Dorset
186 B5 **Abbots Deuglie** P & K
22 F6 **Abbotsham** Devon
7 K3 **Abbotskerswell** Devon
59 H7 **Abbots Langley** Herts
38 D5 **Abbots Leigh** N Som
75 J3 **Abbotsley** Cambs
71 H4 **Abbots Morton** Worcs
89 J7 **Abbots Ripton** Cambs
71 J4 **Abbot's Salford** Warwks
29 J5 **Abbots Worthy** Hants
29 G3 **Abbotts Ann** Hants
15 J3 **Abbott Street** Dorset
83 L6 **Abdon** Shrops
66 B3 **Aberaeron** Cerdgn
52 F7 **Aberaman** Rhondd
81 J2 **Aberangell** Gwynd
202 F1 **Aberarder** Highld
186 B4 **Aberargie** P & K
66 B2 **Aberarth** Cerdgn
51 L7 **Aberavon** Neath
185 J3 **Abercairny** P & K
53 G7 **Abercanaid** Myr Td
37 K2 **Abercarn** Caerph
64 B7 **Abercastle** Pembks
81 H3 **Abercegir** Powys
202 B5 **Aberchalder Lodge** Highld
216 C4 **Aberchirder** Abers
52 C5 **Abercraf** Powys
36 D2 **Abercregan** Neath
52 F7 **Abercwmboi** Rhondd
65 H6 **Abercych** Pembks
37 G2 **Abercynon** Rhondd
185 M4 **Aberdalgie** P & K
52 F7 **Aberdare** Rhondd
94 C7 **Aberdaron** Gwynd
207 H4 **Aberdeen** C Aber
207 G3 Aberdeen Airport C Aber
177 G2 **Aberdour** Fife
52 B7 **Aberdulais** Neath
80 E4 **Aberdyfi** Gwynd
68 C5 **Aberedw** Powys
48 D2 **Abereiddy** Pembks
95 G5 **Abererch** Gwynd
53 G7 **Aberfan** Myr Td
194 D6 **Aberfeldy** P & K
108 D7 **Aberffraw** IoA
124 C3 **Aberford** Leeds
184 C7 **Aberfoyle** Stirlg
53 L5 **Abergavenny** Mons
6 C6 **Abergele** Conwy
D7 **Abergorlech** Carmth
1 **Abergwesyn** Powys

50 F2 **Abergwili** Carmth
36 D2 **Abergwynfi** Neath
109 J6 **Abergwyngregyn**
80 F3 **Abergynolwyn** Gwynd
36 D3 **Aberkenfig** Brdgnd
178 B3 **Aberlady** E Loth
196 E5 **Aberlemno** Angus
81 G2 **Aberllefenni** Gwynd
68 D6 **Aberllynfi** Powys
215 G5 **Aberlour** Moray
82 D5 **Abermule** Powys
50 D2 **Abernant** Carmth
52 F7 **Aber-nant** Rhondd
186 C4 **Abernethy** P & K
186 D2 **Abernyte** P & K
65 J4 **Aberporth** Cerdgn
94 E6 **Abersoch** Gwynd
53 K7 **Abersychan** Torfn
36 F5 **Aberthin** V Glam
53 K7 **Abertillery** Blae G
37 H3 **Abertridwr** Caerph
97 G8 **Abertridwr** Powys
185 K4 **Aberuthven** P & K
80 D6 **Aberystwyth** Cerdgn
41 J2 **Abingdon** Oxon
31 J3 **Abinger** Surrey
31 H2 **Abinger Hammer** Surrey
73 J3 **Abington** Nhants
165 H5 **Abington** S Lans
75 K5 **Abington Pigotts** Cambs
102 B7 **Ab Kettleby** Leics
56 C6 **Ablington** Gloucs
114 D5 **Abney** Derbys
205 L5 **Aboyne** Abers
112 E2 **Abram** Wigan
212 E1 **Abriachan** Highld
45 J2 **Abridge** Essex
175 K3 **Abronhill** N Lans
39 G5 **Abson** S Glos
73 J5 **Abthorpe** Nhants
118 F5 **Aby** Lincs
124 E2 **Acaster Malbis** York
124 E3 **Acaster Selby** N York
121 L5 **Accrington** Lancs
188 F5 **Acha** Ag & B
172 D3 **Achahoish** Ag & B
195 H7 **Achalader** P & K
182 D1 **Achaleven** Ag & B
232 f3 **Acha Mor** W Isls
211 K3 **Achanalt** Highld
222 E6 **Achandunie** Highld
222 D2 **Achany** Highld
190 D3 **Acharacle** Highld
190 E6 **Acharn** Highld
194 B7 **Acharn** P & K
231 H6 **Achavanich** Highld
224 C7 **Achduart** Highld
228 D7 **Achfary** Highld
198 D4 **A'Chill** Highld
224 C6 **Achiltibuie** Highld
161 J6 **Achinhoan** Ag & B
210 E6 **Achintee** Highld
210 C6 **Achintraid** Highld
224 C4 **Achmelvich** Highld
210 D7 **Achmore** Highld
232 f3 **Achmore** W Isls
224 C3 **Achnacarnin** Highld
201 J7 **Achnacarry** Highld
199 J4 **Achnacloich** Highld
202 C2 **Achnaconeran** Highld
191 G2 **Achnacroish** Ag & B
189 L6 **Achnadrish Lodge** Ag & B
185 J3 **Achnafauld** P & K
222 F7 **Achnagarron** Highld
189 L3 **Achnaha** Highld
224 B5 **Achnahaird** Highld
225 L6 **Achnairn** Highld

191 G4 **Achnalea** Highld
172 D2 **Achnamara** Ag & B
211 J3 **Achnasheen** Highld
215 G7 **Achnastank** Moray
189 K3 **Achosnich** Highld
190 E6 **Achranich** Highld
230 E3 **Achreamie** Highld
192 B3 **Achriabhach** Highld
228 C5 **Achriesgill** Highld
229 K3 **Achtoty** Highld
88 E6 **Achurch** Nhants
222 F3 **Achvaich** Highld
231 L5 **Ackergill** Highld
141 L4 **Acklam** Middsb
134 B7 **Acklam** N York
84 D4 **Ackleton** Shrops
159 G2 **Acklington** Nthumb
124 C6 **Ackton** Wakefd
124 C7 **Ackworth Moor Top** Wakefd
93 J2 **Acle** Norfk
85 K6 **Acock's Green** Birm
35 J2 **Acol** Kent
150 B2 **Acomb** Nthumb
124 E1 **Acomb** York
54 D2 **Aconbury** Herefs
98 F2 **Acton** Ches
44 D4 **Acton** Gt Lon
99 J4 **Acton** Staffs
77 K5 **Acton** Suffk
70 E2 **Acton** Worcs
70 C4 **Acton Beauchamp** Herefs
112 E6 **Acton Bridge** Ches
83 K3 **Acton Burnell** Shrops
70 C4 **Acton Green** Herefs
97 M3 **Acton Park** Wrexhm
84 B4 **Acton Round** Shrops
83 J5 **Acton Scott** Shrops
99 L8 **Acton Trussell** Staffs
39 J4 **Acton Turville** S Glos
99 H6 **Adbaston** Staffs
26 E7 **Adber** Dorset
101 L5 **Adbolton** Notts
72 F7 **Adderbury** Oxon
98 F4 **Adderley** Shrops
176 D5 **Addiewell** W Loth
123 G1 **Addingham** Brad
58 C3 **Addington** Bucks
45 G7 **Addington** Gt Lon
33 H2 **Addington** Kent
45 G6 **Addiscombe** Gt Lon
43 H7 **Addlestone** Surrey
119 H7 **Addlethorpe** Lincs
59 H6 **Adeyfield** Herts
82 B4 **Adfa** Powys
69 H1 **Adforton** Herefs
35 G4 **Adisham** Kent
56 E3 **Adlestrop** Gloucs
125 K6 **Adlingfleet** E R Yk
121 J7 **Adlington** Lancs
100 B7 **Admaston** Staffs
84 B2 **Admaston** Wrekin
71 L5 **Admington** Warwks
65 J6 **Adpar** Cerdgn
25 L5 **Adsborough** Somset
25 J4 **Adscombe** Somset
58 C3 **Adstock** Bucks
73 H4 **Adstone** Nhants
31 H6 **Adversane** W Susx
214 D7 **Advie** Highld
124 E8 **Adwick Le Street** Donc
115 J2 **Adwick upon Dearne** Donc
155 H4 **Ae** D & G
155 H5 **Ae Bridgend** D & G
36 D2 **Afan Forest Park** Neath
216 B6 **Affleck** Abers

14 F4 **Affpuddle** Dorset
201 J2 **Affric Lodge** Highld
110 F6 **Afon-wen** Flints
131 K3 **Agglethorpe** N York
111 L4 **Aigburth** Lpool
126 C2 **Aike** E R Yk
148 E5 **Aiketgate** Cumb
148 B4 **Aikton** Cumb
89 G4 **Ailsworth** C Pete
132 E4 **Ainderby Quernhow** N York
132 E2 **Ainderby Steeple** N York
62 D4 **Aingers Green** Essex
120 D7 **Ainsdale** Sefton
148 F5 **Ainstable** Cumb
142 E5 **Ainthorpe** N York
176 B3 **Ainville** W Loth
181 M7 **Aird** Ag & B
144 D3 **Aird** D & G
232 g2 **Aird** W Isls
232 e3 **Aird a Mhulaidh** W Isls
232 e4 **Aird Asaig** W Isls
209 L6 **Aird Dhubh** Highld
182 E2 **Airdeny** Ag & B
181 H2 **Aird of Kinloch** Ag & B
199 J5 **Aird of Sleat** Highld
175 K5 **Airdrie** N Lans
175 K5 **Airdriehill** N Lans
182 E2 **Airds Bay** Ag & B
154 B7 **Airds of Kells** D & G
232 d2 **Aird Uig** W Isls
232 e3 **Airidh a bhruaich** W Isls
146 D4 **Airieland** D & G
195 L6 **Airlie** Angus
125 H5 **Airmyn** E R Yk
186 A1 **Airntully** P & K
199 L4 **Airor** Highld
176 B2 **Airth** Falk
131 G7 **Airton** N York
103 K3 **Aisby** Lincs
116 E3 **Aisby** Lincs
7 G4 **Aish** Devon
7 J4 **Aish** Devon
25 J4 **Aisholt** Somset
134 B3 **Aiskew** N York
134 B3 **Aislaby** N York
143 H5 **Aislaby** N York
141 L5 **Aislaby** S on T
116 F5 **Aisthorpe** Lincs
235 c5 **Aith** Shet
168 E4 **Akeld** Nthumb
73 K6 **Akeley** Bucks
78 D5 **Akenham** Suffk
6 B2 **Albaston** Cnwll
83 G1 **Alberbury** Shrops
19 H3 **Albourne** W Susx
84 E3 **Albrighton** Shrops
98 C8 **Albrighton** Shrops
92 F6 **Alburgh** Norfk
60 C3 **Albury** Herts
31 H2 **Albury** Surrey
31 H3 **Albury Heath** Surrey
212 E3 **Alcaig** Highld
83 J6 **Alcaston** Shrops
71 K3 **Alcester** Warwks
20 B5 **Alciston** E Susx
89 H7 **Alconbury** Cambs
89 H7 **Alconbury Weston** Cambs
132 F6 **Aldborough** N York
106 E5 **Aldborough** Norfk
40 E5 **Aldbourne** Wilts
127 G3 **Aldbrough** E R Yk
140 F5 **Aldbrough St John** N York
58 F5 **Aldbury** Herts
129 K7 **Aldcliffe** Lancs

194 E4 **Aldclune** P & K
79 K3 **Aldeburgh** Suffk
93 J5 **Aldeby** Norfk
43 J2 **Aldenham** Herts
28 D6 **Alderbury** Wilts
106 D8 **Alderford** Norfk
28 C8 **Alderholt** Dorset
39 H3 **Alderley** Gloucs
113 J5 **Alderley Edge** Ches
41 L7 **Aldermaston** W Berk
72 B5 **Alderminster** Warwks
30 E2 **Aldershot** Hants
55 M2 **Alderton** Gloucs
73 K5 **Alderton** Nhants
79 H6 **Alderton** Suffk
39 H4 **Alderton** Wilts
100 F2 **Alderwasley** Derbys
132 D5 **Aldfield** N York
98 B2 **Aldford** Ches
88 E3 **Aldgate** Rutlnd
61 L3 **Aldham** Essex
78 C5 **Aldham** Suffk
18 C5 **Aldingbourne** W Susx
129 G5 **Aldingham** Cumb
34 E7 **Aldington** Kent
71 J5 **Aldington** Worcs
34 E7 **Aldington Corner** Kent
205 H1 **Aldivalloch** Moray
174 C1 **Aldochlay** Ag & B
90 C8 **Aldreth** Cambs
85 J4 **Aldridge** Wsall
79 J3 **Aldringham** Suffk
56 D6 **Aldsworth** Gloucs
215 H8 **Aldunie** Moray
100 E2 **Aldwark** Derbys
133 G6 **Aldwark** N York
18 C6 **Aldwick** W Susx
88 E6 **Aldwincle** Nhants
41 K4 **Aldworth** W Berk
174 D3 **Alexandria** W Duns
25 J4 **Aley** Somset
12 E3 **Alfington** Devon
31 H5 **Alfold** Surrey
31 H4 **Alfold Crossways** Surrey
206 B3 **Alford** Abers
118 F6 **Alford** Lincs
26 E5 **Alford** Somset
101 H2 **Alfreton** Derbys
70 D4 **Alfrick** Worcs
70 D4 **Alfrick Pound** Worcs
20 B5 **Alfriston** E Susx
103 M5 **Algarkirk** Lincs
26 F4 **Alhampton** Somset
125 K6 **Alkborough** N Linc
35 H6 **Alkham** Kent
100 D5 **Alkmonton** Derbys
7 J5 **Allaleigh** Devon
204 D6 **Allanaquoich** Abers
175 L6 **Allanbank** N Lans
179 H7 **Allanton** Border
175 L6 **Allanton** N Lans
175 K7 **Allanton** S Lans
54 F6 **Allaston** Gloucs
29 J7 **Allbrook** Hants
40 B7 **All Cannings** Wilts
149 L4 **Allendale** Nthumb
85 L4 **Allen End** Warwks
149 L6 **Allenheads** Nthumb
60 D5 **Allen's Green** Herts
69 J7 **Allensmore** Herefs
101 G6 **Allenton** C Derb
24 B6 **Aller** Devon
26 B5 **Aller** Somset
147 J6 **Allerby** Cumb
12 D4 **Allercombe** Devon
24 D3 **Allerford** Somset
134 D2 **Allerston** N York
125 J2 **Allerthorpe** E R Yk
123 G4 **Allerton** Brad
213 H2 **Allerton** Highld

111 L4 **Allerton** Lpool
124 C5 **Allerton Bywater** Leeds
132 F7 **Allerton Mauleverer** N York
86 C7 **Allesley** Covtry
101 G5 **Allestree** C Derb
88 B4 **Allexton** Leics
113 L7 **Allgreave** Ches
46 D4 **Allhallows** Medway
210 B4 **Alligin Shuas** Highld
13 L4 **Allington** Dorset
102 E4 **Allington** Lincs
28 D4 **Allington** Wilts
39 K5 **Allington** Wilts
40 B7 **Allington** Wilts
129 J4 **Allithwaite** Cumb
185 J8 **Alloa** Clacks
147 J6 **Allonby** Cumb
163 J5 **Alloway** S Ayrs
26 B8 **Allowenshay** Somset
83 J4 **All Stretton** Shrops
192 C6 **Alltchaorunn** Highld
66 B7 **Alltwalis** Carmth
51 K5 **Alltwen** Neath
66 C5 **Alltyblaca** Cerdgn
26 F8 **Allweston** Dorset
69 G4 **Almeley** Herefs
99 G5 **Almington** Staffs
185 M3 **Almondbank** P & K
123 H7 **Almondbury** Kirk
38 E4 **Almondsbury** S Glos
133 G6 **Alne** N York
222 E6 **Alness** Highld
168 E7 **Alnham** Nthumb
169 J7 **Alnmouth** Nthumb
169 J6 **Alnwick** Nthumb
44 D4 **Alperton** Gt Lon
77 K7 **Alphamstone** Essex
77 K4 **Alpheton** Suffk
11 L6 **Alphington** Devon
114 E8 **Alport** Derbys
98 E1 **Alpraham** Ches
62 C4 **Alresford** Essex
85 L1 **Alrewas** Staffs
99 H2 **Alsager** Ches
100 D2 **Alsop en le Dale** Derbys
149 J5 **Alston** Cumb
13 H2 **Alston** Devon
55 M2 **Alstone** Gloucs
100 C2 **Alstonefield** Staffs
26 B2 **Alston Sutton** Somset
23 L6 **Alswear** Devon
224 B6 **Altandhu** Highld
9 G8 **Altarnun** Cnwll
222 C2 **Altass** Highld
190 D8 **Altcreich** Ag & B
173 H4 **Altgaltraig** Ag & B
61 L7 **Althorne** Essex
125 K8 **Althorpe** N Linc
230 E6 **Altnabreac Station** Highld
182 B2 **Altnacraig** Ag & B
225 M2 **Altnaharra** Highld
115 G8 **Alton** Derbys
30 B4 **Alton** Hants
100 B4 **Alton** Staffs
40 C7 **Alton Barnes** Wilts
14 D3 **Alton Pancras** Dorset
40 C7 **Alton Priors** Wilts
100 B4 **Alton Towers** Staffs
113 H4 **Altrincham** Trafld
184 B6 **Altskeith Hotel** Stirlg
185 J7 **Alva** Clacks
112 D6 **Alvanley** Ches
101 H5 **Alvaston** C Derb
85 J4 **Alvechurch** Worcs
86 B3 **Alvecote** Warwks
27 L6 **Alvediston** Wilts
84 D6 **Alveley** Shrops
23 H6 **Alverdiscott** Devon

17 H3 **Alverstoke** Hants
17 H5 **Alverstone** IoW
123 L6 **Alverthorpe** Wakefd
102 C4 **Alverton** Notts
214 E3 **Alves** Moray
56 F6 **Alvescot** Oxon
38 F3 **Alveston** S Glos
72 B3 **Alveston** Warwks
118 E4 **Alvingham** Lincs
54 E7 **Alvington** Gloucs
89 G4 **Alwalton** C Pete
168 D7 **Alwinton** Nthumb
123 K3 **Alwoodley** Leeds
195 K6 **Alyth** P & K
101 G3 **Ambergate** Derbys
55 J7 **Amberley** Gloucs
18 D3 **Amberley** W Susx
159 G2 **Amble** Nthumb
84 F6 **Amblecote** Dudley
123 G5 **Ambler Thorn** Brad
137 K6 **Ambleside** Cumb
49 G3 **Ambleston** Pembks
57 L4 **Ambrosden** Oxon
125 K7 **Amcotts** N Linc
42 F2 **Amersham** Bucks
42 F2 **Amersham Common** Bucks
42 F2 **Amersham Old Town** Bucks
58 F7 **Amersham on the Hill** Bucks
28 D3 **Amesbury** Wilts
232 d4 **Amhuinnsuidhe** W Isls
86 B3 **Amington** Staffs
155 H5 **Amisfield Town** D & G
108 F3 **Amlwch** IoA
51 J3 **Ammanford** Carmth
134 B5 **Amotherby** N York
29 H6 **Ampfield** Hants
133 J4 **Ampleforth** N York
56 B7 **Ampney Crucis** Gloucs
56 C7 **Ampney St Mary** Gloucs
56 B7 **Ampney St Peter** Gloucs
28 F3 **Amport** Hants
74 F6 **Ampthill** Beds
77 J1 **Ampton** Suffk
49 K6 **Amroth** Pembks
185 J1 **Amulree** P & K
59 K5 **Amwell** Herts
191 G4 **Anaheilt** Highld
103 G4 **Ancaster** Lincs
168 E1 **Ancroft** Nthumb
167 K4 **Ancrum** Border
119 G6 **Anderby** Lincs
29 G3 **Andover** Hants
56 A4 **Andoversford** Gloucs
237 d2 **Andreas** IoM
45 G6 **Anerley** Gt Lon
111 K3 **Anfield** Lpool
3 G4 **Angarrack** Cnwll
83 L7 **Angelbank** Shrops
48 E6 **Angle** Pembks
108 E5 **Anglesey** IoA
18 E5 **Angmering** W Susx
124 D2 **Angram** N York
223 H6 **Ankerville** Highld
126 C5 **Anlaby** E R Yk
105 H6 **Anmer** Norfk
17 J1 **Anmore** Hants
147 L2 **Annan** D & G
210 D4 **Annat** Highld
175 J4 **Annathill** N Lans
29 G3 **Anna Valley** Hants
163 K5 **Annbank** S Ayrs
71 L4 **Anne Hathaway's Cottage** Warwks
101 J2 **Annesley** Notts

101 J2 **Annesley Woodhouse** Notts
150 F5 **Annfield Plain** Dur
174 F5 **Anniesland** C Glas
120 D5 **Ansdell** Lancs
26 F5 **Ansford** Somset
86 C5 **Ansley** Warwks
100 E7 **Anslow** Staffs
100 D7 **Anslow Gate** Staffs
60 C2 **Anstey** Herts
87 G2 **Anstey** Leics
187 J6 **Anstruther** Fife
19 J2 **Ansty** W Susx
86 E6 **Ansty** Warwks
27 L6 **Ansty** Wilts
147 L4 **Anthorn** Cumb
106 F5 **Antingham** Norfk
232 d5 **An t-Ob** W Isls
103 M3 **Anton's Gowt** Lincs
6 B5 **Antony** Cnwll
112 F5 **Antrobus** Ches
103 J3 **Anwick** Lincs
145 M4 **Anwoth** D & G
32 D2 **Aperfield** Gt Lon
88 E4 **Apethorpe** Nhants
117 J6 **Apley** Lincs
115 G5 **Apperknowle** Derbys
55 K3 **Apperley** Gloucs
191 J6 **Appin** Ag & B
126 B7 **Appleby** N Linc
139 G3 **Appleby-in-Westmorland** Cumb
86 C2 **Appleby Magna** Leics
86 C2 **Appleby Parva** Leics
209 L5 **Applecross** Highld
23 G5 **Appledore** Devon
25 G8 **Appledore** Devon
34 C8 **Appledore** Kent
41 K2 **Appleford** Oxon
155 J5 **Applegarth Town** D & G
28 F2 **Appleshaw** Hants
112 D4 **Appleton** Halton
57 H7 **Appleton** Oxon
112 F5 **Appleton** Warrtn
133 L3 **Appleton-le-Moors** N York
134 B5 **Appleton-le-Street** N York
124 E3 **Appleton Roebuck** N York
112 F5 **Appleton Thorn** Warrtn
141 J6 **Appleton Wiske** N York
167 H6 **Appletreehall** Border
131 K7 **Appletreewick** N York
25 G6 **Appley** Somset
121 G8 **Appley Bridge** Lancs
17 G5 **Apse Heath** IoW
59 J2 **Apsley End** Beds
18 A5 **Apuldram** W Susx
223 H6 **Arabella** Highld
196 F7 **Arbirlot** Angus
223 J5 **Arboll** Highld
42 C6 **Arborfield** Wokham
42 C6 **Arborfield Cross** Wokham
197 G7 **Arbroath** Angus
197 K2 **Arbuthnott** Abers
50 F5 **Archddu** Carmth
141 G4 **Archdeacon Newton** Darltn
174 D3 **Archencarroch** W Duns
214 F5 **Archiestown** Moray
99 H1 **Arclid Green** Ches
217 J6 **Ardallie** Abers
182 F3 **Ardanaiseig Hotel** Ag & B
210 C2 **Ardaneaskan** Highld
210 C7 **Ardarroch** Highld

160 D1 **Ardbeg** Ag & B
173 J5 **Ardbeg** Ag & B
173 K2 **Ardbeg** Ag & B
220 F4 **Ardchattan** Highld
180 E4 **Ardchiavaig** Ag & B
182 D5 **Ardchonnel** Ag & B
184 D5 **Ardchullarie More** Stirlg
183 J7 **Arddarroch** Ag & B
201 H7 **Ardechive** Highld
163 H2 **Ardeer** N Ayrs
60 A3 **Ardeley** Herts
210 D8 **Ardelve** Highld
174 C2 **Arden** Ag & B
71 K4 **Ardens Grafton** Warwks
182 B3 **Ardentallen** Ag & B
173 L2 **Ardentinny** Ag & B
173 H4 **Ardentraive** Ag & B
184 E1 **Ardeonaig Hotel** Stirlg
213 J4 **Ardersier** Highld
220 D4 **Ardessie** Highld
182 A6 **Ardfern** Ag & B
222 D4 **Ardgay** Highld
191 K4 **Ardgour** Highld
173 L4 **Ardgowan** Inver
173 K4 **Ardhallow** Ag & B
232 e4 **Ardhasig** W Isls
210 B3 **Ardheslaig** Highld
220 F4 **Ardindrean** Highld
32 C7 **Ardingly** W Susx
41 H3 **Ardington** Oxon
173 G5 **Ardlamont** Ag & B
62 C3 **Ardleigh** Essex
62 C2 **Ardleigh Heath** Essex
195 L7 **Ardler** P & K
57 K3 **Ardley** Oxon
183 K4 **Ardlui** Ag & B
172 B2 **Ardlussa** Ag & B
191 L8 **Ardmaddy** Ag & B
220 E2 **Ardmair** Highld
173 J5 **Ardmaleish** Ag & B
172 B8 **Ardminish** Ag & B
190 E3 **Ardmolich** Highld
174 C3 **Ardmore** Ag & B
222 F4 **Ardmore** Highld
173 K3 **Ardnadam** Ag & B
212 E4 **Ardnagrask** Highld
210 D7 **Ardnarff** Highld
190 F4 **Ardnastang** Highld
183 G5 **Ardno** Ag & B
201 J5 **Ardochy House** Highld
172 C6 **Ardpatrick** Ag & B
172 E2 **Ardrishaig** Ag & B
222 E6 **Ardross** Highld
163 G2 **Ardrossan** N Ayrs
123 K5 **Ardsley East** Leeds
190 B4 **Ardslignish** Highld
171 J7 **Ardtalla** Ag & B
190 C3 **Ardtoe** Highld
182 A5 **Arduaine** Ag & B
212 E2 **Ardullie** Highld
199 K5 **Ardvasar** Highld
184 D3 **Ardvorlich** P & K
232 e3 **Ardvourlie** W Isls
144 D5 **Ardwell** D & G
113 J3 **Ardwick** Manch
70 E1 **Areley Kings** Worcs
190 D3 **Arevegaig** Highld
30 D4 **Arford** Hants
53 J7 **Argoed** Caerph
183 J6 **Argyll Forest Park** Ag & B
232 e3 **Aribruach** W Isls
180 D3 **Aridhglas** Ag & B
188 F5 **Arileod** Ag & B
189 G6 **Arinagour** Ag & B
182 C3 **Ariogan** Ag & B
199 K7 **Arisaig** Highld
199 L7 **Arisaig House** Highld

132 F7 **Arkendale** N York
76 C7 **Arkesden** Essex
130 B5 **Arkholme** Lancs
188 B1 **Arkleton** D & G
44 E2 **Arkley** Gt Lon
115 L1 **Arksey** Donc
115 H7 **Arkwright Town** Derbys
55 L4 **Arle** Gloucs
136 E4 **Arlecdon** Cumb
75 H7 **Arlesey** Beds
84 B2 **Arleston** Wrekin
112 F5 **Arley** Ches
86 C5 **Arley** Warwks
55 G6 **Arlingham** Gloucs
23 K4 **Arlington** Devon
20 B4 **Arlington** E Susx
199 K5 **Armadale** Highld
230 A3 **Armadale** Highld
176 C5 **Armadale** W Loth
137 G2 **Armaside** Cumb
148 E5 **Armathwaite** Cumb
92 F3 **Arminghall** Norfk
85 J1 **Armitage** Staffs
123 K4 **Armley** Leeds
88 F6 **Armston** Nhants
115 L1 **Armthorpe** Donc
188 F4 **Arnabost** Ag & B
131 H5 **Arncliffe** N York
187 H6 **Arncroach** Fife
215 G5 **Arndilly House** Moray
15 H5 **Arne** Dorset
87 H5 **Arnesby** Leics
186 B5 **Arngask** P & K
200 C3 **Arnisdale** Highld
209 J3 **Arnish** Highld
177 K6 **Arniston** Mdloth
232 f1 **Arnol** W Isls
126 E3 **Arnold** E R Yk
101 L4 **Arnold** Notts
184 D7 **Arnprior** Stirlg
129 K4 **Arnside** Cumb
190 B7 **Aros** Ag & B
129 G4 **Arrad Foot** Cumb
126 C2 **Arram** E R Yk
162 B3 **Arran** N Ayrs
132 C2 **Arrathorne** N York
17 G5 **Arreton** IoW
210 B3 **Arrina** Highld
75 K4 **Arrington** Cambs
183 K6 **Arrochar** Ag & B
71 J3 **Arrow** Warwks
83 J2 **Arscott** Shrops
212 F4 **Artafallie** Highld
123 K2 **Arthington** Leeds
87 L7 **Arthingworth** Nhants
217 H6 **Arthrath** Abers
217 J3 **Artrochie** Abers
18 D4 **Arundel** W Susx
136 E3 **Asby** Cumb
173 J5 **Ascog** Ag & B
42 F6 **Ascot** W & M
56 F4 **Ascott-under-Wychwood** Oxon
132 F4 **Asenby** N York
102 B8 **Asfordby** Leics
102 B8 **Asfordby Hill** Leics
103 J4 **Asgarby** Lincs
118 D7 **Asgarby** Lincs
35 H3 **Ash** Kent
45 L6 **Ash** Kent
26 C7 **Ash** Somset
30 E2 **Ash** Surrey
41 K5 **Ashampstead** W Berk
78 E4 **Ashbocking** Suffk
78 E4 **Ashbocking Green** Suffk
100 D3 **Ashbourne** Derbys
25 G6 **Ashbrittle** Somset
7 H2 **Ashburton** Devon
10 D5 **Ashbury** Devon
40 E4 **Ashbury** Oxon

125 L8 **Ashby** N Linc
118 F7 **Ashby by Partney** Lincs
118 F6 **Ashby cum Fenby** NE Lin
103 H2 **Ashby de la Launde** Lincs
86 D1 **Ashby-de-la-Zouch** Leics
87 K2 **Ashby Folville** Leics
87 H5 **Ashby Magna** Leics
87 G5 **Ashby Parva** Leics
118 D7 **Ashby Puerorum** Lincs
73 H2 **Ashby St Ledgers** Nhants
93 G3 **Ashby St Mary** Norfk
55 L2 **Ashchurch** Gloucs
11 L8 **Ashcombe** Devon
37 M7 **Ashcombe** N Som
26 C4 **Ashcott** Somset
76 E6 **Ashdon** Essex
29 K2 **Ashe** Hants
62 A7 **Asheldham** Essex
77 H6 **Ashen** Essex
58 B5 **Ashendon** Bucks
58 F6 **Asheridge** Bucks
185 G6 **Ashfield** Stirlg
78 E3 **Ashfield** Suffk
92 F8 **Ashfield Green** Suffk
7 G6 **Ashford** Devon
23 H4 **Ashford** Devon
34 D6 **Ashford** Kent
43 H6 **Ashford** Surrey
69 K1 **Ashford Bowdler** Shrops
69 K1 **Ashford Carbonel** Shrops
41 K7 **Ashford Hill** Hants
114 D7 **Ashford in the Water** Derbys
175 K7 **Ashgill** S Lans
30 E2 **Ash Green** Surrey
86 D6 **Ash Green** Warwks
12 E1 **Ashill** Devon
91 K3 **Ashill** Norfk
25 L7 **Ashill** Somset
46 E2 **Ashingdon** Essex
159 G5 **Ashington** Nthumb
26 E6 **Ashington** Somset
18 F3 **Ashington** W Susx
167 G5 **Ashkirk** Border
55 J3 **Ashleworth** Gloucs
55 J3 **Ashleworth Quay** Gloucs
77 G3 **Ashley** Cambs
113 H5 **Ashley** Ches
10 F3 **Ashley** Devon
39 L2 **Ashley** Gloucs
16 B4 **Ashley** Hants
29 G5 **Ashley** Hants
35 J5 **Ashley** Kent
87 L5 **Ashley** Nhants
99 H5 **Ashley** Staffs
39 J6 **Ashley** Wilts
58 F6 **Ashley Green** Bucks
98 E4 **Ash Magna** Shrops
41 H8 **Ashmansworth** Hants
22 E7 **Ashmansworthy** Devon
24 C6 **Ash Mill** Devon
27 K7 **Ashmore** Dorset
41 J6 **Ashmore Green** W Berk
72 C3 **Ashorne** Warwks
115 G8 **Ashover** Derbys
72 C1 **Ashow** Warwks
98 E5 **Ash Parva** Shrops
70 B6 **Ashperton** Herefs
7 J4 **Ashprington** Devon
25 J5 **Ash Priors** Somset
10 F3 **Ashreigney** Devon

78 B5 **Ash Street** Suffk
44 D8 **Ashtead** Surrey
12 C1 **Ash Thomas** Devon
113 H2 **Ashton** Ches
3 G5 **Ashton** Cnwll
11 K7 **Ashton** Devon
69 K2 **Ashton** Herefs
173 L3 **Ashton** Inver
73 L5 **Ashton** Nhants
88 F5 **Ashton** Nhants
59 K8 **Ashton Common** Wilts
112 E2 **Ashton-in-Makerfield** Wigan
40 B2 **Ashton Keynes** Wilts
71 H6 **Ashton under Hill** Worcs
113 L2 **Ashton-under-Lyne** Tamesd
16 D1 **Ashurst** Hants
32 F5 **Ashurst** Kent
19 G3 **Ashurst** W Susx
32 D5 **Ashurstwood** W Susx
30 E2 **Ash Vale** Surrey
9 K5 **Ashwater** Devon
75 J6 **Ashwell** Herts
88 C2 **Ashwell** Rutlnd
75 J6 **Ashwell End** Herts
92 D4 **Ashwellthorpe** Norfk
26 F2 **Ashwick** Somset
105 H8 **Ashwicken** Norfk
128 F4 **Askam in Furness** Cumb
124 E7 **Askern** Donc
14 A4 **Askerswell** Dorset
58 D6 **Askett** Bucks
138 D3 **Askham** Cumb
116 C6 **Askham** Notts
124 E2 **Askham Bryan** York
124 E2 **Askham Richard** York
172 F1 **Asknish** Ag & B
131 H2 **Askrigg** N York
123 H2 **Askwith** N York
103 H6 **Aslackby** Lincs
92 D5 **Aslacton** Norfk
102 C4 **Aslockton** Notts
147 K6 **Aspatria** Cumb
60 B3 **Aspenden** Herts
74 D7 **Aspley Guise** Beds
74 D7 **Aspley Heath** Beds
121 J8 **Aspull** Wigan
125 H5 **Asselby** E R Yk
77 L6 **Assington** Suffk
77 H4 **Assington Green** Suffk
99 J1 **Astbury** Ches
73 J4 **Astcote** Nhants
118 C6 **Asterby** Lincs
83 H3 **Asterley** Shrops
83 H5 **Asterton** Shrops
56 F4 **Asthall** Oxon
56 F5 **Asthall Leigh** Oxon
223 G3 **Astle** Highld
98 D8 **Astley** Shrops
86 C5 **Astley** Warwks
113 G2 **Astley** Wigan
70 D2 **Astley** Worcs
84 C4 **Astley Abbots** Shrops
121 K7 **Astley Bridge** Bolton
70 E1 **Astley Cross** Worcs
98 E3 **Aston** Ches
112 E5 **Aston** Ches
114 D5 **Aston** Derbys
111 J7 **Aston** Flints
69 J1 **Aston** Herefs
59 L4 **Aston** Herts
57 G7 **Aston** Oxon
115 J4 **Aston** Rothm
84 E5 **Aston** Shrops
98 D6 **Aston** Shrops
99 H4 **Aston** Staffs
99 K6 **Aston** Staffs

99 K7 **Aston** Staffs
42 C4 **Aston** Wokham
84 B2 **Aston** Wrekin
58 D4 **Aston Abbotts** Bucks
84 B6 **Aston Botterell** Shrops
71 K3 **Aston Cantlow** Warwks
58 E5 **Aston Clinton** Bucks
54 F4 **Aston Crews** Herefs
59 L3 **Aston End** Herts
84 B5 **Aston-Eyre** Shrops
71 G1 **Aston Fields** Worcs
86 F5 **Aston Flamville** Leics
55 G4 **Aston Ingham** Herefs
72 F4 **Aston le Walls** Nhants
71 L7 **Aston Magna** Gloucs
83 K6 **Aston Munslow** Shrops
83 H6 **Aston on Clun** Shrops
83 G3 **Aston Pigott** Shrops
83 G3 **Aston Rogers** Shrops
58 B7 **Aston Rowant** Oxon
71 J6 **Aston Somerville** Worcs
71 K6 **Aston Subedge** Gloucs
41 K3 **Aston Tirrold** Oxon
101 H6 **Aston-upon-Trent** Derbys
41 K3 **Aston Upthorpe** Oxon
75 J6 **Astwick** Beds
74 D5 **Astwood** M Keyn
71 G2 **Astwood** Worcs
71 J3 **Astwood Bank** Worcs
103 H4 **Aswarby** Lincs
118 E7 **Aswardby** Lincs
83 K2 **Atcham** Shrops
14 E4 **Athelhampton** Dorset
78 E1 **Athelington** Suffk
25 M5 **Athelney** Somset
178 C3 **Athelstaneford** E Loth
23 J6 **Atherington** Devon
86 C4 **Atherstone** Warwks
72 B4 **Atherstone on Stour** Warwks
113 G2 **Atherton** Wigan
100 E3 **Atlow** Derbys
210 E6 **Attadale** Highld
117 G3 **Atterby** Lincs
115 G4 **Attercliffe** Sheff
86 D4 **Atterton** Leics
92 C4 **Attleborough** Norfk
86 D5 **Attleborough** Warwks
92 D1 **Attlebridge** Norfk
77 G4 **Attleton Green** Suffk
126 F1 **Atwick** E R Yk
39 J7 **Atworth** Wilts
116 F8 **Aubourn** Lincs
217 G7 **Auchedly** Abers
197 H1 **Auchenblae** Abers
175 L2 **Auchenbowie** Stirlg
146 D5 **Auchencairn** D & G
155 G5 **Auchencairn** D & G
162 D4 **Auchencairn** N Ayrs
179 H6 **Auchencrow** Border
177 H6 **Auchendinny** Mdloth
176 D7 **Auchengray** S Lans
215 J3 **Auchenhalrig** Moray
164 F2 **Auchenheath** S Lans
154 E3 **Auchenhessnane** D & G
173 G4 **Auchenlochan** Ag & B
174 F4 **Auchenmade** N Ayrs
144 F4 **Auchenmalg** D & G
174 C8 **Auchentiber** N Ayrs
184 C8 **Auchentroig** Stirlg
221 G5 **Auchindrean** Highld
216 C5 **Auchininna** Abers
164 B5 **Auchinleck** E Ayrs

175 H4 **Auchinloch** N Lans
175 J3 **Auchinstarry** N Lans
191 L2 **Auchintore** Highld
217 K6 **Auchiries** Abers
207 G6 **Auchlee** Abers
206 C1 **Auchleven** Abers
164 F3 **Auchlochan** S Lans
206 B5 **Auchlossan** Abers
184 B2 **Auchlyne** Stirlg
164 A4 **Auchmillan** E Ayrs
197 G7 **Auchmithie** Angus
216 C6 **Auchmuirbridge** Fife
196 D4 **Auchnacree** Angus
217 H6 **Auchnagatt** Abers
204 F2 **Auchnarrow** Moray
144 B3 **Auchnotteroch** D & G
215 H4 **Auchroisk** Moray
185 K5 **Auchterarder** P & K
202 B4 **Auchteraw** Highld
203 L2 **Auchterblair** Highld
219 J6 **Auchtercairn** Highld
186 C7 **Auchterderran** Fife
196 B8 **Auchterhouse** Angus
216 D6 **Auchterless** Abers
186 D5 **Auchtermuchty** Fife
212 D3 **Auchterneed** Highld
177 H1 **Auchtertool** Fife
210 C8 **Auchtertyre** Highld
184 C4 **Auchtubh** Stirlg
231 L3 **Auckengill** Highld
115 M2 **Auckley** Donc
113 K3 **Audenshaw** Tamesd
98 F4 **Audlem** Ches
99 J3 **Audley** Staffs
76 D6 **Audley End** Essex
76 D6 **Audley End** Essex
77 J4 **Audley End** Suffk
148 A7 **Aughertree** Cumb
125 G3 **Aughton** E R Yk
111 L1 **Aughton** Lancs
115 L6 **Aughton** Lancs
115 J4 **Aughton** Rothm
28 E1 **Aughton** Wilts
112 B1 **Aughton Park** Lancs
213 L4 **Auldearn** Highld
69 J4 **Aulden** Herefs
154 F5 **Auldgirth** D & G
175 H7 **Auldhouse** S Lans
200 E2 **Ault a' chruinn** Highld
219 K4 **Aultbea** Highld
219 H4 **Aultgrishin** Highld
221 J7 **Aultguish Inn** Highld
115 J7 **Ault Hucknall** Derbys
215 J4 **Aultmore** Moray
202 E2 **Aultnagoire** Highld
222 F5 **Aultnamain Inn** Highld
103 H5 **Aunsby** Lincs
38 E3 **Aust** S Glos
116 A3 **Austerfield** Donc
86 C3 **Austrey** Warwks
130 E5 **Austwick** N York
118 E5 **Authorpe** Lincs
40 C6 **Avebury** Wilts
45 L4 **Aveley** Thurr
39 K2 **Avening** Gloucs
102 C2 **Averham** Notts
7 G6 **Aveton Gifford** Devon
203 L3 **Aviemore** Highld
41 G6 **Avington** W Berk
213 G4 **Avoch** Highld
15 L3 **Avon** Hants
176 B4 **Avonbridge** Falk
72 E4 **Avon Dassett** Warwks
38 D5 **Avonmouth** Bristl
7 G4 **Avonwick** Devon
28 F6 **Awbridge** Hants
12 E3 **Awliscombe** Devon
55 G6 **Awre** Gloucs
101 J4 **Awsworth** Notts
26 B1 **Axbridge** Somset
29 L3 **Axford** Hants

40 E6 **Axford** Wilts
13 H3 **Axminster** Devon
13 G4 **Axmouth** Devon
141 G3 **Aycliffe** Dur
150 C2 **Aydon** Nthumb
54 E7 **Aylburton** Gloucs
12 D4 **Aylesbeare** Devon
58 D5 **Aylesbury** Bucks
126 F8 **Aylesby** NE Lin
33 J2 **Aylesford** Kent
35 H4 **Aylesham** Kent
87 H4 **Aylestone** C Leic
106 E5 **Aylmerton** Norfk
106 E6 **Aylsham** Norfk
70 B6 **Aylton** Herefs
56 C4 **Aylworth** Gloucs
69 H2 **Aymestrey** Herefs
57 K2 **Aynho** Nhants
59 K5 **Ayot St Lawrence** Herts
163 J5 **Ayr** S Ayrs
131 J2 **Aysgarth** N York
25 G7 **Ayshford** Devon
129 J3 **Ayside** Cumb
88 C4 **Ayston** Rutlnd
60 F5 **Aythorpe Roding** Essex
179 J6 **Ayton** Border
132 C5 **Azerley** N York

B

7 L3 **Babbacombe** Torbay
60 C5 **Babbs Green** Herts
26 E5 **Babcary** Somset
27 G2 **Babington** Somset
76 D4 **Babraham** Cambs
116 B5 **Babworth** Notts
234 d4 **Backaland** Ork
217 J4 **Backfolds** Abers
111 L6 **Backford** Ches
223 H2 **Backies** Highld
231 H5 **Backlass** Highld
199 K7 **Back of Keppoch** Highld
38 C6 **Backwell** N Som
106 D5 **Baconsthorpe** Norfk
54 A2 **Bacton** Herefs
107 H5 **Bacton** Norfk
78 C2 **Bacton** Suffk
122 C6 **Bacup** Lancs
219 J6 **Badachro** Highld
40 D4 **Badbury** Swindn
73 H3 **Badby** Nhants
228 B7 **Badcall** Highld
228 C4 **Badcall** Highld
220 D3 **Badcaul** Highld
86 B8 **Baddesley Clinton** Warwks
86 C4 **Baddesley Ensor** Warwks
224 D4 **Baddidarrach** Highld
176 F7 **Baddinsgill** Border
216 D6 **Badenscoth** Abers
205 H2 **Badenyon** Abers
84 D4 **Badger** Shrops
55 K4 **Badgeworth** Gloucs
26 B2 **Badgworth** Somset
210 B8 **Badicaul** Highld
79 G2 **Badingham** Suffk
34 D4 **Badlesmere** Kent
165 K5 **Badlieu** Border
231 J5 **Badluarach** Highld
220 C3 **Badluachrach** Highld
223 G3 **Badninish** Highld
220 D3 **Badrallach** Highld
71 J5 **Badsey** Worcs
30 E2 **Badshot Lea** Surrey
124 C7 **Badsworth** Wakefd
78 B2 **Badwell Ash** Suffk

27 H8 **Bagber** Dorset
133 G4 **Bagby** N York
118 E6 **Bag Enderby** Lincs
233 b9 **Bagh a Chaisteil** W Isls
111 H6 **Bagillt** Flints
86 D8 **Baginton** Warwks
51 L6 **Baglan** Neath
98 B6 **Bagley** Shrops
26 C3 **Bagley** Somset
30 A3 **Bagmore** Hants
99 L3 **Bagnall** Staffs
83 L8 **Bagot** Shrops
42 E7 **Bagshot** Surrey
39 G3 **Bagstone** S Glos
86 F2 **Bagworth** Leics
54 C3 **Bagwy Llydiart** Herefs
123 H3 **Baildon** Brad
123 H3 **Baildon Green** Brad
232 f3 **Baile Ailein** W Isls
233 b6 **Baile a Mhanaich** W Isls
180 D3 **Baile Mor** Ag & B
175 J5 **Baillieston** C Glas
131 H2 **Bainbridge** N York
216 B7 **Bainshole** Abers
89 G3 **Bainton** C Pete
126 B1 **Bainton** E R Yk
186 F6 **Baintown** Fife
167 K6 **Bairnkine** Border
114 E7 **Bakewell** Derbys
96 E5 **Bala** Gwynd
232 f3 **Balallan** W Isls
212 C7 **Balbeg** Highld
186 C2 **Balbeggie** P & K
212 D5 **Balblair** Highld
213 G2 **Balblair** Highld
115 K2 **Balby** Donc
146 E5 **Balcary** D & G
212 E5 **Balchraggan** Highld
228 B4 **Balchreick** Highld
32 B6 **Balcombe** W Susx
187 K5 **Balcomie Links** Fife
132 E4 **Baldersby** N York
132 E4 **Baldersby St James** N York
121 J4 **Balderstone** Lancs
102 D3 **Balderton** Notts
187 G5 **Baldinnie** Fife
185 L4 **Baldinnies** P & K
75 J7 **Baldock** Herts
187 G2 **Baldovie** C Dund
237 d5 **Baldrine** IoM
20 F3 **Baldslow** E Susx
106 B5 **Bale** Norfk
186 D2 **Baledgarno** P & K
188 C7 **Balemartine** Ag & B
177 G5 **Balerno** C Edin
186 D6 **Balfarg** Fife
196 E3 **Balfield** Angus
234 C3 **Balfour** Ork
174 F1 **Balfron** Stirlg
216 C6 **Balgaveny** Abers
196 E6 **Balgavies** Angus
185 L8 **Balgonar** Fife
144 D6 **Balgowan** D & G
202 F6 **Balgowan** Highld
218 B7 **Balgown** Highld
144 B3 **Balgracie** D & G
196 C8 **Balgray** Angus
165 H5 **Balgray** S Lans
44 F5 **Balham** Gt Lon
195 L6 **Balhary** P & K
186 B1 **Balholmie** P & K
230 C3 **Baligill** Highld
195 L5 **Balintore** Angus
223 J6 **Balintore** Highld
223 G7 **Balintraid** Highld
233 b6 **Balivanich** W Isls
133 G4 **Balk** N York

196 B7 **Balkeerie** Angus
125 J5 **Balkholme** E R Yk
173 H6 **Ballanlay** Ag & B
152 C5 **Ballantrae** S Ayrs
237 b6 **Ballasalla** IoM
205 J6 **Ballater** Abers
237 c3 **Ballaugh** IoM
223 G6 **Ballchraggan** Highld
178 B3 **Ballencrieff** E Loth
188 B6 **Ballevullin** Ag & B
100 D2 **Ballidon** Derbys
161 L2 **Balliekine** N Ayrs
182 F7 **Balliemore** Ag & B
152 F4 **Balligmorrie** S Ayrs
172 F2 **Ballimore** Ag & B
184 C4 **Ballimore** Stirlg
214 E6 **Ballindalloch** Moray
186 D2 **Ballindean** P & K
58 E7 **Ballinger Common**
      Bucks
54 E2 **Ballingham** Herefs
186 C7 **Ballingry** Fife
194 F6 **Ballinluig** P & K
196 C5 **Ballinshoe** Angus
195 H5 **Ballintuim** P & K
213 H5 **Balloch** Highld
175 K4 **Balloch** N Lans
185 H4 **Balloch** P & K
153 G3 **Balloch** S Ayrs
174 D3 **Balloch** W Duns
206 B6 **Ballogie** Abers
31 G6 **Balls Cross** W Susx
32 E6 **Balls Green** E Susx
189 K7 **Ballygown** Ag & B
171 G5 **Ballygrant** Ag & B
188 F5 **Ballyhaugh** Ag & B
174 B2 **Ballymenoch** Ag & B
154 B6 **Balmaclellan** D & G
146 C6 **Balmae** D & G
174 D1 **Balmaha** Stirlg
186 E5 **Balmalcolm** Fife
146 B5 **Balmangan** D & G
207 H2 **Balmedie** Abers
186 F3 **Balmerino** Fife
162 B3 **Balmichael** N Ayrs
205 G6 **Balmoral Castle**
      Grounds Abers
175 G4 **Balmore** E Duns
223 J5 **Balmuchy** Highld
196 F6 **Balmuir** Angus
177 G2 **Balmule** Fife
187 G4 **Balmullo** Fife
226 E6 **Balnacoil Lodge**
      Highld
210 F5 **Balnacra** Highld
205 G6 **Balnacroft** Abers
213 G7 **Balnafoich** Highld
194 E6 **Balnaguard** P & K
180 F1 **Balnahard** Ag & B
180 F7 **Balnahard** Ag & B
212 C7 **Balnain** Highld
228 F2 **Balnakeil** Highld
223 H7 **Balnapaling** Highld
124 F6 **Balne** N York
185 L1 **Balquharn** P & K
184 C3 **Balquhidder** Stirlg
86 B7 **Balsall Common**
      Solhll
85 J6 **Balsall Heath** Birm
72 E6 **Balscote** Oxon
76 E4 **Balsham** Cambs
235 e1 **Baltasound** Shet
145 J3 **Baltersan** D & G
26 D4 **Baltonsborough**
      Somset
195 G4 **Balvarran** P & K
181 M4 **Balvicar** Ag & B
200 C3 **Balvraid** Highld
213 K7 **Balvraid** Highld
121 H5 **Bamber Bridge** Lancs
60 F4 **Bamber's Green**
      Essex

169 H3 **Bamburgh** Nthumb
169 H3 **Bamburgh Castle**
      Nthumb
195 K6 **Bamff** P & K
114 E5 **Bamford** Derbys
138 D4 **Bampton** Cumb
24 E6 **Bampton** Devon
56 F7 **Bampton** Oxon
138 D4 **Bampton Grange**
      Cumb
191 L2 **Banavie** Highld
72 F6 **Banbury** Oxon
50 F3 **Bancffosfelen**
      Carmth
206 D6 **Banchory** Abers
207 G5 **Banchory-Devenick**
      Abers
50 E3 **Bancycapel** Carmth
50 D2 **Bancyfelin** Carmth
186 C2 **Bandirran** P & K
216 D2 **Banff** Abers
109 H6 **Bangor** Gwynd
98 B4 **Bangor-is-y-coed**
      Wrexhm
9 G5 **Bangors** Cnwll
92 C6 **Bankend** Norfk
16 C2 **Bank** Hants
147 H2 **Bankend** D & G
185 M1 **Bankfoot** P & K
164 C6 **Bankglen** E Ayrs
207 G4 **Bankhead** C Aber
165 J1 **Bankhead** S Lans
175 K3 **Banknock** Falk
120 E6 **Banks** Lancs
155 L5 **Bankshill** D & G
106 F6 **Banningham** Norfk
61 H4 **Bannister Green**
      Essex
175 L1 **Bannockburn** Stirlg
44 E7 **Banstead** Surrey
6 F6 **Bantham** Devon
175 K3 **Banton** N Lans
38 B8 **Banwell** N Som
34 C3 **Bapchild** Kent
27 M4 **Bapton** Wilts
232 F1 **Barabhas** W Isls
163 J3 **Barassie** S Ayrs
223 G6 **Barbaraville** Highld
163 K5 **Barbieston** S Ayrs
130 C3 **Barbon** Cumb
23 L2 **Barbrook** Devon
73 G1 **Barby** Nhants
191 J7 **Barcaldine** Ag & B
72 C6 **Barcheston** Warwks
19 L3 **Barcombe** E Susx
19 L3 **Barcombe Cross**
      E Susx
131 L2 **Barden** N York
33 G4 **Barden Park** Kent
61 G2 **Bardfield End Green**
      Essex
61 G3 **Bardfield Saling**
      Essex
117 J7 **Bardney** Lincs
86 F2 **Bardon** Leics
149 K3 **Bardon Mill** Nthumb
175 G4 **Bardowie** E Duns
174 C4 **Bardrainney** Inver
129 G5 **Bardsea** Cumb
124 B2 **Bardsey** Leeds
91 L8 **Bardwell** Suffk
129 K6 **Bare** Lancs
69 H4 **Barewood** Herefs
145 J8 **Barfad** D & G
92 D3 **Barford** Norfk
72 C3 **Barford** Warwks
57 H2 **Barford St John** Oxon
28 B5 **Barford St Martin**
      Wilts
57 H2 **Barford St Michael**
      Oxon
35 H5 **Barfrestone** Kent

175 J5 **Bargeddie** N Lans
53 J7 **Bargoed** Caerph
153 H6 **Bargrennan** D & G
89 G7 **Barham** Cambs
35 G5 **Barham** Kent
78 D4 **Barham** Suffk
75 L2 **Bar Hill** Cambs
88 F2 **Barholm** Lincs
87 J2 **Barkby** Leics
87 J2 **Barkby Thorpe** Leics
102 C5 **Barkestone-le-Vale**
      Leics
42 C6 **Barkham** Wokham
45 H3 **Barking** Gt Lon
78 C4 **Barking** Suffk
45 H3 **Barkingside** Gt Lon
78 C4 **Barking Tye** Suffk
122 F6 **Barkisland** Calder
3 J2 **Barkla Shop** Cnwll
102 F4 **Barkston** Lincs
124 D4 **Barkston Ash** N York
75 L7 **Barkway** Herts
175 H5 **Barlanark** C Glas
99 K5 **Barlaston** Staffs
18 C3 **Barlavington** W Susx
115 J6 **Barlborough** Derbys
124 F4 **Barlby** N York
86 E3 **Barlestone** Leics
76 B6 **Barley** Herts
122 B3 **Barley** Lancs
88 B2 **Barleythorpe** Rutlnd
46 F3 **Barling** Essex
117 H6 **Barlings** Lincs
146 E4 **Barlochan** D & G
115 G6 **Barlow** Derbys
150 E3 **Barlow** Gatesd
124 F5 **Barlow** N York
125 J2 **Barmby Moor** E R Yk
125 G5 **Barmby on the**
      Marsh E R Yk
161 K1 **Barmollack** Ag & B
80 E1 **Barmouth** Gwynd
141 H4 **Barmpton** Darltn
135 J7 **Barmston** E R Yk
182 E8 **Barnacarry** Ag & B
88 F3 **Barnack** C Pete
140 D4 **Barnard Castle** Dur
57 H6 **Barnard Gate** Oxon
77 G5 **Barnardiston** Suffk
146 E4 **Barnbarroch** D & G
115 J2 **Barnburgh** Donc
93 K5 **Barnby** Suffk
124 F8 **Barnby Dun** Donc
102 E3 **Barnby in the**
      Willows Notts
116 A5 **Barnby Moor** Notts
144 D7 **Barncorkrie** D & G
44 E5 **Barnes** Gt Lon
33 H4 **Barnes Street** Kent
44 E2 **Barnet** Gt Lon
126 C8 **Barnetby le Wold**
      N Linc
106 B6 **Barney** Norfk
91 K7 **Barnham** Suffk
18 C5 **Barnham** W Susx
92 C3 **Barnham Broom**
      Norfk
197 G5 **Barnhead** Angus
187 H2 **Barnhill** C Dund
214 E3 **Barnhill** Moray
152 B7 **Barnhills** D & G
140 D5 **Barningham** Dur
91 L7 **Barningham** Suffk
118 C2 **Barnoldby le Beck**
      NE Lin
122 C2 **Barnoldswick** Lancs
31 J6 **Barns Green** W Susx
115 G1 **Barnsley** Barns
56 B6 **Barnsley** Gloucs
23 J5 **Barnstaple** Devon
61 G4 **Barnston** Essex
111 J5 **Barnston** Wirral

102 B5 **Barnstone** Notts
85 H8 **Barnt Green** Worcs
177 G4 **Barnton** C Edin
112 F6 **Barnton** Ches
88 F6 **Barnwell All Saints**
      Nhants
88 F6 **Barnwell St Andrew**
      Nhants
55 K4 **Barnwood** Gloucs
153 G4 **Barr** S Ayrs
233 b9 **Barra Airport** W Isls
145 H5 **Barrachan** D & G
188 B7 **Barrapoll** Ag & B
158 A7 **Barrasford** Nthumb
174 F6 **Barrhead** E Rens
152 F5 **Barrhill** S Ayrs
76 B5 **Barrington** Cambs
26 B7 **Barrington** Somset
3 H4 **Barripper** Cnwll
174 C7 **Barrmill** N Ayrs
182 B3 **Barrnacarry Bay**
      Ag & B
231 J2 **Barrock** Highld
55 K3 **Barrow** Gloucs
121 L3 **Barrow** Lancs
88 C1 **Barrow** Rutlnd
27 G5 **Barrow** Somset
77 H2 **Barrow** Suffk
168 C7 **Barrow Burn** Nthumb
102 E5 **Barrowby** Lincs
88 D4 **Barrowden** Rutlnd
122 C3 **Barrowford** Lancs
38 D6 **Barrow Gurney**
      N Som
126 D6 **Barrow Haven** N Linc
128 E5 **Barrow-in-Furness**
      Cumb
128 E5 **Barrow Island** Cumb
126 D6 **Barrow-upon-**
      Humber N Linc
101 L8 **Barrow upon Soar**
      Leics
101 G6 **Barrow upon Trent**
      Derbys
187 J1 **Barry** Angus
37 H6 **Barry** V Glam
37 H6 **Barry Island** V Glam
87 K2 **Barsby** Leics
93 H5 **Barsham** Suffk
86 B7 **Barston** Solhll
69 L6 **Bartestree** Herefs
216 F7 **Barthol Chapel** Abers
61 H4 **Bartholomew Green**
      Essex
99 H3 **Barthomley** Ches
28 F8 **Bartley** Hants
85 H6 **Bartley Green** Birm
76 E5 **Bartlow** Cambs
76 B4 **Barton** Cambs
98 C2 **Barton** Ches
56 C3 **Barton** Gloucs
120 E8 **Barton** Lancs
121 G3 **Barton** Lancs
141 G5 **Barton** N York
57 K6 **Barton** Oxon
7 K3 **Barton** Torbay
91 G3 **Barton Bendish** Norfk
39 J2 **Barton End** Gloucs
57 M2 **Barton Hartshorn**
      Bucks
101 K6 **Barton in Fabis** Notts
86 E3 **Barton in the Beans**
      Leics
59 H2 **Barton-le-Clay** Beds
133 L5 **Barton-le-Street**
      N York
133 L6 **Barton-le-Willows**
      N York
91 G8 **Barton Mills** Suffk
16 B4 **Barton-on-Sea** Hants
56 E2 **Barton-on-the-Heath**
      Warwks

26 D5 **Barton St David** Somset	129 G5 **Baycliff** Cumb	95 K3 **Beddgelert** Gwynd
88 C7 **Barton Seagrave** Nhants	40 F5 **Baydon** Wilts	19 L4 **Beddingham** E Susx
29 H3 **Barton Stacey** Hants	60 A6 **Bayford** Herts	44 F6 **Beddington** Gt Lon
23 L4 **Barton Town** Devon	27 G5 **Bayford** Somset	44 F6 **Beddington Corner** Gt Lon
107 H7 **Barton Turf** Norfk	233 b6 **Bayhead** W Isls	
100 D8 **Barton-under-Needwood** Staffs	78 D4 **Baylham** Suffk	78 F2 **Bedfield** Suffk
	54 E3 **Baysham** Herefs	74 F5 **Bedford** Beds
126 C6 **Barton-upon-Humber** N Linc	83 J2 **Bayston Hill** Shrops	17 K2 **Bedhampton** Hants
	77 G6 **Baythorne End** Essex	78 E2 **Bedingfield** Suffk
126 C6 **Barton Waterside** N Linc	84 C8 **Bayton** Worcs	78 E2 **Bedingfield Street** Suffk
232 f1 **Barvas** W Isls	57 J7 **Bayworth** Oxon	
90 D7 **Barway** Cambs	73 L6 **Beachampton** Bucks	132 D7 **Bedlam** N York
86 F4 **Barwell** Leics	91 H3 **Beachamwell** Norfk	34 B5 **Bedlam Lane** Kent
10 E4 **Barwick** Devon	20 C6 **Beachy Head** E Susx	159 G5 **Bedlington** Nthumb
26 E8 **Barwick** Somset	12 F2 **Beacon** Devon	53 H7 **Bedling** Myr Td
124 B3 **Barwick in Elmet** Leeds	62 A3 **Beacon End** Essex	38 E6 **Bedminster** Bristl
	30 E4 **Beacon Hill** Surrey	38 E6 **Bedminster Down** Bristl
98 B7 **Baschurch** Shrops	42 C2 **Beacon's Bottom** Bucks	
72 E2 **Bascote** Warwks		59 J7 **Bedmond** Herts
121 K2 **Bashall Eaves** Lancs	42 F3 **Beaconsfield** Bucks	99 L8 **Bednall** Staffs
46 B3 **Basildon** Essex	133 K3 **Beadlam** N York	167 J5 **Bedrule** Border
29 M2 **Basingstoke** Hants	75 G6 **Beadlow** Beds	83 G7 **Bedstone** Shrops
114 E6 **Baslow** Derbys	169 M4 **Beadnell** Nthumb	37 J3 **Bedwas** Caerph
25 M3 **Bason Bridge** Somset	10 E2 **Beaford** Devon	53 J7 **Bedwellty** Caerph
37 L3 **Bassaleg** Newpt	124 E5 **Beal** N York	86 D6 **Bedworth** Warwks
167 K1 **Bassendean** Border	169 G2 **Beal** Nthumb	87 J2 **Beeby** Leics
137 H2 **Bassenthwaite** Cumb	6 A1 **Bealsmill** Cnwll	30 B4 **Beech** Hants
29 H7 **Bassett** C Sotn	13 L3 **Beaminster** Dorset	99 J5 **Beech** Staffs
75 K5 **Bassingbourn** Cambs	150 F4 **Beamish** Dur	42 B7 **Beech Hill** W Berk
102 E1 **Bassingham** Lincs	131 K8 **Beamsley** N York	40 C8 **Beechingstoke** Wilts
102 F6 **Bassingthorpe** Lincs	39 K7 **Beanacre** Wilts	41 J5 **Beedon** W Berk
60 A3 **Bassus Green** Herts	169 G5 **Beanley** Nthumb	41 J5 **Beedon Hill** W Berk
89 G2 **Baston** Lincs	10 D7 **Beardon** Devon	135 H8 **Beeford** E R Yk
107 J8 **Bastwick** Norfk	12 C3 **Beare** Devon	114 E7 **Beeley** Derbys
43 H2 **Batchworth** Herts	31 K3 **Beare Green** Surrey	117 K2 **Beelsby** NE Lin
14 C2 **Batcombe** Dorset	71 L3 **Bearley** Warwks	6 L8 **Beenham** W Berk
27 G4 **Batcombe** Somset	151 G6 **Bearpark** Dur	13 G5 **Beer** Devon
59 J5 **Batford** Herts	174 F4 **Bearsden** E Duns	26 B5 **Beer** Somset
39 H7 **Bath** BaNES	33 K3 **Bearsted** Kent	25 L7 **Beercrocombe** Somset
39 H7 **Bathampton** BaNES	99 G5 **Bearstone** Shrops	
25 G6 **Bathealton** Somset	85 H6 **Bearwood** Birm	14 B1 **Beer Hackett** Dorset
39 H6 **Batheaston** BaNES	15 K3 **Bearwood** Poole	7 J7 **Beesands** Devon
39 H6 **Bathford** BaNES	155 J2 **Beattock** D & G	118 F5 **Beesby** Lincs
176 D5 **Bathgate** W Loth	60 F6 **Beauchamp Roding** Essex	7 J7 **Beeson** Devon
102 C2 **Bathley** Notts	53 J5 **Beaufort** Blae G	75 H5 **Beeston** Beds
5 L2 **Bathpool** Cnwll	16 E3 **Beaulieu** Hants	98 D2 **Beeston** Ches
25 K6 **Bathpool** Somset	16 E2 **Beaulieu House** Hants	123 K4 **Beeston** Leeds
62 F2 **Bath Side** Essex	212 E5 **Beauly** Highld	91 K1 **Beeston** Norfk
176 C5 **Bathville** W Loth	109 H6 **Beaumaris** IoA	101 K5 **Beeston** Notts
26 E2 **Bathway** Somset	148 C3 **Beaumont** Cumb	106 E4 **Beeston Regis** Norfk
123 J5 **Batley** Kirk	62 E3 **Beaumont** Essex	146 F2 **Beeswing** D & G
71 L7 **Batsford** Gloucs	236 c7 **Beaumont** Jersey	129 K4 **Beetham** Cumb
142 D5 **Battersby** N York	72 B1 **Beausale** Warwks	25 L8 **Beetham** Somset
44 F5 **Battersea** Gt Lon	29 L6 **Beauworth** Hants	106 A8 **Beetley** Norfk
78 B4 **Battisford Tye** Suffk	10 C5 **Beaworthy** Devon	57 J5 **Begbroke** Oxon
20 F3 **Battle** E Susx	61 H3 **Beazley End** Essex	49 J6 **Begelly** Pembks
52 F2 **Battle** Powys	111 K5 **Bebington** Wirral	82 D7 **Beguildy** Powys
196 D5 **Battledykes** Angus	93 J5 **Beccles** Suffk	93 H2 **Beighton** Norfk
103 L2 **Battle of Britain Memorial Flight** Lincs	120 F6 **Becconsall** Lancs	115 H5 **Beighton** Sheff
	84 D6 **Beckbury** Shrops	100 F3 **Beighton Hill** Derbys
46 C2 **Battlesbridge** Essex	45 G6 **Beckenham** Gt Lon	186 B5 **Bein Inn** P & K
24 E6 **Battleton** Somset	117 L3 **Beckering** Lincs	174 C7 **Beith** N Ayrs
70 F6 **Baughton** Worcs	136 E6 **Beckermet** Cumb	35 G4 **Bekesbourne** Kent
41 L7 **Baughurst** Hants	147 J5 **Beckfoot** Cumb	107 G8 **Belaugh** Norfk
206 B6 **Baulds** Abers	71 H7 **Beckford** Worcs	85 G7 **Belbroughton** Worcs
40 F3 **Baulking** Oxon	102 E2 **Beckhampton** Wilts	14 E1 **Belchalwell** Dorset
117 L6 **Baumber** Lincs	116 C4 **Beckingham** Lincs	14 F1 **Belchalwell Street** Dorset
56 A6 **Baunton** Gloucs	116 C4 **Beckingham** Notts	
28 B5 **Baverstock** Wilts	27 J2 **Beckington** Somset	77 J6 **Belchamp Otten** Essex
92 D2 **Bawburgh** Norfk	83 H7 **Beckjay** Shrops	77 H6 **Belchamp St Paul** Essex
106 C7 **Bawdeswell** Norfk	21 G2 **Beckley** E Susx	
25 M4 **Bawdrip** Somset	57 K5 **Beckley** Oxon	77 J6 **Belchamp Walter** Essex
79 H6 **Bawdsey** Suffk	91 G7 **Beck Row** Suffk	
115 M3 **Bawtry** Donc	128 F3 **Beck Side** Cumb	118 D6 **Belchford** Lincs
122 B5 **Baxenden** Lancs	45 H4 **Beckton** Gt Lon	169 G3 **Belford** Nthumb
86 C4 **Baxterley** Warwks	132 D8 **Beckwithshaw** N York	87 H3 **Belgrave** C Leic
208 D4 **Bay** Highld		178 E3 **Belhaven** E Loth
232 g2 **Bayble** W Isls	45 J3 **Becontree** Gt Lon	207 H2 **Belhelvie** Abers
29 K6 **Baybridge** Hants	132 D2 **Bedale** N York	215 K8 **Belhinnie** Abers
	27 J7 **Bedchester** Dorset	205 H3 **Bellabeg** Abers
	37 G4 **Beddau** Rhondd	182 A8 **Bellanoch** Ag & B

195 K4 **Bellaty** Angus	
131 G7 **Bell Busk** N York	
118 E5 **Belleau** Lincs	
85 G7 **Bell End** Worcs	
131 L2 **Bellerby** N York	
148 C4 **Belle Vue** Cumb	
123 L6 **Belle Vue** Wakefd	
164 F3 **Bellfield** S Lans	
165 J5 **Bellfield** S Lans	
58 F6 **Bellingdon** Bucks	
157 L5 **Bellingham** Nthumb	
161 H2 **Belloch** Ag & B	
161 H3 **Bellochantuy** Ag & B	
98 D4 **Bell o' th' Hill** Ches	
175 J6 **Bellshill** N Lans	
175 L6 **Bellside** N Lans	
176 E5 **Bellsquarry** W Loth	
33 G6 **Bells Yew Green** E Susx	
38 E7 **Belluton** BaNES	
213 G3 **Belmaduthie** Highld	
121 K7 **Belmont** Bl w D	
44 E7 **Belmont** Gt Lon	
163 J5 **Belmont** S Ayrs	
235 d2 **Belmont** Shet	
205 J3 **Belnacraig** Abers	
101 G3 **Belper** Derbys	
101 G3 **Belper Lane End** Derbys	
158 D6 **Belsay** Nthumb	
167 J4 **Belses** Border	
7 H4 **Belsford** Devon	
59 G7 **Belsize** Herts	
78 D6 **Belstead** Suffk	
10 F6 **Belstone** Devon	
121 L5 **Belthorn** Lancs	
47 K6 **Beltinge** Kent	
149 K3 **Beltingham** Nthumb	
116 D1 **Beltoft** N Linc	
101 H7 **Belton** Leics	
102 F4 **Belton** Lincs	
116 C1 **Belton** N Linc	
93 K3 **Belton** Norfk	
88 B3 **Belton** Rutlnd	
45 J4 **Belvedere** Gt Lon	
102 D5 **Belvoir** Leics	
102 D5 **Belvoir Castle** Leics	
17 J5 **Bembridge** IoW	
28 C5 **Bemerton** Wilts	
135 J5 **Bempton** E R Yk	
93 K6 **Benacre** Suffk	
233 c6 **Benbecula Airport** W Isls	
154 C3 **Benbuie** D & G	
191 H8 **Benderloch** Ag & B	
33 K6 **Benenden** Kent	
150 D4 **Benfieldside** Dur	
60 A5 **Bengeo** Herts	
71 J5 **Bengeworth** Worcs	
79 H3 **Benhall Green** Suffk	
79 H3 **Benhall Street** Suffk	
197 K3 **Benholm** Abers	
133 H7 **Beningbrough** N York	
59 M4 **Benington** Herts	
104 C3 **Benington** Lincs	
109 G5 **Benllech** IoA	
173 K2 **Benmore** Ag & B	
9 H6 **Bennacott** Cnwll	
162 C5 **Bennan** N Ayrs	
192 B3 **Ben Nevis** Highld	
117 K5 **Benniworth** Lincs	
33 J4 **Benover** Kent	
123 H2 **Ben Rhydding** Brad	
163 J2 **Benslie** N Ayrs	
41 L3 **Benson** Oxon	
206 F5 **Benthoul** C Aber	
115 K1 **Bentley** Donc	
126 C4 **Bentley** E R Yk	
30 C3 **Bentley** Hants	
78 D6 **Bentley** Suffk	
86 C4 **Bentley** Warwks	
23 K4 **Benton** Devon	

156 B4 **Bentpath** D & G
24 B5 **Bentwichen** Devon
30 A4 **Bentworth** Hants
186 E2 **Benvie** Angus
14 A2 **Benville** Dorset
89 L5 **Benwick** Cambs
71 J1 **Beoley** Worcs
199 L6 **Beoraidbeg** Highld
18 B3 **Bepton** W Susx
60 D3 **Berden** Essex
48 D2 **Berea** Pembks
6 C3 **Bere Alston** Devon
6 C3 **Bere Ferrers** Devon
14 F4 **Bere Regis** Dorset
93 G4 **Bergh Apton** Norfk
41 L2 **Berinsfield** Oxon
55 G7 **Berkeley** Gloucs
59 G6 **Berkhamsted** Herts
27 J2 **Berkley** Somset
86 B7 **Berkswell** Solhll
45 G4 **Bermondsey** Gt Lon
200 C2 **Bernera** Highld
183 G8 **Bernice** Ag & B
208 F4 **Bernisdale** Highld
41 L2 **Berrick Prior** Oxon
41 L2 **Berrick Salome** Oxon
227 K4 **Berriedale** Highld
137 L2 **Berrier** Cumb
82 D4 **Berriew** Powys
83 K3 **Berrington** Shrops
69 L2 **Berrington** Worcs
69 L2 **Berrington Green** Worcs
25 L2 **Berrow** Somset
70 D3 **Berrow Green** Worcs
215 L3 **Berryhillock** Moray
215 L4 **Berryhillock** Moray
23 J3 **Berrynarbor** Devon
7 J4 **Berry Pomeroy** Devon
97 L3 **Bersham** Wrexhm
20 B5 **Berwick** E Susx
40 C5 **Berwick Bassett** Wilts
158 F6 **Berwick Hill** Nthumb
28 B4 **Berwick St James** Wilts
27 L6 **Berwick St John** Wilts
27 L5 **Berwick St Leonard** Wilts
179 K7 **Berwick-upon-Tweed** Nthumb
102 D7 **Bescaby** Leics
120 E7 **Bescar** Lancs
71 G5 **Besford** Worcs
115 L2 **Bessacarr** Donc
57 J7 **Bessels Leigh** Oxon
135 J6 **Bessingby** E R Yk
106 E5 **Bessingham** Norfk
92 C4 **Besthorpe** Norfk
116 D8 **Besthorpe** Notts
101 K3 **Bestwood Village** Notts
126 C2 **Beswick** E R Yk
31 K2 **Betchworth** Surrey
62 C3 **Beth Chatto Garden** Essex
109 G7 **Bethel** Gwynd
108 E7 **Bethel** IoA
34 C6 **Bethersden** Kent
109 J7 **Bethesda** Gwynd
49 J4 **Bethesda** Pembks
51 K1 **Bethlehem** Carmth
45 G4 **Bethnal Green** Gt Lon
99 H3 **Betley** Staffs
45 L5 **Betsham** Kent
35 J4 **Betteshanger** Kent
13 K3 **Bettiscombe** Dorset
98 C5 **Bettisfield** Wrexhm
37 L3 **Bettws** Newpt
66 D4 **Bettws Bledrws** Cerdgn
82 C4 **Bettws Cedewain** Powys
65 J5 **Bettws Evan** Cerdgn
54 A6 **Bettws-Newydd** Mons
229 L3 **Bettyhill** Highld
36 D3 **Betws** Brdgnd
97 G3 **Betws Gwerfil Goch** Denbgs
96 C2 **Betws-y-Coed** Conwy
110 C6 **Betws-yn-Rhos** Conwy
65 J5 **Beulah** Cerdgn
67 K4 **Beulah** Powys
116 B6 **Bevercotes** Notts
126 C3 **Beverley** E R Yk
39 K2 **Beverstone** Gloucs
156 F7 **Bewcastle** Cumb
84 D7 **Bewdley** Worcs
132 B6 **Bewerley** N York
126 E1 **Bewholme** E R Yk
20 E4 **Bexhill** E Susx
45 J5 **Bexley** Gt Lon
45 J5 **Bexleyheath** Gt Lon
90 F3 **Bexwell** Norfk
77 L2 **Beyton** Suffk
77 L2 **Beyton Green** Suffk
232 d2 **Bhaltos** W Isls
233 b10 **Bhatarsaigh** W Isls
56 C6 **Bibury** Gloucs
57 L4 **Bicester** Oxon
85 L6 **Bickenhill** Solhll
103 L5 **Bicker** Lincs
112 C2 **Bickerstaffe** Lancs
124 C1 **Bickerton** N York
84 F2 **Bickford** Staffs
7 J2 **Bickington** Devon
23 H5 **Bickington** Devon
6 D4 **Bickleigh** Devon
12 B2 **Bickleigh** Devon
45 H6 **Bickley** Gt Lon
134 C2 **Bickley** N York
98 D3 **Bickley Moss** Ches
61 J7 **Bicknacre** Essex
25 H4 **Bicknoller** Somset
33 L2 **Bicknor** Kent
82 F6 **Bicton** Shrops
83 J1 **Bicton** Shrops
32 F5 **Biddborough** Kent
33 L5 **Biddenden** Kent
74 E4 **Biddenham** Beds
39 K5 **Biddestone** Wilts
26 B2 **Biddisham** Somset
73 J6 **Biddlesden** Bucks
99 K3 **Biddulph** Staffs
99 K2 **Biddulph Moor** Staffs
23 G6 **Bideford** Devon
71 K4 **Bidford-on-Avon** Warwks
125 J2 **Bielby** E R Yk
207 G5 **Bieldside** C Aber
17 G6 **Bierley** IoW
58 D5 **Bierton** Bucks
145 H6 **Big Balcraig** D & G
6 F6 **Bigbury** Devon
6 F6 **Bigbury-on-Sea** Devon
117 H1 **Bigby** Lincs
154 B3 **Big Carlae** D & G
165 K2 **Biggar** S Lans
100 D2 **Biggin** Derbys
100 E3 **Biggin** Derbys
124 E4 **Biggin** N York
32 D2 **Biggin Hill** Gt Lon
45 H7 **Biggin Hill Airport** Gt Lon
75 H5 **Biggleswade** Beds
156 B6 **Bigholms** D & G
230 D3 **Bighouse** Highld
29 L4 **Bighton** Hants
148 A4 **Biglands** Cumb
18 D3 **Bignor** W Susx
53 K6 **Big Pit Blaenavon** Torfn
136 D5 **Bigrigg** Cumb
219 H5 **Big Sand** Highld
235 c7 **Bigton** Shet
101 K4 **Bilborough** C Nott
25 G3 **Bilbrook** Somset
124 E2 **Bilbrough** N York
231 K5 **Bilbster** Highld
140 F3 **Bildershaw** Dur
78 B5 **Bildeston** Suffk
46 B2 **Billericay** Essex
87 K3 **Billesdon** Leics
71 K3 **Billesley** Warwks
103 J5 **Billingborough** Lincs
112 D2 **Billinge** St Hel
92 E7 **Billingford** Norfk
106 B7 **Billingford** Norfk
141 K3 **Billingham** S on T
103 J2 **Billinghay** Lincs
115 H1 **Billingley** Barns
31 H6 **Billingshurst** W Susx
84 C6 **Billingsley** Shrops
58 F4 **Billington** Beds
121 L4 **Billington** Lancs
93 J2 **Billockby** Norfk
150 E7 **Billy Row** Dur
121 G3 **Bilsborrow** Lancs
119 G6 **Bilsby** Lincs
18 D5 **Bilsham** W Susx
34 D7 **Bilsington** Kent
101 M1 **Bilsthorpe** Notts
177 H5 **Bilston** Mdloth
85 G4 **Bilston** Wolves
86 D3 **Bilstone** Leics
126 E4 **Bilton** E R Yk
124 D1 **Bilton** N York
132 D7 **Bilton** N York
86 F8 **Bilton** Warwks
117 K3 **Binbrook** Lincs
14 D5 **Bincombe** Dorset
26 E2 **Binegar** Somset
42 D6 **Binfield** Br For
42 C5 **Binfield Heath** Oxon
158 B7 **Bingfield** Nthumb
102 B4 **Bingham** Notts
14 E3 **Bingham's Melcombe** Dorset
123 G3 **Bingley** Brad
106 B5 **Binham** Norfk
86 E7 **Binley** Covtry
29 H2 **Binley** Hants
86 E7 **Binley Woods** Warwks
15 G5 **Binnegar** Dorset
176 B4 **Binniehill** Falk
30 F3 **Binscombe** Surrey
17 H4 **Binstead** IoW
30 C7 **Binsted** Hants
18 D4 **Binsted** W Susx
71 K4 **Binton** Warwks
106 B7 **Bintree** Norfk
61 M4 **Birch** Essex
105 J5 **Bircham Newton** Norfk
105 J4 **Bircham Tofts** Norfk
60 E4 **Birchanger** Essex
100 C6 **Birch Cross** Staffs
69 J2 **Bircher** Herefs
61 M4 **Birch Green** Essex
37 J4 **Birchgrove** Cardif
51 K5 **Birchgrove** Swans
32 D7 **Birchgrove** W Susx
35 J2 **Birchington** Kent
86 C5 **Birchley Heath** Warwks
100 E1 **Birchover** Derbys
114 A4 **Birch Vale** Derbys
25 K8 **Birch Wood** Somset
112 F4 **Birchwood** Warrtn
115 M3 **Bircotes** Notts
77 G6 **Birdbrook** Essex
133 G4 **Birdforth** N York
17 M3 **Birdham** W Susx
72 E2 **Birdingbury** Warwks
55 L5 **Birdlip** Gloucs
134 C6 **Birdsall** N York
123 J8 **Birds Edge** Kirk
60 F6 **Birds Green** Essex
84 D6 **Birdsgreen** Shrops
13 K3 **Birdsmoorgate** Dorset
115 G2 **Birdwell** Barns
168 B2 **Birgham** Border
223 G3 **Birichin** Highld
141 H6 **Birkby** N York
120 D7 **Birkdale** Sefton
215 L2 **Birkenbog** Abers
111 K4 **Birkenhead** Wirral
216 E5 **Birkenhills** Abers
123 J5 **Birkenshaw** Kirk
205 H6 **Birkhall** Abers
186 F1 **Birkhill** Angus
166 B6 **Birkhill** D & G
124 E5 **Birkin** N York
69 J4 **Birley** Herefs
115 G3 **Birley Carr** Sheff
46 B7 **Birling** Kent
71 G5 **Birlingham** Worcs
85 J6 **Birmingham** Birm
85 L6 **Birmingham Airport** Solhll
195 G7 **Birnam** P & K
217 J7 **Birness** Abers
206 B6 **Birse** Abers
205 L5 **Birsemore** Abers
123 J5 **Birstall** Kirk
87 H2 **Birstall** Leics
132 C7 **Birstwith** N York
151 G4 **Birtley** Gatesd
69 G2 **Birtley** Herefs
157 L6 **Birtley** Nthumb
70 D7 **Birts Street** Worcs
88 C4 **Bisbrooke** Rutlnd
118 C5 **Biscathorpe** Lincs
42 D4 **Bisham** W & M
71 H4 **Bishampton** Worcs
24 B6 **Bish Mill** Devon
140 F2 **Bishop Auckland** Dur
117 G4 **Bishopbridge** Lincs
175 G4 **Bishopbriggs** E Duns
126 B3 **Bishop Burton** E R Yk
141 H2 **Bishop Middleham** Dur
214 F2 **Bishopmill** Moray
132 E6 **Bishop Monkton** N York
117 G3 **Bishop Norton** Lincs
35 G4 **Bishopsbourne** Kent
40 B7 **Bishops Cannings** Wilts
83 G5 **Bishop's Castle** Shrops
27 G8 **Bishop's Caundle** Dorset
55 L3 **Bishop's Cleeve** Gloucs
70 B5 **Bishop's Frome** Herefs
61 G4 **Bishop's Green** Essex
25 J6 **Bishops Hull** Somset
72 E3 **Bishop's Itchington** Warwks
25 J5 **Bishops Lydeard** Somset
55 J3 **Bishop's Norton** Gloucs
24 B6 **Bishop's Nympton** Devon
99 H6 **Bishop's Offley** Staffs
60 D4 **Bishop's Stortford** Herts
29 L5 **Bishop's Sutton** Hants

72 C3 **Bishop's Tachbrook** Warwks
23 J5 **Bishop's Tawton** Devon
7 K2 **Bishopsteignton** Devon
29 J7 **Bishopstoke** Hants
51 H7 **Bishopston** Swans
58 D6 **Bishopstone** Bucks
19 M5 **Bishopstone** E Susx
69 H5 **Bishopstone** Herefs
47 K6 **Bishopstone** Kent
40 E4 **Bishopstone** Swindn
28 B6 **Bishopstone** Wilts
27 K3 **Bishopstrow** Wilts
38 E7 **Bishop Sutton** BaNES
29 K7 **Bishop's Waltham** Hants
25 K8 **Bishopswood** Somset
84 E2 **Bishop's Wood** Staffs
38 E6 **Bishopsworth** Bristl
132 D6 **Bishop Thornton** N York
124 F2 **Bishopthorpe** York
141 J3 **Bishopton** Darltn
174 E4 **Bishopton** Rens
134 C7 **Bishop Wilton** E R Yk
38 B3 **Bishton** Newpt
100 A7 **Bishton** Staffs
55 K6 **Bisley** Gloucs
42 F8 **Bisley** Surrey
3 K3 **Bissoe** Cnwll
15 L3 **Bisterne** Hants
103 G6 **Bitchfield** Lincs
23 J3 **Bittadon** Devon
6 F4 **Bittaford** Devon
83 L7 **Bitterley** Shrops
29 J8 **Bitterne** C Sotn
87 C6 **Bitteswell** Leics
39 G6 **Bitton** S Glos
42 B4 **Bix** Oxon
235 c5 **Bixter** Shet
87 H4 **Blaby** Leics
179 H7 **Blackadder** Border
7 J5 **Blackawton** Devon
12 E1 **Blackborough** Devon
90 F1 **Blackborough End** Norfk
56 F6 **Black Bourton** Oxon
20 B2 **Blackboys** E Susx
101 G3 **Blackbrook** Derbys
112 D3 **Blackbrook** St Hel
99 H5 **Blackbrook** Staffs
206 F3 **Blackburn** Abers
121 K5 **Blackburn** Bl w D
176 D5 **Blackburn** W Loth
150 F2 **Black Callerton** N u Ty
192 E5 **Black Corries Lodge** Highld
164 C7 **Blackcraig** E Ayrs
182 D1 **Black Crofts** Ag & B
207 H3 **Blackdog** Abers
11 J3 **Black Dog** Devon
13 K2 **Blackdown** Dorset
115 G2 **Blacker Hill** Barns
45 J5 **Blackfen** Gt Lon
16 E3 **Blackfield** Hants
185 J5 **Blackford** P & K
26 B2 **Blackford** Somset
26 F6 **Blackford** Somset
101 G8 **Blackfordby** Leics
177 G4 **Blackhall** C Edin
151 K6 **Blackhall Colliery** Dur
166 F2 **Blackhaugh** Border
45 G5 **Blackheath** Gt Lon
85 H6 **Blackheath** Sandw
93 J8 **Blackheath** Suffk
31 G3 **Blackheath** Surrey
217 K3 **Blackhill** Abers
217 K5 **Blackhill** Abers
150 D5 **Blackhill** Dur

217 H5 **Blackhill of Clackriach** Abers
12 C4 **Blackhorse** Devon
165 K7 **Blacklaw** D & G
113 J2 **Blackley** Manch
195 J4 **Blacklunans** P & K
69 K6 **Blackmarstone** Herefs
36 E3 **Blackmill** Brdgnd
30 C5 **Blackmoor** Hants
38 C7 **Blackmoor** N Som
123 G2 **Blackmoorfoot** Kirk
60 F7 **Blackmore** Essex
61 H2 **Blackmore End** Essex
61 H2 **Blackness** Falk
30 D3 **Blacknest** Hants
61 J4 **Black Notley** Essex
122 C3 **Blacko** Lancs
51 J7 **Black Pill** Swans
120 D4 **Blackpool** Bpool
7 K6 **Blackpool** Devon
120 D4 **Blackpool Airport** Lancs
176 B5 **Blackridge** W Loth
121 J7 **Blackrod** Bolton
214 E6 **Blacksboat** Moray
147 J2 **Blackshaw** D & G
122 E5 **Blackshaw Head** Calder
121 K6 **Blacksnape** Bl w D
19 H3 **Blackstone** W Susx
93 K6 **Black Street** Suffk
57 L4 **Blackthorn** Oxon
77 K2 **Blackthorpe** Suffk
125 J5 **Blacktoft** E R Yk
207 G4 **Blacktop** C Aber
10 C4 **Black Torrington** Devon
100 E3 **Blackwall** Derbys
3 J3 **Blackwater** Cnwll
42 D7 **Blackwater** Hants
17 G5 **Blackwater** IoW
25 K7 **Blackwater** Somset
162 A4 **Blackwaterfoot** N Ayrs
148 D4 **Blackwell** Cumb
101 H2 **Blackwell** Derbys
114 C6 **Blackwell** Derbys
72 B5 **Blackwell** Warwks
71 H1 **Blackwell** Worcs
37 J2 **Blackwood** Caerph
154 F5 **Blackwood** D & G
164 F1 **Blackwood** S Lans
111 L7 **Blacon** Ches
145 J4 **Bladnoch** D & G
57 J5 **Bladon** Oxon
65 H5 **Blaenannerch** Cerdgn
96 A4 **Blaenau Ffestiniog** Gwynd
53 K6 **Blaenavon** Torfn
65 H6 **Blaenffos** Pembks
36 D2 **Blaengarw** Brdgnd
52 D6 **Blaengwrach** Neath
36 D2 **Blaengwynfi** Neath
66 E2 **Blaenpennal** Cerdgn
80 D7 **Blaenplwyf** Cerdgn
65 J5 **Blaenporth** Cerdgn
52 E7 **Blaenrhondda** Rhondd
50 B1 **Blaenwaun** Carmth
50 D1 **Blaen-y-Coed** Carmth
52 E7 **Blaen-y-cwm** Rhondd
38 D8 **Blagdon** N Som
25 K7 **Blagdon** Somset
7 K4 **Blagdon** Torbay
25 K7 **Blagdon Hill** Somset
191 K2 **Blaich** Highld
190 D3 **Blain** Highld
53 L8 **Blaina** Blae G
194 D4 **Blair Atholl** P & K
184 F7 **Blair Drummond** Stirlg

195 J7 **Blairgowrie** P & K
176 D2 **Blairhall** Fife
185 K7 **Blairingone** P & K
185 H7 **Blairlogie** Stirlg
173 L2 **Blairmore** Ag & B
228 C4 **Blairmore** Highld
204 F3 **Blairnamarrow** Moray
173 G4 **Blair's Ferry** Ag & B
55 G5 **Blaisdon** Gloucs
84 E7 **Blakebrook** Worcs
84 F7 **Blakedown** Worcs
61 H4 **Blake End** Essex
112 D7 **Blakemere** Ches
69 G6 **Blakemere** Herefs
85 H3 **Blakenall Heath** Wsall
54 F6 **Blakeney** Gloucs
106 B4 **Blakeney** Norfk
99 G3 **Blakenhall** Ches
85 G4 **Blakenhall** Wolves
73 J4 **Blakesley** Nhants
150 B5 **Blanchland** Nthumb
15 G2 **Blandford Forum** Dorset
15 G2 **Blandford St Mary** Dorset
132 C8 **Bland Hill** N York
174 F3 **Blanefield** Stirlg
103 H1 **Blankney** Lincs
175 J6 **Blantyre** S Lans
191 L3 **Blar a' Chaorainn** Highld
202 F6 **Blargie** Highld
191 L3 **Blarmachfoldach** Highld
88 B4 **Blaston** Leics
88 D4 **Blatherwycke** Nhants
129 G2 **Blawith** Cumb
154 B5 **Blawquhairn** D & G
79 H3 **Blaxhall** Suffk
116 A2 **Blaxton** Donc
150 F3 **Blaydon** Gatesd
26 C3 **Bleadney** Somset
25 M1 **Bleadon** N Som
34 F3 **Blean** Kent
102 B3 **Bleasby** Notts
121 H2 **Bleasdale** Lancs
187 G4 **Blebocraigs** Fife
68 E2 **Bleddfa** Powys
56 E4 **Bledington** Gloucs
58 C7 **Bledlow** Bucks
42 D2 **Bledlow Ridge** Bucks
178 B6 **Blegbie** E Loth
138 F2 **Blencarn** Cumb
147 L5 **Blencogo** Cumb
30 B8 **Blendworth** Hants
147 L6 **Blennerhasset** Cumb
57 J4 **Bletchingdon** Oxon
32 B3 **Bletchingley** Surrey
58 E2 **Bletchley** M Keyn
98 F5 **Bletchley** Shrops
49 H4 **Bletherston** Pembks
74 E3 **Bletsoe** Beds
41 K4 **Blewbury** Oxon
106 E6 **Blickling** Norfk
101 L2 **Blidworth** Notts
101 L2 **Blidworth Bottoms** Notts
147 K7 **Blindcrake** Cumb
32 C4 **Blindley Heath** Surrey
5 H2 **Blisland** Cnwll
28 D8 **Blissford** Hants
84 D8 **Bliss Gate** Worcs
73 K4 **Blisworth** Nhants
100 B8 **Blithbury** Staffs
71 L7 **Blockley** Gloucs
93 G2 **Blofield** Norfk
93 G2 **Blofield Heath** Norfk
92 B7 **Blo Norton** Norfk
167 J4 **Bloomfield** Border
99 G5 **Blore** Staffs
100 C3 **Blore** Staffs

72 E7 **Bloxham** Oxon
103 H2 **Bloxholm** Lincs
85 H3 **Bloxwich** Wsall
15 G4 **Bloxworth** Dorset
132 B7 **Blubberhouses** N York
24 F3 **Blue Anchor** Somset
46 C7 **Blue Bell Hill** Kent
114 C5 **Blue John Cavern** Derbys
111 J2 **Blundellsands** Sefton
93 L4 **Blundeston** Suffk
75 H4 **Blunham** Beds
40 C3 **Blunsdon St Andrew** Swindn
84 F8 **Bluntington** Worcs
89 L8 **Bluntisham** Cambs
116 F3 **Blyborough** Lincs
93 J7 **Blyford** Suffk
84 E2 **Blymhill** Staffs
115 L4 **Blyth** Notts
159 H5 **Blyth** Nthumb
165 M1 **Blyth Bridge** Border
93 J7 **Blythburgh** Suffk
178 D7 **Blythe** Border
116 D3 **Blyton** Lincs
187 J5 **Boarhills** Fife
17 H2 **Boarhunt** Hants
57 L5 **Boarstall** Bucks
222 D6 **Boath** Highld
203 L2 **Boat of Garten** Highld
46 E6 **Bobbing** Kent
84 E5 **Bobbington** Staffs
61 J4 **Bocking** Essex
61 J3 **Bocking Churchstreet** Essex
217 L6 **Boddam** Abers
235 C4 **Boddam** Shet
55 K3 **Boddington** Gloucs
108 D5 **Bodedern** IoA
110 D6 **Bodelwyddan** Denbgs
69 K4 **Bodenham** Herefs
28 D6 **Bodenham** Wilts
69 K4 **Bodenham Moor** Herefs
108 E4 **Bodewryd** IoA
110 F7 **Bodfari** Denbgs
108 F6 **Bodffordd** IoA
94 F5 **Bodfuan** Gwynd
106 D4 **Bodham** Norfk
33 K7 **Bodiam** E Susx
33 K7 **Bodiam Castle** E Susx
72 F6 **Bodicote** Oxon
5 H5 **Bodinnick** Cnwll
20 D3 **Bodle Street Green** E Susx
5 G3 **Bodmin** Cnwll
5 J1 **Bodmin Moor** Cnwll
109 M6 **Bodnant Garden** Conwy
34 E3 **Bodsham Green** Kent
5 G4 **Bodwen** Cnwll
212 F4 **Bogallan** Highld
217 J7 **Bogbrae** Abers
163 K3 **Bogend** S Ayrs
177 L4 **Boggs Holdings** E Loth
177 H5 **Boghall** Mdloth
176 D5 **Boghall** W Loth
164 F2 **Boghead** S Lans
215 H2 **Bogmoor** Moray
197 G3 **Bogmuir** Abers
216 B5 **Bogniebrae** Abers
18 C6 **Bognor Regis** W Susx
203 L2 **Bogroy** Highld
154 B6 **Bogue** D & G
3 L5 **Bohortha** Cnwll
201 L8 **Bohuntine** Highld
140 F3 **Bolam** Dur
7 G7 **Bolberry** Devon

85 K5 **Boldmere** Birm
16 C3 **Boldre** Hants
140 C4 **Boldron** Dur
116 C4 **Bole** Notts
100 F2 **Bolehill** Derbys
24 E7 **Bolham** Devon
25 J8 **Bolham Water** Devon
3 K1 **Bolingey** Cnwll
113 L6 **Bollington** Ches
31 L6 **Bolney** W Susx
74 F3 **Bolnhurst** Beds
197 G6 **Bolshan** Angus
115 J7 **Bolsover** Derbys
114 F3 **Bolsterstone** Sheff
133 G3 **Boltby** N York
205 J3 **Boltenstone** Abers
121 L8 **Bolton** Bolton
138 F3 **Bolton** Cumb
178 B4 **Bolton** E Loth
125 J1 **Bolton** E R Yk
169 G6 **Bolton** Nthumb
131 K8 **Bolton Abbey** N York
122 B1 **Bolton by Bowland**
Lancs
148 E2 **Boltonfellend** Cumb
147 M6 **Boltongate** Cumb
129 K6 **Bolton le Sands** Lancs
147 M6 **Bolton Low Houses**
Cumb
141 G7 **Bolton-on-Swale**
N York
124 E3 **Bolton Percy** N York
115 J2 **Bolton Upon Dearne**
Barns
5 J1 **Bolventor** Cnwll
98 C8 **Bomere Heath**
Shrops
222 E3 **Bonar Bridge** Highld
182 E2 **Bonawe** Ag & B
126 C7 **Bonby** N Linc
65 H6 **Boncath** Pembks
167 J6 **Bonchester Bridge**
Border
10 F4 **Bondleigh** Devon
121 G2 **Bonds** Lancs
176 D3 **Bo'ness** Falk
85 J2 **Boney Hay** Staffs
174 D3 **Bonhill** W Duns
84 E3 **Boningale** Shrops
167 K5 **Bonjedward** Border
175 L6 **Bonkle** N Lans
196 F7 **Bonnington** Angus
34 E7 **Bonnington** Kent
186 F6 **Bonnybank** Fife
175 L3 **Bonnybridge** Falk
217 G4 **Bonnykelly** Abers
177 J5 **Bonnyrigg** Mdloth
196 B8 **Bonnyton** Angus
100 F2 **Bonsall** Derbys
155 M7 **Bonshaw Tower**
D & G
81 J4 **Bont-Dolgadfan**
Powys
66 E2 **Bontnewydd** Cerdgn
95 H1 **Bontnewydd** Gwynd
97 G2 **Bontuchel** Denbgs
37 G5 **Bonvilston** V Glam
23 H4 **Boode** Devon
7 K5 **Boohay** Devon
42 D3 **Booker** Bucks
98 E7 **Booley** Shrops
167 J1 **Boon** Border
142 E4 **Boosbeck** R & Cl
61 K2 **Boose's Green** Essex
137 G6 **Boot** Cumb
122 F5 **Booth** Calder
125 H5 **Booth** E R Yk
103 G2 **Boothby Graffoe**
Lincs
102 F6 **Boothby Pagnell**
Lincs
113 G2 **Boothstown** Salfd

128 D2 **Bootle** Cumb
111 K3 **Bootle** Sefton
70 B1 **Boraston** Shrops
236 e2 **Bordeaux** Guern
34 B3 **Borden** Kent
157 G5 **Border Forest Park**
61 J6 **Bordon** Essex
27 K3 **Boreham** Wilts
20 D4 **Boreham Street**
E Susx
44 D7 **Borehamwood** Herts
155 L4 **Boreland** D & G
208 C4 **Boreraig** Highld
232 f1 **Borgh** W Isls
233 b9 **Borgh** W Isls
229 K4 **Borgie** Highld
146 B5 **Borgue** D & G
227 K4 **Borgue** Highld
77 J6 **Borley** Essex
218 B7 **Borneskitaig** Highld
146 A5 **Borness** D & G
132 F6 **Boroughbridge**
N York
33 G2 **Borough Green** Kent
101 H5 **Borrowash** Derbys
132 F7 **Borrowby** N York
176 D3 **Borrowstoun** Falk
46 B6 **Borstal** Medway
80 E5 **Borth** Cerdgn
166 F6 **Borthwickbrae**
Border
166 F6 **Borthwickshiels**
Border
95 K5 **Borth-y-Gest** Gwynd
209 G5 **Borve** Highld
232 d4 **Borve** W Isls
232 f1 **Borve** W Isls
233 b9 **Borve** W Isls
129 L5 **Borwick** Lancs
70 C5 **Bosbury** Herefs
8 E6 **Boscastle** Cnwll
15 L4 **Boscombe** Bmouth
28 D4 **Boscombe** Wilts
17 L2 **Bosham** W Susx
49 G8 **Bosherston** Pembks
113 K7 **Bosley** Ches
4 D4 **Bosoughan** Cnwll
133 L7 **Bossall** N York
8 E6 **Bossiney** Cnwll
34 F5 **Bossingham** Kent
24 D2 **Bossington** Somset
112 F7 **Bostock Green** Ches
104 B4 **Boston** Lincs
124 C2 **Boston Spa** Leeds
4 F7 **Boswinger** Cnwll
2 C5 **Botallack** Cnwll
59 M7 **Botany Bay** Gt Lon
92 C7 **Botesdale** Suffk
159 G5 **Bothal** Nthumb
41 J5 **Bothampstead**
W Berk
116 A6 **Bothamsall** Notts
147 L6 **Bothel** Cumb
13 L4 **Bothenhampton**
Dorset
175 J6 **Bothwell** S Lans
59 G7 **Botley** Bucks
29 K8 **Botley** Hants
57 J6 **Botley** Oxon
58 B3 **Botolph Claydon**
Bucks
19 G4 **Botolphs** W Susx
102 D6 **Bottesford** Leics
116 E1 **Bottesford** N Linc
76 D3 **Bottisham** Cambs
186 F5 **Bottomcraig** Fife
122 D6 **Bottoms** Calder
6 B4 **Botusfleming** Cnwll
94 E6 **Botwnnog** Gwynd
32 E4 **Bough Beech** Kent
68 C6 **Boughrood** Powys
73 L2 **Boughton** Nhants

91 G3 **Boughton** Norfk
116 B7 **Boughton** Notts
34 D5 **Boughton Aluph** Kent
33 K3 **Boughton Green**
Kent
34 B5 **Boughton Malherbe**
Kent
33 K3 **Boughton**
Monchelsea Kent
34 E3 **Boughton Street**
Kent
83 K6 **Bouldon** Shrops
169 K6 **Boulmer** Nthumb
116 F7 **Boultham** Lincs
75 K3 **Bourn** Cambs
103 H7 **Bourne** Lincs
45 J2 **Bournebridge** Essex
85 J6 **Bournebrook** Birm
74 D5 **Bourne End** Beds
42 E3 **Bourne End** Bucks
59 G6 **Bourne End** Herts
15 K4 **Bournemouth**
Bmouth
15 L3 **Bournemouth**
Airport Dorset
46 E3 **Bournes Green**
Sthend
85 G8 **Bournheath** Worcs
85 J7 **Bournville** Birm
27 H5 **Bourton** Dorset
40 E3 **Bourton** Oxon
83 L4 **Bourton** Shrops
40 B7 **Bourton** Wilts
72 E1 **Bourton on**
Dunsmore Warwks
56 D2 **Bourton-on-the-Hill**
Gloucs
56 D4 **Bourton-on-the-**
Water Gloucs
189 G4 **Bousd** Ag & B
129 H3 **Bouth** Cumb
131 L5 **Bouthwaite** N York
184 C2 **Bovain** Stirlg
28 B7 **Boveridge** Dorset
7 J1 **Bovey Tracey** Devon
59 G7 **Bovingdon** Herts
14 F5 **Bovington Tank**
Museum Dorset
11 G4 **Bow** Devon
45 G4 **Bow** Gt Lon
234 b7 **Bow** Ork
74 C7 **Bow Brickhill** M Keyn
55 J6 **Bowbridge** Gloucs
151 H7 **Bowburn** Dur
16 F5 **Bowcombe** IoW
12 E4 **Bowd** Devon
167 H4 **Bowden** Border
39 L6 **Bowden Hill** Wilts
113 H4 **Bowdon** Traffd
231 J3 **Bower** Highld
28 A6 **Bowerchalke** Wilts
231 J3 **Bowermadden**
Highld
99 J5 **Bowers** Staffs
46 C3 **Bowers Gifford** Essex
176 F1 **Bowershall** Fife
124 B5 **Bower's Row** Leeds
140 C4 **Bowes** Dur
121 G2 **Bowgreave** Lancs
147 H2 **Bowhouse** D & G
167 G2 **Bowland** Border
69 K4 **Bowley** Herefs
70 E4 **Bowley Green**
Surrey
123 H4 **Bowling** Brad
174 E4 **Bowling** W Duns
137 J7 **Bowmanstead** Cumb
170 F6 **Bowmore** Ag & B
147 L3 **Bowness-on-Solway**
Cumb
137 L7 **Bowness-on-**
Windermere Cumb

186 E5 **Bow of Fife** Fife
196 E6 **Bowriefauld** Angus
168 E2 **Bowsden** Nthumb
80 E6 **Bow Street** Cerdgn
55 K7 **Box** Gloucs
39 J6 **Box** Wilts
77 L6 **Boxford** Suffk
41 H6 **Boxford** W Berk
18 B4 **Boxgrove** W Susx
33 K2 **Boxley** Kent
59 H6 **Boxmoor** Herts
62 B2 **Boxted** Essex
77 J4 **Boxted** Suffk
59 H6 **Boxmoor** Herts
62 B2 **Boxted Cross** Essex
62 B2 **Boxted Heath** Essex
75 L2 **Boxworth** Cambs
47 L6 **Boyden Gate** Kent
100 D5 **Boylestone** Derbys
216 C2 **Boyndie** Abers
217 G2 **Boyndlie** Abers
135 H6 **Boynton** E R Yk
197 G6 **Boysack** Angus
9 J6 **Boyton** Cnwll
79 H5 **Boyton** Suffk
27 L4 **Boyton** Wilts
61 G6 **Boyton Cross** Essex
77 G5 **Boyton End** Suffk
74 C3 **Bozeat** Nhants
34 E6 **Brabourne** Kent
34 E6 **Brabourne Lees** Kent
231 K2 **Brabstermire** Highld
208 E6 **Bracadale** Highld
88 F2 **Braceborough** Lincs
117 G7 **Bracebridge Heath**
Lincs
116 F7 **Bracebridge Low**
Fields Lincs
103 G5 **Braceby** Lincs
122 C2 **Bracewell** Lancs
101 G2 **Brackenfield** Derbys
175 K5 **Brackenhirst** N Lans
201 J8 **Brackletter** Highld
73 H6 **Brackley** Nhants
42 E6 **Bracknell** Br For
185 H5 **Braco** P & K
215 L4 **Bracobrae** Moray
92 E4 **Bracon Ash** Norfk
199 L6 **Bracora** Highld
199 L6 **Bracorina** Highld
100 D3 **Bradbourne** Derbys
141 H2 **Bradbury** Dur
73 J5 **Bradden** Nhants
42 D2 **Bradenham** Bucks
39 M4 **Bradenstoke** Wilts
12 D1 **Bradfield** Devon
62 D2 **Bradfield** Essex
106 F5 **Bradfield** Norfk
114 F3 **Bradfield** Sheff
41 L6 **Bradfield** W Berk
77 K3 **Bradfield Combust**
Suffk
99 G2 **Bradfield Green** Ches
62 D3 **Bradfield Heath**
Essex
77 K3 **Bradfield St Clare**
Suffk
77 K3 **Bradfield St George**
Suffk
123 H4 **Bradford** Brad
9 L4 **Bradford** Devon
26 E8 **Bradford Abbas**
Dorset
39 J7 **Bradford Leigh** Wilts
39 J7 **Bradford-on-Avon**
Wilts
25 J6 **Bradford-on-Tone**
Somset
14 C4 **Bradford Peverell**
Dorset
23 J5 **Bradiford** Devon
17 H5 **Brading** IoW
100 E4 **Bradley** Derbys

29 M3 **Bradley** Hants
118 C1 **Bradley** NE Lin
99 K8 **Bradley** Staffs
85 G4 **Bradley** Wolves
71 H3 **Bradley** Worcs
71 H3 **Bradley Green** Worcs
100 B4 **Bradley in the Moors** Staffs
38 E4 **Bradley Stoke** S Glos
101 L6 **Bradmore** Notts
12 C2 **Bradninch** Devon
100 A2 **Bradnop** Staffs
13 L4 **Bradpole** Dorset
123 G4 **Bradshaw** Calder
9 K8 **Bradstone** Devon
113 H8 **Bradwall Green** Ches
114 D5 **Bradwell** Derbys
61 K4 **Bradwell** Essex
74 B6 **Bradwell** M Keyn
93 K3 **Bradwell** Norfk
62 B6 **Bradwell-on-Sea** Essex
62 B6 **Bradwell Waterside** Essex
9 J3 **Bradworthy** Devon
213 G2 **Brae** Highld
235 G4 **Brae** Shet
175 K3 **Braeface** Falk
197 H5 **Braehead** Angus
145 J4 **Braehead** D & G
176 C7 **Braehead** S Lans
204 E6 **Braemar** Abers
221 G5 **Braemore** Highld
227 J3 **Braemore** Highld
201 L6 **Brae Roy Lodge** Highld
173 L4 **Braeside** Inver
195 L5 **Braes of Coul** Angus
215 J3 **Braes of Enzie** Moray
234 d4 **Braeswick** Ork
182 D6 **Braevallich** Ag & B
141 H3 **Brafferton** Darltn
132 F5 **Brafferton** N York
74 B3 **Brafield-on-the-Green** Nhants
232 f2 **Bragar** W Isls
59 L4 **Bragbury End** Herts
175 L8 **Braidwood** S Lans
100 E4 **Brailsford** Derbys
61 J4 **Braintree** Essex
78 D1 **Braiseworth** Suffk
29 G6 **Braishfield** Hants
137 H3 **Braithwaite** Cumb
115 K3 **Braithwell** Donc
19 G4 **Bramber** W Susx
86 E5 **Bramcote** Warwks
29 L5 **Bramdean** Hants
93 G3 **Bramerton** Norfk
59 M5 **Bramfield** Herts
93 H8 **Bramfield** Suffk
78 D5 **Bramford** Suffk
113 K5 **Bramhall** Stockp
124 C2 **Bramham** Leeds
123 K2 **Bramhope** Leeds
41 M8 **Bramley** Hants
123 K4 **Bramley** Leeds
115 J3 **Bramley** Rothm
31 G3 **Bramley** Surrey
41 M8 **Bramley Corner** Hants
35 G4 **Bramling** Kent
11 L5 **Brampford Speke** Devon
75 J1 **Brampton** Cambs
138 F3 **Brampton** Cumb
148 F3 **Brampton** Cumb
116 D5 **Brampton** Lincs
106 F7 **Brampton** Norfk
115 H2 **Brampton** Rothm
93 J6 **Brampton** Suffk
54 E3 **Brampton Abbotts** Herefs

87 L6 **Brampton Ash** Nhants
83 G8 **Brampton Bryan** Herefs
115 J4 **Brampton-en-le-Morthen** Rothm
100 B6 **Bramshall** Staffs
28 F7 **Bramshaw** Hants
30 D5 **Bramshott** Hants
26 B5 **Bramwell** Somset
190 B3 **Branault** Highld
105 J4 **Brancaster** Norfk
105 J4 **Brancaster Staithe** Norfk
150 F7 **Brancepeth** Dur
214 D4 **Branchill** Moray
214 F1 **Branderburgh** Moray
126 E2 **Brandesburton** E R Yk
78 D3 **Brandeston** Suffk
106 D7 **Brandiston** Norfk
151 G6 **Brandon** Dur
102 E3 **Brandon** Lincs
91 H6 **Brandon** Suffk
86 E7 **Brandon** Warwks
92 C2 **Brandon Parva** Norfk
133 J5 **Brandsby** N York
117 G3 **Brandy Wharf** Lincs
61 G3 **Bran End** Essex
15 L4 **Branksome** Poole
15 K4 **Branksome Park** Poole
29 H3 **Bransbury** Hants
116 E5 **Bransby** Lincs
12 F5 **Branscombe** Devon
70 E4 **Bransford** Worcs
16 A3 **Bransgore** Hants
126 D4 **Bransholme** C KuH
84 B7 **Bransley** Shrops
102 D6 **Branston** Leics
117 G7 **Branston** Lincs
100 E7 **Branston** Staffs
117 H7 **Branston Booths** Lincs
17 G5 **Branstone** IoW
102 E2 **Brant Broughton** Lincs
78 D7 **Brantham** Suffk
136 E3 **Branthwaite** Cumb
148 B7 **Branthwaite** Cumb
125 L5 **Brantingham** E R Yk
115 M2 **Branton** Donc
168 F6 **Branton** Nthumb
132 F6 **Branton Green** N York
168 D2 **Branxton** Nthumb
100 E2 **Brassington** Derbys
32 E3 **Brasted** Kent
32 E3 **Brasted Chart** Kent
206 D5 **Brathens** Abers
119 G8 **Bratoft** Lincs
116 F5 **Brattleby** Lincs
27 K2 **Bratton** Wilts
10 C6 **Bratton Clovelly** Devon
23 K4 **Bratton Fleming** Devon
26 F5 **Bratton Seymour** Somset
60 C3 **Braughing** Herts
73 G2 **Braunston** Nhants
88 B3 **Braunston** Rutlnd
87 G3 **Braunstone** Leics
23 H4 **Braunton** Devon
134 B4 **Brawby** N York
230 B4 **Brawl** Highld
42 E4 **Bray** W & M
87 L6 **Braybrooke** Nhants
23 L4 **Brayford** Devon
5 M2 **Bray Shop** Cnwll
123 K2 **Braythorn** N York
124 F4 **Brayton** N York
42 E4 **Braywick** W & M

59 J4 **Breachwood Green** Herts
101 G5 **Breadsall** Derbys
55 G7 **Breadstone** Gloucs
3 G5 **Breage** Cnwll
212 D5 **Breakachy** Highld
222 C3 **Brealangwell Lodge** Highld
54 E6 **Bream** Gloucs
28 D7 **Breamore** Hants
25 L1 **Brean** Somset
232 d3 **Breanais** W Isls
132 E7 **Brearton** N York
232 e2 **Breascleit** W Isls
232 e2 **Breaclete** W Isls
101 J5 **Breaston** Derbys
66 C7 **Brechfa** Carmth
196 F4 **Brechin** Angus
91 L5 **Breckles** Norfk
154 E4 **Breckonside** D & G
53 G3 **Brecon** Powys
52 F3 **Brecon Beacons National Park**
113 L3 **Bredbury** Stockp
21 G3 **Brede** E Susx
69 L3 **Bredenbury** Herefs
78 F4 **Bredfield** Suffk
34 B3 **Bredgar** Kent
46 D7 **Bredhurst** Kent
71 G6 **Bredon** Worcs
71 G7 **Bredon's Hardwick** Worcs
71 G7 **Bredon's Norton** Worcs
69 G5 **Bredwardine** Herefs
101 H7 **Breedon on the Hill** Leics
176 C4 **Breich** W Loth
121 L8 **Breightmet** Bolton
125 G4 **Breighton** E R Yk
69 J6 **Breinton** Herefs
39 L5 **Bremhill** Wilts
33 H5 **Brenchley** Kent
24 B2 **Brendon** Devon
172 E2 **Brenfield** Ag & B
232 d3 **Brenish** W Isls
77 L5 **Brent Eleigh** Suffk
44 D5 **Brentford** Gt Lon
102 C8 **Brentingby** Leics
25 M2 **Brent Knoll** Somset
7 G4 **Brent Mill** Devon
60 C2 **Brent Pelham** Herts
45 L2 **Brentwood** Essex
21 K1 **Brenzett** Kent
34 D8 **Brenzett Green** Kent
85 J1 **Brereton** Staffs
113 H8 **Brereton Green** Ches
92 C7 **Bressingham** Norfk
100 F7 **Bretby** Derbys
86 E7 **Bretford** Warwks
71 K5 **Bretforton** Worcs
121 G6 **Bretherton** Lancs
235 d5 **Brettabister** Shet
91 L6 **Brettenham** Norfk
77 L4 **Brettenham** Suffk
111 K8 **Bretton** Flints
84 F2 **Brewood** Staffs
14 F4 **Briantspuddle** Dorset
60 A6 **Brickendon** Herts
59 J7 **Bricket Wood** Herts
114 F5 **Brick Houses** Sheff
71 H6 **Bricklehampton** Worcs
237 e2 **Bride** IoM
147 K7 **Bridekirk** Cumb
10 D6 **Bridestowe** Devon
216 B6 **Brideswell** Abers
11 J7 **Bridford** Devon
3 H3 **Bridge** Cnwll
35 G4 **Bridge** Kent
26 E6 **Bridgehampton** Somset

132 E5 **Bridge Hewick** N York
150 D5 **Bridgehill** Dur
17 H2 **Bridgemary** Hants
215 L7 **Bridgend** Abers
171 G6 **Bridgend** Ag & B
196 E3 **Bridgend** Angus
36 E4 **Bridgend** Brdgnd
165 L7 **Bridgend** D & G
6 E6 **Bridgend** Devon
186 F5 **Bridgend** Fife
215 J7 **Bridgend** Moray
186 B3 **Bridgend** P & K
176 E3 **Bridgend** W Loth
195 L5 **Bridgend of Lintrathen** Angus
206 B2 **Bridge of Alford** Abers
185 G7 **Bridge of Allan** Stirlg
204 E2 **Bridge of Avon** Moray
214 E7 **Bridge of Avon** Moray
193 J6 **Bridge of Balgie** P & K
195 J4 **Bridge of Brewlands** Angus
204 D2 **Bridge of Brown** Highld
195 J6 **Bridge of Cally** P & K
206 C6 **Bridge of Canny** Abers
195 K5 **Bridge of Craigisla** Angus
146 C3 **Bridge of Dee** D & G
207 H4 **Bridge of Don** C Aber
213 L6 **Bridge of Dulsie** Highld
206 C7 **Bridge of Dye** Abers
186 B4 **Bridge of Earn** P & K
193 H5 **Bridge of Ericht** P & K
206 D6 **Bridge of Feugh** Abers
230 F2 **Bridge of Forss** Highld
205 H6 **Bridge of Gairn** Abers
193 H5 **Bridge of Gaur** P & K
216 B4 **Bridge of Marnoch** Abers
192 E7 **Bridge of Orchy** Ag & B
194 D4 **Bridge of Tilt** P & K
215 J3 **Bridge of Tynet** Moray
235 B5 **Bridge of Walls** Shet
174 D5 **Bridge of Weir** Rens
9 H4 **Bridgerule** Devon
69 H6 **Bridge Sollers** Herefs
77 K5 **Bridge Street** Suffk
24 E5 **Bridgetown** Somset
112 C7 **Bridge Trafford** Ches
91 L6 **Bridgham** Norfk
84 C5 **Bridgnorth** Shrops
85 H2 **Bridgtown** Staffs
25 L4 **Bridgwater** Somset
135 J6 **Bridlington** E R Yk
13 L4 **Bridport** Dorset
54 E3 **Bridstow** Herefs
122 C3 **Brierfield** Lancs
124 C7 **Brierley** Barns
54 F5 **Brierley** Gloucs
85 G6 **Brierley Hill** Dudley
117 G1 **Brigg** N Linc
107 G6 **Briggate** Norfk
143 H5 **Briggswath** N York
136 F2 **Brigham** Cumb
135 G8 **Brigham** E R Yk
123 H6 **Brighouse** Calder
16 E5 **Brighstone** IoW
57 G7 **Brighthampton** Oxon
10 E5 **Brightley** Devon
20 D2 **Brightling** E Susx
62 C5 **Brightlingsea** Essex
19 J5 **Brighton** Br & H

111 J2 **Brighton le Sands** Sefton
176 C3 **Brightons** Falk
41 H5 **Brightwalton** W Berk
78 F5 **Brightwell** Suffk
41 M2 **Brightwell Baldwin** Oxon
41 L3 **Brightwell-cum-Sotwell** Oxon
42 A2 **Brightwell Upperton** Oxon
140 D5 **Brignall** Dur
184 C6 **Brig o'Turk** Stirlg
118 C2 **Brigsley** NE Lin
129 K2 **Brigsteer** Cumb
88 D6 **Brigstock** Nhants
58 A5 **Brill** Bucks
3 J5 **Brill** Cnwll
68 F5 **Brilley** Herefs
69 K2 **Brimfield** Herefs
69 K2 **Brimfield Cross** Herefs
115 H6 **Brimington** Derbys
7 J1 **Brimley** Devon
55 L5 **Brimpsfield** Gloucs
41 K7 **Brimpton** W Berk
55 K7 **Brimscombe** Gloucs
111 J5 **Brimstage** Wirral
115 F4 **Brincliffe** Sheff
125 H4 **Brind** E R Yk
235 C5 **Brindister** Shet
121 J5 **Brindle** Lancs
84 E2 **Brineton** Staffs
88 B5 **Bringhurst** Leics
88 F7 **Brington** Cambs
106 C5 **Briningham** Norfk
118 E6 **Brinkhill** Lincs
76 F4 **Brinkley** Cambs
86 E7 **Brinklow** Warwks
40 A4 **Brinkworth** Wilts
121 J6 **Brinscall** Lancs
101 J3 **Brinsley** Notts
115 H4 **Brinsworth** Rothm
106 C5 **Brinton** Norfk
234 c5 **Brinyan** Ork
105 M7 **Brisley** Norfk
38 F6 **Brislington** Bristl
34 C6 **Brissenden Green** Kent
38 E5 **Bristol** Bristl
38 D7 **Bristol Airport** N Som
38 E5 **Bristol Zoo** Bristl
106 C6 **Briston** Norfk
28 D5 **Britford** Wilts
53 J7 **Brithdir** Caerph
96 B8 **Brithdir** Gwynd
33 J2 **British Legion Village** Kent
51 L6 **Briton Ferry** Neath
42 A2 **Britwell Salome** Oxon
7 L5 **Brixham** Torbay
6 E5 **Brixton** Devon
44 F5 **Brixton** Gt Lon
27 K4 **Brixton Deverill** Wilts
73 L1 **Brixworth** Nhants
56 F6 **Brize Norton** Oxon
56 F6 **Brize Norton Airport** Oxon
70 F2 **Broad Alley** Worcs
40 D3 **Broad Blunsdon** Swindn
113 M3 **Broadbottom** Tamesd
17 M2 **Broadbridge** W Susx
31 J5 **Broadbridge Heath** W Susx
71 L6 **Broad Campden** Gloucs
123 G6 **Broad Carr** Calder
28 B6 **Broad Chalke** Wilts
12 C3 **Broadclyst** Devon
174 C4 **Broadfield** Inver
199 K2 **Broadford** Highld

31 H6 **Broadford Bridge** W Susx
166 C7 **Broadgairhill** Border
61 L4 **Broad Green** Essex
70 D4 **Broad Green** Worcs
179 H7 **Broadhaugh** Border
48 E5 **Broad Haven** Pembks
113 H4 **Broadheath** Traffd
12 E2 **Broadhembury** Devon
7 J3 **Broadhempston** Devon
40 C5 **Broad Hinton** Wilts
21 G2 **Broadland Row** E Susx
41 H7 **Broad Laying** Hants
215 J3 **Broadley** Moray
71 K5 **Broad Marston** Worcs
14 D5 **Broadmayne** Dorset
49 J6 **Broadmoor** Pembks
13 K3 **Broadoak** Dorset
20 C2 **Broad Oak** E Susx
21 G2 **Broad Oak** E Susx
54 C4 **Broad Oak** Herefs
35 G3 **Broad Oak** Kent
112 D3 **Broad Oak** St Hel
61 H5 **Broad's Green** Essex
35 G3 **Broadstairs** Kent
15 J4 **Broadstone** Poole
83 K5 **Broadstone** Shrops
21 H3 **Broad Street** E Susx
33 L2 **Broad Street** Kent
40 C5 **Broad Town** Wilts
70 D4 **Broadwas** Worcs
59 L4 **Broadwater** Herts
18 F5 **Broadwater** W Susx
84 E7 **Broadwaters** Worcs
48 E5 **Broadway** Pembks
25 L7 **Broadway** Somset
71 K6 **Broadway** Worcs
54 E5 **Broadwell** Gloucs
56 D3 **Broadwell** Gloucs
56 E6 **Broadwell** Oxon
72 F2 **Broadwell** Warwks
13 K2 **Broadwindsor** Dorset
10 F4 **Broadwood Kelly** Devon
9 K6 **Broadwoodwidger** Devon
209 J5 **Brochel** Highld
70 D4 **Brockamin** Worcs
29 L7 **Brockbridge** Hants
92 E7 **Brockdish** Norfk
16 C3 **Brockenhurst** Hants
164 F2 **Brocketsbrae** S Lans
78 D2 **Brockford Street** Suffk
73 J2 **Brockhall** Nhants
31 K2 **Brockham** Surrey
56 B4 **Brockhampton** Gloucs
17 K2 **Brockhampton** Hants
54 E2 **Brockhampton** Herefs
123 H7 **Brockholes** Kirk
126 E7 **Brocklesby** Lincs
38 C6 **Brockley** N Som
77 J1 **Brockley** Suffk
77 G5 **Brockley Green** Suffk
77 J4 **Brockley Green** Suffk
83 G3 **Brockton** Shrops
83 G6 **Brockton** Shrops
83 L5 **Brockton** Shrops
99 J6 **Brockton** Staffs
54 D7 **Brockweir** Gloucs
55 K5 **Brockworth** Gloucs
99 L8 **Brocton** Staffs
162 C3 **Brodick** N Ayrs
214 B3 **Brodie** Moray
115 H7 **Brodsworth** Donc
218 C7 **Brogaig** Highld
39 K3 **Brokenborough** Wilts

113 K6 **Broken Cross** Ches
27 J2 **Brokerswood** Wilts
111 K5 **Bromborough** Wirral
92 D7 **Brome** Suffk
92 D7 **Brome Street** Suffk
79 G4 **Bromeswell** Suffk
147 L5 **Bromfield** Cumb
83 J7 **Bromfield** Shrops
74 E4 **Bromham** Beds
39 L7 **Bromham** Wilts
45 H6 **Bromley** Gt Lon
84 D4 **Bromley** Shrops
46 C6 **Brompton** Medway
134 E3 **Brompton** N York
141 J7 **Brompton** N York
140 F7 **Brompton-on-Swale** N York
25 G5 **Brompton Ralph** Somset
24 E7 **Brompton Regis** Somset
70 D7 **Bromsberrow** Gloucs
55 G2 **Bromsberrow Heath** Gloucs
71 G1 **Bromsgrove** Worcs
70 B4 **Bromyard** Herefs
66 E2 **Bronant** Cerdgn
65 K5 **Brongest** Cerdgn
98 C4 **Bronington** Wrexhm
68 D7 **Bronllys** Powys
50 E2 **Bronwydd** Carmth
97 K5 **Bronygarth** Shrops
28 F8 **Brook** Hants
16 E5 **Brook** IoW
34 E6 **Brook** Kent
30 F4 **Brook** Surrey
93 G4 **Brooke** Norfk
88 B3 **Brooke** Rutlnd
117 K3 **Brookenby** Lincs
174 D5 **Brookfield** Rens
26 F5 **Brookhampton** Somset
28 F8 **Brook Hill** Hants
129 L6 **Brookhouse** Lancs
115 K4 **Brookhouse** Rothm
99 J1 **Brookhouse Green** Ches
114 B4 **Brookhouses** Derbys
21 K1 **Brookland** Kent
113 H4 **Brooklands** Traffd
59 L7 **Brookmans Park** Herts
45 L2 **Brook Street** Essex
34 C7 **Brook Street** Kent
77 J5 **Brook Street** Suffk
55 J5 **Brookthorpe** Gloucs
42 F8 **Brookwood** Surrey
75 H6 **Broom** Beds
151 G6 **Broom** Dur
115 H3 **Broom** Rothm
71 K4 **Broom** Warwks
93 H5 **Broome** Norfk
83 H7 **Broome** Shrops
84 F7 **Broome** Worcs
113 G4 **Broomedge** Warrtn
61 H5 **Broomfield** Essex
33 L3 **Broomfield** Kent
47 K6 **Broomfield** Kent
25 K5 **Broomfield** Somset
125 K5 **Broomfleet** E R Yk
150 C3 **Broomhaugh** Nthumb
115 H2 **Broom Hill** Barns
101 K3 **Broom Hill** Notts
159 G2 **Broomhill** Nthumb
34 D3 **Broom Street** Kent
226 F7 **Brora** Highld
84 C3 **Broseley** Shrops
150 A7 **Brotherlee** Dur
124 D5 **Brotherton** N York
142 E4 **Brotton** R & Cl
230 F4 **Broubster** Highld

139 H4 **Brough** Cumb
125 L5 **Brough** E R Yk
231 J2 **Brough** Highld
102 D2 **Brough** Notts
230 D4 **Brough** Shet
98 E4 **Broughall** Shrops
235 d2 **Brough Lodge** Shet
139 H5 **Brough Sowerby** Cumb
165 L3 **Broughton** Border
89 K7 **Broughton** Cambs
111 K8 **Broughton** Flints
28 F5 **Broughton** Hants
121 G4 **Broughton** Lancs
74 C6 **Broughton** M Keyn
126 B8 **Broughton** N Linc
122 D1 **Broughton** N York
134 B5 **Broughton** N York
88 B7 **Broughton** Nhants
72 E6 **Broughton** Oxon
113 J2 **Broughton** Salfd
99 H5 **Broughton** Staffs
36 E6 **Broughton** V Glam
87 G5 **Broughton Astley** Leics
39 K7 **Broughton Gifford** Wilts
71 G3 **Broughton Green** Worcs
71 G4 **Broughton Hackett** Worcs
128 F3 **Broughton-in-Furness** Cumb
145 J6 **Broughton Mains** D & G
128 F2 **Broughton Mills** Cumb
147 J7 **Broughton Moor** Cumb
56 E7 **Broughton Poggs** Oxon
187 H2 **Broughty Ferry** C Dund
29 K2 **Brown Candover** Hants
99 K2 **Brown Edge** Staffs
217 G6 **Brownhill** Abers
187 H4 **Brownhills** Fife
85 J3 **Brownhills** Wsall
41 L7 **Browninghill Green** Hants
55 K7 **Browns Hill** Gloucs
7 G5 **Brownston** Devon
134 E2 **Broxa** N York
60 B6 **Broxbourne** Herts
178 E3 **Broxburn** E Loth
176 M4 **Broxburn** W Loth
60 F3 **Broxted** Essex
69 G4 **Broxwood** Herefs
231 K7 **Bruan** Highld
194 C3 **Bruar** P & K
223 K4 **Brucefield** Highld
173 J6 **Bruchag** Ag & B
170 E6 **Bruichladdich** Ag & B
79 G3 **Bruisyard** Suffk
79 G2 **Bruisyard Street** Suffk
125 K8 **Brumby** N Linc
100 C1 **Brund** Staffs
93 G2 **Brundall** Norfk
78 F1 **Brundish** Suffk
78 F1 **Brundish Street** Suffk
159 G7 **Brunswick Village** N u Ty
122 F2 **Brunthwaite** Brad
87 H5 **Bruntingthorpe** Leics
186 E3 **Brunton** Fife
169 J4 **Brunton** Nthumb
28 E1 **Brunton** Wilts
24 E6 **Brushford** Somset
11 G4 **Brushford Barton** Devon

27 G4 **Bruton** Somset
70 F2 **Bryan's Green** Worcs
15 G2 **Bryanston** Dorset
155 L7 **Brydekirk** D & G
26 D7 **Brympton** Somset
51 G5 **Bryn** Carmth
36 C3 **Bryn** Neath
51 K3 **Brynamman** Carmth
64 F7 **Brynberian** Pembks
95 H4 **Bryncir** Gwynd
51 L5 **Bryn-coch** Neath
94 D6 **Bryncroes** Gwynd
80 E3 **Bryncrug** Gwynd
97 H3 **Bryneglwys** Denbgs
111 G6 **Brynford** Flints
112 E2 **Bryn Gates** Wigan
108 D6 **Bryngwran** IoA
54 B6 **Bryngwyn** Mons
68 D5 **Bryngwyn** Powys
64 E6 **Bryn-Henllan** Pembks
65 K4 **Brynhoffnant** Cerdgn
53 J5 **Brynmawr** Blae G
94 D5 **Bryn-mawr** Gwynd
36 D4 **Brynmenyn** Brdgnd
51 J6 **Brynmill** Swans
36 F4 **Brynna** Rhondd
109 H8 **Brynrefail** Gwynd
37 G4 **Brynsadler** Rhondd
97 G3 **Bryn Saith Marchog** Denbgs
108 F7 **Brynsiencyn** IoA
110 B6 **Bryn-y-Maen** Conwy
198 F2 **Bualintur** Highld
86 D8 **Bubbenhall** Warwks
125 H4 **Bubwith** E R Yk
174 E1 **Buchanan Smithy** Stirlg
217 L5 **Buchanhaven** Abers
185 J2 **Buchanty** P & K
184 F6 **Buchany** Stirlg
184 C8 **Buchlyvie** Stirlg
148 C5 **Buckabank** Cumb
75 H2 **Buckden** Cambs
131 N4 **Buckden** N York
93 H3 **Buckenham** Norfk
12 E3 **Buckerell** Devon
7 H3 **Buckfast** Devon
7 H3 **Buckfastleigh** Devon
186 F7 **Buckhaven** Fife
54 D5 **Buckholt** Mons
27 H6 **Buckhorn Weston** Dorset
45 H2 **Buckhurst Hill** Essex
215 J2 **Buckie** Moray
73 K7 **Buckingham** Bucks
58 E5 **Buckland** Bucks
7 G6 **Buckland** Devon
71 J7 **Buckland** Gloucs
75 L7 **Buckland** Herts
35 J6 **Buckland** Kent
41 G2 **Buckland** Oxon
31 K2 **Buckland** Surrey
22 F7 **Buckland Brewer** Devon
58 F6 **Buckland Common** Bucks
27 H2 **Buckland Dinham** Somset
10 C3 **Buckland Filleigh** Devon
7 G2 **Buckland in the Moor** Devon
6 D3 **Buckland Monachorum** Devon
14 D2 **Buckland Newton** Dorset
14 C6 **Buckland Ripers** Dorset
25 L8 **Buckland St Mary** Somset
7 H6 **Buckland-Tout-Saints** Devon

41 K6 **Bucklebury** W Berk
16 E3 **Bucklers Hard** Hants
78 F6 **Bucklesham** Suffk
111 J8 **Buckley** Flints
113 G5 **Bucklow Hill** Ches
102 E7 **Buckminster** Leics
99 K3 **Bucknall** C Stke
117 K7 **Bucknall** Lincs
57 K3 **Bucknell** Oxon
83 G8 **Bucknell** Shrops
215 J2 **Buckpool** Moray
207 G4 **Bucksburn** C Aber
22 E6 **Buck's Cross** Devon
31 H5 **Bucks Green** W Susx
30 D3 **Bucks Horn Oak** Hants
22 E6 **Buck's Mills** Devon
135 J2 **Buckton** E R Yk
169 G2 **Buckton** Nthumb
89 G7 **Buckworth** Cambs
115 L7 **Budby** Notts
187 H2 **Budden** Angus
9 H5 **Budd's Titson** Cnwll
9 G4 **Bude** Cnwll
5 M4 **Budge's Shop** Cnwll
12 D6 **Budleigh Salterton** Devon
3 K5 **Budock Water** Cnwll
99 G4 **Buerton** Ches
73 J3 **Bugbrooke** Nhants
4 F4 **Bugle** Cnwll
27 H6 **Bugley** Dorset
134 B7 **Bugthorpe** E R Yk
84 B3 **Buildwas** Shrops
68 B4 **Builth Wells** Powys
28 C5 **Bulbridge** Wilts
230 E3 **Buldoo** Highld
28 D3 **Bulford** Wilts
98 D2 **Bulkeley** Ches
86 E6 **Bulkington** Warwks
39 L8 **Bulkington** Wilts
9 K3 **Bulkworthy** Devon
42 E6 **Bullbrook** Br For
29 J3 **Bullington** Hants
117 H6 **Bullington** Lincs
77 J6 **Bulmer** Essex
133 L6 **Bulmer** N York
77 J6 **Bulmer Tye** Essex
45 M3 **Bulphan** Thurr
217 H5 **Bulwark** Abers
101 K4 **Bulwell** C Nott
88 D5 **Bulwick** Nhants
60 C6 **Bumble's Green** Essex
199 K7 **Bunacaimb** Highld
201 J7 **Bunarkaig** Highld
98 E2 **Bunbury** Ches
212 F5 **Bunchrew** Highld
210 D8 **Bundalloch** Highld
180 E3 **Bunessan** Ag & B
93 G5 **Bungay** Suffk
171 H4 **Bunnahabhain** Ag & B
101 L6 **Bunny** Notts
212 C7 **Buntait** Highld
60 B3 **Buntingford** Herts
92 D5 **Bunwell** Norfk
92 D5 **Bunwell Street** Norfk
86 F5 **Burbage** Leics
40 F7 **Burbage** Wilts
42 D4 **Burchett's Green** W & M
28 B5 **Burcombe** Wilts
58 E4 **Burcott** Bucks
77 K7 **Bures** Essex
56 E5 **Burford** Oxon
69 L2 **Burford** Shrops
189 J7 **Burg** Ag & B
30 C5 **Burgates** Hants
19 J2 **Burgess Hill** W Susx
78 F4 **Burgh** Suffk
148 B3 **Burgh by Sands** Cumb

93 K3 **Burgh Castle** Norfk
41 J7 **Burghclere** Hants
214 D1 **Burghead** Moray
42 A6 **Burghfield** W Berk
42 A6 **Burghfield Common** W Berk
44 E7 **Burgh Heath** Surrey
69 J5 **Burghill** Herefs
119 G7 **Burgh le Marsh** Lincs
106 F7 **Burgh next Aylsham** Norfk
117 L4 **Burgh on Bain** Lincs
93 J2 **Burgh St Margaret** Norfk
93 K5 **Burgh St Peter** Norfk
124 E7 **Burghwallis** Donc
46 B7 **Burham** Kent
30 C7 **Buriton** Hants
98 E2 **Burland** Ches
4 F2 **Burlawn** Cnwll
55 K7 **Burleigh** Gloucs
25 G7 **Burlescombe** Devon
14 E4 **Burleston** Dorset
16 B2 **Burley** Hants
88 C2 **Burley** Rutlnd
98 E4 **Burleydam** Ches
69 L5 **Burley Gate** Herefs
123 H2 **Burley in Wharfedale** Brad
16 B2 **Burley Street** Hants
123 H2 **Burley Wood Head** Brad
98 C7 **Burlton** Shrops
34 E7 **Burmarsh** Kent
72 C6 **Burmington** Warwks
124 F5 **Burn** N York
113 K3 **Burnage** Manch
100 F6 **Burnaston** Derbys
176 B6 **Burnbrae** N Lans
125 K2 **Burnby** E R Yk
138 D7 **Burneside** Cumb
132 D3 **Burneston** N York
38 F7 **Burnett** BaNES
166 F6 **Burnfoot** Border
167 H6 **Burnfoot** Border
155 G4 **Burnfoot** D & G
156 C3 **Burnfoot** D & G
156 C4 **Burnfoot** D & G
185 K6 **Burnfoot** P & K
42 F4 **Burnham** Bucks
105 J4 **Burnham Deepdale** Norfk
59 L5 **Burnham Green** Herts
105 K4 **Burnham Market** Norfk
105 K4 **Burnham Norton** Norfk
46 F2 **Burnham-on-Crouch** Essex
25 L2 **Burnham-on-Sea** Somset
105 K4 **Burnham Overy** Norfk
105 K4 **Burnham Overy Staithe** Norfk
105 K4 **Burnham Thorpe** Norfk
217 L5 **Burnhaven** Abers
154 E3 **Burnhead** D & G
206 D2 **Burnhervie** Abers
84 E4 **Burnhill Green** Staffs
150 F5 **Burnhope** Dur
174 D7 **Burnhouse** N Ayrs
134 F2 **Burniston** N York
122 C4 **Burnley** Lancs
151 H5 **Burnmoor** Dur
179 K6 **Burnmouth** Border
184 F6 **Burn of Cambus** Stirlg
150 F4 **Burnopfield** Dur
131 J7 **Burnsall** N York
196 C4 **Burnside** Angus

196 E6 **Burnside** Angus
186 B5 **Burnside** Fife
214 E1 **Burnside** Moray
176 E3 **Burnside** W Loth
187 G1 **Burnside of Duntrune** Angus
177 H2 **Burntisland** Fife
85 J2 **Burntwood** Staffs
85 J2 **Burntwood Green** Staffs
132 C7 **Burnt Yates** N York
25 J7 **Burnworthy** Somset
31 G2 **Burpham** Surrey
18 E4 **Burpham** W Susx
168 E7 **Burradon** Nthumb
235 e1 **Burrafirth** Shet
235 d3 **Burravoe** Shet
138 F4 **Burrells** Cumb
195 K8 **Burrelton** P & K
13 H2 **Burridge** Devon
17 G1 **Burridge** Hants
132 C3 **Burrill** N York
125 K8 **Burringham** N Linc
10 F2 **Burrington** Devon
69 J1 **Burrington** Herefs
38 C8 **Burrington** N Som
76 F4 **Burrough Green** Cambs
87 L2 **Burrough on the Hill** Leics
130 C4 **Burrow** Lancs
24 E3 **Burrow** Somset
26 A5 **Burrow Bridge** Somset
42 F7 **Burrowhill** Surrey
50 F7 **Burry Green** Swans
50 F5 **Burry Port** Carmth
120 F7 **Burscough** Lancs
120 F7 **Burscough Bridge** Lancs
125 J4 **Bursea** E R Yk
16 F1 **Bursledon** Hants
99 K3 **Burslem** C Stke
78 D5 **Burstall** Suffk
13 K2 **Burstock** Dorset
92 D6 **Burston** Norfk
32 B5 **Burstow** Surrey
126 F5 **Burstwick** E R Yk
131 G2 **Burtersett** N York
148 F3 **Burtholme** Cumb
77 H2 **Burthorpe Green** Suffk
103 L5 **Burtoft** Lincs
111 K6 **Burton** Ches
112 D8 **Burton** Ches
15 M4 **Burton** Dorset
116 F6 **Burton** Lincs
49 G6 **Burton** Pembks
25 J3 **Burton** Somset
39 J4 **Burton** Wilts
135 H6 **Burton Agnes** E R Yk
13 L4 **Burton Bradstock** Dorset
103 G7 **Burton Coggles** Lincs
126 F4 **Burton Constable Hall** E R Yk
60 E4 **Burton End** Essex
135 G5 **Burton Fleming** E R Yk
86 E5 **Burton Hastings** Warwks
129 L4 **Burton-in-Kendal** Cumb
130 C5 **Burton in Lonsdale** N York
101 M4 **Burton Joyce** Notts
88 C8 **Burton Latimer** Nhants
87 L1 **Burton Lazars** Leics
132 E6 **Burton Leonard** N York

101 L7 **Burton on the Wolds** Leics
87 J4 **Burton Overy** Leics
103 J4 **Burton Pedwardine** Lincs
127 G4 **Burton Pidsea** E R Yk
124 D5 **Burton Salmon** N York
61 K3 **Burton's Green** Essex
125 K6 **Burton upon Stather** N Linc
100 E7 **Burton upon Trent** Staffs
116 F6 **Burton Waters** Lincs
112 E3 **Burtonwood** Warrtn
98 D2 **Burwardsley** Ches
84 B6 **Burwarton** Shrops
33 H7 **Burwash** E Susx
20 D2 **Burwash Common** E Susx
20 D2 **Burwash Weald** E Susx
76 E2 **Burwell** Cambs
118 E5 **Burwell** Lincs
108 L7 **Burwen** IoA
234 c8 **Burwick** Ork
122 B7 **Bury** Bury
89 K6 **Bury** Cambs
24 E6 **Bury** Somset
18 D3 **Bury** W Susx
60 D4 **Bury Green** Herts
77 J2 **Bury St Edmunds** Suffk
134 C6 **Burythorpe** N York
175 G6 **Busby** E Rens
40 E2 **Buscot** Oxon
197 J4 **Bush** Abers
69 J4 **Bush Bank** Herefs
85 J3 **Bushbury** Wolves
43 J2 **Bushey** Herts
43 J3 **Bushey Heath** Herts
45 G2 **Bush Hill Park** Gt Lon
70 F7 **Bushley** Worcs
40 B5 **Bushton** Wilts
55 K7 **Bussage** Gloucs
26 A4 **Bussex** Somset
38 D7 **Butcombe** N Som
26 D5 **Butleigh** Somset
26 D4 **Butleigh Wootton** Somset
72 D4 **Butlers Marston** Warwks
79 H4 **Butley** Suffk
133 L7 **Buttercrambe** N York
179 G5 **Butterdean** Border
140 E3 **Butterknowle** Dur
12 C2 **Butterleigh** Devon
137 G4 **Buttermere** Cumb
123 H5 **Buttershaw** Brad
195 G7 **Butterstone** P & K
99 J4 **Butterton** Staffs
100 B2 **Butterton** Staffs
104 C4 **Butterwick** Lincs
133 L4 **Butterwick** N York
134 F5 **Butterwick** N York
82 E2 **Buttington** Powys
84 D7 **Buttonoak** Shrops
78 B3 **Buxhall** Suffk
20 A2 **Buxted** E Susx
114 B6 **Buxton** Derbys
106 F7 **Buxton** Norfk
106 E7 **Buxton Heath** Norfk
53 J4 **Bwlch** Powys
97 K2 **Bwlchgwyn** Wrexhm
66 D3 **Bwlchllan** Cerdgn
94 E7 **Bwlchtocyn** Gwynd
97 J3 **Bwlch-y-cibau** Powys
82 B4 **Bwlch-y-ffridd** Powys
65 H7 **Bwlch-y-groes** Pembks
82 B8 **Bwlch-y-sarnau** Powys

150 F7 **Byers Green** Dur
73 G4 **Byfield** Nhants
43 H7 **Byfleet** Surrey
69 H6 **Byford** Herefs
151 C3 **Byker** N U Ty
110 D8 **Bylchau** Conwy
113 J4 **Byley** Ches
167 K2 **Byrewalls** Border
157 K2 **Byrness** Nthumb
12 D5 **Bystock** Devon
88 F7 **Bythorn** Cambs
69 G2 **Byton** Herefs
150 D3 **Bywell** Nthumb
31 G7 **Byworth** W Susx

C

117 J2 **Cabourne** Lincs
171 J5 **Cabrach** Ag & B
215 J8 **Cabrach** Moray
121 G2 **Cabus** Lancs
220 F7 **Cabvie Lodge** Highld
11 L4 **Cadbury** Devon
175 G4 **Cadder** E Duns
59 H4 **Caddington** Beds
167 G2 **Caddonfoot** Border
115 K2 **Cadeby** Donc
86 E3 **Cadeby** Leics
11 L4 **Cadeleigh** Devon
20 C2 **Cade Street** E Susx
3 J7 **Cadgwith** Cnwll
186 D6 **Cadham** Fife
113 G3 **Cadishead** Salfd
51 J6 **Cadle** Swans
121 G4 **Cadley** Lancs
28 E2 **Cadley** Wilts
40 E6 **Cadley** Wilts
42 C3 **Cadmore End** Bucks
28 F3 **Cadnam** Hants
117 G2 **Cadney** N Linc
37 H6 **Cadoxton** V Glam
51 L5 **Cadoxton Juxta-Neath** Neath
95 J1 **Caeathro** Gwynd
117 G4 **Caenby** Lincs
66 F6 **Caeo** Carmth
36 D2 **Caerau** Brdgnd
37 H5 **Caerau** Cardif
48 D3 **Caer Farchell** Pembks
108 D5 **Caergeiliog** IoA
97 L2 **Caergwrle** Flints
156 D2 **Caerlanrig** Border
37 M3 **Caerleon** Newpt
37 M3 **Caerleon Roman Amphitheatre** Newpt
108 F8 **Caernarfon** Gwynd
108 F8 **Caernarfon Castle** Gwynd
37 J3 **Caerphilly** Caerph
82 B5 **Caersws** Powys
65 L4 **Caerwedros** Cerdgn
38 C3 **Caerwent** Mons
110 F6 **Caerwys** Flints
233 c6 **Cairinis** W Isls
172 E1 **Cairnbaan** Ag & B
217 J2 **Cairnbulg** Abers
179 J5 **Cairncross** Border
174 C4 **Cairncurran** Inver
183 H5 **Cairndow** Ag & B
176 E2 **Cairneyhill** Fife
215 J3 **Cairnfield House** Moray
144 C4 **Cairngarroch** D & G
204 B5 **Cairngorm Mountains**
215 K5 **Cairnie** Abers
217 G6 **Cairnorrie** Abers
144 C2 **Cairnryan** D & G
215 H4 **Cairnty** Moray
93 L2 **Caister-on-Sea** Norfk

117 J2 **Caistor** Lincs
92 F3 **Caistor St Edmund** Norfk
232 e2 **Calanais** W Isls
16 E5 **Calbourne** IoW
111 G6 **Calcot** Flints
56 C6 **Calcot** Gloucs
42 A6 **Calcot Row** W Berk
215 G2 **Calcots** Moray
148 B6 **Caldbeck** Cumb
75 L3 **Caldecote** Cambs
89 G5 **Caldecote** Cambs
75 J6 **Caldecote** Herts
75 L3 **Caldecote Highfields** Cambs
74 E2 **Caldecott** Nhants
41 J2 **Caldecott** Oxon
88 C5 **Caldecott** Rutlnd
175 K5 **Calderbank** N Lans
136 E6 **Calder Bridge** Cumb
175 L5 **Caldercruix** N Lans
123 L6 **Calder Grove** Wakefd
164 D2 **Caldermill** S Lans
121 G2 **Calder Vale** Lancs
175 H7 **Calderwood** S Lans
38 C3 **Caldicot** Mons
85 H4 **Caldmore** Wsall
140 E5 **Caldwell** N York
234 d4 **Calfsound** Ork
189 J6 **Calgary** Ag & B
214 D3 **Califer** Moray
176 B3 **California** Falk
93 K1 **California** Norfk
101 G7 **Calke** Derbys
209 L4 **Callakille** Highld
184 D5 **Callander** Stirlg
232 e2 **Callanish** W Isls
3 K2 **Callestick** Cnwll
199 K5 **Calligarry** Highld
6 A3 **Callington** Cnwll
69 J7 **Callow** Herefs
70 E4 **Callow End** Worcs
40 B4 **Callow Hill** Wilts
29 G7 **Calmore** Hants
56 B6 **Calmsden** Gloucs
39 M6 **Calne** Wilts
16 F3 **Calshot** Hants
6 C3 **Calstock** Cnwll
40 B6 **Calstone Wellington** Wilts
106 E6 **Calthorpe** Norfk
107 J7 **Calthorpe Street** Norfk
148 E6 **Calthwaite** Cumb
131 G7 **Calton** N York
100 C3 **Calton** Staffs
98 E2 **Calveley** Ches
114 E6 **Calver** Derbys
98 E5 **Calverhall** Shrops
11 L3 **Calverleigh** Devon
73 L6 **Calverton** M Keyn
101 L3 **Calverton** Notts
194 C3 **Calvine** P & K
147 K4 **Calvo** Cumb
165 L3 **Calzeat** Border
55 H7 **Cam** Gloucs
190 F4 **Camasachoirce** Highld
190 F4 **Camasine** Highld
210 E8 **Camas Luinie** Highld
209 H6 **Camastianavaig** Highld
212 D6 **Camault Muir** Highld
21 J2 **Camber** E Susx
42 E7 **Camberley** Surrey
44 F5 **Camberwell** Gt Lon
124 F5 **Camblesforth** N York
158 C5 **Cambo** Nthumb
3 H4 **Camborne** Cnwll
75 K3 **Cambourne** Cambs
76 C3 **Cambridge** Cambs
55 H7 **Cambridge** Gloucs

76 C3 **Cambridge Airport** Cambs
3 H3 **Cambrose** Cnwll
185 H4 **Cambus** Clacks
223 G3 **Cambusavie Platform** Highld
185 G8 **Cambusbarron** Stirlg
185 G8 **Cambuskenneth** Stirlg
175 H6 **Cambuslang** S Lans
205 J5 **Cambus o' May** Abers
165 K2 **Cambuswallace** S Lans
44 F4 **Camden Town** Gt Lon
38 E8 **Cameley** BaNES
8 E7 **Camelford** Cnwll
176 B3 **Camelon** Falk
214 F2 **Camerory** Highld
70 D7 **Camer's Green** Worcs
39 G8 **Camerton** BaNES
136 E2 **Camerton** Cumb
193 J5 **Camghouran** P & K
167 J4 **Camieston** Border
207 G6 **Cammachmore** Abers
116 F5 **Cammeringham** Lincs
223 G4 **Camore** Highld
161 J5 **Campbeltown** Ag & B
161 H5 **Campbeltown Airport** Ag & B
154 F4 **Cample** D & G
195 K8 **Campmuir** P & K
176 E5 **Camps** W Loth
124 E7 **Campsall** Donc
79 G4 **Campsea Ash** Suffk
75 G6 **Campton** Beds
167 K4 **Camptown** Border
48 F4 **Camrose** Pembks
194 C6 **Camserney** P & K
191 L2 **Camusnagaul** Highld
220 D4 **Camusnagaul** Highld
209 L6 **Camusteel** Highld
209 L6 **Camusterrach** Highld
28 F7 **Canada** Hants
205 J4 **Candacraig** Abers
118 F7 **Candlesby** Lincs
165 L2 **Candy Mill** Border
42 B4 **Cane End** Oxon
46 E2 **Canewdon** Essex
15 K5 **Canford Cliffs** Poole
15 J4 **Canford Heath** Poole
15 J3 **Canford Magna** Poole
231 H2 **Canisbay** Highld
86 C7 **Canley** Covtry
27 K7 **Cann** Dorset
211 L7 **Cannich** Highld
25 K4 **Cannington** Somset
45 J4 **Canning Town** Gt Lon
85 H2 **Cannock** Staffs
99 M8 **Cannock Chase** Staffs
69 J4 **Cannon Bridge** Herefs
156 E6 **Canonbie** D & G
70 B5 **Canon Frome** Herefs
69 J5 **Canon Pyon** Herefs
73 H3 **Canons Ashby** Nhants
2 F4 **Canonstown** Cnwll
34 F3 **Canterbury** Kent
34 F3 **Canterbury Cathedral** Kent
93 H3 **Cantley** Norfk
37 J5 **Canton** Cardif
213 J5 **Cantraywood** Highld
130 C5 **Cantsfield** Lancs
46 D4 **Canvey Island** Essex
117 G7 **Canwick** Lincs
9 G6 **Canworthy Water** Cnwll
191 L2 **Caol** Highld
232 e4 **Caolas Scalpaigh** W Isls
188 D6 **Caoles** Ag & B
201 G6 **Caonich** Highld

33 H4 **Capel** Kent
31 K4 **Capel** Surrey
80 E7 **Capel Bangor** Cerdgn
108 F5 **Capel Coch** IoA
96 A2 **Capel Curig** Conwy
50 F2 **Capel Dewi** Carmth
66 B6 **Capel Dewi** Cerdgn
80 E6 **Capel-Dewi** Cerdgn
96 C2 **Capel Garmon** Conwy
51 H4 **Capel Hendre** Carmth
65 J7 **Capel Iwan** Carmth
35 H6 **Capel le Ferne** Kent
108 E6 **Capel Mawr** IoA
79 H5 **Capel St Andrew** Suffk
78 C6 **Capel St Mary** Suffk
80 E7 **Capel Seion** Cerdgn
109 L6 **Capelulo** Conwy
111 K6 **Capenhurst** Ches
158 C6 **Capheaton** Nthumb
174 E6 **Caplaw** E Rens
166 C5 **Cappercleuch** Border
7 J5 **Capton** Devon
195 H7 **Caputh** P & K
174 F3 **Carbeth Inn** Stirlg
2 F4 **Carbis Bay** Cnwll
208 F5 **Carbost** Highld
208 F7 **Carbost** Highld
115 G4 **Carbrook** Sheff
91 L3 **Carbrooke** Norfk
102 B4 **Car Colston** Notts
124 E8 **Carcroft** Donc
186 C7 **Cardenden** Fife
214 F5 **Cardhu** Moray
37 J5 **Cardiff** Cardif
37 G6 **Cardiff Airport** V Glam
65 G5 **Cardigan** Cerdgn
74 F5 **Cardington** Beds
83 K4 **Cardington** Shrops
5 H3 **Cardinham** Cnwll
144 D8 **Cardrain** D & G
166 D2 **Cardrona** Border
174 C3 **Cardross** Ag & B
144 D7 **Cardryne** D & G
147 L3 **Cardurnock** Cumb
88 E1 **Careby** Lincs
196 E4 **Careston** Angus
49 H6 **Carew** Pembks
49 H6 **Carew Cheriton** Pembks
49 H6 **Carew Newton** Pembks
54 E2 **Carey** Herefs
175 K6 **Carfin** N Lans
178 B7 **Carfraemill** Border
93 H2 **Cargate Green** Norfk
155 G7 **Cargen** D & G
155 G6 **Cargenbridge** D & G
195 J8 **Cargill** P & K
148 C3 **Cargo** Cumb
6 C4 **Cargreen** Cnwll
168 B2 **Carham** Nthumb
24 F3 **Carhampton** Somset
3 J3 **Carharrack** Cnwll
193 K5 **Carie** P & K
233 c6 **Carinish** W Isls
16 F5 **Carisbrooke** IoW
129 H4 **Cark** Cumb
6 B4 **Carkeel** Cnwll
232 e2 **Carlabhagh** W Isls
140 F4 **Carlbury** Darltn
88 F2 **Carlby** Lincs
168 C6 **Carlcroft** Nthumb
3 G5 **Carleen** Cnwll
122 E1 **Carleton** N York
92 C3 **Carleton Forehoe** Norfk
92 D5 **Carleton Rode** Norfk
93 H3 **Carleton St Peter** Norfk
216 D5 **Carlincraig** Abers

39 G8 **Carlingcott** BaNES
148 D4 **Carlisle** Cumb
148 E3 **Carlisle Airport** Cumb
177 G6 **Carlops** Border
232 e2 **Carloway** W Isls
124 B7 **Carlton** Barns
74 D4 **Carlton** Beds
76 F4 **Carlton** Cambs
123 L5 **Carlton** Leeds
86 E3 **Carlton** Leics
124 F5 **Carlton** N York
131 K3 **Carlton** N York
133 J3 **Carlton** N York
101 L4 **Carlton** Notts
141 J3 **Carlton** S on T
79 H2 **Carlton** Suffk
93 K5 **Carlton Colville** Suffk
87 K4 **Carlton Curlieu** Leics
76 F4 **Carlton Green** Cambs
133 G4 **Carlton Husthwaite** N York
142 B6 **Carlton-in-Cleveland** N York
115 L5 **Carlton in Lindrick** Notts
102 E2 **Carlton-le-Moorland** Lincs
132 F4 **Carlton Miniott** N York
116 D8 **Carlton-on-Trent** Notts
102 F4 **Carlton Scroop** Lincs
175 L7 **Carluke** S Lans
164 F4 **Carmacoup** S Lans
50 E2 **Carmarthen** Carmth
51 H3 **Carmel** Carmth
111 G6 **Carmel** Flints
95 H2 **Carmel** Gwynd
165 H2 **Carmichael** S Lans
175 G6 **Carmunnock** C Glas
175 H6 **Carmyle** C Glas
196 E7 **Carmyllie** Angus
135 H6 **Carnaby** E R Yk
187 J6 **Carnbee** Fife
185 L6 **Carnbo** P & K
3 H3 **Carn Brea** Cnwll
216 F8 **Carnbrogie** Abers
210 D8 **Carndu** Highld
164 D1 **Carnduff** S Lans
163 L3 **Carnell** E Ayrs
129 K5 **Carnforth** Lancs
200 E2 **Carn-gorm** Highld
3 G4 **Carnhell Green** Cnwll
206 F4 **Carnie** Abers
3 H4 **Carnkie** Cnwll
3 J4 **Carnkie** Cnwll
81 K4 **Carno** Powys
200 D6 **Carnoch** Highld
176 E1 **Carnock** Fife
4 C7 **Carnon Downs** Cnwll
216 C4 **Carnousie** Abers
187 J1 **Carnoustie** Angus
165 J1 **Carnwath** S Lans
86 C7 **Carol Green** Solhll
131 J2 **Carperby** N York
161 K2 **Carradale** Ag & B
203 L2 **Carrbridge** Highld
236 c6 **Carrefour** Jersey
108 E4 **Carreglefn** IoA
123 L5 **Carr Gate** Wakefd
116 C1 **Carrhouse** N Linc
172 F2 **Carrick** Ag & B
183 H8 **Carrick Castle** Ag & B
176 D3 **Carriden** Falk
177 J6 **Carrington** Mdloth
113 H3 **Carrington** Traffd
97 H4 **Carrog** Denbgs
176 B2 **Carron** Falk
214 F6 **Carron** Moray
154 F3 **Carronbridge** D & G
175 K2 **Carron Bridge** Stirlg
176 B2 **Carronshore** Falk

149 K5 **Carr Shield** Nthumb
155 J7 **Carrutherstown** D & G
174 C5 **Carruth House** Inver
151 H6 **Carrville** Dur
181 H3 **Carsaig** Ag & B
196 D5 **Carse Gray** Angus
145 G2 **Carseriggan** D & G
147 H3 **Carsethorn** D & G
44 F6 **Carshalton** Gt Lon
100 E2 **Carsington** Derbys
161 H7 **Carskey** Ag & B
145 K4 **Carsluith** D & G
153 L4 **Carspairn** D & G
165 H1 **Carstairs** S Lans
165 J1 **Carstairs Junction** S Lans
56 F6 **Carterton** Oxon
4 F5 **Carthew** Cnwll
132 D3 **Carthorpe** N York
165 G1 **Cartland** S Lans
129 H4 **Cartmel** Cumb
50 F4 **Carway** Carmth
55 J6 **Cashe's Green** Gloucs
57 J5 **Cassington** Oxon
151 J7 **Cassop Colliery** Dur
236 c3 **Castel** Guern
130 C4 **Casterton** Cumb
91 J1 **Castle Acre** Norfk
74 C3 **Castle Ashby** Nhants
233 b9 **Castlebay** W Isls
131 J2 **Castle Bolton** N York
85 K5 **Castle Bromwich** Solhll
103 G8 **Castle Bytham** Lincs
49 H2 **Castlebythe** Pembks
82 D3 **Castle Caereinion** Powys
76 F6 **Castle Camps** Cambs
148 F4 **Castle Carrock** Cumb
175 K3 **Castlecary** Falk
26 C5 **Castle Cary** Somset
39 J3 **Castle Combe** Wilts
101 H6 **Castle Donington** Leics
146 D3 **Castle Douglas** D & G
40 C2 **Castle Eaton** Swindn
151 K7 **Castle Eden** Dur
124 C5 **Castleford** Wakefd
70 C5 **Castle Frome** Herefs
100 F8 **Castle Gresley** Derbys
77 H7 **Castle Hedingham** Essex
166 C3 **Castlehill** Border
231 H2 **Castlehill** Highld
78 D5 **Castle Hill** Suffk
174 D3 **Castlehill** W Duns
144 D3 **Castle Kennedy** D & G
182 E7 **Castle Lachlan** Ag & B
48 F7 **Castlemartin** Pembks
175 G6 **Castlemilk** C Glas
70 E6 **Castlemorton** Worcs
156 A4 **Castle O'er** D & G
83 H3 **Castle Pulverbatch** Shrops
137 J3 **Castlerigg** Cumb
105 G7 **Castle Rising** Norfk
150 D5 **Castleside** Dur
213 H4 **Castle Stuart** Highld
74 B5 **Castlethorpe** M Keyn
156 E4 **Castleton** Border
114 D5 **Castleton** Derbys
142 E5 **Castleton** N York
37 K4 **Castleton** Newpt
122 D7 **Castleton** Rochdl
231 H3 **Castletown** Highld
237 b7 **Castletown** IoM
151 J4 **Castletown** Sundld
123 K2 **Castley** N York
91 L4 **Caston** Norfk
89 G4 **Castor** C Pete
172 F7 **Catacol** N Ayrs

115 H4 **Catcliffe** Rothm
40 A5 **Catcomb** Wilts
26 B4 **Catcott** Somset
26 B3 **Catcott Burtle** Somset
32 C3 **Caterham** Surrey
107 H7 **Catfield** Norfk
45 G5 **Catford** Gt Lon
121 G4 **Catforth** Lancs
175 G4 **Cathcart** C Glas
53 H3 **Cathedine** Powys
30 B8 **Catherington** Hants
13 J4 **Catherston Leweston** Dorset
17 G2 **Catisfield** Hants
202 F6 **Catlodge** Highld
76 C6 **Catmere End** Essex
41 J4 **Catmore** W Berk
129 L6 **Caton** Lancs
129 L6 **Caton Green** Lancs
164 B4 **Catrine** E Ayrs
20 E3 **Catsfield** E Susx
26 D6 **Catsgore** Somset
85 G8 **Catshill** Worcs
161 H7 **Cattadale** Ag & B
133 G8 **Cattal** N York
62 D2 **Cattawade** Suffk
121 G3 **Catterall** Lancs
141 G7 **Catterick** N York
141 G7 **Catterick Bridge** N York
148 E7 **Catterlen** Cumb
197 L2 **Catterline** Abers
124 D2 **Catterton** N York
31 G3 **Catteshall** Surrey
87 G7 **Catthorpe** Leics
14 B3 **Cattistock** Dorset
132 E4 **Catton** N York
92 F2 **Catton** Norfk
149 L4 **Catton** Nthumb
126 E2 **Catwick** E R Yk
88 F8 **Catworth** Cambs
55 L6 **Caudle Green** Gloucs
57 K3 **Caulcott** Oxon
197 G6 **Cauldcots** Angus
184 E8 **Cauldhame** Stirlg
167 H6 **Cauldmill** Border
100 B3 **Cauldon** Staffs
86 B1 **Cauldwell** Derbys
147 G4 **Caulkerbush** D & G
156 D6 **Caulside** D & G
27 G8 **Caundle Marsh** Dorset
102 C1 **Caunton** Notts
145 J3 **Causeway End** D & G
61 G4 **Causeway End** Essex
165 K3 **Causewayend** S Lans
185 G7 **Causewayhead** Stirlg
207 H2 **Causeyend** Abers
158 F3 **Causey Park Bridge** Nthumb
77 J5 **Cavendish** Suffk
77 H1 **Cavenham** Suffk
57 L3 **Caversfield** Oxon
42 B5 **Caversham** Readg
99 L4 **Caverswall** Staffs
167 L4 **Caverton Mill** Border
213 K4 **Cawdor** Highld
124 E3 **Cawood** N York
6 C5 **Cawsand** Cnwll
106 D7 **Cawston** Norfk
123 K8 **Cawthorne** Barns
75 K3 **Caxton** Cambs
83 K8 **Caynham** Shrops
102 F3 **Caythorpe** Lincs
102 B4 **Caythorpe** Notts
135 G3 **Cayton** N York
233 b6 **Ceann a Bhaigh** W Isls
201 K3 **Ceannacroc Lodge** Highld
232 f3 **Cearsiadar** W Isls
37 L3 **Cefn** Newpt

96 E3 **Cefn-brith** Conwy
36 D4 **Cefn Cribwr** Brdgnd
67 J5 **Cefngorwydd** Powys
97 L4 **Cefn-mawr** Wrexhm
49 K3 **Cefn-y-pant** Carmth
187 J6 **Cellardyke** Fife
99 L3 **Cellarhead** Staffs
108 E3 **Cemaes** IoA
81 H3 **Cemmaes** Powys
81 H3 **Cemmaes Road**
      Powys
65 J6 **Cenarth** Cerdgn
186 F5 **Ceres** Fife
14 C3 **Cerne Abbas** Dorset
40 B2 **Cerney Wick** Gloucs
108 E6 **Cerrigceinwen** IoA
96 E3 **Cerrigydrudion**
      Conwy
95 J1 **Ceunant** Gwynd
55 J2 **Chaceley** Gloucs
3 K3 **Chacewater** Cnwll
73 K7 **Chackmore** Bucks
72 F5 **Chacombe** Nhants
71 H5 **Chadbury** Worcs
113 K1 **Chadderton** Oldham
101 G3 **Chaddesden** C Derb
84 F8 **Chaddesley Corbett**
      Worcs
6 C1 **Chaddlehanger**
      Devon
41 H5 **Chaddleworth**
      W Berk
57 G4 **Chadlington** Oxon
72 D4 **Chadshunt** Warwks
102 C7 **Chadwell** Leics
45 J3 **Chadwell Heath**
      Gt Lon
45 M4 **Chadwell St Mary**
      Thurr
70 E2 **Chadwick** Worcs
86 B8 **Chadwick End** Solhll
13 J1 **Chaffcombe** Somset
11 G7 **Chagford** Devon
19 K2 **Chailey** E Susx
33 J4 **Chainhurst** Kent
32 B3 **Chaldon** Surrey
16 F6 **Chale** IoW
16 F6 **Chale Green** IoW
43 G3 **Chalfont Common**
      Bucks
43 G2 **Chalfont St Giles**
      Bucks
43 G3 **Chalfont St Peter**
      Bucks
55 K7 **Chalford** Gloucs
27 K2 **Chalford** Wilts
41 M2 **Chalgrove** Oxon
46 A5 **Chalk** Kent
34 B2 **Chalkwell** Kent
23 L3 **Challacombe** Devon
145 H2 **Challoch** D & G
34 D5 **Challock** Kent
59 G3 **Chalton** Beds
30 B7 **Chalton** Hants
42 F4 **Chalvey** Slough
20 B4 **Chalvington** E Susx
43 H2 **Chandler's Cross**
      Herts
29 H7 **Chandler's Ford**
      Hants
27 G3 **Chantry** Somset
78 D5 **Chantry** Suffk
186 D8 **Chapel** Fife
123 L3 **Chapel Allerton** Leeds
26 B2 **Chapel Allerton**
      Somset
4 F2 **Chapel Amble** Cnwll
73 K2 **Chapel Brampton**
      Nhants
99 J5 **Chapel Chorlton**
      Staffs
77 G6 **Chapelend Way** Essex

114 B5 **Chapel-en-le-Frith**
      Derbys
72 F3 **Chapel Green** Warwks
124 E5 **Chapel Haddlesey**
      N York
175 K5 **Chapelhall** N Lans
217 K2 **Chapel Hill** Abers
103 K2 **Chapel Hill** Lincs
54 D7 **Chapel Hill** Mons
123 L2 **Chapel Hill** N York
166 C5 **Chapelhope** Border
156 B7 **Chapelknowe** D & G
82 F7 **Chapel Lawn** Shrops
130 E4 **Chapel le Dale** N York
25 H5 **Chapel Leigh** Somset
206 D1 **Chapel of Garioch**
      Abers
144 D6 **Chapel Rossan** D & G
41 L6 **Chapel Row** W Berk
119 H6 **Chapel St Leonards**
      Lincs
137 K6 **Chapel Stile** Cumb
197 G6 **Chapelton** Angus
23 J6 **Chapelton** Devon
175 J8 **Chapelton** S Lans
121 L7 **Chapeltown** Bl w D
204 F2 **Chapeltown** Moray
115 G3 **Chapeltown** Sheff
27 J2 **Chapmanslade** Wilts
9 J6 **Chapmans Well**
      Devon
60 B5 **Chapmore End** Herts
61 L3 **Chappel** Essex
13 H2 **Chard** Somset
13 J2 **Chard Junction**
      Somset
13 H1 **Chardleigh Green**
      Somset
13 H2 **Chardstock** Devon
39 G3 **Charfield** S Glos
34 C5 **Charing** Kent
71 L6 **Charingworth** Gloucs
57 G4 **Charlbury** Oxon
39 H6 **Charlcombe** BaNES
39 M5 **Charlcutt** Wilts
72 C3 **Charlecote** Warwks
85 H5 **Charlemont** Sandw
23 L5 **Charles** Devon
196 C7 **Charleston** Angus
123 H3 **Charlestown** Brad
207 H5 **Charlestown** C Aber
122 E5 **Charlestown** Calder
5 G5 **Charlestown** Cnwll
176 E2 **Charlestown** Fife
213 G5 **Charlestown** Highld
219 J6 **Charlestown** Highld
113 J2 **Charlestown** Salfd
78 B4 **Charles Tye** Suffk
114 A3 **Charlesworth** Derbys
25 K4 **Charlinch** Somset
186 E5 **Charlottetown** Fife
45 H4 **Charlton** Gt Lon
73 G7 **Charlton** Nhants
157 K5 **Charlton** Nthumb
41 H3 **Charlton** Oxon
25 L6 **Charlton** Somset
27 G2 **Charlton** Somset
18 B3 **Charlton** W Susx
27 K6 **Charlton** Wilts
39 L3 **Charlton** Wilts
71 H5 **Charlton** Worcs
83 L2 **Charlton** Wrekin
56 B3 **Charlton Abbots**
      Gloucs
26 D5 **Charlton Adam**
      Somset
28 D6 **Charlton-All-Saints**
      Wilts
14 D4 **Charlton Down**
      Dorset
26 F6 **Charlton Horethorne**
      Somset

55 L4 **Charlton Kings** Gloucs
26 D5 **Charlton Mackrell**
      Somset
15 G2 **Charlton Marshall**
      Dorset
27 G5 **Charlton Musgrove**
      Somset
57 K7 **Charlton-on-Otmoor**
      Oxon
15 G2 **Charlton on the Hill**
      Dorset
28 C1 **Charlton St Peter**
      Wilts
30 A5 **Charlwood** Hants
31 L3 **Charlwood** Surrey
14 D4 **Charminster** Dorset
13 J4 **Charmouth** Dorset
58 A3 **Charndon** Bucks
41 G2 **Charney Bassett**
      Oxon
121 H7 **Charnock Richard**
      Lancs
78 F3 **Charsfield** Suffk
41 L8 **Charter Alley** Hants
179 G8 **Charterhall** Border
26 D1 **Charterhouse** Somset
175 K1 **Chartershall** Stirlg
34 E4 **Chartham** Kent
34 E4 **Chartham Hatch** Kent
58 F7 **Chartridge** Bucks
33 K4 **Chart Sutton** Kent
42 C5 **Charvil** Wokham
73 G4 **Charwelton** Nhants
85 J2 **Chase Terrace** Staffs
85 J2 **Chasetown** Staffs
56 E3 **Chastleton** Oxon
9 J4 **Chasty** Devon
122 B2 **Chatburn** Lancs
99 H5 **Chatcull** Staffs
46 C6 **Chatham** Medway
61 H5 **Chatham Green** Essex
169 J4 **Chathill** Nthumb
114 E7 **Chatsworth House**
      Derbys
46 C5 **Chattenden** Medway
90 B6 **Chatteris** Cambs
122 B6 **Chatterton** Lancs
78 C6 **Chattisham** Suffk
168 B5 **Chatto** Border
168 F4 **Chatton** Nthumb
11 G3 **Chawleigh** Devon
30 B4 **Chawton** Hants
100 A4 **Cheadle** Staffs
113 K4 **Cheadle** Stockp
113 K4 **Cheadle Hulme**
      Stockp
44 E7 **Cheam** Gt Lon
58 B6 **Chearsley** Bucks
99 J6 **Chebsey** Staffs
42 A4 **Checkendon** Oxon
99 G4 **Checkley** Ches
100 B5 **Checkley** Staffs
77 H3 **Chedburgh** Suffk
26 C2 **Cheddar** Somset
58 F4 **Cheddington** Bucks
99 L3 **Cheddleton** Staffs
25 K6 **Cheddon Fitzpaine**
      Somset
93 H4 **Chedgrave** Norfk
13 L2 **Chedington** Dorset
93 H7 **Chediston** Suffk
56 B5 **Chedworth** Gloucs
25 M4 **Chedzoy** Somset
113 J2 **Cheetham Hill** Manch
11 H3 **Cheldon** Devon
113 J6 **Chelford** Ches
101 G6 **Chellaston** C Derb
74 D4 **Chellington** Beds
84 C5 **Chelmarsh** Shrops
78 E6 **Chelmondiston** Suffk
114 C7 **Chelmorton** Derbys
61 H6 **Chelmsford** Essex

85 L6 **Chelmsley Wood**
      Solhll
44 F4 **Chelsea** Gt Lon
45 J7 **Chelsfield** Gt Lon
77 L5 **Chelsworth** Suffk
55 L4 **Cheltenham** Gloucs
74 E1 **Chelveston** Nhants
38 C6 **Chelvey** N Som
38 F7 **Chelwood** BaNES
32 D6 **Chelwood Gate**
      E Susx
40 C2 **Chelworth Lower**
      Green Wilts
40 B2 **Chelworth Upper**
      Green Wilts
83 H6 **Cheney Longville**
      Shrops
43 G2 **Chenies** Bucks
38 D2 **Chepstow** Mons
40 B6 **Cherhill** Wilts
55 K7 **Cherington** Gloucs
72 C6 **Cherington** Warwks
29 L5 **Cheriton** Hants
35 G7 **Cheriton** Kent
50 F6 **Cheriton** Swans
11 H6 **Cheriton Bishop**
      Devon
11 K4 **Cheriton Fitzpaine**
      Devon
49 G7 **Cheriton or**
      Stackpole Elidor
      Pembks
98 F8 **Cherrington** Wrekin
126 B3 **Cherry Burton** E R Yk
76 C3 **Cherry Hinton** Cambs
70 F4 **Cherry Orchard**
      Worcs
117 G6 **Cherry Willingham**
      Lincs
43 H6 **Chertsey** Surrey
14 E3 **Cheselbourne**
      Dorset
58 F7 **Chesham** Bucks
122 B8 **Chesham** Bury
58 F7 **Chesham Bois** Bucks
60 B7 **Cheshunt** Herts
14 B6 **Chesil Beach** Dorset
85 H3 **Cheslyn Hay** Staffs
85 L8 **Chessetts Wood**
      Warwks
44 D7 **Chessington** Gt Lon
44 D7 **Chessington World**
      of Adventures Gt Lon
112 B7 **Chester** Ches
26 F3 **Chesterblade** Somset
112 B7 **Chester Cathedral**
      Ches
115 G7 **Chesterfield** Derbys
177 K5 **Chesterhill** Mdloth
151 G5 **Chester-le-Street** Dur
151 G5 **Chester Moor** Dur
167 J5 **Chesters** Border
167 K7 **Chesters** Border
76 C3 **Chesterton** Cambs
89 G4 **Chesterton** Cambs
56 A7 **Chesterton** Gloucs
57 K4 **Chesterton** Oxon
84 D4 **Chesterton** Shrops
72 D3 **Chesterton Green**
      Warwks
149 L3 **Chesterwood**
      Nthumb
112 B7 **Chester Zoo** Ches
47 J6 **Chestfield** Kent
7 G4 **Cheston** Devon
99 G6 **Cheswardine** Shrops
168 F1 **Cheswick** Nthumb
14 B2 **Chetnole** Dorset
90 D6 **Chettisham** Cambs
27 L8 **Chettle** Dorset
84 B5 **Chetton** Shrops
99 G7 **Chetwynd** Wrekin

99 H8	**Chetwynd Aston** Wrekin	
76 F3	**Cheveley** Cambs	
32 E2	**Chevening** Kent	
77 H3	**Chevington** Suffk	
168 A7	**Cheviot Hills**	
24 F7	**Chevithorne** Devon	
38 E7	**Chew Magna** BaNES	
38 E7	**Chew Stoke** BaNES	
38 F6	**Chewton Keynsham** BaNES	
26 E2	**Chewton Mendip** Somset	
74 C5	**Chicheley** M Keyn	
18 B5	**Chichester** W Susx	
14 C6	**Chickerell** Dorset	
27 K4	**Chicklade** Wilts	
30 A7	**Chidden** Hants	
30 F4	**Chiddingfold** Surrey	
20 B3	**Chiddingly** E Susx	
32 E4	**Chiddingstone** Kent	
32 F4	**Chiddingstone Causeway** Kent	
13 K4	**Chideock** Dorset	
17 L2	**Chidham** W Susx	
123 K6	**Chidswell** Kirk	
41 J5	**Chieveley** W Berk	
61 G6	**Chignall St James** Essex	
61 G5	**Chignall Smealy** Essex	
45 H2	**Chigwell** Essex	
45 J2	**Chigwell Row** Essex	
29 H4	**Chilbolton** Hants	
29 J5	**Chilcomb** Hants	
13 M4	**Chilcombe** Dorset	
26 F2	**Chilcompton** Somset	
86 C2	**Chilcote** Leics	
111 K6	**Childer Thornton** Ches	
27 J8	**Child Okeford** Dorset	
41 G3	**Childrey** Oxon	
98 F7	**Child's Ercall** Shrops	
71 J6	**Childswickham** Worcs	
112 B4	**Childwall** Lpool	
14 B3	**Chilfrome** Dorset	
18 A3	**Chilgrove** W Susx	
34 E4	**Chilham** Kent	
10 C8	**Chillaton** Devon	
35 H4	**Chillenden** Kent	
16 F5	**Chillerton** IoW	
79 H4	**Chillesford** Suffk	
168 F4	**Chillingham** Nthumb	
7 J7	**Chillington** Devon	
13 K1	**Chillington** Somset	
27 L5	**Chilmark** Wilts	
34 C6	**Chilmington Green** Kent	
56 F4	**Chilson** Oxon	
6 B2	**Chilsworthy** Cnwll	
9 J4	**Chilsworthy** Devon	
42 C2	**Chiltern Hills**	
26 D7	**Chilthorne Domer** Somset	
58 B5	**Chilton** Bucks	
141 H2	**Chilton** Dur	
41 J4	**Chilton** Oxon	
29 L4	**Chilton Candover** Hants	
26 E6	**Chilton Cantelo** Somset	
40 F6	**Chilton Foliat** Wilts	
26 B4	**Chilton Polden** Somset	
77 H5	**Chilton Street** Suffk	
25 L4	**Chilton Trinity** Somset	
101 K5	**Chilwell** Notts	
29 H7	**Chilworth** Hants	
31 G3	**Chilworth** Surrey	
57 G7	**Chimney** Oxon	
30 A1	**Chineham** Hants	
45 G2	**Chingford** Gt Lon	
114 B5	**Chinley** Derbys	
58 C7	**Chinnor** Oxon	
99 G6	**Chipnall** Shrops	
76 F1	**Chippenham** Cambs	
39 L5	**Chippenham** Wilts	
59 H7	**Chipperfield** Herts	
60 B2	**Chipping** Herts	
121 J2	**Chipping** Lancs	
71 L6	**Chipping Campden** Gloucs	
56 F3	**Chipping Norton** Oxon	
60 E7	**Chipping Ongar** Essex	
39 G4	**Chipping Sodbury** S Glos	
72 F5	**Chipping Warden** Nhants	
25 G6	**Chipstable** Somset	
32 E3	**Chipstead** Kent	
32 B2	**Chipstead** Surrey	
82 F4	**Chirbury** Shrops	
97 L5	**Chirk** Wrexhm	
40 B8	**Chirton** Wilts	
40 F6	**Chisbury** Wilts	
26 C8	**Chiselborough** Somset	
40 D4	**Chiseldon** Swindn	
57 L7	**Chiselhampton** Oxon	
166 F6	**Chisholme** Border	
45 H6	**Chislehurst** Gt Lon	
47 L6	**Chislet** Kent	
122 F5	**Chisley** Calder	
59 J6	**Chiswell Green** Herts	
44 E4	**Chiswick** Gt Lon	
113 M3	**Chisworth** Derbys	
30 D6	**Chithurst** W Susx	
76 C1	**Chittering** Cambs	
27 M3	**Chitterne** Wilts	
23 K7	**Chittlehamholt** Devon	
10 F3	**Chittlehampton** Devon	
23 K6	**Chittlehampton** Devon	
39 L6	**Chittoe** Wilts	
7 H7	**Chivelstone** Devon	
23 H4	**Chivenor** Devon	
144 D3	**Chlenry** D & G	
42 F7	**Chobham** Surrey	
28 E3	**Cholderton** Wilts	
58 F6	**Cholesbury** Bucks	
158 B7	**Chollerton** Nthumb	
41 L3	**Cholsey** Oxon	
69 J3	**Cholstrey** Herefs	
142 C7	**Chop Gate** N York	
159 G5	**Choppington** Nthumb	
150 E4	**Chopwell** Gatesd	
98 E3	**Chorley** Ches	
121 H6	**Chorley** Lancs	
84 C6	**Chorley** Shrops	
43 H2	**Chorleywood** Herts	
43 G2	**Chorleywood West** Herts	
99 G3	**Chorlton** Ches	
113 J3	**Chorlton-cum-Hardy** Manch	
98 C3	**Choriton Lane** Ches	
83 H5	**Choulton** Shrops	
76 C6	**Chrishall** Essex	
173 L4	**Chrisswell** Inver	
90 C4	**Christchurch** Cambs	
15 M4	**Christchurch** Dorset	
37 M3	**Christchurch** Newpt	
39 L5	**Christian Malford** Wilts	
112 C7	**Christleton** Ches	
38 B8	**Christon** N Som	
169 J5	**Christon Bank** Nthumb	
11 J7	**Christow** Devon	
11 K8	**Chudleigh** Devon	
7 J1	**Chudleigh Knighton** Devon	
11 G3	**Chulmleigh** Devon	
121 L5	**Church** Lancs	
55 H4	**Churcham** Gloucs	
99 H8	**Church Aston** Wrekin	
73 K2	**Church Brampton** Nhants	
100 D5	**Church Broughton** Derbys	
3 J8	**Church Cove** Cnwll	
30 D2	**Church Crookham** Hants	
55 K4	**Churchdown** Gloucs	
99 J8	**Church Eaton** Staffs	
59 G4	**Church End** Beds	
75 H6	**Church End** Beds	
47 G2	**Churchend** Essex	
61 H3	**Church End** Essex	
44 E3	**Church End** Gt Lon	
57 G3	**Church Enstone** Oxon	
124 D3	**Church Fenton** N York	
85 H5	**Churchfield** Sandw	
12 F3	**Church Green** Devon	
57 H5	**Church Hanborough** Oxon	
112 F7	**Church Hill** Ches	
142 E7	**Church Houses** N York	
13 H3	**Churchill** Devon	
38 C7	**Churchill** N Som	
56 F3	**Churchill** Oxon	
71 G4	**Churchill** Worcs	
84 F7	**Churchill** Worcs	
25 K8	**Churchinford** Somset	
15 H6	**Church Knowle** Dorset	
87 K5	**Church Langton** Leics	
86 F7	**Church Lawford** Warwks	
99 J2	**Church Lawton** Ches	
100 A5	**Church Leigh** Staffs	
71 H4	**Church Lench** Worcs	
100 D4	**Church Mayfield** Staffs	
98 F1	**Church Minshull** Ches	
18 B6	**Church Norton** W Susx	
87 G7	**Churchover** Warwks	
83 K4	**Church Preen** Shrops	
83 H3	**Church Pulverbatch** Shrops	
25 J8	**Churchstanton** Somset	
82 F5	**Churchstoke** Powys	
7 G6	**Churchstow** Devon	
73 J3	**Church Stowe** Nhants	
46 B5	**Church Street** Kent	
83 J5	**Church Stretton** Shrops	
5 H1	**Churchtown** Cnwll	
114 E8	**Churchtown** Derbys	
121 G2	**Churchtown** Lancs	
37 G3	**Church Village** Rhondd	
115 K7	**Church Warsop** Notts	
7 K5	**Churston Ferrers** Torbay	
30 D4	**Churt** Surrey	
98 B2	**Churton** Ches	
123 K5	**Churwell** Leeds	
95 G5	**Chwilog** Gwynd	
2 E5	**Chyandour** Cnwll	
2 E4	**Chysauster** Cnwll	
111 G7	**Cilcain** Flints	
66 C3	**Cilcennin** Cerdgn	
52 B7	**Cilfrew** Neath	
37 G3	**Cilfynydd** Rhondd	
65 H6	**Cilgerran** Pembks	
51 L4	**Cilmaengwyn** Neath	
67 L4	**Cilmery** Powys	
51 H2	**Cilsan** Carmth	
96 D4	**Ciltalgarth** Gwynd	
67 G6	**Cilycwm** Carmth	
36 B2	**Cimla** Neath	
54 F5	**Cinderford** Gloucs	
42 F4	**Cippenham** Slough	
56 A7	**Cirencester** Gloucs	
45 G4	**City** Gt Lon	
45 H4	**City Airport** Gt Lon	
188 F5	**Clabhach** Ag & B	
173 J3	**Clachaig** Ag & B	
172 C6	**Clachan** Ag & B	
182 A4	**Clachan** Ag & B	
191 D7	**Clachan** Ag & B	
209 H6	**Clachan** Highld	
233 c6	**Clachan-a-Luib** W Isls	
153 H3	**Clachaneasy** D & G	
188 C6	**Clachan Mor** Ag & B	
233 c6	**Clachan na Luib** W Isls	
175 G3	**Clachan of Campsie** E Duns	
181 M4	**Clachan-Seil** Ag & B	
213 G5	**Clachnaharry** Highld	
224 C3	**Clachtoll** Highld	
195 J4	**Clackavoid** P & K	
185 J8	**Clackmannan** Clacks	
214 F3	**Clackmarras** Moray	
62 E5	**Clacton-on-Sea** Essex	
182 F3	**Cladich** Ag & B	
71 J3	**Cladswell** Worcs	
190 E6	**Claggan** Highld	
208 C4	**Claigan** Highld	
30 B7	**Clanfield** Hants	
56 F7	**Clanfield** Oxon	
28 F2	**Clanville** Hants	
26 F5	**Clanville** Somset	
172 E6	**Claonaig** Ag & B	
60 C3	**Clapgate** Herts	
74 F4	**Clapham** Beds	
44 F5	**Clapham** Gt Lon	
130 E5	**Clapham** N York	
18 F4	**Clapham** W Susx	
13 K2	**Clapton** Somset	
26 F2	**Clapton** Somset	
38 C5	**Clapton-in-Gordano** N Som	
56 D4	**Clapton-on-the-Hill** Gloucs	
150 E3	**Claravale** Gatesd	
49 H3	**Clarbeston** Pembks	
49 H4	**Clarbeston Road** Pembks	
116 B5	**Clarborough** Notts	
77 H5	**Clare** Suffk	
146 F3	**Clarebrand** D & G	
147 J2	**Clarencefield** D & G	
150 C2	**Clarewood** Nthumb	
167 H5	**Clarilaw** Border	
175 G6	**Clarkston** E Rens	
223 G4	**Clashmore** Highld	
224 C3	**Clashmore** Highld	
224 C3	**Clashnessie** Highld	
204 F2	**Clashnoir** Moray	
185 K4	**Clathy** P & K	
185 L5	**Clathymore** P & K	
205 L1	**Clatt** Abers	
81 L5	**Clatter** Powys	
25 J5	**Clatworthy** Somset	
121 G3	**Claughton** Lancs	
130 B6	**Claughton** Lancs	
111 J4	**Claughton** Wirral	
71 L2	**Claverdon** Warwks	
38 C6	**Claverham** N Som	
60 D2	**Clavering** Essex	
84 E5	**Claverley** Shrops	
39 H7	**Claverton** BaNES	
37 G5	**Clawdd-coch** V Glam	

97 G3 **Clawdd-newydd** Denbgs
9 J5 **Clawton** Devon
117 J3 **Claxby** Lincs
133 L7 **Claxton** N York
93 H3 **Claxton** Norfk
86 F5 **Claybrooke Magna** Leics
87 H7 **Clay Coton** Nhants
115 H8 **Clay Cross** Derbys
72 F4 **Claydon** Oxon
78 D5 **Claydon** Suffk
156 D6 **Claygate** D & G
33 J4 **Claygate** Kent
44 D7 **Claygate** Surrey
45 H3 **Clayhall** Gt Lon
24 F6 **Clayhanger** Devon
25 J7 **Clayhidon** Devon
21 G2 **Clayhill** E Susx
231 H4 **Clayock** Highld
55 H6 **Claypits** Gloucs
102 D3 **Claypole** Lincs
123 G4 **Clayton** Brad
124 C8 **Clayton** Donc
19 J3 **Clayton** W Susx
121 L4 **Clayton-le-Moors** Lancs
121 H6 **Clayton-le-Woods** Lancs
123 K7 **Clayton West** Kirk
116 B4 **Clayworth** Notts
199 G7 **Cleadale** Highld
151 J3 **Cleadon** S Tyne
6 D3 **Clearbrook** Devon
54 E6 **Clearwell** Gloucs
141 G5 **Cleasby** N York
234 c8 **Cleat** Ork
140 E4 **Cleatlam** Dur
136 D4 **Cleator** Cumb
136 E4 **Cleator Moor** Cumb
123 J5 **Cleehill** Shrops
175 K6 **Cleekhimin** N Lans
83 L6 **Clee St Margaret** Shrops
127 H8 **Cleethorpes** NE Lin
84 B7 **Cleeton St Mary** Shrops
38 C7 **Cleeve** N Som
41 L4 **Cleeve** Oxon
55 M3 **Cleeve Hill** Gloucs
71 J5 **Cleeve Prior** Worcs
178 D2 **Cleghornie** E Loth
69 J6 **Clehonger** Herefs
186 A7 **Cleish** P & K
175 L6 **Cleland** N Lans
182 C2 **Clenamacrie** Ag & B
104 F7 **Clenchwarton** Norfk
216 E3 **Clenerty** Abers
85 G7 **Clent** Worcs
84 C7 **Cleobury Mortimer** Shrops
84 B6 **Cleobury North** Shrops
161 H3 **Cleongart** Ag & B
213 J4 **Clephanton** Highld
156 A3 **Clerkhill** D & G
154 E3 **Cleuch-head** D & G
40 B5 **Clevancy** Wilts
38 B6 **Clevedon** N Som
120 D2 **Cleveleys** Lancs
39 L4 **Cleverton** Wilts
26 C2 **Clewer** Somset
106 C4 **Cley next the Sea** Norfk
138 E3 **Cliburn** Cumb
29 M2 **Cliddesden** Hants
46 C5 **Cliffe** Medway
125 G4 **Cliffe** N York
140 F4 **Cliffe** N York
21 H3 **Cliff End** E Susx
46 C5 **Cliffe Woods** Medway

68 E5 **Clifford** Herefs
124 C2 **Clifford** Leeds
71 L4 **Clifford Chambers** Warwks
55 G4 **Clifford's Mesne** Gloucs
75 H4 **Clifton** Beds
38 E5 **Clifton** Bristl
101 K5 **Clifton** C Nott
123 H4 **Clifton** Calder
138 D2 **Clifton** Cumb
100 D4 **Clifton** Derbys
115 K3 **Clifton** Donc
120 F4 **Clifton** Lancs
123 J2 **Clifton** N York
57 J2 **Clifton** Oxon
70 F5 **Clifton** Worcs
133 J8 **Clifton** York
86 B2 **Clifton Campville** Staffs
41 K2 **Clifton Hampden** Oxon
74 C4 **Clifton Reynes** M Keyn
87 G7 **Clifton upon Dunsmore** Warwks
70 C3 **Clifton upon Teme** Worcs
35 K1 **Cliftonville** Kent
18 D5 **Climping** W Susx
27 L4 **Clink** Somset
132 D7 **Clint** N York
206 F3 **Clinterty** C Aber
92 B2 **Clint Green** Norfk
167 J3 **Clintmains** Border
93 J2 **Clippesby** Norfk
88 D1 **Clipsham** Rutlnd
87 K7 **Clipston** Nhants
101 M5 **Clipston** Notts
58 F3 **Clipstone** Beds
115 L8 **Clipstone** Notts
121 L3 **Clitheroe** Lancs
98 D7 **Clive** Shrops
117 J2 **Clixby** Lincs
39 M3 **Cloatley** Wilts
97 G2 **Clocaenog** Denbgs
215 J3 **Clochan** Moray
196 D5 **Clochtow** Angus
53 L3 **Clodock** Herefs
217 J5 **Clola** Abers
74 F6 **Clophill** Beds
88 F7 **Clopton** Nhants
78 F4 **Clopton** Suffk
78 F4 **Clopton Corner** Suffk
236 d2 **Clos du Valle** Guern
154 F4 **Closeburn** D & G
154 F3 **Closeburnmill** D & G
14 B1 **Closworth** Somset
59 L2 **Clothall** Herts
112 D8 **Clotton** Ches
122 D5 **Clough Foot** Calder
123 G6 **Clough Head** Calder
143 K7 **Cloughton** N York
235 c5 **Clousta** Shet
196 B2 **Clova** Angus
22 E6 **Clovelly** Devon
167 G3 **Clovenfords** Border
191 K4 **Clovulin** Highld
122 C5 **Clow Bridge** Lancs
115 J6 **Clowne** Derbys
70 C1 **Clows Top** Worcs
201 G3 **Cluanie Inn** Highld
201 G3 **Cluanie Lodge** Highld
145 H4 **Clugston** D & G
82 F7 **Clun** Shrops
213 K5 **Clunas** Highld
83 G7 **Clunbury** Shrops
49 J4 **Clunderwen** Carmth
203 J1 **Clune** Highld
201 J7 **Clunes** Highld
83 H7 **Clungunford** Shrops
216 C4 **Clunie** Abers

195 H7 **Clunie** P & K
83 G7 **Clunton** Shrops
186 D7 **Cluny** Fife
38 F8 **Clutton** BaNES
98 C2 **Clutton** Ches
38 F8 **Clutton Hill** BaNES
53 K5 **Clydach** Mons
51 K5 **Clydach** Swans
36 F2 **Clydach Vale** Rhondd
174 F4 **Clydebank** W Duns
40 B5 **Clyffe Pypard** Wilts
174 A2 **Clynder** Ag & B
52 C7 **Clyne** Neath
95 G3 **Clynnog-fawr** Gwynd
68 E5 **Clyro** Powys
12 C4 **Clyst Honiton** Devon
12 D3 **Clyst Hydon** Devon
12 C5 **Clyst St George** Devon
12 D3 **Clyst St Lawrence** Devon
12 C4 **Clyst St Mary** Devon
232 g2 **Cnoc** W Isls
80 F8 **Cnwch Coch** Cerdgn
5 L1 **Coad's Green** Cnwll
164 F2 **Coalburn** S Lans
150 E3 **Coalburns** Gatesd
55 H7 **Coaley** Gloucs
61 J7 **Coalhill** Essex
84 F4 **Coalpit Heath** S Glos
84 C3 **Coalport** Wrekin
185 J7 **Coalsnaughton** Clacks
186 D7 **Coaltown of Balgonie** Fife
186 E7 **Coaltown of Wemyss** Fife
86 E2 **Coalville** Leics
149 H3 **Coanwood** Nthumb
26 C7 **Coat** Somset
175 J5 **Coatbridge** N Lans
175 K5 **Coatdyke** N Lans
40 D4 **Coate** Swindn
40 B7 **Coate** Wilts
89 K4 **Coates** Cambs
55 L7 **Coates** Gloucs
116 E5 **Coates** Lincs
18 D3 **Coates** W Susx
23 K6 **Cobbaton** Devon
55 L5 **Coberley** Gloucs
46 A6 **Cobham** Kent
43 J7 **Cobham** Surrey
69 J3 **Cobnash** Herefs
236 c2 **Cobo** Guern
217 H2 **Coburby** Abers
75 J5 **Cockayne Hatley** Beds
205 G4 **Cock Bridge** Abers
179 G4 **Cockburnspath** Border
61 K7 **Cock Clarks** Essex
177 L4 **Cockenzie and Port Seton** E Loth
120 F1 **Cockerham** Lancs
136 F2 **Cockermouth** Cumb
59 J4 **Cockernhoe Green** Herts
51 J6 **Cockett** Swans
140 E3 **Cockfield** Dur
77 K4 **Cockfield** Suffk
44 F2 **Cockfosters** Gt Lon
61 H4 **Cock Green** Essex
18 B3 **Cocking** W Susx
18 B2 **Cocking Causeway** W Susx
7 K3 **Cockington** Torbay
26 C2 **Cocklake** Somset
158 F4 **Cockle Park** Nthumb
91 H3 **Cockley Cley** Norfk
21 H2 **Cock Marling** E Susx
42 D4 **Cockpole Green** Wokham

98 B6 **Cockshutt** Shrops
106 B4 **Cockthorpe** Norfk
12 C6 **Cockwood** Devon
114 B5 **Cockyard** Derbys
78 D4 **Coddenham** Suffk
70 C6 **Coddington** Herefs
102 D2 **Coddington** Notts
27 L4 **Codford St Mary** Wilts
27 L4 **Codford St Peter** Wilts
59 K4 **Codicote** Herts
31 H7 **Codmore Hill** W Susx
101 H7 **Codnor** Derbys
39 G5 **Codrington** S Glos
84 F3 **Codsall** Staffs
84 F3 **Codsall Wood** Staffs
108 F5 **Coedana** IoA
97 L3 **Coedpoeth** Wrexhm
97 L2 **Coed Talon** Flints
53 M7 **Coed-y-paen** Mons
7 K3 **Coffinswell** Devon
12 C6 **Cofton** Devon
85 H7 **Cofton Hackett** Worcs
37 J6 **Cogan** V Glam
74 B3 **Cogenhoe** Nhants
61 K4 **Coggeshall** Essex
203 H2 **Coignafearn** Highld
205 H6 **Coilacriech** Abers
184 D6 **Coilantogle** Stirlg
208 E6 **Coillore** Highld
202 B4 **Coiltry** Highld
36 E4 **Coity** Brdgnd
232 g2 **Col** W Isls
225 L6 **Colaboll** Highld
4 D4 **Colan** Cnwll
12 D5 **Colaton Raleigh** Devon
208 C5 **Colbost** Highld
140 F7 **Colburn** N York
138 F3 **Colby** Cumb
237 b6 **Colby** IoM
62 B3 **Colchester** Essex
41 K6 **Cold Ash** W Berk
87 J7 **Cold Ashby** Nhants
39 H6 **Cold Ashton** S Glos
56 C4 **Cold Aston** Gloucs
229 J4 **Coldbackie** Highld
74 D4 **Cold Brayfield** M Keyn
19 J4 **Coldean** Br & H
7 J2 **Coldeast** Devon
122 E5 **Colden** Calder
29 J6 **Colden Common** Hants
79 J3 **Coldfair Green** Suffk
117 G5 **Cold Hanworth** Lincs
31 J3 **Coldharbour** Surrey
73 J4 **Cold Higham** Nhants
179 J5 **Coldingham** Border
133 H3 **Cold Kirby** N York
99 J6 **Coldmeece** Staffs
61 K7 **Cold Norton** Essex
88 B2 **Cold Overton** Leics
35 H5 **Coldred** Kent
11 G4 **Coldridge** Devon
168 C2 **Coldstream** Border
18 D3 **Coldwaltham** W Susx
69 H7 **Coldwell** Herefs
217 H6 **Coldwells** Abers
26 F5 **Cole** Somset
83 G6 **Colebatch** Shrops
12 C6 **Colebrook** Devon
11 H5 **Colebrooke** Devon
102 F1 **Coleby** Lincs
125 L6 **Coleby** N Linc
11 H5 **Coleford** Devon
54 E6 **Coleford** Gloucs
27 G2 **Coleford** Somset
25 H5 **Coleford Water** Somset
92 E6 **Colegate End** Norfk

15 J3 **Colehill** Dorset
32 D6 **Coleman's Hatch** E Susx
98 B6 **Colemere** Shrops
30 B5 **Colemore** Hants
186 B2 **Colenden** P & K
39 J6 **Colerne** Wilts
56 A5 **Colesbourne** Gloucs
42 F2 **Coleshill** Bucks
40 E2 **Coleshill** Oxon
85 L5 **Coleshill** Warwks
26 E1 **Coley** BaNES
31 L5 **Colgate** W Susx
187 H6 **Colinsburgh** Fife
177 H5 **Colinton** C Edin
173 H4 **Colintraive** Ag & B
105 L7 **Colkirk** Norfk
186 C2 **Collace** P & K
235 C3 **Collafirth** Shet
7 G7 **Collaton** Devon
7 K4 **Collaton St Mary** Torbay
214 E2 **College of Roseisle** Moray
42 D7 **College Town** Br For
186 E5 **Collessie** Fife
45 J2 **Collier Row** Gt Lon
60 B4 **Collier's End** Herts
33 J4 **Collier Street** Kent
217 K8 **Collieston** Abers
155 H6 **Collin** D & G
28 E2 **Collingbourne Ducis** Wilts
28 E1 **Collingbourne Kingston** Wilts
124 B2 **Collingham** Leeds
102 D1 **Collingham** Notts
70 B3 **Collington** Herefs
73 L4 **Collingtree** Nhants
112 E3 **Collins Green** Warrtn
196 F7 **Colliston** Angus
12 E2 **Colliton** Devon
88 E3 **Collyweston** Nhants
152 D5 **Colmonell** S Ayrs
75 G3 **Colmworth** Beds
43 G5 **Colnbrook** Slough
89 L7 **Colne** Cambs
122 D3 **Colne** Lancs
61 K3 **Colne Engaine** Essex
92 E3 **Colney** Norfk
59 K6 **Colney Heath** Herts
56 B6 **Coln Rogers** Gloucs
56 C6 **Coln St Aldwyns** Gloucs
56 B5 **Coln St Dennis** Gloucs
216 C7 **Colpy** Abers
166 E2 **Colquhar** Border
102 F7 **Colsterworth** Lincs
102 B5 **Colston Bassett** Notts
214 D2 **Coltfield** Moray
106 F8 **Coltishall** Norfk
129 C5 **Colton** Cumb
124 B4 **Colton** Leeds
124 E2 **Colton** N York
92 D2 **Colton** Norfk
100 B7 **Colton** Staffs
33 H4 **Colt's Hill** Kent
146 F4 **Colvend** D & G
70 D6 **Colwall** Herefs
158 B6 **Colwell** Nthumb
100 A7 **Colwich** Staffs
36 E5 **Colwinston** V Glam
18 C5 **Colworth** W Susx
110 B5 **Colwyn Bay** Conwy
13 G4 **Colyford** Devon
13 G4 **Colyton** Devon
57 H5 **Combe** Oxon
41 G2 **Combe** W Berk
39 H7 **Combe Down** BaNES
7 J3 **Combe Fishacre** Devon

25 J5 **Combe Florey** Somset
39 G7 **Combe Hay** BaNES
7 K2 **Combeinteignhead** Devon
23 J3 **Combe Martin** Devon
12 F3 **Combe Raleigh** Devon
112 F6 **Comberbach** Ches
85 L3 **Comberford** Staffs
75 L4 **Comberton** Cambs
69 K2 **Comberton** Herefs
13 H1 **Combe St Nicholas** Somset
72 C4 **Combrook** Warwks
114 B6 **Combs** Derbys
78 C3 **Combs** Suffk
78 C3 **Combs Ford** Suffk
25 K3 **Combwich** Somset
206 D4 **Comers** Abers
70 E2 **Comhampton** Worcs
49 K4 **Commercial** Pembks
81 J3 **Commins Coch** Powys
142 E5 **Commondale** N York
136 D3 **Common End** Cumb
5 K2 **Common Moor** Cnwll
113 L4 **Compstall** Stockp
146 B4 **Compstonend** D & G
7 K3 **Compton** Devon
29 J6 **Compton** Hants
84 E6 **Compton** Staffs
30 F3 **Compton** Surrey
41 K4 **Compton** W Berk
30 C7 **Compton** W Susx
28 C2 **Compton** Wilts
27 K7 **Compton Abbas** Dorset
56 B5 **Compton Abdale** Gloucs
40 B6 **Compton Bassett** Wilts
40 F3 **Compton Beauchamp** Oxon
26 B1 **Compton Bishop** Somset
28 B5 **Compton Chamberlayne** Wilts
38 F7 **Compton Dando** BaNES
26 C5 **Compton Dundon** Somset
26 B7 **Compton Durville** Somset
38 E4 **Compton Greenfield** S Glos
38 D8 **Compton Martin** BaNES
26 F6 **Compton Pauncefoot** Somset
14 B4 **Compton Valence** Dorset
176 D1 **Comrie** Fife
185 K3 **Comrie** P & K
191 K3 **Conaglen House** Highld
210 D8 **Conchra** Highld
195 H7 **Concraigie** P & K
71 G6 **Conderton** Worcs
56 D3 **Condicote** Gloucs
175 K4 **Condorrat** N Lans
83 J3 **Condover** Shrops
55 J4 **Coney Hill** Gloucs
31 J6 **Coneyhurst Common** W Susx
133 L5 **Coneysthorpe** N York
91 L7 **Coney Weston** Suffk
5 L1 **Congdon's Shop** Cnwll
86 D3 **Congerstone** Leics
105 H7 **Congham** Norfk
113 J8 **Congleton** Ches
38 C7 **Congresbury** N Som

147 H2 **Conheath** D & G
214 B4 **Conicavel** Moray
103 L2 **Coningsby** Lincs
75 K2 **Conington** Cambs
89 H6 **Conington** Cambs
115 K2 **Conisbrough** Donc
118 E3 **Conisholme** Lincs
137 J7 **Coniston** Cumb
126 E4 **Coniston** E R Yk
131 G8 **Coniston Cold** N York
131 J6 **Conistone** N York
111 J7 **Connah's Quay** Flints
182 C1 **Connel** Ag & B
164 C6 **Connel Park** E Ayrs
3 G4 **Connor Downs** Cnwll
212 E4 **Conon Bridge** Highld
122 E2 **Cononley** N York
99 M3 **Consall** Staffs
150 E5 **Consett** Dur
132 B2 **Constable Burton** N York
3 J5 **Constantine** Cnwll
4 D2 **Constantine Bay** Cnwll
212 C3 **Contin** Highld
109 L6 **Conwy** Conwy
77 K2 **Conyer's Green** Suffk
20 E4 **Cooden** E Susx
9 K4 **Cookbury** Devon
42 E4 **Cookham** W & M
42 E4 **Cookham Dean** W & M
42 E4 **Cookham Rise** W & M
71 J3 **Cookhill** Worcs
93 H7 **Cookley** Suffk
84 E7 **Cookley** Worcs
42 B3 **Cookley Green** Oxon
207 G6 **Cookney** Abers
62 E4 **Cook's Green** Essex
77 L4 **Cooks Green** Suffk
61 G6 **Cooksmill Green** Essex
31 J6 **Coolham** W Susx
46 C5 **Cooling** Medway
7 L2 **Coombe** Devon
12 E4 **Coombe** Devon
39 H2 **Coombe** Gloucs
30 A7 **Coombe** Hants
28 C6 **Coombe Bissett** Wilts
7 K2 **Coombe Cellars** Devon
25 G5 **Coombe End** Somset
55 K3 **Coombe Hill** Gloucs
14 F5 **Coombe Keynes** Dorset
7 L3 **Coombe Pafford** Torbay
19 G4 **Coombes** W Susx
69 G2 **Coombes-Moor** Herefs
60 D7 **Coopersale Common** Essex
78 D6 **Copdock** Suffk
61 L4 **Copford Green** Essex
132 E6 **Copgrove** N York
235 d3 **Copister** Shet
75 G5 **Cople** Beds
140 D3 **Copley** Dur
124 E2 **Copmanthorpe** York
99 J6 **Copmere End** Staffs
120 F3 **Copp** Lancs
9 G5 **Coppathorne** Cnwll
99 K8 **Coppenhall** Staffs
2 F4 **Copperhouse** Cnwll
89 H7 **Coppingford** Cambs
11 H4 **Copplestone** Devon
121 H7 **Coppull** Lancs
31 K6 **Copsale** W Susx
121 K4 **Copster Green** Lancs
86 F5 **Copston Magna** Warwks
35 J3 **Cop Street** Kent

132 E5 **Copt Hewick** N York
32 B5 **Copthorne** W Susx
86 F2 **Copt Oak** Leics
28 F8 **Copythorne** Hants
45 K3 **Corbets Tey** Gt Lon
236 a7 **Corbiere** Jersey
150 C3 **Corbridge** Nthumb
88 C5 **Corby** Nhants
103 G7 **Corby Glen** Lincs
162 D4 **Cordon** N Ayrs
84 B8 **Coreley** Shrops
25 K7 **Corfe** Somset
15 H6 **Corfe Castle** Dorset
15 J3 **Corfe Mullen** Dorset
83 J6 **Corfton** Shrops
205 G4 **Corgarff** Abers
29 L7 **Corhampton** Hants
86 C6 **Corley** Warwks
86 C6 **Corley Ash** Warwks
195 L3 **Cormuir** Angus
77 K6 **Cornard Tye** Suffk
151 H7 **Cornforth** Dur
216 B3 **Cornhill** Abers
168 C2 **Cornhill-on-Tweed** Nthumb
122 D5 **Cornholme** Calder
188 C6 **Cornoigmore** Ag & B
150 E6 **Cornsay** Dur
150 F6 **Cornsay Colliery** Dur
212 E3 **Corntown** Highld
36 E5 **Corntown** V Glam
56 F3 **Cornwell** Oxon
6 E4 **Cornwood** Devon
7 J4 **Cornworthy** Devon
191 L2 **Corpach** Highld
106 D6 **Corpusty** Norfk
205 K4 **Corrachree** Abers
191 K4 **Corran** Highld
200 C4 **Corran** Highld
155 L5 **Corrie** D & G
162 C2 **Corrie** N Ayrs
162 B5 **Corriecravie** N Ayrs
162 D3 **Corriegills** N Ayrs
201 K6 **Corriegour Lodge Hotel** Highld
212 B2 **Corriemoille** Highld
212 B2 **Corrimony** Highld
116 E4 **Corringham** Lincs
46 B4 **Corringham** Thurr
81 G2 **Corris** Gwynd
81 G2 **Corris Uchaf** Gwynd
183 H7 **Corrow** Ag & B
199 K1 **Corry** Highld
10 F5 **Corscombe** Devon
13 M2 **Corscombe** Dorset
55 H3 **Corse** Gloucs
55 J2 **Corse Lawn** Gloucs
39 K6 **Corsham** Wilts
206 D4 **Corsindae** Abers
27 J3 **Corsley** Wilts
27 J3 **Corsley Heath** Wilts
154 D6 **Corsock** D & G
39 G7 **Corston** BaNES
39 L4 **Corston** Wilts
177 G4 **Corstorphine** C Edin
196 C4 **Cortachy** Angus
93 L4 **Corton** Suffk
27 L4 **Corton** Wilts
26 F6 **Corton Denham** Somset
191 L3 **Coruanan Lodge** Highld
97 G4 **Corwen** Denbgs
10 C7 **Coryton** Devon
46 C4 **Coryton** Thurr
87 G4 **Cosby** Leics
85 G5 **Coseley** Dudley
73 L6 **Cosgrove** Nhants
17 J2 **Cosham** C Port
49 G6 **Cosheston** Pembks
194 C6 **Coshieville** P & K
101 J4 **Cossall** Notts

87 H2 **Cossington** Leics
26 A4 **Cossington** Somset
92 E2 **Costessey** Norfk
102 D7 **Coston** Leics
92 C3 **Coston** Norfk
57 G7 **Cote** Oxon
112 E2 **Cotebrook** Ches
148 E5 **Cotehill** Cumb
101 K7 **Cotes** Leics
87 G6 **Cotesbach** Leics
25 J6 **Cotford St Luke** Somset
101 M5 **Cotgrave** Notts
207 G3 **Cothal** Abers
102 C3 **Cotham** Notts
140 C4 **Cotherstone** Dur
57 J7 **Cothill** Oxon
13 G3 **Cotleigh** Devon
101 J4 **Cotmanhay** Derbys
76 B3 **Coton** Cambs
73 J1 **Coton** Nhants
99 J7 **Coton** Staffs
99 K7 **Coton Clanford** Staffs
83 J2 **Coton Hill** Shrops
86 B1 **Coton in the Elms** Derbys
55 M6 **Cotswolds**
7 H4 **Cott** Devon
121 G4 **Cottam** Lancs
116 D5 **Cottam** Notts
76 C2 **Cottenham** Cambs
60 A3 **Cottered** Herts
88 F5 **Cotterstock** Nhants
87 K8 **Cottesbrooke** Nhants
88 C2 **Cottesmore** Rutlnd
126 C4 **Cottingham** E R Yk
88 B5 **Cottingham** Nhants
123 G3 **Cottingley** Brad
57 L2 **Cottisford** Oxon
78 C2 **Cotton** Suffk
206 E3 **Cottown** Abers
215 L8 **Cottown** Abers
216 F6 **Cottown of Gight** Abers
6 C3 **Cotts** Devon
71 J3 **Coughton** Warwks
172 C5 **Coulaghailtro** Ag & B
210 E5 **Coulags** Highld
205 L3 **Coull** Abers
173 L2 **Coulport** Ag & B
32 B2 **Coulsdon** Gt Lon
27 L2 **Coulston** Wilts
165 K3 **Coulter** S Lans
133 K5 **Coulton** N York
186 F3 **Coultra** Fife
83 L3 **Cound** Shrops
141 G2 **Coundon** Dur
131 H2 **Countersett** N York
12 B4 **Countess Wear** Devon
87 H4 **Countesthorpe** Leics
24 B2 **Countisbury** Devon
195 K7 **Coupar Angus** P & K
168 D3 **Coupland** Nthumb
172 D8 **Cour** Ag & B
155 J4 **Courance** D & G
199 L6 **Courteachan** Highld
73 L4 **Courteenhall** Nhants
51 H2 **Court Henry** Carmth
47 G2 **Courtsend** Essex
25 J5 **Courtway** Somset
177 K6 **Cousland** Mdloth
33 H6 **Cousley Wood** E Susx
173 L2 **Cove** Ag & B
179 G4 **Cove** Border
24 E7 **Cove** Devon
30 E1 **Cove** Hants
219 J3 **Cove** Highld
207 H5 **Cove Bay** C Aber
93 L6 **Covehithe** Suffk
85 G3 **Coven** Staffs

90 C6 **Coveney** Cambs
118 D3 **Covenham St Bartholomew** Lincs
118 D7 **Covenham St Mary** Lincs
86 D7 **Coventry** Covtry
86 D8 **Coventry Airport** Warwks
3 K7 **Coverack** Cnwll
3 H5 **Coverack Bridges** Cnwll
131 L3 **Coverham** N York
74 F1 **Covington** Cambs
165 J2 **Covington** S Lans
130 C4 **Cowan Bridge** Lancs
20 C3 **Cowbeech** E Susx
103 L8 **Cowbit** Lincs
36 F5 **Cowbridge** V Glam
32 K5 **Cowden** Kent
177 L1 **Cowdenbeath** Fife
100 F3 **Cowers Lane** Derbys
16 F3 **Cowes** IoW
133 G2 **Cowesby** N York
31 K6 **Cowfold** W Susx
38 E3 **Cowhill** S Glos
71 K5 **Cow Honeybourne** Worcs
175 L1 **Cowie** Stirlg
11 K5 **Cowley** Devon
55 L5 **Cowley** Gloucs
43 H4 **Cowley** Gt Lon
57 K7 **Cowley** Oxon
121 H6 **Cowling** Lancs
122 E2 **Cowling** N York
132 C3 **Cowling** N York
77 G4 **Cowlinge** Suffk
159 H5 **Cowpen** Nthumb
17 K1 **Cowplain** Hants
149 L6 **Cowshill** Dur
38 C7 **Cowslip Green** N Som
132 F8 **Cowthorpe** N York
98 F4 **Coxbank** Ches
101 G4 **Coxbench** Derbys
8 F5 **Coxford** Cnwll
105 K6 **Coxford** Norfk
33 J3 **Coxheath** Kent
151 H7 **Coxhoe** Dur
26 D3 **Coxley** Somset
26 D3 **Coxley Wick** Somset
45 K2 **Coxtie Green** Essex
133 H4 **Coxwold** N York
36 E4 **Coychurch** Brdgnd
163 K5 **Coylton** S Ayrs
203 L3 **Coylumbridge** Highld
36 D4 **Coytrahen** Brdgnd
71 J2 **Crabbs Cross** Worcs
31 K6 **Crabtree** W Susx
138 F3 **Crackenthorpe** Cumb
8 F5 **Crackington Haven** Cnwll
84 D2 **Crackleybank** Shrops
131 J7 **Cracoe** N York
25 G8 **Craddock** Devon
85 G6 **Cradley** Dudley
70 D5 **Cradley** Herefs
85 G6 **Cradley Heath** Sandw
52 F2 **Cradoc** Powys
6 B5 **Crafthole** Cnwll
58 E4 **Crafton** Bucks
204 C1 **Craggan** Highld
122 E5 **Cragg Vale** Calder
150 F5 **Craghead** Dur
52 D7 **Crai** Powys
215 L3 **Craibstone** Moray
196 E6 **Craichie** Angus
197 H5 **Craig** Angus
211 G4 **Craig** Highld
164 C6 **Craigbank** E Ayrs
177 H7 **Craigburn** Border
156 C5 **Craigcleuch** D & G
216 F7 **Craigdam** Abers
182 B6 **Craigdhu** Ag & B

206 D3 **Craigearn** Abers
215 G5 **Craigellachie** Moray
186 B4 **Craigend** P & K
174 E4 **Craigend** Rens
174 C3 **Craigendoran** Ag & B
145 G3 **Craighlaw** D & G
171 K5 **Craighouse** Ag & B
195 H7 **Craigie** P & K
163 K3 **Craigie** S Ayrs
217 H2 **Craigiefold** Abers
146 D4 **Craigley** D & G
51 K4 **Craig Llangiwg** Neath
177 H4 **Craiglockhart** C Edin
215 H4 **Craiglug** Moray
177 J4 **Craigmillar** C Edin
154 D5 **Craigneston** D & G
175 K5 **Craigneuk** N Lans
175 K6 **Craigneuk** N Lans
190 E8 **Craignure** Ag & B
197 H4 **Craigo** Angus
186 F5 **Craigrothie** Fife
184 B4 **Craigruie** Stirlg
196 E8 **Craigton** Angus
206 F5 **Craigton** C Aber
174 F7 **Craigton** E Rens
196 B6 **Craigton of Airlie** Angus
187 K5 **Crail** Fife
167 L4 **Crailing** Border
116 C2 **Craiselound** N Linc
132 C2 **Crakehall** N York
133 L6 **Crambe** N York
159 G6 **Cramlington** Nthumb
177 G3 **Cramond** C Edin
177 G4 **Cramond Bridge** C Edin
113 H7 **Cranage** Ches
99 J5 **Cranberry** Staffs
28 B8 **Cranborne** Dorset
33 K6 **Cranbrook** Kent
74 D6 **Cranfield** Beds
43 J5 **Cranford** Gt Lon
88 D7 **Cranford St Andrew** Nhants
88 D7 **Cranford St John** Nhants
55 K5 **Cranham** Gloucs
112 D2 **Crank** St Hel
31 H4 **Cranleigh** Surrey
26 F3 **Cranmore** Somset
87 L4 **Cranoe** Leics
79 G2 **Cransford** Suffk
178 E6 **Cranshaws** Border
4 C4 **Crantock** Cnwll
103 G3 **Cranwell** Lincs
91 H4 **Cranwich** Norfk
92 B3 **Cranworth** Norfk
182 A6 **Craobh Haven** Ag & B
182 E7 **Crarae** Ag & B
225 L4 **Crask Inn** Highld
212 D6 **Crask of Aigas** Highld
169 K5 **Craster** Nthumb
93 G7 **Cratfield** Suffk
206 E6 **Crathes** Abers
206 D6 **Crathes Castle** Abers
205 K6 **Crathie** Abers
202 E6 **Crathie** Highld
141 K5 **Crathorne** N York
83 H6 **Craven Arms** Shrops
150 E3 **Crawcrook** Gatesd
165 J5 **Crawford** S Lans
165 G5 **Crawfordjohn** S Lans
164 F1 **Crawick** D & G
29 H4 **Crawley** Hants
57 G5 **Crawley** Oxon
31 L4 **Crawley** W Susx
32 C5 **Crawley Down** W Susx
122 B5 **Crawshawbooth** Lancs
197 L1 **Crawton** Abers
131 H4 **Cray** N York

45 K5 **Crayford** Gt Lon
133 H5 **Crayke** N York
46 B2 **Crays Hill** Essex
24 E8 **Craze Lowman** Devon
24 C7 **Creacombe** Devon
191 J7 **Creagan Inn** Ag & B
233 c7 **Creag Ghoraidh** W Isls
233 c7 **Creagorry** W Isls
192 E3 **Creaguaineach Lodge** Highld
73 K1 **Creaton** Nhants
155 M7 **Creca** D & G
69 J5 **Credenhill** Herefs
11 J5 **Crediton** Devon
153 H6 **Creebank** D & G
145 J2 **Creebridge** D & G
25 L6 **Creech Heathfield** Somset
25 L6 **Creech St Michael** Somset
4 E6 **Creed** Cnwll
45 J4 **Creekmouth** Gt Lon
78 D3 **Creeting St Mary** Suffk
103 G8 **Creeton** Lincs
145 K3 **Creetown** D & G
237 a7 **Cregneash** IoM
186 E3 **Creich** Fife
37 G4 **Creigiau** Cardif
6 C5 **Cremyll** Cnwll
83 L3 **Cressage** Shrops
114 D6 **Cressbrook** Derbys
49 H6 **Cresselly** Pembks
42 D3 **Cressex** Bucks
61 J4 **Cressing** Essex
159 H4 **Cresswell** Nthumb
49 H6 **Cresswell** Pembks
99 L5 **Cresswell** Staffs
115 K6 **Creswell** Derbys
78 F3 **Cretingham** Suffk
172 C5 **Cretshengan** Ag & B
98 B2 **Crewe** Ches
99 G2 **Crewe** Ches
99 G2 **Crewe Green** Ches
83 G1 **Crew Green** Powys
13 K1 **Crewkerne** Somset
101 G5 **Crewton** C Derb
183 L3 **Crianlarich** Stirlg
38 E4 **Cribbs Causeway** S Glos
66 C4 **Cribyn** Cerdgn
95 J5 **Criccieth** Gwynd
101 G2 **Crich** Derbys
177 K6 **Crichton** Mdloth
87 H8 **Crick** Nhants
68 C6 **Crickadarn** Powys
13 J2 **Cricket St Thomas** Somset
53 K4 **Crickhowell** Powys
40 C2 **Cricklade** Wilts
44 E3 **Cricklewood** Gt Lon
124 D6 **Cridling Stubbs** N York
185 H3 **Crieff** P & K
82 F1 **Criggion** Powys
123 L7 **Crigglestone** Wakefd
217 K3 **Crimond** Abers
90 F3 **Crimplesham** Norfk
72 B5 **Crimscote** Warwks
212 C6 **Crinaglack** Highld
182 A8 **Crinan** Ag & B
175 L6 **Crindledyke** N Lans
92 E3 **Cringleford** Norfk
49 J5 **Crinow** Pembks
213 G8 **Croachy** Highld
154 F6 **Crochmore House** D & G
45 K6 **Crockenhill** Kent
42 B3 **Crocker End** Oxon
11 H6 **Crockernwell** Devon
27 K3 **Crockerton** Wilts
154 E7 **Crocketford** D & G

32 D3 **Crockham Hill** Kent
36 D2 **Croeserw** Neath
48 D2 **Croes-goch** Pembks
65 L5 **Croes-lan** Cerdgn
95 L4 **Croesor** Gwynd
50 E3 **Croesyceiliog** Carmth
37 L2 **Croesyceiliog** Torfn
87 G4 **Croft** Leics
104 E1 **Croft** Lincs
112 F4 **Croft** Warrtn
174 E2 **Croftamie** Stirlg
124 B6 **Crofton** Wakefd
141 H5 **Croft-on-Tees** N York
146 C2 **Crofts** D & G
215 G4 **Crofts** Moray
215 H3 **Crofts of Dipple** Moray
217 K3 **Crofts of Savoch** Abers
51 G6 **Crofty** Swans
181 L3 **Croggan** Ag & B
148 F5 **Croglin** Cumb
222 B3 **Croik** Highld
223 H7 **Cromarty** Highld
176 E2 **Crombie** Fife
214 D8 **Cromdale** Highld
59 M3 **Cromer** Herts
106 F4 **Cromer** Norfk
100 F2 **Cromford** Derbys
39 G3 **Cromhall** S Glos
232 f3 **Cromor** W Isls
102 D1 **Cromwell** Notts
164 C5 **Cronberry** E Ayrs
30 C2 **Crondall** Hants
112 C4 **Cronton** Knows
138 C7 **Crook** Cumb
150 E7 **Crook** Dur
163 L3 **Crookedholm** E Ayrs
148 E3 **Crooked Holme** Cumb
168 D2 **Crookham** Nthumb
41 K7 **Crookham** W Berk
30 C2 **Crookham Village** Hants
165 L4 **Crook Inn** Border
129 L3 **Crooklands** Cumb
185 L7 **Crook of Devon** P & K
72 F5 **Cropredy** Oxon
87 G2 **Cropston** Leics
71 H5 **Cropthorne** Worcs
134 B2 **Cropton** N York
102 B5 **Cropwell Bishop** Notts
102 B5 **Cropwell Butler** Notts
232 g1 **Cros** W Isls
173 L7 **Crosbie** N Ayrs
232 f3 **Crosbost** W Isls
147 J7 **Crosby** Cumb
237 C5 **Crosby** IoM
125 K7 **Crosby** N Linc
111 J2 **Crosby** Sefton
139 G5 **Crosby Garret** Cumb
138 F4 **Crosby Ravensworth** Cumb
26 E3 **Croscombe** Somset
26 B1 **Cross** Somset
172 E7 **Crossaig** Ag & B
188 C7 **Crossapoll** Ag & B
54 B4 **Cross Ash** Mons
33 K4 **Cross-at-Hand** Kent
147 J6 **Crosscanonby** Cumb
106 F5 **Crossdale Street** Norfk
123 G3 **Cross Flatts** Brad
176 E2 **Crossford** Fife
175 L8 **Crossford** S Lans
177 K5 **Crossgatehall** E Loth
163 J1 **Crossgates** E Ayrs
176 F1 **Crossgates** Fife
124 B4 **Cross Gates** Leeds
134 F3 **Crossgates** N York
129 L6 **Crossgill** Lancs

123 L4 **Cross Green** Leeds
77 J4 **Cross Green** Suffk
77 K4 **Cross Green** Suffk
78 B4 **Cross Green** Suffk
51 H3 **Cross Hands** Carmth
163 L4 **Crosshands** E Ayrs
186 C7 **Crosshill** Fife
163 J7 **Crosshill** S Ayrs
163 K2 **Crosshouse** E Ayrs
83 K3 **Cross Houses** Shrops
20 B2 **Cross in Hand** E Susx
65 L3 **Cross Inn** Cerdgn
174 C2 **Cross Keys** Ag & B
37 K3 **Crosskeys** Caerph
230 F2 **Crosskirk** Highld
129 H2 **Crosslands** Cumb
17 G4 **Cross Lane** IoW
84 C4 **Cross Lane Head** Shrops
174 D5 **Crosslee** Rens
146 C2 **Crossmichael** D & G
216 E7 **Cross of Jackston** Abers
100 F4 **Cross o' th' hands** Derbys
206 B4 **Crossroads** Abers
206 E6 **Crossroads** Abers
92 E7 **Cross Street** Suffk
196 E5 **Crosston** Angus
113 H5 **Cross Town** Ches
70 E2 **Crossway Green** Worcs
14 E5 **Crossways** Dorset
64 F6 **Crosswell** Pembks
129 J2 **Crosthwaite** Cumb
121 G6 **Croston** Lancs
92 F1 **Crostwick** Norfk
44 F3 **Crouch End** Gt Lon
28 B6 **Croucheston** Wilts
14 D1 **Crouch Hill** Dorset
73 G7 **Croughton** Nhants
216 F2 **Crovie** Abers
3 H4 **Crowan** Cnwll
32 F6 **Crowborough** E Susx
25 H4 **Crowcombe** Somset
114 C7 **Crowdecote** Derbys
114 D2 **Crow Edge** Barns
58 C7 **Crowell** Oxon
78 D3 **Crowfield** Suffk
178 F4 **Crowhill** E Loth
54 F3 **Crow Hill** Herefs
20 F3 **Crowhurst** E Susx
32 D4 **Crowhurst** Surrey
89 J2 **Crowland** Lincs
78 B1 **Crowland** Suffk
2 F5 **Crowlas** Cnwll
125 J7 **Crowle** N Linc
71 G4 **Crowle** Worcs
71 G3 **Crowle Green** Worcs
41 L3 **Crowmarsh Gifford** Oxon
78 F1 **Crown Corner** Suffk
6 C4 **Crownhill** C Plym
92 C3 **Crownthorpe** Norfk
3 H5 **Crowntown** Cnwll
2 D5 **Crows-an-Wra** Cnwll
42 D7 **Crowthorne** Wokham
112 E6 **Crowton** Ches
151 G7 **Croxdale** Dur
100 B5 **Croxden** Staffs
43 H2 **Croxley Green** Herts
75 J3 **Croxton** Cambs
126 D7 **Croxton** N Linc
91 K6 **Croxton** Norfk
106 B6 **Croxton** Norfk
99 H6 **Croxton** Staffs
102 D6 **Croxton Kerrial** Leics
213 J4 **Croy** Highld
175 J3 **Croy** N Lans
23 G4 **Croyde** Devon
75 K5 **Croydon** Cambs
44 F6 **Croydon** Gt Lon

203 G7 **Crubenmore** Highld
83 H2 **Cruckmeole** Shrops
83 H2 **Cruckton** Shrops
217 K6 **Cruden Bay** Abers
98 F8 **Crudgington** Wrekin
39 L2 **Crudwell** Wilts
37 K2 **Crumlin** Caerph
5 K5 **Crumplehorn** Cnwll
113 J2 **Crumpsall** Manch
34 E5 **Crundale** Kent
49 K5 **Crunwear** Pembks
29 H1 **Crux Easton** Hants
50 F3 **Crwbin** Carmth
42 E2 **Cryers Hill** Bucks
65 G7 **Crymmych** Pembks
52 C6 **Crynant** Neath
45 G5 **Crystal Palace** Gt Lon
209 L3 **Cuaig** Highld
181 L4 **Cuan Ferry Village** Ag & B
72 D2 **Cubbington** Warwks
4 C4 **Cubert** Cnwll
58 D4 **Cublington** Bucks
69 H6 **Cublington** Herefs
32 B7 **Cuckfield** W Susx
27 H6 **Cucklington** Somset
115 K7 **Cuckney** Notts
57 L7 **Cuddesdon** Oxon
58 C5 **Cuddington** Bucks
112 E7 **Cuddington** Ches
98 C3 **Cuddington Heath** Ches
32 D2 **Cudham** Gt Lon
10 D8 **Cudliptown** Devon
15 K3 **Cudnell** Bmouth
124 B8 **Cudworth** Barns
13 J1 **Cudworth** Somset
59 M7 **Cuffley** Herts
191 J5 **Cuil** Highld
212 F3 **Culbokie** Highld
212 D6 **Culburnie** Highld
213 G5 **Culcabock** Highld
213 K4 **Culcharry** Highld
112 F3 **Culcheth** Warrtn
215 L7 **Culdrain** Abers
209 L6 **Culduie** Highld
77 J1 **Culford** Suffk
138 E2 **Culgaith** Cumb
41 J2 **Culham** Oxon
224 C2 **Culkein** Highld
224 D2 **Culkein Drumbeg** Highld
39 L2 **Culkerton** Gloucs
215 L2 **Cullen** Moray
159 J7 **Cullercoats** N Tyne
206 E5 **Cullerlie** Abers
213 G2 **Cullicudden** Highld
123 G3 **Cullingworth** Brad
199 G2 **Cuillin Hills** Highld
181 L5 **Cullipool House** Ag & B
235 d2 **Cullivoe** Shet
213 H5 **Culloden** Highld
12 C2 **Cullompton** Devon
25 H7 **Culm Davy** Devon
83 J6 **Culmington** Shrops
25 H8 **Culmstock** Devon
224 C7 **Culnacraig** Highld
146 D5 **Culnaightrie** D & G
209 H2 **Culnaknock** Highld
222 D3 **Culrain** Highld
176 D2 **Culross** Fife
163 H6 **Culroy** S Ayrs
216 C7 **Culsalmond** Abers
145 K5 **Culscadden** D & G
145 G5 **Culshabbin** D & G
235 b6 **Culswick** Shet
207 H1 **Cultercullen** Abers
207 G5 **Cults** C Aber
45 M7 **Culverstone Green** Kent
103 G4 **Culverthorpe** Lincs

73 G5 **Culworth** Nhants
163 G7 **Culzean Castle** S Ayrs
175 K4 **Cumbernauld** N Lans
175 K3 **Cumbernauld Village** N Lans
119 G6 **Cumberworth** Lincs
216 F4 **Cuminestown** Abers
179 G7 **Cumledge** Border
148 D4 **Cummersdale** Cumb
147 K2 **Cummertrees** D & G
214 E1 **Cummingston** Moray
164 B5 **Cumnock** E Ayrs
57 J7 **Cumnor** Oxon
148 F5 **Cumrew** Cumb
155 J5 **Cumrue** D & G
148 D4 **Cumwhinton** Cumb
148 E4 **Cumwhitton** Cumb
132 F5 **Cundall** N York
163 J2 **Cunninghamhead** N Ayrs
235 c7 **Cunningsburgh** Shet
186 F4 **Cupar** Fife
186 F5 **Cupar Muir** Fife
114 E6 **Curbar** Derbys
17 G1 **Curbridge** Hants
57 G6 **Curbridge** Oxon
29 K8 **Curdridge** Hants
85 L5 **Curdworth** Warwks
25 L7 **Curland** Somset
41 J6 **Curridge** W Berk
177 G5 **Currie** C Edin
25 L6 **Curry Mallet** Somset
26 B6 **Curry Rivel** Somset
33 J5 **Curtisden Green** Kent
7 H5 **Curtisknowle** Devon
3 H6 **Cury** Cnwll
205 L3 **Cushnie** Abers
145 J7 **Cutcloy** D & G
24 E4 **Cutcombe** Somset
223 G4 **Cuthill** Highld
70 F2 **Cutnall Green** Worcs
56 C3 **Cutsdean** Gloucs
115 G6 **Cutthorpe** Derbys
42 A2 **Cuxham** Oxon
46 B6 **Cuxton** Medway
117 K2 **Cuxwold** Lincs
110 E6 **Cwm** Denbgs
36 B3 **Cwmafan** Neath
52 F7 **Cwmaman** Rhondd
50 B1 **Cwmbach** Carmth
68 D6 **Cwmbach** Powys
52 F7 **Cwmbach** Rhondd
68 B4 **Cwmbach Llechryd** Powys
37 L2 **Cwmbran** Torfn
37 K2 **Cwmcarn** Caerph
54 C6 **Cwmcarvan** Mons
65 J6 **Cwm-cou** Cerdgn
53 H4 **Cwm Crawnon** Powys
52 F7 **Cwmdare** Rhondd
53 J4 **Cwmdu** Powys
51 J6 **Cwmdu** Swans
65 L7 **Cwmduad** Carmth
36 D3 **Cwmfelin** Brdgnd
53 H7 **Cwmfelin** Myr Td
49 K4 **Cwmfelin Boeth** Carmth
37 J3 **Cwmfelinfach** Caerph
50 E3 **Cwmffrwd** Carmth
52 C5 **Cwmgiedd** Powys
51 K4 **Cwmgorse** Carmth
51 H4 **Cwmgwili** Carmth
65 K6 **Cwmhiraeth** Carmth
81 J2 **Cwm Llinau** Powys
51 L3 **Cwmllynfell** Neath
51 G3 **Cwmmawr** Carmth
36 E2 **Cwmparc** Rhondd
65 K6 **Cwmpengraig** Carmth
66 B5 **Cwmsychbant** Cerdgn
53 K6 **Cwmtillery** Blae G

51	H3	Cwm-y-glo Carmth
109	H8	Cwm-y-glo Gwynd
81	H8	Cwmystwyth Cerdgn
66	C5	Cwrt-newydd Cerdgn
51	L3	Cyllioebyn Fcudn
36	D2	Cymer Neath
36	F3	Cymmer Rhondd
67	H6	Cynghordy Carmth
36	C2	Cynonville Neath
97	G4	Cynwyd Denbgs
65	L8	Cynwyl Elfed Carmth

D

7	K3	Daccombe Devon
138	C2	Dacre Cumb
132	B7	Dacre N York
132	B6	Dacre Banks N York
149	M7	Daddry Shield Dur
73	J6	Dadford Bucks
86	E4	Dadlington Leics
45	J3	Dagenham Gt Lon
55	M6	Daglingworth Gloucs
59	G5	Dagnall Bucks
152	F2	Dailly S Ayrs
187	G4	Dairsie Fife
233	b8	Dalabrog W Isls
182	D5	Dalavich Ag & B
146	E3	Dalbeattie D & G
237	b5	Dalby IoM
133	K5	Dalby N York
194	F5	Dalcapon P & K
226	F7	Dalchalm Highld
201	L3	Dalchreichart Highld
184	F4	Dalchruin P & K
185	L2	Dalcrue P & K
12	D5	Dalditch Devon
101	H5	Dale Derbys
48	D6	Dale Pembks
163	H1	Dalgarven N Ayrs
177	G2	Dalgety Bay Fife
164	B6	Dalgig E Ayrs
185	G3	Dalginross P & K
194	F6	Dalguise P & K
230	C5	Dalhalvaig Highld
77	G3	Dalham Suffk
233	b8	Daliburgh W Isls
177	K5	Dalkeith Mdloth
214	D4	Dallas Moray
78	F4	Dallinghoo Suffk
20	D2	Dallington E Susx
73	K3	Dallington Nhants
183	H3	Dalmally Ag & B
184	C7	Dalmary Stirlg
153	K2	Dalmellington E Ayrs
176	F3	Dalmeny C Edin
203	H2	Dalmigavie Highld
203	H2	Dalmigavie Lodge Highld
222	F7	Dalmore Highld
174	E4	Dalmuir W Duns
190	E3	Dalnabreck Highld
194	B3	Dalnacardoch P & K
203	K2	Dalnahaitnach Highld
193	K2	Dalnaspidal P & K
230	F7	Dalnawillan Lodge Highld
194	C5	Daloist P & K
186	A6	Dalqueich P & K
153	G3	Dalquhairn S Ayrs
226	D6	Dalreavoch Lodge Highld
174	B7	Dalry N Ayrs
163	J6	Dalrymple E Ayrs
175	L7	Dalserf S Lans
161	G4	Dalsmeran Ag & B
148	C5	Dalston Cumb
45	G3	Dalston Gt Lon
155	G3	Dalswinton D & G
155	K7	Dalton D & G

132	F4	Dalton N York
140	E5	Dalton N York
158	E7	Dalton Nthumb
128	F5	Dalton-in-Furness Cumb
151	K5	Dalton-le-Dale Dur
141	H5	Dalton-on-Tees N York
141	L2	Dalton Piercy Hartpl
165	G7	Dalveen D & G
184	D3	Dalveich Stirlg
202	F7	Dalwhinnie Highld
13	G3	Dalwood Devon
28	C7	Damerham Hants
93	J2	Damgate Norfk
61	J6	Danbury Essex
142	F5	Danby N York
141	H7	Danby Wiske N York
215	G5	Dandaleith Moray
177	J4	Danderhall Mdloth
113	L7	Danebridge Ches
60	B4	Dane End Herts
32	D7	Danehill E Susx
87	H3	Dane Hills C Leic
34	E4	Dane Street Kent
216	D3	Danshillock Abers
178	C5	Danskine E Loth
45	K5	Darenth Kent
112	E5	Daresbury Halton
115	H1	Darfield Barns
34	E3	Dargate Kent
5	K3	Darite Cnwll
85	H4	Darlaston Wsall
85	H4	Darlaston Green Wsall
132	C7	Darley N York
101	G5	Darley Abbey C Derb
100	E1	Darley Bridge Derbys
114	F8	Darley Dale Derbys
85	L8	Darley Green Solhll
59	J4	Darleyhall Herts
132	B7	Darley Head N York
72	B6	Darlingscott Warwks
141	M4	Darlington Darltn
116	C6	Darlton Notts
167	H3	Darnick Border
81	H3	Darowen Powys
216	E5	Darra Abers
9	G2	Darracott Devon
23	G4	Darracott Devon
158	E7	Darras Hall Nthumb
124	D6	Darrington Wakefd
79	J1	Darsham Suffk
26	E3	Darshill Somset
45	K5	Dartford Kent
7	H4	Dartington Devon
11	G8	Dartmoor National Park Devon
7	K5	Dartmouth Devon
123	L7	Darton Barns
164	B2	Darvel E Ayrs
121	K6	Darwen Bl w D
43	G5	Datchet W & M
59	L4	Datchworth Herts
121	K8	Daubhill Bolton
39	M4	Dauntsey Wilts
214	C6	Dava Highld
112	F7	Davenham Ches
73	H3	Daventry Nhants
177	G4	Davidson's Mains C Edin
8	F7	Davidstow Cnwll
155	M2	Davington D & G
34	D3	Davington Hill Kent
216	E8	Daviot Abers
213	H6	Daviot Highld
213	H6	Daviot House Highld
215	K4	Davoch of Grange Moray
31	K3	Dawesgreen Surrey
84	C2	Dawley Wrekin
12	B6	Dawlish Devon

12	C6	Dawlish Warren Devon
110	B6	Dawn Conwy
101	L4	Daybrook Notts
88	B7	Daylesford Gloucs
35	K4	Deal Kent
136	E3	Dean Cumb
7	H3	Dean Devon
23	L2	Dean Devon
29	K7	Dean Hants
57	G4	Dean Oxon
26	F3	Dean Somset
45	L6	Dean Bottom Kent
166	F6	Deanburnhaugh Border
7	G3	Deancombe Devon
57	J6	Dean Court Oxon
121	K8	Deane Bolton
29	K2	Deane Hants
122	F7	Deanhead Kirk
27	M7	Deanland Dorset
7	H3	Dean Prior Devon
149	L3	Deanraw Nthumb
176	D5	Deans W Loth
136	F2	Deanscales Cumb
73	L6	Deanshanger Nhants
215	H4	Deanshaugh Moray
184	F6	Deanston Stirlg
147	J7	Dearham Cumb
78	F4	Debach Suffk
45	H2	Debden Essex
60	E2	Debden Essex
78	E2	Debenham Suffk
70	E5	Deblin's Green Worcs
176	E4	Dechmont W Loth
176	D4	Dechmont Road W Loth
57	J2	Deddington Oxon
62	C2	Dedham Essex
42	F5	Dedworth W & M
88	D5	Deene Nhants
88	D5	Deenethorpe Nhants
114	F3	Deepcar Sheff
89	G2	Deeping Gate C Pete
89	H2	Deeping St James Lincs
89	J1	Deeping St Nicholas Lincs
55	K3	Deerhurst Gloucs
71	G5	Defford Worcs
52	E3	Defynnog Powys
109	L5	Deganwy Conwy
182	A5	Degnish Ag & B
141	J6	Deighton N York
124	F2	Deighton York
109	H8	Deiniolen Gwynd
8	E7	Delabole Cnwll
112	E7	Delamere Ches
207	H2	Delfrigs Abers
214	D7	Delliefure Highld
18	A5	Dell Quay W Susx
204	E3	Delnabo Moray
214	E7	Delnashaugh Inn Moray
223	G6	Delny Highld
122	E8	Delph Oldham
150	E5	Delves Dur
195	H7	Delvine P & K
103	H5	Dembleby Lincs
115	J2	Denaby Donc
110	E7	Denbigh Denbgs
186	F4	Denbrae Fife
7	J3	Denbury Devon
101	H4	Denby Derbys
123	J8	Denby Dale Kirk
41	G3	Denchworth Oxon
128	F5	Dendron Cumb
185	K4	Denfield P & K
88	E7	Denford Nhants
62	B7	Dengie Essex
43	H3	Denham Bucks
77	H3	Denham Suffk

92	E8	Denham Suffk
43	H3	Denham Green Bucks
217	J4	Denhead Abers
187	G5	Denhead Fife
186	F0	Denhead of Gray C Dund
167	J5	Denholm Border
123	G4	Denholme Brad
30	A8	Denmead Hants
207	H3	Denmore C Aber
79	G2	Dennington Suffk
175	L2	Denny Falk
175	L3	Dennyloanhead Falk
186	D4	Den of Lindores Fife
122	E7	Denshaw Oldham
206	F6	Denside Abers
35	G6	Densole Kent
77	H4	Denston Suffk
100	C4	Denstone Staffs
34	E3	Denstroude Kent
130	D3	Dent Cumb
89	G6	Denton Cambs
140	F4	Denton Darltn
19	L5	Denton E Susx
35	G5	Denton Kent
102	E6	Denton Lincs
123	H2	Denton N York
74	B3	Denton Nhants
93	G5	Denton Norfk
113	L3	Denton Tamesd
90	E3	Denver Norfk
169	J6	Denwick Nthumb
92	C4	Deopham Norfk
92	C4	Deopham Green Norfk
77	H3	Depden Suffk
45	G4	Deptford Gt Lon
28	A4	Deptford Wilts
101	G5	Derby C Derb
23	J5	Derby Devon
237	b7	Derbyhaven IoM
194	D5	Derculich P & K
92	B2	Dereham Norfk
53	H7	Deri Caerph
35	G5	Derringstone Kent
99	K7	Derrington Staffs
39	L6	Derry Hill Wilts
125	J8	Derrythorpe N Linc
105	H6	Dersingham Norfk
189	K6	Dervaig Ag & B
97	G3	Derwen Denbgs
80	F4	Derwenlas Powys
137	J3	Derwent Water Cumb
88	B6	Desborough Nhants
86	F3	Desford Leics
215	L3	Deskford Moray
33	K2	Detling Kent
54	C7	Devauden Mons
81	G7	Devil's Bridge Cerdgn
40	A7	Devizes Wilts
6	C5	Devonport C Plym
185	J7	Devonside Clacks
4	C7	Devoran Cnwll
177	K5	Dewarton Mdloth
14	E3	Dewlish Dorset
123	K6	Dewsbury Kirk
97	K8	Deytheur Powys
121	L4	Dial Hall Lancs
18	F2	Dial Post W Susx
16	E2	Dibden Hants
16	E2	Dibden Purlieu Hants
92	E6	Dickleburgh Norfk
56	B2	Didbrook Gloucs
41	K3	Didcot Oxon
41	K3	Didcot Railway Centre Oxon
75	H2	Diddington Cambs
83	K6	Diddlebury Shrops
18	A3	Didling W Susx
39	J3	Didmarton Gloucs
113	J3	Didsbury Manch

103 H2	**Digby** Lincs	
218 C7	**Digg** Highld	
122 F8	**Diggle** Oldham	
112 C1	**Digmoor** Lancs	
66 C4	**Dihewyd** Cerdgn	
107 G7	**Dilham** Norfk	
99 L4	**Dilhorne** Staffs	
75 C3	**Dillington** Cambs	
150 B3	**Dilston** Nthumb	
27 K2	**Dilton** Wilts	
27 J2	**Dilton Marsh** Wilts	
69 H4	**Dilwyn** Herefs	
94 E5	**Dinas** Gwynd	
64 E6	**Dinas** Pembks	
81 J1	**Dinas-Mawddwy** Gwynd	
37 J6	**Dinas Powys** V Glam	
26 E3	**Dinder** Somset	
69 K6	**Dinedor** Herefs	
54 C6	**Dingestow** Mons	
111 K4	**Dingle** Lpool	
87 L6	**Dingley** Nhants	
212 K3	**Dingwall** Highld	
205 K5	**Dinnet** Abers	
158 F7	**Dinnington** N u Ty	
115 K4	**Dinnington** Rothm	
26 B8	**Dinnington** Somset	
95 K1	**Dinorwic** Gwynd	
58 C5	**Dinton** Bucks	
28 A5	**Dinton** Wilts	
155 K4	**Dinwoodie** D & G	
9 J2	**Dinworthy** Devon	
25 J6	**Dipford** Somset	
161 K2	**Dippen** Ag & B	
162 D5	**Dippen** N Ayrs	
10 C7	**Dippertown** Devon	
215 H3	**Dipple** Moray	
152 E2	**Dipple** S Ayrs	
7 G4	**Diptford** Devon	
150 E4	**Dipton** Dur	
178 B2	**Dirleton** E Loth	
149 L5	**Dirt Pot** Nthumb	
101 J7	**Diseworth** Leics	
132 F5	**Dishforth** N York	
113 L5	**Disley** Ches	
92 D7	**Diss** Norfk	
136 D3	**Distington** Cumb	
28 C5	**Ditchampton** Wilts	
169 H5	**Ditchburn** Nthumb	
26 F4	**Ditcheat** Somset	
93 G5	**Ditchingham** Norfk	
19 J3	**Ditchling** E Susx	
83 K2	**Ditherington** Shrops	
39 J6	**Ditteridge** Wilts	
7 K5	**Dittisham** Devon	
112 D4	**Ditton** Halton	
33 J2	**Ditton** Kent	
76 F3	**Ditton Green** Cambs	
83 L5	**Ditton Priors** Shrops	
55 M2	**Dixton** Gloucs	
54 D5	**Dixton** Mons	
113 M1	**Dobcross** Oldham	
5 K3	**Dobwalls** Cnwll	
11 H7	**Doccombe** Devon	
212 F6	**Dochgarroch** Highld	
130 B5	**Docker** Lancs	
105 J3	**Docking** Norfk	
69 L3	**Docklow** Herefs	
137 L3	**Dockray** Cumb	
60 F7	**Doddinghurst** Essex	
90 A3	**Doddington** Cambs	
34 C4	**Doddington** Kent	
116 E7	**Doddington** Lincs	
168 E3	**Doddington** Nthumb	
84 B7	**Doddington** Shrops	
11 K7	**Doddiscombsleigh** Devon	
98 E4	**Dodd's Green** Ches	
73 H3	**Dodford** Nhants	
85 G8	**Dodford** Worcs	
39 H4	**Dodington** S Glos	
25 J4	**Dodington** Somset	
98 A1	**Dodleston** Ches	
174 F7	**Dodside** E Rens	
100 A5	**Dod's Leigh** Staffs	
114 F1	**Dodworth** Barns	
103 K2	**Dogdyke** Lincs	
30 C2	**Dogmersfield** Hants	
82 B2	**Dolanog** Powys	
95 J4	**Dolbenmaen** Gwynd	
81 K3	**Dolfach** Powys	
82 C6	**Dolfor** Powys	
109 L7	**Dolgarrog** Conwy	
96 B8	**Dolgellau** Gwynd	
226 F7	**Doll** Highld	
185 K7	**Dollar** Clacks	
185 K7	**Dollarfield** Clacks	
111 H6	**Dolphin** Flints	
129 L8	**Dolphinholme** Lancs	
176 F8	**Dolphinton** S Lans	
10 E3	**Dolton** Devon	
110 B6	**Dolwen** Conwy	
96 B3	**Dolwyddelan** Conwy	
97 L8	**Domgay** Powys	
115 L2	**Doncaster** Donc	
27 K6	**Donhead St Andrew** Wilts	
27 K6	**Donhead St Mary** Wilts	
177 G2	**Donibristle** Fife	
25 G3	**Doniford** Somset	
103 K5	**Donington** Lincs	
118 C5	**Donington on Bain** Lincs	
86 C2	**Donisthorpe** Leics	
56 D3	**Donnington** Gloucs	
83 L2	**Donnington** Shrops	
41 J6	**Donnington** W Berk	
18 B5	**Donnington** W Susx	
84 C2	**Donnington** Wrekin	
25 M8	**Donyatt** Somset	
163 H5	**Doonfoot** S Ayrs	
163 J6	**Doonholm** S Ayrs	
204 D3	**Dorback Lodge** Highld	
14 D4	**Dorchester** Dorset	
41 L2	**Dorchester** Oxon	
86 C4	**Dordon** Warwks	
114 F5	**Dore** Sheff	
212 F7	**Dores** Highld	
31 K2	**Dorking** Surrey	
32 D5	**Dormans Land** Surrey	
69 L6	**Dormington** Herefs	
71 H3	**Dormston** Worcs	
42 F5	**Dorney** Bucks	
200 D1	**Dornie** Highld	
223 H4	**Dornoch** Highld	
147 M2	**Dornock** D & G	
230 F5	**Dorrery** Highld	
85 L8	**Dorridge** Solhll	
103 H2	**Dorrington** Lincs	
83 J3	**Dorrington** Shrops	
99 G4	**Dorrington** Shrops	
71 K4	**Dorsington** Warwks	
69 G6	**Dorstone** Herefs	
58 B5	**Dorton** Bucks	
237 d6	**Douglas** IoM	
165 G4	**Douglas** S Lans	
187 G2	**Douglas and Angus** C Dund	
165 G3	**Douglas Castle** S Lans	
183 H7	**Douglas Pier** Ag & B	
196 C6	**Douglastown** Angus	
165 G3	**Douglas Water** S Lans	
164 F3	**Douglas West** S Lans	
26 F3	**Doulting** Somset	
234 b5	**Dounby** Ork	
221 L2	**Doune** Highld	
184 F6	**Doune** Stirlg	
152 E3	**Dounepark** S Ayrs	
222 D4	**Dounie** Highld	
114 B6	**Dove Holes** Derbys	
147 J7	**Dovenby** Cumb	
35 J6	**Dover** Kent	
35 J6	**Dover Castle** Kent	
62 F2	**Dovercourt** Essex	
70 F2	**Doverdale** Worcs	
100 C5	**Doveridge** Derbys	
31 L2	**Doversgreen** Surrey	
194 F6	**Dowally** P & K	
55 M4	**Dowdeswell** Gloucs	
53 G6	**Dowlais** Myr Td	
10 E3	**Dowland** Devon	
26 A8	**Dowlish Wake** Somset	
40 C2	**Down Ampney** Gloucs	
5 L5	**Downderry** Cnwll	
45 H7	**Downe** Gt Lon	
39 J2	**Downend** Gloucs	
38 F5	**Downend** S Glos	
186 F2	**Downfield** C Dund	
5 L2	**Downgate** Cnwll	
6 A2	**Downgate** Cnwll	
46 B2	**Downham** Essex	
45 H5	**Downham** Gt Lon	
122 B2	**Downham** Lancs	
90 E3	**Downham Market** Norfk	
55 K4	**Down Hatherley** Gloucs	
26 E6	**Downhead** Somset	
27 G3	**Downhead** Somset	
186 A2	**Downhill** P & K	
140 E7	**Downholme** N York	
207 H6	**Downies** Abers	
42 D2	**Downley** Bucks	
11 H4	**Down St Mary** Devon	
43 J8	**Downside** Surrey	
6 D6	**Down Thomas** Devon	
16 C4	**Downton** Hants	
28 D6	**Downton** Wilts	
83 H8	**Downton on the Rock** Herefs	
103 J6	**Dowsby** Lincs	
39 G5	**Doynton** S Glos	
37 K3	**Draethen** Caerph	
164 F1	**Draffan** S Lans	
116 B4	**Drakeholes** Notts	
174 B7	**Drakemyre** N Ayrs	
71 G5	**Drakes Broughton** Worcs	
131 K8	**Draughton** N York	
87 L7	**Draughton** Nhants	
125 G5	**Drax** N York	
72 F1	**Draycote** Warwks	
101 H6	**Draycott** Derbys	
71 L7	**Draycott** Gloucs	
26 C2	**Draycott** Somset	
100 D6	**Draycott in the Clay** Staffs	
99 M4	**Draycott in the Moors** Staffs	
17 J2	**Drayton** C Port	
88 B5	**Drayton** Leics	
92 E2	**Drayton** Norfk	
41 J2	**Drayton** Oxon	
72 E6	**Drayton** Oxon	
26 B6	**Drayton** Somset	
85 G7	**Drayton** Worcs	
85 L4	**Drayton Bassett** Staffs	
58 E5	**Drayton Beauchamp** Bucks	
85 L4	**Drayton Manor Park** Staffs	
58 D3	**Drayton Parslow** Bucks	
41 L2	**Drayton St Leonard** Oxon	
48 F5	**Dreen Hill** Pembks	
51 G3	**Drefach** Carmth	
65 K6	**Drefach** Carmth	
66 C5	**Drefach** Cerdgn	
163 J2	**Dreghorn** N Ayrs	
35 H6	**Drellingore** Kent	
178 B3	**Drem** E Loth	
11 H6	**Drewsteignton** Devon	
118 E6	**Driby** Lincs	
134 F7	**Driffield** E R Yk	
56 B7	**Driffield** Gloucs	
2 D5	**Drift** Cnwll	
136 E7	**Drigg** Cumb	
123 J5	**Drighlington** Leeds	
190 B5	**Drimnin** Highld	
13 K2	**Drimpton** Dorset	
191 J1	**Drimsallie** Highld	
124 E2	**Dringhouses** York	
77 L3	**Drinkstone** Suffk	
77 L3	**Drinkstone Green** Suffk	
100 A6	**Drointon** Staffs	
70 F2	**Droitwich** Worcs	
186 B4	**Dron** P & K	
115 G5	**Dronfield** Derbys	
163 K5	**Drongan** E Ayrs	
186 E1	**Dronley** Angus	
14 E2	**Droop** Dorset	
29 L7	**Droxford** Hants	
113 K2	**Droylsden** Tamesd	
97 G4	**Druid** Denbgs	
48 E4	**Druidston** Pembks	
192 B6	**Druimachoish** Highld	
191 L3	**Druimarbin** Highld	
172 C4	**Druimdrishaig** Ag & B	
199 L7	**Druimindarroch** Highld	
172 F3	**Drum** Ag & B	
185 L7	**Drum** P & K	
165 H2	**Drumalbin** S Lans	
224 B3	**Drumbeg** Highld	
216 B6	**Drumblade** Abers	
144 C6	**Drumbreddon** D & G	
210 B7	**Drumbuie** Highld	
148 A3	**Drumburgh** Cumb	
146 F4	**Drumburn** D & G	
174 F4	**Drumchapel** C Glas	
193 L5	**Drumchastle** P & K	
164 C2	**Drumclog** S Lans	
187 G6	**Drumeldrie** Fife	
165 M3	**Drumelzier** Border	
199 L3	**Drumfearn** Highld	
206 D5	**Drumfrennie** Abers	
196 C6	**Drumgley** Angus	
203 J5	**Drumguish** Highld	
214 E7	**Drumin** Moray	
153 L3	**Drumjohn** D & G	
153 G6	**Drumlamford** S Ayrs	
206 C4	**Drumlasie** Abers	
148 A5	**Drumleaning** Cumb	
161 H5	**Drumlemble** Ag & B	
197 J1	**Drumlithie** Abers	
145 H6	**Drummoddie** D & G	
144 D7	**Drummore** D & G	
215 J5	**Drummuir** Moray	
212 D7	**Drumnadrochit** Highld	
144 D7	**Drumnaglaur** D & G	
215 L4	**Drumnagorrach** Moray	
154 F6	**Drumpark** D & G	
224 F2	**Drumrunie Lodge** Highld	
163 G6	**Drumshang** S Ayrs	
209 G5	**Drumuie** Highld	
204 B2	**Drumuillie** Highld	
184 E6	**Drumvaich** Stirlg	
186 B5	**Drunzie** P & K	
138 F4	**Drybeck** Cumb	
215 K2	**Drybridge** Moray	
163 J3	**Drybridge** N Ayrs	
54 F4	**Drybrook** Gloucs	
167 J3	**Dryburgh** Border	
102 D3	**Dry Doddington** Lincs	
75 L3	**Dry Drayton** Cambs	
3 G5	**Drym** Cnwll	

174 E2 **Drymen** Stirlg
217 G5 **Drymuir** Abers
208 F7 **Drynoch** Highld
216 F2 **Dubford** Abers
225 J5 **Duchally** Highld
57 G6 **Ducklington** Oxon
76 C7 **Duddenhoe End**
Essex
177 J4 **Duddingston** C Edin
88 E4 **Duddington** Nhants
25 K7 **Duddlestone** Somset
84 B6 **Duddlewick** Shrops
168 D2 **Duddo** Nthumb
112 D8 **Duddon** Ches
97 M5 **Duddleston** Shrops
85 G5 **Dudley** Dudley
159 G7 **Dudley** N Tyne
85 G5 **Dudley Port** Sandw
15 K3 **Dudsbury** Dorset
101 G4 **Duffield** Derbys
36 C2 **Duffryn** Neath
215 H6 **Dufftown** Moray
214 E2 **Duffus** Moray
139 G3 **Dufton** Cumb
134 D6 **Duggleby** N York
210 B7 **Duirinish** Highld
199 L3 **Duisdalemore** Highld
191 K2 **Duisky** Highld
78 C6 **Duke Street** Suffk
113 L2 **Dukinfield** Tamesd
26 E3 **Dulcote** Somset
12 D2 **Dulford** Devon
194 C6 **Dull** P & K
175 K3 **Dullatur** N Lans
76 F3 **Dullingham** Cambs
76 F3 **Dullingham Ley**
Cambs
204 B1 **Dulnain Bridge** Highld
75 H3 **Duloe** Beds
5 K4 **Duloe** Cnwll
24 E5 **Dulverton** Somset
45 G5 **Dulwich** Gt Lon
174 D4 **Dumbarton** W Duns
71 H7 **Dumbleton** Gloucs
155 G6 **Dumfries** D & G
174 F2 **Dumgoyne** Stirlg
29 L3 **Dummer** Hants
35 K2 **Dumpton** Kent
197 G4 **Dun** Angus
193 L5 **Dunalastair** P & K
173 K4 **Dunan** Ag & B
209 J8 **Dunan** Highld
193 G5 **Dunan** P & K
161 H7 **Dunaverty** Ag & B
25 L3 **Dunball** Somset
178 E3 **Dunbar** E Loth
227 L3 **Dunbeath** Highld
182 C2 **Dunbeg** Ag & B
185 G6 **Dunblane** Stirlg
186 E4 **Dunbog** Fife
212 F3 **Duncanston** Highld
216 B8 **Duncanstone** Abers
11 K7 **Dunchideock** Devon
72 F1 **Dunchurch** Warwks
155 G5 **Duncow** D & G
186 B5 **Duncrievie** P & K
18 C3 **Duncton** W Susx
186 F2 **Dundee** C Dund
186 F2 **Dundee Airport**
C Dund
26 C5 **Dundon** Somset
163 J3 **Dundonald** S Ayrs
220 E4 **Dundonnell** Highld
147 L5 **Dundraw** Cumb
201 L3 **Dundreggan** Highld
146 D5 **Dundrennan** D & G
38 E6 **Dundry** N Som
206 E4 **Dunecht** Abers
176 F2 **Dunfermline** Fife
40 C2 **Dunfield** Gloucs
164 D3 **Dungavel** S Lans
21 L3 **Dungeness** Kent

116 D6 **Dunham** Notts
112 C6 **Dunham-on-the-Hill**
Ches
70 F2 **Dunhampton** Worcs
113 H4 **Dunham Town** Traffd
113 G4 **Dunham**
Woodhouses Traffd
117 G5 **Dunholme** Lincs
187 J5 **Dunino** Fife
175 L2 **Dunipace** Falk
195 G7 **Dunkeld** P & K
39 G8 **Dunkerton** BaNES
12 E1 **Dunkeswell** Devon
123 L2 **Dunkeswick** N York
34 E3 **Dunkirk** Kent
39 H4 **Dunkirk** S Glos
33 G3 **Dunk's Green** Kent
196 F3 **Dunlappie** Angus
70 E2 **Dunley** Worcs
174 D8 **Dunlop** E Ayrs
202 F2 **Dunmaglass** Highld
176 B1 **Dunmore** Falk
231 J2 **Dunnet** Highld
196 E6 **Dunnichen** Angus
185 L4 **Dunning** P & K
126 E1 **Dunnington** E R Yk
71 J4 **Dunnington** Warwks
133 K8 **Dunnington** York
122 B5 **Dunnockshaw** Lancs
173 K3 **Dunoon** Ag & B
214 C5 **Dunphail** Moray
144 E4 **Dunragit** D & G
179 G7 **Duns** Border
103 J6 **Dunsby** Lincs
154 F5 **Dunscore** D & G
124 F8 **Dunscroft** Donc
142 D4 **Dunsdale** R & Cl
42 C5 **Dunsden Green** Oxon
9 J3 **Dunsdon** Devon
31 G4 **Dunsfold** Surrey
11 J6 **Dunsford** Devon
186 D5 **Dunshalt** Fife
217 J5 **Dunshillock** Abers
101 J1 **Dunsill** Notts
143 H5 **Dunsley** N York
84 F6 **Dunsley** Staffs
58 E6 **Dunsmore** Bucks
121 K1 **Dunsop Bridge**
Lancs
59 G4 **Dunstable** Beds
100 D7 **Dunstall** Staffs
169 K5 **Dunstan** Nthumb
24 F3 **Dunster** Somset
57 J3 **Duns Tew** Oxon
151 G3 **Dunston** Gatesd
117 H8 **Dunston** Lincs
92 F3 **Dunston** Norfk
99 L8 **Dunston** Staffs
6 E5 **Dunstone** Devon
7 G2 **Dunstone** Devon
124 F8 **Dunsville** Donc
126 D4 **Dunswell** E R Yk
176 E8 **Dunsyre** S Lans
6 B1 **Dunterton** Devon
55 L6 **Duntisbourne**
Abbots Gloucs
55 M6 **Duntisbourne Rouse**
Gloucs
14 D2 **Duntish** Dorset
174 E4 **Duntocher** W Duns
75 J5 **Dunton** Beds
58 D3 **Dunton** Bucks
105 L6 **Dunton** Norfk
87 G5 **Dunton Bassett** Leics
32 F2 **Dunton Green** Kent
218 C6 **Duntulm** Highld
163 G6 **Dunure** S Ayrs
51 H6 **Dunvant** Swans
208 D5 **Dunvegan** Highld
79 K1 **Dunwich** Suffk
3 K5 **Durgan** Cnwll
151 G6 **Durham** Dur

151 G6 **Durham Cathedral**
Dur
141 J5 **Durham Tees Valley**
Airport S on T
154 F2 **Durisdeer** D & G
154 F2 **Durisdeermill** D & G
25 L4 **Durleigh** Somset
29 K7 **Durley** Hants
40 E7 **Durley** Wilts
29 K7 **Durley Street** Hants
35 H3 **Durlock** Kent
35 J2 **Durlock** Kent
228 F3 **Durness** Highld
216 D8 **Durno** Abers
191 K5 **Duror** Highld
182 D5 **Durran** Ag & B
18 F5 **Durrington** W Susx
28 D3 **Durrington** Wilts
206 E6 **Durris** Abers
39 H2 **Dursley** Gloucs
55 G4 **Dursley Cross** Gloucs
25 L5 **Durston** Somset
15 G2 **Durweston** Dorset
73 K3 **Duston** Nhants
203 L1 **Duthil** Highld
112 E5 **Dutton** Ches
76 C5 **Duxford** Cambs
57 G7 **Duxford** Oxon
76 C5 **Duxford Aircraft**
Museum Cambs
109 L6 **Dwygyfylchi** Conwy
108 F7 **Dwyran** IoA
207 G3 **Dyce** C Aber
95 K7 **Dyffryn Ardudwy**
Gwynd
52 D6 **Dyffryn Cellwen**
Neath
103 J7 **Dyke** Lincs
214 B3 **Dyke** Moray
195 K5 **Dykehead** Angus
196 C4 **Dykehead** Angus
176 B6 **Dykehead** N Lans
184 D7 **Dykehead** Stirlg
197 H3 **Dykelands** Abers
195 K5 **Dykends** Angus
216 D5 **Dykeside** Abers
34 E8 **Dymchurch** Kent
55 G2 **Dymock** Gloucs
39 H5 **Dyrham** S Glos
186 E8 **Dysart** Fife
110 E5 **Dyserth** Denbgs

E

120 F2 **Eagland Hill** Lancs
116 E7 **Eagle** Lincs
141 K4 **Eaglescliffe** S on T
136 F2 **Eaglesfield** Cumb
155 M7 **Eaglesfield** D & G
175 G7 **Eaglesham** E Rens
121 L7 **Eagley** Bolton
102 A1 **Eakring** Notts
125 J7 **Ealand** N Linc
44 D4 **Ealing** Gt Lon
149 H4 **Eals** Nthumb
138 D2 **Eamont Bridge** Cumb
122 D2 **Earby** Lancs
84 C5 **Eardington** Shrops
69 H3 **Eardisland** Herefs
68 F5 **Eardisley** Herefs
98 A7 **Eardiston** Shrops
70 C2 **Eardiston** Worcs
89 L8 **Earith** Cambs
112 E3 **Earlestown** St Hel
42 C6 **Earley** Wokham
208 F3 **Earlish** Highld
74 C2 **Earls Barton** Nhants
61 K3 **Earls Colne** Essex
71 G3 **Earls Common** Worcs
70 F6 **Earl's Croome** Worcs

86 D7 **Earlsdon** Covtry
187 H7 **Earlsferry** Fife
44 E5 **Earlsfield** Gt Lon
216 F7 **Earlsford** Abers
123 K6 **Earlsheaton** Kirk
86 F4 **Earl Shilton** Leics
78 F2 **Earl Soham** Suffk
114 C7 **Earl Sterndale** Derbys
167 J2 **Earlston** Border
163 K3 **Earlston** E Ayrs
32 B4 **Earlswood** Surrey
85 K8 **Earlswood** Warwks
17 M3 **Earnley** W Susx
159 H7 **Earsdon** N Tyne
158 F4 **Earsdon** Nthumb
93 G5 **Earsham** Norfk
18 C4 **Eartham** W Susx
142 C5 **Easby** N York
181 L4 **Easdale** Ag & B
30 E6 **Easebourne** W Susx
86 F7 **Easenhall** Warwks
30 F3 **Eashing** Surrey
58 B6 **Easington** Bucks
151 K6 **Easington** Dur
127 J6 **Easington** E R Yk
142 F4 **Easington** R & Cl
151 K6 **Easington Colliery**
Dur
133 K6 **Easingwold** N York
196 B7 **Eassie and Nevay**
Angus
37 G8 **East Aberthaw**
V Glam
7 H6 **East Allington** Devon
24 D6 **East Anstey** Devon
17 H5 **East Ashey** IoW
17 M2 **East Ashling** W Susx
134 F3 **East Ayton** N York
117 K5 **East Barkwith** Lincs
33 J3 **East Barming** Kent
143 G5 **East Barnby** N York
44 F2 **East Barnet** Gt Lon
178 F3 **East Barns** E Loth
105 L5 **East Barsham** Norfk
106 E4 **East Beckham** Norfk
43 H5 **East Bedfont** Gt Lon
78 C7 **East Bergholt** Suffk
106 A8 **East Bilney** Norfk
20 A5 **East Blatchington**
E Susx
151 J3 **East Boldon** S Tyne
16 D3 **East Boldre** Hants
141 H4 **Eastbourne** Darltn
20 C5 **Eastbourne** E Susx
91 L2 **East Bradenham**
Norfk
25 M2 **East Brent** Somset
79 J2 **Eastbridge** Suffk
102 B4 **East Bridgford** Notts
23 L5 **East Buckland** Devon
12 D5 **East Budleigh** Devon
122 F2 **Eastburn** Brad
43 J2 **Eastbury** Herts
41 G5 **Eastbury** W Berk
116 D1 **East Butterwick**
N Linc
131 J8 **Eastby** N York
92 E3 **East Calder** W Loth
92 E3 **East Carleton** Norfk
123 J2 **East Carlton** Leeds
88 B5 **East Carlton** Nhants
14 E5 **East Chaldon**
(Chaldon Herring)
Dorset
41 G3 **East Challow** Oxon
7 H7 **East Charleton** Devon
14 A2 **East Chelborough**
Dorset
19 K3 **East Chiltington**
E Susx
26 C8 **East Chinnock**
Somset

28 C2 **East Chisenbury** Wilts
47 G5 **Eastchurch** Kent
31 H2 **East Clandon** Surrey
58 C3 **East Claydon** Bucks
D8 **East Coker** Somset
55 K6 **Eastcombe** Gloucs
25 J5 **East Combe** Somset
26 E3 **East Compton** Somset
7 J5 **East Cornworthy** Devon
43 J3 **Eastcote** Gt Lon
73 K4 **Eastcote** Nhants
85 L7 **Eastcote** Solhll
28 A1 **Eastcott** Wilts
125 G3 **East Cottingwith** E R Yk
39 L2 **Eastcourt** Wilts
40 E7 **Eastcourt** Wilts
16 F4 **East Cowes** IoW
125 G6 **East Cowick** E R Yk
141 H6 **East Cowton** N York
27 G3 **East Cranmore** Somset
15 H6 **East Creech** Dorset
20 B6 **East Dean** E Susx
54 F4 **East Dean** Gloucs
28 F6 **East Dean** Hants
18 B3 **East Dean** W Susx
23 J3 **East Down** Devon
116 C6 **East Drayton** Notts
45 G5 **East Dulwich** Gt Lon
38 E7 **East Dundry** N Som
126 C5 **East Ella** C KuH
46 F2 **Eastend** Essex
16 D3 **East End** Hants
41 H7 **East End** Hants
33 L6 **East End** Kent
57 H5 **East End** Oxon
165 J2 **Eastend** S Lans
26 F3 **East End** Somset
205 G6 **Easter Balmoral** Abers
38 E4 **Easter Compton** S Glos
213 H4 **Easter Dalziel** Highld
18 C5 **Eastergate** W Susx
175 J5 **Easterhouse** C Glas
177 H5 **Easter Howgate** Mdloth
212 E4 **Easter Kinkell** Highld
212 E5 **Easter Moniack** Highld
86 C7 **Eastern Green** Covtry
206 F4 **Easter Ord** Abers
187 J6 **Easter Pitkierie** Fife
235 c6 **Easter Skeld** Shet
168 A3 **Easter Softlaw** Border
213 G4 **Easter Suddie** Highld
28 A1 **Easterton** Wilts
28 D2 **Easterton** Wilts
33 J3 **East Farleigh** Kent
87 K6 **East Farndon** Nhants
116 D2 **East Ferry** Lincs
176 B5 **Eastfield** N Lans
135 G3 **Eastfield** N York
178 C3 **East Fortune** E Loth
41 G5 **East Garston** W Berk
150 B7 **Eastgate** Dur
106 D7 **Eastgate** Norfk
87 J2 **East Goscote** Leics
40 E7 **East Grafton** Wilts
28 E5 **East Grimstead** Wilts
32 D5 **East Grinstead** W Susx
21 J2 **East Guldeford** E Susx
73 J2 **East Haddon** Nhants
41 K3 **East Hagbourne** Oxon
126 E6 **East Halton** N Linc

45 H4 **East Ham** Gt Lon
42 E6 **Easthampstead** Br For
69 H2 **Easthampton** Herefs
41 H2 **East Hanney** Oxon
61 J7 **East Hanningfield** Essex
124 C3 **East Hardwick** Wakefd
92 B6 **East Harling** Norfk
141 K7 **East Harlsey** N York
28 C5 **East Harnham** Wilts
26 E1 **East Harptree** BaNES
141 K4 **East Hartburn** S on T
30 D7 **East Harting** W Susx
27 L5 **East Hatch** Wilts
75 K4 **East Hatley** Cambs
132 B2 **East Hauxwell** N York
187 J1 **East Haven** Angus
103 K4 **East Heckington** Lincs
150 E6 **East Hedleyhope** Dur
227 H5 **East Helmsdale** Highld
41 J3 **East Hendred** Oxon
134 E4 **East Heslerton** N York
20 B3 **East Hoathly** E Susx
15 G5 **East Holme** Dorset
83 L4 **Easthope** Shrops
61 L4 **Easthorpe** Essex
26 E3 **East Horrington** Somset
31 H2 **East Horsley** Surrey
15 K4 **East Howe** Bmouth
25 M3 **East Huntspill** Somset
41 J4 **East Ilsley** W Berk
11 H3 **Eastington** Devon
55 H6 **Eastington** Gloucs
56 C5 **Eastington** Gloucs
118 E8 **East Keal** Lincs
40 C6 **East Kennett** Wilts
124 B2 **East Keswick** Leeds
175 H7 **East Kilbride** S Lans
118 D3 **East Kirkby** Lincs
14 F5 **East Knighton** Dorset
27 K5 **East Knoyle** Wilts
26 B7 **East Lambrook** Somset
154 E1 **Eastlands** D & G
35 J5 **East Langdon** Kent
87 K5 **East Langton** Leics
191 L5 **East Laroch** Highld
18 B4 **East Lavant** W Susx
18 C3 **East Lavington** W Susx
140 E5 **East Layton** N York
56 D6 **Eastleach Martin** Gloucs
56 D6 **Eastleach Turville** Gloucs
101 K7 **East Leake** Notts
7 H4 **East Leigh** Devon
11 G4 **East Leigh** Devon
23 H5 **Eastleigh** Devon
29 J7 **Eastleigh** Hants
105 K8 **East Lexham** Norfk
34 C4 **Eastling** Kent
178 D3 **East Linton** E Loth
41 H3 **East Lockinge** Oxon
116 C2 **East Lound** N Linc
15 G6 **East Lulworth** Dorset
134 E5 **East Lutton** N York
26 E5 **East Lydford** Somset
33 J2 **East Malling** Kent
30 D8 **East Marden** W Susx
116 C6 **East Markham** Notts
28 B7 **East Martin** Hants
122 D1 **East Marton** N York
30 B6 **East Meon** Hants
62 C5 **East Mersea** Essex
43 J6 **East Molesey** Surrey
15 G4 **East Morden** Dorset

123 G3 **East Morton** Brad
154 F3 **East Morton** D & G
133 L4 **East Ness** N York
17 J3 **Eastney** C Port
70 D6 **Eastnor** Herefs
87 L4 **East Norton** Leics
125 J7 **Eastoft** N Linc
7 J2 **East Ogwell** Devon
75 G1 **Easton** Cambs
148 B3 **Easton** Cumb
11 G6 **Easton** Devon
14 D7 **Easton** Dorset
29 K5 **Easton** Hants
102 F6 **Easton** Lincs
92 D2 **Easton** Norfk
26 D3 **Easton** Somset
79 G3 **Easton** Suffk
39 K6 **Easton** Wilts
39 K3 **Easton Grey** Wilts
38 D5 **Easton-in-Gordano** N Som
74 C3 **Easton Maudit** Nhants
88 E3 **Easton on the Hill** Nhants
40 D7 **Easton Royal** Wilts
27 J7 **East Orchard** Dorset
33 H4 **East Peckham** Kent
49 G6 **East Pennar** Pembks
26 E4 **East Pennard** Somset
75 G2 **East Perry** Cambs
7 H7 **East Portlemouth** Devon
7 H8 **East Prawle** Devon
18 E5 **East Preston** W Susx
14 D1 **East Pulham** Dorset
9 K2 **East Putford** Devon
25 H3 **East Quantoxhead** Somset
151 H5 **East Rainton** Sundld
118 C2 **East Ravendale** NE Lin
105 L7 **East Raynham** Norfk
89 K4 **Eastrea** Cambs
147 M2 **Eastriggs** D & G
124 B2 **East Rigton** Leeds
125 J4 **Eastrington** E R Yk
40 D2 **Eastrop** Swindn
141 K6 **East Rounton** N York
105 K6 **East Rudham** Norfk
106 E4 **East Runton** Norfk
107 H6 **East Ruston** Norfk
35 J4 **Eastry** Kent
178 B5 **East Saltoun** E Loth
44 D5 **East Sheen** Gt Lon
41 H5 **East Shefford** W Berk
116 C3 **East Stockwith** Lincs
15 G5 **East Stoke** Dorset
102 C3 **East Stoke** Notts
27 J6 **East Stour** Dorset
35 H3 **East Stourmouth** Kent
23 K6 **East Stowford** Devon
29 K4 **East Stratton** Hants
35 J5 **East Studdal** Kent
5 J3 **East Taphouse** Cnwll
23 G6 **East-the-Water** Devon
158 F3 **East Thirston** Nthumb
46 B5 **East Tilbury** Thurr
30 B5 **East Tisted** Hants
117 J5 **East Torrington** Lincs
92 C2 **East Tuddenham** Norfk
28 F5 **East Tytherley** Hants
39 L5 **East Tytherton** Wilts
11 J4 **East Village** Devon
38 E5 **Eastville** Bristl
104 C2 **Eastville** Lincs
83 K5 **East Wall** Shrops
91 G1 **East Walton** Norfk

26 D2 **East Water** Somset
10 F6 **East Week** Devon
102 C6 **Eastwell** Leics
28 F7 **East Wellow** Hants
186 E7 **East Wemyss** Fife
176 C5 **East Whitburn** W Loth
60 C5 **Eastwick** Herts
45 J5 **East Wickham** Gt Lon
49 J6 **East Williamston** Pembks
91 G1 **East Winch** Norfk
28 E5 **East Winterslow** Wilts
17 L3 **East Wittering** W Susx
131 L3 **East Witton** N York
122 E5 **Eastwood** Calder
101 J3 **Eastwood** Notts
46 D3 **Eastwood** Sthend
158 A5 **East Woodburn** Nthumb
41 H7 **East Woodhay** Hants
30 C4 **East Worldham** Hants
91 K5 **East Wretham** Norfk
9 H2 **East Youlstone** Devon
72 E2 **Eathorpe** Warwks
112 E8 **Eaton** Ches
113 K7 **Eaton** Ches
102 D6 **Eaton** Leics
92 E3 **Eaton** Norfk
116 B6 **Eaton** Notts
57 H7 **Eaton** Oxon
83 K5 **Eaton** Shrops
58 F4 **Eaton Bray** Beds
83 L3 **Eaton Constantine** Shrops
58 F4 **Eaton Green** Beds
56 E7 **Eaton Hastings** Oxon
83 K3 **Eaton Mascott** Shrops
75 J4 **Eaton Socon** Cambs
98 F7 **Eaton upon Tern** Shrops
134 D3 **Ebberston** N York
27 M6 **Ebbesborne Wake** Wilts
53 J6 **Ebbw Vale** Blae G
150 D4 **Ebchester** Dur
12 C5 **Ebford** Devon
55 J6 **Ebley** Gloucs
98 C3 **Ebnal** Ches
71 H4 **Ebrington** Gloucs
41 J8 **Ecchinswell** Hants
178 F5 **Ecclaw** Border
155 L7 **Ecclefechan** D & G
168 A2 **Eccles** Border
46 B7 **Eccles** Kent
113 H2 **Eccles** Salfd
114 F5 **Ecclesall** Sheff
115 G3 **Ecclesfield** Sheff
99 J6 **Eccleshall** Staffs
123 H4 **Eccleshill** Brad
176 E4 **Ecclesmachan** W Loth
92 B5 **Eccles Road** Norfk
112 B8 **Eccleston** Ches
121 G6 **Eccleston** Lancs
112 C3 **Eccleston** St Hel
206 E4 **Echt** Abers
167 L4 **Eckford** Border
115 H5 **Eckington** Derbys
71 G6 **Eckington** Worcs
74 B2 **Ecton** Nhants
114 C4 **Edale** Derbys
234 d4 **Eday Airport** Ork
19 H4 **Edburton** W Susx
222 F4 **Edderton** Highld
177 H8 **Eddleston** Border
175 J2 **Eddlewood** S Lans
32 D4 **Edenbridge** Kent
122 B6 **Edenfield** Lancs
138 E2 **Edenhall** Cumb

103 H7 **Edenham** Lincs
45 G6 **Eden Park** Gt Lon
114 E7 **Edensor** Derbys
183 K8 **Frientaggart** Ag & B
115 L1 **Edenthorpe** Donc
94 E5 **Edern** Gwynd
85 J6 **Edgbaston** Birm
58 B4 **Edgcott** Bucks
24 D4 **Edgcott** Somset
55 J6 **Edge** Gloucs
83 H2 **Edge** Shrops
106 C5 **Edgefield** Norfk
106 D5 **Edgefield Green** Norfk
123 H6 **Edgerton** Kirk
55 L6 **Edgeworth** Gloucs
99 G8 **Edgmond** Wrekin
83 H6 **Edgton** Shrops
44 D2 **Edgware** Gt Lon
121 L6 **Edgworth** Bl w D
208 E4 **Edinbane** Highld
177 H4 **Edinburgh** C Edin
176 F4 **Edinburgh Airport** C Edin
177 H4 **Edinburgh Castle** C Edin
177 H4 **Edinburgh Royal Botanic Gardens** C Edin
177 G4 **Edinburgh Zoo** C Edin
86 B2 **Edingale** Staffs
146 E3 **Edingham** D & G
102 A2 **Edingley** Notts
107 G6 **Edingthorpe** Norfk
107 G6 **Edingthorpe Green** Norfk
179 J7 **Edington** Border
158 E5 **Edington** Nthumb
26 B4 **Edington** Somset
27 L2 **Edington** Wilts
26 B3 **Edington Burtle** Somset
26 A2 **Edingworth** Somset
25 L2 **Edithmead** Somset
88 D3 **Edith Weston** Rutlnd
58 F4 **Edlesborough** Bucks
169 G8 **Edlingham** Nthumb
118 C7 **Edlington** Lincs
15 K1 **Edmondsham** Dorset
151 G6 **Edmondsley** Dur
102 E8 **Edmondthorpe** Leics
45 G2 **Edmonton** Gt Lon
150 C5 **Edmundbyers** Dur
167 L2 **Ednam** Border
194 D6 **Edradynate** P & K
179 H7 **Edrom** Border
98 D6 **Edstaston** Shrops
71 L3 **Edstone** Warwks
101 L5 **Edwalton** Notts
115 L7 **Edwinstowe** Notts
75 J6 **Edworth** Beds
70 B3 **Edwyn Ralph** Herefs
196 F3 **Edzell** Angus
197 G3 **Edzell Woods** Abers
36 B2 **Efail-fach** Neath
37 G4 **Efail Isaf** Rhondd
94 F5 **Efailnewydd** Gwynd
49 K3 **Efailwen** Carmth
97 H2 **Efenechtyd** Denbgs
156 B4 **Effgill** D & G
31 J2 **Effingham** Surrey
11 K5 **Efford** Devon
121 K7 **Egerton** Bolton
34 B5 **Egerton** Kent
6 D4 **Eggbuckland** C Plym
11 L3 **Eggesford** Devon
58 F3 **Eggington** Beds
100 E6 **Egginton** Derbys
141 K4 **Egglescliffe** S on T
140 C3 **Eggleston** Dur
43 G6 **Egham** Surrey
88 C3 **Egleton** Rutlnd

169 G5 **Eglingham** Nthumb
4 F2 **Egloshayle** Cnwll
9 H7 **Egloskerry** Cnwll
109 M7 **Eglwysbach** Conwy
98 C4 **Eglwys Cross** Wrexhm
65 G6 **Eglwyswrw** Pembks
116 B7 **Egmanton** Notts
136 D5 **Egremont** Cumb
111 K3 **Egremont** Wirral
143 G6 **Egton** N York
143 G6 **Egton Bridge** N York
61 M3 **Eight Ash Green** Essex
200 C2 **Eilanreach** Highld
67 K2 **Elan Village** Powys
38 E3 **Elberton** S Glos
6 D5 **Elburton** C Plym
40 C4 **Elcombe** Swindn
55 H2 **Eldersfield** Worcs
174 E5 **Elderslie** Rens
141 G2 **Eldon** Dur
206 F7 **Elfhill** Abers
85 L2 **Elford** Staffs
214 F2 **Elgin** Moray
199 H3 **Elgol** Highld
35 G6 **Elham** Kent
187 H7 **Elie** Fife
108 D4 **Elim** IoA
29 G8 **Eling** Hants
116 B6 **Elkesley** Notts
55 L5 **Elkstone** Gloucs
216 C3 **Ella** Abers
7 L3 **Ellacombe** Torbay
181 L4 **Ellanbeich** Ag & B
123 G6 **Elland** Calder
172 C3 **Ellary** Ag & B
100 C4 **Ellastone** Staffs
129 K7 **Ellel** Lancs
178 F6 **Ellemford** Border
99 J7 **Ellenhall** Staffs
31 H4 **Ellen's Green** Surrey
141 K7 **Ellerbeck** N York
143 G3 **Ellerby** N York
98 F7 **Ellerdine Heath** Wrekin
191 K6 **Elleric** Ag & B
125 L5 **Ellerker** E R Yk
125 G3 **Ellerton** E R Yk
141 G7 **Ellerton** N York
58 D6 **Ellesborough** Bucks
98 B5 **Ellesmere** Shrops
111 L6 **Ellesmere Port** Ches
93 H5 **Ellingham** Norfk
169 H4 **Ellingham** Nthumb
132 B3 **Ellingstring** N York
75 H1 **Ellington** Cambs
159 G4 **Ellington** Nthumb
27 J3 **Elliots Green** Somset
29 M3 **Ellisfield** Hants
209 H3 **Ellishader** Highld
86 E2 **Ellistown** Leics
217 H7 **Ellon** Abers
148 D7 **Ellonby** Cumb
126 B5 **Elloughton** E R Yk
54 E6 **Ellwood** Gloucs
90 C3 **Elm** Cambs
70 F2 **Elmbridge** Worcs
76 C6 **Elmdon** Essex
85 L6 **Elmdon** Solhll
45 G6 **Elmers End** Gt Lon
86 F4 **Elmesthorpe** Leics
85 K2 **Elmhurst** Staffs
71 H6 **Elmley Castle** Worcs
70 F1 **Elmley Lovett** Worcs
55 H5 **Elmore** Gloucs
55 H5 **Elmore Back** Gloucs
45 K3 **Elm Park** Gt Lon
78 C5 **Elmsett** Suffk
62 C3 **Elmstead Market** Essex
34 H7 **Elmsted Court** Kent
35 H3 **Elmstone** Kent

55 K3 **Elmstone Hardwicke** Gloucs
134 F7 **Elmswell** E R Yk
78 B2 **Elmswell** Suffk
115 J6 **Elmton** Derbys
224 F6 **Elphin** Highld
177 K4 **Elphinstone** E Loth
206 F4 **Elrick** Abers
145 G5 **Elrig** D & G
149 L3 **Elrington** Nthumb
158 B4 **Elsdon** Nthumb
60 E3 **Elsenham** Essex
57 K6 **Elsfield** Oxon
126 C7 **Elsham** N Linc
92 C1 **Elsing** Norfk
122 D2 **Elslack** N York
17 H3 **Elson** Hants
165 K2 **Elsrickle** S Lans
30 E3 **Elstead** Surrey
30 D7 **Elsted** W Susx
103 H7 **Elsthorpe** Lincs
102 C3 **Elston** Notts
11 G2 **Elstone** Devon
74 F5 **Elstow** Beds
44 D2 **Elstree** Herts
126 F4 **Elstronwick** E R Yk
120 F3 **Elswick** Lancs
151 G3 **Elsworth** N u Ty
75 K2 **Elsworth** Cambs
137 K6 **Elterwater** Cumb
45 H5 **Eltham** Gt Lon
75 J3 **Eltisley** Cambs
88 F5 **Elton** Cambs
112 C6 **Elton** Ches
100 E1 **Elton** Derbys
69 J1 **Elton** Herefs
102 C3 **Elton** Notts
141 J4 **Elton** S on T
150 D3 **Eltringham** Nthumb
165 J6 **Elvanfoot** S Lans
101 H6 **Elvaston** Derbys
91 J7 **Elveden** Suffk
30 D1 **Elvetham Heath** Hants
178 A4 **Elvingston** E Loth
35 H5 **Elvington** Kent
125 G2 **Elvington** York
141 K2 **Elwick** Hartpl
99 H1 **Elworth** Ches
25 G4 **Elworthy** Somset
90 D7 **Ely** Cambs
37 H5 **Ely** Cardif
74 C5 **Emberton** M Keyn
169 J5 **Embleton** Nthumb
223 H3 **Embo** Highld
26 E2 **Emborough** Somset
223 H3 **Embo Street** Highld
131 J8 **Embsay** N York
16 C2 **Emery Down** Hants
123 K7 **Emley** Kirk
58 C7 **Emmington** Oxon
90 C3 **Emneth** Norfk
90 D3 **Emneth Hungate** Norfk
88 D2 **Empingham** Rutlnd
30 C5 **Empshott** Hants
17 K2 **Emsworth** Hants
41 H7 **Enborne** W Berk
41 H7 **Enborne Row** W Berk
87 G4 **Enderby** Leics
129 L3 **Endmoor** Cumb
99 L2 **Endon** Staffs
99 L2 **Endon Bank** Staffs
60 B7 **Enfield** Gt Lon
60 B7 **Enfield Lock** Gt Lon
60 B7 **Enfield Wash** Gt Lon
28 C2 **Enford** Wilts
39 G4 **Engine Common** S Glos
41 L6 **Englefield** W Berk
43 G6 **Englefield Green** Surrey

54 E5 **English Bicknor** Gloucs
39 G7 **Englishcombe** BaNES
98 C6 **English Frankton** Shrops
29 G2 **Enham-Alamein** Hants
25 K4 **Enmore** Somset
27 J6 **Enmore Green** Dorset
136 E4 **Ennerdale Bridge** Cumb
195 G4 **Enochdhu** P & K
189 K8 **Ensay** Ag & B
15 K3 **Ensbury** Bmouth
83 H1 **Ensdon** Shrops
23 J6 **Ensis** Devon
57 G3 **Enstone** Oxon
154 K2 **Enterkinfoot** D & G
84 E6 **Enville** Staffs
233 b9 **Eolaigearraidh** W Isls
55 H5 **Epney** Gloucs
101 M3 **Epperstone** Notts
60 D7 **Epping** Essex
60 D7 **Epping Green** Essex
60 C6 **Epping Upland** Essex
140 F5 **Eppleby** N York
44 E7 **Epsom** Surrey
72 D6 **Epwell** Oxon
116 C2 **Epworth** N Linc
97 M4 **Erbistock** Wrexhm
85 K5 **Erdington** Birm
32 F6 **Eridge Green** E Susx
172 K4 **Erines** Ag & B
191 H7 **Eriska** Ag & B
91 G7 **Eriswell** Suffk
45 K4 **Erith** Gt Lon
27 L2 **Erlestoke** Wilts
6 F5 **Ermington** Devon
106 E6 **Erpingham** Norfk
202 E2 **Errogie** Highld
186 D3 **Errol** P & K
174 E4 **Erskine** Rens
144 B2 **Ervie** D & G
78 F7 **Erwarton** Suffk
68 C6 **Erwood** Powys
141 H5 **Eryholme** N York
97 J2 **Eryrys** Denbgs
140 F2 **Escomb** Dur
124 F2 **Escrick** N York
81 G3 **Esgairgeiliog** Powys
150 F6 **Esh** Dur
43 J7 **Esher** Surrey
158 F3 **Eshott** Nthumb
150 F6 **Esh Winning** Dur
212 C6 **Eskadale** Highld
177 J5 **Eskbank** Mdloth
137 G6 **Eskdale Green** Cumb
156 A3 **Eskdalemuir** D & G
120 E3 **Esprick** Lancs
88 F2 **Essendine** Rutlnd
59 L6 **Essendon** Herts
213 G6 **Essich** Highld
85 G3 **Essington** Staffs
217 H7 **Esslemont** Abers
142 C4 **Eston** R & Cl
168 D2 **Etal** Nthumb
40 B7 **Etchilhampton** Wilts
33 J7 **Etchingham** E Susx
34 F6 **Etchinghill** Kent
100 B8 **Etchinghill** Staffs
42 F5 **Eton** W & M
42 F5 **Eton Wick** W & M
99 K3 **Etruria** C Stke
203 G6 **Etteridge** Highld
139 K2 **Ettersgill** Dur
99 G1 **Ettiley Heath** Ches
85 G4 **Ettingshall** Wolves
72 C5 **Ettington** Warwks
89 G3 **Etton** C Pete
126 B2 **Etton** E R Yk
166 D6 **Ettrick** Border
166 F4 **Ettrickbridge** Border

166 C6 **Ettrickhill** Border
100 F6 **Etwall** Derbys
91 K7 **Euston** Suffk
121 H6 **Euxton** Lancs
212 F2 **Evanton** Highld
103 H3 **Evedon** Lincs
223 G4 **Evelix** Highld
68 F3 **Evenjobb** Powys
73 H7 **Evenley** Nhants
56 E3 **Evenlode** Gloucs
140 E3 **Evenwood** Dur
26 F4 **Evercreech** Somset
125 J3 **Everingham** E R Yk
28 D2 **Everleigh** Wilts
59 G2 **Eversholt** Beds
14 B2 **Evershot** Dorset
42 C7 **Eversley** Hants
42 C7 **Eversley Cross** Hants
125 L4 **Everthorpe** E R Yk
75 H4 **Everton** Beds
16 C4 **Everton** Hants
111 K3 **Everton** Lpool
116 B4 **Everton** Notts
156 C6 **Evertown** D & G
70 C5 **Evesbatch** Herefs
71 J5 **Evesham** Worcs
87 J3 **Evington** C Leic
114 F3 **Ewden Village** Sheff
44 E7 **Ewell** Surrey
35 H6 **Ewell Minnis** Kent
41 M3 **Ewelme** Oxon
40 A2 **Ewen** Gloucs
36 D5 **Ewenny** V Glam
103 J3 **Ewerby** Lincs
158 D4 **Ewesley** Nthumb
31 H4 **Ewhurst** Surrey
20 F2 **Ewhurst Green** E Susx
31 H4 **Ewhurst Green** Surrey
111 J7 **Ewloe** Flints
10 C6 **Eworthy** Devon
30 D2 **Ewshot** Hants
54 B3 **Ewyas Harold** Herefs
10 E4 **Exbourne** Devon
16 E3 **Exbury** Hants
24 E6 **Exebridge** Somset
132 D3 **Exelby** N York
11 L6 **Exeter** Devon
12 C4 **Exeter Airport** Devon
24 D4 **Exford** Somset
83 J3 **Exfordsgreen** Shrops
71 K4 **Exhall** Warwks
86 D4 **Exhall** Warwks
42 A4 **Exlade Street** Oxon
12 B5 **Exminster** Devon
24 D4 **Exmoor National Park**
12 C6 **Exmouth** Devon
76 E2 **Exning** Suffk
35 G5 **Exted** Kent
12 C5 **Exton** Devon
29 L7 **Exton** Hants
88 D2 **Exton** Rutlnd
24 E5 **Exton** Somset
11 K6 **Exwick** Devon
114 E6 **Eyam** Derbys
73 G4 **Eydon** Nhants
89 J3 **Eye** C Pete
69 J2 **Eye** Herefs
92 D8 **Eye** Suffk
179 K5 **Eyemouth** Border
75 J5 **Eyeworth** Beds
33 L3 **Eyhorne Street** Kent
79 G4 **Eyke** Suffk
75 H3 **Eynesbury** Cambs
45 K6 **Eynsford** Kent
57 H6 **Eynsham** Oxon
13 L4 **Eype** Dorset
208 F4 **Eyre** Highld
35 H5 **Eythorne** Kent
69 J3 **Eyton** Herefs

83 G6 **Eyton** Shrops
98 C7 **Eyton** Shrops
83 L3 **Eyton on Severn** Shrops
84 B1 **Eyton upon the Weald Moors** Wrekin

F

41 H8 **Faccombe** Hants
141 L6 **Faceby** N York
82 B1 **Fachwen** Powys
98 E3 **Faddiley** Ches
133 K2 **Fadmoor** N York
51 K5 **Faerdre** Swans
174 H4 **Faifley** W Duns
38 D6 **Failand** N Som
163 L4 **Failford** S Ayrs
113 K2 **Failsworth** Oldham
80 E2 **Fairbourne** Gwynd
124 D5 **Fairburn** N York
114 B6 **Fairfield** Derbys
85 G7 **Fairfield** Worcs
56 D7 **Fairford** Gloucs
146 F4 **Fairgirth** D & G
120 D5 **Fairhaven** Lancs
173 L7 **Fairlie** N Ayrs
21 G4 **Fairlight** E Susx
12 E3 **Fairmile** Devon
43 J7 **Fairmile** Surrey
167 G3 **Fairnilee** Border
29 J7 **Fair Oak** Hants
99 H6 **Fairoak** Staffs
42 A7 **Fair Oak Green** Hants
45 L7 **Fairseat** Kent
61 J5 **Fairstead** Essex
32 E7 **Fairwarp** E Susx
37 H5 **Fairwater** Cardif
22 F6 **Fairy Cross** Devon
105 L6 **Fakenham** Norfk
91 K7 **Fakenham Magna** Suffk
177 L6 **Fala** Mdloth
177 L6 **Fala Dam** Mdloth
177 L7 **Falahill** Border
117 H5 **Faldingworth** Lincs
236 e7 **Faldouet** Jersey
39 G2 **Falfield** S Glos
79 G6 **Falkenham** Suffk
176 B3 **Falkirk** Falk
186 D6 **Falkland** Fife
185 H8 **Fallin** Stirlg
169 J5 **Falloden** Nthumb
113 J3 **Fallowfield** Manch
150 B2 **Fallowfield** Nthumb
182 E5 **Falls of Blarghour** Ag & B
19 L4 **Falmer** E Susx
3 K5 **Falmouth** Cnwll
156 D2 **Falnash** Border
134 F2 **Falsgrave** N York
157 J5 **Falstone** Nthumb
228 B5 **Fanagmore** Highld
59 G3 **Fancott** Beds
212 D5 **Fanellan** Highld
142 C7 **Fangdale Beck** N York
134 B8 **Fangfoss** E R Yk
189 K7 **Fanmore** Ag & B
211 L8 **Fannich Lodge** Highld
167 J2 **Fans** Border
74 C7 **Far Bletchley** M Keyn
89 H5 **Farcet** Cambs
73 L3 **Far Cotton** Nhants
17 H2 **Fareham** Hants
137 J7 **Far End** Cumb
85 J2 **Farewell** Staffs
55 H7 **Far Green** Gloucs
40 F2 **Faringdon** Oxon
121 H5 **Farington** Lancs
185 L1 **Farkhill** P & K

148 F3 **Farlam** Cumb
38 D6 **Farleigh** N Som
32 C2 **Farleigh** Surrey
39 J8 **Farleigh Hungerford** Somset
29 L3 **Farleigh Wallop** Hants
119 G6 **Farlesthorpe** Lincs
129 L4 **Farleton** Cumb
130 B6 **Farleton** Lancs
100 B4 **Farley** Staffs
28 E5 **Farley** Wilts
77 G4 **Farley Green** Suffk
31 H3 **Farley Green** Surrey
42 C7 **Farley Hill** Wokham
55 H5 **Farleys End** Gloucs
17 J2 **Farlington** C Port
133 J6 **Farlington** N York
84 B7 **Farlow** Shrops
38 F7 **Farmborough** BaNES
56 B3 **Farmcote** Gloucs
66 E5 **Farmers** Carmth
56 C5 **Farmington** Gloucs
57 J6 **Farmoor** Oxon
112 D2 **Far Moor** Wigan
215 L4 **Farmtown** Moray
45 H7 **Farnborough** Gt Lon
30 E2 **Farnborough** Hants
41 H4 **Farnborough** W Berk
72 E5 **Farnborough** Warwks
30 E1 **Farnborough Park** Hants
30 E1 **Farnborough Street** Hants
31 G3 **Farncombe** Surrey
74 D2 **Farndish** Beds
98 B2 **Farndon** Ches
102 C3 **Farndon** Notts
169 K2 **Farne Islands** Nthumb
197 G5 **Farnell** Angus
27 L7 **Farnham** Dorset
60 D3 **Farnham** Essex
132 E7 **Farnham** N York
79 H3 **Farnham** Suffk
30 D3 **Farnham** Surrey
42 F4 **Farnham Common** Bucks
42 F4 **Farnham Royal** Bucks
45 K6 **Farningham** Kent
123 K4 **Farnley** Leeds
123 J2 **Farnley** N York
123 H7 **Farnley Tyas** Kirk
101 M2 **Farnsfield** Notts
113 G1 **Farnworth** Bolton
112 D4 **Farnworth** Halton
55 L7 **Far Oakridge** Gloucs
203 K5 **Farr** Highld
213 G7 **Farr** Highld
229 L3 **Farr** Highld
202 E2 **Farraline** Highld
12 C4 **Farringdon** Devon
26 F1 **Farrington Gurney** BaNES
137 K7 **Far Sawrey** Cumb
73 G6 **Farthinghoe** Nhants
73 H4 **Farthingstone** Nhants
118 C6 **Far Thorpe** Lincs
123 H6 **Fartown** Kirk
123 J4 **Fartown** Leeds
12 F4 **Farway Street** Devon
191 K6 **Fasnacloich** Ag & B
211 L8 **Fasnakyle** Highld
191 K2 **Fassfern** Highld
151 H4 **Fatfield** Sundld
176 C6 **Fauldhouse** W Loth
61 J5 **Faulkbourne** Essex
27 H1 **Faulkland** Somset
98 E6 **Fauls** Shrops
34 D3 **Faversham** Kent
132 F5 **Fawdington** N York

151 G2 **Fawdon** N u Ty
168 F6 **Fawdon** Nthumb
45 L6 **Fawkham Green** Kent
57 G4 **Fawler** Oxon
42 C3 **Fawley** Bucks
16 F2 **Fawley** Hants
41 H4 **Fawley** W Berk
125 K5 **Faxfleet** E R Yk
31 K5 **Faygate** W Susx
111 K3 **Fazakerley** Lpool
85 L3 **Fazeley** Staffs
132 B4 **Fearby** N York
223 H6 **Fearn** Highld
194 B7 **Fearnan** P & K
210 B3 **Fearnbeg** Highld
209 L3 **Fearnmore** Highld
172 F3 **Fearnoch** Ag & B
85 G3 **Featherstone** Staffs
124 C6 **Featherstone** Wakefd
71 H3 **Feckenham** Worcs
61 L4 **Feering** Essex
140 C7 **Feetham** N York
32 C5 **Felbridge** Surrey
106 E5 **Felbrigg** Norfk
32 C5 **Felcourt** Surrey
51 G2 **Felindre** Carmth
65 K6 **Felindre** Carmth
82 D7 **Felindre** Powys
51 J5 **Felindre** Swans
64 F6 **Felindre Farchog** Pembks
51 G2 **Felin gwm Isaf** Carmth
51 G1 **Felin gwm Uchaf** Carmth
133 G3 **Felixkirk** N York
79 G7 **Felixstowe** Suffk
151 G3 **Felling** Gatesd
74 E3 **Felmersham** Beds
106 F6 **Felmingham** Norfk
18 C5 **Felpham** W Susx
77 L3 **Felsham** Suffk
61 G4 **Felsted** Essex
43 J5 **Feltham** Gt Lon
43 H6 **Felthamhill** Surrey
106 E8 **Felthorpe** Norfk
69 L5 **Felton** Herefs
38 D7 **Felton** N Som
158 F3 **Felton** Nthumb
98 E3 **Felton Butler** Shrops
91 G5 **Feltwell** Norfk
122 C3 **Fence** Lancs
115 H4 **Fence** Rothm
132 D2 **Fencote** N York
57 L5 **Fencott** Oxon
104 D1 **Fendike Corner** Lincs
76 C3 **Fen Ditton** Cambs
75 J2 **Fen Drayton** Cambs
121 J5 **Feniscowles** Bl w D
12 E3 **Feniton** Devon
84 D6 **Fenn Green** Shrops
46 D5 **Fenn Street** Medway
100 D7 **Fenny Bentley** Derbys
12 E3 **Fenny Bridges** Devon
72 E4 **Fenny Compton** Warwks
86 D3 **Fenny Drayton** Leics
75 K2 **Fenstanton** Cambs
92 B4 **Fen Street** Norfk
99 K4 **Fenton** C Stke
89 K7 **Fenton** Cambs
148 E4 **Fenton** Cumb
102 E3 **Fenton** Lincs
116 D6 **Fenton** Lincs
116 C5 **Fenton** Notts
168 E3 **Fenton** Nthumb
178 B3 **Fenton Barns** E Loth
124 F7 **Fenwick** Donc
163 L2 **Fenwick** E Ayrs
158 D7 **Fenwick** Nthumb
169 G2 **Fenwick** Nthumb

4 C7 **Feock** Cnwll
171 H4 **Feolin Ferry** Ag & B
163 J2 **Fergushill** N Ayrs
208 B4 **Feriniquarrie** Highld
196 D4 **Fern** Angus
36 F2 **Ferndale** Rhondd
15 K3 **Ferndown** Dorset
214 B5 **Ferness** Highld
40 F3 **Fernham** Oxon
70 F3 **Fernhill Heath** Worcs
30 E5 **Fernhurst** W Susx
186 E4 **Fernie** Fife
175 K7 **Ferniegair** S Lans
208 F7 **Fernilea** Highld
114 A5 **Fernilee** Derbys
102 D3 **Fernwood** Notts
132 E7 **Ferrensby** N York
199 K4 **Ferrindonald** Highld
18 F5 **Ferring** W Susx
197 H5 **Ferryden** Angus
141 H2 **Ferryhill** Dur
223 G4 **Ferry Point** Highld
50 D4 **Ferryside** Carmth
223 G4 **Ferrytown** Highld
92 C6 **Fersfield** Norfk
192 F2 **Fersit** Highld
203 K4 **Feshiebridge** Highld
31 J1 **Fetcham** Surrey
217 J4 **Fetterangus** Abers
197 G2 **Fettercairn** Abers
132 B8 **Fewston** N York
51 J2 **Ffairfach** Carmth
67 G2 **Ffair Rhos** Cerdgn
96 A4 **Ffestiniog** Gwynd
95 L4 **Ffestiniog Railway** Gwynd
51 H5 **Fforest** Carmth
51 J6 **Fforest Fach** Swans
65 L5 **Ffostrasol** Cerdgn
97 L2 **Ffrith** Flints
111 G5 **Ffynnongroyw** Flints
225 K3 **Fiag Lodge** Highld
32 C2 **Fickleshole** Surrey
55 L2 **Fiddington** Gloucs
25 K4 **Fiddington** Somset
27 J8 **Fiddleford** Dorset
4 C5 **Fiddlers Green** Cnwll
100 A5 **Field** Staffs
129 J3 **Field Broughton** Cumb
106 B5 **Field Dalling** Norfk
86 F2 **Field Head** Leics
27 H6 **Fifehead Magdalen** Dorset
14 E1 **Fifehead Neville** Dorset
14 E1 **Fifehead St Quintin** Dorset
215 J4 **Fife Keith** Moray
56 E4 **Fifield** Oxon
42 E5 **Fifield** W & M
28 D3 **Figheldean** Wilts
93 K2 **Filby** Norfk
135 H4 **Filey** N York
74 C5 **Filgrave** M Keyn
56 E6 **Filkins** Oxon
11 H3 **Filleigh** Devon
23 K5 **Filleigh** Devon
116 F4 **Fillingham** Lincs
86 C6 **Fillongley** Warwks
38 E5 **Filton** S Glos
134 D7 **Fimber** E R Yk
196 D5 **Finavon** Angus
91 G3 **Fincham** Norfk
42 D7 **Finchampstead** Wokham
182 C6 **Fincharn** Ag & B
30 C8 **Finchdean** Hants
61 G2 **Finchingfield** Essex
44 F2 **Finchley** Gt Lon
100 F6 **Findern** Derbys
214 C2 **Findhorn** Moray

213 J8 **Findhorn Bridge** Highld
215 K2 **Findochty** Moray
185 L4 **Findo Gask** P & K
207 H6 **Findon** Abers
18 F4 **Findon** W Susx
212 F3 **Findon Mains** Highld
206 B4 **Findrack House** Abers
74 D1 **Finedon** Nhants
78 F1 **Fingal Street** Suffk
186 C4 **Fingask** P & K
42 C3 **Fingest** Bucks
132 B2 **Finghall** N York
164 E6 **Fingland** D & G
35 J4 **Finglesham** Kent
62 B4 **Fingringhoe** Essex
184 C1 **Finlarig** Stirlg
57 M2 **Finmere** Oxon
193 H5 **Finnart** P & K
78 C1 **Finningham** Suffk
116 A2 **Finningley** Donc
232 d5 **Finsbay** W Isls
71 H1 **Finstall** Worcs
129 H2 **Finsthwaite** Cumb
57 G5 **Finstock** Oxon
234 b6 **Finstown** Ork
216 E4 **Fintry** Abers
175 H7 **Fintry** Stirlg
206 B6 **Finzean** Abers
180 D3 **Fionnphort** Ag & B
232 d5 **Fionnsbhagh** W Isls
130 C2 **Firbank** Cumb
115 K4 **Firbeck** Rothm
132 D3 **Firby** N York
134 B6 **Firby** N York
118 F8 **Firsby** Lincs
150 E7 **Fir Tree** Dur
17 G4 **Fishbourne** IoW
18 A5 **Fishbourne** W Susx
18 A5 **Fishbourne Roman Palace** W Susx
141 J2 **Fishburn** Dur
185 J7 **Fishcross** Clacks
216 C7 **Fisherford** Abers
177 K4 **Fisherrow** E Loth
29 J7 **Fisher's Pond** Hants
213 H4 **Fisherton** Highld
163 H6 **Fisherton** S Ayrs
27 M4 **Fisherton de la Mere** Wilts
64 D6 **Fishguard** Pembks
125 G7 **Fishlake** Donc
190 D7 **Fishnish Pier** Ag & B
38 F5 **Fishponds** Bristl
104 B4 **Fishtoft** Lincs
104 A3 **Fishtoft Drove** Lincs
208 E7 **Fiskavaig** Highld
117 H6 **Fiskerton** Lincs
102 C3 **Fiskerton** Notts
28 D2 **Fittleton** Wilts
18 D2 **Fittleworth** W Susx
98 C8 **Fitz** Shrops
25 H5 **Fitzhead** Somset
124 C7 **Fitzwilliam** Wakefd
19 M2 **Five Ash Down** E Susx
32 F7 **Five Ashes** E Susx
26 A6 **Fivehead** Somset
9 G8 **Fivelanes** Cnwll
33 H4 **Five Oak Green** Kent
236 d7 **Five Oaks** Jersey
31 H5 **Five Oaks** W Susx
42 E3 **Flackwell Heath** Bucks
71 H5 **Fladbury** Worcs
235 c6 **Fladdabister** Shet
114 C7 **Flagg** Derbys
135 K5 **Flamborough** E R Yk
135 K5 **Flamborough Head** E R Yk
134 B4 **Flamingo Land Theme Park** N York

59 H5 **Flamstead** Herts
18 C5 **Flansham** W Susx
123 L6 **Flanshaw** Wakefd
131 H7 **Flasby** N York
114 A7 **Flash** Staffs
208 E4 **Flashader** Highld
59 G7 **Flaunden** Herts
102 C4 **Flawborough** Notts
133 G6 **Flawith** N York
38 D6 **Flax Bourton** N Som
132 F7 **Flaxby** N York
55 G5 **Flaxley** Gloucs
25 H4 **Flaxpool** Somset
133 K6 **Flaxton** N York
87 J5 **Fleckney** Leics
73 G2 **Flecknoe** Warwks
116 B6 **Fledborough** Notts
14 C6 **Fleet** Dorset
30 D2 **Fleet** Hants
104 C7 **Fleet** Lincs
104 C7 **Fleet Hargate** Lincs
120 D2 **Fleetwood** Lancs
36 F6 **Flemingston** V Glam
175 H6 **Flemington** S Lans
77 J1 **Flempton** Suffk
147 L6 **Fletchertown** Cumb
19 L2 **Fletching** E Susx
9 G4 **Flexbury** Cnwll
30 F2 **Flexford** Surrey
147 H7 **Flimby** Cumb
33 J6 **Flimwell** E Susx
111 H6 **Flint** Flints
102 C4 **Flintham** Notts
126 E7 **Flinton** E R Yk
105 H6 **Flitcham** Norfk
74 F7 **Flitton** Beds
74 F7 **Flitwick** Beds
125 K7 **Flixborough** N Linc
125 K7 **Flixborough Stather** N Linc
135 G4 **Flixton** N York
93 G6 **Flixton** Suffk
113 H3 **Flixton** Traffd
123 J7 **Flockton** Kirk
123 K7 **Flockton Green** Kirk
218 C6 **Flodigarry** Highld
129 H4 **Flookburgh** Cumb
92 E4 **Flordon** Norfk
73 J3 **Flore** Nhants
78 C5 **Flowton** Suffk
3 L4 **Flushing** Cnwll
12 E4 **Fluxton** Devon
71 H4 **Flyford Flavell** Worcs
46 B4 **Fobbing** Thurr
215 H3 **Fochabers** Moray
125 K6 **Fockerby** N Linc
26 E5 **Foddington** Somset
81 L2 **Foel** Powys
125 H3 **Foggathorpe** E R Yk
179 G8 **Fogo** Border
214 F3 **Fogwatt** Moray
195 J4 **Folda** Angus
100 B5 **Fole** Staffs
86 D6 **Foleshill** Covtry
26 F8 **Folke** Dorset
35 H7 **Folkestone** Kent
103 H5 **Folkingham** Lincs
20 B5 **Folkington** E Susx
89 G5 **Folksworth** Cambs
135 G4 **Folkton** N York
216 D7 **Folla Rule** Abers
132 E8 **Follifoot** N York
10 E5 **Folly Gate** Devon
27 L5 **Fonthill Bishop** Wilts
27 L5 **Fonthill Gifford** Wilts
27 K7 **Fontmell Magna** Dorset
27 J8 **Fontmell Parva** Dorset
18 C4 **Fontwell** W Susx
114 D6 **Foolow** Derbys

205 H3 **Forbestown** Abers
140 F5 **Forcett** N York
182 C6 **Ford** Ag & B
58 C6 **Ford** Bucks
113 H3 **Ford** Derbys
7 J7 **Ford** Devon
22 F6 **Ford** Devon
56 C3 **Ford** Gloucs
168 E2 **Ford** Nthumb
25 H5 **Ford** Somset
100 B2 **Ford** Staffs
18 D5 **Ford** W Susx
39 J5 **Ford** Wilts
32 F5 **Fordcombe** Kent
177 G2 **Fordell** Fife
82 E5 **Forden** Powys
61 G5 **Ford End** Essex
7 H3 **Forder Green** Devon
76 F1 **Fordham** Cambs
61 L3 **Fordham** Essex
90 E4 **Fordham** Norfk
28 D8 **Fordingbridge** Hants
135 G4 **Fordon** E R Yk
197 J3 **Fordoun** Abers
61 L3 **Fordstreet** Essex
25 J7 **Ford Street** Somset
35 G3 **Fordwich** Kent
216 B2 **Fordyce** Abers
99 L7 **Forebridge** Staffs
101 G7 **Foremark** Derbys
236 c4 **Forest** Guern
122 B1 **Forest Becks** Lancs
113 L6 **Forest Chapel** Ches
45 H3 **Forest Gate** Gt Lon
31 J3 **Forest Green** Surrey
151 G2 **Forest Hall** N Tyne
45 J5 **Forest Hill** Gt Lon
57 L6 **Forest Hill** Oxon
132 E7 **Forest Lane Head** N York
192 D7 **Forest Lodge** Ag & B
185 K3 **Forest Mill** Clacks
54 F5 **Forest of Dean** Gloucs
32 D6 **Forest Row** E Susx
30 C8 **Forestside** W Susx
196 D5 **Forfar** Angus
186 A4 **Forgandenny** P & K
37 L2 **Forge Hammer** Torfn
215 J4 **Forgie** Moray
215 J4 **Forgieside** Moray
216 B5 **Forgue** Abers
111 J1 **Formby** Sefton
92 D5 **Forncett End** Norfk
92 E5 **Forncett St Mary** Norfk
92 E5 **Forncett St Peter** Norfk
77 J2 **Fornham All Saints** Suffk
77 J2 **Fornham St Martin** Suffk
213 L4 **Fornighty** Highld
214 C3 **Forres** Moray
99 L4 **Forsbrook** Staffs
227 M2 **Forse** Highld
227 M2 **Forse House** Highld
230 E4 **Forsinard** Highld
202 B4 **Fort Augustus** Highld
185 L4 **Forteviot** P & K
176 C7 **Forth** S Lans
55 K2 **Forthampton** Gloucs
194 B6 **Fortingall** P & K
29 H3 **Forton** Hants
121 G2 **Forton** Lancs
83 H1 **Forton** Shrops
13 J2 **Forton** Somset
99 H7 **Forton** Staffs
216 C2 **Fortrie** Abers
213 H3 **Fortrose** Highld
14 D7 **Fortuneswell** Dorset
191 L2 **Fort William** Highld

60 B7 **Forty Hill** Gt Lon
40 F8 **Fosbury** Wilts
56 E4 **Foscot** Oxon
104 A5 **Fosdyke** Lincs
194 C5 **Foss** P & K
56 B5 **Fossebridge** Gloucs
60 D6 **Foster Street** Essex
100 D6 **Foston** Derbys
87 H4 **Foston** Leics
102 E4 **Foston** Lincs
133 L6 **Foston** N York
135 H7 **Foston on the Wolds** E R Yk
118 D3 **Fotherby** Lincs
88 F5 **Fotheringhay** Nhants
179 J7 **Foulden** Border
91 H4 **Foulden** Norfk
86 B4 **Foul End** Warwks
122 D3 **Foulridge** Lancs
106 B7 **Foulsham** Norfk
177 **Fountainhall** Border
78 B1 **Four Ashes** Suffk
97 K8 **Four Crosses** Powys
32 E4 **Four Elms** Kent
25 K4 **Four Forks** Somset
90 C1 **Four Gotes** Cambs
3 J4 **Four Lanes** Cnwll
30 A4 **Four Marks** Hants
108 C5 **Four Mile Bridge** IoA
86 B7 **Four Oaks** Solhll
223 H3 **Fourpenny** Highld
50 F4 **Four Roads** Carmth
149 M2 **Fourstones** Nthumb
33 K7 **Four Throws** Kent
28 A5 **Fovant** Wilts
207 H2 **Foveran** Abers
5 H5 **Fowey** Cnwll
33 J4 **Fowlhall** Kent
186 E2 **Fowlis** Angus
185 J3 **Fowlis Wester** P & K
76 B5 **Fowlmere** Cambs
69 L7 **Fownhope** Herefs
174 E6 **Foxbar** Rens
27 L2 **Foxcote** Somset
237 b5 **Foxdale** IoM
77 J5 **Foxearth** Essex
128 E4 **Foxfield** Cumb
4 F5 **Foxhole** Cnwll
134 F5 **Foxholes** N York
106 C7 **Foxley** Norfk
100 B3 **Foxt** Staffs
76 B5 **Foxton** Cambs
87 K5 **Foxton** Leics
141 K7 **Foxton** N York
84 B7 **Foxwood** Shrops
54 E3 **Foy** Herefs
202 D2 **Foyers** Highld
213 L4 **Foynesfield** Highld
4 E4 **Fraddon** Cnwll
85 L2 **Fradley** Staffs
99 M6 **Fradswell** Staffs
135 J7 **Fraisthorpe** E R Yk
20 A2 **Framfield** E Susx
92 F3 **Framingham Earl** Norfk
92 F3 **Framingham Pigot** Norfk
79 G2 **Framlingham** Suffk
14 C4 **Frampton** Dorset
104 B5 **Frampton** Lincs
38 F4 **Frampton Cotterell** S Glos
55 L7 **Frampton Mansell** Gloucs
55 H6 **Frampton on Severn** Gloucs
78 E3 **Framsden** Suffk
151 G6 **Framwellgate Moor** Dur
121 J3 **Frances Green** Lancs
84 E7 **Franche** Worcs
111 H4 **Frankby** Wirral

85 H7 **Frankley** Worcs
72 E1 **Frankton** Warwks
33 G6 **Frant** E Susx
217 J2 **Fraserburgh** Abers
62 C4 **Frating** Essex
62 C4 **Frating Green** Essex
17 J3 **Fratton** C Port
6 B5 **Freathy** Cnwll
76 F1 **Freckenham** Suffk
120 F5 **Freckleton** Lancs
102 D7 **Freeby** Leics
29 J2 **Freefolk** Hants
57 H5 **Freeland** Oxon
93 J3 **Freethorpe** Norfk
93 J3 **Freethorpe Common** Norfk
104 B4 **Freiston** Lincs
23 H5 **Fremington** Devon
140 D7 **Fremington** N York
38 F5 **Frenchay** S Glos
194 C5 **Frenich** P & K
30 D3 **Frensham** Surrey
120 C8 **Freshfield** Sefton
39 H7 **Freshford** Wilts
16 D5 **Freshwater** IoW
92 F7 **Fressingfield** Suffk
78 E6 **Freston** Suffk
231 L3 **Freswick** Highld
55 G6 **Fretherne** Gloucs
106 F8 **Frettenham** Norfk
186 E6 **Freuchie** Fife
49 G5 **Freystrop** Pembks
85 H4 **Friar Park** Sandw
90 C3 **Friday Bridge** Cambs
79 H3 **Friday Street** Suffk
134 D7 **Fridaythorpe** E R Yk
44 F2 **Friern Barnet** Gt Lon
188 F5 **Friesland Bay** Ag & B
117 H5 **Friesthorpe** Lincs
102 F3 **Frieston** Lincs
42 D3 **Frieth** Bucks
41 H2 **Frilford** Oxon
41 K5 **Frilsham** W Berk
42 E4 **Frimley** Surrey
46 C6 **Frindsbury** Medway
105 H5 **Fring** Norfk
57 L3 **Fringford** Oxon
34 B4 **Frinsted** Kent
62 F4 **Frinton-on-Sea** Essex
196 F6 **Friockheim** Angus
102 B8 **Frisby on the Wreake** Leics
104 D2 **Friskney** Lincs
20 B6 **Friston** E Susx
79 J3 **Friston** Suffk
101 G3 **Fritchley** Derbys
28 E8 **Fritham** Hants
23 G7 **Frithelstock** Devon
23 G7 **Frithelstock Stone** Devon
104 A3 **Frithville** Lincs
33 K5 **Frittenden** Kent
7 J6 **Frittiscombe** Devon
92 F5 **Fritton** Norfk
93 K4 **Fritton** Norfk
57 K3 **Fritwell** Oxon
123 H4 **Frizinghall** Brad
136 E4 **Frizington** Cumb
55 H7 **Frocester** Gloucs
83 K3 **Frodesley** Shrops
112 D6 **Frodsham** Ches
168 B4 **Frogden** Border
76 B5 **Frog End** Cambs
114 E6 **Froggatt** Derbys
100 A3 **Froghall** Staffs
7 H7 **Frogmore** Devon
89 H2 **Frognall** Lincs
70 E2 **Frog Pool** Worcs
6 A3 **Frogwell** Cnwll
87 G5 **Frolesworth** Leics
27 H2 **Frome** Somset

14 B2 **Frome St Quintin** Dorset
70 C5 **Fromes Hill** Herefs
97 K4 **Froncysyllte** Denbgs
96 D5 **Fron-goch** Gwynd
97 L4 **Fron Isaf** Wrexhm
150 C7 **Frosterley** Dur
40 F6 **Froxfield** Wilts
30 B6 **Froxfield Green** Hants
29 H7 **Fryern Hill** Hants
61 G7 **Fryerning** Essex
190 C6 **Fuinary** Highld
102 F3 **Fulbeck** Lincs
76 D4 **Fulbourn** Cambs
56 E5 **Fulbrook** Oxon
29 J5 **Fulflood** Hants
25 K5 **Fulford** Somset
99 L5 **Fulford** Staffs
124 F2 **Fulford** York
44 E5 **Fulham** Gt Lon
19 H4 **Fulking** W Susx
163 H2 **Fullarton** N Ayrs
61 H5 **Fuller Street** Essex
29 G4 **Fullerton** Hants
118 D6 **Fulletby** Lincs
72 C5 **Fullready** Warwks
134 B7 **Full Sutton** E R Yk
174 E7 **Fullwood** E Ayrs
43 G4 **Fulmer** Bucks
106 B6 **Fulmodeston** Norfk
117 H5 **Fulnetby** Lincs
103 L7 **Fulney** Lincs
118 D3 **Fulstow** Lincs
57 G4 **Fulwell** Oxon
151 J3 **Fulwell** Sundld
121 H4 **Fulwood** Lancs
114 F4 **Fulwood** Sheff
92 D4 **Fundenhall** Norfk
17 L2 **Funtington** W Susx
184 F3 **Funtullich** P & K
13 H2 **Furley** Devon
182 E7 **Furnace** Ag & B
51 G5 **Furnace** Carmth
114 A5 **Furness Vale** Derbys
60 C3 **Furneux Pelham** Herts
28 F7 **Furzley** Hants
60 F6 **Fyfield** Essex
28 F3 **Fyfield** Hants
57 H7 **Fyfield** Oxon
40 C6 **Fyfield** Wilts
40 D7 **Fyfield** Wilts
143 J6 **Fylingthorpe** N York
30 D6 **Fyning** W Susx
216 E6 **Fyvie** Abers

G

174 E7 **Gabroc Hill** E Ayrs
87 K2 **Gaddesby** Leics
59 H5 **Gaddesden Row** Herts
163 K5 **Gadgirth** S Ayrs
38 C2 **Gaer-llwyd** Mons
108 F7 **Gaerwen** IoA
163 H3 **Gailes** N Ayrs
85 G2 **Gailey** Staffs
140 F4 **Gainford** Dur
116 D4 **Gainsborough** Lincs
77 G7 **Gainsford End** Essex
219 J6 **Gairloch** Highld
201 J8 **Gairlochy** Highld
186 B7 **Gairneybridge** P & K
123 H3 **Gaisby** Brad
148 C5 **Gaitsgill** Cumb
167 G3 **Galashiels** Border
129 K7 **Galgate** Lancs
26 F5 **Galhampton** Somset
182 B3 **Gallanach** Ag & B

186 E8 **Gallatown** Fife
61 H7 **Galleywood** Essex
202 E7 **Gallovie** Highld
153 J5 **Galloway Forest Park**
196 D7 **Gallowfauld** Angus
186 B1 **Gallowhill** P & K
200 C2 **Galltair** Highld
7 G7 **Galmpton** Devon
7 K5 **Galmpton** Torbay
132 C5 **Galphay** N York
163 L3 **Galston** E Ayrs
14 E5 **Galton** Dorset
149 G6 **Gamblesby** Cumb
75 J4 **Gamlingay** Cambs
75 J4 **Gamlingay Great Heath** Cambs
216 F2 **Gamrie** Abers
101 L5 **Gamston** Notts
116 B6 **Gamston** Notts
182 B2 **Ganavan Bay** Ag & B
96 B7 **Ganllwyd** Gwynd
196 F3 **Gannachy** Angus
126 E4 **Ganstead** E R Yk
133 L5 **Ganthorpe** N York
134 F4 **Ganton** N York
215 H4 **Garbity** Moray
92 B7 **Garboldisham** Norfk
205 G4 **Garchory** Abers
42 D6 **Gardeners Green** Wokham
216 F2 **Gardenstown** Abers
114 E2 **Garden Village** Sheff
235 H2 **Garderhouse** Shet
27 H4 **Gare Hill** Somset
173 L1 **Garelochhead** Ag & B
41 H2 **Garford** Oxon
124 B4 **Garforth** Leeds
131 H4 **Gargrave** N York
184 F8 **Gargunnock** Stirlg
92 E6 **Garlic Street** Norfk
145 K5 **Garlieston** D & G
35 J2 **Garlinge** Kent
34 F4 **Garlinge Green** Kent
206 E4 **Garlogie** Abers
216 F4 **Garmond** Abers
215 H2 **Garmouth** Moray
83 L3 **Garmston** Shrops
95 J4 **Garn-Dolbenmaen** Gwynd
175 J5 **Garnkirk** N Lans
232 g2 **Garrabost** W Isls
164 B5 **Garrallan** E Ayrs
3 J6 **Garras** Cnwll
95 K4 **Garreg** Gwynd
149 J6 **Garrigill** Cumb
153 M6 **Garroch** D & G
144 D7 **Garrochtrie** D & G
173 J7 **Garrochty** Ag & B
209 H4 **Garros** Highld
130 E2 **Garsdale Head** Cumb
39 L3 **Garsdon** Wilts
99 L5 **Garshall Green** Staffs
57 L7 **Garsington** Oxon
121 G2 **Garstang** Lancs
59 J7 **Garston** Herts
112 B5 **Garston** Lpool
171 J6 **Gartachossan** Ag & B
175 J5 **Gartcosh** N Lans
67 K5 **Garth** Powys
97 K4 **Garth** Wrexhm
175 H5 **Garthamlock** C Glas
82 E4 **Garthmyl** Powys
102 D7 **Garthorpe** Leics
125 K6 **Garthorpe** N Linc
80 E6 **Garth Penrhyncoch** Cerdgn
138 D7 **Garth Row** Cumb
215 L7 **Gartly** Abers
184 C7 **Gartmore** Stirlg
175 K5 **Gartness** N Lans
174 F2 **Gartness** Stirlg

174 D2 **Gartocharn** W Duns
127 G4 **Garton** E R Yk
134 F7 **Garton-on-the-Wolds** E R Yk
227 H5 **Gartymore** Highld
178 D4 **Garvald** E Loth
191 J2 **Garvan** Highld
171 G1 **Garvard** Ag & B
212 B3 **Garve** Highld
92 B3 **Garvestone** Norfk
174 B4 **Garvock** Inver
54 C4 **Garway** Herefs
54 C4 **Garway Common** Herefs
232 f3 **Garyvard** W Isls
27 H5 **Gasper** Wilts
39 K6 **Gastard** Wilts
91 L7 **Gasthorpe** Norfk
60 D5 **Gaston Green** Essex
16 F5 **Gatcombe** IoW
116 D5 **Gate Burton** Lincs
124 E5 **Gateforth** N York
163 K3 **Gatehead** E Ayrs
133 L7 **Gate Helmsley** N York
157 K4 **Gatehouse** Nthumb
145 M4 **Gatehouse of Fleet** D & G
106 A7 **Gateley** Norfk
132 E3 **Gatenby** N York
168 B5 **Gateshaw** Border
151 J3 **Gateshead** Gatesd
196 D7 **Gateside** Angus
174 E6 **Gateside** E Rens
186 C5 **Gateside** Fife
174 C7 **Gateside** N Ayrs
154 F2 **Gateslack** D & G
113 J4 **Gatley** Stockp
167 H3 **Gattonside** Border
32 B5 **Gatwick Airport** W Susx
87 K4 **Gaulby** Leics
186 F3 **Gauldry** Fife
195 K6 **Gauldswell** P & K
117 K6 **Gautby** Lincs
179 G7 **Gavinton** Border
58 B2 **Gawcott** Bucks
113 K7 **Gawsworth** Ches
130 D3 **Gawthrop** Cumb
129 G3 **Gawthwaite** Cumb
72 D4 **Gaydon** Warwks
74 B5 **Gayhurst** M Keyn
131 G2 **Gayle** N York
140 E5 **Gayles** N York
73 K4 **Gayton** Nhants
105 H8 **Gayton** Norfk
99 M6 **Gayton** Staffs
118 F5 **Gayton le Marsh** Lincs
105 H8 **Gayton Thorpe** Norfk
105 G7 **Gaywood** Norfk
77 G2 **Gazeley** Suffk
232 f3 **Gearraidh Bhaird** W Isls
208 D3 **Geary** Highld
77 L3 **Gedding** Suffk
35 H5 **Geddinge** Kent
88 C6 **Geddington** Nhants
101 L4 **Gedling** Notts
104 C7 **Gedney** Lincs
104 C7 **Gedney Broadgate** Lincs
104 D6 **Gedney Drove End** Lincs
104 C7 **Gedney Dyke** Lincs
89 L2 **Gedney Hill** Lincs
88 E3 **Geeston** Rutlnd
93 H5 **Geldeston** Norfk
110 F8 **Gellifor** Denbgs
37 H2 **Gelligaer** Caerph
95 M4 **Gellilydan** Gwynd
51 K5 **Gellinudd** Neath
195 H8 **Gellyburn** P & K

50 C2 **Gellywen** Carmth
146 D3 **Gelston** D & G
102 E4 **Gelston** Lincs
135 H7 **Gembling** E R Yk
85 J2 **Gentleshaw** Staffs
156 B4 **Georgefield** D & G
43 G4 **George Green** Bucks
23 G4 **Georgeham** Devon
23 L6 **George Nympton** Devon
234 b5 **Georth** Ork
10 C6 **Germansweek** Devon
4 D8 **Gerrans** Cnwll
43 G3 **Gerrards Cross** Bucks
142 E5 **Gerrick** R & Cl
77 J6 **Gestingthorpe** Essex
82 E2 **Geuffordd** Powys
45 K3 **Gidea Park** Gt Lon
175 G6 **Giffnock** E Rens
178 C5 **Gifford** E Loth
186 E5 **Giffordtown** Fife
130 F6 **Giggleswick** N York
125 K5 **Gilberdyke** E R Yk
178 B5 **Gilchriston** E Loth
147 K7 **Gilcrux** Cumb
123 K5 **Gildersome** Leeds
115 K4 **Gildingwells** Rothm
151 H6 **Gilesgate Moor** Dur
36 F6 **Gileston** V Glam
53 J7 **Gilfach** Caerph
36 F3 **Gilfach Goch** Brdgnd
65 L3 **Gilfachrheda** Cerdgn
136 E3 **Gilgarran** Cumb
133 K2 **Gillamoor** N York
208 D3 **Gillen** Highld
155 K4 **Gillesbie** D & G
133 J4 **Gilling East** N York
27 J6 **Gillingham** Dorset
46 C6 **Gillingham** Medway
93 J5 **Gillingham** Norfk
140 F6 **Gilling West** N York
231 J4 **Gillock** Highld
231 K2 **Gills** Highld
166 E5 **Gilmanscleuch** Border
177 J5 **Gilmerton** C Edin
185 J3 **Gilmerton** P & K
140 C5 **Gilmonby** Dur
87 H6 **Gilmorton** Leics
149 G2 **Gilsland** Cumb
177 L6 **Gilston** Border
60 D5 **Gilston** Herts
53 K5 **Gilwern** Mons
107 G5 **Gimingham** Norfk
78 C2 **Gipping** Suffk
103 M3 **Gipsey Bridge** Lincs
163 J2 **Girdle Toll** N Ayrs
235 c5 **Girlsta** Shet
141 J5 **Girsby** N York
146 A4 **Girthon** D & G
76 B3 **Girton** Cambs
116 D7 **Girton** Notts
152 E3 **Girvan** S Ayrs
122 C2 **Gisburn** Lancs
93 K5 **Gisleham** Suffk
78 C1 **Gislingham** Suffk
92 D6 **Gissing** Norfk
12 E3 **Gittisham** Devon
68 E4 **Gladestry** Powys
177 M4 **Gladsmuir** E Loth
51 K5 **Glais** Swans
143 G6 **Glaisdale** N York
196 C6 **Glamis** Angus
51 J3 **Glanaman** Carmth
106 C4 **Glandford** Norfk
49 K2 **Glandwr** Pembks
80 F4 **Glandyfi** Cerdgn
36 D3 **Glanllynfi** Brdgnd
169 G6 **Glanton** Nthumb
14 D2 **Glanvilles Wootton** Dorset
111 G5 **Glan-y-don** Flints
88 E5 **Glapthorn** Nhants

115 J7 **Glapwell** Derbys
68 D6 **Glasbury** Powys
68 D4 **Glascwm** Powys
96 E3 **Glasfryn** Conwy
175 G5 **Glasgow** C Glas
174 E5 **Glasgow Airport** Rens
175 G5 **Glasgow Science Centre** C Glas
109 H7 **Glasinfryn** Gwynd
199 L6 **Glasnacardoch Bay** Highld
199 H3 **Glasnakille** Highld
145 J7 **Glasserton** D & G
175 J8 **Glassford** S Lans
55 G4 **Glasshouse** Gloucs
132 B6 **Glasshouses** N York
148 A3 **Glasson** Cumb
129 K7 **Glasson** Lancs
149 G7 **Glassonby** Cumb
196 F6 **Glasterlaw** Angus
88 C4 **Glaston** Rutlnd
26 D4 **Glastonbury** Somset
89 H6 **Glatton** Cambs
113 G3 **Glazebrook** Warrtn
112 F3 **Glazebury** Warrtn
84 C5 **Glazeley** Shrops
128 F5 **Gleaston** Cumb
202 D2 **Glebe** Highld
123 L3 **Gledhow** Leeds
146 B5 **Gledpark** D & G
97 L5 **Gledrid** Shrops
77 J5 **Glemsford** Suffk
215 G6 **Glenallachie** Moray
199 K6 **Glenancross** Highld
190 B7 **Glenaros House** Ag & B
237 d3 **Glen Auldyn** IoM
161 H3 **Glenbarr** Ag & B
216 B4 **Glenbarry** Abers
190 C4 **Glenbeg** Highld
214 C8 **Glenbeg** Highld
197 J1 **Glenbervie** Abers
175 J5 **Glenboig** N Lans
190 C4 **Glenborrodale** Highld
183 G7 **Glenbranter** Ag & B
165 K5 **Glenbreck** Border
198 F2 **Glenbrittle House** Highld
164 E4 **Glenbuck** E Ayrs
196 B4 **Glencally** Angus
147 H2 **Glencaple** D & G
211 G4 **Glencarron Lodge** Highld
186 C3 **Glencarse** P & K
192 B6 **Glenceitlin** Highld
204 E8 **Glen Clunie Lodge** Abers
191 L5 **Glencoe** Highld
165 L4 **Glencothe** Border
186 C7 **Glencraig** Fife
154 D4 **Glencrosh** D & G
208 B4 **Glendale** Highld
173 G2 **Glendaruel** Ag & B
185 K6 **Glendevon** P & K
202 C4 **Glendoe Lodge** Highld
186 C3 **Glendoick** P & K
186 D4 **Glenduckie** Fife
185 J5 **Gleneagles** Ag & B
185 J5 **Gleneagles Hotel** P & K
170 F7 **Glenegedale** Ag & B
200 C2 **Glenelg** Highld
214 C5 **Glenerney** Moray
186 B5 **Glenfarg** P & K
203 K6 **Glenfeshie Lodge** Highld
87 G3 **Glenfield** Leics
191 H1 **Glenfinnan** Highld
201 K7 **Glenfintaig Lodge** Highld
186 C4 **Glenfoot** P & K

183 H4 **Glenfyne Lodge** Ag & B
174 C7 **Glengarnock** N Ayrs
231 G3 **Glengolly** Highld
189 K5 **Glengorm Castle** Ag & B
209 G5 **Glengrasco** Highld
165 L3 **Glenholm** Border
154 A5 **Glenhoul** D & G
195 K4 **Glenisla** Angus
173 K3 **Glenkin** Ag & B
205 K3 **Glenkindie** Abers
214 F8 **Glenlivet** Moray
146 C3 **Glenlochar** D & G
186 C6 **Glenlomond** P & K
144 E4 **Glenluce** D & G
173 J2 **Glenmassen** Ag & B
175 K5 **Glenmavis** N Lans
237 b5 **Glen Maye** IoM
209 G6 **Glenmore** Highld
204 B4 **Glenmore Lodge** Highld
192 B3 **Glen Nevis House** Highld
185 H7 **Glenochil** Clacks
87 H4 **Glen Parva** Leics
196 C4 **Glenquiech** Angus
172 E5 **Glenralloch** Ag & B
137 J4 **Glenridding** Cumb
186 D7 **Glenrothes** Fife
185 K1 **Glenshee** P & K
202 E6 **Glenshero Lodge** Highld
173 J3 **Glenstriven** Ag & B
117 G4 **Glentham** Lincs
203 J6 **Glentromie Lodge** Highld
153 J6 **Glen Trool Lodge** D & G
153 H6 **Glentrool Village** D & G
203 G6 **Glentruim House** Highld
116 F4 **Glentworth** Lincs
190 D2 **Glenuig** Highld
191 K6 **Glenure** Ag & B
209 G6 **Glenvarragill** Highld
152 E7 **Glenwhilly** D & G
164 F4 **Glespin** S Lans
54 E4 **Glewstone** Herefs
89 H3 **Glinton** C Pete
87 L4 **Glooston** Leics
114 B3 **Glossop** Derbys
159 G2 **Gloster Hill** Nthumb
55 J4 **Gloucester** Gloucs
55 K4 **Gloucestershire Airport** Gloucs
122 F2 **Glusburn** N York
227 H2 **Glutt Lodge** Highld
4 E3 **Gluvian** Cnwll
57 H4 **Glympton** Oxon
65 K5 **Glynarthen** Cerdgn
97 J5 **Glyn Ceiriog** Wrexhm
97 J5 **Glyncorrwg** Neath
19 L4 **Glynde** E Susx
97 J4 **Glyndyfrdwy** Denbgs
52 D6 **Glynneath** Neath
52 D5 **Glyntawe** Powys
65 K6 **Glynteg** Carmth
99 J7 **Gnosall** Staffs
99 J7 **Gnosall Heath** Staffs
87 L4 **Goadby** Leics
102 C7 **Goadby Marwood** Leics
40 A5 **Goatacre** Wilts
182 E7 **Goatfield** Ag & B
26 F7 **Goathill** Dorset
143 H6 **Goathland** N York
25 K5 **Goathurst** Somset
97 L5 **Gobowen** Shrops
30 F3 **Godalming** Surrey

33 L6 **Goddard's Green** Kent
75 J1 **Godmanchester** Cambs
14 C3 **Godmanstone** Dorset
34 E5 **Godmersham** Kent
26 C3 **Godney** Somset
3 G5 **Godolphin Cross** Cnwll
51 L4 **Godre'r-graig** Neath
17 G6 **Godshill** IoW
32 C3 **Godstone** Surrey
53 L6 **Goetre** Mons
60 B7 **Goff's Oak** Herts
53 K5 **Gofilon** Mons
177 G4 **Gogar** C Edin
80 F7 **Goginan** Cerdgn
95 J4 **Golan** Gwynd
5 H5 **Golant** Cnwll
5 M2 **Golberdon** Cnwll
112 E3 **Golborne** Wigan
123 G7 **Golcar** Kirk
38 A4 **Goldcliff** Newpt
33 H4 **Golden Green** Kent
30 B3 **Golden Pot** Hants
44 E3 **Golders Green** Gt Lon
61 L6 **Goldhanger** Essex
74 F4 **Goldington** Beds
132 F7 **Goldsborough** N York
143 H4 **Goldsborough** N York
2 F5 **Goldsithney** Cnwll
43 G8 **Goldsworth Park** Surrey
115 J2 **Goldthorpe** Barns
22 F6 **Goldworthy** Devon
213 J4 **Gollanfield** Highld
223 H2 **Golspie** Highld
28 D4 **Gomeldon** Wilts
31 H2 **Gomshall** Surrey
102 B3 **Gonalston** Notts
235 c4 **Gonfirth** Shet
60 F5 **Good Easter** Essex
91 H3 **Gooderstone** Norfk
23 J5 **Goodleigh** Devon
125 K2 **Goodmanham** E R Yk
45 J3 **Goodmayes** Gt Lon
34 D3 **Goodnestone** Kent
35 H4 **Goodnestone** Kent
54 E4 **Goodrich** Herefs
54 E4 **Goodrich Castle** Herefs
7 K4 **Goodrington** Torbay
122 B5 **Goodshaw Fold** Lancs
64 C6 **Goodwick** Pembks
29 G3 **Goodworth Clatford** Hants
125 H5 **Goole** E R Yk
71 H4 **Goom's Hill** Worcs
3 J2 **Goonbell** Cnwll
3 K1 **Goonhavern** Cnwll
3 J2 **Goonvrea** Cnwll
206 E8 **Goosecruives** Abers
11 G6 **Gooseford** Devon
62 D3 **Goose Green** Essex
62 D3 **Goose Green** Essex
38 F5 **Goose Green** S Glos
41 G3 **Goosey** Oxon
121 H3 **Goosnargh** Lancs
113 H7 **Goostrey** Ches
167 K2 **Gordon** Border
166 D4 **Gordon Arms Hotel** Border
216 B3 **Gordonstown** Abers
216 D6 **Gordonstown** Abers
177 K6 **Gorebridge** Mdloth
90 B2 **Gorefield** Cambs
40 C8 **Gores** Wilts
236 e7 **Corey** Jersey
41 L4 **Goring** Oxon
18 F5 **Goring-by-Sea** W Susx
93 L3 **Gorleston on Sea** Norfk

216 E3 **Gorrachie** Abers
4 F7 **Gorran** Cnwll
4 F7 **Gorran Haven** Cnwll
111 G6 **Gorsedd** Flints
40 D3 **Gorse Hill** Swindn
51 H5 **Gorseinon** Swans
66 C4 **Gorsgoch** Cerdgn
51 H3 **Gorslas** Carmth
55 G3 **Gorsley** Gloucs
54 F3 **Gorsley Common** Herefs
212 B2 **Gorstan** Highld
98 A1 **Gorstella** Ches
100 C6 **Gorsty Hill** Staffs
181 L2 **Gorten** Ag & B
202 E2 **Gorthleck** Highld
113 K3 **Gorton** Manch
78 D4 **Gosbeck** Suffk
103 L6 **Gosberton** Lincs
61 J3 **Gosfield** Essex
136 E6 **Gosforth** Cumb
151 G2 **Gosforth** N u Ty
84 F5 **Gospel End** Staffs
17 H3 **Gosport** Hants
55 H7 **Gossington** Gloucs
101 K6 **Gotham** Notts
55 L3 **Gotherington** Gloucs
25 K5 **Gotton** Somset
33 J5 **Goudhurst** Kent
118 C5 **Goulceby** Lincs
216 E6 **Gourdas** Abers
186 F2 **Gourdie** C Dund
197 K3 **Gourdon** Abers
173 L3 **Gourock** Inver
174 F5 **Govan** C Glas
7 H6 **Goveton** Devon
124 F6 **Gowdall** E R Yk
212 D3 **Gower** Highld
51 G7 **Gower** Swans
51 H6 **Gowerton** Swans
176 E1 **Gowkhall** Fife
126 F2 **Goxhill** E R Yk
126 D6 **Goxhill** N Linc
232 f3 **Grabhair** W Isls
18 C3 **Graffham** W Susx
75 H2 **Grafham** Cambs
31 G3 **Grafham** Surrey
132 F6 **Grafton** N York
56 F7 **Grafton** Oxon
98 B8 **Grafton** Shrops
71 H6 **Grafton** Worcs
71 G4 **Grafton Flyford** Worcs
73 L5 **Grafton Regis** Nhants
88 D7 **Grafton Underwood** Nhants
34 D3 **Grafty Green** Kent
109 M6 **Graig** Conwy
97 J2 **Graig-fechan** Denbgs
46 E5 **Grain** Medway
118 C2 **Grainsby** Lincs
118 E3 **Grainthorpe** Lincs
4 E6 **Grampound** Cnwll
4 E5 **Grampound Road** Cnwll
233 c6 **Gramsdal** W Isls
233 c6 **Gramsdale** W Isls
58 C3 **Granborough** Bucks
102 C5 **Granby** Notts
72 F2 **Grandborough** Warwks
236 d7 **Grand Chemins** Jersey
236 c2 **Grandes Rocques** Guern
101 H7 **Grand Prix Collection** Donington Leics
194 E5 **Grandtully** P & K
137 H4 **Grange** Cumb
46 D6 **Grange** Medway
186 D3 **Grange** P & K

215 K4 **Grange Crossroads** Moray
214 C3 **Grange Hall** Moray
165 J2 **Grangehall** S Lans
45 H2 **Grange Hill** Essex
100 E2 **Grangemill** Derbys
123 J7 **Grange Moor** Kirk
176 C3 **Grangemouth** Falk
186 D4 **Grange of Lindores** Fife
129 J4 **Grange-over-Sands** Cumb
176 D3 **Grangepans** Falk
142 C3 **Grangetown** R & Cl
151 K4 **Grangetown** Sundld
151 G4 **Grange Villa** Dur
135 H7 **Gransmoor** E R Yk
64 C7 **Granston** Pembks
76 B4 **Grantchester** Cambs
102 E5 **Grantham** Lincs
177 H3 **Granton** C Edin
214 C8 **Grantown-on-Spey** Highld
179 G5 **Grantshouse** Border
117 H1 **Grasby** Lincs
137 K5 **Grasmere** Cumb
113 L1 **Grasscroft** Oldham
111 L4 **Grassendale** Lpool
131 J6 **Grassington** N York
115 H7 **Grassmoor** Derbys
116 C7 **Grassthorpe** Notts
28 F3 **Grateley** Hants
75 J2 **Graveley** Cambs
59 L3 **Graveley** Herts
34 E3 **Graveney** Kent
46 A5 **Gravesend** Kent
232 f3 **Gravir** W Isls
116 F3 **Grayingham** Lincs
138 E7 **Grayrigg** Cumb
45 L4 **Grays** Thurr
30 E4 **Grayshott** Hants
30 E4 **Grayswood** Surrey
115 H3 **Greasbrough** Rothm
111 H4 **Greasby** Wirral
101 J3 **Greasley** Notts
76 B5 **Great Abington** Cambs
88 D7 **Great Addington** Nhants
71 K3 **Great Alne** Warwks
111 K1 **Great Altcar** Lancs
60 B5 **Great Amwell** Herts
138 F5 **Great Asby** Cumb
78 B2 **Great Ashfield** Suffk
142 C5 **Great Ayton** N York
61 H6 **Great Baddow** Essex
39 J4 **Great Badminton** S Glos
61 G2 **Great Bardfield** Essex
75 G4 **Great Barford** Beds
85 J4 **Great Barr** Sandw
56 E5 **Great Barrington** Gloucs
112 C7 **Great Barrow** Ches
77 K2 **Great Barton** Suffk
134 B4 **Great Barugh** N York
158 C6 **Great Bavington** Nthumb
78 F5 **Great Bealings** Suffk
40 F7 **Great Bedwyn** Wilts
62 D4 **Great Bentley** Essex
74 B3 **Great Billing** Nhants
105 J6 **Great Bircham** Norfk
78 D4 **Great Blakenham** Suffk
138 C2 **Great Blencow** Cumb
98 F7 **Great Bolas** Wrekin
31 J1 **Great Bookham** Surrey
2 D4 **Great Bosullow** Cnwll
72 F5 **Great Bourton** Oxon
87 L5 **Great Bowden** Leics

76 F4 **Great Bradley** Suffk
61 K5 **Great Braxted** Essex
78 C4 **Great Bricett** Suffk
58 E3 **Great Brickhill** Bucks
99 K6 **Great Bridgeford** Staffs
73 J2 **Great Brington** Nhants
62 C3 **Great Bromley** Essex
136 E2 **Great Broughton** Cumb
142 C6 **Great Broughton** N York
112 F6 **Great Budworth** Ches
141 H4 **Great Burdon** Darltn
46 B2 **Great Burstead** Essex
142 B6 **Great Busby** N York
118 E4 **Great Carlton** Lincs
88 E2 **Great Casterton** Rutlnd
39 K7 **Great Chalfield** Wilts
34 C6 **Great Chart** Kent
84 E1 **Great Chatwell** Staffs
76 D6 **Great Chesterford** Essex
27 M1 **Great Cheverell** Wilts
76 B6 **Great Chishill** Cambs
62 E5 **Great Clacton** Essex
136 E2 **Great Clifton** Cumb
126 F8 **Great Coates** NE Lin
71 G6 **Great Comberton** Worcs
148 E4 **Great Corby** Cumb
77 K6 **Great Cornard** Suffk
126 F3 **Great Cowden** E R Yk
40 F2 **Great Coxwell** Oxon
88 B7 **Great Cransley** Nhants
91 J3 **Great Cressingham** Norfk
137 J3 **Great Crosthwaite** Cumb
100 D5 **Great Cubley** Derbys
87 L2 **Great Dalby** Leics
74 C2 **Great Doddington** Nhants
91 K1 **Great Dunham** Norfk
61 G4 **Great Dunmow** Essex
28 C4 **Great Durnford** Wilts
60 F3 **Great Easton** Essex
88 B5 **Great Easton** Leics
120 F3 **Great Eccleston** Lancs
92 B4 **Great Ellingham** Norfk
27 H2 **Great Elm** Somset
7 H2 **Great Englebourne** Devon
73 H3 **Great Everdon** Nhants
75 L4 **Great Eversden** Cambs
78 B3 **Great Finborough** Suffk
88 F2 **Greatford** Lincs
91 K2 **Great Fransham** Norfk
59 G5 **Great Gaddesden** Herts
100 B4 **Greatgate** Staffs
89 G6 **Great Gidding** Cambs
134 C8 **Great Givendale** E R Yk
79 H3 **Great Glemham** Suffk
87 J4 **Great Glen** Leics
102 E5 **Great Gonerby** Lincs
75 J4 **Great Gransden** Cambs
75 K5 **Great Green** Cambs
77 K4 **Great Green** Suffk
134 B4 **Great Habton** N York
103 J4 **Great Hale** Lincs

60 E4 **Great Hallingbury** Essex
30 C5 **Greatham** Hants
141 L2 **Greatham** Hartpl
18 E3 **Greatham** W Susx
58 D7 **Great Hampden** Bucks
74 C1 **Great Harrowden** Nhants
121 L4 **Great Harwood** Lancs
57 M7 **Great Haseley** Oxon
126 F3 **Great Hatfield** E R Yk
99 M7 **Great Haywood** Staffs
124 E6 **Great Heck** N York
77 K6 **Great Henny** Essex
39 K8 **Great Hinton** Wilts
91 L5 **Great Hockham** Norfk
62 E4 **Great Holland** Essex
62 B2 **Great Horkesley** Essex
60 C3 **Great Hormead** Herts
123 H4 **Great Horton** Brad
58 C2 **Great Horwood** Bucks
115 H1 **Great Houghton** Barns
73 L3 **Great Houghton** Nhants
114 D6 **Great Hucklow** Derbys
135 H7 **Great Kelk** E R Yk
58 D6 **Great Kimble** Bucks
42 E2 **Great Kingshill** Bucks
137 J6 **Great Langdale** Cumb
141 H7 **Great Langton** N York
61 H4 **Great Leighs** Essex
126 E8 **Great Limber** Lincs
74 C6 **Great Linford** M Keyn
77 K1 **Great Livermere** Suffk
114 D6 **Great Longstone** Derbys
151 H5 **Great Lumley** Dur
70 D5 **Great Malvern** Worcs
77 J7 **Great Maplestead** Essex
120 D4 **Great Marton** Bpool
105 J7 **Great Massingham** Norfk
57 L7 **Great Milton** Oxon
58 E7 **Great Missenden** Bucks
121 K3 **Great Mitton** Lancs
35 K4 **Great Mongeham** Kent
92 E5 **Great Moulton** Norfk
139 H4 **Great Musgrave** Cumb
98 B8 **Great Ness** Shrops
54 B6 **Great Oak** Mons
62 E3 **Great Oakley** Essex
88 C6 **Great Oakley** Nhants
59 J3 **Great Offley** Herts
139 G4 **Great Ormside** Cumb
148 B4 **Great Orton** Cumb
133 L6 **Great Ouseburn** N York
87 K6 **Great Oxendon** Nhants
61 G6 **Great Oxney Green** Essex
75 H2 **Great Paxton** Cambs
120 E4 **Great Plumpton** Lancs
93 G2 **Great Plumstead** Norfk
102 F6 **Great Ponton** Lincs
124 B5 **Great Preston** Leeds
89 J7 **Great Raveley** Cambs

56 D5 **Great Rissington** Gloucs
56 F2 **Great Rollright** Oxon
106 A6 **Great Ryburgh** Norfk
168 F6 **Great Ryle** Nthumb
83 J3 **Great Ryton** Shrops
61 H3 **Great Saling** Essex
148 F7 **Great Salkeld** Cumb
76 F7 **Great Sampford** Essex
111 K7 **Great Saughall** Ches
41 G5 **Great Shefford** W Berk
76 C4 **Great Shelford** Cambs
141 H6 **Great Smeaton** N York
105 M5 **Great Snoring** Norfk
39 L4 **Great Somerford** Wilts
99 G6 **Great Soudley** Shrops
141 H3 **Great Stainton** Darltn
46 E2 **Great Stambridge** Essex
75 G2 **Great Staughton** Cambs
118 F8 **Great Steeping** Lincs
38 F4 **Great Stoke** S Glos
21 L2 **Greatstone-on-Sea** Kent
138 D3 **Great Strickland** Cumb
89 J8 **Great Stukeley** Cambs
117 K6 **Great Sturton** Lincs
158 B6 **Great Swinburne** Nthumb
57 H3 **Great Tew** Oxon
61 L3 **Great Tey** Essex
23 H7 **Great Torrington** Devon
158 C3 **Great Tosson** Nthumb
61 K5 **Great Totham** Essex
61 L5 **Great Totham** Essex
129 G5 **Great Urswick** Cumb
46 F3 **Great Wakering** Essex
77 K5 **Great Waldingfield** Suffk
105 M5 **Great Walsingham** Norfk
61 H5 **Great Waltham** Essex
45 L2 **Great Warley** Essex
71 H7 **Great Washbourne** Gloucs
11 G7 **Great Weeke** Devon
88 D5 **Great Weldon** Nhants
78 C6 **Great Wenham** Suffk
158 C7 **Great Whittington** Nthumb
62 A5 **Great Wigborough** Essex
76 D3 **Great Wilbraham** Cambs
28 B4 **Great Wishford** Wilts
55 K5 **Great Witcombe** Gloucs
70 D2 **Great Witley** Worcs
72 B7 **Great Wolford** Warwks
73 G6 **Greatworth** Nhants
77 G5 **Great Wratting** Suffk
59 K3 **Great Wymondley** Herts
85 H3 **Great Wyrley** Staffs
93 L3 **Great Yarmouth** Norfk
77 H6 **Great Yeldham** Essex
176 C6 **Greenburn** W Loth
60 B2 **Green End** Herts
60 B4 **Green End** Herts
173 M1 **Greenfield** Ag & B
74 F7 **Greenfield** Beds

111 H6 **Greenfield** Flints
201 J5 **Greenfield** Highld
113 M2 **Greenfield** Oldham
43 J4 **Greenford** Gt Lon
175 K4 **Greengairs** N Lans
123 J3 **Greengates** Brad
120 E4 **Greenhalgh** Lancs
25 G7 **Greenham** Somset
133 G7 **Green Hammerton** N York
157 K5 **Greenhaugh** Nthumb
149 H3 **Greenhead** Nthumb
85 H2 **Green Heath** Staffs
155 J6 **Greenhill** D & G
175 L3 **Greenhill** Falk
47 K6 **Greenhill** Kent
165 H3 **Greenhill** S Lans
45 L5 **Greenhithe** Kent
164 B3 **Greenholm** E Ayrs
167 H5 **Greenhouse** Border
131 L6 **Greenhow Hill** N York
231 J3 **Greenland** Highld
115 H4 **Greenland** Sheff
167 L1 **Greenlaw** Border
155 H6 **Greenlea** D & G
185 H6 **Greenloaning** P & K
122 B7 **Greenmount** Bury
174 B3 **Greenock** Inver
129 G3 **Greenodd** Cumb
26 E2 **Green Ore** Somset
138 C6 **Green Quarter** Cumb
165 K2 **Greenshields** S Lans
150 E3 **Greenside** Gatesd
123 H7 **Greenside** Kirk
73 J4 **Greens Norton** Nhants
62 B3 **Greenstead** Essex
61 K3 **Greenstead Green** Essex
59 K7 **Green Street** Herts
60 D4 **Green Street** Herts
45 L6 **Green Street Green** Kent
60 C4 **Green Tye** Herts
25 L6 **Greenway** Somset
45 G4 **Greenwich** Gt Lon
56 B3 **Greet** Gloucs
69 L1 **Greete** Shrops
118 D7 **Greetham** Lincs
88 D2 **Greetham** Rutlnd
123 G6 **Greetland** Calder
26 B4 **Greinton** Somset
237 b6 **Grenaby** IoM
74 C3 **Grendon** Nhants
86 C4 **Grendon** Warwks
58 B4 **Grendon Underwood** Bucks
115 G3 **Grenoside** Sheff
232 e4 **Greosabhagh** W Isls
97 M2 **Gresford** Wrexhm
106 E5 **Gresham** Norfk
208 E4 **Greshornish House Hotel** Highld
91 L1 **Gressenhall** Norfk
91 L1 **Gressenhall Green** Norfk
130 B5 **Gressingham** Lancs
140 D5 **Greta Bridge** Dur
148 B2 **Gretna** D & G
148 B2 **Gretna Green** D & G
56 A2 **Gretton** Gloucs
88 C5 **Gretton** Nhants
83 K4 **Gretton** Shrops
132 C4 **Grewelthorpe** N York
155 J4 **Greyrigg** D & G
42 M2 **Greys Green** Oxon
136 E2 **Greysouthen** Cumb
138 C2 **Greystoke** Cumb
196 E7 **Greystone** Angus
30 B2 **Greywell** Hants
86 D5 **Griff** Warwks
53 L7 **Griffithstown** Torfn

121 J7 **Grimeford Village** Lancs
115 G4 **Grimesthorpe** Sheff
124 C8 **Grimethorpe** Barns
70 E3 **Grimley** Worcs
163 H7 **Grimmet** S Ayrs
118 E4 **Grimoldby** Lincs
98 A7 **Grimpo** Shrops
121 H4 **Grimsargh** Lancs
127 G7 **Grimsby** NE Lin
73 J4 **Grimscote** Nhants
9 H4 **Grimscott** Cnwll
232 f3 **Grimshader** W Isls
103 H7 **Grimsthorpe** Lincs
102 B7 **Grimston** Leics
105 L7 **Grimston** Norfk
14 C4 **Grimston** Dorset
77 L2 **Grimstone End** Suffk
135 H5 **Grindale** E R Yk
114 E6 **Grindleford** Derbys
121 L2 **Grindleton** Lancs
98 D4 **Grindley Brook** Shrops
114 D6 **Grindlow** Derbys
100 B2 **Grindon** Staffs
151 J4 **Grindon** Sundld
116 C4 **Gringley on the Hill** Notts
148 C4 **Grinsdale** Cumb
98 D7 **Grinshill** Shrops
140 D7 **Grinton** N York
232 f3 **Griomaisiader** W Isls
233 c6 **Griomsaigh** W Isls
188 F4 **Grishipoll** Ag & B
135 H3 **Gristhorpe** N York
91 L4 **Griston** Norfk
234 d6 **Gritley** Ork
40 B4 **Grittenham** Wilts
39 K4 **Grittleton** Wilts
128 F3 **Grizebeck** Cumb
137 K7 **Grizedale** Cumb
87 G3 **Groby** Leics
110 D8 **Groes** Conwy
37 G4 **Groes-faen** Rhondd
37 H3 **Groes-Wen** Caerph
233 b7 **Grogarry** W Isls
161 K1 **Grogport** Ag & B
233 b7 **Groigearraidh** W Isls
110 F5 **Gronant** Flints
32 F5 **Groombridge** E Susx
232 e4 **Grosebay** W Isls
54 B3 **Grosmont** Mons
143 H6 **Grosmont** N York
77 L6 **Groton** Suffk
236 e7 **Grouville** Jersey
116 C5 **Grove** Notts
41 H3 **Grove** Oxon
33 K3 **Grove Green** Kent
45 H5 **Grove Park** Gt Lon
51 H5 **Grovesend** Swans
219 L4 **Gruinard** Highld
170 F5 **Gruinart** Ag & B
208 F8 **Grula** Highld
190 B7 **Gruline** Ag & B
78 F4 **Grundisburgh** Suffk
235 c5 **Gruting** Shet
192 B7 **Gualachulain** Highld
187 G4 **Guardbridge** Fife
70 E5 **Guarlford** Worcs
194 F6 **Guay** P & K
236 c3 **Guernsey Airport** Guern
21 G3 **Guestling Green** E Susx
21 G3 **Guestling Thorn** E Susx
106 E6 **Guestwick** Norfk
121 K5 **Guide** Bl w D
159 G5 **Guide Post** Nthumb
75 K5 **Guilden Morden** Cambs
112 C7 **Guilden Sutton** Ches

31 G2 **Guildford** Surrey
186 B2 **Guildtown** P & K
87 J8 **Guilsborough** Nhants
82 E2 **Guilsfield** Powys
163 J7 **Guiltreehill** S Ayrs
23 J4 **Guineaford** Devon
142 D4 **Guisborough** R & Cl
123 J3 **Guiseley** Leeds
106 B7 **Guist** Norfk
56 C3 **Guiting Power** Gloucs
178 B2 **Gullane** E Loth
2 E5 **Gulval** Cnwll
6 C2 **Gulworthy** Devon
49 J7 **Gumfreston** Pembks
87 K5 **Gumley** Leics
102 E7 **Gunby** Lincs
118 F7 **Gunby** Lincs
29 L5 **Gundleton** Hants
20 C3 **Gun Hill** E Susx
23 K5 **Gunn** Devon
139 L7 **Gunnerside** N York
158 A7 **Gunnerton** Nthumb
125 K7 **Gunness** N Linc
6 C2 **Gunnislake** Cnwll
235 d6 **Gunnista** Shet
116 D3 **Gunthorpe** N Linc
106 B5 **Gunthorpe** Norfk
102 B4 **Gunthorpe** Notts
3 H6 **Gunwalloe** Cnwll
16 F4 **Gurnard** IoW
26 F2 **Gurney Slade** Somset
52 B6 **Gurnos** Powys
15 J1 **Gussage All Saints**
Dorset
27 L8 **Gussage St Andrew**
Dorset
15 J1 **Gussage St Michael**
Dorset
35 J5 **Guston** Kent
235 d2 **Gutcher** Shet
196 F6 **Guthrie** Angus
90 B3 **Guyhirn** Cambs
158 F2 **Guyzance** Nthumb
110 F5 **Gwaenysgor** Flints
108 E6 **Gwalchmai** IoA
51 K3 **Gwaun-Cae-Gurwen**
Carmth
3 J6 **Gweek** Cnwll
68 B6 **Gwenddwr** Powys
3 J4 **Gwennap** Cnwll
111 H7 **Gwernaffield** Flints
54 B7 **Gwernesney** Mons
66 C7 **Gwernogle** Carmth
111 H8 **Gwernymynydd**
Flints
110 F5 **Gwespyr** Flints
3 G4 **Gwinear** Cnwll
3 G3 **Gwithian** Cnwll
97 G3 **Gwyddelwern**
Denbgs
66 B7 **Gwyddgrug** Carmth
96 D1 **Gwytherin** Conwy

H

83 H3 **Habberley** Shrops
84 E7 **Habberley** Worcs
122 B4 **Habergham** Lancs
119 G7 **Habertoft** Lincs
126 E7 **Habrough** NE Lin
103 J7 **Hacconby** Lincs
103 G5 **Haceby** Lincs
79 G3 **Hacheston** Suffk
44 F6 **Hackbridge** Gt Lon
115 H5 **Hackenthorpe** Sheff
92 C3 **Hackford** Norfk
132 C2 **Hackforth** N York
234 c5 **Hackland** Ork
74 B4 **Hackleton** Nhants
35 J4 **Hacklinge** Kent

134 F2 **Hackness** N York
45 J3 **Hackney** Gt Lon
117 G5 **Hackthorn** Lincs
138 D3 **Hackthorpe** Cumb
168 B3 **Hadden** Border
58 C6 **Haddenham** Bucks
90 C7 **Haddenham** Cambs
178 B4 **Haddington** E Loth
116 E8 **Haddington** Lincs
93 J4 **Haddiscoe** Norfk
216 F6 **Haddo** Abers
89 G5 **Haddon** Cambs
114 A3 **Hadfield** Derbys
60 C4 **Hadham Ford** Herts
46 D3 **Hadleigh** Essex
78 B6 **Hadleigh** Suffk
70 F2 **Hadley** Worcs
100 C7 **Hadley End** Staffs
44 E1 **Hadley Wood** Gt Lon
33 H3 **Hadlow** Kent
20 B2 **Hadlow Down**
E Susx
98 D7 **Hadnall** Shrops
76 D5 **Hadstock** Essex
71 G3 **Hadzor** Worcs
235 c5 **Haggersta** Shet
168 F2 **Haggerston** Nthumb
175 K3 **Haggs** Falk
69 L6 **Hagley** Herefs
85 G7 **Hagley** Worcs
118 D7 **Hagworthingham**
Lincs
136 E5 **Haile** Cumb
57 G5 **Hailey** Oxon
20 C4 **Hailsham** E Susx
75 H3 **Hail Weston** Cambs
45 J2 **Hainault** Gt Lon
106 F8 **Hainford** Norfk
117 K5 **Hainton** Lincs
135 H6 **Haisthorpe** E R Yk
48 F6 **Hakin** Pembks
102 A3 **Halam** Notts
176 F1 **Halbeath** Fife
24 F8 **Halberton** Devon
231 J4 **Halcro** Highld
129 K4 **Hale** Cumb
112 C5 **Hale** Halton
28 D7 **Hale** Hants
30 D2 **Hale** Surrey
113 H4 **Hale** Traffd
20 B3 **Hale Green** E Susx
93 H4 **Hales** Norfk
99 G5 **Hales** Staffs
85 G6 **Halesowen** Dudley
34 F3 **Hales Place** Kent
33 H4 **Hale Street** Kent
93 H7 **Halesworth** Suffk
112 C4 **Halewood** Knows
7 J2 **Halford** Devon
72 C5 **Halford** Warwks
84 E5 **Halfpenny Green**
Staffs
83 J7 **Halfway House**
Shrops
46 F5 **Halfway Houses** Kent
123 G5 **Halifax** Calder
231 G4 **Halkirk** Highld
111 H7 **Halkyn** Flints
174 D7 **Hall** E Rens
20 A3 **Halland** E Susx
87 L4 **Hallaton** Leics
38 F8 **Hallatrow** BaNES
149 G3 **Hallbankgate** Cumb
137 H7 **Hall Dunnerdale**
Cumb
38 D4 **Hallen** S Glos
151 H6 **Hallgarth** Dur
176 B3 **Hall Glen** Falk
85 K7 **Hall Green** Birm
208 D3 **Hallin** Highld
46 B7 **Halling** Medway
118 D4 **Hallington** Lincs

158 C6 **Hallington** Nthumb
121 K7 **Halliwell** Bolton
102 B3 **Halloughton** Notts
70 E3 **Hallow** Worcs
7 J7 **Hallsands** Devon
59 L3 **Hall's Green** Herts
166 B2 **Hallyne** Border
55 G7 **Halmore** Gloucs
18 B4 **Halnaker** W Susx
120 E7 **Halsall** Lancs
73 H6 **Halse** Nhants
25 H5 **Halse** Somset
2 E4 **Halsetown** Cnwll
127 G5 **Halsham** E R Yk
61 K2 **Halstead** Essex
45 J7 **Halstead** Kent
87 L3 **Halstead** Leics
14 A2 **Halstock** Dorset
25 H4 **Halsway** Somset
118 C8 **Haltham** Lincs
58 E6 **Halton** Bucks
129 K6 **Halton** Lancs
123 L4 **Halton** Leeds
150 C2 **Halton** Nthumb
97 L4 **Halton** Wrexhm
131 K8 **Halton East** N York
131 G4 **Halton Gill** N York
118 F7 **Halton Holegate**
Lincs
149 H4 **Halton Lea Gate**
Nthumb
150 C2 **Halton Shields**
Nthumb
130 B7 **Halton West** N York
149 J3 **Haltwhistle** Nthumb
93 J3 **Halvergate** Norfk
7 H5 **Halwell** Devon
10 C5 **Halwill** Devon
10 C5 **Halwill Junction**
Devon
13 G3 **Ham** Devon
55 G7 **Ham** Gloucs
44 D5 **Ham** Gt Lon
35 J4 **Ham** Kent
25 L6 **Ham** Somset
41 G7 **Ham** Wilts
42 C3 **Hambleden** Bucks
29 M7 **Hambledon** Hants
30 F4 **Hambledon** Surrey
16 F2 **Hamble-le-Rice**
Hants
120 E3 **Hambleton** Lancs
124 E4 **Hambleton** N York
26 B6 **Hambridge** Somset
17 L2 **Hambrook** W Susx
118 D7 **Hameringham** Lincs
89 G7 **Hamerton** Cambs
71 H2 **Ham Green** Worcs
175 J7 **Hamilton** S Lans
14 B2 **Hamlet** Dorset
44 E4 **Hammersmith** Gt Lon
85 J3 **Hammerwich** Staffs
27 J8 **Hammoon** Dorset
235 c6 **Hamnavoe** Shet
20 C5 **Hampden Park**
E Susx
56 C5 **Hampnett** Gloucs
124 D7 **Hampole** Donc
15 K3 **Hampreston** Dorset
44 E3 **Hampstead** Gt Lon
41 K5 **Hampstead Norrey's**
W Berk
132 C2 **Hampsthwaite**
N York
89 H5 **Hampton** C Pete
43 J6 **Hampton** Gt Lon
47 K6 **Hampton** Kent
84 D6 **Hampton** Shrops
40 D3 **Hampton** Swindn
71 H5 **Hampton** Worcs
69 L6 **Hampton Bishop**
Herefs

44 D6 **Hampton Court**
Palace & Gardens
Gt Lon
98 D3 **Hampton Heath** Ches
86 B7 **Hampton in Arden**
Solhll
70 F2 **Hampton Lovett**
Worcs
72 B3 **Hampton Lucy**
Warwks
72 C2 **Hampton Magna**
Warwks
57 J5 **Hampton Poyle** Oxon
44 D6 **Hampton Wick** Gt Lon
28 E7 **Hamptworth** Wilts
19 L3 **Hamsey** E Susx
100 C8 **Hamstall Ridware**
Staffs
41 H7 **Hamstead Marshall**
W Berk
140 E2 **Hamsterley** Dur
150 E4 **Hamsterley** Dur
34 D7 **Hamstreet** Kent
26 D4 **Ham Street** Somset
15 J4 **Hamworthy** Poole
100 D6 **Hanbury** Staffs
71 G2 **Hanbury** Worcs
99 J4 **Hanchurch** Staffs
12 D4 **Hand and Pen** Devon
112 B7 **Handbridge** Ches
31 L5 **Handcross** W Susx
113 J5 **Handforth** Ches
98 C2 **Handley** Ches
101 G1 **Handley** Derbys
85 J5 **Handsworth** Birm
115 H4 **Handsworth** Sheff
123 K6 **Hanging Heaton** Kirk
87 L8 **Hanging Houghton**
Nhants
28 B4 **Hanging Langford**
Wilts
19 H4 **Hangleton** Br & H
38 F6 **Hanham** S Glos
98 C4 **Hankelow** Ches
39 L3 **Hankerton** Wilts
99 K3 **Hanley** C Stke
99 K3 **Hanley** C Stke
70 E6 **Hanley Castle** Worcs
70 B2 **Hanley Child** Worcs
70 E6 **Hanley Swan** Worcs
70 C2 **Hanley William** Worcs
131 G7 **Hanlith** N York
98 C4 **Hanmer** Wrexhm
23 J5 **Hannaford** Devon
29 K1 **Hannington** Hants
74 B1 **Hannington** Nhants
40 D2 **Hannington** Swindn
40 D2 **Hannington Wick**
Swindn
74 B5 **Hanslope** M Keyn
103 H7 **Hanthorpe** Lincs
44 D4 **Hanwell** Gt Lon
72 E5 **Hanwell** Oxon
83 J2 **Hanwood** Shrops
43 J6 **Hanworth** Gt Lon
106 E5 **Hanworth** Norfk
165 G3 **Happendon** S Lans
107 H6 **Happisburgh** Norfk
107 H6 **Happisburgh**
Common Norfk
112 C6 **Hapsford** Ches
122 B4 **Hapton** Lancs
92 E4 **Hapton** Norfk
7 H4 **Harberton** Devon
7 H5 **Harbertonford** Devon
34 F3 **Harbledown** Kent
85 H6 **Harborne** Birm
86 F7 **Harborough Magna**
Warwks
158 B2 **Harbottle** Nthumb
7 G4 **Harbourneford**
Devon

72 D3 **Harbury** Warwks
102 C6 **Harby** Leics
116 E7 **Harby** Notts
11 K8 **Harcombe** Devon
12 F4 **Harcombe** Devon
13 J4 **Harcombe Bottom** Devon
123 G3 **Harden** Brad
85 H4 **Harden** Wsall
206 E5 **Hardgate** Abers
146 E2 **Hardgate** D & G
174 F4 **Hardgate** W Duns
18 E3 **Hardham** W Susx
92 C3 **Hardingham** Norfk
73 L3 **Hardingstone** Nhants
27 H2 **Hardington** Somset
13 M1 **Hardington Mandeville** Somset
13 M1 **Hardington Marsh** Somset
26 D8 **Hardington Moor** Somset
22 C7 **Hardisworthy** Devon
16 E2 **Hardley** Hants
93 H4 **Hardley Street** Norfk
131 G2 **Hardraw** N York
115 H8 **Hardstoft** Derbys
17 H3 **Hardway** Hants
27 G5 **Hardway** Somset
58 D4 **Hardwick** Bucks
75 L3 **Hardwick** Cambs
74 B1 **Hardwick** Nhants
92 F5 **Hardwick** Norfk
57 G6 **Hardwick** Oxon
57 L3 **Hardwick** Oxon
55 H5 **Hardwicke** Gloucs
55 K3 **Hardwicke** Gloucs
61 M4 **Hardy's Green** Essex
118 D7 **Hareby** Lincs
123 G4 **Hare Croft** Brad
43 H3 **Harefield** Gt Lon
62 D3 **Hare Green** Essex
42 D5 **Hare Hatch** Wokham
100 D5 **Harehill** Derbys
123 L4 **Harehills** Leeds
167 H5 **Harelaw** Border
156 D6 **Harelaw** D & G
55 J6 **Harescombe** Gloucs
55 J6 **Haresfield** Gloucs
29 J5 **Harestock** Hants
60 C6 **Hare Street** Essex
60 C3 **Hare Street** Herts
123 L2 **Harewood** Leeds
54 D3 **Harewood End** Herefs
6 F4 **Harford** Devon
98 C1 **Hargrave** Ches
74 F1 **Hargrave** Nhants
77 H3 **Hargrave Green** Suffk
78 E7 **Harkstead** Suffk
86 B2 **Harlaston** Staffs
102 E6 **Harlaxton** Lincs
95 K6 **Harlech** Gwynd
83 K1 **Harlescott** Shrops
44 E4 **Harlesden** Gt Lon
115 J6 **Harlesthorpe** Derbys
7 J6 **Harleston** Devon
92 F6 **Harleston** Norfk
78 B3 **Harleston** Suffk
73 K2 **Harlestone** Nhants
122 C4 **Harle Syke** Lancs
115 G2 **Harley** Rothm
83 L3 **Harley** Shrops
59 G2 **Harlington** Beds
115 J2 **Harlington** Donc
43 H5 **Harlington** Gt Lon
208 D6 **Harlosh** Highld
60 D6 **Harlow** Essex
150 D2 **Harlow Hill** Nthumb
125 H3 **Harlthorpe** E R Yk
76 B4 **Harlton** Cambs
4 D2 **Harlyn** Cnwll

15 J6 **Harman's Cross** Dorset
131 L2 **Harmby** N York
59 L5 **Harmer Green** Herts
98 C7 **Harmer Hill** Shrops
116 F8 **Harmston** Lincs
83 L3 **Harnage** Shrops
56 B7 **Harnhill** Gloucs
45 K2 **Harold Hill** Gt Lon
48 E4 **Haroldston West** Pembks
235 e1 **Haroldswick** Shet
45 K3 **Harold Wood** Gt Lon
133 K3 **Harome** N York
59 J5 **Harpenden** Herts
12 E4 **Harpford** Devon
135 H7 **Harpham** E R Yk
105 J7 **Harpley** Norfk
70 C3 **Harpley** Worcs
73 K3 **Harpole** Nhants
231 G4 **Harpsdale** Highld
116 F4 **Harpswell** Lincs
113 K2 **Harpurhey** Manch
148 D4 **Harraby** Cumb
23 J6 **Harracott** Devon
199 K2 **Harrapool** Highld
185 K2 **Harrietfield** P & K
33 L3 **Harrietsham** Kent
44 F3 **Harringay** Gt Lon
136 D3 **Harrington** Cumb
118 E6 **Harrington** Lincs
87 L7 **Harrington** Nhants
88 D4 **Harringworth** Nhants
132 D8 **Harrogate** N York
74 D3 **Harrold** Beds
44 D3 **Harrow** Gt Lon
6 B2 **Harrowbarrow** Cnwll
77 J4 **Harrow Green** Suffk
44 D3 **Harrow on the Hill** Gt Lon
44 D2 **Harrow Weald** Gt Lon
76 B4 **Harston** Cambs
102 D6 **Harston** Leics
125 J3 **Harswell** E R Yk
151 L7 **Hart** Hartpl
158 D5 **Hartburn** Nthumb
77 J4 **Hartest** Suffk
32 E6 **Hartfield** E Susx
89 J8 **Hartford** Cambs
112 F6 **Hartford** Ches
42 C8 **Hartfordbridge** Hants
61 G4 **Hartford End** Essex
140 F6 **Harthill** N York
27 J7 **Hartgrove** Dorset
98 D2 **Harthill** Ches
176 B5 **Harthill** N Lans
115 J5 **Harthill** Rothm
100 C1 **Hartington** Derbys
22 D6 **Hartland** Devon
22 C6 **Hartland Quay** Devon
70 E1 **Hartlebury** Worcs
151 L7 **Hartlepool** Hartpl
139 H5 **Hartley** Cumb
33 K6 **Hartley** Kent
45 L6 **Hartley** Kent
42 B8 **Hartley Wespall** Hants
30 C1 **Hartley Wintney** Hants
46 D7 **Hartlip** Kent
133 L6 **Harton** N York
151 J2 **Harton** S Tyne
55 J3 **Hartpury** Gloucs
123 H6 **Hartshead** Kirk
99 K4 **Hartshill** C Stke
86 D5 **Hartshill** Warwks
100 F7 **Hartshorne** Derbys
168 E6 **Hartside** Nthumb
73 L4 **Hartwell** Nhants
132 C6 **Hartwith** N York
175 L6 **Hartwood** N Lans

166 F4 **Hartwoodmyres** Border
46 A7 **Harvel** Kent
71 J5 **Harvington** Worcs
84 F8 **Harvington** Worcs
116 B3 **Harwell** Notts
41 J3 **Harwell** Oxon
62 F2 **Harwich** Essex
143 K7 **Harwood Dale** N York
115 L3 **Harworth** Notts
85 G6 **Hasbury** Dudley
31 G4 **Hascombe** Surrey
87 K7 **Haselbech** Nhants
13 L1 **Haselbury Plucknett** Somset
72 B2 **Haseley** Warwks
71 K3 **Haselor** Warwks
55 J3 **Hasfield** Gloucs
120 E8 **Haskayne** Lancs
78 F4 **Hasketon** Suffk
30 E5 **Haslemere** Surrey
122 B6 **Haslingden** Lancs
76 B4 **Haslingfield** Cambs
99 G3 **Haslington** Ches
93 H3 **Hassingham** Norfk
19 J3 **Hassocks** W Susx
114 E6 **Hassop** Derbys
231 K5 **Haster** Highld
34 E2 **Hastingleigh** Kent
21 G4 **Hastings** E Susx
60 E2 **Hastingwood** Essex
58 F6 **Hastoe** Herts
151 J6 **Haswell** Dur
151 J6 **Haswell Plough** Dur
25 L7 **Hatch Beauchamp** Somset
43 J3 **Hatch End** Gt Lon
112 D6 **Hatchmere** Ches
117 K2 **Hatcliffe** NE Lin
125 G8 **Hatfield** Donc
69 L3 **Hatfield** Herefs
59 L6 **Hatfield** Herts
60 E5 **Hatfield Broad Oak** Essex
60 E5 **Hatfield Heath** Essex
61 J5 **Hatfield Peverel** Essex
125 G8 **Hatfield Woodhouse** Donc
41 G2 **Hatford** Oxon
29 G2 **Hatherden** Hants
10 D4 **Hatherleigh** Devon
101 J7 **Hathern** Leics
56 D6 **Hatherop** Gloucs
114 E5 **Hathersage** Derbys
114 E5 **Hathersage Booths** Derbys
99 G3 **Hatherton** Ches
85 G2 **Hatherton** Staffs
75 K4 **Hatley St George** Cambs
6 B4 **Hatt** Cnwll
113 M3 **Hattersley** Tamesd
217 K6 **Hatton** Abers
196 D7 **Hatton** Angus
100 E6 **Hatton** Derbys
43 J5 **Hatton** Gt Lon
117 K6 **Hatton** Lincs
83 J5 **Hatton** Shrops
112 E5 **Hatton** Warrtn
72 B2 **Hatton** Warwks
206 F3 **Hatton of Fintray** Abers
163 L4 **Haugh** E Ayrs
118 D5 **Haugham** Lincs
175 G3 **Haughhead** E Duns
78 B3 **Haughley** Suffk
78 B2 **Haughley Green** Suffk
215 J6 **Haugh of Glass** Moray
146 E2 **Haugh of Urr** D & G
84 D2 **Haughton** Shrops
98 B6 **Haughton** Shrops

99 K7 **Haughton** Staffs
141 H4 **Haughton le Skerne** Darltn
98 E2 **Haughton Moss** Ches
60 B4 **Haultwick** Herts
86 B2 **Haunton** Staffs
76 B4 **Hauxton** Cambs
17 K2 **Havant** Hants
17 G4 **Havenstreet** IoW
124 B7 **Havercroft** Wakefd
48 F4 **Haverfordwest** Pembks
76 F5 **Haverhill** Suffk
128 E4 **Haverigg** Cumb
45 K2 **Havering-atte-Bower** Gt Lon
74 B6 **Haversham** M Keyn
129 H3 **Haverthwaite** Cumb
38 C7 **Havyat** N Som
111 J7 **Hawarden** Flints
61 J4 **Hawbush Green** Essex
65 K5 **Hawen** Cerdgn
131 G2 **Hawes** N York
92 F4 **Hawe's Green** Norfk
70 E3 **Hawford** Worcs
167 G6 **Hawick** Border
13 J3 **Hawkchurch** Devon
77 H4 **Hawkedon** Suffk
27 K2 **Hawkeridge** Wilts
39 H3 **Hawkesbury** S Glos
39 H3 **Hawkesbury Upton** S Glos
33 K6 **Hawkhurst** Kent
35 G6 **Hawkinge** Kent
30 C5 **Hawkley** Hants
24 D5 **Hawkridge** Somset
137 K7 **Hawkshead** Cumb
137 K7 **Hawkshead Hill** Cumb
165 G2 **Hawksland** S Lans
61 G2 **Hawkspur Green** Essex
98 E6 **Hawkstone** Shrops
131 H5 **Hawkswick** N York
123 H3 **Hawksworth** Leeds
102 C4 **Hawksworth** Notts
46 E2 **Hawkwell** Essex
42 E8 **Hawley** Hants
56 B4 **Hawling** Gloucs
133 H2 **Hawnby** N York
122 F3 **Haworth** Brad
77 J3 **Hawstead** Suffk
151 K5 **Hawthorn** Dur
103 K2 **Hawthorn Hill** Lincs
102 C3 **Hawton** Notts
133 J7 **Haxby** York
116 C2 **Haxey** N Linc
112 E3 **Haydock** St Hel
149 L2 **Haydon Bridge** Nthumb
40 C3 **Haydon Wick** Swindn
43 J3 **Hayes** Gt Lon
45 H6 **Hayes** Gt Lon
43 H4 **Hayes End** Gt Lon
182 E3 **Hayfield** Ag & B
114 B4 **Hayfield** Derbys
196 E7 **Hayhillock** Angus
2 F4 **Hayle** Cnwll
85 G6 **Hayley Green** Dudley
17 K3 **Hayling Island** Hants
11 H7 **Hayne** Devon
24 E7 **Hayne** Devon
74 F6 **Haynes (Church End)** Beds
75 G6 **Haynes (Northwood End)** Beds
75 G6 **Haynes (Silver End)** Beds
74 F6 **Haynes (West End)** Beds
68 E6 **Hay-on-Wye** Powys

48 F3	**Hayscastle** Pembks	
48 F3	**Hayscastle Cross** Pembks	
60 C3	**Hay Street** Herts	
147 K6	**Hayton** Cumb	
148 E4	**Hayton** Cumb	
125 J2	**Hayton** E R Yk	
116 B5	**Hayton** Notts	
7 H1	**Haytor Vale** Devon	
9 K3	**Haytown** Devon	
19 J2	**Haywards Heath** W Susx	
124 E7	**Haywood** Donc	
165 G1	**Hazelbank** S Lans	
14 E2	**Hazelbury Bryan** Dorset	
61 K7	**Hazeleigh** Essex	
113 L4	**Hazel Grove** Stockp	
186 E3	**Hazelton Walls** Fife	
101 G4	**Hazelwood** Derbys	
42 E2	**Hazlemere** Bucks	
159 G2	**Hazlerigg** N u Ty	
56 B4	**Hazleton** Gloucs	
105 G5	**Heacham** Norfk	
29 J5	**Headbourne Worthy** Hants	
33 L4	**Headcorn** Kent	
123 K4	**Headingley** Leeds	
57 K6	**Headington** Oxon	
140 F4	**Headlam** Dur	
176 B6	**Headlesscross** N Lans	
71 J2	**Headless Cross** Worcs	
30 D4	**Headley** Hants	
41 K7	**Headley** Hants	
31 K1	**Headley** Surrey	
30 D4	**Headley Down** Hants	
116 C6	**Headon** Notts	
175 J8	**Heads** S Lans	
148 E4	**Heads Nook** Cumb	
101 G3	**Heage** Derbys	
124 D2	**Healaugh** N York	
140 C7	**Healaugh** N York	
113 J4	**Heald Green** Stockp	
25 K7	**Heale** Somset	
26 B6	**Heale** Somset	
132 B4	**Healey** N York	
150 D5	**Healeyfield** Dur	
126 F7	**Healing** NE Lin	
2 E5	**Heamoor** Cnwll	
101 H3	**Heanor** Derbys	
23 H4	**Heanton Punchardon** Devon	
116 E4	**Heapham** Lincs	
24 B5	**Heasley Mill** Devon	
199 K2	**Heast** Highld	
115 J7	**Heath** Derbys	
123 L6	**Heath** Wakefd	
58 F3	**Heath and Reach** Beds	
100 D1	**Heathcote** Derbys	
30 D2	**Heath End** Surrey	
86 E2	**Heather** Leics	
20 C2	**Heathfield** E Susx	
25 J6	**Heathfield** Somset	
71 J1	**Heath Green** Worcs	
155 H6	**Heath Hall** D & G	
85 H2	**Heath Hayes & Wimblebury** Staffs	
84 D2	**Heath Hill** Shrops	
43 H5	**Heathrow Airport** Gt Lon	
84 E5	**Heathton** Shrops	
85 G4	**Heath Town** Wolves	
100 B6	**Heatley** Staffs	
113 G4	**Heatley** Warrtn	
123 H4	**Heaton** Brad	
151 G2	**Heaton** N u Ty	
113 L8	**Heaton** Staffs	
120 E7	**Heaton's Bridge** Lancs	
33 G2	**Heaverham** Kent	
12 B4	**Heavitree** Devon	

151 H3	**Hebburn** S Tyne	
131 J6	**Hebden** N York	
122 E5	**Hebden Bridge** Calder	
60 A4	**Hebing End** Herts	
49 K3	**Hebron** Carmth	
158 F4	**Hebron** Nthumb	
42 B7	**Heckfield** Hants	
92 E7	**Heckfield Green** Suffk	
61 M4	**Heckfordbridge** Essex	
103 J4	**Heckington** Lincs	
123 J5	**Heckmondwike** Kirk	
39 M6	**Heddington** Wilts	
150 E2	**Heddon-on-the-Wall** Nthumb	
93 G5	**Hedenham** Norfk	
29 J8	**Hedge End** Hants	
42 F3	**Hedgerley** Bucks	
25 L5	**Hedging** Somset	
150 D3	**Hedley on the Hill** Nthumb	
85 H2	**Hednesford** Staffs	
126 F5	**Hedon** E R Yk	
42 E3	**Hedsor** Bucks	
235 c5	**Heglibister** Shet	
141 G3	**Heighington** Darltn	
117 G7	**Heighington** Lincs	
70 D1	**Heightington** Worcs	
167 L4	**Heiton** Border	
12 C2	**Hele** Devon	
23 H3	**Hele** Devon	
25 J6	**Hele** Somset	
174 B2	**Helensburgh** Ag & B	
163 J4	**Helenton** S Ayrs	
3 K6	**Helford** Cnwll	
3 K6	**Helford Passage** Cnwll	
105 K7	**Helhoughton** Norfk	
76 F6	**Helions Bumpstead** Essex	
5 G2	**Helland** Cnwll	
9 H6	**Hellescott** Cnwll	
92 E2	**Hellesdon** Norfk	
73 G3	**Hellidon** Nhants	
131 G7	**Hellifield** N York	
20 C4	**Hellingly** E Susx	
158 F3	**Helm** Nthumb	
73 H5	**Helmdon** Nhants	
123 G7	**Helme** Kirk	
78 E3	**Helmingham** Suffk	
227 H5	**Helmsdale** Highld	
122 B6	**Helmshore** Lancs	
133 J3	**Helmsley** N York	
133 G5	**Helperby** N York	
134 E5	**Helperthorpe** N York	
103 J4	**Helpringham** Lincs	
89 G3	**Helpston** C Pete	
112 C6	**Helsby** Ches	
3 H5	**Helston** Cnwll	
8 E8	**Helstone** Cnwll	
138 D3	**Helton** Cumb	
59 H6	**Hemel Hempstead** Herts	
6 E4	**Hemerdon** Devon	
125 G4	**Hemingbrough** N York	
118 C6	**Hemingby** Lincs	
75 K1	**Hemingford Abbots** Cambs	
75 K1	**Hemingford Grey** Cambs	
78 D4	**Hemingstone** Suffk	
101 J6	**Hemington** Leics	
88 F6	**Hemington** Nhants	
27 G2	**Hemington** Somset	
79 G6	**Hemley** Suffk	
142 B4	**Hemlington** Middsb	
92 F5	**Hempnall** Norfk	
92 F5	**Hempnall Green** Norfk	
214 D2	**Hempriggs** Moray	
76 F6	**Hempstead** Essex	

106 D5	**Hempstead** Norfk	
107 J6	**Hempstead** Norfk	
105 L6	**Hempton** Norfk	
57 H2	**Hempton** Oxon	
107 K8	**Hemsby** Norfk	
116 F4	**Hemswell** Lincs	
116 F4	**Hemswell Cliff** Lincs	
124 C7	**Hemsworth** Wakefd	
25 H8	**Hemyock** Devon	
167 L3	**Hendersyde Park** Border	
44 E3	**Hendon** Gt Lon	
151 K4	**Hendon** Sundld	
51 H5	**Hendy** Carmth	
19 G3	**Henfield** W Susx	
37 J2	**Hengoed** Caerph	
68 E4	**Hengoed** Powys	
77 J2	**Hengrave** Suffk	
60 E3	**Henham** Essex	
82 C2	**Heniarth** Powys	
25 L6	**Henlade** Somset	
14 D2	**Henley** Dorset	
26 B5	**Henley** Somset	
78 E4	**Henley** Suffk	
30 E6	**Henley** W Susx	
71 L2	**Henley-in-Arden** Warwks	
42 C4	**Henley-on-Thames** Oxon	
20 E3	**Henley's Down** E Susx	
65 K6	**Henllan** Cerdgn	
110 E7	**Henllan** Denbgs	
37 K3	**Henllys** Torfn	
75 H6	**Henlow** Beds	
11 J8	**Hennock** Devon	
77 K6	**Henny Street** Essex	
109 L6	**Henryd** Conwy	
49 H3	**Henry's Moat (Castell Hendre)** Pembks	
124 F5	**Hensall** N York	
149 K3	**Henshaw** Nthumb	
136 D4	**Hensingham** Cumb	
93 K6	**Henstead** Suffk	
29 J6	**Hensting** Hants	
27 G7	**Henstridge** Somset	
27 G7	**Henstridge Ash** Somset	
58 C7	**Henton** Oxon	
26 C3	**Henton** Somset	
70 E4	**Henwick** Worcs	
5 L2	**Henwood** Cnwll	
36 E4	**Heol-y-Cyw** Brdgnd	
158 C2	**Hepple** Nthumb	
158 F5	**Hepscott** Nthumb	
122 E5	**Heptonstall** Calder	
114 D1	**Hepworth** Kirk	
92 B8	**Hepworth** Suffk	
48 E6	**Herbrandston** Pembks	
69 K6	**Hereford** Herefs	
35 K2	**Hereson** Kent	
218 B7	**Heribusta** Highld	
177 L7	**Heriot** Border	
177 G4	**Hermiston** C Edin	
156 E3	**Hermitage** Border	
14 C2	**Hermitage** Dorset	
41 J5	**Hermitage** W Berk	
65 K7	**Hermon** Carmth	
49 L2	**Hermon** Pembks	
47 K6	**Herne** Kent	
47 K6	**Herne Bay** Kent	
44 F5	**Herne Hill** Gt Lon	
33 H3	**Herne Pound** Kent	
23 J6	**Herner** Devon	
34 E3	**Hernhill** Kent	
5 K4	**Herodsfoot** Cnwll	
152 D5	**Heronsford** S Ayrs	
30 A3	**Herriard** Hants	
93 K4	**Herringfleet** Suffk	
77 G1	**Herringswell** Suffk	
115 J3	**Herringthorpe** Rothm	
151 H4	**Herrington** Sundld	

35 G3	**Hersden** Kent	
43 J7	**Hersham** Surrey	
20 D3	**Herstmonceux** E Susx	
234 c7	**Herston** Ork	
60 B5	**Hertford** Herts	
60 B5	**Hertford Heath** Herts	
60 A5	**Hertingfordbury** Herts	
120 F5	**Hesketh Bank** Lancs	
121 J3	**Hesketh Lane** Lancs	
148 C7	**Hesket Newmarket** Cumb	
151 K7	**Hesleden** Dur	
124 F1	**Heslington** York	
133 H8	**Hessay** York	
5 L4	**Hessenford** Cnwll	
77 L3	**Hessett** Suffk	
126 C5	**Hessle** E R Yk	
124 C6	**Hessle** Wakefd	
129 K6	**Hest Bank** Lancs	
43 J5	**Heston** Gt Lon	
234 b5	**Hestwall** Ork	
111 J5	**Heswall** Wirral	
57 L3	**Hethe** Oxon	
92 D3	**Hethersett** Norfk	
148 E2	**Hethersgill** Cumb	
168 D4	**Hethpool** Nthumb	
151 G7	**Hett** Dur	
131 H7	**Hetton** N York	
151 J5	**Hetton-le-Hole** Sundld	
158 D7	**Heugh** Nthumb	
205 J3	**Heughhead** Abers	
179 H6	**Heugh Head** Border	
93 G8	**Heveningham** Suffk	
32 K4	**Hever** Kent	
129 K3	**Heversham** Cumb	
106 E7	**Hevingham** Norfk	
4 F6	**Hewas Water** Cnwll	
54 E7	**Hewelsfield** Gloucs	
13 K2	**Hewish** Somset	
13 J2	**Hewood** Dorset	
150 B3	**Hexham** Nthumb	
45 K6	**Hextable** Kent	
115 K2	**Hexthorpe** Donc	
59 J2	**Hexton** Herts	
9 K8	**Hexworthy** Cnwll	
6 F2	**Hexworthy** Devon	
61 G7	**Heybridge** Essex	
61 K6	**Heybridge** Essex	
6 D6	**Heybrook Bay** Devon	
76 B6	**Heydon** Cambs	
106 D6	**Heydon** Norfk	
103 G5	**Heydour** Lincs	
188 C7	**Heylipoll** Ag & B	
235 c3	**Heylor** Shet	
129 J7	**Heysham** Lancs	
18 B3	**Heyshott** W Susx	
27 L3	**Heytesbury** Wilts	
57 G3	**Heythrop** Oxon	
122 C7	**Heywood** Rochdl	
27 K2	**Heywood** Wilts	
116 F2	**Hibaldstow** N Linc	
115 J1	**Hickleton** Donc	
107 J7	**Hickling** Norfk	
102 B6	**Hickling** Notts	
107 J7	**Hickling Green** Norfk	
31 L7	**Hickstead** W Susx	
71 L6	**Hidcote Bartrim** Gloucs	
71 L6	**Hidcote Boyce** Gloucs	
124 C6	**High Ackworth** Wakefd	
114 F1	**Higham** Barns	
101 H2	**Higham** Derbys	
33 G4	**Higham** Kent	
46 B5	**Higham** Kent	
122 B3	**Higham** Lancs	
77 H2	**Higham** Suffk	
78 B7	**Higham** Suffk	
158 E6	**Higham Dykes** Nthumb	

74 D2 **Higham Ferrers** Nhants
59 J2 **Higham Gobion** Beds
45 G3 **Higham Hill** Gt Lon
86 E4 **Higham on the Hill** Leics
10 C4 **Highampton** Devon
45 H2 **Highams Park** Gt Lon
144 C6 **High Ardwell** D & G
154 F5 **High Auldgirth** D & G
148 F6 **High Bankhill** Cumb
60 C7 **High Beach** Essex
130 C5 **High Bentham** N York
23 J7 **High Bickington** Devon
130 B4 **High Biggins** Cumb
175 J6 **High Blantyre** S Lans
175 L3 **High Bonnybridge** Falk
23 L5 **High Bray** Devon
25 L3 **Highbridge** Somset
32 C7 **Highbrook** W Susx
33 G5 **High Brooms** Kent
123 J7 **Highburton** Kirk
44 F3 **Highbury** Gt Lon
27 G2 **Highbury** Somset
130 C4 **High Casterton** Cumb
133 L8 **High Catton** E R Yk
41 H8 **Highclere** Hants
16 B4 **Highcliffe** Dorset
141 G4 **High Coniscliffe** Darltn
148 E3 **High Crosby** Cumb
163 K1 **High Cross** E Ayrs
30 B6 **High Cross** Hants
60 B4 **High Cross** Herts
71 L2 **High Cross** Warwks
144 D7 **High Drummore** D & G
60 F5 **High Easter** Essex
132 B3 **High Ellington** N York
14 E2 **Higher Ansty** Dorset
121 G4 **Higher Bartle** Lancs
14 D4 **Higher Bockhampton** Dorset
7 L5 **Higher Brixham** Torbay
98 E8 **Higher Ercall** Wrekin
13 K1 **Higher Chillington** Somset
113 G2 **Higher Folds** Wigan
7 L3 **Higher Gabwell** Devon
129 J7 **Higher Heysham** Lancs
113 G3 **Higher Irlam** Salfd
97 L1 **Higher Kinnerton** Flints
23 J4 **Higher Muddiford** Devon
121 G5 **Higher Penwortham** Lancs
4 C6 **Higher Town** Cnwll
4 F4 **Higher Town** Cnwll
2 b1 **Higher Town** IoS
121 H5 **Higher Walton** Lancs
112 E4 **Higher Walton** Warrtn
13 H2 **Higher Wambrook** Somset
14 D4 **Higher Waterston** Dorset
121 J6 **Higher Wheelton** Lancs
112 F5 **Higher Whitley** Ches
14 B3 **Higher Wraxhall** Dorset
98 C4 **Higher Wych** Ches
140 F2 **High Etherley** Dur
150 E3 **Highfield** Gatesd
174 C7 **Highfield** N Ayrs
61 J3 **High Garrett** Essex
44 F3 **Highgate** Gt Lon

132 C5 **High Grantley** N York
92 D3 **High Green** Norfk
92 E5 **High Green** Norfk
115 G3 **High Green** Sheff
76 F5 **High Green** Worcs
34 B7 **High Halden** Kent
46 C5 **High Halstow** Medway
26 B5 **High Ham** Somset
132 D7 **High Harrogate** N York
98 E7 **High Hatton** Shrops
159 G2 **High Hauxley** Nthumb
143 J5 **High Hawsker** N York
148 E6 **High Hesket** Cumb
123 K8 **High Hoyland** Barns
32 E7 **High Hurstwood** E Susx
134 B5 **High Hutton** N York
147 M7 **High Ireby** Cumb
133 H4 **High Kilburn** N York
140 E3 **High Lands** Dur
203 J4 **Highland Wildlife Park** Highld
115 H5 **Highlane** Derbys
113 L4 **High Lane** Stockp
3 G4 **High Lanes** Cnwll
55 H4 **Highleadon** Gloucs
113 G5 **High Legh** Ches
18 A6 **Highleigh** W Susx
141 K5 **High Leven** S on T
84 D6 **Highley** Shrops
38 F8 **High Littleton** BaNES
137 G3 **High Lorton** Cumb
116 D7 **High Marnham** Notts
115 K2 **High Melton** Donc
150 D3 **High Mickley** Nthumb
42 B4 **Highmoor** Oxon
42 B4 **Highmoor Cross** Oxon
55 H4 **Highnam** Gloucs
151 J4 **High Newport** Sundld
129 J3 **High Newton** Cumb
129 G2 **High Nibthwaite** Cumb
99 H7 **High Offley** Staffs
60 E7 **High Ongar** Essex
84 E1 **High Onn** Staffs
62 C4 **High Park Corner** Essex
163 L7 **High Pennyvenie** E Ayrs
60 F4 **High Roding** Essex
18 F4 **High Salvington** W Susx
150 E3 **High Spen** Gatesd
34 B3 **Highsted** Kent
4 F5 **High Street** Cnwll
34 E3 **Highstreet** Kent
79 J4 **High Street** Suffk
31 G4 **Highstreet Green** Surrey
155 J6 **Hightae** D & G
111 J2 **Hightown** Sefton
77 L4 **Hightown Green** Suffk
118 C7 **High Toynton** Lincs
158 C2 **High Trewhitt** Nthumb
151 G4 **High Urpeth** Dur
176 D2 **High Valleyfield** Fife
7 J2 **Highweek** Devon
44 E2 **Highwood Hill** Gt Lon
40 D2 **Highworth** Swindn
137 K7 **High Wray** Cumb
60 D5 **High Wych** Herts
42 E3 **High Wycombe** Bucks
91 J4 **Hilborough** Norfk
40 C8 **Hilcott** Wilts
32 F4 **Hildenborough** Kent
33 G4 **Hilden Park** Kent

76 D5 **Hildersham** Cambs
99 L5 **Hilderstone** Staffs
135 J6 **Hilderthorpe** E R Yk
14 C2 **Hilfield** Dorset
90 E4 **Hilgay** Norfk
38 F2 **Hill** S Glos
72 F2 **Hill** Warwks
124 D5 **Hillam** N York
30 C6 **Hill Brow** Hants
15 J3 **Hillbutts** Dorset
99 H5 **Hill Chorlton** Staffs
100 F3 **Hillclifflane** Derbys
25 H6 **Hill Common** Somset
104 B3 **Hill Dyke** Lincs
176 F2 **Hillend** Fife
185 L7 **Hill End** Fife
70 F6 **Hill End** Gloucs
177 H5 **Hillend** Mdloth
175 L5 **Hillend** N Lans
58 B3 **Hillesden** Bucks
39 H3 **Hillesley** Gloucs
25 J6 **Hillfarrance** Somset
46 D7 **Hill Green** Kent
17 G2 **Hill Head** Hants
165 J2 **Hillhead** S Lans
217 K5 **Hillhead of Cocklaw** Abers
231 H3 **Hilliclay** Highld
43 H3 **Hillingdon** Gt Lon
174 F5 **Hillington** C Glas
105 H7 **Hillington** Norfk
87 G8 **Hillmorton** Warwks
176 F1 **Hill of Beath** Fife
223 H4 **Hill of Fearn** Highld
186 F5 **Hill of Tarvit Mansion House** Fife
146 D3 **Hillowton** D & G
100 B8 **Hill Ridware** Staffs
207 H5 **Hillside** Abers
197 H4 **Hillside** Angus
123 H6 **Hill Side** Kirk
115 J7 **Hills Town** Derbys
29 G7 **Hillstreet** Hants
235 C3 **Hillswick** Shet
123 L7 **Hill Top** Wakefd
10 D8 **Hilltown** Devon
177 J4 **Hilltown** Mdloth
235 C8 **Hillwell** Shet
40 A5 **Hilmarton** Wilts
39 K8 **Hilperton** Wilts
17 J2 **Hilsea** C Port
127 G4 **Hilston** E R Yk
179 H7 **Hilton** Border
75 K2 **Hilton** Cambs
139 G2 **Hilton** Cumb
100 E6 **Hilton** Derbys
14 E2 **Hilton** Dorset
140 F3 **Hilton** Dur
223 J6 **Hilton** Highld
141 K5 **Hilton** S on T
84 D4 **Hilton** Shrops
71 G3 **Himbleton** Worcs
84 F5 **Himley** Staffs
129 L3 **Hincaster** Cumb
44 D6 **Hinchley Wood** Surrey
86 E5 **Hinckley** Leics
92 E5 **Hinderclay** Suffk
143 G4 **Hinderwell** N York
30 E4 **Hindhead** Surrey
112 F1 **Hindley** Wigan
70 F3 **Hindlip** Worcs
106 C6 **Hindolveston** Norfk
27 K5 **Hindon** Wilts
106 B5 **Hindringham** Norfk
92 B3 **Hingham** Norfk
99 G7 **Hinstock** Shrops
78 C5 **Hintlesham** Suffk
69 G6 **Hinton** Herefs
39 G5 **Hinton** S Glos
83 H2 **Hinton** Shrops
29 L6 **Hinton Ampner** Hants

26 E1 **Hinton Blewett** BaNES
39 H8 **Hinton Charterhouse** BaNES
73 H0 **Hinton in the Hedges** Nhants
15 J2 **Hinton Martell** Dorset
71 H6 **Hinton on the Green** Worcs
40 E4 **Hinton Parva** Swindn
26 B8 **Hinton St George** Somset
27 H7 **Hinton St Mary** Dorset
57 G7 **Hinton Waldrist** Oxon
85 L3 **Hints** Staffs
74 D3 **Hinwick** Beds
34 D6 **Hinxhill** Kent
76 C5 **Hinxton** Cambs
75 J6 **Hinxworth** Herts
123 H5 **Hipperholme** Calder
140 F7 **Hipswell** N York
206 B5 **Hirn** Abers
97 G7 **Hirnant** Powys
159 G5 **Hirst** Nthumb
124 F5 **Hirst Courtney** N York
52 E6 **Hirwaun** Rhondd
23 J6 **Hiscott** Devon
76 B2 **Histon** Cambs
78 B4 **Hitcham** Suffk
78 B4 **Hitcham Causeway** Suffk
78 B4 **Hitcham Street** Suffk
59 K3 **Hitchin** Herts
45 H5 **Hither Green** Gt Lon
11 H5 **Hittisleigh** Devon
125 J4 **Hive** E R Yk
100 A7 **Hixon** Staffs
35 H3 **Hoaden** Kent
100 C7 **Hoar Cross** Staffs
54 D3 **Hoarwithy** Herefs
47 K7 **Hoath** Kent
82 F7 **Hobarris** Shrops
167 J7 **Hobkirk** Border
150 F4 **Hobson** Dur
102 A8 **Hoby** Leics
92 C2 **Hockering** Norfk
102 B2 **Hockerton** Notts
46 D2 **Hockley** Essex
85 L8 **Hockley Heath** Solhll
58 F3 **Hockliffe** Beds
91 G6 **Hockwold cum Wilton** Norfk
25 G7 **Hockworthy** Devon
60 B6 **Hoddesdon** Herts
121 L6 **Hoddlesden** Bl w D
155 L7 **Hoddom Cross** D & G
155 K7 **Hoddom Mains** D & G
49 H7 **Hodgeston** Pembks
98 E6 **Hodnet** Shrops
45 L7 **Hodsall Street** Kent
115 L4 **Hodsock** Notts
40 D4 **Hodson** Swindn
115 K6 **Hodthorpe** Derbys
92 B1 **Hoe** Norfk
34 D4 **Hogben's Hill** Kent
58 D3 **Hoggeston** Bucks
86 B5 **Hoggrill's End** Warwks
121 J5 **Hoghton** Lancs
100 E3 **Hognaston** Derbys
119 H6 **Hogsthorpe** Lincs
104 B7 **Holbeach** Lincs
104 B6 **Holbeach Bank** Lincs
104 B6 **Holbeach Clough** Lincs
89 K2 **Holbeach Drove** Lincs
104 C6 **Holbeach Hurn** Lincs
104 B8 **Holbeach St Johns** Lincs
104 B6 **Holbeach St Mark's** Lincs

104 C6 **Holbeach St Matthew** Lincs
115 K6 **Holbeck** Notts
71 H3 **Holberrow Green** Worcs
6 F5 **Holbeton** Devon
44 F4 **Holborn** Gt Lon
101 G4 **Holbrook** Derbys
78 E6 **Holbrook** Suffk
16 E2 **Holbury** Hants
12 B7 **Holcombe** Devon
26 F2 **Holcombe** Somset
25 G7 **Holcombe Rogus** Devon
73 L1 **Holcot** Nhants
122 B1 **Holden** Lancs
73 K2 **Holdenby** Nhants
61 G3 **Holder's Green** Essex
83 L5 **Holdgate** Shrops
103 H3 **Holdingham** Lincs
13 J2 **Holditch** Dorset
10 B4 **Hole** Devon
25 J3 **Holford** Somset
124 E1 **Holgate** York
129 H4 **Holker** Cumb
105 L4 **Holkham** Norfk
105 L4 **Holkham Hall** Norfk
9 K4 **Hollacombe** Devon
103 L3 **Holland Fen** Lincs
62 E5 **Holland-on-Sea** Essex
234 e3 **Hollandstoun** Ork
148 A2 **Hollee** D & G
79 H5 **Hollesley** Suffk
7 K4 **Hollicombe** Torbay
33 L3 **Hollingbourne** Kent
19 J4 **Hollingbury** Br & H
58 E3 **Hollingdon** Bucks
100 E5 **Hollington** Derbys
100 B5 **Hollington** Staffs
114 A3 **Hollingworth** Tamesd
114 B7 **Hollinsclough** Staffs
115 G5 **Hollins End** Sheff
113 G4 **Hollins Green** Warrtn
10 F3 **Hollocombe** Devon
100 F2 **Holloway** Derbys
44 F3 **Holloway** Gt Lon
73 K1 **Hollowell** Nhants
112 C7 **Hollowmoor Heath** Ches
156 C6 **Hollows** D & G
53 J7 **Hollybush** Caerph
163 K6 **Hollybush** E Ayrs
70 D6 **Hollybush** Herefs
70 F6 **Holly Green** Worcs
127 H5 **Hollym** E R Yk
114 C1 **Holmbridge** Kirk
31 J3 **Holmbury St Mary** Surrey
5 G5 **Holmbush** Cnwll
99 K7 **Holmcroft** Staffs
89 H6 **Holme** Cambs
129 L4 **Holme** Cumb
114 C1 **Holme** Kirk
132 E3 **Holme** N York
102 D2 **Holme** Notts
122 C5 **Holme Chapel** Lancs
124 E3 **Holme Green** N York
91 K3 **Holme Hale** Norfk
69 L7 **Holme Lacy** Herefs
69 G4 **Holme Marsh** Herefs
105 H4 **Holme next the Sea** Norfk
126 B2 **Holme on the Wolds** E R Yk
101 L5 **Holme Pierrepont** Notts
69 K6 **Holmer** Herefs
42 E2 **Holmer Green** Bucks
147 J5 **Holme St Cuthbert** Cumb
113 H7 **Holmes Chapel** Ches
114 F6 **Holmesfield** Derbys

120 F6 **Holmeswood** Lancs
32 B3 **Holmethorpe** Surrey
125 J3 **Holme upon Spalding Moor** E R Yk
115 H7 **Holmewood** Derbys
123 H8 **Holmfirth** Kirk
164 B5 **Holmhead** E Ayrs
127 J5 **Holmpton** E R Yk
136 E7 **Holmrook** Cumb
150 F5 **Holmside** Dur
7 G3 **Holne** Devon
14 C1 **Holnest** Dorset
24 E3 **Holnicote** Somset
9 J4 **Holsworthy** Devon
9 K3 **Holsworthy Beacon** Devon
15 J2 **Holt** Dorset
106 C5 **Holt** Norfk
39 K7 **Holt** Wilts
70 E3 **Holt** Worcs
98 B2 **Holt** Wrexhm
133 K8 **Holtby** York
71 J1 **Holt End** Worcs
70 E2 **Holt Heath** Worcs
57 L6 **Holton** Oxon
27 G6 **Holton** Somset
93 J7 **Holton** Suffk
117 J5 **Holton cum Beckering** Lincs
118 C2 **Holton le Clay** Lincs
117 H3 **Holton le Moor** Lincs
78 C6 **Holton St Mary** Suffk
14 D1 **Holwell** Dorset
59 K2 **Holwell** Herts
102 B7 **Holwell** Leics
56 E6 **Holwell** Oxon
139 K2 **Holwick** Dur
30 B4 **Holybourne** Hants
108 C5 **Holyhead** IoA
108 C5 **Holy Island** IoA
169 H6 **Holy Island** Nthumb
115 G7 **Holymoorside** Derbys
42 E5 **Holyport** W & M
158 B2 **Holystone** Nthumb
175 K6 **Holytown** N Lans
59 G5 **Holywell** Beds
75 L1 **Holywell** Cambs
4 B4 **Holywell** Cnwll
14 B2 **Holywell** Dorset
111 G6 **Holywell** Flints
123 G6 **Holywell Green** Calder
25 H7 **Holywell Lake** Somset
91 G7 **Holywell Row** Suffk
155 G6 **Holywood** D & G
155 G6 **Holywood Village** D & G
84 B3 **Homer** Shrops
111 K4 **Homer Green** Sefton
93 G6 **Homersfield** Suffk
28 C6 **Homington** Wilts
71 K5 **Honeybourne** Worcs
10 H3 **Honeychurch** Devon
40 C7 **Honeystreet** Wilts
77 L7 **Honey Tye** Suffk
86 B8 **Honiley** Warwks
107 G6 **Honing** Norfk
92 D2 **Honingham** Norfk
102 F4 **Honington** Lincs
91 K8 **Honington** Suffk
72 C6 **Honington** Warwks
12 F3 **Honiton** Devon
123 H7 **Honley** Kirk
6 D5 **Hooe** C Plym
20 E4 **Hooe** E Susx
113 L6 **Hoo Green** Ches
120 D3 **Hoohill** Bpool
125 H5 **Hook** E R Yk
44 D1 **Hook** Gt Lon
30 B1 **Hook** Hants
49 L6 **Hook** Pembks
40 B4 **Hook** Wilts

14 A3 **Hooke** Dorset
33 H6 **Hook Green** Kent
45 L6 **Hook Green** Kent
57 G2 **Hook Norton** Oxon
11 K5 **Hookway** Devon
32 B3 **Hooley** Surrey
46 C5 **Hoo St Werburgh** Medway
115 K3 **Hooton Levitt** Rothm
124 D8 **Hooton Pagnell** Donc
115 J3 **Hooton Roberts** Rothm
114 D5 **Hope** Derbys
7 G7 **Hope** Devon
97 L2 **Hope** Flints
83 L8 **Hope** Shrops
100 C2 **Hope** Staffs
83 J5 **Hope Bowdler** Shrops
166 D6 **Hopehouse** Border
214 E1 **Hopeman** Moray
54 F4 **Hope Mansell** Herefs
83 H6 **Hopesay** Shrops
69 K4 **Hope under Dinmore** Herefs
133 K8 **Hopgrove** York
132 F7 **Hopperton** N York
84 D5 **Hopstone** Shrops
100 E2 **Hopton** Derbys
99 L7 **Hopton** Staffs
92 B7 **Hopton** Suffk
83 K7 **Hopton Cangeford** Shrops
83 G7 **Hopton Castle** Shrops
83 H7 **Hoptonheath** Shrops
93 L4 **Hopton on Sea** Norfk
84 B7 **Hopton Wafers** Shrops
85 L3 **Hopwas** Staffs
85 J7 **Hopwood** Worcs
20 C3 **Horam** E Susx
103 J5 **Horbling** Lincs
123 K6 **Horbury** Wakefd
151 K6 **Horden** Dur
16 C4 **Hordle** Hants
98 B6 **Hordley** Shrops
38 E5 **Horfield** Bristl
92 E8 **Horham** Suffk
62 B3 **Horkesley Heath** Essex
126 B6 **Horkstow** N Linc
72 E5 **Horley** Oxon
32 B5 **Horley** Surrey
26 E5 **Hornblotton Green** Somset
130 B5 **Hornby** Lancs
132 C2 **Hornby** N York
141 J6 **Hornby** N York
118 C7 **Horncastle** Lincs
45 K3 **Hornchurch** Gt Lon
179 J7 **Horncliffe** Nthumb
179 J8 **Horndean** Border
30 B8 **Horndean** Hants
10 D8 **Horndon** Devon
46 A4 **Horndon on the Hill** Thurr
32 C4 **Horne** Surrey
24 D3 **Horner** Somset
107 H8 **Horning** Norfk
88 B4 **Horninghold** Leics
100 E7 **Horninglow** Staffs
76 C3 **Horningsea** Cambs
27 J3 **Horningsham** Wilts
105 M7 **Horningtoft** Norfk
22 F5 **Horns Cross** Devon
126 F2 **Hornsea** E R Yk
44 F3 **Hornsey** Gt Lon
72 E5 **Hornton** Oxon
235 d2 **Horra** Shet
6 D2 **Horrabridge** Devon
7 H2 **Horridge** Devon
77 J3 **Horringer** Suffk
121 L2 **Horrocksford** Lancs

6 B2 **Horsebridge** Devon
20 C4 **Horsebridge** E Susx
29 G5 **Horsebridge** Hants
83 G3 **Horsebridge** Shrops
76 E5 **Horseheath** Cambs
131 K4 **Horsehouse** N York
43 G8 **Horsell** Surrey
98 C4 **Horseman's Green** Wrexhm
107 K7 **Horsey** Norfk
25 L4 **Horsey** Somset
92 E1 **Horsford** Norfk
123 J3 **Horsforth** Leeds
31 K5 **Horsham** W Susx
70 D3 **Horsham** Worcs
92 E1 **Horsham St Faith** Norfk
117 K7 **Horsington** Lincs
27 G6 **Horsington** Somset
101 G4 **Horsley** Derbys
39 J2 **Horsley** Gloucs
150 D2 **Horsley** Nthumb
157 L3 **Horsley** Nthumb
62 D3 **Horsleycross Street** Essex
167 K6 **Horsleyhill** Border
101 H4 **Horsley Woodhouse** Derbys
33 J5 **Horsmonden** Kent
57 L6 **Horspath** Oxon
106 F8 **Horstead** Norfk
32 C7 **Horsted Keynes** W Susx
58 F4 **Horton** Bucks
15 J2 **Horton** Dorset
122 C1 **Horton** Lancs
74 B4 **Horton** Nhants
39 H4 **Horton** S Glos
25 L7 **Horton** Somset
99 L2 **Horton** Staffs
50 F7 **Horton** Swans
43 G5 **Horton** W & M
40 B7 **Horton** Wilts
84 C1 **Horton** Wrekin
57 L5 **Horton-cum-Studley** Oxon
98 C3 **Horton Green** Ches
130 F5 **Horton in Ribblesdale** N York
45 K6 **Horton Kirby** Kent
121 J7 **Horwich** Bolton
23 H6 **Horwood** Devon
166 F6 **Hoscote** Border
102 B6 **Hose** Leics
185 H3 **Hosh** P & K
235 C7 **Hoswick** Shet
125 L4 **Hotham** E R Yk
34 C5 **Hothfield** Kent
101 L7 **Hoton** Leics
157 K5 **Hott** Nthumb
99 G3 **Hough** Ches
102 E4 **Hougham** Lincs
112 C4 **Hough Green** Halton
102 F3 **Hough-on-the-Hill** Lincs
75 K1 **Houghton** Cambs
29 G5 **Houghton** Hants
49 G6 **Houghton** Pembks
18 D4 **Houghton** W Susx
74 F6 **Houghton Conquest** Beds
21 H2 **Houghton Green** E Susx
151 H5 **Houghton-le-Spring** Sundld
87 J3 **Houghton on the Hill** Leics
59 G4 **Houghton Regis** Beds
105 L5 **Houghton St Giles** Norfk
42 B8 **Hound Green** Hants
178 D8 **Houndslow** Border

179 H5 **Houndwood** Border
43 J5 **Hounslow** Gt Lon
61 G4 **Hounslow Green** Essex
213 L4 **Househill** Highld
123 J6 **Houses Hill** Kirk
149 K2 **Housesteads Roman Fort** Nthumb
207 G1 **Housieside** Abers
174 D5 **Houston** Rens
227 K2 **Houstry** Highld
234 b6 **Houton** Ork
19 J5 **Hove** Br & H
102 B3 **Hoveringham** Notts
107 G8 **Hoveton** Norfk
133 K4 **Hovingham** N York
54 E3 **How Caple** Herefs
125 H5 **Howden** E R Yk
150 E7 **Howden-le-Wear** Dur
231 K3 **Howe** Highld
132 E4 **Howe** N York
92 F4 **Howe** Norfk
61 J7 **Howe Green** Essex
61 K7 **Howegreen** Essex
103 J4 **Howell** Lincs
216 E5 **Howe of Teuchar** Abers
147 L2 **Howes** D & G
61 H5 **Howe Street** Essex
77 G7 **Howe Street** Essex
68 B3 **Howey** Powys
136 D3 **Howgate** Cumb
177 H6 **Howgate** Mdloth
169 K5 **Howick** Nthumb
140 D3 **Howle** Dur
99 G7 **Howle** Wrekin
54 E4 **Howle Hill** Herefs
76 E7 **Howlett End** Essex
13 H1 **Howley** Somset
148 E4 **How Mill** Cumb
233 b7 **Howmore** W Isls
168 B5 **Hownam** Border
117 H2 **Howsham** N Linc
133 L6 **Howsham** N York
168 D3 **Howtel** Nthumb
174 D6 **Howwood** Rens
92 E7 **Hoxne** Suffk
111 H4 **Hoylake** Wirral
115 G2 **Hoyland Nether** Barns
114 E1 **Hoyland Swaine** Barns
48 E6 **Hubberston** Pembks
123 K2 **Huby** N York
133 J6 **Huby** N York
55 K4 **Hucclecote** Gloucs
33 L2 **Hucking** Kent
101 K3 **Hucknall** Notts
123 H7 **Huddersfield** Kirk
71 G3 **Huddington** Worcs
140 E7 **Hudswell** N York
134 D7 **Huggate** E R Yk
42 E2 **Hughenden Valley** Bucks
83 L4 **Hughley** Shrops
2 b2 **Hugh Town** IoS
10 D3 **Huish** Devon
40 C7 **Huish** Wilts
25 G5 **Huish Champflower** Somset
26 B6 **Huish Episcopi** Somset
58 D5 **Hulcott** Bucks
12 C5 **Hulham** Devon
100 E3 **Hulland** Derbys
100 E3 **Hulland Ward** Derbys
39 K4 **Hullavington** Wilts
46 D2 **Hullbridge** Essex
113 J3 **Hulme** Manch
99 L4 **Hulme** Staffs
112 E4 **Hulme** Warrtn
100 C2 **Hulme End** Staffs

113 J7 **Hulme Walfield** Ches
16 E5 **Hulverstone** IoW
93 K6 **Hulver Street** Suffk
126 D7 **Humberside Airport** N Linc
118 D1 **Humberston** NE Lin
87 J3 **Humberstone** C Leic
178 B5 **Humbie** E Loth
126 F4 **Humbleton** E R Yk
103 G6 **Humby** Lincs
167 L2 **Hume** Border
158 A7 **Humshaugh** Nthumb
231 L2 **Huna** Highld
87 G4 **Huncote** Leics
167 K5 **Hundalee** Border
140 C3 **Hunderthwaite** Dur
118 E7 **Hundleby** Lincs
49 G7 **Hundleton** Pembks
77 G5 **Hundon** Suffk
120 F6 **Hundred End** Lancs
68 C4 **Hundred House** Powys
87 K3 **Hungarton** Leics
25 G4 **Hungerford** Somset
41 G6 **Hungerford** W Berk
41 G6 **Hungerford Newtown** W Berk
69 J7 **Hungerstone** Herefs
135 H4 **Hunmanby** N York
72 D2 **Hunningham** Warwks
73 K3 **Hunsbury Hill** Nhants
60 C5 **Hunsdon** Herts
132 F8 **Hunsingore** N York
123 L4 **Hunslet** Leeds
149 G7 **Hunsonby** Cumb
105 G4 **Hunstanton** Norfk
150 B5 **Hunstanworth** Dur
99 G4 **Hunsterson** Ches
77 L2 **Hunston** Suffk
18 B5 **Hunston** W Susx
38 F7 **Hunstrete** BaNES
123 J5 **Hunsworth** Kirk
173 K3 **Hunter's Quay** Ag & B
25 M6 **Huntham** Somset
196 D3 **Hunthill Lodge** Angus
75 J1 **Huntingdon** Cambs
93 G8 **Huntingfield** Suffk
112 B8 **Huntington** Ches
178 B4 **Huntington** E Loth
68 E4 **Huntington** Herefs
85 H2 **Huntington** Staffs
133 J7 **Huntington** York
55 L6 **Huntley** Gloucs
215 L6 **Huntly** Abers
29 J4 **Hunton** Hants
33 J4 **Hunton** Kent
132 B2 **Hunton** N York
24 E3 **Huntscott** Somset
24 F7 **Huntsham** Devon
23 H6 **Huntshaw** Devon
25 L3 **Huntspill** Somset
25 K5 **Huntstile** Somset
25 L4 **Huntworth** Somset
140 F2 **Hunwick** Dur
106 C5 **Hunworth** Norfk
28 D5 **Hurdcott** Wilts
113 L6 **Hurdsfield** Ches
42 D4 **Hurley** W & M
86 B4 **Hurley** Warwks
86 B4 **Hurley Common** Warwks
163 L3 **Hurlford** E Ayrs
15 L3 **Hurn** Dorset
29 H6 **Hursley** Hants
42 C5 **Hurst** Wokham
29 H3 **Hurstbourne Priors** Hants
29 G2 **Hurstbourne Tarrant** Hants
33 J7 **Hurst Green** E Susx
62 C5 **Hurst Green** Essex
121 J5 **Hurst Green** Lancs

32 D3 **Hurst Green** Surrey
19 J3 **Hurstpierpoint** W Susx
122 C4 **Hurstwood** Lancs
234 c6 **Hurtiso** Ork
141 H5 **Hurworth-on-Tees** Darltn
141 H5 **Hurworth Place** Darltn
87 J6 **Husbands Bosworth** Leics
74 D7 **Husborne Crawley** Beds
133 H4 **Husthwaite** N York
101 J2 **Huthwaite** Notts
119 G6 **Huttoft** Lincs
179 J7 **Hutton** Border
134 F8 **Hutton** E R Yk
45 M2 **Hutton** Essex
121 G5 **Hutton** Lancs
37 M8 **Hutton** N Som
141 H7 **Hutton Bonville** N York
134 F3 **Hutton Buscel** N York
132 E5 **Hutton Conyers** N York
126 C1 **Hutton Cranswick** E R Yk
148 D7 **Hutton End** Cumb
151 K7 **Hutton Henry** Dur
133 L2 **Hutton-le-Hole** N York
142 D4 **Hutton Lowcross** R & Cl
140 E5 **Hutton Magna** Dur
130 B4 **Hutton Roof** Cumb
148 C7 **Hutton Roof** Cumb
141 K6 **Hutton Rudby** N York
133 G4 **Hutton Sessay** N York
124 D1 **Hutton Wandesley** N York
12 B3 **Huxham** Devon
98 D1 **Huxley** Ches
112 C4 **Huyton** Knows
128 D2 **Hycemoor** Cumb
113 L3 **Hyde** Tamesd
58 F7 **Hyde Heath** Bucks
99 K8 **Hyde Lea** Staffs
165 H2 **Hyndford Bridge** S Lans
188 C8 **Hynish** Ag & B
82 F5 **Hyssington** Powys
16 E2 **Hythe** Hants
34 F7 **Hythe** Kent
43 G6 **Hythe End** W & M

I

14 E2 **Ibberton** Dorset
100 E2 **Ible** Derbys
15 L1 **Ibsley** Hants
86 E2 **Ibstock** Leics
42 C2 **Ibstone** Bucks
29 G2 **Ibthorpe** Hants
143 H5 **Iburndale** N York
29 K1 **Ibworth** Hants
91 J4 **Ickburgh** Norfk
43 H3 **Ickenham** Gt Lon
57 M6 **Ickford** Bucks
35 G3 **Ickham** Kent
59 K2 **Ickleford** Herts
21 H3 **Icklesham** E Susx
76 C5 **Ickleton** Cambs
91 H8 **Icklingham** Suffk
122 E2 **Ickornshaw** N York
75 G5 **Ickwell Green** Beds
77 J3 **Ickworth** Suffk
56 E4 **Icomb** Gloucs
56 E4 **Idbury** Oxon
10 E3 **Iddesleigh** Devon

11 K6 **Ide** Devon
7 K1 **Ideford** Devon
32 E3 **Ide Hill** Kent
21 H2 **Iden** E Susx
33 J5 **Iden Green** Kent
33 K6 **Iden Green** Kent
123 H3 **Idle** Brad
4 C6 **Idless** Cnwll
72 C5 **Idlicote** Warwks
28 D4 **Idmiston** Wilts
50 E3 **Idole** Carmth
100 F3 **Idridgehay** Derbys
208 F2 **Idrigill** Highld
40 E4 **Idstone** Oxon
57 K7 **Iffley** Oxon
31 L4 **Ifield** W Susx
15 L4 **Iford** Bmouth
19 L4 **Iford** E Susx
38 C3 **Ifton** Mons
98 E5 **Ightfield** Shrops
33 G2 **Ightham** Kent
79 J4 **Iken** Suffk
100 C3 **Ilam** Staffs
26 D6 **Ilchester** Somset
168 F5 **Ilderton** Nthumb
45 H3 **Ilford** Gt Lon
26 A7 **Ilford** Somset
23 H7 **Ilfracombe** Devon
101 J4 **Ilkeston** Derbys
93 H6 **Ilketshall St Andrew** Suffk
93 H6 **Ilketshall St Margaret** Suffk
123 H2 **Ilkley** Brad
5 L1 **Illand** Cnwll
85 H7 **Illey** Dudley
3 H3 **Illogan** Cnwll
87 K4 **Illston on the Hill** Leics
58 C6 **Ilmer** Bucks
72 B5 **Ilmington** Warwks
26 A8 **Ilminster** Somset
7 H2 **Ilsington** Devon
51 H7 **Ilston** Swans
132 B4 **Ilton** N York
25 M7 **Ilton** Somset
161 L2 **Imachar** N Ayrs
126 F7 **Immingham** NE Lin
126 F7 **Immingham Dock** NE Lin
76 C2 **Impington** Cambs
112 C6 **Ince** Ches
111 K2 **Ince Blundell** Sefton
112 E1 **Ince-in-Makerfield** Wigan
221 K7 **Inchbae Lodge Hotel** Highld
196 F4 **Inchbare** Angus
215 G4 **Inchberry** Moray
211 G3 **Incheril** Highld
174 E5 **Inchinnan** Rens
201 J5 **Inchlaggan** Highld
186 D3 **Inchmichael** P & K
202 B3 **Inchnacardoch Hotel** Highld
224 F4 **Inchnadamph** Highld
186 D2 **Inchture** P & K
211 K6 **Inchvuilt** Highld
186 C4 **Inchyra** P & K
4 E4 **Indian Queens** Cnwll
61 G7 **Ingatestone** Essex
114 E1 **Ingbirchworth** Barns
99 L7 **Ingestre** Staffs
116 F5 **Ingham** Lincs
107 H7 **Ingham** Norfk
77 J1 **Ingham** Suffk
107 H6 **Ingham Corner** Norfk
101 G6 **Ingleby** Derbys
141 K6 **Ingleby Arncliffe** N York
141 K4 **Ingleby Barwick** S on T

142 C6 **Ingleby Greenhow** N York
10 E4 **Ingleigh Green** Devon
39 G7 **Inglesbatch** BaNES
56 D7 **Inglesham** Swindn
147 G2 **Ingleston** D & G
140 F3 **Ingleton** Dur
130 D7 **Ingleton** N York
121 H3 **Inglewhite** Lancs
158 C7 **Ingoe** Nthumb
121 G4 **Ingol** Lancs
105 G6 **Ingoldisthorpe** Norfk
119 H7 **Ingoldmells** Lincs
103 G6 **Ingoldsby** Lincs
168 F6 **Ingram** Nthumb
45 M2 **Ingrave** Essex
122 F3 **Ingrow** Brad
138 C7 **Ings** Cumb
38 E3 **Ingst** S Glos
88 E2 **Ingthorpe** Rutlnd
106 E6 **Ingworth** Norfk
71 H3 **Inkberrow** Worcs
217 H6 **Inkhorn** Abers
41 G7 **Inkpen** W Berk
231 J2 **Inkstack** Highld
173 K4 **Innellan** Ag & B
166 E3 **Innerleithen** Border
186 F7 **Innerleven** Fife
144 F3 **Innermessan** D & G
178 F4 **Innerwick** E Loth
215 G2 **Innesmill** Moray
216 C8 **Insch** Abers
203 J5 **Insh** Highld
120 F3 **Inskip** Lancs
23 G5 **Instow** Devon
115 H5 **Intake** Sheff
204 F6 **Inver** Abers
223 J5 **Inver** Highld
194 F7 **Inver** P & K
190 F1 **Inverailort** Highld
210 C3 **Inverailigin** Highld
217 K2 **Inverallochy** Abers
222 D2 **Inveran** Highld
182 F5 **Inveraray** Ag & B
209 J7 **Inverarish** Highld
196 D7 **Inverarity** Angus
183 K4 **Inverarnan** Stirlg
219 J4 **Inverasdale** Highld
176 C3 **Inveravon** Falk
182 E2 **Inverawe** Ag & B
183 K7 **Inverbeg** Ag & B
197 K2 **Inverbervie** Abers
216 C2 **Inver-boyndie** Abers
220 F5 **Inverbroom** Highld
191 K6 **Invercreran House Hotel** Ag & B
203 L3 **Inverdruie** Highld
177 K4 **Inveresk** E Loth
182 E1 **Inveresragan** Ag & B
219 K5 **Inverewe Garden** Highld
204 D7 **Inverey** Abers
202 D2 **Inverfarigaig** Highld
191 J7 **Inverfolla** Ag & B
201 L5 **Invergarry** Highld
184 F2 **Invergeldie** P & K
201 K7 **Invergloy** Highld
222 F7 **Invergordon** Highld
186 F2 **Invergowrie** P & K
200 B4 **Inverguseran** Highld
193 L5 **Inverhadden** P & K
183 L3 **Inverherive Hotel** Stirlg
200 B5 **Inverie** Highld
182 E4 **Inverinan** Ag & B
200 E2 **Inverinate** Highld
197 G6 **Inverkeilor** Angus
176 F2 **Inverkeithing** Fife
216 C5 **Inverkeithny** Abers
173 L4 **Inverkip** Inver
224 C4 **Inverkirkaig** Highld
220 F4 **Inverlael** Highld

192 E1 **Inverlair** Highld
182 C6 **Inverliever Lodge** Ag & B
183 H2 **Inverlochy** Ag & B
196 D1 **Invermark** Angus
215 J6 **Invermarkie** Abers
202 C3 **Invermoriston** Highld
213 G5 **Inverness** Highld
213 J4 **Inverness Dalcross Airport** Highld
183 G7 **Invernoaden** Ag & B
192 D7 **Inveroran Hotel** Ag & B
196 C5 **Inverquharity** Angus
217 J5 **Inverquhomery** Abers
201 K8 **Inverroy** Highld
191 J4 **Inversanda** Highld
200 E2 **Invershiel** Highld
222 D3 **Invershin** Highld
231 J8 **Invershore** Highld
183 K5 **Inversnaid Hotel** Stirlg
217 L5 **Inverugie** Abers
183 K5 **Inveruglas** Ag & B
203 J5 **Inveruglass** Highld
206 E2 **Inverurie** Abers
10 E5 **Inwardleigh** Devon
61 L4 **Inworth** Essex
233 b7 **Iochdar** W Isls
180 C3 **Iona** Ag & B
30 D6 **Iping** W Susx
7 J3 **Ipplepen** Devon
41 M4 **Ipsden** Oxon
100 A3 **Ipstones** Staffs
78 E5 **Ipswich** Suffk
111 J5 **Irby** Wirral
118 F8 **Irby in the Marsh** Lincs
117 K1 **Irby upon Humber** NE Lin
74 D2 **Irchester** Nhants
147 M7 **Ireby** Cumb
130 C4 **Ireby** Lancs
128 F4 **Ireleth** Cumb
149 L4 **Ireshopeburn** Dur
100 F3 **Ireton Wood** Derbys
113 G3 **Irlam** Salfd
103 G7 **Irnham** Lincs
39 G4 **Iron Acton** S Glos
84 C3 **Ironbridge** Wrekin
84 C3 **Iron Bridge Museum** Wrekin
154 B6 **Ironmacannie** D & G
101 H3 **Ironville** Derbys
107 H7 **Irstead** Norfk
148 E3 **Irthington** Cumb
74 D1 **Irthlingborough** Nhants
134 F3 **Irton** N York
163 H2 **Irvine** N Ayrs
163 H2 **Irvine Maritime Centre** N Ayrs
230 E3 **Isauld** Highld
235 c2 **Isbister** Shet
235 d4 **Isbister** Shet
19 L3 **Isfield** E Susx
88 C8 **Isham** Nhants
30 C3 **Islington** Hants
170 F7 **Islay Airport** Ag & B
26 A7 **Isle Abbotts** Somset
26 A7 **Isle Brewers** Somset
90 F8 **Isleham** Cambs
45 G4 **Isle of Dogs** Gt Lon
237 b7 **Isle of Man Ronaldsway Airport** IoM
15 J5 **Isle of Purbeck** Dorset
46 F6 **Isle of Sheppey** Kent
145 K7 **Isle of Whithorn** D & G

17 G5 **Isle of Wight** IoW
199 L3 **Isleornsay** Highld
2 b2 **Isles of Scilly St Mary's Airport** IoS
155 G7 **Islesteps** D & G
44 D5 **Isleworth** Gt Lon
101 H7 **Isley Walton** Leics
232 d3 **Islibhig** W Isls
44 F3 **Islington** Gt Lon
88 E7 **Islip** Nhants
57 K5 **Islip** Oxon
232 d3 **Islivig** W Isls
83 L2 **Isombridge** Wrekin
29 K5 **Itchen Abbas** Hants
29 K5 **Itchen Stoke** Hants
31 J5 **Itchingfield** W Susx
106 D6 **Itteringham** Norfk
11 G5 **Itton** Devon
38 C2 **Itton** Mons
148 D6 **Ivegill** Cumb
43 G4 **Iver** Bucks
43 G4 **Iver Heath** Bucks
150 E5 **Iveston** Dur
58 F5 **Ivinghoe** Bucks
58 F4 **Ivinghoe Aston** Bucks
69 J3 **Ivington** Herefs
69 J4 **Ivington Green** Herefs
6 F5 **Ivybridge** Devon
21 K1 **Ivychurch** Kent
33 G3 **Ivy Hatch** Kent
46 E6 **Iwade** Kent
27 K8 **Iwerne Courtney or Shroton** Dorset
27 K8 **Iwerne Minster** Dorset
77 L1 **Ixworth** Suffk
91 K8 **Ixworth Thorpe** Suffk

J

12 C4 **Jack-in-the-Green** Devon
175 J7 **Jackton** S Lans
9 G7 **Jacobstow** Cnwll
10 E4 **Jacobstowe** Devon
49 H7 **Jameston** Pembks
212 D3 **Jamestown** Highld
174 D3 **Jamestown** W Duns
227 L3 **Janetstown** Highld
231 L5 **Janets-town** Highld
155 J3 **Jardine Hall** D & G
151 H3 **Jarrow** S Tyne
61 H3 **Jasper's Green** Essex
175 L4 **Jawcraig** Falk
62 D5 **Jaywick** Essex
167 K5 **Jedburgh** Border
49 J6 **Jeffreyston** Pembks
213 H2 **Jemimaville** Highld
236 d4 **Jerbourg** Guern
236 b7 **Jersey Airport** Jersey
151 G2 **Jesmond** N u Ty
20 B5 **Jevington** E Susx
59 H5 **Jockey End** Herts
148 D7 **Johnby** Cumb
112 B5 **John Lennon Airport** Lpool
231 L2 **John o' Groats** Highld
197 J3 **Johnshaven** Abers
48 F5 **Johnston** Pembks
155 M3 **Johnstone** D & G
174 D5 **Johnstone** Rens
155 J4 **Johnstonebridge** D & G
50 E2 **Johnstown** Carmth
97 L4 **Johnstown** Wrexhm
177 J4 **Joppa** C Edin
66 D2 **Joppa** Cerdgn
163 K5 **Joppa** S Ayrs
64 C7 **Jordanston** Pembks

45 K5 **Joyden's Wood** Kent
150 B3 **Juniper** Nthumb
177 G5 **Juniper Green** C Edin
237 c2 **Jurby** IoM

K

139 H5 **Kaber** Cumb
165 J1 **Kaimend** S Lans
173 G4 **Kames** Ag & B
164 D4 **Kames** E Ayrs
4 C7 **Kea** Cnwll
125 K7 **Keadby** N Linc
104 B1 **Keal Cotes** Lincs
113 H1 **Kearsley** Bolton
158 C6 **Kearsley** Nthumb
35 H6 **Kearsney** Kent
130 B4 **Kearstwick** Cumb
77 G5 **Kedington** Suffk
100 F4 **Kedleston** Derbys
126 E8 **Keelby** Lincs
99 J4 **Keele** Staffs
123 G4 **Keelham** Brad
48 F4 **Keeston** Pembks
39 L8 **Keevil** Wilts
101 J7 **Kegworth** Leics
3 G3 **Kehelland** Cnwll
206 B2 **Keig** Abers
122 F3 **Keighley** Brad
185 J8 **Keilarsbrae** Clacks
185 K3 **Keillour** P & K
204 E6 **Keiloch** Abers
171 K5 **Keils** Ag & B
26 D5 **Keinton Mandeville** Somset
154 E4 **Keir Mill** D & G
139 G3 **Keisley** Cumb
231 L4 **Keiss** Highld
215 J4 **Keith** Moray
195 K8 **Keithick** P & K
196 F4 **Keithock** Angus
212 E3 **Keithtown** Highld
122 D2 **Kelbrook** Lancs
173 L6 **Kelburn** N Ayrs
103 G4 **Kelby** Lincs
139 K6 **Keld** N York
124 F3 **Kelfield** N York
102 C2 **Kelham** Notts
147 K2 **Kelhead** D & G
120 E5 **Kellamergh** Lancs
187 G1 **Kellas** Angus
214 E4 **Kellas** Moray
7 J7 **Kellaton** Devon
106 C4 **Kelling** Norfk
124 E5 **Kellington** N York
151 J7 **Kelloe** Dur
164 E6 **Kelloholm** D & G
9 K8 **Kelly** Devon
87 K7 **Kelmarsh** Nhants
56 E7 **Kelmscott** Oxon
79 H2 **Kelsale** Suffk
112 D7 **Kelsall** Ches
75 K7 **Kelshall** Herts
147 L5 **Kelsick** Cumb
167 L3 **Kelso** Border
115 G8 **Kelstedge** Derbys
118 C4 **Kelstern** Lincs
39 G6 **Kelston** BaNES
194 B6 **Keltneyburn** P & K
155 H7 **Kelton** D & G
186 B8 **Kelty** Fife
61 K4 **Kelvedon** Essex
60 F7 **Kelvedon Hatch** Essex
2 C5 **Kelynack** Cnwll
187 G4 **Kemback** Fife
84 D3 **Kemberton** Shrops
39 M2 **Kemble** Gloucs
71 G6 **Kemerton** Worcs

53 M6 **Kemeys Commander** Mons
206 E3 **Kemnay** Abers
54 F3 **Kempley** Gloucs
55 U3 **Kempley Green** Gloucs
70 F5 **Kempsey** Worcs
40 D2 **Kempsford** Gloucs
29 L2 **Kempshott** Hants
74 F5 **Kempston** Beds
83 G6 **Kempton** Shrops
19 J5 **Kemp Town** Br & H
32 F2 **Kemsing** Kent
34 C7 **Kenardington** Kent
69 J6 **Kenchester** Herefs
56 E6 **Kencot** Oxon
129 L2 **Kendal** Cumb
36 C4 **Kenfig** Brdgnd
72 C1 **Kenilworth** Warwks
32 B2 **Kenley** Gt Lon
83 L4 **Kenley** Shrops
210 B3 **Kenmore** Highld
194 B7 **Kenmore** P & K
11 L7 **Kenn** Devon
38 B6 **Kenn** N Som
172 D5 **Kennacraig** Ag & B
11 J4 **Kennerleigh** Devon
111 L2 **Kennessee Green** Sefton
176 C1 **Kennet** Clacks
215 L8 **Kennethmont** Abers
77 G2 **Kennett** Cambs
11 L7 **Kennford** Devon
92 C6 **Kenninghall** Norfk
34 D5 **Kennington** Kent
57 K7 **Kennington** Oxon
186 F6 **Kennoway** Fife
25 L7 **Kenny** Somset
90 F7 **Kennyhill** Suffk
134 C6 **Kennythorpe** N York
188 C6 **Kenovay** Ag & B
208 F4 **Kensaleyre** Highld
44 E4 **Kensington** Gt Lon
59 G4 **Kensworth Common** Beds
191 K5 **Kentallen** Highld
54 B3 **Kentchurch** Herefs
77 G2 **Kentford** Suffk
35 J2 **Kent International Airport** Kent
12 D2 **Kentisbeare** Devon
23 K3 **Kentisbury** Devon
44 F3 **Kentish Town** Gt Lon
138 C6 **Kentmere** Cumb
12 B5 **Kenton** Devon
44 D3 **Kenton** Gt Lon
150 F2 **Kenton** N u Ty
78 E2 **Kenton** Suffk
190 D3 **Kentra** Highld
55 H4 **Kent's Green** Gloucs
28 F6 **Kent's Oak** Hants
4 C6 **Kenwyn** Cnwll
228 F3 **Keoldale** Highld
200 D1 **Keppoch** Highld
133 G2 **Kepwick** N York
86 D6 **Keresley** Covtry
2 D5 **Kerris** Cnwll
82 D5 **Kerry** Powys
173 J6 **Kerrycroy** Ag & B
116 B8 **Kersall** Notts
12 D5 **Kersbrook** Devon
78 B5 **Kersey** Suffk
232 f3 **Kershader** W Isls
12 D2 **Kerswell** Devon
70 F5 **Kerswell Green** Worcs
78 F5 **Kesgrave** Suffk
93 L6 **Kessingland** Suffk
4 F6 **Kestle** Cnwll
4 D4 **Kestle Mill** Cnwll
45 H7 **Keston** Gt Lon
137 J3 **Keswick** Cumb
92 E3 **Keswick** Norfk

118 E6 **Ketsby** Lincs
88 C7 **Kettering** Nhants
92 E3 **Ketteringham** Norfk
195 K8 **Kettins** P & K
77 L4 **Kettlebaston** Suffk
186 E6 **Kettlebridge** Fife
86 B3 **Kettlebrook** Staffs
78 F3 **Kettleburgh** Suffk
155 K6 **Kettleholm** D & G
113 M5 **Kettleshulme** Ches
132 C7 **Kettlesing** N York
132 C7 **Kettlesing Bottom** N York
106 A6 **Kettlestone** Norfk
116 D6 **Kettlethorpe** Lincs
234 d4 **Kettletoft** Ork
131 H5 **Kettlewell** N York
88 E3 **Ketton** Rutlnd
44 D5 **Kew** Gt Lon
44 D5 **Kew Gardens** Gt Lon
37 M7 **Kewstoke** N Som
116 E4 **Kexby** Lincs
125 G1 **Kexby** York
113 K8 **Key Green** Ches
87 J3 **Keyham** Leics
16 C4 **Keyhaven** Hants
127 G5 **Keyingham** E R Yk
19 J3 **Keymer** W Susx
38 F6 **Keynsham** BaNES
74 F3 **Keysoe** Beds
74 F3 **Keysoe Row** Beds
88 F7 **Keyston** Cambs
101 L6 **Keyworth** Notts
151 G4 **Kibblesworth** Gatesd
87 K5 **Kibworth Beauchamp** Leics
87 K5 **Kibworth Harcourt** Leics
45 H5 **Kidbrooke** Gt Lon
84 E7 **Kidderminster** Worcs
57 J5 **Kidlington** Oxon
42 B5 **Kidmore End** Oxon
145 J7 **Kidsdale** D & G
99 J2 **Kidsgrove** Staffs
50 E4 **Kidwelly** Carmth
191 H8 **Kiel Crofts** Ag & B
157 G4 **Kielder** Nthumb
171 H5 **Kiells** Ag & B
174 D5 **Kilbarchan** Rens
199 K4 **Kilbeg** Highld
172 C5 **Kilberry** Ag & B
174 C7 **Kilbirnie** N Ayrs
172 C3 **Kilbride** Ag & B
173 H5 **Kilbride** Ag & B
182 B3 **Kilbride** Ag & B
214 D3 **Kilbuiack** Moray
101 G4 **Kilburn** Derbys
44 E4 **Kilburn** Gt Lon
133 H4 **Kilburn** N York
87 J4 **Kilby** Leics
172 D6 **Kilchamaig** Ag & B
173 J7 **Kilchattan** Ag & B
180 E7 **Kilchattan** Ag & B
191 G8 **Kilcheran** Ag & B
189 L4 **Kilchoan** Highld
170 D5 **Kilchoman** Ag & B
182 E3 **Kilchrenan** Ag & B
187 H6 **Kilconquhar** Fife
55 G3 **Kilcot** Gloucs
212 E4 **Kilcoy** Highld
173 L3 **Kilcreggan** Ag & B
142 D5 **Kildale** N York
161 J5 **Kildalloig** Ag & B
223 G6 **Kildary** Highld
173 G5 **Kildavaig** Ag & B
173 H5 **Kildavanan** Ag & B
227 G4 **Kildonan** Highld
162 D5 **Kildonan** N Ayrs
226 F4 **Kildonan Lodge** Highld
199 G7 **Kildonnan** Highld

144 C4 **Kildrochet House** D & G
205 K2 **Kildrummy** Abers
122 F2 **Kildwick** N York
174 F4 **Kilfinan** Ag & B
201 K6 **Kilfinnan** Highld
49 J6 **Kilgetty** Pembks
152 F2 **Kilgrammie** S Ayrs
38 C2 **Kilgwrrwg Common** Mons
135 G6 **Kilham** E R Yk
188 B7 **Kilkenneth** Ag & B
161 H4 **Kilkenzie** Ag & B
161 J5 **Kilkerran** Ag & B
9 H3 **Kilkhampton** Cnwll
115 J5 **Killamarsh** Derbys
51 H6 **Killay** Swans
174 F2 **Killearn** Stirlg
213 G3 **Killen** Highld
140 F3 **Killerby** Darltn
12 C3 **Killerton** Devon
193 J5 **Killichonan** P & K
190 B7 **Killiechronan** Ag & B
194 E4 **Killiecrankie** P & K
210 E7 **Killilan** Highld
184 C2 **Killin** Stirlg
132 D7 **Killinghall** N York
130 C2 **Killington** Cumb
159 G7 **Killingworth** N Tyne
167 G1 **Killochyett** Border
174 C4 **Kilmacolm** Inver
184 D5 **Kilmahog** Stirlg
182 A8 **Kilmahumaig** Ag & B
218 C6 **Kilmaluag** Highld
186 F3 **Kilmany** Fife
163 K2 **Kilmarnock** E Ayrs
182 B7 **Kilmartin** Ag & B
163 K2 **Kilmaurs** E Ayrs
182 B5 **Kilmelford** Ag & B
27 G2 **Kilmersdon** Somset
29 L6 **Kilmeston** Hants
161 H5 **Kilmichael** Ag & B
182 B8 **Kilmichael Glassary** Ag & B
172 D2 **Kilmichael of Inverlussa** Ag & B
13 H3 **Kilmington** Devon
27 H4 **Kilmington** Wilts
27 H4 **Kilmington Common** Wilts
27 H4 **Kilmington Street** Wilts
212 D5 **Kilmorack** Highld
182 C3 **Kilmore** Ag & B
199 K4 **Kilmore** Highld
172 C4 **Kilmory** Ag & B
190 B3 **Kilmory** Highld
162 B5 **Kilmory** N Ayrs
208 D5 **Kilmuir** Highld
213 G4 **Kilmuir** Highld
218 B7 **Kilmuir** Highld
223 G6 **Kilmuir** Highld
173 K3 **Kilmun** Ag & B
170 F4 **Kilnave** Ag & B
176 B8 **Kilncadzow** S Lans
33 J6 **Kilndown** Kent
182 B3 **Kilninver** Ag & B
150 C4 **Kiln Pit Hill** Nthumb
127 J7 **Kilnsea** E R Yk
131 H6 **Kilnsey** N York
126 C1 **Kilnwick** E R Yk
180 E7 **Kiloran** Ag & B
162 A4 **Kilpatrick** N Ayrs
54 C3 **Kilpeck** Herefs
125 J5 **Kilpin** E R Yk
187 J6 **Kilrenny** Fife
73 H1 **Kilsby** Nhants
186 D5 **Kilspindie** P & K
144 D7 **Kilstay** D & G
175 J3 **Kilsyth** N Lans
212 D6 **Kiltarlity** Highld
142 E4 **Kilton** R & Cl

142 E4 **Kilton Thorpe** R & Cl
218 B7 **Kilvaxter** Highld
25 H3 **Kilve** Somset
102 D4 **Kilvington** Notts
92 C3 **Kimberley** Norfk
101 J4 **Kimberley** Notts
115 H3 **Kimberworth** Rothm
151 G5 **Kimblesworth** Dur
75 G2 **Kimbolton** Cambs
69 K3 **Kimbolton** Herefs
87 H6 **Kimcote** Leics
15 H4 **Kimmeridge** Dorset
28 F3 **Kimpton** Hants
59 K4 **Kimpton** Herts
226 F3 **Kinbrace** Highld
185 G6 **Kinbuck** Stirlg
187 G4 **Kincaple** Fife
176 C2 **Kincardine** Fife
222 E4 **Kincardine** Highld
206 B5 **Kincardine O'Neil** Abers
195 J8 **Kinclaven** P & K
207 H5 **Kincorth** C Aber
214 C3 **Kincorth House** Moray
203 K4 **Kincraig** Highld
194 F6 **Kincraigie** P & K
194 F6 **Kindallachan** P & K
172 B7 **Kinerarach** Ag & B
56 C3 **Kineton** Gloucs
72 D4 **Kineton** Warwks
186 C3 **Kinfauns** P & K
163 H3 **Kinfold** S Ayrs
173 J6 **Kingarth** Ag & B
81 G3 **King Arthur's Labyrinth** Gwynd
207 G5 **Kingcausie** Abers
54 B6 **Kingcoed** Mons
117 H3 **Kingerby** Lincs
9 H4 **Kingford** Devon
56 E3 **Kingham** Oxon
155 G7 **Kingholm Quay** D & G
177 H2 **Kinghorn** Fife
186 D7 **Kinglassie** Fife
196 B5 **Kingoldrum** Angus
186 E2 **Kingoodie** P & K
6 C5 **Kingsand** Cnwll
187 K5 **Kingsbarns** Fife
7 H6 **Kingsbridge** Devon
24 F4 **Kingsbridge** Somset
85 K1 **King's Bromley** Staffs
208 F4 **Kingsburgh** Highld
44 D3 **Kingsbury** Gt Lon
86 B4 **Kingsbury** Warwks
26 B7 **Kingsbury Episcopi** Somset
54 E3 **Kings Caple** Herefs
41 K8 **Kingsclere** Hants
46 K4 **King's Cliffe** Nhants
39 J2 **Kingscote** Gloucs
23 H7 **Kingscott** Devon
71 J3 **King's Coughton** Warwks
162 D4 **Kingscross** N Ayrs
26 D4 **Kingsdon** Somset
35 K5 **Kingsdown** Kent
40 D3 **Kingsdown** Swindn
39 J6 **Kingsdown** Wilts
176 F1 **Kingseat** Fife
58 C6 **Kingsey** Bucks
31 K4 **Kingsfold** W Susx
206 F4 **Kingsford** C Aber
174 E8 **Kingsford** E Ayrs
35 K1 **Kingsgate** Kent
77 K3 **Kingshall Street** Suffk
23 J4 **Kingsheanton** Devon
85 J7 **King's Heath** Birm
33 H3 **Kings Hill** Kent
84 H4 **King's Hill** Wsall
192 D5 **Kings House Hotel** Highld

184 C4 **Kingshouse Hotel** Stirlg
7 K3 **Kingskerswell** Devon
186 E5 **Kingskettle** Fife
69 J3 **Kingsland** Herefs
108 C5 **Kingsland** IoA
59 H7 **Kings Langley** Herts
112 D6 **Kingsley** Ches
30 C4 **Kingsley** Hants
100 A3 **Kingsley** Staffs
30 E5 **Kingsley Green** W Susx
73 L3 **Kingsley Park** Nhants
104 F8 **King's Lynn** Norfk
138 E3 **Kings Meaburn** Cumb
236 c3 **King's Mills** Guern
196 D6 **Kingsmuir** Angus
166 C2 **Kings Muir** Border
187 J5 **Kingsmuir** Fife
86 F7 **Kings Newnham** Warwks
34 D6 **Kingsnorth** Kent
85 J7 **King's Norton** Birm
87 K4 **King's Norton** Leics
23 L7 **King's Nympton** Devon
69 J4 **King's Pyon** Herefs
89 J7 **Kings Ripton** Cambs
29 G5 **King's Somborne** Hants
14 D1 **King's Stag** Dorset
55 J7 **King's Stanley** Gloucs
72 F7 **King's Sutton** Nhants
85 J4 **Kingstanding** Birm
7 K2 **Kingsteignton** Devon
54 D2 **Kingsthorne** Herefs
73 L2 **Kingsthorpe** Nhants
75 L4 **Kingston** Cambs
6 C4 **Kingston** Cnwll
6 F6 **Kingston** Devon
14 E1 **Kingston** Dorset
15 H6 **Kingston** Dorset
178 C3 **Kingston** E Loth
16 F6 **Kingston** IoW
35 G4 **Kingston** Kent
57 H7 **Kingston Bagpuize** Oxon
58 C7 **Kingston Blount** Oxon
27 J4 **Kingston Deverill** Wilts
69 H7 **Kingstone** Herefs
26 B8 **Kingstone** Somset
100 B6 **Kingstone** Staffs
40 F3 **Kingston Lisle** Oxon
19 K4 **Kingston near Lewes** E Susx
101 J6 **Kingston on Soar** Notts
215 H2 **Kingston on Spey** Moray
14 B4 **Kingston Russell** Dorset
25 K5 **Kingston St Mary** Somset
38 B6 **Kingston Seymour** N Som
126 D5 **Kingston upon Hull** C KuH
44 D6 **Kingston upon Thames** Gt Lon
59 K4 **King's Walden** Herts
7 K5 **Kingswear** Devon
207 G4 **Kingswells** C Aber
38 D5 **Kings Weston** Bristl
84 F5 **Kingswinford** Dudley
58 B4 **Kingswood** Bucks
39 H3 **Kingswood** Gloucs
38 F5 **Kingswood** S Glos
25 H4 **Kingswood** Somset
31 L1 **Kingswood** Surrey
71 L1 **Kingswood** Warwks

84 E3 **Kingswood Common** Staffs
29 J5 **Kings Worthy** Hants
117 J6 **Kingthorpe** Lincs
68 F3 **Kington** Herefs
38 F3 **Kington** S Glos
71 H4 **Kington** Worcs
39 L5 **Kington Langley** Wilts
27 H6 **Kington Magna** Dorset
39 K5 **Kington St Michael** Wilts
203 H5 **Kingussie** Highld
26 D5 **Kingweston** Somset
217 H7 **Kinharrachie** Abers
147 G2 **Kinharvie** D & G
185 J4 **Kinkell Bridge** P & K
217 J2 **Kinknockie** Abers
177 G5 **Kinleith** C Edin
84 C7 **Kinlet** Shrops
198 F5 **Kinloch** Highld
225 H2 **Kinloch** Highld
229 H5 **Kinloch** Highld
195 J7 **Kinloch** P & K
195 L7 **Kinloch** P & K
184 B6 **Kinlochard** Stirlg
228 C4 **Kinlochbervie** Highld
191 J1 **Kinlocheil** Highld
210 F3 **Kinlochewe** Highld
200 B8 **Kinloch Hourn** Highld
202 E7 **Kinlochlaggan** Highld
192 C4 **Kinlochleven** Highld
190 E2 **Kinlochmoidart** Highld
200 B8 **Kinlochnanuagh** Highld
193 L5 **Kinloch Rannoch** P & K
214 C3 **Kinloss** Moray
110 D5 **Kinmel Bay** Conwy
206 F2 **Kinmuck** Abers
207 G2 **Kinmundy** Abers
160 B2 **Kinnabus** Ag & B
217 J6 **Kinnadie** Abers
194 F5 **Kinnaird** P & K
197 G5 **Kinnaird Castle** Angus
214 F1 **Kinneddar** Moray
197 K2 **Kinneff** Abers
155 H2 **Kinnelhead** D & G
196 F6 **Kinnell** Angus
97 M7 **Kinnerley** Shrops
69 G5 **Kinnersley** Herefs
70 F5 **Kinnersley** Worcs
68 E2 **Kinnerton** Powys
186 C6 **Kinnesswood** P & K
140 D3 **Kinninvie** Dur
196 B5 **Kinnordy** Angus
102 B6 **Kinoulton** Notts
186 B6 **Kinross** P & K
186 C2 **Kinrossie** P & K
69 G2 **Kinsham** Herefs
71 J7 **Kinsham** Worcs
124 C7 **Kinsley** Wakefd
15 K3 **Kinson** Bmouth
200 F2 **Kintail** Highld
41 G6 **Kintbury** W Berk
214 B3 **Kintessack** Moray
186 B4 **Kintillo** P & K
83 H8 **Kinton** Herefs
98 A8 **Kinton** Shrops
206 E3 **Kintore** Abers
171 H7 **Kintour** Ag & B
180 D3 **Kintra** Ag & B
182 B6 **Kintraw** Ag & B
161 J2 **Kintyre** Ag & B
203 L2 **Kinveachy** Highld
84 E6 **Kinver** Staffs
124 C4 **Kippax** Leeds
184 E7 **Kippen** Stirlg
146 E4 **Kippford or Scaur** D & G

33 H5 **Kipping's Cross** Kent
234 b6 **Kirbister** Ork
93 G3 **Kirby Bedon** Norfk
102 B8 **Kirby Bellars** Leics
93 H5 **Kirby Cane** Norfk
62 E4 **Kirby Cross** Essex
87 G3 **Kirby Fields** Leics
134 D6 **Kirby Grindalythe** N York
132 F5 **Kirby Hill** N York
140 E6 **Kirby Hill** N York
133 G3 **Kirby Knowle** N York
62 F4 **Kirby le Soken** Essex
134 B4 **Kirby Misperton** N York
87 G3 **Kirby Muxloe** Leics
93 H5 **Kirby Row** Norfk
141 K7 **Kirby Sigston** N York
134 C7 **Kirby Underdale** E R Yk
132 E3 **Kirby Wiske** N York
31 G6 **Kirdford** W Susx
231 K4 **Kirk** Highld
235 d6 **Kirkabister** Shet
146 A5 **Kirkandrews** D & G
148 C4 **Kirkandrews upon Eden** Cumb
148 B4 **Kirkbampton** Cumb
147 G3 **Kirkbean** D & G
124 F7 **Kirk Bramwith** Donc
147 M4 **Kirkbride** Cumb
196 E7 **Kirkbuddo** Angus
166 D2 **Kirkburn** Border
134 F7 **Kirkburn** E R Yk
123 J7 **Kirkburton** Kirk
111 L2 **Kirkby** Knows
117 H3 **Kirkby** Lincs
142 C6 **Kirkby** N York
141 G7 **Kirkby Fleetham** N York
103 H2 **Kirkby Green** Lincs
101 J2 **Kirkby in Ashfield** Notts
128 F3 **Kirkby-in-Furness** Cumb
103 J4 **Kirkby la Thorpe** Lincs
130 B4 **Kirkby Lonsdale** Cumb
131 G7 **Kirkby Malham** N York
86 F4 **Kirkby Mallory** Leics
132 C5 **Kirkby Malzeard** N York
133 L3 **Kirkbymoorside** N York
118 C8 **Kirkby on Bain** Lincs
123 L2 **Kirkby Overblow** N York
139 H5 **Kirkby Stephen** Cumb
138 F3 **Kirkby Thore** Cumb
103 H6 **Kirkby Underwood** Lincs
124 D3 **Kirkby Wharf** N York
186 D3 **Kirkcaldy** Fife
148 F2 **Kirkcambeck** Cumb
146 B5 **Kirkchrist** D & G
144 B2 **Kirkcolm** D & G
164 E6 **Kirkconnel** D & G
146 B3 **Kirkconnell** D & G
147 G2 **Kirkconnell** D & G
145 G3 **Kirkcowan** D & G
146 B5 **Kirkcudbright** D & G
111 K3 **Kirkdale** Lpool
124 B1 **Kirk Deighton** N York
126 C5 **Kirk Ella** E R Yk
165 G2 **Kirkfieldbank** S Lans
146 F2 **Kirkgunzeon** D & G
101 J4 **Kirk Hallam** Derbys
120 F4 **Kirkham** Lancs
134 B6 **Kirkham** N York

123 K6 **Kirkhamgate** Wakefd
133 G7 **Kirk Hammerton** N York
158 C5 **Kirkharle** Nthumb
149 H5 **Kirkhaugh** Nthumb
123 H6 **Kirkheaton** Kirk
158 C6 **Kirkheaton** Nthumb
212 E5 **Kirkhill** Highld
165 J7 **Kirkhope** S Lans
199 H2 **Kirkibost** Highld
195 L7 **Kirkinch** P & K
145 J5 **Kirkinner** D & G
175 H4 **Kirkintilloch** E Duns
100 E3 **Kirk Ireton** Derbys
136 E4 **Kirkland** Cumb
154 E4 **Kirkland** D & G
155 H4 **Kirkland** D & G
164 E6 **Kirkland** D & G
100 F5 **Kirk Langley** Derbys
142 D3 **Kirkleatham** R & Cl
141 K5 **Kirklevington** S on T
93 L5 **Kirkley** Suffk
132 D4 **Kirklington** N York
102 B2 **Kirklington** Notts
148 D2 **Kirklinton** Cumb
176 F4 **Kirkliston** C Edin
145 K4 **Kirkmabreck** D & G
144 D7 **Kirkmaiden** D & G
141 G2 **Kirk Merrington** Dur
237 c4 **Kirk Michael** IoM
195 H4 **Kirkmichael** P & K
163 J7 **Kirkmichael** S Ayrs
164 F2 **Kirkmuirhill** S Lans
168 D4 **Kirknewton** Nthumb
176 F5 **Kirknewton** W Loth
215 L7 **Kirkney** Abers
175 L5 **Kirk of Shotts** N Lans
148 F6 **Kirkoswald** Cumb
163 G7 **Kirkoswald** S Ayrs
154 F4 **Kirkpatrick** D & G
154 D7 **Kirkpatrick Durham** D & G
156 B7 **Kirkpatrick-Fleming** D & G
124 F8 **Kirk Sandall** Donc
128 D4 **Kirksanton** Cumb
124 D7 **Kirk Smeaton** N York
123 K4 **Kirkstall** Leeds
103 K1 **Kirkstead** Lincs
215 L7 **Kirkstile** Abers
156 C4 **Kirkstile** D & G
231 L2 **Kirkstyle** Highld
124 B6 **Kirkthorpe** Wakefd
206 C1 **Kirkton** Abers
216 F5 **Kirkton** Abers
155 G6 **Kirkton** D & G
186 F3 **Kirkton** Fife
210 C8 **Kirkton** Highld
210 D6 **Kirkton** Highld
185 K4 **Kirkton** P & K
166 C2 **Kirkton Manor** Border
195 L6 **Kirkton of Airlie** Angus
196 B8 **Kirkton of Auchterhouse** Angus
213 K5 **Kirkton of Barevan** Highld
186 C2 **Kirkton of Collace** P & K
205 J3 **Kirkton of Glenbuchat** Abers
217 J7 **Kirkton of Logie Buchan** Abers
196 E4 **Kirkton of Menmuir** Angus
196 E8 **Kirkton of Monikie** Angus
216 D7 **Kirkton of Rayne** Abers
206 F2 **Kirkton of Skene** Abers

186 F1 **Kirkton of Strathmartine** Angus
196 C8 **Kirkton of Tealing** Angus
206 C3 **Kirkton of Tough** Abers
217 J2 **Kirktown** Abers
217 K4 **Kirktown** Abers
216 D3 **Kirktown of Alvah** Abers
206 F1 **Kirktown of Bourtie** Abers
206 F7 **Kirktown of Fetteresso** Abers
215 H6 **Kirktown of Mortlach** Moray
217 K8 **Kirktown of Slains** Abers
165 M1 **Kirkurd** Border
234 c6 **Kirkwall** Ork
234 c6 Kirkwall Airport Ork
158 C5 **Kirkwhelpington** Nthumb
168 C4 **Kirk Yetholm** Border
126 D7 **Kirmington** N Linc
117 K3 **Kirmond le Mire** Lincs
173 K3 **Kirn** Ag & B
196 C5 **Kirriemuir** Angus
93 G4 **Kirstead Green** Norfk
155 M7 **Kirtlebridge** D & G
77 G3 **Kirtling** Cambs
76 F4 **Kirtling Green** Cambs
57 J4 **Kirtlington** Oxon
229 M3 **Kirtomy** Highld
104 A5 **Kirton** Lincs
116 B7 **Kirton** Notts
78 F6 **Kirton** Suffk
174 D4 **Kirtonhill** W Duns
116 F2 **Kirton in Lindsey** N Linc
145 J4 **Kirwaugh** D & G
210 C6 **Kishorn** Highld
73 K3 **Kislingbury** Nhants
25 G6 **Kittisford** Somset
207 H4 **Kittybrewster** C Aber
54 C2 **Kivernoll** Herefs
115 J5 **Kiveton Park** Rothm
116 D5 **Knaith** Lincs
27 J6 **Knap Corner** Dorset
42 F8 **Knaphill** Surrey
25 L6 **Knapp** Somset
134 D4 **Knapton** N York
107 G5 **Knapton** Norfk
124 E1 **Knapton** York
75 K2 **Knapwell** Cambs
132 E7 **Knaresborough** N York
149 H4 **Knarsdale** Nthumb
217 G5 **Knaven** Abers
132 F2 **Knayton** N York
59 L4 **Knebworth** Herts
125 H5 **Knedlington** E R Yk
116 B8 **Kneesall** Notts
75 L5 **Kneesworth** Cambs
102 B4 **Kneeton** Notts
50 F7 **Knelston** Swans
99 L5 **Knenhall** Staffs
72 E4 **Knightcote** Warwks
99 J7 **Knightley** Staffs
87 H4 **Knighton** C Leic
14 C1 **Knighton** Dorset
82 F8 **Knighton** Powys
25 J3 **Knighton** Somset
99 G4 **Knighton** Staffs
99 H6 **Knighton** Staffs
70 B1 **Knighton on Teme** Worcs
70 D4 **Knightwick** Worcs
68 F3 **Knill** Herefs
102 D6 **Knipton** Leics
100 E3 **Kniveton** Derbys
138 F2 **Knock** Cumb

199 K4 **Knock** Highld
215 L4 **Knock** Moray
232 g2 **Knock** W Isls
227 K3 **Knockally** Highld
224 F6 **Knockan** Highld
214 F6 **Knockando** Moray
212 E5 **Knockbain** Highld
212 F3 **Knockbain** Highld
173 L5 **Knock Castle** N Ayrs
231 H4 **Knockdee** Highld
39 J3 **Knockdown** Wilts
153 G3 **Knockeen** S Ayrs
162 D4 **Knockenkelly** N Ayrs
163 K2 **Knockentiber** E Ayrs
32 E2 **Knockholt** Kent
32 E2 **Knockholt Pound** Kent
97 M7 **Knockin** Shrops
163 K2 **Knockinlaw** E Ayrs
144 B3 **Knocknain** D & G
153 M5 **Knocksheen** D & G
154 D7 **Knockvennie Smithy** D & G
79 J3 **Knodishall** Suffk
26 C6 **Knole** Somset
113 J5 **Knolls Green** Ches
98 B5 **Knolton** Wrexhm
27 L3 **Knook** Wilts
88 B2 **Knossington** Leics
120 E2 **Knott End-on-Sea** Lancs
74 E2 **Knotting** Beds
74 E3 **Knotting Green** Beds
124 D5 **Knottingley** Wakefd
112 B3 **Knotty Ash** Lpool
83 L7 **Knowbury** Shrops
153 G7 **Knowe** D & G
154 A4 **Knowehead** D & G
163 G6 **Knoweside** S Ayrs
38 E6 **Knowle** Bristl
11 H5 **Knowle** Devon
12 C2 **Knowle** Devon
12 D6 **Knowle** Devon
23 H4 **Knowle** Devon
83 L8 **Knowle** Shrops
85 L7 **Knowle** Solhll
24 E3 **Knowle** Somset
148 D4 **Knowlefield** Cumb
121 J3 **Knowle Green** Lancs
13 J1 **Knowle St Giles** Somset
42 D4 **Knowl Hill** W & M
112 C3 **Knowsley** Knows
112 C3 **Knowsley Safari Park** Knows
24 C6 **Knowstone** Devon
33 K5 **Knox Bridge** Kent
82 F8 **Knucklas** Powys
74 D2 **Knuston** Nhants
113 H5 **Knutsford** Ches
122 F6 **Krumlin** Calder
3 J7 **Kuggar** Cnwll
200 B1 **Kyleakin** Highld
210 B8 **Kyle of Lochalsh** Highld
200 B2 **Kylerhea** Highld
224 F2 **Kylesku** Highld
200 C6 **Kylesmorar** Highld
232 e4 **Kyles Scalpay** W Isls
224 F2 **Kylestrome** Highld
84 C1 **Kynnersley** Wrekin
69 L2 **Kyrewood** Worcs

L

232 f3 **Lacasaigh** W Isls
232 f2 **Lacasdal** W Isls
117 K1 **Laceby** NE Lin
58 D7 **Lacey Green** Bucks
113 G6 **Lach Dennis** Ches

77 H1 **Lackford** Suffk
77 H1 **Lackford Green** Suffk
39 K6 **Lacock** Wilts
72 E3 **Ladbroke** Warwks
33 J4 **Laddingford** Kent
4 D5 **Ladock** Cnwll
234 d4 **Lady** Ork
186 E5 **Ladybank** Fife
165 H4 **Ladygill** S Lans
128 E3 **Lady Hall** Cumb
179 J8 **Ladykirk** Border
85 J6 **Ladywood** Birm
70 F3 **Ladywood** Worcs
236 e1 **La Fontenelle** Guern
154 F5 **Lag** D & G
190 D4 **Laga** Highld
160 C1 **Lagavulin** Ag & B
162 B5 **Lagg** N Ayrs
201 L6 **Laggan** Highld
202 F6 **Laggan** Highld
236 b5 **La Greve de Lecq** Jersey
228 F4 **Laid** Highld
219 L3 **Laide** Highld
199 G7 **Laig** Highld
174 E8 **Laigh Clunch** E Ayrs
163 L2 **Laigh Fenwick** E Ayrs
164 C5 **Laigh Glenmuir** E Ayrs
175 J7 **Laighstonehall** S Lans
46 B3 **Laindon** Essex
225 M7 **Lairg** Highld
123 J4 **Laisterdyke** Brad
17 H5 **Lake** IoW
15 J4 **Lake** Poole
28 C4 **Lake** Wilts
137 H5 **Lake District National Park** Cumb
91 G6 **Lakenheath** Suffk
90 D7 **Lakesend** Norfk
36 D4 **Laleston** Brdgnd
177 G7 **Lamancha** Border
77 K7 **Lamarsh** Essex
106 F7 **Lamas** Norfk
167 L2 **Lambden** Border
33 H6 **Lamberhurst** Kent
33 H6 **Lamberhurst Down** Kent
179 K6 **Lamberton** Border
44 F4 **Lambeth** Gt Lon
77 G4 **Lambfair Green** Suffk
101 M4 **Lambley** Notts
149 H4 **Lambley** Nthumb
40 F5 **Lambourn** W Berk
45 J2 **Lambourne End** Essex
31 L4 **Lambs Green** W Susx
6 C1 **Lamerton** Devon
151 G4 **Lamesley** Gatesd
165 J3 **Lamington** S Lans
162 C3 **Lamlash** N Ayrs
148 D7 **Lamonby** Cumb
2 E6 **Lamorna** Cnwll
4 D7 **Lamorran** Cnwll
66 D5 **Lampeter** Cerdgn
49 K5 **Lampeter Velfrey** Pembks
49 H7 **Lamphey** Pembks
136 F3 **Lamplugh** Cumb
87 L8 **Lamport** Nhants
26 F4 **Lamyatt** Somset
165 G2 **Lanark** S Lans
129 K7 **Lancaster** Lancs
150 F5 **Lanchester** Dur
19 G5 **Lancing** W Susx
236 d1 **L'Ancresse** Guern
76 C2 **Landbeach** Cambs
23 G6 **Landcross** Devon
206 E4 **Landerberry** Abers
28 E7 **Landford** Wilts
227 L2 **Land-hallow** Highld
50 D7 **Landimore** Swans
23 J5 **Landkey** Devon

23 J5 **Landkey Town** Devon
51 J6 **Landore** Swans
6 B4 **Landrake** Cnwll
7 H3 **Landscove** Devon
2 C6 **Land's End** Cnwll
2 C5 Land's End Airport Cnwll
6 C4 **Landulph** Cnwll
4 C4 **Lane** Cnwll
9 G7 **Laneast** Cnwll
42 D3 **Lane End** Bucks
27 J3 **Lane End** Wilts
100 E5 **Lane Ends** Derbys
128 D2 **Lane End Waberthwaite** Cumb
116 D6 **Laneham** Notts
140 E5 **Lane Head** Dur
149 L6 **Lanehead** Dur
25 K6 **Langaller** Somset
102 B5 **Langar** Notts
174 D4 **Langbank** Rens
123 G1 **Langbar** N York
130 F6 **Langcliffe** N York
134 E2 **Langdale End** N York
16 E2 **Langdown** Hants
186 E6 **Langdyke** Fife
62 B4 **Langenhoe** Essex
75 H6 **Langford** Beds
12 D2 **Langford** Devon
61 K6 **Langford** Essex
102 D2 **Langford** Notts
56 E7 **Langford** Oxon
25 H6 **Langford Budville** Somset
62 B2 **Langham** Essex
106 B4 **Langham** Norfk
88 B2 **Langham** Rutlnd
77 L1 **Langham** Suffk
121 K4 **Langho** Lancs
156 C5 **Langholm** D & G
167 H3 **Langlee** Border
16 F3 **Langley** Hants
59 K4 **Langley** Herts
33 K3 **Langley** Kent
149 L3 **Langley** Nthumb
43 G5 **Langley** Slough
25 G5 **Langley** Somset
30 D5 **Langley** W Susx
71 L3 **Langley** Warwks
39 L5 **Langley Burrell** Wilts
61 L4 **Langley Green** Essex
25 G5 **Langley Marsh** Somset
150 F6 **Langley Park** Dur
93 H3 **Langley Street** Norfk
76 C7 **Langley Upper Green** Essex
20 D5 **Langney** E Susx
115 L4 **Langold** Notts
9 J7 **Langore** Cnwll
26 B6 **Langport** Somset
103 L3 **Langrick** Lincs
39 H6 **Langridge** BaNES
147 K5 **Langrigg** Cumb
30 B6 **Langrish** Hants
114 E2 **Langsett** Barns
185 G5 **Langside** P & K
17 K2 **Langstone** Hants
132 C2 **Langthorne** N York
132 F6 **Langthorpe** N York
140 C6 **Langthwaite** N York
134 F6 **Langtoft** E R Yk
89 G2 **Langtoft** Lincs
140 F4 **Langton** Dur
118 C7 **Langton** Lincs
118 E7 **Langton** Lincs
134 C6 **Langton** N York
117 J6 **Langton by Wragby** Lincs
32 F5 **Langton Green** Kent
14 C6 **Langton Herring** Dorset

15 J6 **Langton Matravers** Dorset
10 C2 **Langtree** Devon
148 F7 **Langwathby** Cumb
227 K4 **Langwell House** Highld
117 H6 **Langworth** Lincs
5 H3 **Lanhydrock House & Gardens** Cnwll
5 G3 **Lanivet** Cnwll
5 H2 **Lank** Cnwll
5 G4 **Lanlivery** Cnwll
3 J4 **Lanner** Cnwll
5 J4 **Lanreath** Cnwll
5 J5 **Lansallos** Cnwll
8 E7 **Lanteglos** Cnwll
5 J5 **Lanteglos Highway** Cnwll
167 J5 **Lanton** Border
168 D3 **Lanton** Nthumb
11 H3 **Lapford** Devon
160 C1 **Laphroaig** Ag & B
84 F2 **Lapley** Staffs
71 L1 **Lapworth** Warwks
190 E6 **Larachbeg** Highld
176 B3 **Larbert** Falk
216 B7 **Largie** Abers
172 F2 **Largiemore** Ag & B
187 H5 **Largoward** Fife
173 L6 **Largs** N Ayrs
162 D5 **Largybeg** N Ayrs
162 D5 **Largymore** N Ayrs
173 L4 **Larkfield** Inver
33 J2 **Larkfield** Kent
175 K7 **Larkhall** S Lans
28 C3 **Larkhill** Wilts
92 B5 **Larling** Norfk
236 e8 **La Rocque** Jersey
140 C4 **Lartington** Dur
30 A3 **Lasham** Hants
99 K2 **Lask Edge** Staffs
186 B8 **Lassodie** Fife
177 J5 **Lasswade** Mdloth
133 L2 **Lastingham** N York
61 L7 **Latchingdon** Essex
6 B2 **Latchley** Cnwll
74 C5 **Lathbury** M Keyn
227 L2 **Latheron** Highld
227 L3 **Latheronwheel** Highld
187 H5 **Lathones** Fife
59 G7 **Latimer** Bucks
38 F4 **Latteridge** S Glos
27 G6 **Lattiford** Somset
40 C2 **Latton** Wilts
178 C8 **Lauder** Border
50 C4 **Laugharne** Carmth
116 D6 **Laughterton** Lincs
20 A3 **Laughton** E Susx
87 J5 **Laughton** Leics
103 H6 **Laughton** Lincs
116 D3 **Laughton** Lincs
115 K4 **Laughton-en-le-Morthen** Rothm
9 H4 **Launcells** Cnwll
9 J7 **Launceston** Cnwll
57 L4 **Launton** Oxon
197 H3 **Laurencekirk** Abers
146 B3 **Laurieston** D & G
176 B3 **Laurieston** Falk
74 D4 **Lavendon** M Keyn
77 K5 **Lavenham** Suffk
37 J6 **Lavernock** V Glam
148 E3 **Laversdale** Cumb
28 D5 **Laverstock** Wilts
29 J2 **Laverstoke** Hants
71 J7 **Laverton** Gloucs
132 C5 **Laverton** N York
27 H2 **Laverton** Somset
236 d4 **La Villette** Guern
98 A2 **Lavister** Wrexhm
175 L7 **Law** S Lans

193 L7 **Lawers** P & K
62 C2 **Lawford** Essex
25 H4 **Lawford** Somset
186 A3 **Lawgrove** P & K
175 L7 **Law Hill** S Lans
9 J7 **Lawhitton** Cnwll
130 E6 **Lawkland** N York
49 H6 **Lawrenny** Pembks
77 K4 **Lawshall** Suffk
232 F3 **Laxay** W Isls
232 f2 **Laxdale** W Isls
237 d4 **Laxey** IoM
93 G8 **Laxfield** Suffk
228 C6 **Laxford Bridge** Highld
235 d4 **Laxo** Shet
125 J5 **Laxton** E R Yk
88 D4 **Laxton** Nhants
116 B7 **Laxton** Notts
122 F3 **Laycock** Brad
61 M4 **Layer Breton** Essex
62 A4 **Layer-de-la-Haye** Essex
61 L4 **Layer Marney** Essex
78 B6 **Layham** Suffk
13 K2 **Laymore** Dorset
125 H3 **Laytham** E R Yk
147 M4 **Laythes** Cumb
148 F6 **Lazonby** Cumb
101 G2 **Lea** Derbys
54 F4 **Lea** Herefs
116 D4 **Lea** Lincs
83 G5 **Lea** Shrops
39 L3 **Lea** Wilts
212 F5 **Leachkin** Highld
177 H7 **Leadburn** Border
102 F3 **Leadenham** Lincs
60 F5 **Leaden Roding** Essex
150 E5 **Leadgate** Dur
165 G6 **Leadhills** S Lans
56 F5 **Leafield** Oxon
59 H4 **Leagrave** Luton
104 C3 **Leake Common Side** Lincs
142 F5 **Lealholm** N York
209 H3 **Lealt** Highld
86 B5 **Lea Marston** Warwks
72 F2 **Leamington Hastings** Warwks
72 D2 **Leamington Spa** Warwks
20 C4 **Leap Cross** E Susx
129 K3 **Leasgill** Cumb
103 H3 **Leasingham** Lincs
141 G2 **Leasingthorne** Dur
31 K1 **Leatherhead** Surrey
123 J2 **Leathley** N York
98 C8 **Leaton** Shrops
34 D4 **Leaveland** Kent
77 L6 **Leavenheath** Suffk
134 C6 **Leavening** N York
45 H7 **Leaves Green** Gt Lon
135 G2 **Lebberston** N York
236 c4 **Le Bourg** Guern
56 E7 **Lechlade on Thames** Gloucs
170 E5 **Lecht Gruinart** Ag & B
130 C4 **Leck** Lancs
193 L7 **Leckbuie** P & K
29 G4 **Leckford** Hants
73 K6 **Leckhampstead** Bucks
41 H5 **Leckhampstead** W Berk
41 H5 **Leckhampstead Thicket** W Berk
55 L4 **Leckhampton** Gloucs
220 F4 **Leckmelm** Highld
126 C2 **Leconfield** E R Yk
191 H8 **Ledaig** Ag & B
58 E4 **Ledburn** Bucks
70 C6 **Ledbury** Herefs

69 H4 **Ledgemoor** Herefs
224 F6 **Ledmore Junction** Highld
124 C4 **Ledsham** Leeds
124 C5 **Ledston** Leeds
57 H3 **Ledwell** Oxon
23 H3 **Lee** Devon
45 H5 **Lee** Gt Lon
83 J4 **Leebotwood** Shrops
98 D6 **Lee Brockhurst** Shrops
128 F5 **Leece** Cumb
46 B3 **Lee Chapel** Essex
58 E6 **Lee Clump** Bucks
33 L3 **Leeds** Kent
123 K4 **Leeds** Leeds
33 L3 **Leeds Castle** Kent
3 G4 **Leedstown** Cnwll
99 M2 **Leek** Staffs
72 C2 **Leek Wootton** Warwks
6 E5 **Lee Mill** Devon
132 D2 **Leeming** N York
132 D2 **Leeming Bar** N York
17 G3 **Lee-on-the-Solent** Hants
100 E5 **Lees** Derbys
113 L2 **Lees** Oldham
100 E5 **Lees Green** Derbys
87 L2 **Leesthorpe** Leics
97 K1 **Leeswood** Flints
186 C3 **Leetown** P & K
112 F6 **Leftwich** Ches
118 E5 **Legbourne** Lincs
167 J2 **Legerwood** Border
42 F5 **Legoland** W & M
117 J4 **Legsby** Lincs
87 H3 **Leicester** C Leic
87 G3 **Leicester Forest East** Leics
14 C2 **Leigh** Dorset
55 K3 **Leigh** Gloucs
32 F4 **Leigh** Kent
31 L3 **Leigh** Surrey
112 F2 **Leigh** Wigan
40 B3 **Leigh** Wilts
70 D4 **Leigh** Worcs
46 D4 **Leigh Beck** Essex
39 K5 **Leigh Delamere** Wilts
34 B7 **Leigh Green** Kent
175 H7 **Leigh Knoweglass** S Lans
46 D3 **Leigh-on-Sea** Sthend
15 J3 **Leigh Park** Dorset
70 D4 **Leigh Sinton** Worcs
85 J3 **Leighswood** Wsall
39 J3 **Leighterton** Gloucs
82 E3 **Leighton** Powys
84 B3 **Leighton** Shrops
89 G7 **Leighton Bromswold** Cambs
58 F3 **Leighton Buzzard** Beds
27 G3 **Leigh upon Mendip** Somset
38 E6 **Leigh Woods** N Som
69 J2 **Leinthall Earls** Herefs
69 J1 **Leinthall Starkes** Herefs
83 H8 **Leintwardine** Herefs
87 G5 **Leire** Leics
79 J3 **Leiston** Suffk
195 L7 **Leitfie** P & K
177 H3 **Leith** C Edin
168 B1 **Leitholm** Border
2 F4 **Lelant** Cnwll
126 F4 **Lelley** E R Yk
168 B3 **Lempitlaw** Border
232 f3 **Lemreway** W Isls
59 L5 **Lemsford** Herts

71 J5 **Lenchwick** Worcs
152 D4 **Lendalfoot** S Ayrs
184 C6 **Lendrick** Stirlg
217 L6 **Lendrum Terrace** Abers
34 B4 **Lenham** Kent
34 B5 **Lenham Heath** Kent
202 D1 **Lenie** Highld
168 C2 **Lennel** Border
146 A5 **Lennox Plunton** D & G
175 H3 **Lennoxtown** E Duns
101 K5 **Lenton** C Nott
103 G6 **Lenton** Lincs
106 D8 **Lenwade** Norfk
175 H4 **Lenzie** E Duns
205 L4 **Leochel-Cushnie** Abers
69 K3 **Leominster** Herefs
55 J7 **Leonard Stanley** Gloucs
208 B4 **Lephin** Highld
134 B7 **Leppington** N York
123 J7 **Lepton** Kirk
236 b3 **L'Eree** Guern
5 J4 **Lerryn** Cnwll
235 d6 **Lerwick** Shet
169 J6 **Lesbury** Nthumb
206 B1 **Leslie** Abers
186 D6 **Leslie** Fife
164 F2 **Lesmahagow** S Lans
8 F6 **Lesnewth** Cnwll
236 d2 **Les Quartiers** Guern
236 b7 **Les Quennevais** Jersey
107 H6 **Lessingham** Norfk
147 L5 **Lessonhall** Cumb
144 B3 **Leswalt** D & G
236 a6 **L'Etacq** Jersey
43 J2 **Letchmore Heath** Herts
59 L2 **Letchworth Garden City** Herts
41 G4 **Letcombe Bassett** Oxon
41 G3 **Letcombe Regis** Oxon
196 E6 **Letham** Angus
167 K7 **Letham** Border
176 B2 **Letham** Falk
186 E4 **Letham** Fife
197 G7 **Letham Grange** Angus
195 H7 **Lethendy** P & K
206 B2 **Lethenty** Abers
216 F6 **Lethenty** Abers
78 F3 **Letheringham** Suffk
106 C5 **Letheringsett** Norfk
219 L7 **Letterewe** Highld
200 D2 **Letterfearn** Highld
201 K6 **Letterfinlay Lodge Hotel** Highld
199 M7 **Lettermorar** Highld
220 F4 **Letters** Highld
165 H5 **Lettershaw** S Lans
48 F2 **Letterston** Pembks
204 C2 **Lettoch** Highld
214 D7 **Lettoch** Highld
69 G5 **Letton** Herefs
59 M5 **Letty Green** Herts
115 K4 **Letwell** Rothm
187 G3 **Leuchars** Fife
232 f3 **Leumrabhagh** W Isls
232 f3 **Leurbost** W Isls
84 F1 **Levedale** Staffs
126 D2 **Leven** E R Yk
186 F7 **Leven** Fife
129 K3 **Levens** Cumb
60 B4 **Levens Green** Herts
113 K3 **Levenshulme** Manch
235 c7 **Levenwick** Shet
232 d5 **Leverburgh** W Isls
90 C2 **Leverington** Cambs

59 H6 **Leverstock Green** Herts
104 C3 **Leverton** Lincs
236 C2 **Le Villocq** Guern
78 F6 **Levington** Suffk
134 C2 **Levisham** N York
56 F6 **Lew** Oxon
9 H8 **Lewannick** Cnwll
10 C7 **Lewdown** Devon
19 L4 **Lewes** E Susx
48 F3 **Leweston** Pembks
45 G5 **Lewisham** Gt Lon
212 D8 **Lewiston** Highld
36 E3 **Lewistown** Brdgnd
42 B2 **Lewknor** Oxon
34 C3 **Lewson Street** Kent
10 C7 **Lewtrenchard** Devon
62 A3 **Lexden** Essex
25 K4 **Lexworthy** Somset
33 H2 **Leybourne** Kent
131 L2 **Leyburn** N York
59 K3 **Leygreen** Herts
59 G7 **Ley Hill** Bucks
121 H6 **Leyland** Lancs
206 E3 **Leylodge** Abers
217 J4 **Leys** Abers
195 K8 **Leys** P & K
47 G6 **Leysdown-on-Sea** Kent
196 F6 **Leysmill** Angus
196 C6 **Leys of Cossans** Angus
69 L2 **Leysters** Herefs
45 G3 **Leyton** Gt Lon
45 H3 **Leytonstone** Gt Lon
5 M1 **Lezant** Cnwll
237 d3 **Lezayre** IoM
215 G3 **Lhanbryde** Moray
52 F3 **Libanus** Powys
165 J2 **Libberton** S Lans
177 J4 **Liberton** C Edin
85 K2 **Lichfield** Staffs
85 H7 **Lickey** Worcs
85 H8 **Lickey End** Worcs
30 F6 **Lickfold** W Susx
190 F4 **Liddesdale** Highld
40 E4 **Liddington** Swindn
77 G3 **Lidgate** Suffk
74 E6 **Lidlington** Beds
186 E2 **Liff** Angus
85 J7 **Lifford** Birm
9 K7 **Lifton** Devon
9 K7 **Liftondown** Devon
72 D4 **Lighthorne** Warwks
72 D4 **Lighthorne Heath** Warwks
42 F7 **Lightwater** Surrey
87 H7 **Lilbourne** Nhants
84 D1 **Lilleshall** Wrekin
59 J3 **Lilley** Herts
167 H4 **Lilliesleaf** Border
73 K6 **Lillingstone Dayrell** Bucks
73 K6 **Lillingstone Lovell** Bucks
26 F8 **Lillington** Dorset
15 K4 **Lilliput** Poole
25 J3 **Lilstock** Somset
59 H3 **Limbury** Luton
175 J7 **Limekilnburn** S Lans
176 E2 **Limekilns** Fife
176 B4 **Limerigg** Falk
16 E6 **Limerstone** IoW
55 J2 **Lime Street** Worcs
26 D6 **Limington** Somset
164 C4 **Limmerhaugh** E Ayrs
93 H3 **Limpenhoe** Norfk
39 H7 **Limpley Stoke** Wilts
32 D3 **Limpsfield** Surrey
32 D3 **Limpsfield Chart** Surrey
101 K3 **Linby** Notts

30 E5 **Linchmere** W Susx
155 G6 **Lincluden** D & G
116 F7 **Lincoln** Lincs
70 E2 **Lincomb** Worcs
129 J4 **Lindale** Cumb
128 F4 **Lindal in Furness** Cumb
32 C7 **Lindfield** W Susx
30 D4 **Lindford** Hants
123 G6 **Lindley** Kirk
123 J2 **Lindley Green** N York
70 C2 **Lindridge** Worcs
61 G3 **Lindsell** Essex
77 L5 **Lindsey** Suffk
78 B5 **Lindsey Tye** Suffk
142 E4 **Lingdale** R & Cl
69 G2 **Lingen** Herefs
32 C4 **Lingfield** Surrey
93 H2 **Lingwood** Norfk
218 B7 **Linicro** Highld
55 J2 **Linkend** Worcs
41 G8 **Linkenholt** Hants
5 L2 **Linkinhorne** Cnwll
177 J1 **Linktown** Fife
214 F3 **Linkwood** Moray
83 G5 **Linley** Shrops
70 C4 **Linley Green** Herefs
84 C4 **Linleygreen** Shrops
176 D3 **Linlithgow** W Loth
222 D2 **Linsidemore** Highld
58 E3 **Linslade** Beds
93 G7 **Linstead Parva** Suffk
148 D4 **Linstock** Cumb
85 H8 **Linthurst** Worcs
123 H7 **Linthwaite** Kirk
179 H6 **Lintlaw** Border
215 L2 **Lintmill** Moray
168 B4 **Linton** Border
76 E5 **Linton** Cambs
86 C1 **Linton** Derbys
54 F3 **Linton** Herefs
33 K3 **Linton** Kent
124 B2 **Linton** Leeds
131 J6 **Linton** N York
54 F3 **Linton Hill** Herefs
133 G7 **Linton-on-Ouse** N York
117 J4 **Linwood** Lincs
174 E5 **Linwood** Rens
233 b7 **Lionacleit** W Isls
232 g1 **Lional** W Isls
30 D5 **Liphook** Hants
111 J3 **Liscard** Wirral
24 D5 **Liscombe** Somset
5 K3 **Liskeard** Cnwll
30 C5 **Liss** Hants
135 H7 **Lissett** E R Yk
117 J5 **Lissington** Lincs
37 J4 **Lisvane** Cardif
37 M3 **Liswerry** Newpt
105 L8 **Litcham** Norfk
73 J4 **Litchborough** Nhants
29 J2 **Litchfield** Hants
111 K2 **Litherland** Sefton
75 K6 **Litlington** Cambs
20 B5 **Litlington** E Susx
76 D5 **Little Abington** Cambs
88 D8 **Little Addington** Nhants
145 J5 **Little Airies** D & G
71 K3 **Little Alne** Warwks
111 J1 **Little Altcar** Sefton
60 B5 **Little Amwell** Herts
139 G5 **Little Asby** Cumb
85 K4 **Little Aston** Staffs
142 C5 **Little Ayton** N York
61 J6 **Little Baddow** Essex
39 J4 **Little Badminton** S Glos
148 A4 **Little Bampton** Cumb
61 G2 **Little Bardfield** Essex

75 H3 **Little Barford** Beds
106 D5 **Little Barningham** Norfk
56 D5 **Little Barrington** Gloucs
112 C7 **Little Barrow** Ches
158 C6 **Little Bavington** Nthumb
40 F7 **Little Bedwyn** Wilts
62 D3 **Little Bentley** Essex
59 M6 **Little Berkhamsted** Herts
74 B3 **Little Billing** Nhants
58 F4 **Little Billington** Beds
54 D2 **Little Birch** Herefs
78 D5 **Little Blakenham** Suffk
148 E7 **Little Blencow** Cumb
31 G7 **Little Bognor** W Susx
100 F2 **Little Bolehill** Derbys
113 G4 **Little Bollington** Ches
31 J1 **Little Bookham** Surrey
116 D5 **Littleborough** Notts
122 D7 **Littleborough** Rochdl
35 G3 **Littlebourne** Kent
72 F5 **Little Bourton** Oxon
77 G4 **Little Bradley** Suffk
61 K5 **Little Braxted** Essex
196 F4 **Little Brechin** Angus
14 B5 **Littlebredy** Dorset
58 E2 **Little Brickhill** M Keyn
73 J2 **Little Brington** Nhants
62 C3 **Little Bromley** Essex
112 E7 **Little Budworth** Ches
212 F4 **Littleburn** Highld
46 A2 **Little Burstead** Essex
76 D6 **Littlebury** Essex
76 C6 **Littlebury Green** Essex
103 G8 **Little Bytham** Lincs
118 E4 **Little Carlton** Lincs
88 E2 **Little Casterton** Rutlnd
118 E5 **Little Cawthorpe** Lincs
43 G2 **Little Chalfont** Bucks
34 C5 **Little Chart** Kent
76 D6 **Little Chesterford** Essex
27 M2 **Little Cheverell** Wilts
76 B6 **Little Chishill** Cambs
62 E4 **Little Clacton** Essex
136 E2 **Little Clifton** Cumb
71 G5 **Little Comberton** Worcs
20 E4 **Little Common** E Susx
56 E3 **Little Compton** Warwks
77 K6 **Little Cornard** Suffk
69 L4 **Little Cowarne** Herefs
40 F2 **Little Coxwell** Oxon
132 C2 **Little Crakehall** N York
91 K4 **Little Cressingham** Norfk
111 K2 **Little Crosby** Sefton
100 D5 **Little Cubley** Derbys
87 L2 **Little Dalby** Leics
54 F5 **Littledean** Gloucs
217 K5 **Little Dens** Abers
54 D2 **Little Dewchurch** Herefs
76 F3 **Little Ditton** Cambs
90 D6 **Little Downham** Cambs
134 F7 **Little Driffield** E R Yk
91 K2 **Little Dunham** Norfk
195 G7 **Little Dunkeld** P & K
61 G4 **Little Dunmow** Essex
28 C5 **Little Durnford** Wilts

60 F3 **Little Easton** Essex
101 G4 **Little Eaton** Derbys
92 B4 **Little Ellingham** Norfk
73 H3 **Little Everdon** Nhants
75 L4 **Little Eversden** Cambs
56 E7 **Little Faringdon** Oxon
132 D2 **Little Fencote** N York
124 D4 **Little Fenton** N York
91 K2 **Little Fransham** Norfk
59 G5 **Little Gaddesden** Herts
79 H3 **Little Glemham** Suffk
55 G3 **Little Gorsley** Herefs
75 J4 **Little Gransden** Cambs
27 G2 **Little Green** Somset
118 D3 **Little Grimsby** Lincs
60 C4 **Little Hadham** Herts
103 J4 **Little Hale** Lincs
101 J4 **Little Hallam** Derbys
60 D4 **Little Hallingbury** Essex
12 D6 **Littleham** Devon
23 G6 **Littleham** Devon
18 D5 **Littlehampton** W Susx
74 C1 **Little Harrowden** Nhants
57 M7 **Little Haseley** Oxon
126 E2 **Little Hatfield** E R Yk
48 E5 **Little Haven** Pembks
31 K5 **Littlehaven** W Susx
85 K3 **Little Hay** Staffs
100 A7 **Little Haywood** Staffs
86 D6 **Little Heath** Covtry
7 J4 **Littlehempston** Devon
69 K2 **Little Hereford** Herefs
62 A2 **Little Horkesley** Essex
60 C3 **Little Hormead** Herts
19 M3 **Little Horsted** E Susx
123 H4 **Little Horton** Brad
58 C2 **Little Horwood** Bucks
115 H1 **Little Houghton** Barns
74 B3 **Little Houghton** Nhants
114 D5 **Little Hucklow** Derbys
133 G4 **Little Hutton** N York
74 C2 **Little Irchester** Nhants
27 H3 **Little Keyford** Somset
58 D6 **Little Kimble** Bucks
72 D4 **Little Kineton** Warwks
58 E7 **Little Kingshill** Bucks
146 E3 **Little Knox** D & G
137 J6 **Little Langdale** Cumb
28 B4 **Little Langford** Wilts
9 K4 **Little Lashbrook** Devon
112 F6 **Little Leigh** Ches
61 H5 **Little Leighs** Essex
121 L8 **Little Lever** Bolton
74 B5 **Little Linford** M Keyn
26 C6 **Little Load** Somset
20 C2 **Little London** E Susx
29 G2 **Little London** Hants
41 L8 **Little London** Hants
114 D6 **Little Longstone** Derbys
70 D6 **Little Malvern** Worcs
77 J7 **Little Maplestead** Essex
70 C7 **Little Marcle** Herefs
42 E3 **Little Marlow** Bucks
105 J7 **Little Massingham** Norfk
92 E3 **Little Melton** Norfk

205 H6 **Littlemill** Abers
213 L4 **Littlemill** Highld
53 L7 **Little Mill** Mons
57 L7 **Little Milton** Oxon
58 F7 **Little Missenden** Bucks
57 K7 **Littlemore** Oxon
139 H5 **Little Musgrave** Cumb
98 B8 **Little Ness** Shrops
49 G2 **Little Newcastle** Pembks
140 E4 **Little Newsham** Dur
26 C7 **Little Norton** Somset
62 F3 **Little Oakley** Essex
88 C6 **Little Oakley** Nhants
84 E1 **Little Onn** Staffs
148 C4 **Little Orton** Cumb
101 G5 **Littleover** C Derb
86 B6 **Little Packington** Warwks
75 H3 **Little Paxton** Cambs
4 E2 **Little Petherick** Cnwll
93 G2 **Little Plumstead** Norfk
102 F6 **Little Ponton** Lincs
90 E6 **Littleport** Cambs
73 H4 **Little Preston** Nhants
89 J7 **Little Raveley** Cambs
125 J6 **Little Reedness** E R Yk
132 F8 **Little Ribston** N York
56 D4 **Little Rissington** Gloucs
56 F3 **Little Rollright** Oxon
106 A6 **Little Ryburgh** Norfk
148 F7 **Little Salkeld** Cumb
76 F7 **Little Sampford** Essex
111 K7 **Little Saughall** Ches
77 H2 **Little Saxham** Suffk
212 B3 **Little Scatwell** Highld
133 G5 **Little Sessay** N York
76 G4 **Little Shelford** Cambs
11 K5 **Little Silver** Devon
120 E3 **Little Singleton** Lancs
125 G3 **Little Skipwith** N York
124 D6 **Little Smeaton** N York
106 A6 **Little Snoring** Norfk
39 H4 **Little Sodbury** S Glos
29 G5 **Little Somborne** Hants
39 L4 **Little Somerford** Wilts
99 G6 **Little Soudley** Shrops
141 J3 **Little Stainton** Darltn
112 B6 **Little Stanney** Ches
75 G3 **Little Staughton** Beds
118 F8 **Little Steeping** Lincs
21 L2 **Littlestone-on-Sea** Kent
78 D3 **Little Stonham** Suffk
87 J4 **Little Stretton** Leics
83 J5 **Little Stretton** Shrops
138 E4 **Little Strickland** Cumb
89 H7 **Little Stukeley** Cambs
99 J6 **Little Sugnall** Staffs
158 B6 **Little Swinburne** Nthumb
146 C4 **Little Sypland** D & G
57 G3 **Little Tew** Oxon
61 L4 **Little Tey** Essex
90 D7 **Little Thetford** Cambs
151 K6 **Little Thorpe** Dur
87 G4 **Littlethorpe** Leics
132 E5 **Littlethorpe** N York
77 G4 **Little Thurlow Green** Suffk
45 L4 **Little Thurrock** Thurr
196 B6 **Littleton** Angus
112 C7 **Littleton** Ches
146 B4 **Littleton** D & G

29 J5 **Littleton** Hants
26 C5 **Littleton** Somset
43 H6 **Littleton** Surrey
39 J4 **Littleton Drew** Wilts
38 E3 **Littleton-on-Severn** S Glos
27 M2 **Littleton Pannell** Wilts
10 D2 **Little Torrington** Devon
136 E8 **Littletown** Dur
121 K4 **Little Town** Lancs
128 F5 **Little Urswick** Cumb
46 F3 **Little Wakering** Essex
76 D6 **Little Walden** Essex
77 K5 **Little Waldingfield** Suffk
105 M5 **Little Walsingham** Norfk
61 H5 **Little Waltham** Essex
55 M2 **Little Washbourne** Gloucs
126 B4 **Little Weighton** E R Yk
88 D5 **Little Weldon** Nhants
78 C6 **Little Wenham** Suffk
84 B3 **Little Wenlock** Wrekin
26 F6 **Little Weston** Somset
17 H4 **Little Whitefield** IoW
42 D4 **Littlewick Green** W & M
76 D3 **Little Wilbraham** Cambs
55 K5 **Little Witcombe** Gloucs
70 D2 **Little Witley** Worcs
41 K2 **Little Wittenham** Oxon
72 C7 **Little Wolford** Warwks
44 F7 **Little Woodcote** Gt Lon
40 F2 **Littleworth** Oxon
99 L7 **Littleworth** Staffs
70 F4 **Littleworth** Worcs
77 G5 **Little Wratting** Suffk
74 D2 **Little Wymington** Beds
59 K3 **Little Wymondley** Herts
85 H3 **Little Wyrley** Staffs
77 H6 **Little Yeldham** Essex
61 H4 **Littley Green** Essex
114 D6 **Litton** Derbys
131 G5 **Litton** N York
26 E1 **Litton** Somset
14 A4 **Litton Cheney** Dorset
232 f2 **Liurbost** W Isls
111 K4 **Liverpool** Lpool
123 J5 **Liversedge** Kirk
7 J2 **Liverton** Devon
142 F4 **Liverton** R & Cl
176 E5 **Livingston** W Loth
176 E5 **Livingston Village** W Loth
7 G5 **Lixton** Devon
111 G7 **Lixwm** Flints
3 J8 **Lizard** Cnwll
95 G4 **Llanaelhaearn** Gwynd
66 F1 **Llanafan** Cerdgn
109 G4 **Llanallgo** IoA
97 J6 **Llanarmon Dyffryn Ceiriog** Wrexhm
97 J2 **Llanarmon-yn-Ial** Denbgs
65 L3 **Llanarth** Cerdgn
54 B5 **Llanarth** Mons
51 G2 **Llanarthne** Carmth
110 F5 **Llanasa** Flints
80 E7 **Llanbadarn Fawr** Cerdgn
82 C7 **Llanbadarn Fynydd** Powys

54 B7 **Llanbadoc** Mons
38 B3 **Llanbeder** Newpt
95 K7 **Llanbedr** Gwynd
53 K4 **Llanbedr** Powys
97 H2 **Llanbedr-Dyffryn-Clwyd** Denbgs
109 G5 **Llanbedrgoch** IoA
94 F6 **Llanbedrog** Gwynd
109 L7 **Llanbedr-y-Cennin** Conwy
95 K1 **Llanberis** Gwynd
37 G6 **Llanbethery** V Glam
82 C8 **Llanbister** Powys
36 F5 **Llanblethian** V Glam
49 L3 **Llanboidy** Carmth
37 J3 **Llanbradach** Caerph
81 J3 **Llanbrynmair** Powys
37 G6 **Llancadle** V Glam
37 G6 **Llancarfan** V Glam
54 D4 **Llancloudy** Herefs
37 J5 **Llandaff** Cardif
95 K6 **Llandanwg** Gwynd
109 G7 **Llanddaniel Fab** IoA
51 G3 **Llanddarog** Carmth
66 D1 **Llanddeiniol** Cerdgn
109 H7 **Llanddeiniolen** Gwynd
96 F5 **Llandderfel** Gwynd
108 D4 **Llanddeusant** IoA
53 G2 **Llanddew** Powys
50 F7 **Llanddewi** Swans
66 F4 **Llanddewi Brefi** Cerdgn
53 M5 **Llanddewi Rhydderch** Mons
49 K4 **Llanddewi Velfrey** Pembks
68 C2 **Llanddewi Ystradenni** Powys
109 M8 **Llanddoget** Conwy
109 H5 **Llanddona** IoA
50 B3 **Llanddowror** Carmth
110 C6 **Llanddulas** Conwy
95 K7 **Llanddwywe** Gwynd
109 G5 **Llanddyfnan** IoA
53 H3 **Llandefaelog-Tre'r-Graig** Powys
68 C7 **Llandefalle** Powys
109 H6 **Llandegfan** IoA
68 D2 **Llandegley** Powys
37 M2 **Llandegveth** Mons
51 J2 **Llandeilo** Carmth
68 C5 **Llandeilo Graban** Powys
48 E3 **Llandeloy** Pembks
54 B7 **Llandenny** Mons
38 B3 **Llandevaud** Newpt
38 B3 **Llandevenny** Mons
82 B5 **Llandinam** Powys
49 J3 **Llandissilio** Pembks
54 D7 **Llandogo** Mons
36 F6 **Llandough** V Glam
37 J3 **Llandough** V Glam
67 G7 **Llandovery** Carmth
36 E5 **Llandow** V Glam
66 F6 **Llandre** Carmth
80 E6 **Llandre** Cerdgn
49 J2 **Llandre Isaf** Pembks
97 G5 **Llandrillo** Denbgs
110 B5 **Llandrillo-yn-Rhos** Conwy
68 B3 **Llandrindod Wells** Powys
97 L8 **Llandrinio** Powys
109 L5 **Llandudno** Conwy
109 M6 **Llandudno Junction** Conwy
94 E5 **Llandudwen** Gwynd
67 J6 **Llandulas** Powys
95 H2 **Llandwrog** Gwynd
51 J3 **Llandybie** Carmth
50 E3 **Llandyfaelog** Carmth

65 K6 **Llandyfriog** Cerdgn
109 H7 **Llandygai** Gwynd
65 H5 **Llandygwydd** Cerdgn
110 F8 **Llandyrnog** Denbgs
82 E4 **Llandyssil** Powys
65 L6 **Llandysul** Cerdgn
37 K4 **Llanedeyrn** Cardif
68 B6 **Llaneglwys** Powys
80 D3 **Llanegryn** Gwynd
51 G2 **Llanegwad** Carmth
108 F3 **Llaneilian** IoA
110 B6 **Llanelian-yn-Rhos** Conwy
97 H3 **Llanelidan** Denbgs
68 D7 **Llanelieu** Powys
53 L5 **Llanellen** Mons
51 G5 **Llanelli** Carmth
96 A8 **Llanelltyd** Gwynd
68 B4 **Llanelwedd** Powys
95 K7 **Llanenddwyn** Gwynd
94 E6 **Llanengan** Gwynd
108 E5 **Llanerchymedd** IoA
82 B2 **Llanerfyl** Powys
108 D5 **Llanfachraeth** IoA
96 B7 **Llanfachreth** Gwynd
108 D6 **Llanfaelog** IoA
94 D6 **Llanfaelrhys** Gwynd
108 D4 **Llanfaethlu** IoA
95 K6 **Llanfair** Gwynd
82 C3 **Llanfair Caereinion** Powys
66 E4 **Llanfair Clydogau** Cerdgn
97 H2 **Llanfair Dyffryn Clwyd** Denbgs
109 K6 **Llanfairfechan** Conwy
109 G7 **Llanfair-is-gaer** Gwynd
109 G6 **Llanfair P G** IoA
110 C7 **Llanfair Talhaiarn** Conwy
82 E7 **Llanfair Waterdine** Shrops
108 F7 **Llanfair-y-Cwmwd** IoA
108 D4 **Llanfairynghornwy** IoA
108 C6 **Llanfair-yn-Neubwll** IoA
49 K4 **Llanfallteg** Carmth
49 K4 **Llanfallteg West** Carmth
80 D7 **Llanfarian** Cerdgn
97 J7 **Llanfechain** Powys
108 E3 **Llanfechell** IoA
97 J1 **Llanferres** Denbgs
66 B6 **Llanfihangel-ar-arth** Carmth
96 F3 **Llanfihangel Glyn Myfyr** Conwy
67 K7 **Llanfihangel Nant Bran** Powys
68 D2 **Llanfihangel Rhydithon** Powys
38 C3 **Llanfihangel Rogiet** Mons
80 F7 **Llanfihangel-y-Creuddyn** Cerdgn
82 C1 **Llanfihangel-yng-Ngwynfa** Powys
108 D6 **Llanfihangel yn Nhowyn** IoA
95 K5 **Llanfihangel-y-tra-ethau** Gwynd
53 H2 **Llanfilo** Powys
53 L5 **Llanfoist** Mons
96 E5 **Llanfor** Gwynd
37 L2 **Llanfrechfa** Torfn
53 G3 **Llanfrynach** Powys
97 H2 **Llanfwrog** Denbgs
108 C5 **Llanfwrog** IoA
97 H8 **Llanfyllin** Powys

66 D8 Llanfynydd Carmth
97 L2 Llanfynydd Flints
49 L2 Llanfyrnach Pembks
81 L2 Llangadfan Powys
66 F8 Llangadog Carmth
108 E7 Llangadwaladr IoA
108 F7 Llangaffo IoA
67 K5 Llangammarch Wells Powys
36 E5 Llangan V Glam
54 D4 Llangarron Herefs
51 H2 Llangathen Carmth
53 K4 Llangattock Powys
54 A4 Llangattock Lingoed Mons
97 J7 Llangedwyn Powys
108 F6 Llangefni IoA
36 E3 Llangeinor Brdgnd
108 F7 Llangeinwen IoA
66 E3 Llangeitho Cerdgn
65 L6 Llangeler Carmth
80 D3 Llangelynin Gwynd
50 F3 Llangendeirne Carmth
51 H5 Llangennech Carmth
50 E7 Llangennith Swans
110 B7 Llangernyw Conwy
94 E6 Llangian Gwynd
64 C7 Llangloffan Pembks
49 K3 Llanglydwen Carmth
109 J5 Llangoed IoA
97 K4 Llangollen Denbgs
49 J3 Llangolman Pembks
53 H3 Llangors Powys
96 D6 Llangower Gwynd
65 K4 Llangranog Cerdgn
108 F6 Llangristiolus IoA
54 D4 Llangrove Herefs
68 E1 Llangunllo Powys
50 E2 Llangunnor Carmth
81 K7 Llangurig Powys
96 F4 Llangwm Conwy
54 B7 Llangwm Mons
49 G5 Llangwm Pembks
54 B7 Llangwm-isaf Mons
94 D6 Llangwnnadl Gwynd
66 D1 Llangwyryfon Cerdgn
66 E4 Llangybi Cerdgn
95 G4 Llangybi Gwynd
38 A2 Llangybi Mons
110 F8 Llangynhafal Denbgs
53 J4 Llangynidr Powys
50 B2 Llangynin Carmth
50 D3 Llangynog Carmth
97 G7 Llangynog Powys
36 D3 Llangynwyd Brdgnd
53 H3 Llanhamlach Powys
36 F4 Llanharan Rhondd
36 F4 Llanharry Rhondd
38 A2 Llanhennock Mons
53 K7 Llanhilleth Blae G
81 K6 Llanidloes Powys
94 E5 Llaniestyn Gwynd
68 E6 Llanigon Powys
80 E8 Llanilar Cerdgn
36 F4 Llanilid Rhondd
65 L3 Llanina Cerdgn
37 J4 Llanishen Cardif
54 C7 Llanishen Mons
109 J7 Llanllechid Gwynd
54 B7 Llanllowell Mons
82 B3 Llanllugan Powys
50 E2 Llanllwch Carmth
82 C5 Llanllwchaiarn Powys
66 C6 Llanllwni Carmth
95 H3 Llanllyfni Gwynd
50 F6 Llanmadoc Swans
36 F6 Llanmaes V Glam
38 B3 Llanmartin Newpt
50 B4 Llanmiloe Carmth
110 D7 Llannefydd Conwy
51 G4 Llannon Carmth

94 F5 Llannor Gwynd
66 C2 Llanon Cerdgn
53 L6 Llanover Mons
65 L8 Llanpumsaint Carmth
97 H7 Llanrhaeadr-ym-Mochnant Powys
48 D2 Llanrhian Pembks
50 F6 Llanrhidian Swans
96 B1 Llanrhychwyn Conwy
108 D4 Llanrhyddlad IoA
66 C1 Llanrhystud Cerdgn
54 C4 Llanrothal Herefs
109 G8 Llanrug Gwynd
37 K4 Llanrumney Cardif
96 C1 Llanrwst Conwy
50 C4 Llansadurnen Carmth
66 F7 Llansadwrn Carmth
109 H6 Llansadwrn IoA
50 E4 Llansaint Carmth
51 K6 Llansamlet Swans
109 M6 Llansanffraid Glan Conwy Conwy
110 C7 Llansannan Conwy
53 H4 Llansantffraed Powys
67 L2 Llansantffraed-Cwmdeuddwr Powys
68 C4 Llansantffraed-in-Elvel Powys
66 C2 Llansantffraid Cerdgn
97 K7 Llansantffraid-ym-Mechain Powys
66 E7 Llansawel Carmth
97 K6 Llansilin Powys
54 C7 Llansoy Mons
52 F3 Llanspyddid Powys
48 F6 Llanstadwell Pembks
50 D4 Llansteffan Carmth
37 L2 Llantarnam Torfn
49 K5 Llanteg Pembks
53 M5 Llanthewy Skirrid Mons
53 L3 Llanthony Mons
54 B5 Llantilio-Crossenny Mons
53 L5 Llantilio Pertholey Mons
38 B2 Llantrisant Mons
37 G4 Llantrisant Rhondd
37 G6 Llantrithyd V Glam
37 G3 Llantwit Fardre Rhondd
36 F6 Llantwit Major V Glam
96 D6 Llanuwchllyn Gwynd
38 B3 Llanvaches Newpt
38 C3 Llanvair Discoed Mons
54 A5 Llanvapley Mons
54 A5 Llanvetherine Mons
53 L4 Llanvihangel Crucorney Mons
96 F8 Llanwddyn Powys
66 C5 Llanwenog Cerdgn
38 A3 Llanwern Newpt
50 C1 Llanwinio Carmth
95 H2 Llanwnda Gwynd
64 C6 Llanwnda Pembks
66 C5 Llanwnnen Cerdgn
82 B5 Llanwnog Powys
66 F7 Llanwrda Carmth
81 H3 Llanwrin Powys
67 L2 Llanwrthwl Powys
67 J5 Llanwrtyd Wells Powys
82 C4 Llanwyddelan Powys
97 K7 Llanyblodwel Shrops
50 D3 Llanybri Carmth
66 C5 Llanybydder Carmth
49 J3 Llanycefn Pembks
64 D7 Llanychaer Bridge Pembks

96 D8 Llanymawddwy Gwynd
97 K7 Llanymynech Powys
108 D5 Llanynghenedl IoA
110 F8 Llanynys Denbgs
68 B3 Llanyre Powys
95 H5 Llanystumdwy Gwynd
53 H3 Llanywern Powys
49 H4 Llawhaden Pembks
81 K5 Llawryglyn Powys
97 M2 Llay Wrexhm
53 H6 Llechrhyd Caerph
65 H5 Llechryd Cerdgn
66 E1 Lledrod Cerdgn
94 E5 Lleyn Peninsula Gwynd
94 F4 Llithfaen Gwynd
111 G6 Lloc Flints
68 D6 Llowes Powys
52 F6 Llwydcoed Rhondd
82 B1 Llwydiarth Powys
66 B3 Llwyncelyn Cerdgn
65 L4 Llwyndafydd Cerdgn
80 D2 Llwyngwril Gwynd
97 K5 Llwynmawr Wrexhm
36 F2 Llwynypia Rhondd
97 L7 Llynclys Shrops
108 E5 Llynfaes IoA
110 B6 Llysfaen Conwy
68 C6 Llyswen Powys
36 E5 Llysworney V Glam
49 H3 Llys-y-fran Pembks
52 D3 Llywel Powys
176 D3 Loan Falk
177 J5 Loanhead Mdloth
147 G4 Loaningfoot D & G
163 J3 Loans S Ayrs
10 C7 Lobhillcross Devon
200 B8 Lochailort Highld
190 D7 Lochaline Highld
144 C4 Lochans D & G
155 H6 Locharbriggs D & G
182 D4 Lochavich Ag & B
183 G2 Lochawe Ag & B
233 C8 Loch Baghasdail W Isls
233 G8 Lochboisdale W Isls
181 J3 Lochbuie Ag & B
210 D6 Lochcarron Highld
181 L2 Lochdon Ag & B
181 L2 Lochdonhead Ag & B
172 D3 Lochead Ag & B
184 D3 Lochearnhead Stirlg
186 F2 Lochee C Dund
191 K2 Locheilside Station Highld
212 F6 Lochend Highld
233 c6 Locheport W Isls
233 c6 Loch Euphort W Isls
154 F7 Lochfoot D & G
172 F1 Lochgair Ag & B
186 C8 Lochgelly Fife
172 E2 Lochgilphead Ag & B
183 H6 Lochgoilhead Ag & B
186 D5 Lochieheads Fife
215 G2 Lochill Moray
214 B7 Lochindorb Lodge Highld
224 D4 Lochinver Highld
183 L8 Loch Lomond
211 L2 Lochluichart Highld
155 J5 Lochmaben D & G
233 c6 Lochmaddy W Isls
219 L7 Loch Maree Hotel Highld
233 c8 Loch nam Madadh W Isls
202 E1 Loch Ness Highld
186 F5 Lochore Fife
172 F7 Lochranza N Ayrs
197 H4 Lochside Abers

155 G6 Lochside D & G
213 J4 Lochside Highld
152 F6 Lochton S Ayrs
196 E4 Lochty Angus
187 H5 Lochty Fife
190 F5 Lochuisge Highld
174 C6 Lochwinnoch Rens
155 J3 Lochwood D & G
5 G4 Lockengate Cnwll
155 K5 Lockerbie D & G
40 C6 Lockeridge Wilts
28 F5 Lockerley Hants
38 A8 Locking N Som
112 F3 Locking Stumps Warrtn
126 B2 Lockington E R Yk
99 G6 Lockleywood Shrops
45 H6 Locksbottom Gt Lon
17 G2 Locks Heath Hants
134 C2 Lockton N York
87 L3 Loddington Leics
88 B7 Loddington Nhants
7 G6 Loddiswell Devon
93 H4 Loddon Norfk
76 D3 Lode Cambs
85 L7 Lode Heath Solhll
13 L4 Loders Dorset
30 F6 Lodsworth W Susx
123 L5 Lofthouse Leeds
131 L5 Lofthouse N York
123 L5 Lofthouse Gate Wakefd
142 F4 Loftus R & Cl
164 C5 Logan E Ayrs
176 C6 Loganlea W Loth
99 G5 Loggerheads Staffs
197 H4 Logie Angus
186 F4 Logie Fife
214 C4 Logie Moray
205 K4 Logie Coldstone Abers
197 G4 Logie Pert Angus
194 B7 Logierait P & K
217 H8 Logierieve Abers
49 K3 Login Carmth
75 L2 Lolworth Cambs
209 L4 Lonbain Highld
125 K2 Londesborough E R Yk
44 F4 London Gt Lon
4 F6 London Apprentice Cnwll
59 K7 London Colney Herts
132 D3 Londonderry N York
102 F5 Londonthorpe Lincs
219 K5 Londubh Highld
219 J6 Lonemore Highld
38 D6 Long Ashton N Som
84 D8 Long Bank Worcs
102 D4 Long Bennington Lincs
151 G2 Longbenton N Tyne
56 D3 Longborough Gloucs
14 M4 Long Bredy Dorset
85 H7 Longbridge Birm
27 K4 Longbridge Deverill Wilts
73 J2 Long Buckby Nhants
26 F8 Longburton Dorset
102 B6 Long Clawson Leics
100 E2 Longcliffe Derbys
7 J4 Longcombe Devon
99 J7 Long Compton Staffs
56 F2 Long Compton Warwks
40 F3 Longcot Oxon
58 B6 Long Crendon Bucks
15 J1 Long Crichel Dorset
83 J3 Longden Shrops
44 D6 Long Ditton Surrey
85 J2 Longdon Staffs
70 E7 Longdon Worcs

85 J2 **Longdon Green** Staffs
84 B1 **Longdon upon Tern** Wrekin
11 K6 **Longdown** Devon
3 J4 **Longdowns** Cnwll
115 H7 **Long Duckmanton** Derbys
101 J5 **Long Eaton** Derbys
45 L6 **Longfield** Kent
100 E5 **Longford** Derbys
55 J4 **Longford** Gloucs
98 F5 **Longford** Shrops
99 G8 **Longford** Wrekin
186 E2 **Longforgan** P & K
178 E6 **Longformacus** Border
158 E3 **Longframlington** Nthumb
112 C7 **Long Green** Ches
55 J2 **Long Green** Worcs
15 K3 **Longham** Dorset
91 L1 **Longham** Norfk
57 H5 **Long Hanborough** Oxon
217 L6 **Longhaven** Abers
158 F4 **Longhirst** Nthumb
55 G4 **Longhope** Gloucs
234 b7 **Longhope** Ork
158 E4 **Longhorsley** Nthumb
169 J6 **Longhoughton** Nthumb
72 E2 **Long Itchington** Warwks
100 E5 **Longlane** Derbys
86 F7 **Long Lawford** Warwks
27 J3 **Longleat Safari Park** Wilts
55 J4 **Longlevens** Gloucs
122 F6 **Longley** Calder
195 L7 **Longleys** P & K
26 C6 **Long Load** Somset
216 E2 **Longmanhill** Abers
58 E5 **Long Marston** Herts
124 D1 **Long Marston** N York
71 L5 **Long Marston** Warwks
138 F3 **Long Marton** Cumb
77 J5 **Long Melford** Suffk
30 C5 **Longmoor Camp** Hants
214 F3 **Longmorn** Moray
113 K6 **Longmoss** Ches
39 K3 **Long Newnton** Gloucs
167 J4 **Longnewton** Border
178 B5 **Long Newton** E Loth
141 J4 **Longnewton** S on T
55 H5 **Longney** Gloucs
177 L3 **Longniddry** E Loth
83 J4 **Longnor** Shrops
114 C8 **Longnor** Staffs
29 H3 **Longparish** Hants
130 F2 **Long Preston** N York
121 J3 **Longridge** Lancs
176 C5 **Longridge** W Loth
175 L4 **Longriggend** N Lans
126 E3 **Long Riston** E R Yk
2 E5 **Longrock** Cnwll
99 L2 **Longsdon** Staffs
217 K5 **Longside** Abers
76 B2 **Longstanton** Cambs
29 G4 **Longstock** Hants
75 K4 **Longstowe** Cambs
92 E5 **Long Stratton** Norfk
74 B5 **Long Street** M Keyn
28 C2 **Longstreet** Wilts
30 C3 **Long Sutton** Hants
104 C7 **Long Sutton** Lincs
26 C5 **Long Sutton** Somset
89 H4 **Longthorpe** C Pete
78 B2 **Long Thurlow** Suffk

138 B3 **Longthwaite** Cumb
99 K4 **Longton** C Stke
121 G5 **Longton** Lancs
148 C2 **Longtown** Cumb
53 L3 **Longtown** Herefs
236 d7 **Longueville** Jersey
83 K5 **Longville in the Dale** Shrops
84 B1 **Long Waste** Wrekin
101 J7 **Long Whatton** Leics
58 C6 **Longwick** Bucks
41 K2 **Long Wittenham** Oxon
158 A5 **Longwitton** Nthumb
146 C3 **Longwood** D & G
57 G7 **Longworth** Oxon
178 C5 **Longyester** E Loth
217 J3 **Lonmay** Abers
208 D5 **Lonmore** Highld
5 K5 **Looe** Cnwll
33 K3 **Loose** Kent
58 D7 **Loosley Row** Bucks
216 B4 **Lootcherbrae** Abers
26 B8 **Lopen** Somset
98 C6 **Loppington** Shrops
46 C7 **Lords Wood** Medway
195 J6 **Lornty** P & K
101 H3 **Loscoe** Derbys
214 F1 **Lossiemouth** Moray
4 F6 **Lost Gardens of Heligan** Cnwll
113 G6 **Lostock Gralam** Ches
113 G6 **Lostock Green** Ches
5 H4 **Lostwithiel** Cnwll
227 G6 **Lothbeg** Highld
122 E2 **Lothersdale** N York
227 G6 **Lothmore** Highld
101 K8 **Loughborough** Leics
51 H6 **Loughor** Swans
45 H2 **Loughton** Essex
74 B6 **Loughton** M Keyn
84 B6 **Loughton** Shrops
103 H8 **Lound** Lincs
116 B4 **Lound** Notts
93 K4 **Lound** Suffk
101 G8 **Lount** Leics
118 D4 **Louth** Lincs
122 B5 **Love Clough** Lancs
30 B8 **Lovedean** Hants
28 E7 **Lover** Wilts
115 L2 **Loversall** Donc
61 G6 **Loves Green** Essex
49 J5 **Loveston** Pembks
26 E5 **Lovington** Somset
124 C6 **Low Ackworth** Wakefd
144 B2 **Low Barbeth** D & G
130 C5 **Low Bentham** N York
130 B4 **Low Biggins** Cumb
138 E6 **Low Borrowbridge** Cumb
114 E3 **Low Bradfield** Sheff
122 F2 **Low Bradley** N York
116 C2 **Low Burnham** N Linc
136 D3 **Lowca** Cumb
133 L8 **Low Catton** E R Yk
148 D3 **Low Crosby** Cumb
102 A3 **Lowdham** Notts
141 J5 **Low Dinsdale** Darltn
124 E5 **Low Eggborough** N York
132 C3 **Low Ellington** N York
25 J4 **Lower Aisholt** Somset
14 E2 **Lower Ansty** Dorset
55 J3 **Lower Apperley** Gloucs
11 J7 **Lower Ashton** Devon
42 C4 **Lower Assendon** Oxon
121 G4 **Lower Bartle** Lancs
41 L5 **Lower Basildon** W Berk

31 L6 **Lower Beeding** W Susx
88 E5 **Lower Benefield** Nhants
71 H2 **Lower Bentley** Worcs
72 F4 **Lower Boddington** Nhants
30 D3 **Lower Bourne** Surrey
72 C6 **Lower Brailes** Warwks
199 L2 **Lower Breakish** Highld
70 E3 **Lower Broadheath** Worcs
70 C4 **Lower Brockhampton Manor** Herefs
69 K6 **Lower Bullingham** Herefs
28 D7 **Lower Burgate** Hants
75 H5 **Lower Caldecote** Beds
55 H7 **Lower Cam** Gloucs
68 B7 **Lower Chapel** Powys
27 L5 **Lower Chicksgrove** Wilts
28 F2 **Lower Chute** Wilts
45 G3 **Lower Clapton** Gt Lon
85 G7 **Lower Clent** Worcs
123 J8 **Lower Cumberworth** Kirk
74 F2 **Lower Dean** Beds
210 C3 **Lower Diabaig** Highld
20 B4 **Lower Dicker** E Susx
83 G6 **Lower Down** Shrops
133 G6 **Lower Dunsforth** N York
70 B5 **Lower Egleton** Herefs
74 D6 **Lower End** M Keyn
35 H5 **Lower Eythorne** Kent
38 D5 **Lower Failand** N Som
30 B4 **Lower Farringdon** Hants
43 H6 **Lower Feltham** Gt Lon
30 C3 **Lower Froyle** Hants
7 L2 **Lower Gabwell** Devon
222 D4 **Lower Gledfield** Highld
26 C3 **Lower Godney** Somset
75 G7 **Lower Gravenhurst** Beds
32 F5 **Lower Green** Kent
33 G5 **Lower Green** Kent
43 H6 **Lower Halliford** Surrey
46 E6 **Lower Halstow** Kent
15 J4 **Lower Hamworthy** Poole
34 F4 **Lower Hardres** Kent
58 C5 **Lower Hartwell** Bucks
68 F4 **Lower Hergest** Herefs
57 J3 **Lower Heyford** Oxon
123 H7 **Lower Houses** Kirk
113 G3 **Lower Irlam** Salfd
160 A2 **Lower Killeyan** Ag & B
97 M1 **Lower Kinnerton** Ches
38 C7 **Lower Langford** N Som
187 G6 **Lower Largo** Fife
100 A5 **Lower Leigh** Staffs
23 K4 **Lower Loxhore** Devon
54 E5 **Lower Lydbrook** Gloucs
69 H2 **Lower Lye** Herefs
37 K3 **Lower Machen** Newpt
25 J4 **Lower Merridge** Somset

73 G6 **Lower Middleton Cheney** Nhants
71 H5 **Lower Moor** Worcs
38 F3 **Lower Morton** S Glos
60 C6 **Lower Nazeing** Essex
37 J6 **Lower Penarth** V Glam
84 F4 **Lower Penn** Staffs
113 H6 **Lower Peover** Ches
71 L5 **Lower Quinton** Warwks
78 C6 **Lower Raydon** Suffk
25 G4 **Lower Roadwater** Somset
39 L4 **Lower Seagry** Wilts
74 E6 **Lower Shelton** Beds
42 C4 **Lower Shiplake** Oxon
72 F3 **Lower Shuckburgh** Warwks
56 D4 **Lower Slaughter** Gloucs
35 H6 **Lower Standen** Kent
39 L4 **Lower Stanton St Quintin** Wilts
46 D5 **Lower Stoke** Medway
38 F2 **Lower Stone** Gloucs
91 L5 **Lower Stow Bedon** Norfk
106 F5 **Lower Street** Norfk
78 D4 **Lower Street** Suffk
59 H3 **Lower Sundon** Beds
16 F1 **Lower Swanwick** Hants
56 D3 **Lower Swell** Gloucs
100 A5 **Lower Tean** Staffs
7 G2 **Lower Town** Devon
64 D6 **Lower Town** Pembks
72 D5 **Lower Tysoe** Warwks
11 K8 **Lower Upcott** Devon
29 K7 **Lower Upham** Hants
25 H4 **Lower Vexford** Somset
26 B2 **Lower Weare** Somset
71 G6 **Lower Westmancote** Worcs
27 H3 **Lower Whatley** Somset
112 E5 **Lower Whitley** Ches
29 M4 **Lower Wield** Hants
20 C5 **Lower Willingdon** E Susx
113 J7 **Lower Withington** Ches
28 C4 **Lower Woodford** Wilts
14 B3 **Lower Wraxhall** Dorset
87 K3 **Lowesby** Leics
93 L5 **Lowestoft** Suffk
137 G3 **Loweswater** Cumb
151 G3 **Low Fell** Gatesd
31 L4 **Lowfield Heath** W Susx
174 E2 **Low Gartachorrans** Stirlg
132 C5 **Low Grantley** N York
26 B5 **Low Ham** Somset
132 D7 **Low Harrogate** N York
148 E5 **Low Hesket** Cumb
134 B6 **Low Hutton** N York
88 E7 **Lowick** Nhants
168 F2 **Lowick** Nthumb
129 G3 **Lowick Green** Cumb
137 G3 **Low Lorton** Cumb
116 D7 **Low Marnham** Notts
142 E7 **Low Mill** N York
151 H5 **Low Moorsley** Sundld
134 D6 **Low Mowthorpe** N York
129 J3 **Low Newton** Cumb
149 G3 **Low Row** Cumb

140 B7 **Low Row** N York
144 B2 **Low Salchrie** D & G
125 L7 **Low Santon** N Linc
71 L2 **Lowsonford** Warwks
92 E4 **Low Tharston** Norfk
138 D3 **Lowther** Cumb
135 G7 **Lowthorpe** E R Yk
25 J7 **Lowton** Somset
176 D2 **Low Torry** Fife
141 J5 **Low Worsall** N York
137 K6 **Low Wray** Cumb
11 L2 **Loxbeare** Devon
31 G4 **Loxhill** Surrey
23 K4 **Loxhore** Devon
72 C4 **Loxley** Warwks
26 A1 **Loxton** N Som
31 H5 **Loxwood** W Susx
229 J6 **Loyal Lodge** Highld
87 K6 **Lubenham** Leics
24 E3 **Luccombe** Somset
17 H6 **Luccombe Village** IoW
169 H4 **Lucker** Nthumb
6 B2 **Luckett** Cnwll
77 J7 **Lucking Street** Essex
39 J4 **Luckington** Wilts
24 E4 **Luckwell Bridge** Somset
69 J2 **Lucton** Herefs
233 d9 **Ludag** W Isls
118 D3 **Ludborough** Lincs
6 F5 **Ludbrook** Devon
49 K5 **Ludchurch** Pembks
122 F5 **Luddenden** Calder
122 F5 **Luddenden Foot** Calder
46 A6 **Luddesdown** Kent
125 J7 **Luddington** N Linc
71 L4 **Luddington** Warwks
89 G6 **Luddington in the Brook** Nhants
117 K4 **Ludford** Lincs
83 K8 **Ludford** Shrops
58 A4 **Ludgershall** Bucks
28 E2 **Ludgershall** Wilts
2 E5 **Ludgvan** Cnwll
107 H8 **Ludham** Norfk
83 K7 **Ludlow** Shrops
26 B8 **Ludney** Somset
27 K6 **Ludwell** Wilts
151 J6 **Ludworth** Dur
9 J6 **Luffincott** Devon
178 B3 **Luffness** E Loth
164 C5 **Lugar** E Ayrs
178 D4 **Luggate Burn** E Loth
175 K4 **Luggiebank** N Lans
174 D7 **Lugton** E Ayrs
69 K6 **Lugwardine** Herefs
209 J8 **Luib** Highld
69 H6 **Lulham** Herefs
86 B2 **Lullington** Derbys
27 H2 **Lullington** Somset
38 D7 **Lulsgate Bottom** N Som
70 D4 **Lulsley** Worcs
122 F6 **Lumb** Calder
122 C5 **Lumb** Lancs
124 D4 **Lumby** N York
175 H4 **Lumloch** E Duns
206 B4 **Lumphanan** Abers
186 C8 **Lumphinnans** Fife
205 K2 **Lumsden** Abers
197 H6 **Lunan** Angus
196 D6 **Lunanhead** Angus
186 A2 **Luncarty** P & K
126 B2 **Lund** E R Yk
125 G4 **Lund** N York
186 E1 **Lundie** Angus
184 F6 **Lundie** Stirlg
187 G6 **Lundin Links** Fife
187 G6 **Lundin Mill** Fife
235 d4 **Lunna** Shet

33 J2 **Lunsford** Kent
20 E4 **Lunsford's Cross** E Susx
111 K2 **Lunt** Sefton
12 F2 **Luppitt** Devon
7 G5 **Lupridge** Devon
123 L6 **Lupset** Wakefd
129 L4 **Lupton** Cumb
30 F6 **Lurgashall** W Susx
11 L2 **Lurley** Devon
7 J4 **Luscombe** Devon
183 L8 **Luss** Ag & B
208 D3 **Lusta** Highld
11 H8 **Lustleigh** Devon
69 J2 **Luston** Herefs
197 G3 **Luthermuir** Abers
186 E4 **Luthrie** Fife
7 K1 **Luton** Devon
12 D2 **Luton** Devon
59 H4 **Luton** Luton
46 C6 **Luton** Medway
59 J4 **Luton Airport** Luton
87 G6 **Lutterworth** Leics
6 E4 **Lutton** Devon
7 G4 **Lutton** Devon
104 C7 **Lutton** Lincs
89 G6 **Lutton** Nhants
24 F4 **Luxborough** Somset
5 G4 **Luxulyan** Cnwll
231 J7 **Lybster** Highld
83 G6 **Lydbury North** Shrops
21 K2 **Lydd** Kent
21 L2 **Lydd Airport** Kent
35 H5 **Lydden** Kent
35 K2 **Lydden** Kent
88 C4 **Lyddington** Rutlnd
25 H5 **Lydeard St Lawrence** Somset
10 D7 **Lydford** Devon
26 E5 **Lydford on Fosse** Somset
122 D5 **Lydgate** Calder
83 G5 **Lydham** Shrops
40 C3 **Lydiard Millicent** Wilts
40 C4 **Lydiard Tregoze** Swindn
111 K2 **Lydiate** Sefton
85 H7 **Lydiate Ash** Worcs
27 H8 **Lydlinch** Dorset
54 F7 **Lydney** Gloucs
49 J7 **Lydstep** Pembks
85 G6 **Lye** Dudley
32 F6 **Lye Green** E Susx
71 L2 **Lye Green** Warwks
27 J3 **Lye's Green** Wilts
41 H2 **Lyford** Oxon
34 F6 **Lymbridge Green** Kent
13 J4 **Lyme Regis** Dorset
34 F6 **Lyminge** Kent
16 C4 **Lymington** Hants
18 D5 **Lyminster** W Susx
113 G4 **Lymm** Warrtn
34 F7 **Lympne** Kent
25 M1 **Lympsham** Somset
12 C5 **Lympstone** Devon
203 J5 **Lynchat** Highld
92 D3 **Lynch Green** Norfk
16 C2 **Lyndhurst** Hants
88 C3 **Lyndon** Rutlnd
166 B2 **Lyne** Border
43 G7 **Lyne** Surrey
98 C6 **Lyneal** Shrops
56 F4 **Lyneham** Oxon
40 A5 **Lyneham** Wilts
40 A5 **Lyneham Airport** Wilts
206 E4 **Lyne of Skene** Abers
234 b7 **Lyness** Ork
106 C8 **Lyng** Norfk
25 M5 **Lyng** Somset
23 L2 **Lynmouth** Devon

214 F7 **Lynn of Shenval** Moray
34 C3 **Lynsted** Kent
23 L2 **Lynton** Devon
14 C2 **Lyon's Gate** Dorset
69 G4 **Lyonshall** Herefs
15 H4 **Lytchett Matravers** Dorset
15 H4 **Lytchett Minster** Dorset
231 K5 **Lyth** Highld
120 E5 **Lytham** Lancs
120 D5 **Lytham St Anne's** Lancs
143 H5 **Lythe** N York
230 F3 **Lythmore** Highld

M

3 K4 **Mabe Burnthouse** Cnwll
155 G7 **Mabie** D & G
119 G4 **Mablethorpe** Lincs
113 K6 **Macclesfield** Ches
216 D2 **Macduff** Abers
161 J7 **Macharioch** Ag & B
37 K3 **Machen** Caerph
162 A3 **Machrie** N Ayrs
161 G5 **Machrihanish** Ag & B
180 E8 **Machrins** Ag & B
81 G4 **Machynlleth** Powys
51 G5 **Machynys** Carmth
100 F5 **Mackworth** Derbys
177 L4 **Macmerry** E Loth
10 D6 **Maddaford** Devon
185 K3 **Madderty** P & K
176 C3 **Maddiston** Falk
99 H4 **Madeley** Staffs
76 B3 **Madingley** Cambs
69 H6 **Madley** Herefs
70 E5 **Madresfield** Worcs
2 E5 **Madron** Cnwll
49 J3 **Maenclochog** Pembks
36 F5 **Maendy** V Glam
95 L4 **Maentwrog** Gwynd
65 L3 **Maen-y-groes** Cerdgn
99 H5 **Maer** Staffs
36 F2 **Maerdy** Rhondd
97 L7 **Maesbrook** Shrops
97 L7 **Maesbury** Shrops
97 L7 **Maesbury Marsh** Shrops
65 K5 **Maesllyn** Cerdgn
36 D3 **Maesteg** Brdgnd
51 H3 **Maesybont** Carmth
37 J2 **Maesycwmmer** Caerph
215 H5 **Maggieknockater** Moray
20 C4 **Magham Down** E Susx
111 K2 **Maghull** Sefton
38 B3 **Magor** Mons
32 B6 **Maidenbower** W Susx
27 J4 **Maiden Bradley** Wilts
7 L3 **Maidencombe** Torbay
13 H4 **Maidenhayne** Devon
38 E6 **Maiden Head** N Som
42 E4 **Maidenhead** W & M
14 B3 **Maiden Newton** Dorset
163 G7 **Maidens** S Ayrs
118 D5 **Maidenwell** Lincs
49 G7 **Maiden Wells** Pembks
73 H4 **Maidford** Nhants
73 K4 **Maids Moreton** Bucks
33 K3 **Maidstone** Kent
87 L7 **Maidwell** Nhants
235 d6 **Mail** Shet
37 L3 **Maindee** Newpt

141 H2 **Mainsforth** Dur
196 E4 **Mains of Balhall** Angus
197 G2 **Mains of Balnakettle** Abers
214 D7 **Mains of Dalvey** Highld
197 H2 **Mains of Haulkerton** Abers
147 G4 **Mainsriddle** D & G
82 F6 **Mainstone** Shrops
55 J4 **Maisemore** Gloucs
101 G4 **Makeney** Derbys
7 G7 **Malborough** Devon
61 K6 **Maldon** Essex
131 G6 **Malham** N York
199 L6 **Mallaig** Highld
199 L5 **Mallaigvaig** Highld
177 G5 **Malleny Mills** C Edin
108 E7 **Malltraeth** IoA
81 J2 **Mallwyd** Gwynd
39 L3 **Malmesbury** Wilts
24 C2 **Malmsmead** Devon
98 C3 **Malpas** Ches
4 D7 **Malpas** Cnwll
37 L3 **Malpas** Newpt
115 K8 **Maltby** Rothm
141 L5 **Maltby** S on T
118 F5 **Maltby le Marsh** Lincs
34 B6 **Maltman's Hill** Kent
134 C5 **Malton** N York
70 D5 **Malvern Hills**
70 E5 **Malvern Link** Worcs
70 D6 **Malvern Wells** Worcs
145 J4 **Malzie** D & G
70 C1 **Mamble** Worcs
53 L7 **Mamhilad** Mons
3 K6 **Manaccan** Cnwll
82 C3 **Manafon** Powys
232 d5 **Manais** W Isls
11 H8 **Manaton** Devon
118 E4 **Manby** Lincs
86 D4 **Mancetter** Warwks
113 J3 **Manchester** Manch
113 J5 **Manchester Airport** Manch
111 K7 **Mancot** Flints
201 K4 **Mandally** Highld
179 G7 **Manderston House** Border
90 C5 **Manea** Cambs
85 K4 **Maney** Birm
140 F4 **Manfield** N York
38 F5 **Mangotsfield** S Glos
232 d5 **Manish** W Isls
112 D7 **Manley** Ches
53 J7 **Manmoel** Caerph
188 C7 **Mannel** Ag & B
40 C8 **Manningford Bohune** Wilts
40 C8 **Manningford Bruce** Wilts
123 H4 **Manningham** Brad
31 K5 **Manning's Heath** W Susx
15 K2 **Mannington** Dorset
62 D2 **Manningtree** Essex
207 H4 **Mannofield** C Aber
49 H7 **Manorbier** Pembks
49 H7 **Manorbier Newton** Pembks
167 K3 **Manorhill** Border
64 C7 **Manorowen** Pembks
45 H3 **Manor Park** Gt Lon
69 H5 **Mansell Gamage** Herefs
69 H5 **Mansell Lacy** Herefs
164 C6 **Mansfield** E Ayrs
101 K1 **Mansfield** Notts
115 K8 **Mansfield Woodhouse** Notts
27 J7 **Manston** Dorset

124 B4 **Manston** Leeds
15 J2 **Manswood** Dorset
88 F1 **Manthorpe** Lincs
116 F2 **Manton** N Linc
88 C3 **Manton** Rutlnd
40 D6 **Manton** Wilts
60 D3 **Manuden** Essex
26 F6 **Maperton** Somset
102 B1 **Maplebeck** Notts
42 A5 **Mapledurham** Oxon
30 D3 **Mapledurwell** Hants
31 K6 **Maplehurst** W Susx
45 K7 **Maplescombe** Kent
100 D3 **Mapleton** Derbys
101 H4 **Mapperley** Derbys
101 L4 **Mapperley Park** C Nott
13 L3 **Mapperton** Dorset
71 J2 **Mappleborough Green** Warwks
126 F2 **Mappleton** E R Yk
123 L7 **Mapplewell** Barns
14 E2 **Mappowder** Dorset
4 C5 **Marazanvose** Cnwll
2 F5 **Marazion** Cnwll
98 E4 **Marbury** Ches
90 B4 **March** Cambs
165 J6 **March** S Lans
41 J2 **Marcham** Oxon
98 E6 **Marchamley** Shrops
100 C6 **Marchington** Staffs
94 F7 **Marchros** Gwynd
98 A3 **Marchwiel** Wrexhm
16 D1 **Marchwood** Hants
36 B6 **Marcross** V Glam
69 K5 **Marden** Herefs
33 J4 **Marden** Kent
40 C8 **Marden** Wilts
33 K5 **Marden Thorn** Kent
53 L5 **Mardy** Mons
103 L1 **Mareham le Fen** Lincs
118 C7 **Mareham on the Hill** Lincs
18 E3 **Marehill** W Susx
19 M2 **Maresfield** E Susx
126 E5 **Marfleet** C KuH
98 A2 **Marford** Wrexhm
36 B3 **Margam** Neath
27 J7 **Margaret Marsh** Dorset
61 G7 **Margaretting** Essex
61 G7 **Margaretting Tye** Essex
35 K1 **Margate** Kent
162 D3 **Margnaheglish** N Ayrs
145 M5 **Margrie** D & G
142 E4 **Margrove Park** R & Cl
91 G2 **Marham** Norfk
9 G4 **Marhamchurch** Cnwll
89 G3 **Marholm** C Pete
24 B6 **Mariansleigh** Devon
46 F5 **Marine Town** Kent
206 D3 **Marionburgh** Abers
209 H2 **Marishader** Highld
6 C3 **Maristow** Devon
155 J5 **Marjoriebanks** D & G
26 B2 **Mark** Somset
32 E5 **Markbeech** Kent
119 G5 **Markby** Lincs
33 G6 **Mark Cross** E Susx
86 E3 **Market Bosworth** Leics
89 G2 **Market Deeping** Lincs
98 F5 **Market Drayton** Shrops
87 K6 **Market Harborough** Leics
28 A1 **Market Lavington** Wilts
88 C1 **Market Overton** Rutlnd

117 J4 **Market Rasen** Lincs
118 C5 **Market Stainton** Lincs
115 K7 **Market Warsop** Notts
125 K3 **Market Weighton** E R Yk
92 B7 **Market Weston** Suffk
86 F2 **Markfield** Leics
53 J7 **Markham** Caerph
116 B6 **Markham Moor** Notts
186 E6 **Markinch** Fife
132 D6 **Markington** N York
178 C3 **Markle** E Loth
38 F7 **Marksbury** BaNES
61 L4 **Marks Tey** Essex
59 H5 **Markyate** Herts
40 D6 **Marlborough** Wilts
71 K4 **Marlcliff** Warwks
7 K3 **Marldon** Devon
79 G3 **Marlesford** Suffk
92 D2 **Marlingford** Norfk
48 D5 **Marloes** Pembks
42 D3 **Marlow** Bucks
42 D3 **Marlow Bottom** Bucks
32 D4 **Marlpit Hill** Kent
27 H7 **Marnhull** Dorset
113 L4 **Marple** Stockp
115 K1 **Marr** Donc
140 D7 **Marrick** N York
122 F7 **Marsden** Kirk
151 J3 **Marsden** S Tyne
59 K6 **Marshalswick** Herts
106 E7 **Marsham** Norfk
57 K7 **Marsh Baldon** Oxon
35 J3 **Marshborough** Kent
83 J5 **Marshbrook** Shrops
118 E2 **Marsh Chapel** Lincs
37 K4 **Marshfield** Newpt
39 H5 **Marshfield** S Glos
8 F6 **Marshgate** Cnwll
57 M4 **Marsh Gibbon** Bucks
12 D4 **Marsh Green** Devon
32 D4 **Marsh Green** Kent
90 D2 **Marshland St James** Norfk
115 H5 **Marsh Lane** Derbys
24 F3 **Marsh Street** Somset
13 J3 **Marshwood** Dorset
140 D6 **Marske** N York
142 D3 **Marske-by-the-Sea** R & Cl
69 G3 **Marston** Herefs
102 E4 **Marston** Lincs
57 K6 **Marston** Oxon
99 L6 **Marston** Staffs
27 L1 **Marston** Wilts
85 L6 **Marston Green** Solhll
26 E6 **Marston Magna** Somset
40 C2 **Marston Meysey** Wilts
100 C5 **Marston Montgomery** Derbys
74 E6 **Marston Moretaine** Beds
100 E6 **Marston on Dove** Derbys
73 G6 **Marston St Lawrence** Nhants
87 K6 **Marston Trussell** Nhants
54 D4 **Marstow** Herefs
58 F5 **Marsworth** Bucks
40 F7 **Marten** Wilts
113 J6 **Marthall** Ches
107 J8 **Martham** Norfk
28 B7 **Martin** Hants
35 J5 **Martin** Kent
103 J1 **Martin** Lincs
118 C7 **Martin** Lincs
23 L2 **Martinhoe** Devon

70 F3 **Martin Hussingtree** Worcs
14 C5 **Martinstown** Dorset
78 F5 **Martlesham** Suffk
78 F5 **Martlesham Heath** Suffk
49 H5 **Martletwy** Pembks
70 D3 **Martley** Worcs
26 C7 **Martock** Somset
113 J7 **Marton** Ches
126 F3 **Marton** E R Yk
116 D5 **Marton** Lincs
142 B4 **Marton** Middsb
132 F6 **Marton** N York
134 B3 **Marton** N York
82 F3 **Marton** Shrops
72 E2 **Marton** Warwks
132 E5 **Marton-le-Moor** N York
29 K5 **Martyr Worthy** Hants
234 b5 **Marwick** Ork
23 H4 **Marwood** Devon
212 D4 **Marybank** Highld
212 E3 **Maryburgh** Highld
207 G5 **Maryculter** Abers
179 G6 **Marygold** Border
216 F5 **Maryhill** Abers
175 G4 **Maryhill** C Glas
197 H3 **Marykirk** Abers
44 F4 **Marylebone** Gt Lon
121 H8 **Marylebone** Wigan
214 F6 **Marypark** Moray
147 H7 **Maryport** Cumb
144 D7 **Maryport** D & G
10 C7 **Marystow** Devon
6 D1 **Mary Tavy** Devon
197 H5 **Maryton** Angus
206 B6 **Marywell** Abers
207 H5 **Marywell** Abers
197 G7 **Marywell** Angus
132 C4 **Masham** N York
130 C4 **Mashbury** Essex
115 J6 **Mastin Moor** Derbys
60 E5 **Matching Green** Essex
60 E5 **Matching Tye** Essex
158 C7 **Matfen** Nthumb
33 H5 **Matfield** Kent
38 D3 **Mathern** Mons
70 D5 **Mathon** Herefs
48 E2 **Mathry** Pembks
106 D5 **Matlask** Norfk
100 F1 **Matlock** Derbys
100 F2 **Matlock Bath** Derbys
55 J3 **Matson** Gloucs
116 B4 **Mattersey** Notts
42 B8 **Mattingley** Hants
92 C2 **Mattishall** Norfk
92 C2 **Mattishall Burgh** Norfk
163 L4 **Mauchline** E Ayrs
217 H5 **Maud** Abers
236 d6 **Maufant** Jersey
56 D3 **Maugersbury** Gloucs
237 e3 **Maughold** IoM
212 C6 **Mauld** Highld
74 F6 **Maulden** Beds
138 F4 **Maulds Meaburn** Cumb
132 E3 **Maunby** N York
69 L4 **Maund Bryan** Herefs
25 G5 **Maundown** Somset
93 K2 **Mautby** Norfk
85 J1 **Mavesyn Ridware** Staffs
118 C7 **Mavis Enderby** Lincs
147 J5 **Mawbray** Cumb
121 G7 **Mawdesley** Lancs
36 C4 **Mawdlam** Brdgnd
3 J6 **Mawgan** Cnwll
4 D3 **Mawgan Porth** Cnwll
3 J3 **Mawla** Cnwll

3 K5 **Mawnan** Cnwll
3 K5 **Mawnan Smith** Cnwll
88 B7 **Mawsley** Nhants
89 G2 **Maxey** C Pete
86 B6 **Maxstoke** Warwks
34 F5 **Maxted Street** Kent
167 J4 **Maxton** Border
35 J6 **Maxton** Kent
155 G6 **Maxwell Town** D & G
9 H6 **Maxworthy** Cnwll
99 J3 **May Bank** Staffs
163 H7 **Maybole** S Ayrs
43 G8 **Maybury** Surrey
33 G7 **Mayfield** E Susx
177 K5 **Mayfield** Mdloth
100 D4 **Mayfield** Staffs
31 G1 **Mayford** Surrey
55 G4 **May Hill** Gloucs
61 L7 **Mayland** Essex
61 L7 **Maylandsea** Essex
20 C3 **Maynard's Green** E Susx
93 J4 **Maypole Green** Norfk
77 K3 **Maypole Green** Suffk
39 G8 **Meadgate** BaNES
58 D6 **Meadle** Bucks
151 G6 **Meadowfield** Dur
9 K8 **Meadwell** Devon
147 K5 **Mealrigg** Cumb
123 K5 **Meanwood** Leeds
26 C3 **Meare** Somset
25 L6 **Meare Green** Somset
25 M6 **Meare Green** Somset
174 F7 **Mearns** E Rens
74 B2 **Mears Ashby** Nhants
86 D2 **Measham** Leics
129 J4 **Meathop** Cumb
6 D3 **Meavy** Devon
88 B5 **Medbourne** Leics
115 L7 **Meden Vale** Notts
42 D4 **Medmenham** Bucks
150 E4 **Medomsley** Dur
30 A4 **Medstead** Hants
99 M1 **Meerbrook** Staffs
60 C2 **Meesden** Herts
10 E3 **Meeth** Devon
107 G6 **Meeting House Hill** Norfk
50 C2 **Meidrim** Carmth
82 D2 **Meifod** Powys
195 L7 **Meigle** P & K
164 F6 **Meikle Carco** D & G
175 J7 **Meikle Earnock** S Lans
173 H6 **Meikle Kilmory** Ag & B
195 G8 **Meikle Obney** P & K
195 J7 **Meikleour** P & K
216 D7 **Meikle Wartle** Abers
50 F4 **Meinciau** Carmth
99 L4 **Meir** C Stke
75 L5 **Melbourn** Cambs
101 G2 **Melbourne** Derbys
125 H2 **Melbourne** E R Yk
27 K7 **Melbury Abbas** Dorset
14 B2 **Melbury Bubb** Dorset
14 B2 **Melbury Osmond** Dorset
74 E2 **Melchbourne** Beds
14 E2 **Melcombe Bingham** Dorset
10 E6 **Meldon** Devon
158 C6 **Meldon** Nthumb
75 L5 **Meldreth** Cambs
184 F7 **Meldrum** Stirlg
182 B5 **Melfort** Ag & B
196 E5 **Melgund Castle** Angus
110 E5 **Meliden** Denbgs
97 G3 **Melin-y-wig** Denbgs
138 D3 **Melkinthorpe** Cumb

149 J3 **Melkridge** Nthumb
39 K7 **Melksham** Wilts
130 B5 **Melling** Lancs
111 L2 **Melling** Sefton
92 C8 **Mellis** Suffk
219 K3 **Mellon Charles** Highld
219 K3 **Mellon Udrigle** Highld
121 J4 **Mellor** Lancs
113 M4 **Mellor** Stockp
121 J4 **Mellor Brook** Lancs
27 G2 **Mells** Somset
149 G7 **Melmerby** Cumb
131 K3 **Melmerby** N York
132 E4 **Melmerby** N York
229 J3 **Melness** Highld
13 L3 **Melplash** Dorset
167 H3 **Melrose** Border
234 B7 **Melsetter** Ork
140 F5 **Melsonby** N York
123 G7 **Meltham** Kirk
126 B5 **Melton** E R Yk
79 G4 **Melton** Suffk
106 C6 **Melton Constable** Norfk
102 C8 **Melton Mowbray** Leics
126 D7 **Melton Ross** N Linc
219 H4 **Melvaig** Highld
83 G1 **Melverley** Shrops
230 C3 **Melvich** Highld
13 H2 **Membury** Devon
217 H2 **Memsie** Abers
196 C5 **Memus** Angus
109 H6 **Menai Bridge** IoA
92 F6 **Mendham** Suffk
26 D2 **Mendip Hills**
78 D2 **Mendlesham** Suffk
78 D2 **Mendlesham Green** Suffk
5 L4 **Menheniot** Cnwll
164 F7 **Mennock** D & G
123 H2 **Menston** Brad
185 H7 **Menstrie** Clacks
58 E4 **Mentmore** Bucks
200 C7 **Meoble** Highld
83 J2 **Meole Brace** Shrops
29 L7 **Meonstoke** Hants
45 M6 **Meopham** Kent
90 B7 **Mepal** Cambs
75 G2 **Meppershall** Beds
113 G5 **Mere** Ches
27 J5 **Mere** Wilts
120 F6 **Mere Brow** Lancs
122 C4 **Mereclough** Lancs
33 H3 **Mereworth** Kent
86 B6 **Meriden** Solhll
208 F7 **Merkadale** Highld
48 F7 **Merrion** Pembks
26 C8 **Merriott** Somset
31 G2 **Merrow** Surrey
43 J2 **Merry Hill** Herts
84 F4 **Merryhill** Wolves
5 L3 **Merrymeet** Cnwll
34 E6 **Mersham** Kent
32 B3 **Merstham** Surrey
18 B5 **Merston** W Susx
17 G5 **Merstone** IoW
4 D6 **Merther** Cnwll
67 L6 **Merthyr Cynog** Powys
36 D5 **Merthyr Mawr** Brdgnd
53 G6 **Merthyr Tydfil** Myr Td
53 G7 **Merthyr Vale** Myr Td
10 D3 **Merton** Devon
44 E6 **Merton** Gt Lon
91 K4 **Merton** Norfk
57 L4 **Merton** Oxon
24 B7 **Meshaw** Devon
61 L4 **Messing** Essex
116 E2 **Messingham** N Linc
93 G7 **Metfield** Suffk

6 B3 **Metherell** Cnwll
103 H1 **Metheringham** Lincs
186 F7 **Methil** Fife
186 F7 **Methilhill** Fife
124 B5 **Methley** Leeds
217 G6 **Methlick** Abers
185 L3 **Methven** P & K
91 G4 **Methwold** Norfk
91 G4 **Methwold Hythe** Norfk
93 H5 **Mettingham** Suffk
106 E5 **Metton** Norfk
4 F6 **Mevagissey** Cnwll
115 J2 **Mexborough** Donc
231 K2 **Mey** Highld
94 D6 **Meyllteyrn** Gwynd
56 C7 **Meysey Hampton** Gloucs
232 d2 **Miabhig** W Isls
232 d2 **Miavaig** W Isls
54 D3 **Michaelchurch** Herefs
69 G7 **Michaelchurch Escley** Herefs
37 K4 **Michaelstone-y-Fedw** Newpt
37 J5 **Michaelston-le-Pit** V Glam
5 G1 **Michaelstow** Cnwll
29 K4 **Micheldever** Hants
29 K3 **Micheldever Station** Hants
29 G6 **Michelmersh** Hants
78 D3 **Mickfield** Suffk
115 K3 **Micklebring** Donc
143 G5 **Mickleby** N York
124 C4 **Micklefield** Leeds
31 K2 **Mickleham** Surrey
100 F5 **Mickleover** C Derb
140 B3 **Mickleton** Dur
71 L5 **Mickleton** Gloucs
124 B5 **Mickletown** Leeds
112 C7 **Mickle Trafford** Ches
132 C4 **Mickley** N York
77 J3 **Mickley Green** Suffk
150 D3 **Mickley Square** Nthumb
217 H2 **Mid Ardlaw** Abers
234 c4 **Midbea** Ork
206 C5 **Mid Beltie** Abers
176 E5 **Mid Calder** W Loth
231 K7 **Mid Clyth** Highld
57 J3 **Middle Aston** Oxon
57 H3 **Middle Barton** Oxon
155 L6 **Middlebie** D & G
194 D3 **Middlebridge** P & K
26 C8 **Middle Chinnock** Somset
58 B3 **Middle Claydon** Bucks
55 M6 **Middle Duntisbourne** Gloucs
131 L3 **Middleham** N York
115 H6 **Middle Handley** Derbys
39 J6 **Middlehill** Wilts
83 K5 **Middlehope** Shrops
172 F1 **Middle Kames** Ag & B
71 J5 **Middle Littleton** Worcs
14 C2 **Middlemarsh** Dorset
100 C4 **Middle Mayfield** Staffs
117 H4 **Middle Rasen** Lincs
7 K2 **Middle Rocombe** Devon
141 L4 **Middlesbrough** Middsb
129 L2 **Middleshaw** Cumb
131 K5 **Middlesmoor** N York
46 D5 **Middle Stoke** Medway
141 G2 **Middlestone** Dur
123 K6 **Middlestown** Wakefd
167 K2 **Middlethird** Border

188 B7 **Middleton** Ag & B
100 F2 **Middleton** Derbys
114 D8 **Middleton** Derbys
77 K6 **Middleton** Essex
29 H3 **Middleton** Hants
69 K1 **Middleton** Herefs
123 L5 **Middleton** Leeds
174 D7 **Middleton** N Ayrs
123 G2 **Middleton** N York
134 B3 **Middleton** N York
88 B5 **Middleton** Nhants
90 F1 **Middleton** Norfk
158 D5 **Middleton** Nthumb
186 B6 **Middleton** P & K
113 K1 **Middleton** Rochdl
83 K7 **Middleton** Shrops
79 J2 **Middleton** Suffk
50 E7 **Middleton** Swans
85 L4 **Middleton** Warwks
73 G6 **Middleton Cheney** Nhants
139 L3 **Middleton-in-Teesdale** Dur
79 J2 **Middleton Moor** Suffk
141 J5 **Middleton One Row** Darltn
18 C5 **Middleton-on-Sea** W Susx
69 K2 **Middleton on the Hill** Herefs
125 L2 **Middleton on the Wolds** E R Yk
132 E4 **Middleton Quernhow** N York
141 J5 **Middleton St George** Darltn
84 C6 **Middleton Scriven** Shrops
57 K4 **Middleton Stoney** Oxon
141 G6 **Middleton Tyas** N York
2 a2 **Middle Town** IoS
82 F2 **Middletown** Powys
72 D5 **Middle Tysoe** Warwks
28 F4 **Middle Wallop** Hants
113 G7 **Middlewich** Ches
28 E5 **Middle Winterslow** Wilts
5 L2 **Middlewood** Cnwll
28 C4 **Middle Woodford** Wilts
78 D3 **Middlewood Green** Suffk
163 M3 **Middleyard** E Ayrs
26 B5 **Middlezoy** Somset
39 H7 **Midford** BaNES
41 K6 **Midgham** W Berk
122 F5 **Midgley** Calder
123 K7 **Midgley** Wakefd
114 E2 **Midhopestones** Sheff
30 E6 **Midhurst** W Susx
18 B4 **Mid Lavant** W Susx
167 H4 **Midlem** Border
212 C6 **Mid Mains** Highld
173 H6 **Midpark** Ag & B
26 F1 **Midsomer Norton** BaNES
229 J4 **Midtown** Highld
235 d3 **Mid Yell** Shet
205 K4 **Migvie** Abers
26 F7 **Milborne Port** Somset
14 F3 **Milborne St Andrew** Dorset
26 F7 **Milborne Wick** Somset
158 E6 **Milbourne** Nthumb
39 L3 **Milbourne** Wilts
138 F2 **Milburn** Cumb
38 F3 **Milbury Heath** S Glos
132 F6 **Milby** N York
72 E7 **Milcombe** Oxon

77 L5 **Milden** Suffk
91 G8 **Mildenhall** Suffk
40 E6 **Mildenhall** Wilts
105 L8 **Mileham** Norfk
19 H4 **Mile Oak** Br & H
176 E2 **Milesmark** Fife
113 J2 **Miles Platting** Manch
46 F5 **Mile Town** Kent
168 D3 **Milfield** Nthumb
101 G4 **Milford** Derbys
22 C6 **Milford** Devon
99 L7 **Milford** Staffs
30 F3 **Milford** Surrey
48 F6 **Milford Haven** Pembks
16 C4 **Milford on Sea** Hants
54 E6 **Milkwall** Gloucs
30 D5 **Milland** W Susx
122 F6 **Mill Bank** Calder
217 J5 **Millbreck** Abers
216 F5 **Millbrex** Abers
30 D3 **Millbridge** Surrey
74 E6 **Millbrook** Beds
29 G8 **Millbrook** C Sotn
6 B5 **Millbrook** Cnwll
236 C7 **Millbrook** Jersey
113 L4 **Mill Brow** Stockp
206 F4 **Millbuie** Abers
212 E4 **Millbuie** Highld
163 K4 **Millburn** S Ayrs
21 G2 **Millcorner** E Susx
222 E7 **Millcraig** Highld
100 C2 **Milldale** Staffs
42 C4 **Mill End** Bucks
60 B2 **Mill End** Herts
177 J4 **Millerhill** Mdloth
114 C6 **Miller's Dale** Derbys
175 H5 **Millerston** C Glas
76 F5 **Mill Green** Cambs
61 G7 **Mill Green** Essex
103 L7 **Mill Green** Lincs
77 L6 **Mill Green** Suffk
78 B3 **Mill Green** Suffk
78 D3 **Mill Green** Suffk
68 F5 **Millhalf** Herefs
175 K7 **Millheugh** S Lans
44 E2 **Mill Hill** Gt Lon
173 G4 **Millhouse** Ag & B
155 K5 **Millhousebridge** D & G
114 E2 **Millhouse Green** Barns
115 G5 **Millhouses** Sheff
174 D6 **Milliken Park** Rens
125 J1 **Millington** E R Yk
99 J5 **Mill Meece** Staffs
185 H4 **Mill of Drummond** P & K
174 D2 **Mill of Haldane** W Duns
128 E4 **Milom** Cumb
173 K7 **Millport** N Ayrs
78 C1 **Mill Street** Suffk
130 C2 **Millthrop** Cumb
207 G5 **Milltimber** C Aber
205 G4 **Milltown** Abers
205 K3 **Milltown** Abers
156 C6 **Milltown** D & G
23 J4 **Milltown** Devon
206 C5 **Milltown of Campfield** Abers
215 G6 **Milltown of Edinvillie** Moray
206 C5 **Milltown of Learney** Abers
186 B6 **Milnathort** P & K
175 H4 **Milngavie** E Duns
122 D7 **Milnrow** Rochdl
129 K3 **Milnthorpe** Cumb
208 B4 **Milovaig** Highld
84 B8 **Milson** Shrops
34 B3 **Milstead** Kent

28 D3 **Milston** Wilts
73 H5 **Milthorpe** Nhants
76 C2 **Milton** Cambs
148 F3 **Milton** Cumb
144 F4 **Milton** D & G
154 E7 **Milton** D & G
100 F7 **Milton** Derbys
209 L5 **Milton** Highld
212 D7 **Milton** Highld
212 E4 **Milton** Highld
223 G6 **Milton** Highld
231 L5 **Milton** Highld
174 C5 **Milton** Inver
46 A5 **Milton** Kent
204 E2 **Milton** Moray
215 L2 **Milton** Moray
37 M7 **Milton** N Som
116 B6 **Milton** Notts
41 J3 **Milton** Oxon
72 F7 **Milton** Oxon
195 H5 **Milton** P & K
49 H6 **Milton** Pembks
26 C6 **Milton** Somset
184 B6 **Milton** Stirlg
174 D4 **Milton** W Duns
14 F3 **Milton Abbas** Dorset
9 K8 **Milton Abbot** Devon
177 H5 **Milton Bridge** Mdloth
58 F7 **Milton Bryan** Beds
26 F4 **Milton Clevedon**
Somset
6 D3 **Milton Combe** Devon
9 K3 **Milton Damerel**
Devon
74 E4 **Milton Ernest** Beds
98 C2 **Milton Green** Ches
41 J3 **Milton Hill** Oxon
74 C6 **Milton Keynes**
M Keyn
40 D7 **Milton Lilbourne** Wilts
73 K4 **Milton Malsor** Nhants
184 D1 **Milton Morenish**
P & K
206 B5 **Milton of**
Auchinhove Abers
186 E7 **Milton of Balgonie**
Fife
174 E1 **Milton of Buchanan**
Stirlg
175 H3 **Milton of Campsie**
E Duns
213 G6 **Milton of Leys** Highld
205 J6 **Milton of Tullich**
Abers
27 J5 **Milton on Stour**
Dorset
46 E6 **Milton Regis** Kent
56 E4 **Milton-under-**
Wychwood Oxon
25 H6 **Milverton** Somset
72 C2 **Milverton** Warwks
99 L6 **Milwich** Staffs
182 D7 **Minard** Ag & B
55 K7 **Minchinhampton**
Gloucs
24 F3 **Minehead** Somset
97 L3 **Minera** Wrexhm
40 A3 **Minety** Wilts
95 K5 **Minffordd** Gwynd
190 D3 **Mingarrypark** Highld
118 D8 **Miningsby** Lincs
5 L2 **Minions** Cnwll
163 J6 **Minishant** S Ayrs
81 J2 **Minllyn** Gwynd
145 J2 **Minnigaff** D & G
216 E3 **Minnonie** Abers
132 F6 **Minskip** N York
16 C1 **Minstead** Hants
30 D7 **Minsted** W Susx
35 J2 **Minster** Kent
46 F5 **Minster** Kent
83 G3 **Minsterley** Shrops

56 F5 **Minster Lovell** Oxon
55 H5 **Minsterworth** Gloucs
14 C2 **Minterne Magna**
Dorset
117 K6 **Minting** Lincs
217 J5 **Mintlaw** Abers
167 H5 **Minto** Border
83 H5 **Minton** Shrops
136 D4 **Mirehouse** Cumb
123 J6 **Mirfield** Kirk
55 L6 **Miserden** Gloucs
37 G4 **Miskin** Rhondd
116 B3 **Misson** Notts
87 G6 **Misterton** Leics
116 C3 **Misterton** Notts
13 L2 **Misterton** Somset
62 D2 **Mistley** Essex
44 F6 **Mitcham** Gt Lon
54 F4 **Mitcheldean** Gloucs
4 D5 **Mitchell** Cnwll
155 G3 **Mitchellslacks** D & G
54 C6 **Mitchel Troy** Mons
158 F5 **Mitford** Nthumb
3 J2 **Mithian** Cnwll
73 H7 **Mixbury** Oxon
113 H5 **Mobberley** Ches
100 A4 **Mobberley** Staffs
82 B5 **Mochdre** Powys
145 H5 **Mochrum** D & G
33 J4 **Mockbeggar** Kent
136 F3 **Mockerkin** Cumb
6 F5 **Modbury** Devon
99 L5 **Moddershall** Staffs
109 G4 **Moelfre** IoA
97 J6 **Moelfre** Powys
155 J2 **Moffat** D & G
75 G5 **Mogerhanger** Beds
86 C1 **Moira** Leics
34 D4 **Molash** Kent
199 G3 **Mol-chlach** Highld
111 H8 **Mold** Flints
123 H7 **Moldgreen** Kirk
60 E3 **Molehill Green** Essex
126 C3 **Molescroft** E R Yk
88 F7 **Molesworth** Cambs
24 C5 **Molland** Devon
111 L7 **Mollington** Ches
72 F5 **Mollington** Oxon
175 J4 **Mollinsburn** N Lans
197 J1 **Mondynes** Abers
78 F3 **Monewden** Suffk
185 M2 **Moneydie** P & K
154 D4 **Moniaive** D & G
187 H2 **Monifieth** Angus
196 E8 **Monikie** Angus
186 E5 **Monimail** Fife
44 E1 **Monken Hadley**
Gt Lon
124 D5 **Monk Fryston** N York
70 B5 **Monkhide** Herefs
148 C3 **Monkhill** Cumb
84 B5 **Monkhopton** Shrops
69 J3 **Monkland** Herefs
23 G7 **Monkleigh** Devon
36 E6 **Monknash** V Glam
10 E4 **Monkokehampton**
Devon
159 H7 **Monkseaton** N Tyne
77 L5 **Monks Eleigh** Suffk
31 K6 **Monk's Gate** W Susx
113 J6 **Monks Heath** Ches
29 L1 **Monk Sherborne**
Hants
34 F6 **Monks Horton** Kent
25 G4 **Monksilver** Somset
86 F6 **Monks Kirby** Warwks
78 E2 **Monk Soham** Suffk
58 D6 **Monks Risborough**
Bucks
118 F7 **Monksthorpe** Lincs
60 F3 **Monk Street** Essex
53 M7 **Monkswood** Mons

12 F2 **Monkton** Devon
47 M6 **Monkton** Kent
163 J4 **Monkton** S Ayrs
151 H3 **Monkton** S Tyne
39 H7 **Monkton Combe**
BaNES
27 J4 **Monkton Deverill**
Wilts
39 J7 **Monkton Farleigh**
Wilts
25 K6 **Monkton Heathfield**
Somset
13 J3 **Monkton Wyld**
Dorset
151 J4 **Monkwearmouth**
Sundld
30 A5 **Monkwood** Hants
85 G4 **Monmore Green**
Wolves
54 D5 **Monmouth** Mons
69 G5 **Monnington on Wye**
Herefs
145 H6 **Monreith** D & G
26 D7 **Montacute** Somset
83 H1 **Montford** Shrops
83 H1 **Montford Bridge**
Shrops
206 B2 **Montgarrie** Abers
164 A4 **Montgarswood**
E Ayrs
82 E4 **Montgomery** Powys
197 H5 **Montrose** Angus
236 b3 **Mont Saint** Guern
28 F3 **Monxton** Hants
114 D7 **Monyash** Derbys
206 D3 **Monymusk** Abers
185 H3 **Monzie** P & K
175 J4 **Moodiesburn** N Lans
186 E4 **Moonzie** Fife
123 L3 **Moor Allerton** Leeds
118 D8 **Moorby** Lincs
15 J2 **Moor Crichel** Dorset
15 K4 **Moordown** Bmouth
112 E5 **Moore** Halton
122 F5 **Moor End** Calder
125 G7 **Moorends** Donc
101 J3 **Moorgreen** Notts
123 H3 **Moorhead** Brad
148 B4 **Moorhouse** Cumb
116 C7 **Moorhouse** Notts
32 D3 **Moorhouse Bank**
Surrey
26 B4 **Moorlinch** Somset
133 H7 **Moor Monkton**
N York
142 E4 **Moorsholm** R & Cl
27 H7 **Moorside** Dorset
5 K3 **Moorswater** Cnwll
124 C7 **Moorthorpe** Wakefd
123 K3 **Moortown** Leeds
117 H2 **Moortown** Lincs
223 G5 **Morangie** Highld
199 L6 **Morar** Highld
89 G5 **Morborne** Cambs
11 H4 **Morchard Bishop**
Devon
13 K4 **Morcombelake**
Dorset
88 D4 **Morcott** Rutlnd
97 L6 **Morda** Shrops
15 H4 **Morden** Dorset
44 E6 **Morden** Gt Lon
69 L6 **Mordiford** Herefs
141 H2 **Mordon** Dur
83 G5 **More** Shrops
24 E6 **Morebath** Devon
168 B4 **Morebattle** Border
129 J6 **Morecambe** Lancs
40 C3 **Moredon** Swindn
220 E3 **Morefield** Highld
35 G7 **Morehall** Kent
7 H5 **Moreleigh** Devon

184 D1 **Morenish** P & K
29 K6 **Morestead** Hants
14 F4 **Moreton** Dorset
60 E6 **Moreton** Essex
69 K2 **Moreton** Herefs
58 B6 **Moreton** Oxon
111 J4 **Moreton** Wirral
98 E7 **Moreton Corbet**
Shrops
11 H7 **Moretonhampstead**
Devon
56 D2 **Moreton-in-Marsh**
Gloucs
69 L5 **Moreton Jeffries**
Herefs
72 C4 **Moreton Morrell**
Warwks
69 K5 **Moreton on Lugg**
Herefs
73 H5 **Moreton Pinkney**
Nhants
98 F5 **Moreton Say** Shrops
55 H6 **Moreton Valence**
Gloucs
94 E4 **Morfa Nefyn** Gwynd
178 C4 **Morham** E Loth
138 E3 **Morland** Cumb
113 J5 **Morley** Ches
101 H4 **Morley** Derbys
123 K5 **Morley** Leeds
113 J5 **Morley Green** Ches
92 C4 **Morley St Botolph**
Norfk
177 H4 **Morningside** C Edin
175 L7 **Morningside** N Lans
92 F5 **Morningthorpe** Norfk
158 F5 **Morpeth** Nthumb
197 H4 **Morphie** Abers
100 C8 **Morrey** Staffs
51 J6 **Morriston** Swans
106 B4 **Morston** Norfk
23 G3 **Mortehoe** Devon
115 J4 **Morthen** Rothm
41 M7 **Mortimer** W Berk
41 M7 **Mortimer West End**
Hants
44 E5 **Mortlake** Gt Lon
148 C4 **Morton** Cumb
101 H1 **Morton** Derbys
103 H7 **Morton** Lincs
116 D3 **Morton** Lincs
102 B3 **Morton** Notts
97 L7 **Morton** Shrops
132 E2 **Morton-on-Swale**
N York
92 D1 **Morton on the Hill**
Norfk
2 D4 **Morvah** Cnwll
5 K4 **Morval** Cnwll
200 E2 **Morvich** Highld
84 C5 **Morville** Shrops
6 C2 **Morwellham Quay**
Devon
9 G2 **Morwenstow** Cnwll
115 H5 **Mosborough** Sheff
163 L2 **Moscow** E Ayrs
85 J6 **Moseley** Birm
85 G4 **Moseley** Wolves
70 E3 **Moseley** Worcs
188 B7 **Moss** Ag & B
124 F7 **Moss** Donc
205 K2 **Mossat** Abers
235 d4 **Mossbank** Shet
112 D3 **Moss Bank** St Hel
136 D2 **Mossbay** Cumb
163 K4 **Mossblown** S Ayrs
167 K6 **Mossburnford** Border
154 B7 **Mossdale** D & G
153 K2 **Mossdale** E Ayrs
120 F2 **Moss Edge** Lancs
175 K6 **Mossend** N Lans
113 L2 **Mossley** Tamesd

156 D3 **Mosspaul Hotel** Border
213 K4 **Moss-side** Highld
215 H3 **Mosstodloch** Moray
145 L5 **Mossyard** D & G
121 H7 **Mossy Lea** Lancs
13 L2 **Mosterton** Dorset
113 K2 **Moston** Manch
111 G5 **Mostyn** Flints
27 J6 **Motcombe** Dorset
6 F6 **Mothecombe** Devon
138 B2 **Motherby** Cumb
175 K6 **Motherwell** N Lans
44 E6 **Motspur Park** Gt Lon
45 H5 **Mottingham** Gt Lon
28 F6 **Mottisfont** Hants
16 E5 **Mottistone** IoW
113 M3 **Mottram in Longdendale** Tamesd
113 K5 **Mottram St Andrew** Ches
112 D7 **Mouldsworth** Ches
194 E4 **Moulin** P & K
19 J4 **Moulsecoomb** Br & H
41 L4 **Moulsford** Oxon
74 C6 **Moulsoe** M Keyn
222 E7 **Moultavie** Highld
112 F7 **Moulton** Ches
104 A7 **Moulton** Lincs
141 G6 **Moulton** N York
73 L2 **Moulton** Nhants
77 G2 **Moulton** Suffk
37 G6 **Moulton** V Glam
103 M8 **Moulton Chapel** Lincs
93 H3 **Moulton St Mary** Norfk
104 A6 **Moulton Seas End** Lincs
5 J3 **Mount** Cnwll
123 G4 **Mountain** Brad
53 G7 **Mountain Ash** Rhondd
176 F8 **Mountain Cross** Border
3 J3 **Mount Ambrose** Cnwll
61 L2 **Mount Bures** Essex
20 E2 **Mountfield** E Susx
212 E3 **Mountgerald House** Highld
3 J2 **Mount Hawke** Cnwll
4 D4 **Mountjoy** Cnwll
177 H6 **Mount Lothian** Mdloth
60 F8 **Mountnessing** Essex
38 D2 **Mounton** Mons
101 G3 **Mount Pleasant** Derbys
77 G5 **Mount Pleasant** Suffk
87 H2 **Mountsorrel** Leics
122 F5 **Mount Tabor** Calder
30 F3 **Mousehill** Surrey
2 E6 **Mousehole** Cnwll
155 J7 **Mouswald** D & G
168 B5 **Mowhaugh** Border
87 J5 **Mowsley** Leics
202 C8 **Moy** Highld
213 J7 **Moy** Highld
200 D2 **Moye** Highld
64 F5 **Moylgrove** Pembks
161 H2 **Muasdale** Ag & B
207 G6 **Muchalls** Abers
54 D3 **Much Birch** Herefs
70 B5 **Much Cowarne** Herefs
54 C2 **Much Dewchurch** Herefs
26 B6 **Muchelney** Somset
26 C6 **Muchelney Ham** Somset
60 C4 **Much Hadham** Herts
120 F6 **Much Hoole** Lancs

5 K5 **Muchlarnick** Cnwll
54 F2 **Much Marcle** Herefs
84 B4 **Much Wenlock** Shrops
106 D4 **Muckleburgh Collection** Norfk
99 G5 **Mucklestone** Staffs
118 E5 **Muckton** Lincs
23 J4 **Muddiford** Devon
20 B3 **Muddles Green** E Susx
16 A4 **Mudeford** Dorset
26 E7 **Mudford** Somset
26 E7 **Mudford Sock** Somset
175 D4 **Mugdock** Stirlg
209 G6 **Mugeary** Highld
100 F4 **Mugginton** Derbys
216 D4 **Muirden** Abers
196 F8 **Muirdrum** Angus
216 D5 **Muiresk** Abers
186 E1 **Muirhead** Angus
186 E6 **Muirhead** Fife
175 J4 **Muirhead** N Lans
164 D4 **Muirkirk** E Ayrs
175 J2 **Muirmill** Stirlg
206 B3 **Muir of Fowlis** Abers
214 E3 **Muir of Miltonduff** Moray
212 E4 **Muir of Ord** Highld
195 G8 **Muir of Thorn** P & K
192 B1 **Muirshearlich** Highld
217 J6 **Muirtack** Abers
185 J5 **Muirton** P & K
212 C4 **Muirton Mains** Highld
195 J7 **Muirton of Ardblair** P & K
139 K7 **Muker** N York
92 E4 **Mulbarton** Norfk
215 H4 **Mulben** Moray
181 J1 **Mull** Ag & B
3 H7 **Mullion** Cnwll
3 H7 **Mullion Cove** Cnwll
119 G6 **Mumby** Lincs
70 B4 **Munderfield Row** Herefs
70 B4 **Munderfield Stocks** Herefs
107 G5 **Mundesley** Norfk
91 H5 **Mundford** Norfk
93 G4 **Mundham** Norfk
61 K7 **Mundon Hill** Essex
137 K2 **Mungrisdale** Cumb
213 G4 **Munlochy** Highld
174 B8 **Munnoch** N Ayrs
70 B6 **Munsley** Herefs
83 K6 **Munslow** Shrops
11 G7 **Murchington** Devon
57 L5 **Murcott** Oxon
231 H2 **Murkle** Highld
200 F6 **Murlaggan** Highld
187 G1 **Murroes** Angus
89 L3 **Murrow** Cambs
58 D3 **Mursley** Bucks
196 D5 **Murthill** Angus
195 H8 **Murthly** P & K
139 G3 **Murton** Cumb
151 J5 **Murton** Dur
179 K8 **Murton** Nthumb
133 K8 **Murton** York
13 H4 **Musbury** Devon
177 K4 **Musselburgh** E Loth
102 D5 **Muston** Leics
135 H4 **Muston** N York
44 F3 **Muswell Hill** Gt Lon
146 C5 **Mutehill** D & G
93 K6 **Mutford** Suffk
185 H4 **Muthill** P & K
231 H5 **Mybster** Highld
52 B3 **Myddfai** Carmth
98 C7 **Myddle** Shrops
66 B4 **Mydroilyn** Cerdgn

4 C8 **Mylor** Cnwll
4 C8 **Mylor Bridge** Cnwll
49 K2 **Mynachlog ddu** Pembks
83 H5 **Myndtown** Shrops
38 C2 **Mynydd-bach** Mons
51 J6 **Mynydd-Bach** Swans
206 E5 **Myrebird** Abers
157 G3 **Myredykes** Border
30 E1 **Mytchett** Surrey
122 E5 **Mytholm** Calder
122 F5 **Mytholmroyd** Calder
132 F6 **Myton-on-Swale** N York

N

219 J5 **Naast** Highld
232 d4 **Na Buirgh** W Isls
124 F2 **Naburn** York
34 H4 **Nackington** Kent
78 F6 **Nacton** Suffk
135 G7 **Nafferton** E R Yk
25 K5 **Nailsbourne** Somset
38 C6 **Nailsea** N Som
86 E3 **Nailstone** Leics
55 J7 **Nailsworth** Gloucs
213 K3 **Nairn** Highld
111 G7 **Nannerch** Flints
87 G1 **Nanpantan** Leics
4 F5 **Nanpean** Cnwll
5 G3 **Nanstallon** Cnwll
65 L3 **Nanternis** Cerdgn
50 F2 **Nantgaredig** Carmth
96 F1 **Nantglyn** Denbgs
68 B2 **Nantmel** Powys
95 K4 **Nantmor** Gwynd
95 K2 **Nant Peris** Gwynd
98 F3 **Nantwich** Ches
53 J6 **Nantyglo** Blae G
36 E2 **Nant-y-moel** Brdgnd
42 D2 **Naphill** Bucks
72 F3 **Napton on the Hill** Warwks
49 J4 **Narberth** Pembks
87 G4 **Narborough** Leics
91 H2 **Narborough** Norfk
95 H3 **Nasareth** Gwynd
87 K7 **Naseby** Nhants
73 L7 **Nash** Bucks
37 M4 **Nash** Newpt
69 L1 **Nash** Shrops
30 A3 **Nash's Green** Hants
88 F4 **Nassington** Nhants
139 H6 **Nateby** Cumb
120 F2 **Nateby** Lancs
87 H3 **National Space Science Centre** C Leic
129 L2 **Natland** Cumb
78 B5 **Naughton** Suffk
56 C4 **Naunton** Gloucs
70 F6 **Naunton** Worcs
71 G4 **Naunton Beauchamp** Worcs
103 G2 **Navenby** Lincs
45 K1 **Navestock** Essex
60 E8 **Navestock Side** Essex
227 J5 **Navidale House Hotel** Highld
213 J2 **Navity** Highld
133 K3 **Nawton** N York
77 L7 **Nayland** Suffk
60 C6 **Nazeing** Essex
235 d5 **Neap** Shet
100 B4 **Near Cotton** Staffs
137 K7 **Near Sawrey** Cumb
44 E3 **Neasden** Gt Lon
141 H5 **Neasham** Darltn
51 L6 **Neath** Neath
30 C4 **Neatham** Hants

107 H7 **Neatishead** Norfk
66 D2 **Nebo** Cerdgn
96 C2 **Nebo** Conwy
95 H3 **Nebo** Gwynd
108 F4 **Nebo** IoA
91 K2 **Necton** Norfk
224 D3 **Nedd** Highld
78 B5 **Nedging** Suffk
78 B4 **Nedging Tye** Suffk
92 F6 **Needham** Norfk
78 C4 **Needham Market** Suffk
75 L1 **Needingworth** Cambs
84 C7 **Neen Savage** Shrops
84 B8 **Neen Sollars** Shrops
84 B6 **Neenton** Shrops
94 E4 **Nefyn** Gwynd
174 E6 **Neilston** E Rens
37 H2 **Nelson** Caerph
122 C3 **Nelson** Lancs
165 G1 **Nemphlar** S Lans
38 D7 **Nempnett Thrubwell** BaNES
149 K6 **Nenthead** Cumb
167 K2 **Nenthorn** Border
97 K1 **Nercwys** Flints
170 E7 **Nereabolls** Ag & B
175 H6 **Nerston** S Lans
168 E3 **Nesbit** Nthumb
123 G1 **Nesfield** N York
111 J6 **Ness Botanic Gardens** Ches
98 B8 **Nesscliffe** Shrops
111 J6 **Neston** Ches
39 K6 **Neston** Wilts
84 B5 **Netchwood** Shrops
113 J6 **Nether Alderley** Ches
28 D2 **Netheravon** Wilts
167 H2 **Nether Blainslie** Border
216 F3 **Netherbrae** Abers
102 B7 **Nether Broughton** Leics
175 L8 **Netherburn** S Lans
13 L3 **Netherbury** Dorset
123 L2 **Netherby** N York
14 C3 **Nether Cerne** Dorset
155 K5 **Nethercleuch** D & G
26 E7 **Nether Compton** Dorset
206 F2 **Nether Crimond** Abers
215 H2 **Nether Dallachy** Moray
54 E7 **Netherend** Gloucs
11 L5 **Nether Exe** Devon
20 E2 **Netherfield** E Susx
20 E3 **Netherfield Road** E Susx
165 H7 **Nether Fingland** S Lans
28 C5 **Netherhampton** Wilts
196 B7 **Nether Handwick** Angus
115 H3 **Nether Haugh** Rothm
13 K2 **Netherhay** Dorset
116 C6 **Nether Headon** Notts
101 G3 **Nether Heage** Derbys
73 J3 **Nether Heyford** Nhants
165 K6 **Nether Howcleugh** S Lans
129 K6 **Nether Kellet** Lancs
217 K5 **Nether Kinmundy** Abers
115 K7 **Nether Langwith** Notts
146 C6 **Netherlaw** D & G
207 G6 **Netherley** Abers
155 H5 **Nethermill** D & G
115 G7 **Nether Moor** Derbys
217 G5 **Nethermuir** Abers

32 B3 **Netherne-on-the-Hill** Surrey
123 H6 **Netheroyd Hill** Kirk
114 E6 **Nether Padley** Derbys
174 F7 **Netherplace** E Rens
133 J8 **Nether Poppleton** York
86 C2 **Netherseal** Derbys
133 C2 **Nether Silton** N York
25 J4 **Nether Stowey** Somset
123 H8 **Netherthong** Kirk
196 E5 **Netherton** Angus
7 K2 **Netherton** Devon
85 G6 **Netherton** Dudley
123 H7 **Netherton** Kirk
175 K7 **Netherton** N Lans
168 E7 **Netherton** Nthumb
195 J6 **Netherton** P & K
84 D6 **Netherton** Shrops
175 G3 **Netherton** Stirlg
123 K6 **Netherton** Wakefd
136 D5 **Nethertown** Cumb
231 L1 **Nethertown** Highld
100 C8 **Nethertown** Staffs
165 L1 **Netherurd** Border
28 F4 **Nether Wallop** Hants
136 F6 **Nether Wasdale** Cumb
56 E4 **Nether Westcote** Gloucs
86 B5 **Nether Whitacre** Warwks
165 G5 **Nether Whitecleuch** S Lans
58 B5 **Nether Winchendon** Bucks
158 D4 **Netherwitton** Nthumb
204 B2 **Nethy Bridge** Highld
16 F2 **Netley** Hants
29 G8 **Netley Marsh** Hants
42 B3 **Nettlebed** Oxon
26 F2 **Nettlebridge** Somset
13 M4 **Nettlecombe** Dorset
59 G6 **Nettleden** Herts
117 G6 **Nettleham** Lincs
33 H3 **Nettlestead** Kent
33 H3 **Nettlestead Green** Kent
17 H4 **Nettlestone** IoW
151 G5 **Nettlesworth** Dur
117 J2 **Nettleton** Lincs
39 J5 **Nettleton** Wilts
28 C4 **Netton** Wilts
64 F6 **Nevern** Pembks
88 B5 **Nevill Holt** Leics
147 G2 **New Abbey** D & G
217 G2 **New Aberdour** Abers
45 G7 **New Addington** Gt Lon
123 J2 **Newall** Leeds
29 L5 **New Alresford** Hants
195 K6 **New Alyth** P & K
234 e4 **Newark** Ork
102 D2 **Newark-on-Trent** Notts
175 K6 **Newarthill** N Lans
45 L6 **New Ash Green** Kent
102 D3 **New Balderton** Notts
45 L6 **New Barn** Kent
44 F2 **New Barnet** Gt Lon
177 J5 **Newbattle** Mdloth
169 G5 **New Bewick** Nthumb
147 L3 **Newbie** D & G
138 C2 **Newbiggin** Cumb
138 F2 **Newbiggin** Cumb
148 F5 **Newbiggin** Cumb
139 K2 **Newbiggin** Dur
131 J3 **Newbiggin** N York
159 H5 **Newbiggin-by-the-Sea** Nthumb

187 H1 **Newbigging** Angus
195 L7 **Newbigging** Angus
196 C8 **Newbigging** Angus
165 K1 **Newbigging** S Lans
139 G6 **Newbiggin-on-Lune** Cumb
86 F7 **New Bilton** Warwks
115 G6 **Newbold** Derbys
86 F7 **Newbold on Avon** Warwks
72 B5 **Newbold on Stour** Warwks
72 C3 **Newbold Pacey** Warwks
86 F3 **Newbold Verdon** Leics
104 A2 **New Bolingbroke** Lincs
89 H3 **Newborough** C Pete
108 E7 **Newborough** IoA
100 C7 **Newborough** Staffs
116 F7 **New Boultham** Lincs
78 F6 **Newbourne** Suffk
74 B6 **New Bradwell** M Keyn
115 G7 **New Brampton** Derbys
151 G6 **New Brancepeth** Dur
176 F4 **Newbridge** C Edin
37 K2 **Newbridge** Caerph
2 D5 **Newbridge** Cnwll
155 G6 **Newbridge** D & G
28 F7 **Newbridge** Hants
16 E5 **Newbridge** IoW
70 E6 **Newbridge Green** Worcs
67 L3 **Newbridge on Wye** Powys
111 J3 **New Brighton** Wirral
149 L2 **Newbrough** Nthumb
92 C5 **New Buckenham** Norfk
11 J4 **Newbuildings** Devon
207 J1 **Newburgh** Abers
217 H3 **Newburgh** Abers
186 D4 **Newburgh** Fife
121 G7 **Newburgh** Lancs
133 H4 **Newburgh Priory** N York
150 F2 **Newburn** N u Ty
27 G2 **Newbury** Somset
41 J6 **Newbury** W Berk
45 J3 **Newbury Park** Gt Lon
138 E3 **Newby** Cumb
122 B2 **Newby** Lancs
130 D5 **Newby** N York
142 B5 **Newby** N York
129 H3 **Newby Bridge** Cumb
148 E4 **Newby East** Cumb
216 F4 **New Byth** Abers
148 C4 **Newby West** Cumb
132 E3 **Newby Wiske** N York
54 C5 **Newcastle** Mons
82 E6 **Newcastle** Shrops
158 F7 **Newcastle Airport** Nthumb
65 J6 **Newcastle Emlyn** Carmth
156 E5 **Newcastleton** Border
99 J4 **Newcastle-under-Lyme** Staffs
151 G3 **Newcastle upon Tyne** N u Ty
65 H6 **Newchapel** Pembks
32 C5 **Newchapel** Surrey
17 G5 **Newchurch** IoW
34 E7 **Newchurch** Kent
38 C2 **Newchurch** Mons
68 E4 **Newchurch** Powys
100 D7 **Newchurch** Staffs
92 E2 **New Costessey** Norfk
177 J4 **Newcraighall** C Edin
124 B6 **New Crofton** Wakefd

45 G5 **New Cross** Gt Lon
26 B7 **New Cross** Somset
164 C6 **New Cumnock** E Ayrs
217 G5 **New Deer** Abers
43 H4 **New Denham** Bucks
31 K3 **Newdigate** Surrey
73 K3 **New Duston** Nhants
133 J7 **New Earswick** York
115 K2 **New Edlington** Donc
214 F3 **New Elgin** Moray
126 E3 **New Ellerby** E R Yk
42 E6 **Newell Green** Br For
45 H5 **New Eltham** Gt Lon
71 J3 **New End** Worcs
33 L7 **Newenden** Kent
89 H4 **New England** C Pete
55 G3 **Newent** Gloucs
150 F7 **Newfield** Dur
223 H6 **Newfield** Highld
89 H4 **New Fletton** C Pete
16 C2 **New Forest** Hants
48 E3 **Newgale** Pembks
154 B6 **New Galloway** D & G
59 M6 **Newgate Street** Herts
187 G5 **New Gilston** Fife
2 a1 **New Grimsby** IoS
98 E4 **Newhall** Ches
159 H6 **New Hartley** Nthumb
177 H3 **Newhaven** C Edin
19 L5 **Newhaven** E Susx
43 H7 **New Haw** Surrey
126 D5 **New Holland** N Linc
143 H5 **Newholm** N York
115 J7 **New Houghton** Derbys
105 J6 **New Houghton** Norfk
175 L6 **Newhouse** N Lans
130 B2 **New Hutton** Cumb
19 L2 **Newick** E Susx
35 G7 **Newington** Kent
46 E6 **Newington** Kent
41 L2 **Newington** Oxon
66 B6 **New Inn** Carmth
53 L7 **New Inn** Torfn
82 F7 **New Invention** Shrops
165 G2 **New Lanark** S Lans
126 D4 **Newland** C KuH
54 D6 **Newland** Gloucs
125 G5 **Newland** N York
24 C4 **Newland** Somset
70 E5 **Newland** Worcs
177 K6 **Newlandrig** Mdloth
156 E4 **Newlands** Border
150 D4 **Newlands** Nthumb
215 G4 **Newlands of Dundurcas** Moray
156 C5 **New Langholm** D & G
104 C2 **New Leake** Lincs
217 J4 **New Leeds** Abers
123 L8 **New Lodge** Barns
121 G5 **New Longton** Lancs
144 E3 **New Luce** D & G
2 E5 **Newlyn** Cnwll
4 C5 **Newlyn East** Cnwll
207 G2 **Newmachar** Abers
175 L6 **Newmains** N Lans
44 E6 **New Malden** Gt Lon
77 K5 **Newman's Green** Suffk
76 F2 **Newmarket** Suffk
232 f2 **Newmarket** W Isls
142 D3 **New Marske** R & Cl
57 K6 **New Marston** Oxon
206 E8 **New Mill** Abers
167 G7 **Newmill** Border
2 E4 **New Mill** Cnwll
123 H8 **New Mill** Kirk
215 K4 **Newmill** Moray
123 L7 **Newmillerdam** Wakefd

196 C4 **Newmill of Inshewan** Angus
177 G5 **Newmills** C Edin
4 D5 **New Mills** Cnwll
113 M4 **New Mills** Derbys
176 D2 **Newmills** Fife
54 D6 **Newmills** Mons
82 C4 **New Mills** Powys
186 B2 **Newmiln** P & K
164 B2 **Newmilns** E Ayrs
16 B4 **New Milton** Hants
62 D2 **New Mistley** Essex
49 H3 **New Moat** Pembks
61 G6 **Newney Green** Essex
55 G5 **Newnham** Gloucs
30 B2 **Newnham** Hants
75 J6 **Newnham** Herts
34 C3 **Newnham** Kent
73 H3 **Newnham** Nhants
70 B2 **Newnham** Worcs
116 A7 **New Ollerton** Notts
217 G3 **New Pitsligo** Abers
9 J7 **Newport** Cnwll
23 J5 **Newport** Devon
125 K4 **Newport** E R Yk
76 D7 **Newport** Essex
39 G2 **Newport** Gloucs
227 K4 **Newport** Highld
16 F5 **Newport** IoW
37 L3 **Newport** Newpt
64 E6 **Newport** Pembks
99 H8 **Newport** Wrekin
187 G2 **Newport-on-Tay** Fife
74 C5 **Newport Pagnell** M Keyn
163 J4 **New Prestwick** S Ayrs
65 L3 **New Quay** Cerdgn
4 C4 **Newquay** Cnwll
4 D3 **Newquay Airport** Cnwll
93 G2 **New Rackheath** Norfk
68 E3 **New Radnor** Powys
150 D3 **New Ridley** Nthumb
21 L2 **New Romney** Kent
115 L2 **New Rossington** Donc
185 J7 **New Sauchie** Clacks
216 D7 **Newseat** Abers
121 G4 **Newsham** Lancs
132 E3 **Newsham** N York
140 E5 **Newsham** N York
159 H6 **Newsham** Nthumb
124 B6 **New Sharlston** Wakefd
125 H5 **Newsholme** E R Yk
151 J4 **New Silksworth** Sundld
123 H7 **Newsome** Kirk
102 F5 **New Somerby** Lincs
167 H3 **Newstead** Border
101 K3 **Newstead** Notts
169 H4 **Newstead** Nthumb
175 K6 **New Stevenston** N Lans
215 K5 **Newtack** Moray
124 C4 **Newthorpe** N York
101 J4 **Newthorpe** Notts
182 F7 **Newton** Ag & B
75 J5 **Newton** Beds
167 J5 **Newton** Border
36 C5 **Newton** Brdgnd
76 B5 **Newton** Cambs
90 B1 **Newton** Cambs
98 D1 **Newton** Ches
112 B7 **Newton** Ches
128 F5 **Newton** Cumb
101 H2 **Newton** Derbys
53 M2 **Newton** Herefs
69 K4 **Newton** Herefs
212 F4 **Newton** Highld
213 H5 **Newton** Highld

213 J2 **Newton** Highld
121 K1 **Newton** Lancs
103 H5 **Newton** Lincs
214 E2 **Newton** Moray
215 H2 **Newton** Moray
88 C6 **Newton** Nhants
91 J1 **Newton** Norfk
102 B4 **Newton** Notts
150 C3 **Newton** Nthumb
165 H3 **Newton** S Lans
175 H6 **Newton** S Lans
25 H4 **Newton** Somset
100 B7 **Newton** Staffs
77 K6 **Newton** Suffk
176 E3 **Newton** W Loth
87 G7 **Newton** Warwks
7 K2 **Newton Abbot** Devon
147 L4 **Newton Arlosh** Cumb
141 G3 **Newton Aycliffe** Dur
141 K2 **Newton Bewley**
Hartpl
74 D4 **Newton Blossomville**
M Keyn
74 E2 **Newton Bromswold**
Nhants
86 D2 **Newton Burgoland**
Leics
169 J4 **Newton-by-the-Sea**
Nthumb
117 H4 **Newton by Toft** Lincs
6 A3 **Newton Ferrers** Cnwll
6 E6 **Newton Ferrers**
Devon
232 C5 **Newton Ferry** W Isls
92 E4 **Newton Flotman**
Norfk
216 B7 **Newtongarry Croft**
Abers
177 J5 **Newtongrange**
Mdloth
87 J4 **Newton Harcourt**
Leics
113 K2 **Newton Heath**
Manch
207 G6 **Newtonhill** Abers
124 C2 **Newton Kyme** N York
132 C2 **Newton-le-Willows**
N York
112 E3 **Newton-le-Willows**
St Hel
177 J5 **Newtonloan** Mdloth
58 D2 **Newton Longville**
Bucks
174 F7 **Newton Mearns**
E Rens
196 F4 **Newtonmill** Angus
203 H5 **Newtonmore** Highld
141 G5 **Newton Morrell**
N York
186 B5 **Newton of**
Balcanquhal P & K
187 H6 **Newton of Balcormo**
Fife
133 H7 **Newton on Ouse**
N York
134 C2 **Newton-on-**
Rawcliffe N York
158 F2 **Newton-on-the-**
Moor Nthumb
116 D6 **Newton on Trent**
Lincs
12 E4 **Newton Poppleford**
Devon
57 L3 **Newton Purcell** Oxon
86 C3 **Newton Regis**
Warwks
138 C2 **Newton Reigny**
Cumb
231 L5 **Newton Row** Highld
11 K5 **Newton St Cyres**
Devon

92 F1 **Newton St Faith**
Norfk
39 G7 **Newton St Loe** BaNES
100 F7 **Newton Solney**
Derbys
29 H4 **Newton Stacey** Hants
145 J3 **Newton Stewart**
D & G
28 E4 **Newton Tony** Wilts
23 H6 **Newton Tracey**
Devon
142 C5 **Newton under**
Roseberry R & Cl
125 H2 **Newton upon**
Derwent E R Yk
30 B5 **Newton Valence**
Hants
155 K3 **Newton Wamphray**
D & G
120 F4 **Newton with Scales**
Lancs
98 F3 **Newtown** Ches
147 J5 **Newtown** Cumb
148 E3 **Newtown** Cumb
164 F7 **Newtown** D & G
12 D3 **Newtown** Devon
24 B6 **Newtown** Devon
27 L7 **New Town** Dorset
27 M7 **New Town** Dorset
19 M2 **New Town** E Susx
54 F7 **Newtown** Gloucs
29 L8 **Newtown** Hants
70 B5 **Newtown** Herefs
70 C6 **Newtown** Herefs
202 B4 **Newtown** Highld
16 E4 **Newtown** IoW
158 C3 **Newtown** Nthumb
168 F4 **Newtown** Nthumb
15 K4 **Newtown** Poole
82 C5 **Newtown** Powys
98 B7 **Newtown** Shrops
98 C6 **Newtown** Shrops
25 L8 **Newtown** Somset
99 K1 **Newtown** Staffs
112 E1 **Newtown** Wigan
70 F4 **Newtown** Worcs
87 G2 **Newtown Linford**
Leics
174 D6 **Newtown of**
Beltrees Rens
167 J3 **Newtown St**
Boswells Border
53 H7 **New Tredegar** Caerph
164 F2 **New Trows** S Lans
195 L7 **Newtyle** Angus
90 C2 **New Walsoken**
Cambs
118 C1 **New Waltham** NE Lin
177 L4 **New Winton** E Loth
182 D5 **Newyork** Ag & B
103 L2 **New York** Lincs
49 G6 **Neyland** Pembks
25 H7 **Nicholashayne** Devon
51 G7 **Nicholaston** Swans
132 D7 **Nidd** N York
207 H5 **Nigg** C Aber
223 H6 **Nigg** Highld
24 D6 **Nightcott** Somset
149 K4 **Ninebanks** Nthumb
40 C3 **Nine Elms** Swindn
70 B2 **Nineveh** Worcs
20 E3 **Ninfield** E Susx
16 E5 **Ningwood** IoW
167 K4 **Nisbet** Border
179 G7 **Nisbet Hill** Border
17 F6 **Niton** IoW
174 F6 **Nitshill** C Glas
117 H8 **Nocton** Lincs
57 K5 **Noke** Oxon
48 E4 **Nolton** Pembks

48 E4 **Nolton Haven**
Pembks
98 D3 **No Man's Heath** Ches
Warwks
11 J3 **Nomansland** Devon
28 E7 **Nomansland** Wilts
98 C6 **Noneley** Shrops
35 H4 **Nonington** Kent
129 L3 **Nook** Cumb
44 D6 **Norbiton** Gt Lon
98 E3 **Norbury** Ches
100 C4 **Norbury** Derbys
44 F6 **Norbury** Gt Lon
83 G5 **Norbury** Shrops
99 H7 **Norbury** Staffs
70 F2 **Norchard** Worcs
90 D4 **Nordelph** Norfk
84 C4 **Nordley** Shrops
93 K2 **Norfolk Broads** Norfk
179 J8 **Norham** Nthumb
123 G6 **Norland Town** Calder
112 E6 **Norley** Ches
16 D3 **Norleywood** Hants
117 G4 **Normanby** Lincs
125 K7 **Normanby** N Linc
134 B3 **Normanby** N York
142 C4 **Normanby** R & Cl
117 J3 **Normanby le Wold**
Lincs
30 F2 **Normandy** Surrey
12 D2 **Norman's Green**
Devon
101 G5 **Normanton** C Derb
102 D4 **Normanton** Leics
102 F4 **Normanton** Lincs
102 B2 **Normanton** Notts
124 B6 **Normanton** Wakefd
86 D2 **Normanton le Heath**
Leics
101 K7 **Normanton on Soar**
Notts
101 L6 **Normanton on the**
Wolds Notts
116 C7 **Normanton on Trent**
Notts
58 F4 **Northall** Bucks
141 J7 **Northallerton** N York
29 H8 **Northam** C Sotn
23 G5 **Northam** Devon
73 L3 **Northampton** Nhants
70 E2 **Northampton** Worcs
115 K5 **North Anston** Rothm
42 E6 **North Ascot** Br For
57 J3 **North Aston** Oxon
59 L7 **Northaw** Herts
13 H1 **Northay** Somset
29 H7 **North Baddesley**
Hants
191 L4 **North Ballachulish**
Highld
26 E5 **North Barrow** Somset
105 L5 **North Barsham** Norfk
46 C3 **North Benfleet** Essex
18 C5 **North Bersted** W Susx
178 C2 **North Berwick** E Loth
17 H1 **North Boarhunt**
Hants
89 H3 **Northborough** C Pete
35 J4 **Northbourne** Kent
11 H7 **North Bovey** Devon
27 J1 **North Bradley** Wilts
10 C8 **North Brentor** Devon
27 G4 **North Brewham**
Somset
29 K4 **Northbrook** Hants
23 G4 **North Buckland**
Devon
93 H2 **North Burlingham**
Norfk
26 F6 **North Cadbury**
Somset

116 F6 **North Carlton** Lincs
115 L4 **North Carlton** Notts
125 K4 **North Cave** E R Yk
19 K2 **North Chailey** E Susx
30 F5 **Northchapel** W Susx
28 D7 **North Charford** Hants
169 H5 **North Charlton**
Nthumb
44 E6 **North Cheam** Gt Lon
27 G6 **North Cheriton**
Somset
13 K4 **North Chideock**
Dorset
58 F6 **Northchurch** Herts
125 K3 **North Cliffe** E R Yk
116 D6 **North Clifton** Notts
118 E4 **North Cockerington**
Lincs
182 C1 **North Connel** Ag & B
36 C4 **North Cornelly**
Brdgnd
191 G5 **North Corry** Highld
118 E5 **North Cotes** Lincs
9 J6 **Northcott** Devon
57 J7 **Northcourt** Oxon
93 K5 **North Cove** Suffk
141 G6 **North Cowton** N York
74 D5 **North Crawley**
M Keyn
105 K5 **North Creake** Norfk
25 L6 **North Curry** Somset
125 L1 **North Dalton** E R Yk
124 B1 **North Deighton**
N York
35 K2 **Northdown** Kent
34 B4 **North Downs**
125 G3 **North Duffield** N York
218 C6 **North Duntulm**
Highld
35 G5 **North Elham** Kent
106 B7 **North Elmham** Norfk
124 D7 **North Elmsall** Wakefd
17 J3 **North End** C Port
61 G4 **North End** Essex
28 C7 **North End** Hants
74 D2 **North End** Nhants
18 D5 **North End** W Susx
72 E4 **Northend** Warwks
113 J4 **Northenden** Manch
219 H5 **North Erradale** Highld
87 J3 **North Evington**
C Leic
61 K7 **North Fambridge**
Essex
126 B5 **North Ferriby** E R Yk
85 H7 **Northfield** Birm
207 G4 **Northfield** C Aber
126 C5 **Northfield** E R Yk
88 E2 **Northfields** Lincs
45 M5 **Northfleet** Kent
135 H8 **North Frodingham**
E R Yk
15 M1 **North Gorley** Hants
79 G3 **North Green** Suffk
117 G6 **North Greetwell** Lincs
134 C6 **North Grimston**
N York
17 K2 **North Hayling** Hants
5 L1 **North Hill** Cnwll
43 H4 **North Hillingdon**
Gt Lon
57 K7 **North Hinksey** Oxon
31 K3 **North Holmwood**
Surrey
7 G5 **North Huish** Devon
116 F7 **North Hykeham** Lincs
21 G2 **Northiam** E Susx
75 G5 **Northill** Beds
29 K4 **Northington** Hants
117 H2 **North Kelsey** Lincs
213 G5 **North Kessock** Highld

126 E6 **North Killingholme** N Linc
132 F3 **North Kilvington** N York
87 H6 **North Kilworth** Leics
103 J3 **North Kyme** Lincs
135 K5 **North Landing** E R Yk
104 B2 **Northlands** Lincs
56 C5 **Northleach** Gloucs
58 D6 **North Lee** Bucks
12 F3 **Northleigh** Devon
23 J4 **Northleigh** Devon
57 H5 **North Leigh** Oxon
116 C5 **North Leverton with Habblesthorpe** Notts
10 D5 **Northlew** Devon
71 J5 **North Littleton** Worcs
92 C6 **North Lopham** Norfk
88 D3 **North Luffenham** Rutlnd
30 D7 **North Marden** W Susx
58 C4 **North Marston** Bucks
177 K6 **North Middleton** Mdloth
144 C4 **North Milmain** D & G
24 B5 **North Molton** Devon
57 H7 **Northmoor** Oxon
41 K3 **North Moreton** Oxon
196 C5 **Northmuir** Angus
18 B5 **North Mundham** W Susx
102 D2 **North Muskham** Notts
125 L3 **North Newbald** E R Yk
72 E6 **North Newington** Oxon
40 C8 **North Newnton** Wilts
25 L5 **North Newton** Somset
17 K2 **Northney** Hants
39 H2 **North Nibley** Gloucs
43 J4 **Northolt** Gt Lon
111 H7 **Northop** Flints
111 J7 **Northop Hall** Flints
142 B4 **North Ormesby** Middsb
118 C3 **North Ormsby** Lincs
103 K5 **Northorpe** Lincs
116 E3 **Northorpe** Lincs
132 E2 **North Otterington** N York
117 H3 **North Owersby** Lincs
123 G5 **Northowram** Calder
13 L1 **North Perrott** Somset
25 L5 **North Petherton** Somset
9 H6 **North Petherwin** Cnwll
91 J3 **North Pickenham** Norfk
71 G4 **North Piddle** Worcs
7 H7 **North Pool** Devon
13 M3 **North Poorton** Dorset
15 H5 **Northport** Dorset
176 F3 **North Queensferry** Fife
24 B5 **North Radworthy** Devon
103 G3 **North Rauceby** Lincs
106 F5 **Northrepps** Norfk
118 E5 **North Reston** Lincs
123 K1 **North Rigton** N York
113 K7 **North Rode** Ches
234 e3 **North Ronaldsay Airport** Ork
90 F1 **North Runcton** Norfk
116 D7 **North Scarle** Lincs
191 H7 **North Shian** Ag & B
151 J2 **North Shields** N Tyne

46 F3 **North Shoebury** Sthend
120 D3 **North Shore** Bpool
89 K4 **North Side** C Pete
118 F3 **North Somercotes** Lincs
132 D4 **North Stainley** N York
45 L4 **North Stifford** Thurr
39 G6 **North Stoke** BaNES
41 L3 **North Stoke** Oxon
18 D4 **North Stoke** W Susx
34 D3 **North Street** Kent
41 M6 **North Street** W Berk
169 J3 **North Sunderland** Nthumb
9 J5 **North Tamerton** Cnwll
10 F4 **North Tawton** Devon
175 K1 **North Third** Stirlg
118 D2 **North Thoresby** Lincs
232 d5 **Northton** W Isls
10 D3 **North Town** Devon
26 E3 **North Town** Somset
42 E4 **North Town** W & M
92 C2 **North Tuddenham** Norfk
157 L2 **Northumberland National Park** Nthumb
107 G6 **North Walsham** Norfk
29 K3 **North Waltham** Hants
30 B2 **North Warnborough** Hants
25 M5 **Northway** Somset
60 D7 **North Weald Bassett** Essex
116 C4 **North Wheatley** Notts
112 F6 **Northwich** Ches
70 E3 **Northwick** Worcs
38 E8 **North Widcombe** BaNES
117 K4 **North Willingham** Lincs
115 H8 **North Wingfield** Derbys
102 F7 **North Witham** Lincs
91 H4 **Northwold** Norfk
43 H3 **Northwood** Gt Lon
16 F4 **Northwood** IoW
98 C6 **Northwood** Shrops
55 G5 **Northwood Green** Gloucs
26 F8 **North Wootton** Dorset
105 K2 **North Wootton** Norfk
26 E3 **North Wootton** Somset
39 J5 **North Wraxall** Wilts
142 F6 **North York Moors National Park**
124 E7 **Norton** Donc
19 M5 **Norton** E Susx
55 J3 **Norton** Gloucs
134 C5 **Norton** N York
73 H2 **Norton** Nhants
115 L6 **Norton** Notts
68 F2 **Norton** Powys
141 K3 **Norton** S on T
84 D4 **Norton** Shrops
77 L2 **Norton** Suffk
18 C4 **Norton** W Susx
39 K4 **Norton** Wilts
70 F4 **Norton** Worcs
71 J5 **Norton** Worcs
27 K3 **Norton Bavant** Wilts
99 K6 **Norton Bridge** Staffs
85 H2 **Norton Canes** Staffs
69 H5 **Norton Canon** Herefs
102 E2 **Norton Disney** Lincs
25 J6 **Norton Fitzwarren** Somset

16 D5 **Norton Green** IoW
38 E7 **Norton Hawkfield** BaNES
60 F6 **Norton Heath** Essex
99 G5 **Norton in Hales** Shrops
86 D3 **Norton-Juxta-Twycross** Leics
132 F5 **Norton-le-Clay** N York
72 B2 **Norton Lindsey** Warwks
77 L2 **Norton Little Green** Suffk
38 E7 **Norton Malreward** BaNES
27 H1 **Norton St Philip** Somset
93 J4 **Norton Subcourse** Norfk
26 C7 **Norton sub Hamdon** Somset
69 G5 **Norton Wood** Herefs
102 C1 **Norwell** Notts
116 B8 **Norwell Woodhouse** Notts
92 F2 **Norwich** Norfk
92 E2 **Norwich Airport** Norfk
92 F2 **Norwich Cathedral** Norfk
235 e1 **Norwick** Shet
185 J8 **Norwood** Clacks
43 J5 **Norwood Green** Gt Lon
31 L3 **Norwood Hill** Surrey
87 K4 **Noseley** Leics
6 E6 **Noss Mayo** Devon
132 D4 **Nosterfield** N York
210 D8 **Nostie** Highld
56 C4 **Notgrove** Gloucs
36 C5 **Nottage** Brdgnd
6 B4 **Notter** Cnwll
101 L5 **Nottingham** C Nott
101 J7 **Nottingham East Midlands Airport** Leics
123 L7 **Notton** Wakefd
39 K6 **Notton** Wilts
70 E2 **Noutard's Green** Worcs
83 H2 **Nox** Shrops
42 A3 **Nuffield** Oxon
125 K2 **Nunburnholme** E R Yk
86 D5 **Nuneaton** Warwks
57 K7 **Nuneham Courtenay** Oxon
45 G5 **Nunhead** Gt Lon
126 E1 **Nunkeeling** E R Yk
133 H7 **Nun Monkton** N York
27 G3 **Nunney** Somset
133 K4 **Nunnington** N York
127 G8 **Nunsthorpe** NE Lin
142 C4 **Nunthorpe** Middsb
124 F1 **Nunthorpe** York
142 C5 **Nunthorpe Village** Middsb
28 D6 **Nunton** Wilts
132 E5 **Nunwick** N York
29 G7 **Nursling** Hants
17 L2 **Nutbourne** W Susx
18 E3 **Nutbourne** W Susx
32 B3 **Nutfield** Surrey
101 K4 **Nuthall** Notts
76 B7 **Nuthampstead** Herts
31 K6 **Nuthurst** W Susx
32 D7 **Nutley** E Susx
231 L3 **Nybster** Highld
18 B6 **Nyetimber** W Susx
30 D6 **Nyewood** W Susx

11 G4 **Nymet Rowland** Devon
11 G5 **Nymet Tracey** Devon
55 J7 **Nympsfield** Gloucs
18 C5 **Nyton** W Susx

O

87 J4 **Oadby** Leics
34 B3 **Oad Street** Kent
100 B4 **Oakamoor** Staffs
176 E5 **Oakbank** W Loth
10 D5 **Oak Cross** Devon
37 J2 **Oakdale** Caerph
25 J6 **Oake** Somset
84 F3 **Oaken** Staffs
121 H2 **Oakenclough** Lancs
84 C2 **Oakengates** Wrekin
150 F7 **Oakenshaw** Dur
123 H5 **Oakenshaw** Kirk
100 F1 **Oaker Side** Derbys
66 B3 **Oakford** Cerdgn
24 E6 **Oakford** Devon
88 C2 **Oakham** Rutlnd
30 C4 **Oakhanger** Hants
26 F3 **Oakhill** Somset
76 B2 **Oakington** Cambs
55 H4 **Oakle Street** Gloucs
74 E4 **Oakley** Beds
57 M5 **Oakley** Bucks
176 D1 **Oakley** Fife
29 K2 **Oakley** Hants
92 E7 **Oakley** Suffk
55 K7 **Oakridge** Gloucs
39 M2 **Oaksey** Wilts
86 D2 **Oakthorpe** Leics
101 G5 **Oakwood** C Derb
31 J4 **Oakwoodhill** Surrey
122 F3 **Oakworth** Brad
34 D3 **Oare** Kent
24 C3 **Oare** Somset
40 D7 **Oare** Wilts
103 G5 **Oasby** Lincs
26 B6 **Oath** Somset
196 D5 **Oathlaw** Angus
43 H7 **Oatlands Park** Surrey
182 B2 **Oban** Ag & B
83 G7 **Obley** Shrops
195 G8 **Obney** P & K
26 F7 **Oborne** Dorset
78 D1 **Occold** Suffk
231 J7 **Occumster** Highld
163 L5 **Ochiltree** E Ayrs
101 H5 **Ockbrook** Derbys
31 H1 **Ockham** Surrey
190 B3 **Ockle** Highld
31 J4 **Ockley** Surrey
69 L5 **Ocle Pychard** Herefs
26 D7 **Odcombe** Somset
39 H7 **Odd Down** BaNES
71 G3 **Oddingley** Worcs
56 E3 **Oddington** Gloucs
57 K5 **Oddington** Oxon
74 D3 **Odell** Beds
30 C2 **Odiham** Hants
123 H5 **Odsal** Brad
75 K6 **Odsey** Cambs
28 D6 **Odstock** Wilts
86 E3 **Odstone** Leics
72 D2 **Offchurch** Warwks
71 J5 **Offenham** Worcs
113 K4 **Offerton** Stockp
19 L3 **Offham** E Susx
33 H2 **Offham** Kent
18 D4 **Offham** W Susx
75 J2 **Offord Cluny** Cambs
75 J2 **Offord Darcy** Cambs
78 C5 **Offton** Suffk
12 F3 **Offwell** Devon

40 D6 **Ogbourne Maizey** Wilts
40 D6 **Ogbourne St Andrew** Wilts
40 D5 **Ogbourne St George** Wilts
158 E6 **Ogle** Nthumb
112 C5 **Oglet** Lpool
36 C5 **Ogmore** V Glam
36 D5 **Ogmore-by-Sea** V Glam
36 E3 **Ogmore Vale** Brdgnd
14 F1 **Okeford Fitzpaine** Dorset
10 E5 **Okehampton** Devon
87 L8 **Old** Nhants
207 H4 **Old Aberdeen** C Aber
29 L5 **Old Alresford** Hants
224 D2 **Oldany** Highld
154 D3 **Old Auchenbrack** D & G
101 K4 **Old Basford** C Nott
30 A2 **Old Basing** Hants
106 A8 **Old Beetley** Norfk
71 K2 **Oldberrow** Warwks
169 G5 **Old Bewick** Nthumb
118 E8 **Old Bolingbroke** Lincs
123 J2 **Old Bramhope** Leeds
115 G6 **Old Brampton** Derbys
146 D2 **Old Bridge of Urr** D & G
92 C5 **Old Buckenham** Norfk
41 J8 **Old Burghclere** Hants
85 H5 **Oldbury** Sandw
84 C5 **Oldbury** Shrops
86 C5 **Oldbury** Warwks
38 E2 **Oldbury-on-Severn** S Glos
39 J3 **Oldbury on the Hill** Gloucs
133 H3 **Old Byland** N York
115 L2 **Old Cantley** Donc
53 L3 **Oldcastle** Mons
127 G8 **Old Clee** NE Lin
25 G3 **Old Cleeve** Somset
115 L8 **Old Clipstone** Notts
115 L4 **Oldcotes** Notts
152 F3 **Old Dailly** S Ayrs
102 A7 **Old Dalby** Leics
217 J5 **Old Deer** Abers
115 K3 **Old Edlington** Donc
126 E3 **Old Ellerby** E R Yk
79 G7 **Old Felixstowe** Suffk
70 E2 **Oldfield** Worcs
89 H4 **Old Fletton** C Pete
27 H2 **Oldford** Somset
54 E4 **Old Forge** Herefs
2 a1 **Old Grimsby** IoS
60 B4 **Old Hall Green** Herts
113 L1 **Oldham** Oldham
178 F4 **Oldhamstocks** E Loth
60 D5 **Old Harlow** Essex
105 G4 **Old Hunstanton** Norfk
89 K7 **Old Hurst** Cambs
130 B2 **Old Hutton** Cumb
4 D7 **Old Kea** Cnwll
174 E4 **Old Kilpatrick** W Duns
59 L4 **Old Knebworth** Herts
38 F6 **Oldland** S Glos
121 K4 **Old Langho** Lancs
104 C3 **Old Leake** Lincs
134 C3 **Old Malton** N York
216 F8 **Oldmeldrum** Abers
124 C4 **Old Micklefield** Leeds
6 B2 **Oldmill** Cnwll
72 C2 **Old Milverton** Warwks
37 M8 **Oldmixon** N Som
78 C3 **Old Newton** Suffk
68 E3 **Old Radnor** Powys
216 D8 **Old Rayne** Abers

21 K2 **Old Romney** Kent
19 G4 **Old Shoreham** W Susx
228 C4 **Oldshoremore** Highld
20 H8 **Old Sodbury** S Glos
102 F5 **Old Somerby** Lincs
133 H4 **Oldstead** N York
73 L6 **Old Stratford** Nhants
84 F6 **Old Swinford** Dudley
132 F2 **Old Thirsk** N York
130 B3 **Old Town** Cumb
20 C5 **Old Town** E Susx
2 b2 **Old Town** IoS
113 J3 **Old Trafford** Traffd
148 E3 **Oldwall** Cumb
50 F6 **Oldwalls** Swans
75 G5 **Old Warden** Beds
89 G7 **Old Weston** Cambs
231 L5 **Old Wick** Highld
43 G5 **Old Windsor** W & M
34 E4 **Old Wives Lees** Kent
43 G8 **Old Woking** Surrey
100 C8 **Olive Green** Staffs
165 L4 **Oliver** Border
29 J6 **Oliver's Battery** Hants
235 C3 **Ollaberry** Shet
209 H6 **Ollach** Highld
116 H6 **Ollerton** Ches
116 A7 **Ollerton** Notts
98 F7 **Ollerton** Shrops
74 C4 **Olney** M Keyn
231 H3 **Olrig House** Highld
85 K6 **Olton** Solhll
38 E3 **Olveston** S Glos
70 E2 **Ombersley** Worcs
116 B7 **Ompton** Notts
237 d5 **Onchan** IoM
100 B2 **Onecote** Staffs
83 J7 **Onibury** Shrops
191 K4 **Onich** Highld
52 C6 **Onllwyn** Neath
99 H4 **Onneley** Staffs
31 G2 **Onslow Village** Surrey
112 E6 **Onston** Ches
219 H6 **Opinan** Highld
215 G3 **Orbliston** Moray
208 D5 **Orbost** Highld
119 G7 **Orby** Lincs
25 K6 **Orchard Portman** Somset
28 B3 **Orcheston** Wilts
54 C3 **Orcop** Herefs
54 C3 **Orcop Hill** Herefs
216 C3 **Ord** Abers
206 C3 **Ordhead** Abers
205 K5 **Ordie** Abers
215 H3 **Ordiequish** Moray
150 B3 **Ordley** Nthumb
116 B5 **Ordsall** Notts
21 G4 **Ore** E Susx
79 J4 **Orford** Suffk
112 E4 **Orford** Warrtn
15 H4 **Organford** Dorset
34 D7 **Orlestone** Kent
69 J2 **Orleton** Herefs
70 C2 **Orleton** Worcs
74 C1 **Orlingbury** Nhants
142 C4 **Ormesby** R & Cl
93 K1 **Ormesby St Margaret** Norfk
93 K1 **Ormesby St Michael** Norfk
219 K4 **Ormiscaig** Highld
177 L4 **Ormiston** E Loth
189 L4 **Ormsaigmore** Highld
172 C4 **Ormsary** Ag & B
120 F8 **Ormskirk** Lancs
171 G2 **Oronsay** Ag & B
234 b6 **Orphir** Ork
45 J6 **Orpington** Gt Lon
111 K3 **Orrell** Sefton
112 D2 **Orrell** Wigan
146 D5 **Orroland** D & G

45 M4 **Orsett** Thurr
84 E1 **Orslow** Staffs
102 C4 **Orston** Notts
178 F5 **Orton** Cumb
88 B7 **Orton** Nhants
84 F4 **Orton** Staffs
89 H4 **Orton Longueville** C Pete
86 C3 **Orton-on-the-Hill** Leics
89 H4 **Orton Waterville** C Pete
75 L4 **Orwell** Cambs
121 J4 **Osbaldeston** Lancs
124 F1 **Osbaldwick** York
86 E3 **Osbaston** Leics
97 L7 **Osbaston** Shrops
17 G4 **Osborne House** IoW
103 H5 **Osbournby** Lincs
112 D7 **Oscroft** Ches
208 E6 **Ose** Highld
101 H8 **Osgathorpe** Leics
117 H3 **Osgodby** Lincs
124 F7 **Osgodby** N York
135 G3 **Osgodby** N York
209 H6 **Oskaig** Highld
189 L7 **Oskamull** Ag & B
100 D4 **Osmaston** Derbys
14 D5 **Osmington** Dorset
14 E6 **Osmington Mills** Dorset
123 L4 **Osmondthorpe** Leeds
141 K7 **Osmotherley** N York
57 J6 **Osney** Oxon
34 D3 **Ospringe** Kent
123 K6 **Ossett** Wakefd
116 C8 **Ossington** Notts
44 D5 **Osterley** Gt Lon
133 K4 **Oswaldkirk** N York
121 L5 **Oswaldtwistle** Lancs
97 L6 **Oswestry** Shrops
32 F2 **Otford** Kent
33 K3 **Otham** Kent
26 B5 **Othery** Somset
123 J2 **Otley** Leeds
78 E4 **Otley** Suffk
29 J6 **Otterbourne** Hants
131 G7 **Otterburn** N York
157 M4 **Otterburn** Nthumb
172 F2 **Otter Ferry** Ag & B
8 F6 **Otterham** Cnwll
25 K3 **Otterhampton** Somset
232 c5 **Otternish** W Isls
43 G7 **Ottershaw** Surrey
235 d3 **Otterswick** Shet
12 E5 **Otterton** Devon
6 C2 **Ottery** Devon
12 E4 **Ottery St Mary** Devon
34 F6 **Ottinge** Kent
127 G5 **Ottringham** E R Yk
147 K6 **Oughterside** Cumb
114 F3 **Oughtibridge** Sheff
113 G4 **Oughtrington** Warrtn
133 H5 **Oulston** N York
147 M5 **Oulton** Cumb
106 D6 **Oulton** Norfk
99 K5 **Oulton** Staffs
93 L5 **Oulton** Suffk
93 L5 **Oulton Broad** Suffk
106 D6 **Oulton Street** Norfk
88 F6 **Oundle** Nhants
84 F5 **Ounsdale** Staffs
149 G2 **Ousby** Cumb
77 G3 **Ousden** Suffk
125 K6 **Ousefleet** E R Yk
151 G4 **Ouston** Dur
137 K7 **Outgate** Cumb
139 H6 **Outhgill** Cumb
71 K2 **Outhill** Warwks
123 G6 **Outlane** Kirk
120 E3 **Out Rawcliffe** Lancs

90 D3 **Outwell** Norfk
32 B4 **Outwood** Surrey
99 H8 **Outwoods** Staffs
115 L5 **Ouzlewell Green** Leeds
75 L1 **Over** Cambs
71 G6 **Overbury** Worcs
14 D6 **Overcombe** Dorset
26 E7 **Over Compton** Dorset
114 D7 **Over Haddon** Derbys
129 L5 **Over Kellet** Lancs
57 H4 **Over Kiddington** Oxon
26 C4 **Overleigh** Somset
56 F3 **Over Norton** Oxon
113 H6 **Over Peover** Ches
111 L6 **Overpool** Ches
225 J4 **Overscaig Hotel** Highld
86 C1 **Overseal** Derbys
133 G2 **Over Silton** N York
34 E3 **Oversland** Kent
74 B2 **Overstone** Nhants
25 J4 **Over Stowey** Somset
106 F4 **Overstrand** Norfk
26 B7 **Over Stratton** Somset
72 F6 **Overthorpe** Nhants
207 G3 **Overton** C Aber
29 K2 **Overton** Hants
129 J7 **Overton** Lancs
133 H7 **Overton** N York
69 K1 **Overton** Shrops
50 F7 **Overton** Swans
123 K7 **Overton** Wakefd
98 A4 **Overton** Wrexhm
130 C4 **Overtown** Lancs
175 L7 **Overtown** N Lans
28 F4 **Over Wallop** Hants
86 B5 **Over Whitacre** Warwks
57 H3 **Over Worton** Oxon
58 C4 **Oving** Bucks
18 B5 **Oving** W Susx
19 K5 **Ovingdean** Br & H
150 D3 **Ovingham** Nthumb
140 E4 **Ovington** Dur
77 H6 **Ovington** Essex
29 K5 **Ovington** Hants
91 K3 **Ovington** Norfk
150 D3 **Ovington** Nthumb
28 F7 **Ower** Hants
14 E5 **Owermoigne** Dorset
115 G4 **Owlerton** Sheff
42 D7 **Owlsmoor** Br For
58 C6 **Owlswick** Bucks
117 G4 **Ownby** Lincs
117 H1 **Ownby** Lincs
29 K6 **Owslebury** Hants
124 E7 **Owston** Donc
87 L3 **Owston** Leics
116 D2 **Owston Ferry** N Linc
127 G4 **Owstwick** E R Yk
127 H5 **Owthorne** E R Yk
102 A5 **Owthorpe** Notts
91 G3 **Oxborough** Norfk
13 L3 **Oxbridge** Dorset
118 D6 **Oxcombe** Lincs
61 G3 **Oxen End** Essex
129 L2 **Oxenholme** Cumb
122 F4 **Oxenhope** Brad
129 G3 **Oxen Park** Cumb
26 C3 **Oxenpill** Somset
55 L2 **Oxenton** Gloucs
40 F8 **Oxenwood** Wilts
57 K6 **Oxford** Oxon
43 J2 **Oxhey** Herts
72 C5 **Oxhill** Warwks
84 F3 **Oxley** Wolves
61 L5 **Oxley Green** Essex
90 C6 **Oxlode** Cambs
167 L5 **Oxnam** Border
106 F7 **Oxnead** Norfk

43 J7 **Oxshott** Surrey
114 F2 **Oxspring** Barns
32 C3 **Oxted** Surrey
178 B7 **Oxton** Border
124 D2 **Oxton** N York
101 M3 **Oxton** Notts
51 G7 **Oxwich** Swans
50 F7 **Oxwich Green** Swans
221 K2 **Oykel Bridge Hotel** Highld
206 D1 **Oyne** Abers
51 H7 **Oystermouth** Swans

P

232 g2 **Pabail** W Isls
86 D1 **Packington** Leics
196 C6 **Padanaram** Angus
58 B2 **Padbury** Bucks
44 F4 **Paddington** Gt Lon
35 G6 **Paddlesworth** Kent
46 B7 **Paddlesworth** Kent
33 H4 **Paddock Wood** Kent
122 B4 **Padiham** Lancs
132 B7 **Padside** N York
4 E2 **Padstow** Cnwll
41 L7 **Padworth** W Berk
18 B6 **Pagham** W Susx
46 F2 **Paglesham** Essex
7 K4 **Paignton** Torbay
86 F6 **Pailton** Warwks
68 D5 **Painscastle** Powys
150 D3 **Painshawfield** Nthumb
134 C7 **Painsthorpe** E R Yk
55 K6 **Painswick** Gloucs
34 D3 **Painter's Forstal** Kent
174 E5 **Paisley** Rens
93 L5 **Pakefield** Suffk
77 L2 **Pakenham** Suffk
42 E5 **Paley Street** W & M
85 H4 **Palfrey** Wsall
92 D7 **Palgrave** Suffk
14 E4 **Pallington** Dorset
163 L5 **Palmerston** E Ayrs
146 E4 **Palnackie** D & G
145 J3 **Palnure** D & G
115 J7 **Palterton** Derbys
41 L8 **Pamber End** Hants
41 L8 **Pamber Green** Hants
41 L7 **Pamber Heath** Hants
55 L2 **Pamington** Gloucs
15 J3 **Pamphill** Dorset
76 C5 **Pampisford** Cambs
187 J1 **Panbride** Angus
9 H4 **Pancrasweek** Devon
53 M4 **Pandy** Mons
110 B8 **Pandy Tudur** Conwy
61 H3 **Panfield** Essex
41 M5 **Pangbourne** W Berk
19 J4 **Pangdean** W Susx
123 L1 **Pannal** N York
132 D8 **Pannal Ash** N York
205 J6 **Pannanich Wells Hotel** Abers
97 L7 **Pant** Shrops
111 G6 **Pantasaph** Flints
36 E4 **Pant-ffrwyth** Brdgnd
95 H3 **Pant Glas** Gwynd
81 G4 **Pantglas** Powys
117 K5 **Panton** Lincs
81 L8 **Pant-y-dwr** Powys
111 H8 **Pant-y-mwyn** Flints
93 H2 **Panxworth** Norfk
234 c3 **Papa Westray Airport** Ork
136 E2 **Papcastle** Cumb
231 L5 **Papigoe** Highld
178 D4 **Papple** E Loth
101 K3 **Papplewick** Notts

75 K3 **Papworth Everard** Cambs
75 J2 **Papworth St Agnes** Cambs
5 G5 **Par** Cnwll
121 G7 **Parbold** Lancs
26 E4 **Parbrook** Somset
96 D5 **Parc** Gwynd
38 B3 **Parc Seymour** Newpt
136 F3 **Pardshaw** Cumb
79 G3 **Parham** Suffk
206 E5 **Park** Abers
154 F4 **Park** D & G
149 H3 **Park** Nthumb
42 B3 **Park Corner** Oxon
54 E6 **Parkend** Gloucs
33 G4 **Parkers Green** Kent
34 D6 **Park Farm** Kent
111 J6 **Parkgate** Ches
155 H4 **Parkgate** D & G
17 G2 **Park Gate** Hants
123 J3 **Park Gate** Leeds
31 K3 **Parkgate** Surrey
174 E4 **Parkhall** W Duns
22 F6 **Parkham** Devon
207 G3 **Parkhill House** Abers
51 G7 **Parkmill** Swans
44 D4 **Park Royal** Gt Lon
151 K5 **Parkside** Dur
175 L6 **Parkside** N Lans
15 J4 **Parkstone** Poole
59 J6 **Park Street** Herts
60 C6 **Parndon** Essex
23 L3 **Parracombe** Devon
89 L2 **Parson Drove** Cambs
62 B3 **Parson's Heath** Essex
174 F5 **Partick** C Glas
113 G3 **Partington** Traffd
118 F7 **Partney** Lincs
136 D3 **Parton** Cumb
19 G2 **Partridge Green** W Susx
100 D2 **Parwich** Derbys
73 L6 **Passenham** Nhants
107 G5 **Paston** Norfk
19 J4 **Patcham** Br & H
18 E4 **Patching** W Susx
38 E4 **Patchway** S Glos
132 B6 **Pateley Bridge** N York
186 E8 **Pathhead** Fife
177 K5 **Pathhead** Mdloth
185 M5 **Path of Condie** P & K
163 K7 **Patna** E Ayrs
40 B8 **Patney** Wilts
237 b5 **Patrick** IoM
132 C2 **Patrick Brompton** N York
113 H2 **Patricroft** Salfd
127 H6 **Patrington** E R Yk
127 H6 **Patrington Haven** E R Yk
35 G4 **Patrixbourne** Kent
137 L4 **Patterdale** Cumb
84 E4 **Pattingham** Staffs
73 J4 **Pattishall** Nhants
61 K3 **Pattiswick Green** Essex
2 E5 **Paul** Cnwll
73 K5 **Paulerspury** Nhants
126 E5 **Paull** E R Yk
28 C5 **Paul's Dene** Wilts
26 F1 **Paulton** BaNES
158 D3 **Pauperhaugh** Nthumb
74 E4 **Pavenham** Beds
25 L3 **Pawlett** Somset
71 L6 **Paxford** Gloucs
179 J7 **Paxton** Border
12 E3 **Payhembury** Devon
122 C1 **Paythorne** Lancs
19 L5 **Peacehaven** E Susx

114 D3 **Peak District National Park**
114 C5 **Peak Forest** Derbys
89 H3 **Peakirk** C Pete
190 E1 **Peanmeanach** Highld
39 G8 **Peasedown St John** BaNES
92 C1 **Peaseland Green** Norfk
41 J5 **Peasemore** W Berk
79 H2 **Peasenhall** Suffk
31 L5 **Pease Pottage** W Susx
31 H3 **Peaslake** Surrey
112 D3 **Peasley Cross** St Hel
21 H2 **Peasmarsh** E Susx
217 H2 **Peathill** Abers
187 G5 **Peat Inn** Fife
87 H5 **Peatling Magna** Leics
87 H5 **Peatling Parva** Leics
77 J7 **Pebmarsh** Essex
71 K5 **Pebworth** Worcs
122 E5 **Pecket Well** Calder
98 D2 **Peckforton** Ches
45 G5 **Peckham** Gt Lon
86 F4 **Peckleton** Leics
34 F7 **Pedlinge** Kent
85 G6 **Pedmore** Dudley
26 B4 **Pedwell** Somset
166 C2 **Peebles** Border
237 b4 **Peel** IoM
35 G6 **Peene** Kent
59 J2 **Pegsdon** Beds
159 G5 **Pegswood** Nthumb
35 K2 **Pegwell** Kent
209 H7 **Peinchorran** Highld
208 F3 **Peinlich** Highld
62 B5 **Peldon** Essex
85 H3 **Pelsall** Wsall
151 G4 **Pelton** Dur
5 K5 **Pelynt** Cnwll
51 G5 **Pemberton** Carmth
112 D2 **Pemberton** Wigan
50 E5 **Pembrey** Carmth
69 H3 **Pembridge** Herefs
49 G7 **Pembroke** Pembks
49 G6 **Pembroke Dock** Pembks
48 E4 **Pembrokeshire Coast National Park** Pembks
33 G5 **Pembury** Kent
54 D6 **Penallt** Mons
49 J7 **Penally** Pembks
54 E3 **Penalt** Herefs
37 J6 **Penarth** V Glam
80 F6 **Pen-bont Rhydybeddau** Cerdgn
65 J4 **Penbryn** Cerdgn
66 B7 **Pencader** Carmth
177 L5 **Pencaitland** E Loth
108 D6 **Pencarnisiog** IoA
66 C5 **Pencarreg** Carmth
53 H3 **Pencelli** Powys
51 G6 **Penclawdd** Swans
36 E4 **Pencoed** Brdgnd
69 L4 **Pencombe** Herefs
54 E4 **Pencraig** Herefs
97 G6 **Pencraig** Powys
2 C4 **Pendeen** Cnwll
52 E6 **Penderyn** Rhondd
50 B4 **Pendine** Carmth
113 H2 **Pendlebury** Salfd
121 L3 **Pendleton** Lancs
55 H2 **Pendock** Worcs
8 D8 **Pendoggett** Cnwll
13 M1 **Pendomer** Somset
37 G5 **Pendoylan** V Glam
81 G4 **Penegoes** Powys
49 J3 **Pen-ffordd** Pembks
37 J2 **Pengam** Caerph
37 K5 **Pengam** Cardif

45 G6 **Penge** Gt Lon
8 E7 **Pengelly** Cnwll
4 F6 **Pengrugla** Cnwll
3 K2 **Penhallow** Cnwll
3 J4 **Penhalvean** Cnwll
40 D3 **Penhill** Swindn
38 B3 **Penhow** Newpt
177 H6 **Penicuik** Mdloth
209 G6 **Penifiler** Highld
161 J4 **Peninver** Ag & B
114 E2 **Penistone** Barns
152 F3 **Penkill** S Ayrs
85 G2 **Penkridge** Staffs
9 G5 **Penlean** Cnwll
98 B4 **Penley** Wrexhm
36 F5 **Penllyn** V Glam
96 C3 **Penmachno** Conwy
37 J2 **Penmaen** Caerph
51 G7 **Penmaen** Swans
109 K6 **Penmaenmawr** Conwy
95 M8 **Penmaenpool** Gwynd
37 G6 **Penmark** V Glam
95 J4 **Penmorfa** Gwynd
109 G6 **Penmynydd** IoA
42 F2 **Penn** Bucks
80 F4 **Pennal** Gwynd
216 F2 **Pennan** Abers
81 J4 **Pennant** Powys
83 G4 **Pennerley** Shrops
122 E4 **Pennines**
128 F4 **Pennington** Cumb
53 H3 **Pennorth** Powys
42 F2 **Penn Street** Bucks
129 G3 **Penny Bridge** Cumb
181 G3 **Pennycross** Ag & B
181 H3 **Pennyghael** Ag & B
163 H7 **Pennyglen** S Ayrs
11 K3 **Pennymoor** Devon
65 H5 **Penparc** Cerdgn
53 L6 **Penperlleni** Mons
5 J5 **Penpoll** Cnwll
3 H4 **Penponds** Cnwll
154 E4 **Penpont** D & G
65 H6 **Pen-rhiw** Pembks
37 G2 **Penrhiwceiber** Rhondd
51 L4 **Pen Rhiwfawr** Neath
65 K6 **Penrhiwllan** Cerdgn
65 K5 **Penrhiw-pal** Cerdgn
94 F5 **Penrhos** Gwynd
54 B5 **Penrhos** Mons
110 B5 **Penrhyn Bay** Conwy
109 H6 **Penrhyn Castle** Gwynd
95 K5 **Penrhyndeudraeth** Gwynd
50 F7 **Penrice** Swans
161 L1 **Penrioch** N Ayrs
138 D2 **Penrith** Cumb
4 D2 **Penrose** Cnwll
138 B2 **Penruddock** Cumb
3 K4 **Penryn** Cnwll
50 E2 **Pensarn** Carmth
110 C5 **Pensarn** Conwy
70 C2 **Pensax** Worcs
27 H5 **Penselwood** Somset
38 F7 **Pensford** BaNES
71 G5 **Pensham** Worcs
151 H4 **Penshaw** Sundld
32 F4 **Penshurst** Kent
5 L2 **Pensilva** Cnwll
4 F6 **Pentewan** Cnwll
109 H7 **Pentir** Gwynd
4 C4 **Pentire** Cnwll
77 J5 **Pentlow** Essex
91 G2 **Pentney** Norfk
156 D6 **Pentonbridge** Cumb
29 G3 **Penton Mewsey** Hants
109 G5 **Pentraeth** IoA
36 F2 **Pentre** Rhondd

98 A8 **Pentre** Shrops
53 G7 **Pentrebach** Myr Td
52 E2 **Pentre-bach** Powys
108 F6 **Pentre Berw** IoA
97 J2 **Pentre-celyn** Denbgs
81 J3 **Pentre-celyn** Powys
51 J6 **Pentre-chwyth** Swans
65 L6 **Pentre-cwrt** Carmth
97 J3 **Pentredwr** Denbgs
95 J5 **Pentrefelin** Gwynd
96 D3 **Pentrefoelas** Conwy
65 K4 **Pentregat** Cerdgn
51 H3 **Pentre-Gwenlais** Carmth
83 G7 **Pentre Hodrey** Shrops
110 F8 **Pentre Llanrhaeadr** Denbgs
36 E5 **Pentre Meyrick** V Glam
96 C1 **Pentre-tafarn-y-fedw** Conwy
101 G3 **Pentrich** Derbys
28 B7 **Pentridge Hill** Dorset
54 D6 **Pen-twyn** Mons
37 J2 **Pentwynmaur** Caerph
37 H4 **Pentyrch** Cardif
5 G5 **Penwithick** Cnwll
51 H2 **Penybanc** Carmth
68 C2 **Penybont** Powys
97 K7 **Pen-y-bont** Powys
97 G7 **Pen-y-bont-fawr** Powys
65 G6 **Pen-y-bryn** Pembks
97 L4 **Penycae** Wrexhm
54 C6 **Pen-y-clawdd** Mons
37 G3 **Pen-y-coedcae** Rhondd
48 E3 **Pen-y-cwn** Pembks
111 G7 **Pen-y-felin** Flints
97 L1 **Penyffordd** Flints
97 H7 **Pen-y-Garnedd** Powys
94 D5 **Pen-y-graig** Gwynd
36 F3 **Penygraig** Rhondd
51 H3 **Penygroes** Carmth
95 H2 **Penygroes** Gwynd
108 F4 **Penysarn** IoA
97 J3 **Pen-y-stryt** Denbgs
52 F6 **Penywaun** Rhondd
2 E5 **Penzance** Cnwll
2 E5 **Penzance Heliport** Cnwll
71 G4 **Peopleton** Worcs
98 F7 **Peplow** Shrops
163 J2 **Perceton** N Ayrs
217 H2 **Percyhorner** Abers
28 E2 **Perham Down** Wilts
24 E3 **Periton** Somset
44 D4 **Perivale** Gt Lon
12 D4 **Perkins Village** Devon
115 M7 **Perlethorpe** Notts
3 K4 **Perranarworthal** Cnwll
3 K1 **Perranporth** Cnwll
2 F5 **Perranuthnoe** Cnwll
3 K4 **Perranwell** Cnwll
3 K2 **Perranzabuloe** Cnwll
85 J5 **Perry Barr** Birm
39 L3 **Perry Green** Wilts
99 J6 **Pershall** Staffs
71 G5 **Pershore** Worcs
74 F2 **Pertenhall** Beds
186 B3 **Perth** P & K
98 A5 **Perthy** Shrops
69 L6 **Perton** Herefs
84 F4 **Perton** Staffs
89 H4 **Peterborough** C Pete
69 G6 **Peterchurch** Herefs
206 F5 **Peterculter** C Aber

217 L5 **Peterhead** Abers
151 K6 **Peterlee** Dur
30 C6 **Petersfield** Hants
59 J4 **Peter's Green** Herts
44 D5 **Petersham** Gt Lon
10 C3 **Peters Marland** Devon
37 K4 **Peterstone Wentlooge** Newpt
37 G5 **Peterston-super-Ely** V Glam
54 E3 **Peterstow** Herefs
6 D1 **Peter Tavy** Devon
34 F4 **Petham** Kent
9 H6 **Petherwin Gate** Cnwll
10 D3 **Petrockstow** Devon
21 H3 **Pett** E Susx
78 E3 **Pettaugh** Suffk
196 C7 **Petterden** Angus
165 J2 **Pettinain** S Lans
79 G4 **Pettistree** Suffk
24 F6 **Petton** Devon
45 J6 **Petts Wood** Gt Lon
177 H2 **Pettycur** Fife
207 G1 **Pettymuk** Abers
31 G6 **Petworth** W Susx
20 D5 **Pevensey** E Susx
40 D7 **Pewsey** Wilts
71 G3 **Phepson** Worcs
22 D6 **Philham** Devon
166 F4 **Philiphaugh** Border
2 F4 **Phillack** Cnwll
4 D7 **Philleigh** Cnwll
176 E3 **Philpstoun** W Loth
30 C1 **Phoenix Green** Hants
203 G6 **Phoines** Highld
26 C6 **Pibsbury** Somset
136 E3 **Pica** Cumb
115 K1 **Pickburn** Donc
134 C3 **Pickering** N York
86 C6 **Pickford** Covtry
132 E3 **Pickhill** N York
83 J4 **Picklescott** Shrops
113 G6 **Pickmere** Ches
25 J5 **Pickney** Somset
121 K6 **Pickup Bank** Bl w D
87 L2 **Pickwell** Leics
103 H5 **Pickworth** Lincs
88 E2 **Pickworth** Rutlnd
206 E3 **Pictillum** Abers
112 B7 **Picton** Ches
141 K5 **Picton** N York
19 L5 **Piddinghoe** E Susx
74 B4 **Piddington** Nhants
57 M5 **Piddington** Oxon
14 D3 **Piddlehinton** Dorset
14 D3 **Piddletrenthide** Dorset
89 K7 **Pidley** Cambs
140 F4 **Piercebridge** Darltn
234 c3 **Pierowall** Ork
45 L2 **Pilgrims Hatch** Essex
116 E3 **Pilham** Lincs
6 A3 **Pillaton** Cnwll
72 C5 **Pillerton Hersey** Warwks
72 C5 **Pillerton Priors** Warwks
115 G2 **Pilley** Barns
16 D3 **Pilley** Hants
120 E2 **Pilling** Lancs
38 D4 **Pilning** S Glos
114 C8 **Pilsbury** Derbys
13 K3 **Pilsdon** Dorset
101 H1 **Pilsley** Derbys
114 E7 **Pilsley** Derbys
93 H2 **Pilson Green** Norfk
19 L2 **Piltdown** E Susx
23 J5 **Pilton** Devon
88 E6 **Pilton** Nhants
88 D3 **Pilton** Rutlnd
26 E3 **Pilton** Somset

15 G1 **Pimperne** Dorset
103 L7 **Pinchbeck** Lincs
59 L3 **Pin Green** Herts
12 C4 **Pinhoe** Devon
72 B2 **Pinley Green** Warwks
152 E4 **Pinminnoch** S Ayrs
152 E4 **Pinmore** S Ayrs
12 E5 **Pinn** Devon
43 J3 **Pinner** Gt Lon
43 J3 **Pinner Green** Gt Lon
71 G5 **Pinvin** Worcs
152 E5 **Pinwherry** S Ayrs
101 J2 **Pinxton** Derbys
69 K5 **Pipe and Lyde** Herefs
99 G4 **Pipe Gate** Shrops
213 K4 **Piperhill** Highld
88 B6 **Pipewell** Nhants
30 F1 **Pirbright** Surrey
167 K4 **Pirnie** Border
161 L1 **Pirnmill** N Ayrs
59 J2 **Pirton** Herts
70 F5 **Pirton** Worcs
42 B3 **Pishill** Oxon
94 F4 **Pistyll** Gwynd
194 C3 **Pitagowan** P & K
217 J2 **Pitblae** Abers
185 M3 **Pitcairngreen** P & K
223 H6 **Pitcalnie** Highld
206 D1 **Pitcaple** Abers
196 B4 **Pitcarity** Angus
55 J6 **Pitchcombe** Gloucs
58 C4 **Pitchcott** Bucks
83 K3 **Pitchford** Shrops
58 C7 **Pitch Green** Bucks
214 E6 **Pitchroy** Moray
26 F5 **Pitcombe** Somset
178 E4 **Pitcox** E Loth
206 D3 **Pitfichie** Abers
216 D5 **Pitglassie** Abers
223 H3 **Pitgrudy** Highld
196 E5 **Pitkennedy** Angus
186 E5 **Pitlessie** Fife
194 E5 **Pitlochry** P & K
216 C8 **Pitmachie** Abers
203 H5 **Pitmain** Highld
217 G8 **Pitmedden** Abers
217 G8 **Pitmedden Garden** Abers
25 K7 **Pitminster** Somset
196 F6 **Pitmuies** Angus
206 C3 **Pitmunie** Abers
26 C5 **Pitney** Somset
186 C3 **Pitroddie** P & K
187 G5 **Pitscottie** Fife
46 C3 **Pitsea** Essex
73 L2 **Pitsford** Nhants
58 F5 **Pitstone** Bucks
25 G7 **Pitt** Devon
197 H2 **Pittarrow** Abers
187 J6 **Pittenweem** Fife
186 D7 **Pitteuchar** Fife
151 H6 **Pittington** Dur
206 D1 **Pittodrie House Hotel** Abers
28 E5 **Pitton** Wilts
217 H2 **Pittulie** Abers
151 G5 **Pity Me** Dur
31 K2 **Pixham** Surrey
175 L5 **Plains** N Lans
83 K4 **Plaish** Shrops
101 G2 **Plaistow** Derbys
45 H4 **Plaistow** Gt Lon
31 G5 **Plaistow** W Susx
28 F7 **Plaitford** Hants
108 C6 **Plas Cymyran** IoA
33 G2 **Platt** Kent
151 G5 **Plawsworth** Dur
33 G3 **Plaxtol** Kent
21 H2 **Playden** E Susx
78 F5 **Playford** Suffk
42 C5 **Play Hatch** Oxon
55 H2 **Playley Green** Gloucs

83 H3 **Plealey** Shrops
175 L2 **Plean** Stirlg
186 D5 **Pleasance** Fife
121 J5 **Pleasington** Bl w D
115 J8 **Pleasley** Derbys
112 C7 **Plemstall** Ches
61 G5 **Pleshey** Essex
210 E2 **Plockton** Highld
83 H6 **Plowden** Shrops
83 G3 **Plox Green** Shrops
34 B5 **Pluckley** Kent
34 B5 **Pluckley Thorne** Kent
147 K6 **Plumbland** Cumb
113 G6 **Plumley** Ches
148 E7 **Plumpton** Cumb
19 K3 **Plumpton** E Susx
73 H5 **Plumpton** Nhants
19 K3 **Plumpton Green** E Susx
45 J4 **Plumstead** Gt Lon
106 D5 **Plumstead** Norfk
101 L6 **Plumtree** Notts
102 C5 **Plungar** Leics
34 C7 **Plurenden** Kent
14 D3 **Plush** Dorset
65 K4 **Plwmp** Cerdgn
6 C5 **Plymouth** C Plym
6 D4 **Plymouth Airport** C Plym
6 D5 **Plympton** C Plym
6 D5 **Plymstock** C Plym
12 D2 **Plymtree** Devon
133 K3 **Pockley** N York
125 J2 **Pocklington** E R Yk
26 D6 **Podimore** Somset
74 D3 **Podington** Beds
99 H5 **Podmore** Staffs
103 J6 **Pointon** Lincs
15 L4 **Pokesdown** Bmouth
224 B6 **Polbain** Highld
6 A4 **Polbathic** Cnwll
176 D5 **Polbeth** W Loth
3 H5 **Poldark Mine** Cnwll
88 F6 **Polebrook** Nhants
32 B5 **Polegate** E Susx
86 C3 **Polesworth** Warwks
224 C6 **Polglass** Highld
4 F5 **Polgooth** Cnwll
154 C2 **Polgown** D & G
18 E5 **Poling** W Susx
18 E5 **Poling Corner** W Susx
5 H5 **Polkerris** Cnwll
124 F7 **Pollington** E R Yk
190 F3 **Polloch** Highld
175 G6 **Pollokshaws** C Glas
175 G5 **Pollokshields** C Glas
4 F6 **Polmassick** Cnwll
176 C3 **Polmont** Falk
200 B8 **Polnish** Highld
5 K5 **Polperro** Cnwll
5 K5 **Polruan** Cnwll
78 B6 **Polstead** Suffk
182 B7 **Poltalloch** Ag & B
12 C3 **Poltimore** Devon
177 J5 **Polton** Mdloth
178 F7 **Polwarth** Border
9 H7 **Polyphant** Cnwll
4 E1 **Polzeath** Cnwll
177 H6 **Pomathorn** Mdloth
89 J5 **Pondersbridge** Cambs
45 G2 **Ponders End** Gt Lon
3 K4 **Ponsanooth** Cnwll
7 G2 **Ponsworthy** Devon
50 F3 **Pontamman** Carmth
51 K5 **Pontantwn** Carmth
51 H5 **Pontardawe** Neath
51 H5 **Pontarddulais** Swans
51 G2 **Pont-ar-gothi** Carmth
66 B8 **Pontarsais** Carmth
97 L1 **Pontblyddyn** Flints
124 C6 **Pontefract** Wakefd
158 F7 **Ponteland** Nthumb

81 G7 **Ponterwyd** Cerdgn
83 H3 **Pontesbury** Shrops
83 H3 **Pontesford** Shrops
97 K5 **Pontfadog** Wrexhm
64 E7 **Pontfaen** Pembks
67 L7 **Pont-faen** Powys
65 K4 **Pontgarreg** Cerdgn
50 F4 **Ponthenry** Carmth
37 M2 **Ponthir** Torfn
65 J5 **Ponthirwaun** Cerdgn
37 J2 **Pontllanfraith** Caerph
51 H5 **Pontlliw** Swans
53 H6 **Pontlottyn** Caerph
95 G3 **Pontlyfni** Gwynd
52 D6 **Pontneddfechan**
     Neath
37 L2 **Pontnewydd** Torfn
150 E4 **Pontop** Dur
67 G2 **Pontrhydfendigaid**
     Cerdgn
36 C2 **Pont-rhyd-y-fen**
     Neath
81 G8 **Pontrhydygroes**
     Cerdgn
54 B3 **Pontrilas** Herefs
82 C2 **Pont Robert** Powys
20 D3 **Ponts Green** E Susx
66 B5 **Pontshaen** Cerdgn
54 F4 **Pontshill** Herefs
53 G5 **Pontsticill** Myr Td
65 L6 **Pontwelly** Carmth
50 F4 **Pontyates** Carmth
51 G4 **Pontyberem** Carmth
97 L2 **Pontybodkin** Flints
37 G4 **Pontyclun** Rhondd
36 D3 **Pontycymer** Brdgnd
96 B2 **Pont-y-pant** Conwy
53 L7 **Pontypool** Torfn
37 G3 **Pontypridd** Rhondd
37 K2 **Pontywaun** Caerph
3 H3 **Pool** Cnwll
123 J2 **Pool** Leeds
15 J4 **Poole** Poole
39 M2 **Poole Keynes** Gloucs
219 K3 **Poolewe** Highld
138 C3 **Pooley Bridge** Cumb
99 K1 **Poolfold** Staffs
55 G5 **Poolhill** Gloucs
185 L7 **Pool of Muckhart**
     Clacks
77 H6 **Pool Street** Essex
45 G4 **Poplar** Gt Lon
16 F4 **Porchfield** IoW
92 F3 **Poringland** Norfk
3 J5 **Porkellis** Cnwll
24 D3 **Porlock** Somset
24 D2 **Porlock Weir** Somset
172 E6 **Portachoillan** Ag & B
210 B7 **Port-an-Eorna** Highld
191 H7 **Port Appin** Ag & B
171 H5 **Port Askaig** Ag & B
172 F4 **Portavadie** Ag & B
173 J5 **Port Bannatyne**
     Ag & B
38 D5 **Portbury** N Som
147 M3 **Port Carlisle** Cumb
170 E6 **Port Charlotte** Ag & B
17 H2 **Portchester** Hants
173 G4 **Port Driseach** Ag & B
50 F7 **Port Einon** Swans
160 C3 **Port Ellen** Ag & B
206 E2 **Port Elphinstone**
     Abers
152 B7 **Portencalzie** D & G
173 K8 **Portencross** N Ayrs
237 a6 **Port Erin** IoM
14 B5 **Portesham** Dorset
215 K2 **Portessie** Moray
48 F4 **Portfield Gate**
     Pembks
10 B7 **Portgate** Devon
8 D8 **Port Gaverne** Cnwll

174 C4 **Port Glasgow** Inver
215 J2 **Portgordon** Moray
227 H5 **Portgower** Highld
4 C4 **Porth** Cnwll
36 F3 **Porth** Rhondd
3 K6 **Porthallow** Cnwll
5 K5 **Porthallow** Cnwll
36 C5 **Porthcawl** Brdgnd
4 D2 **Porthcothan** Cnwll
2 C6 **Porthcurno** Cnwll
219 H6 **Port Henderson**
     Highld
64 A7 **Porthgain** Pembks
2 C6 **Porthgwarra** Cnwll
37 G6 **Porthkerry** V Glam
3 H6 **Porthleven** Cnwll
95 K5 **Porthmadog** Gwynd
3 K5 **Porth Navas** Cnwll
3 K6 **Porthoustock** Cnwll
5 G5 **Porthpean** Cnwll
3 J2 **Porthtowan** Cnwll
51 G3 **Porthyrhyd** Carmth
183 J8 **Portincaple** Ag & B
125 J4 **Portington** E R Yk
182 D5 **Portinnisherrich**
     Ag & B
137 H3 **Portinscale** Cumb
8 D8 **Port Isaac** Cnwll
38 C5 **Portishead** N Som
215 K2 **Portknockie** Moray
14 D7 **Portland** Dorset
207 H6 **Portlethen** Abers
146 F4 **Portling** D & G
4 E7 **Portloe** Cnwll
144 D6 **Port Logan** D & G
223 K5 **Portmahomack**
     Highld
95 K5 **Portmeirion** Gwynd
4 F6 **Portmellon** Cnwll
189 K1 **Port Mor** Highld
191 H6 **Portnacroish** Ag & B
232 g2 **Portnaguran** W Isls
170 D7 **Portnahaven** Ag & B
208 E7 **Portnalong** Highld
232 g2 **Port nan Giuran**
     W Isls
232 c5 **Port nan Long** W Isls
232 g1 **Port Nis** W Isls
177 J4 **Portobello** C Edin
85 G4 **Portobello** Wolves
184 D6 **Port of Menteith**
     Stirlg
232 g1 **Port of Ness** W Isls
28 D4 **Porton** Wilts
144 B4 **Portpatrick** D & G
8 C8 **Port Quin** Cnwll
191 H7 **Port Ramsay** Ag & B
3 H3 **Portreath** Cnwll
209 G5 **Portree** Highld
237 b7 **Port St Mary** IoM
4 D8 **Portscatho** Cnwll
17 J3 **Portsea** C Port
230 C3 **Portskerra** Highld
38 D3 **Portskewett** Mons
19 H4 **Portslade** Br & H
19 H5 **Portslade-by-Sea**
     Br & H
144 B3 **Portslogan** D & G
17 J3 **Portsmouth** C Port
122 D5 **Portsmouth** Calder
237 c6 **Port Soderick** IoM
182 F3 **Portsonachan Hotel**
     Ag & B
216 B2 **Portsoy** Abers
111 K5 **Port Sunlight** Wirral
29 H8 **Portswood** C Sotn
36 B3 **Port Talbot** Neath
189 K3 **Portuairk** Highld
85 J8 **Portway** Worcs
170 D7 **Port Wemyss** Ag & B
145 H6 **Port William** D & G
6 A5 **Portwrinkle** Cnwll

145 K7 **Portyerrock** D & G
77 H5 **Poslingford** Suffk
166 B3 **Posso** Border
10 F8 **Postbridge** Devon
58 B7 **Postcombe** Oxon
34 F6 **Postling** Kent
93 G2 **Postwick** Norfk
206 B6 **Potarch** Abers
58 F3 **Potsgrove** Beds
59 G6 **Potten End** Herts
134 F4 **Potter Brompton**
     N York
117 H7 **Potterhanworth**
     Lincs
117 H7 **Potterhanworth**
     Booths Lincs
107 J8 **Potter Heigham**
     Norfk
39 M8 **Potterne** Wilts
39 M8 **Potterne Wick** Wilts
59 L7 **Potters Bar** Herts
59 J6 **Potters Crouch** Herts
87 G4 **Potters Marston** Leics
73 L6 **Potterspury** Nhants
207 H3 **Potterton** Abers
141 L6 **Potto** N York
75 J5 **Potton** Beds
113 L5 **Pott Shrigley** Ches
9 G4 **Poughill** Cnwll
11 K3 **Poughill** Devon
15 M2 **Poulner** Hants
39 L7 **Poulshot** Wilts
56 C7 **Poulton** Gloucs
120 D3 **Poulton-le-Fylde**
     Lancs
51 H6 **Poundffald** Swans
20 B2 **Pound Green** E Susx
77 G4 **Pound Green** Suffk
32 B5 **Pound Hill** W Susx
57 M3 **Poundon** Bucks
7 G2 **Poundsgate** Devon
9 G5 **Poundstock** Cnwll
145 K5 **Pouton** D & G
31 L3 **Povey Cross** Surrey
168 F6 **Powburn** Nthumb
12 C5 **Powderham** Devon
13 M3 **Powerstock** Dorset
147 K2 **Powfoot** D & G
147 M4 **Powhill** Cumb
70 E4 **Powick** Worcs
185 L7 **Powmill** P & K
14 E5 **Poxwell** Dorset
43 G5 **Poyle** Slough
19 H4 **Poynings** W Susx
26 F7 **Poyntington** Dorset
113 L5 **Poynton** Ches
98 E8 **Poynton Green**
     Wrekin
3 G5 **Praa Sands** Cnwll
45 J7 **Pratt's Bottom**
     Gt Lon
3 H4 **Praze-an-Beeble**
     Cnwll
98 D5 **Prees** Shrops
120 E2 **Preesall** Lancs
98 E6 **Prees Green** Shrops
168 E6 **Prendwick** Nthumb
65 L5 **Pren-gwyn** Cerdgn
95 K4 **Prenteg** Gwynd
112 C3 **Prescot** Knows
25 H8 **Prescott** Devon
195 J3 **Presnerb** Angus
110 E5 **Prestatyn** Denbgs
113 K6 **Prestbury** Ches
55 L4 **Prestbury** Gloucs
69 G2 **Presteigne** Powys
26 F4 **Prestleigh** Somset
179 G6 **Preston** Border
19 J4 **Preston** Br & H
7 K2 **Preston** Devon
14 D5 **Preston** Dorset
126 F4 **Preston** E R Yk

56 B7 **Preston** Gloucs
59 K3 **Preston** Herts
34 D3 **Preston** Kent
35 H3 **Preston** Kent
121 H4 **Preston** Lancs
169 H4 **Preston** Nthumb
88 C3 **Preston** Rutlnd
25 H4 **Preston** Somset
77 L4 **Preston** Suffk
7 K4 **Preston** Torbay
40 B5 **Preston** Wilts
71 L2 **Preston Bagot**
     Warwks
58 A3 **Preston Bissett** Bucks
25 H6 **Preston Bowyer**
     Somset
98 D7 **Preston Brockhurst**
     Shrops
112 E5 **Preston Brook** Halton
29 L3 **Preston Candover**
     Hants
73 M4 **Preston Capes**
     Nhants
71 L2 **Preston Green**
     Warwks
98 C8 **Preston Gubbals**
     Shrops
72 B4 **Preston on Stour**
     Warwks
112 E5 **Preston on the Hill**
     Halton
69 H6 **Preston on Wye**
     Herefs
177 K4 **Prestonpans** E Loth
129 L3 **Preston Patrick**
     Cumb
26 D7 **Preston Plucknett**
     Somset
131 K2 **Preston-under-Scar**
     N York
84 C1 **Preston upon the**
     Weald Moors Wrekin
69 L5 **Preston Wynne**
     Herefs
113 J1 **Prestwich** Bury
163 J4 **Prestwick** S Ayrs
163 J4 **Prestwick Airport**
     S Ayrs
58 E7 **Prestwood** Bucks
90 E6 **Prickwillow** Cambs
26 D2 **Priddy** Somset
129 L5 **Priest Hutton** Lancs
164 B2 **Priestland** E Ayrs
82 F4 **Priest Weston** Shrops
179 G6 **Primrosehill** Border
168 B4 **Primsidemill** Border
58 D7 **Princes Risborough**
     Bucks
72 E1 **Princethorpe** Warwks
6 E2 **Princetown** Devon
72 F4 **Priors Hardwick**
     Warwks
72 F3 **Priors Marston**
     Warwks
55 K3 **Priors Norton** Gloucs
40 C4 **Priory Vale** Swindn
39 G7 **Priston** BaNES
46 E3 **Prittlewell** Sthend
30 B6 **Privett** Hants
4 E6 **Probus** Cnwll
178 C3 **Prora** E Loth
147 K6 **Prospect** Cumb
3 H5 **Prospidnick** Cnwll
216 F2 **Protstonhill** Abers
150 D3 **Prudhoe** Nthumb
38 F7 **Publow** BaNES
60 C4 **Puckeridge** Herts
26 B7 **Puckington** Somset
39 G5 **Pucklechurch** S Glos
111 K6 **Puddington** Ches
11 J3 **Puddington** Devon
14 E4 **Puddletown** Dorset

123 J4 **Pudsey** Leeds
18 E3 **Pulborough** W Susx
98 A2 **Pulford** Ches
14 D2 **Pulham** Dorset
92 E6 **Pulham Market** Norfk
92 E6 **Pulham St Mary** Norfk
74 F7 **Pulloxhill** Beds
176 E4 **Pumpherston** W Loth
66 E6 **Pumsaint** Carmth
49 G2 **Puncheston** Pembks
14 A5 **Puncknowle** Dorset
20 C2 **Punnett's Town** E Susx
17 J2 **Purbrook** Hants
45 K4 **Purfleet** Thurr
25 L3 **Puriton** Somset
61 K7 **Purleigh** Essex
44 F7 **Purley** Gt Lon
42 A5 **Purley** W Berk
27 G7 **Purse Caundle** Dorset
13 K2 **Purtington** Somset
54 F6 **Purton** Gloucs
55 G7 **Purton** Gloucs
40 C3 **Purton** Wilts
40 C3 **Purton Stoke** Wilts
73 K5 **Pury End** Nhants
41 G2 **Pusey** Oxon
70 B6 **Putley** Herefs
70 B6 **Putley Green** Herefs
55 H6 **Putloe** Gloucs
44 E5 **Putney** Gt Lon
30 F2 **Puttenham** Surrey
73 L6 **Puxley** Nhants
38 B7 **Puxton** N Som
50 F5 **Pwll** Carmth
97 H2 **Pwll-glas** Denbgs
68 B7 **Pwllgloyw** Powys
94 F5 **Pwllheli** Gwynd
38 D2 **Pwllmeyric** Mons
50 C3 **Pwll Trap** Carmth
36 C2 **Pwll-y-glaw** Neath
101 H3 **Pye Bridge** Derbys
19 J3 **Pyecombe** W Susx
36 C4 **Pyle** Brdgnd
25 H5 **Pyleigh** Somset
26 E4 **Pylle** Somset
90 C6 **Pymoor** Cambs
13 L4 **Pymore** Dorset
43 H8 **Pyrford** Surrey
42 B2 **Pyrton** Oxon
88 C8 **Pytchley** Nhants
9 J4 **Pyworthy** Devon

Q

103 L6 **Quadring** Lincs
58 C4 **Quainton** Bucks
25 J4 **Quantock Hills** Somset
235 c6 **Quarff** Shet
28 F3 **Quarley** Hants
101 G4 **Quarndon** Derbys
174 C5 **Quarrier's Village** Inver
103 L6 **Quarrington** Lincs
151 H7 **Quarrington Hill** Dur
85 G6 **Quarry Bank** Dudley
214 E2 **Quarrywood** Moray
173 L6 **Quarter** N Ayrs
175 J7 **Quarter** S Lans
84 D5 **Quatford** Shrops
84 D6 **Quatt** Shrops
150 F6 **Quebec** Dur
55 J5 **Quedgeley** Gloucs
90 E7 **Queen Adelaide** Cambs
46 E5 **Queenborough** Kent
26 E6 **Queen Camel** Somset

38 F6 **Queen Charlton** BaNES
184 B6 **Queen Elizabeth Forest Park** Stirlg
70 F6 **Queenhill** Worcs
27 H5 **Queen Oak** Dorset
17 H5 **Queen's Bower** IoW
123 G4 **Queensbury** Brad
111 K7 **Queensferry** Flints
175 H5 **Queenslie** C Glas
33 H4 **Queen Street** Kent
175 J3 **Queenzieburn** N Lans
60 E3 **Quendon** Essex
87 J2 **Queniborough** Leics
56 C7 **Quenington** Gloucs
85 J4 **Queslett** Birm
5 L3 **Quethiock** Cnwll
92 B6 **Quidenham** Norfk
28 C5 **Quidhampton** Wilts
73 L4 **Quinton** Nhants
4 D4 **Quintrell Downs** Cnwll
10 C8 **Quither** Devon
179 G5 **Quixwood** Border
9 K5 **Quoditch** Devon
185 H3 **Quoig** P & K
87 H1 **Quorn** Leics
165 J2 **Quothquan** S Lans
234 c6 **Quoyburray** Ork
234 b5 **Quoyloo** Ork

R

165 L3 **Rachan Mill** Border
109 J7 **Rachub** Gwynd
24 D7 **Rackenford** Devon
18 E3 **Rackham** W Susx
93 G1 **Rackheath** Norfk
155 H7 **Racks** D & G
234 a7 **Rackwick** Ork
100 F5 **Radbourne** Derbys
113 H1 **Radcliffe** Bury
159 G2 **Radcliffe** Nthumb
101 M5 **Radcliffe on Trent** Notts
73 J7 **Radclive** Bucks
213 H3 **Raddery** Highld
187 G5 **Radernie** Fife
72 D2 **Radford Semele** Warwks
59 K7 **Radlett** Herts
57 K7 **Radley** Oxon
60 F6 **Radley Green** Essex
42 C2 **Radnage** Bucks
27 G1 **Radstock** BaNES
73 H6 **Radstone** Nhants
72 D5 **Radway** Warwks
74 E3 **Radwell** Beds
75 J7 **Radwell** Herts
76 E6 **Radwinter** Essex
37 H4 **Radyr** Cardif
214 C3 **Rafford** Moray
102 A8 **Ragdale** Leics
54 B6 **Raglan** Mons
116 D6 **Ragnall** Notts
213 J8 **Raigbeg** Highld
70 F4 **Rainbow Hill** Worcs
112 C2 **Rainford** St Hel
45 K4 **Rainham** Gt Lon
46 D6 **Rainham** Medway
112 C4 **Rainhill** St Hel
112 D4 **Rainhill Stoops** St Hel
113 L6 **Rainow** Ches
132 E4 **Rainton** N York
101 L2 **Rainworth** Notts
134 D7 **Raisthorpe** N York
186 D3 **Rait** P & K
118 D5 **Raithby** Lincs
118 E7 **Raithby** Lincs
30 D5 **Rake** Hants

203 H5 **Ralia** Highld
208 B5 **Ramasaig** Highld
3 J4 **Rame** Cnwll
6 B6 **Rame** Cnwll
14 B3 **Rampisham** Dorset
128 F6 **Rampside** Cumb
76 B2 **Rampton** Cambs
116 D5 **Rampton** Notts
122 B6 **Ramsbottom** Bury
40 F6 **Ramsbury** Wilts
227 K3 **Ramscraigs** Highld
30 B6 **Ramsdean** Hants
41 L8 **Ramsdell** Hants
57 G5 **Ramsden** Oxon
46 B2 **Ramsden Bellhouse** Essex
89 K6 **Ramsey** Cambs
62 E2 **Ramsey** Essex
237 e3 **Ramsey** IoM
89 K6 **Ramsey Forty Foot** Cambs
89 J6 **Ramsey Heights** Cambs
61 M6 **Ramsey Island** Essex
89 K5 **Ramsey Mereside** Cambs
89 J6 **Ramsey St Mary's** Cambs
35 K2 **Ramsgate** Kent
131 L5 **Ramsgill** N York
157 J2 **Ramshope** Nthumb
100 B4 **Ramshorn** Staffs
30 F5 **Ramsnest Common** Surrey
118 B5 **Ranby** Lincs
116 A5 **Ranby** Notts
117 J5 **Rand** Lincs
55 J6 **Randwick** Gloucs
174 D5 **Ranfurly** Rens
100 D7 **Rangemore** Staffs
39 G3 **Rangeworthy** S Glos
163 L6 **Rankinston** E Ayrs
121 K5 **Rann** Bl w D
193 G5 **Rannoch Station** P & K
24 E3 **Ranscombe** Somset
116 A4 **Ranskill** Notts
99 J7 **Ranton** Staffs
99 J7 **Ranton Green** Staffs
93 H1 **Ranworth** Norfk
185 G7 **Raploch** Stirlg
234 c4 **Rapness** Ork
146 D5 **Rascarrel** D & G
173 K2 **Rashfield** Ag & B
71 G2 **Rashwood** Worcs
133 G5 **Raskelf** N York
123 H6 **Rastrick** Calder
200 E2 **Ratagan** Highld
87 G3 **Ratby** Leics
86 D4 **Ratcliffe Culey** Leics
101 J6 **Ratcliffe on Soar** Notts
87 J1 **Ratcliffe on the Wreake** Leics
217 J3 **Rathen** Abers
186 F3 **Rathillet** Fife
130 F7 **Rathmell** N York
176 F4 **Ratho** C Edin
176 F4 **Ratho Station** C Edin
215 K2 **Rathven** Moray
72 E5 **Ratley** Warwks
35 H4 **Ratling** Kent
83 H4 **Ratlinghope** Shrops
231 J2 **Rattar** Highld
7 H4 **Rattery** Devon
77 L3 **Rattlesden** Suffk
20 C5 **Ratton Village** E Susx
195 J7 **Rattray** P & K
88 E8 **Raunds** Nhants
115 J3 **Ravenfield** Rothm
136 F7 **Ravenglass** Cumb
93 H4 **Raveningham** Norfk

143 K6 **Ravenscar** N York
74 F4 **Ravensden** Beds
101 K2 **Ravenshead** Notts
123 J6 **Ravensthorpe** Kirk
73 J1 **Ravensthorpe** Nhants
86 E2 **Ravenstone** Leics
74 B4 **Ravenstone** M Keyn
139 G6 **Ravenstonedale** Cumb
165 H1 **Ravenstruther** S Lans
140 E5 **Ravensworth** N York
125 G6 **Rawcliffe** E R Yk
133 J8 **Rawcliffe** York
123 J3 **Rawdon** Leeds
34 B3 **Rawling Street** Kent
115 H3 **Rawmarsh** Rothm
46 C2 **Rawreth** Essex
12 F2 **Rawridge** Devon
122 B6 **Rawtenstall** Lancs
78 C6 **Raydon** Suffk
46 D2 **Rayleigh** Essex
61 H4 **Rayne** Essex
44 E6 **Raynes Park** Gt Lon
76 E2 **Reach** Cambs
122 B4 **Read** Lancs
42 B5 **Reading** Readg
34 B8 **Reading Street** Kent
35 K2 **Reading Street** Kent
138 E4 **Reagill** Cumb
223 G3 **Rearquhar** Highld
87 J2 **Rearsby** Leics
230 D3 **Reay** Highld
47 L6 **Reculver** Kent
25 H7 **Red Ball** Devon
49 J6 **Redberth** Pembks
59 J5 **Redbourn** Herts
116 F2 **Redbourne** N Linc
54 D6 **Redbrook** Gloucs
98 D4 **Redbrook** Wrexhm
34 C7 **Redbrook Street** Kent
213 L5 **Redburn** Highld
142 D3 **Redcar** R & Cl
146 E2 **Redcastle** D & G
212 E4 **Redcastle** Highld
176 C3 **Redding** Falk
176 C3 **Reddingmuirhead** Falk
71 J2 **Redditch** Worcs
77 J4 **Rede** Suffk
92 F6 **Redenhall** Norfk
157 L5 **Redesmouth** Nthumb
197 J3 **Redford** Abers
196 F7 **Redford** Angus
30 E6 **Redford** W Susx
166 E6 **Redfordgreen** Border
186 A2 **Redgorton** P & K
92 C7 **Redgrave** Suffk
206 E4 **Redhill** Abers
15 K4 **Red Hill** Bmouth
59 M2 **Redhill** Herts
38 D7 **Redhill** N Som
32 B3 **Redhill** Surrey
71 K4 **Red Hill** Warwks
93 J6 **Redisham** Suffk
38 E5 **Redland** Bristl
234 b5 **Redland** Ork
78 E1 **Redlingfield** Suffk
78 E1 **Redlingfield Green** Suffk
77 L7 **Red Lodge** Suffk
27 G5 **Redlynch** Somset
28 D7 **Redlynch** Wilts
70 D2 **Redmarley** Worcs
55 H2 **Redmarley D'Abitot** Gloucs
141 J3 **Redmarshall** S on T
102 D5 **Redmile** Leics
131 K2 **Redmire** N York
197 J2 **Redmyre** Abers
98 A6 **Rednal** Shrops
167 J3 **Redpath** Border

219 H7	**Redpoint** Highld
49 L5	**Red Roses** Carmth
159 G3	**Red Row** Nthumb
3 J3	**Redruth** Cnwll
186 C1	**Redstone** P & K
109 G5	**Red Wharf Bay** IoA
38 B4	**Redwick** Newpt
38 D3	**Redwick** S Glos
141 G3	**Redworth** Darltn
75 L7	**Reed** Herts
93 J3	**Reedham** Norfk
125 J6	**Reedness** E R Yk
117 H6	**Reepham** Lincs
106 D7	**Reepham** Norfk
140 C7	**Reeth** N York
86 C7	**Reeves Green** Solhll
224 B5	**Reiff** Highld
31 L2	**Reigate** Surrey
135 H4	**Reighton** N York
207 G2	**Reisque** Abers
231 L5	**Reiss** Highld
2 F5	**Relubbus** Cnwll
214 B5	**Relugas** Moray
42 C4	**Remenham** Wokham
42 C4	**Remenham Hill** Wokham
101 L7	**Rempstone** Notts
56 A6	**Rendcomb** Gloucs
79 H2	**Rendham** Suffk
79 H4	**Rendlesham** Suffk
174 F5	**Renfrew** Rens
74 F4	**Renhold** Beds
115 J6	**Renishaw** Derbys
169 J5	**Rennington** Nthumb
174 D3	**Renton** W Duns
149 G6	**Renwick** Cumb
93 J1	**Repps** Norfk
100 F6	**Repton** Derbys
213 H5	**Resaurie** Highld
4 F7	**Rescassa** Cnwll
190 E4	**Resipole** Highld
3 H3	**Reskadinnick** Cnwll
213 G2	**Resolis** Highld
52 C7	**Resolven** Neath
183 J6	**Rest and be thankful** Ag & B
179 H6	**Reston** Border
196 E6	**Reswallie** Angus
116 B5	**Retford** Notts
61 J7	**Rettendon** Essex
103 M1	**Revesby** Lincs
12 B3	**Rewe** Devon
16 F4	**Rew Street** IoW
93 K7	**Reydon** Suffk
92 B3	**Reymerston** Norfk
49 J5	**Reynalton** Pembks
50 F7	**Reynoldston** Swans
6 A1	**Rezare** Cnwll
67 H5	**Rhandirmwyn** Carmth
67 L2	**Rhayader** Powys
212 D5	**Rhenigidale** Highld
111 G7	**Rhes-y-cae** Flints
97 H1	**Rhewl** Denbgs
97 J4	**Rhewl** Denbgs
224 D4	**Rhicarn** Highld
228 C5	**Rhiconich** Highld
222 F6	**Rhicullen** Highld
52 E6	**Rhigos** Rhondd
220 D3	**Rhireavach** Highld
223 H2	**Rhives** Highld
37 J4	**Rhiwbina** Cardif
37 K3	**Rhiwderyn** Newpt
109 H7	**Rhiwlas** Gwynd
33 H4	**Rhoden Green** Kent
34 F6	**Rhodes Minnis** Kent
48 C3	**Rhodiad-y-brenin** Pembks
146 C3	**Rhonehouse** D & G
37 G6	**Rhoose** V Glam
65 L7	**Rhos** Carmth
51 L5	**Rhos** Neath
108 E3	**Rhosbeirio** IoA
108 C6	**Rhoscolyn** IoA
48 F6	**Rhoscrowther** Pembks
111 H7	**Rhosesmor** Flints
68 D5	**Rhosgoch** Powys
65 H6	**Rhoshill** Pembks
94 D6	**Rhoshirwaun** Gwynd
80 D3	**Rhoslefain** Gwynd
97 L3	**Rhosllanerchrugog** Wrexhm
108 F6	**Rhosmeirch** IoA
108 D6	**Rhosneigr** IoA
110 B5	**Rhos-on-Sea** Conwy
50 E7	**Rhossili** Swans
95 H2	**Rhostryfan** Gwynd
97 L3	**Rhostyllen** Wrexhm
108 F4	**Rhosybol** IoA
96 E5	**Rhos-y-gwaliau** Gwynd
97 L4	**Rhosymedre** Wrexhm
174 B2	**Rhu** Ag & B
110 F6	**Rhuallt** Denbgs
173 H4	**Rhubodach** Ag & B
110 E6	**Rhuddlan** Denbgs
172 C8	**Rhunahaorine** Ag & B
95 L4	**Rhyd** Gwynd
50 F1	**Rhydargaeau** Carmth
66 D6	**Rhydcymerau** Carmth
95 K3	**Rhyd-Ddu** Gwynd
65 K5	**Rhydlewis** Cerdgn
66 B5	**Rhydowen** Cerdgn
96 D5	**Rhyd-uchaf** Gwynd
94 F5	**Rhyd-y-clafdy** Gwynd
110 C6	**Rhyd-y-foel** Conwy
51 K4	**Rhydyfro** Neath
109 H7	**Rhyd-y-groes** Gwynd
80 E6	**Rhyd-y pennau** Cerdgn
110 D5	**Rhyl** Denbgs
53 H6	**Rhymney** Caerph
186 B4	**Rhynd** P & K
215 L8	**Rhynie** Abers
223 J5	**Rhynie** Highld
84 D8	**Ribbesford** Worcs
121 H4	**Ribbleton** Lancs
121 J4	**Ribchester** Lancs
126 F8	**Riby** Lincs
124 F3	**Riccall** N York
156 F3	**Riccarton** Border
163 K3	**Riccarton** E Ayrs
69 J1	**Richards Castle** Herefs
44 D5	**Richmond** Gt Lon
140 F6	**Richmond** N York
115 H4	**Richmond** Sheff
99 L7	**Rickerscote** Staffs
38 C8	**Rickford** N Som
7 H7	**Rickham** Devon
92 C7	**Rickinghall** Suffk
60 E3	**Rickling Green** Essex
43 H2	**Rickmansworth** Herts
167 H4	**Riddell** Border
10 F3	**Riddlecombe** Devon
123 G3	**Riddlesden** Brad
15 H5	**Ridge** Dorset
59 K7	**Ridge** Herts
27 L5	**Ridge** Wilts
38 D7	**Ridgehill** N Som
86 C4	**Ridge Lane** Warwks
115 H5	**Ridgeway** Derbys
77 G6	**Ridgewell** Essex
19 M2	**Ridgewood** E Susx
74 E7	**Ridgmont** Beds
150 C3	**Riding Mill** Nthumb
107 H6	**Ridlington** Norfk
88 B3	**Ridlington** Rutlnd
158 A5	**Ridsdale** Nthumb
133 J3	**Rievaulx** N York
133 J3	**Rievaulx Abbey** N York
148 B2	**Rigg** D & G
175 K4	**Riggend** N Lans
213 K4	**Righoul** Highld
118 F6	**Rigsby** Lincs
165 G3	**Rigside** S Lans
121 J5	**Riley Green** Lancs
5 L2	**Rilla Mill** Cnwll
134 D5	**Rillington** N York
122 B2	**Rimington** Lancs
26 E6	**Rimpton** Somset
127 H5	**Rimswell** E R Yk
49 G3	**Rinaston** Pembks
84 D4	**Rindleford** Shrops
146 C3	**Ringford** D & G
92 D2	**Ringland** Norfk
19 L3	**Ringmer** E Susx
6 F6	**Ringmore** Devon
7 L2	**Ringmore** Devon
215 G3	**Ringorm** Moray
93 J5	**Ringsfield** Suffk
93 J6	**Ringsfield Corner** Suffk
59 G5	**Ringshall** Herts
78 D4	**Ringshall** Suffk
78 C4	**Ringshall Stocks** Suffk
88 B2	**Ringstead** Nhants
105 H4	**Ringstead** Norfk
15 L2	**Ringwood** Hants
35 K5	**Ringwould** Kent
20 B4	**Ripe** E Susx
101 H3	**Ripley** Derbys
15 M3	**Ripley** Hants
132 D7	**Ripley** N York
31 H1	**Ripley** Surrey
30 A6	**Riplington** Hants
132 D5	**Ripon** N York
103 H6	**Rippingale** Lincs
35 J5	**Ripple** Kent
70 F6	**Ripple** Worcs
122 F6	**Ripponden** Calder
160 B2	**Risabus** Ag & B
69 K4	**Risbury** Herefs
77 H2	**Risby** Suffk
37 K3	**Risca** Caerph
126 E3	**Rise** E R Yk
103 K6	**Risegate** Lincs
74 F3	**Riseley** Beds
42 B7	**Riseley** Wokham
78 E2	**Rishangles** Suffk
121 L4	**Rishton** Lancs
122 F6	**Rishworth** Calder
101 J5	**Risley** Derbys
112 F3	**Risley** Warrtn
132 C5	**Risplith** N York
35 J6	**River** Kent
30 F6	**River** W Susx
212 E4	**Riverford** Highld
32 F3	**Riverhead** Kent
121 J7	**Rivington** Lancs
73 L4	**Roade** Nhants
176 B7	**Roadmeetings** S Lans
164 B5	**Roadside** E Ayrs
231 H4	**Roadside** Highld
25 J2	**Roadwater** Somset
208 D5	**Roag** Highld
153 G2	**Roan of Craigoch** S Ayrs
37 J5	**Roath** Cardif
166 F7	**Roberton** Border
165 H4	**Roberton** S Lans
20 E2	**Robertsbridge** E Susx
123 J6	**Roberttown** Kirk
49 J4	**Robeston Wathen** Pembks
155 M7	**Robgill Tower** D & G
116 A2	**Robin Hood** Doncaster Sheffield Airport Donc
143 K6	**Robin Hood's Bay** N York
6 D4	**Roborough** Devon
10 E2	**Roborough** Devon
112 B4	**Roby** Knows
100 C5	**Rocester** Staffs
48 E3	**Roch** Pembks
122 D7	**Rochdale** Rochdl
4 F4	**Roche** Cnwll
46 C6	**Rochester** Medway
157 L3	**Rochester** Nthumb
46 E3	**Rochford** Essex
70 B2	**Rochford** Worcs
4 E2	**Rock** Cnwll
169 J5	**Rock** Nthumb
70 D1	**Rock** Worcs
12 C4	**Rockbeare** Devon
28 C7	**Rockbourne** Hants
148 C3	**Rockcliffe** Cumb
146 E4	**Rockcliffe** D & G
7 L4	**Rockend** Torbay
111 K4	**Rock Ferry** Wirral
223 K5	**Rockfield** Highld
54 C5	**Rockfield** Mons
24 B2	**Rockford** Devon
38 F2	**Rockhampton** S Glos
82 F7	**Rockhill** Shrops
88 C5	**Rockingham** Nhants
92 B4	**Rockland All Saints** Norfk
93 G3	**Rockland St Mary** Norfk
92 B4	**Rockland St Peter** Norfk
116 B6	**Rockley** Notts
40 D6	**Rockley** Wilts
173 L1	**Rockville** Ag & B
42 D3	**Rockwell End** Bucks
55 J6	**Rodborough** Gloucs
40 C4	**Rodbourne** Swindn
39 L4	**Rodbourne** Wilts
14 B5	**Rodden** Dorset
27 J2	**Rode** Somset
99 J2	**Rode Heath** Ches
232 d5	**Rodel** W Isls
83 L1	**Roden** Wrekin
24 H4	**Rodhuish** Somset
83 L1	**Rodington** Wrekin
83 L1	**Rodington Heath** Wrekin
55 H5	**Rodley** Gloucs
39 L2	**Rodmarton** Gloucs
19 L4	**Rodmell** E Susx
34 B3	**Rodmersham** Kent
34 B3	**Rodmersham Green** Kent
26 C2	**Rodney Stoke** Somset
100 D4	**Rodsley** Derbys
132 E6	**Roecliffe** N York
59 K6	**Roe Green** Herts
75 K7	**Roe Green** Herts
44 E5	**Roehampton** Gt Lon
31 K5	**Roffey** W Susx
226 C7	**Rogart** Highld
30 D6	**Rogate** W Susx
37 L3	**Rogerstone** Newpt
232 d5	**Roghadal** W Isls
38 C3	**Rogiet** Mons
41 L2	**Roke** Oxon
151 J3	**Roker** Sundld
93 J1	**Rollesby** Norfk
87 K4	**Rolleston** Leics
102 C3	**Rolleston** Notts
100 E6	**Rolleston** Staffs
126 F2	**Rolston** E R Yk
33 L6	**Rolvenden** Kent
33 L7	**Rolvenden Layne** Kent
140 C3	**Romaldkirk** Dur
39 H7	**Roman Baths & Pump Room** BaNES

132 E2 **Romanby** N York
177 G8 **Romanno Bridge** Border
34 B7 **Romansleigh** Devon
208 F4 **Romesdal** Highld
15 K1 **Romford** Dorset
45 K3 **Romford** Gt Lon
113 L4 **Romiley** Stockp
29 G6 **Romsey** Hants
84 D6 **Romsley** Shrops
85 G7 **Romsley** Worcs
172 C7 **Ronachan** Ag & B
150 B6 **Rookhope** Dur
17 G5 **Rookley** IoW
26 A2 **Rooks Bridge** Somset
25 H5 **Rooks Nest** Somset
132 C3 **Rookwith** N York
127 G4 **Roos** E R Yk
75 G3 **Roothams Green** Beds
29 M5 **Ropley** Hants
29 L5 **Ropley Dean** Hants
103 G5 **Ropsley** Lincs
217 K4 **Rora** Abers
82 F4 **Rorrington** Shrops
215 J4 **Rosarie** Moray
3 K1 **Rose** Cnwll
24 C6 **Rose Ash** Devon
175 L2 **Rosebank** S Lans
49 J2 **Rosebush** Pembks
142 F7 **Rosedale Abbey** N York
61 L3 **Rose Green** Essex
77 L5 **Rose Green** Suffk
77 L6 **Rose Green** Suffk
18 B5 **Rose Green** W Susx
225 K7 **Rosehall** Highld
217 H2 **Rosehearty** Abers
122 C4 **Rose Hill** Lancs
214 E2 **Roseisle** Moray
20 C5 **Roselands** E Susx
49 G5 **Rosemarket** Pembks
213 H3 **Rosemarkie** Highld
25 J7 **Rosemary Lane** Devon
195 J7 **Rosemount** P & K
4 E3 **Rosenannon** Cnwll
177 J6 **Rosewell** Mdloth
141 K3 **Roseworth** S on T
138 D4 **Rosgill** Cumb
208 D5 **Roskhill** Highld
148 B6 **Rosley** Cumb
177 H5 **Roslin** Mdloth
86 B1 **Rosliston** Derbys
174 B2 **Rosneath** Ag & B
146 B6 **Ross** D & G
98 A2 **Rossett** Wrexhm
132 D8 **Rossett Green** N York
115 L2 **Rossington** Donc
174 E4 **Rossland** Rens
54 E4 **Ross-on-Wye** Herefs
231 J7 **Roster** Highld
113 H5 **Rostherne** Ches
137 H4 **Rosthwaite** Cumb
100 C4 **Roston** Derbys
176 F2 **Rosyth** Fife
158 D2 **Rothbury** Nthumb
87 J1 **Rotherby** Leics
32 F7 **Rotherfield** E Susx
42 B4 **Rotherfield Greys** Oxon
42 B4 **Rotherfield Peppard** Oxon
115 H3 **Rotherham** Rothm
73 K3 **Rothersthorpe** Nhants
30 B1 **Rotherwick** Hants
215 G4 **Rothes** Moray
173 J5 **Rothesay** Ag & B
216 E6 **Rothiebrisbane** Abers
215 M5 **Rothiemay** Moray

204 B4 **Rothiemurchus Lodge** Highld
216 D7 **Rothienorman** Abers
87 H2 **Rothley** Leics
216 D7 **Rothmaise** Abers
123 L5 **Rothwell** Leeds
117 J2 **Rothwell** Lincs
88 B7 **Rothwell** Nhants
196 B3 **Rottal Lodge** Angus
19 K5 **Rottingdean** Br & H
136 D5 **Rottington** Cumb
155 H6 **Roucan** D & G
105 K7 **Rougham** Norfk
77 K3 **Rougham Green** Suffk
34 F3 **Rough Common** Kent
205 H3 **Roughpark** Abers
118 C8 **Roughton** Lincs
106 F5 **Roughton** Norfk
84 D5 **Roughton** Shrops
60 F5 **Roundbush Green** Essex
13 K1 **Roundham** Somset
123 L3 **Roundhay** Leeds
40 A7 **Roundway** Wilts
196 C6 **Roundyhill** Angus
13 H4 **Rousdon** Devon
57 J3 **Rousham** Oxon
71 H4 **Rous Lench** Worcs
173 L6 **Rousternburn** N Ayrs
126 D3 **Routh** E R Yk
129 K2 **Row** Cumb
156 D6 **Rowanburn** D & G
183 L7 **Rowardennan Hotel** Stirlg
183 L7 **Rowardennan Lodge** Stirlg
114 A4 **Rowarth** Derbys
38 C8 **Rowberrow** Somset
39 L7 **Rowde** Wilts
109 L6 **Rowen** Conwy
149 H3 **Rowfoot** Nthumb
62 B4 **Rowhedge** Essex
72 B2 **Rowington** Warwks
114 E6 **Rowland** Derbys
17 K1 **Rowland's Castle** Hants
150 E4 **Rowland's Gill** Gatesd
30 D3 **Rowledge** Surrey
150 D5 **Rowley** Dur
126 B4 **Rowley** E R Yk
86 D6 **Rowley Green** Covtry
85 H6 **Rowley Regis** Sandw
54 A3 **Rowlstone** Herefs
31 H4 **Rowly** Surrey
17 H3 **Rowner** Hants
71 J1 **Rowney Green** Worcs
29 G7 **Rownhams** Hants
136 E4 **Rowrah** Cumb
58 D4 **Rowsham** Bucks
114 E7 **Rowsley** Derbys
103 H2 **Rowston** Lincs
112 C8 **Rowton** Ches
98 E8 **Rowton** Wrekin
167 L4 **Roxburgh** Border
125 L6 **Roxby** N Linc
75 G4 **Roxton** Beds
61 G6 **Roxwell** Essex
192 D1 **Roy Bridge** Highld
60 C6 **Roydon** Essex
92 D7 **Roydon** Norfk
105 H7 **Roydon** Norfk
60 C6 **Roydon Hamlet** Essex
124 B7 **Royston** Barns
75 L6 **Royston** Herts
122 D8 **Royton** Oldham
236 e6 **Rozel** Jersey
97 L4 **Ruabon** Wrexhm
188 D6 **Ruaig** Ag & B
4 D7 **Ruan Lanihorne** Cnwll
3 J7 **Ruan Major** Cnwll
3 J7 **Ruan Minor** Cnwll

54 F4 **Ruardean** Gloucs
54 F5 **Ruardean Hill** Gloucs
54 F5 **Ruardean Woodside** Gloucs
85 H7 **Rubery** Birm
233 c9 **Rubha Ban** W Isls
69 J6 **Ruckhall** Herefs
34 D7 **Ruckinge** Kent
83 K4 **Ruckley** Shrops
141 L6 **Rudby** N York
150 E2 **Rudchester** Nthumb
101 L6 **Ruddington** Notts
27 J2 **Rudge** Somset
38 F3 **Rudgeway** S Glos
31 H5 **Rudgwick** W Susx
112 F6 **Rudheath** Ches
61 K7 **Rudley Green** Essex
39 J6 **Rudloe** Wilts
37 J3 **Rudry** Caerph
135 H6 **Rudston** E R Yk
99 L2 **Rudyard** Staffs
167 J5 **Ruecastle** Border
120 F7 **Rufford** Lancs
124 D1 **Rufforth** York
87 G7 **Rugby** Warwks
100 B8 **Rugeley** Staffs
25 K6 **Ruishton** Somset
43 H3 **Ruislip** Gt Lon
215 J4 **Rumbach** Moray
185 L7 **Rumbling Bridge** P & K
93 H7 **Rumburgh** Suffk
4 D2 **Rumford** Cnwll
176 C3 **Rumford** Falk
37 K5 **Rumney** Cardif
112 D5 **Runcorn** Halton
18 B5 **Runcton** W Susx
90 E2 **Runcton Holme** Norfk
30 E3 **Runfold** Surrey
92 C3 **Runhall** Norfk
93 K2 **Runham** Norfk
25 H6 **Runnington** Somset
143 G4 **Runswick** N York
195 L3 **Runtaleave** Angus
46 C2 **Runwell** Essex
42 D5 **Ruscombe** Wokham
70 B7 **Rushall** Herefs
92 E6 **Rushall** Norfk
28 C1 **Rushall** Wilts
77 K3 **Rushbrooke** Suffk
83 K5 **Rushbury** Shrops
60 A2 **Rushden** Herts
74 D2 **Rushden** Nhants
91 K7 **Rushford** Norfk
62 E5 **Rush Green** Essex
45 K3 **Rush Green** Gt Lon
20 D3 **Rushlake Green** E Susx
93 K6 **Rushmere** Suffk
30 E4 **Rushmoor** Surrey
70 F1 **Rushock** Worcs
113 J3 **Rusholme** Manch
112 E8 **Rushton** Ches
88 B6 **Rushton** Nhants
113 L8 **Rushton Spencer** Staffs
70 E4 **Rushwick** Worcs
141 G2 **Rushyford** Dur
184 D7 **Ruskie** Stirlg
103 H3 **Ruskington** Lincs
129 H2 **Rusland** Cumb
31 K4 **Rusper** W Susx
54 F5 **Ruspidge** Gloucs
42 B3 **Russell's Water** Oxon
31 L4 **Russ Hill** Surrey
32 F5 **Rusthall** Kent
18 E5 **Rustington** W Susx
134 E3 **Ruston** N York
135 G6 **Ruston Parva** E R Yk
143 H5 **Ruswarp** N York
167 K4 **Rutherford** Border

175 H6 **Rutherglen** S Lans
4 F3 **Ruthernbridge** Cnwll
97 H2 **Ruthin** Denbgs
207 H4 **Ruthrieston** C Aber
215 L5 **Ruthven** Abers
195 L6 **Ruthven** Angus
203 H5 **Ruthven** Highld
195 L6 **Ruthven House** Angus
4 E4 **Ruthvoes** Cnwll
147 J2 **Ruthwell** D & G
98 B7 **Ruyton-XI-Towns** Shrops
158 C7 **Ryal** Nthumb
13 K4 **Ryall** Dorset
70 F6 **Ryall** Worcs
33 H2 **Ryarsh** Kent
137 K6 **Rydal** Cumb
17 H4 **Ryde** IoW
21 H2 **Rye** E Susx
21 H2 **Rye Foreign** E Susx
70 D7 **Rye Street** Worcs
88 F2 **Ryhall** Rutlnd
124 B7 **Ryhill** Wakefd
151 K4 **Ryhope** Sundld
117 G5 **Ryland** Lincs
101 K5 **Rylands** Notts
131 H7 **Rylstone** N York
14 B1 **Ryme Intrinseca** Dorset
124 E3 **Ryther** N York
150 E3 **Ryton** Gatesd
84 D3 **Ryton** Shrops
86 E8 **Ryton-on-Dunsmore** Warwks

S

122 B3 **Sabden** Lancs
60 B4 **Sacombe** Herts
151 G5 **Sacriston** Dur
141 H4 **Sadberge** Darltn
161 K3 **Saddell** Ag & B
87 J5 **Saddington** Leics
90 E1 **Saddle Bow** Norfk
19 H4 **Saddlescombe** W Susx
76 D6 **Saffron Walden** Essex
49 H6 **Sageston** Pembks
91 K3 **Saham Hills** Norfk
91 K3 **Saham Toney** Norfk
98 C1 **Saighton** Ches
179 J5 **St Abbs** Border
178 E5 **St Agnes** Border
3 J2 **St Agnes** Cnwll
59 J6 **St Albans** Herts
4 C5 **St Allen** Cnwll
236 c3 **St Andrew** Guern
187 H4 **St Andrews** Fife
187 H4 **St Andrew's Botanic Gardens** Fife
37 H6 **St Andrew's Major** V Glam
13 L4 **St Andrews Well** Dorset
120 D5 **St Anne's** Lancs
155 J4 **St Ann's** D & G
6 B2 **St Ann's Chapel** Cnwll
6 F6 **St Ann's Chapel** Devon
3 K6 **St Anthony** Cnwll
20 D5 **St Anthony's Hill** E Susx
38 D2 **St Arvans** Mons
110 E6 **St Asaph** Denbgs
36 F6 **St Athan** V Glam
236 b7 **St Aubin** Jersey
4 F5 **St Austell** Cnwll
136 D5 **St Bees** Cumb
5 G5 **St Blazey** Cnwll

167 J3 **St Boswells** Border
236 b7 **St Brelade** Jersey
236 b7 **St Brelade's Bay** Jersey
4 F2 **St Breock** Cnwll
5 H1 **St Breward** Cnwll
54 E6 **St Briavels** Gloucs
36 D5 **St Bride's Major** V Glam
37 H5 **St Brides super-Ely** V Glam
37 L4 **St Brides Wentlooge** Newpt
6 C4 **St Budeaux** C Plym
71 K6 **Saintbury** Gloucs
2 D6 **St Buryan** Cnwll
183 G6 **St Catherines** Ag & B
55 J7 **St Chloe** Gloucs
50 C3 **St Clears** Carmth
5 K3 **St Cleer** Cnwll
4 D6 **St Clement** Cnwll
236 e8 **St Clement** Jersey
9 G7 **St Clether** Cnwll
173 H5 **St Colmac** Ag & B
4 E3 **St Columb Major** Cnwll
4 D4 **St Columb Minor** Cnwll
4 E4 **St Columb Road** Cnwll
217 K2 **St Combs** Abers
93 G6 **St Cross South Elmham** Suffk
197 J4 **St Cyrus** Abers
185 K4 **St David's** P & K
48 C3 **St David's** Pembks
3 J3 **St Day** Cnwll
4 E4 **St Dennis** Cnwll
65 G5 **St Dogmaels** Pembks
6 B3 **St Dominick** Cnwll
36 E6 **St Donats** V Glam
4 F1 **St Endellion** Cnwll
4 D4 **St Enoder** Cnwll
4 D6 **St Erme** Cnwll
6 B4 **St Erney** Cnwll
2 F4 **St Erth** Cnwll
3 G4 **St Erth Praze** Cnwll
4 D2 **St Ervan** Cnwll
4 F6 **St Ewe** Cnwll
37 H5 **St Fagans** Cardif
37 H5 **St Fagans Welsh Life Museum** Cardif
217 K4 **St Fergus** Abers
184 F3 **St Fillans** P & K
49 J7 **St Florence** Pembks
8 F5 **St Gennys** Cnwll
110 D6 **St George** Conwy
38 B7 **St Georges** N Som
37 H5 **St George's** V Glam
6 A4 **St Germans** Cnwll
23 H7 **St Giles in the Wood** Devon
9 K6 **St Giles-on-the-Heath** Devon
81 L8 **St Harmon** Powys
140 F2 **St Helen Auckland** Dur
17 J5 **St Helens** IoW
112 D3 **St Helens** St Hel
44 E6 **St Helier** Gt Lon
236 d7 **St Helier** Jersey
2 F5 **St Hilary** Cnwll
36 F5 **St Hilary** V Glam
59 K3 **St Ippollitts** Herts
48 E6 **St Ishmael's** Pembks
4 E2 **St Issey** Cnwll
5 L3 **St Ive** Cnwll
75 K1 **St Ives** Cambs
2 F3 **St Ives** Cnwll
73 L3 **St James's End** Nhants

93 G7 **St James South Elmham** Suffk
6 B5 **St John** Cnwll
236 c5 **St John** Jersey
237 b5 **St John's** IoM
32 F3 **St Johns** Kent
43 G8 **St Johns** Surrey
70 E4 **St Johns** Worcs
23 H5 **St John's Chapel** Devon
149 M7 **St John's Chapel** Dur
90 D2 **St John's Fen End** Norfk
165 J3 **St John's Kirk** S Lans
154 B6 **St John's Town of Dalry** D & G
44 F4 **St John's Wood** Gt Lon
237 d3 **St Jude's** IoM
2 C5 **St Just** Cnwll
4 D8 **St Just-in-Roseland** Cnwll
216 F7 **St Katherines** Abers
3 K6 **St Keverne** Cnwll
5 G1 **St Kew** Cnwll
5 G2 **St Kew Highway** Cnwll
5 K4 **St Keyne** Cnwll
62 A6 **St Lawrence** Essex
17 G6 **St Lawrence** IoW
236 c6 **St Lawrence** Jersey
35 K2 **St Lawrence** Kent
58 E6 **St Leonards** Bucks
15 L2 **St Leonards** Dorset
20 F4 **St Leonards** E Susx
2 C6 **St Levan** Cnwll
37 H6 **St Lythans** V Glam
5 G2 **St Mabyn** Cnwll
186 C3 **St Madoes** P & K
69 G7 **St Margarets** Herefs
60 B5 **St Margarets** Herts
35 K5 **St Margaret's at Cliffe** Kent
234 C7 **St Margaret's Hope** Ork
93 G6 **St Margaret South Elmham** Suffk
237 c6 **St Marks** IoM
5 K5 **St Martin** Cnwll
236 d3 **St Martin** Guern
236 e6 **St Martin** Jersey
186 B2 **St Martin's** P & K
97 L5 **St Martins** Shrops
236 b6 **St Mary** Jersey
29 H2 **St Mary Bourne** Hants
7 L3 **St Marychurch** Torbay
36 F6 **St Mary Church** V Glam
45 J6 **St Mary Cray** Gt Lon
21 L1 **St Mary in the Marsh** Kent
234 c6 **St Mary's** Ork
21 L1 **St Mary's Bay** Kent
46 D5 **St Mary's Hoo** Medway
54 C5 **St Maughans Green** Mons
3 L5 **St Mawes** Cnwll
4 D3 **St Mawgan** Cnwll
6 B3 **St Mellion** Cnwll
37 K4 **St Mellons** Cardif
4 D2 **St Merryn** Cnwll
4 F5 **St Mewan** Cnwll
4 F7 **St Michael Caerhays** Cnwll
25 L5 **St Michael Church** Somset
4 D7 **St Michael Penkevil** Cnwll
34 B7 **St Michaels** Kent
69 L2 **St Michaels** Worcs

120 F3 **St Michael's on Wyre** Lancs
4 F1 **St Minver** Cnwll
187 H6 **St Monans** Fife
5 J3 **St Neot** Cnwll
75 H3 **St Neots** Cambs
64 C7 **St Nicholas** Pembks
37 H5 **St Nicholas** V Glam
47 L6 **St Nicholas at Wade** Kent
185 G8 **St Ninians** Stirlg
93 J4 **St Olaves** Norfk
62 D5 **St Osyth** Essex
236 b6 **St Ouen** Jersey
54 D3 **St Owens Cross** Herefs
45 J6 **St Pauls Cray** Gt Lon
59 K4 **St Paul's Walden** Herts
236 b6 **St Peter** Jersey
236 d3 **St Peter Port** Guern
236 b3 **St Peter's** Guern
35 K2 **St Peter's** Kent
5 J3 **St Pinnock** Cnwll
163 J5 **St Quivox** S Ayrs
236 d2 **St Sampson** Guern
236 c3 **St Saviour** Guern
236 d7 **St Saviour** Jersey
4 E5 **St Stephen** Cnwll
6 B4 **St Stephens** Cnwll
9 J7 **St Stephens** Cnwll
4 E5 **St Stephen's Coombe** Cnwll
8 E8 **St Teath** Cnwll
5 G1 **St Tudy** Cnwll
48 F7 **St Twynnells** Pembks
5 J5 **St Veep** Cnwll
197 G7 **St Vigeans** Angus
4 F3 **St Wenn** Cnwll
54 D3 **St Weonards** Herefs
191 L6 **Salachail** Ag & B
7 H7 **Salcombe** Devon
12 F5 **Salcombe Regis** Devon
61 M5 **Salcott-cum-Virley** Essex
113 H3 **Sale** Traffd
118 F5 **Saleby** Lincs
71 G3 **Sale Green** Worcs
20 F2 **Salehurst** E Susx
80 F6 **Salem** Cerdgn
95 J2 **Salem** Gwynd
190 C7 **Salen** Ag & B
190 D4 **Salen** Highld
74 D6 **Salford** Beds
56 F3 **Salford** Oxon
113 J2 **Salford** Salfd
71 J4 **Salford Priors** Warwks
32 B4 **Salfords** Surrey
93 G1 **Salhouse** Norfk
185 L8 **Saline** Fife
28 C5 **Salisbury** Wilts
28 C5 **Salisbury Cathedral** Wilts
28 B3 **Salisbury Plain** Wilts
148 F7 **Salkeld Dykes** Cumb
106 D7 **Salle** Norfk
118 D6 **Salmonby** Lincs
56 B4 **Salperton** Gloucs
175 L5 **Salsburgh** N Lans
99 L6 **Salt** Staffs
123 H3 **Saltaire** Brad
6 B4 **Saltash** Cnwll
223 G7 **Saltburn** Highld
142 E3 **Saltburn-by-the-Sea** R & Cl
102 D7 **Saltby** Leics
163 G2 **Saltcoats** N Ayrs
19 K5 **Saltdean** Br & H
136 D3 **Salterbeck** Cumb
122 D2 **Salterforth** Lancs
28 C4 **Salterton** Wilts

118 F3 **Saltfleet** Lincs
118 F4 **Saltfleetby All Saints** Lincs
118 F3 **Saltfleetby St Clement** Lincs
118 F4 **Saltfleetby St Peter** Lincs
39 G6 **Salford** BaNES
106 C4 **Salthouse** Norfk
125 J3 **Saltmarshe** E R Yk
111 L8 **Saltney** Flints
133 L4 **Salton** N York
23 G6 **Saltrens** Devon
34 F7 **Saltwood** Kent
18 F5 **Salvington** W Susx
70 F3 **Salwarpe** Worcs
13 L3 **Salwayash** Dorset
71 J3 **Sambourne** Warwks
99 G7 **Sambrook** Wrekin
121 H4 **Samlesbury** Lancs
25 H7 **Sampford Arundel** Somset
25 G3 **Sampford Brett** Somset
10 F5 **Sampford Courtenay** Devon
25 H7 **Sampford Moor** Somset
25 G8 **Sampford Peverell** Devon
6 D2 **Sampford Spiney** Devon
234 G5 **Samsonlane** Ork
178 B4 **Samuelston** E Loth
170 E4 **Sanaigmore** Ag & B
2 D5 **Sancreed** Cnwll
125 L3 **Sancton** E R Yk
199 L5 **Sandaig** Highld
123 L6 **Sandal Magna** Wakefd
199 G7 **Sandavore** Highld
234 d4 **Sanday Airport** Ork
99 H1 **Sandbach** Ches
173 K3 **Sandbank** Ag & B
15 K5 **Sandbanks** Poole
216 B2 **Sandend** Abers
45 G7 **Sanderstead** Gt Lon
139 G4 **Sandford** Cumb
11 J4 **Sandford** Devon
15 H5 **Sandford** Dorset
15 M3 **Sandford** Hants
17 G6 **Sandford** IoW
38 B8 **Sandford** N Som
164 E2 **Sandford** S Lans
57 K7 **Sandford-on-Thames** Oxon
26 F7 **Sandford Orcas** Dorset
57 H3 **Sandford St Martin** Oxon
35 G7 **Sandgate** Kent
217 H2 **Sandhaven** Abers
144 D5 **Sandhead** D & G
124 B3 **Sand Hills** Leeds
57 K6 **Sandhills** Oxon
30 F4 **Sandhills** Surrey
150 B2 **Sandhoe** Nthumb
182 E7 **Sandhole** Ag & B
125 J3 **Sand Hole** E R Yk
125 J4 **Sandholme** E R Yk
42 F7 **Sandhurst** Br For
55 J4 **Sandhurst** Gloucs
33 K7 **Sandhurst** Kent
132 F3 **Sandhutton** N York
133 L2 **Sand Hutton** N York
101 J5 **Sandiacre** Derbys
119 G5 **Sandilands** Lincs
28 C7 **Sandleheath** Hants
57 J7 **Sandleigh** Oxon
27 H6 **Sandley** Dorset
235 H6 **Sandness** Shet
61 H6 **Sandon** Essex

75 K7	**Sandon** Herts	
99 L6	**Sandon** Staffs	
99 L6	**Sandon Bank** Staffs	
17 H5	**Sandown** IoW	
5 K4	**Sandplace** Cnwll	
59 K6	**Sandridge** Herts	
105 H6	**Sandringham** Norfk	
143 H5	**Sandsend** N York	
125 H8	**Sandtoft** N Linc	
34 B5	**Sandway** Kent	
35 J3	**Sandwich** Kent	
235 C7	**Sandwick** Shet	
232 g2	**Sandwick** W Isls	
136 D4	**Sandwith** Cumb	
75 H5	**Sandy** Beds	
155 L4	**Sandyford** D & G	
7 K2	**Sandygate** Devon	
237 d3	**Sandygate** IoM	
146 F4	**Sandyhills** D & G	
129 J6	**Sandylands** Lancs	
39 L6	**Sandy Lane** Wilts	
11 G6	**Sandy Park** Devon	
228 F3	**Sangobeg** Highld	
228 F3	**Sangomore** Highld	
70 E2	**Sankyn's Green** Worcs	
189 K3	**Sanna Bay** Highld	
232 g2	**Sanndabhaig** W Isls	
162 C1	**Sannox** N Ayrs	
164 F7	**Sanquhar** D & G	
136 F6	**Santon Bridge** Cumb	
91 J6	**Santon Downham** Suffk	
86 F5	**Sapcote** Leics	
70 C2	**Sapey Common** Herefs	
91 K7	**Sapiston** Suffk	
55 L7	**Sapperton** Gloucs	
103 G5	**Sapperton** Lincs	
104 B6	**Saracen's Head** Lincs	
231 L6	**Sarclet** Highld	
17 G2	**Sarisbury** Hants	
94 D6	**Sarn** Gwynd	
81 K4	**Sarn** Powys	
82 E5	**Sarn** Powys	
65 K4	**Sarnau** Cerdgn	
82 E1	**Sarnau** Powys	
69 H4	**Sarnesfield** Herefs	
51 H3	**Saron** Carmth	
109 G7	**Saron** Gwynd	
59 H7	**Sarratt** Herts	
47 L6	**Sarre** Kent	
56 F4	**Sarsden** Oxon	
150 E6	**Satley** Dur	
23 L6	**Satterleigh** Devon	
129 H2	**Satterthwaite** Cumb	
206 D3	**Sauchen** Abers	
186 C2	**Saucher** P & K	
197 G3	**Sauchieburn** Abers	
55 H6	**Saul** Gloucs	
116 C4	**Saundby** Notts	
49 K6	**Saundersfoot** Pembks	
58 C7	**Saunderton** Bucks	
23 G4	**Saunton** Devon	
118 E7	**Sausthorpe** Lincs	
123 K6	**Savile Town** Kirk	
73 G2	**Sawbridge** Warwks	
60 D5	**Sawbridgeworth** Herts	
134 E3	**Sawdon** N York	
122 B2	**Sawley** Lancs	
132 C6	**Sawley** N York	
76 C5	**Sawston** Cambs	
89 H6	**Sawtry** Cambs	
102 D8	**Saxby** Leics	
117 G4	**Saxby** Lincs	
126 B7	**Saxby All Saints** N Linc	
102 B7	**Saxelbye** Leics	
78 C3	**Saxham Street** Suffk	
116 E6	**Saxilby** Lincs	
106 B5	**Saxlingham** Norfk	
92 F4	**Saxlingham Green** Norfk	
92 F4	**Saxlingham Nethergate** Norfk	
92 E4	**Saxlingham Thorpe** Norfk	
79 H2	**Saxmundham** Suffk	
102 B4	**Saxondale** Notts	
76 F3	**Saxon Street** Cambs	
78 F2	**Saxtead** Suffk	
78 F2	**Saxtead Green** Suffk	
78 F2	**Saxtead Little Green** Suffk	
106 D6	**Saxthorpe** Norfk	
124 D3	**Saxton** N York	
19 H3	**Sayers Common** W Susx	
133 K5	**Scackleton** N York	
137 H5	**Scafell Pike** Cumb	
116 A3	**Scaftworth** Notts	
134 C5	**Scagglethorpe** N York	
180 E8	**Scalasaig** Ag & B	
125 K5	**Scalby** E R Yk	
134 F2	**Scalby** N York	
73 L1	**Scaldwell** Nhants	
148 D3	**Scaleby** Cumb	
148 D3	**Scalebyhill** Cumb	
129 G5	**Scales** Cumb	
137 K2	**Scales** Cumb	
102 C7	**Scalford** Leics	
142 F4	**Scaling** N York	
235 c6	**Scalloway** Shet	
118 C5	**Scamblesby** Lincs	
191 G2	**Scamodale** Highld	
134 D4	**Scampston** N York	
116 F5	**Scampton** Lincs	
212 F6	**Scaniport** Highld	
123 G7	**Scapegoat Hill** Kirk	
135 G2	**Scarborough** N York	
4 E5	**Scarcewater** Cnwll	
115 J7	**Scarcliffe** Derbys	
124 B3	**Scarcroft** Leeds	
231 J2	**Scarfskerry** Highld	
140 D5	**Scargill** Dur	
188 D7	**Scarinish** Ag & B	
120 E7	**Scarisbrick** Lancs	
91 L2	**Scarning** Norfk	
102 B4	**Scarrington** Notts	
118 C1	**Scartho** NE Lin	
235 c4	**Scatsta Airport** Shet	
116 F1	**Scawby** N Linc	
115 K1	**Scawsby** Donc	
115 K1	**Scawthorpe** Donc	
133 H3	**Scawton** N York	
19 K2	**Scayne's Hill** W Susx	
53 H3	**Scethrog** Powys	
123 H8	**Scholes** Kirk	
124 B3	**Scholes** Leeds	
115 H3	**Scholes** Rothm	
112 E1	**Scholes** Wigan	
123 K7	**Scissett** Kirk	
64 C7	**Scleddau** Pembks	
115 L5	**Scofton** Notts	
92 D7	**Scole** Norfk	
186 B3	**Scone** P & K	
209 H7	**Sconser** Highld	
186 F6	**Scoonie** Fife	
103 H2	**Scopwick** Lincs	
220 C3	**Scoraig** Highld	
126 C2	**Scorborough** E R Yk	
3 J3	**Scorrier** Cnwll	
121 G7	**Scorton** Lancs	
141 G7	**Scorton** N York	
148 D4	**Scotby** Cumb	
140 F6	**Scotch Corner** N York	
129 K7	**Scotforth** Lancs	
117 G6	**Scothern** Lincs	
186 C6	**Scotlandwell** P & K	
231 G4	**Scotscalder Station** Highld	
158 C5	**Scot's Gap** Nthumb	
206 B2	**Scotsmill** Abers	
174 F5	**Scotstoun** C Glas	
150 F3	**Scotswood** N u Ty	
116 E2	**Scotter** Lincs	
116 E2	**Scotterthorpe** Lincs	
116 E2	**Scotton** Lincs	
132 E7	**Scotton** N York	
140 F7	**Scotton** N York	
92 B4	**Scoulton** Norfk	
228 B6	**Scourie** Highld	
228 B6	**Scourie More** Highld	
235 C7	**Scousburgh** Shet	
231 G2	**Scrabster** Highld	
167 K5	**Scraesburgh** Border	
104 C4	**Scrane End** Lincs	
87 J3	**Scraptoft** Leics	
93 K1	**Scratby** Norfk	
133 L7	**Scrayingham** N York	
103 H4	**Scredington** Lincs	
118 F7	**Scremby** Lincs	
179 L8	**Scremerston** Nthumb	
102 B4	**Screveton** Notts	
132 E7	**Scriven** N York	
115 M4	**Scrooby** Notts	
100 D6	**Scropton** Derbys	
103 L2	**Scrub Hill** Lincs	
195 K5	**Scruschloch** Angus	
132 D2	**Scruton** N York	
229 J4	**Scullomie** Highld	
105 L6	**Sculthorpe** Norfk	
125 K7	**Scunthorpe** N Linc	
13 L2	**Seaborough** Dorset	
35 G7	**Seabrook** Kent	
151 J3	**Seaburn** Sundld	
124 B4	**Seacroft** Leeds	
209 G5	**Seafield** Highld	
176 B5	**Seafield** W Loth	
20 A6	**Seaford** E Susx	
111 K3	**Seaforth** Sefton	
101 L8	**Seagrave** Leics	
151 K5	**Seaham** Dur	
169 J2	**Seahouses** Nthumb	
32 F2	**Seal** Kent	
30 E2	**Seale** Surrey	
134 F3	**Seamer** N York	
142 B5	**Seamer** N York	
173 L8	**Seamill** N Ayrs	
107 J6	**Sea Palling** Norfk	
117 H1	**Searby** Lincs	
47 H6	**Seasalter** Kent	
136 E6	**Seascale** Cumb	
137 H7	**Seathwaite** Cumb	
137 H3	**Seatoller** Cumb	
5 L5	**Seaton** Cnwll	
136 E2	**Seaton** Cumb	
13 G4	**Seaton** Devon	
126 E2	**Seaton** E R Yk	
35 G3	**Seaton** Kent	
159 H6	**Seaton** Nthumb	
88 C4	**Seaton** Rutlnd	
142 B2	**Seaton Carew** Hartpl	
159 H6	**Seaton Delaval** Nthumb	
125 J3	**Seaton Ross** E R Yk	
159 H6	**Seaton Sluice** Nthumb	
13 K4	**Seatown** Dorset	
142 C7	**Seave Green** N York	
17 J4	**Seaview** IoW	
147 K4	**Seaville** Cumb	
26 B7	**Seavington St Mary** Somset	
26 B7	**Seavington St Michael** Somset	
148 C6	**Sebergham** Cumb	
86 C3	**Seckington** Warwks	
130 C2	**Sedbergh** Cumb	
38 D2	**Sedbury** Gloucs	
131 G2	**Sedbusk** N York	
71 H6	**Sedgeberrow** Worcs	
102 D5	**Sedgebrook** Lincs	
141 J2	**Sedgefield** Dur	
105 H5	**Sedgeford** Norfk	
27 K5	**Sedgehill** Wilts	
85 G5	**Sedgley** Dudley	
129 L3	**Sedgwick** Cumb	
20 F3	**Sedlescombe** E Susx	
58 D5	**Sedrup** Bucks	
39 L7	**Seend** Wilts	
39 L7	**Seend Cleeve** Wilts	
42 F3	**Seer Green** Bucks	
93 G4	**Seething** Norfk	
111 K2	**Sefton** Sefton	
99 K7	**Seighford** Staffs	
109 H7	**Seion** Gwynd	
84 E4	**Seisdon** Staffs	
97 K5	**Selattyn** Shrops	
30 C5	**Selborne** Hants	
124 F4	**Selby** N York	
30 F7	**Selham** W Susx	
45 G6	**Selhurst** Gt Lon	
167 G4	**Selkirk** Border	
54 E3	**Sellack** Herefs	
235 d2	**Sellafirth** Shet	
34 E6	**Sellindge** Kent	
34 D4	**Selling** Kent	
39 L7	**Sells Green** Wilts	
85 J6	**Selly Oak** Birm	
20 B4	**Selmeston** E Susx	
45 G7	**Selsdon** Gt Lon	
55 J7	**Selsey** Gloucs	
18 B6	**Selsey** W Susx	
130 E4	**Selside** N York	
35 G5	**Selsted** Kent	
101 J2	**Selston** Notts	
24 E3	**Selworthy** Somset	
78 B5	**Semer** Suffk	
39 K7	**Semington** Wilts	
27 K6	**Semley** Wilts	
31 G1	**Send** Surrey	
37 H3	**Senghenydd** Caerph	
2 C6	**Sennen** Cnwll	
2 C6	**Sennen Cove** Cnwll	
52 E3	**Sennybridge** Powys	
133 G4	**Sessay** N York	
90 F2	**Setchey** Norfk	
177 L4	**Seton Mains** E Loth	
130 F6	**Settle** N York	
134 C5	**Settrington** N York	
25 J5	**Seven Ash** Somset	
56 B4	**Sevenhampton** Gloucs	
40 E3	**Sevenhampton** Swindn	
45 J3	**Seven Kings** Gt Lon	
32 F3	**Sevenoaks** Kent	
32 F3	**Sevenoaks Weald** Kent	
52 C6	**Seven Sisters** Neath	
61 M3	**Seven Star Green** Essex	
71 K7	**Seven Wells** Gloucs	
38 D4	**Severn Beach** S Glos	
70 F5	**Severn Stoke** Worcs	
34 D6	**Sevington** Kent	
76 E6	**Sewards End** Essex	
59 G4	**Sewell** Beds	
135 J5	**Sewerby** E R Yk	
3 J5	**Seworgan** Cnwll	
102 E7	**Sewstern** Leics	
232 g1	**Sgiogarstaigh** W Isls	
58 A6	**Shabbington** Bucks	
86 D3	**Shackerstone** Leics	
30 F3	**Shackleford** Surrey	
232 f1	**Shader** W Isls	
151 H6	**Shadforth** Dur	
93 J6	**Shadingfield** Suffk	
34 C7	**Shadoxhurst** Kent	
91 L6	**Shadwell** Norfk	
76 B6	**Shaftenhoe End** Herts	
27 K6	**Shaftesbury** Dorset	
124 F3	**Shafton** Barns	
113 G2	**Shakerley** Wigan	

40 F7	**Shalbourne** Wilts
30 B3	**Shalden** Hants
7 L2	**Shaldon** Devon
16 E5	**Shalfleet** IoW
61 H3	**Shalford** Essex
31 G3	**Shalford** Surrey
61 H3	**Shalford Green** Essex
34 E4	**Shalmsford Street** Kent
73 J7	**Shalstone** Bucks
31 G3	**Shamley Green** Surrey
196 D4	**Shandford** Angus
174 B2	**Shandon** Ag & B
223 J6	**Shandwick** Highld
87 K4	**Shangton** Leics
17 H6	**Shanklin** IoW
138 E4	**Shap** Cumb
15 H3	**Shapwick** Dorset
26 B4	**Shapwick** Somset
101 H6	**Shardlow** Derbys
85 G3	**Shareshill** Staffs
124 B6	**Sharlston** Wakefd
74 E3	**Sharnbrook** Beds
86 F5	**Sharnford** Leics
121 G4	**Sharoe Green** Lancs
132 E5	**Sharow** N York
59 H2	**Sharpenhoe** Beds
158 B2	**Sharperton** Nthumb
54 F7	**Sharpness** Gloucs
106 C5	**Sharrington** Norfk
84 E7	**Shatterford** Worcs
6 D3	**Shaugh Prior** Devon
99 G3	**Shavington** Ches
122 D8	**Shaw** Oldham
41 J6	**Shaw** W Berk
39 K7	**Shaw** Wilts
232 e2	**Shawbost** W Isls
98 E7	**Shawbury** Shrops
87 G7	**Shawell** Leics
29 J6	**Shawford** Hants
154 F6	**Shawhead** D & G
132 C6	**Shaw Mills** N York
175 K7	**Shawsburn** S Lans
147 H2	**Shearington** D & G
87 J5	**Shearsby** Leics
25 L5	**Shearston** Somset
10 C3	**Shebbear** Devon
99 H7	**Shebdon** Staffs
230 E3	**Shebster** Highld
175 G6	**Sheddens** E Rens
29 K8	**Shedfield** Hants
100 C1	**Sheen** Staffs
123 H6	**Sheepridge** Kirk
123 L4	**Sheepscar** Leeds
55 K6	**Sheepscombe** Gloucs
6 E3	**Sheepstor** Devon
10 C4	**Sheepwash** Devon
86 D3	**Sheepy Magna** Leics
86 D3	**Sheepy Parva** Leics
60 E5	**Sheering** Essex
46 F5	**Sheerness** Kent
43 H7	**Sheerwater** Surrey
30 C6	**Sheet** Hants
115 G4	**Sheffield** Sheff
75 G6	**Shefford** Beds
228 B4	**Sheigra** Highld
83 L3	**Sheinton** Shrops
83 H7	**Shelderton** Shrops
85 L6	**Sheldon** Birm
114 D7	**Sheldon** Derbys
12 E2	**Sheldon** Devon
34 D4	**Sheldwich** Kent
92 D6	**Shelfanger** Norfk
102 A4	**Shelford** Notts
123 J7	**Shelley** Kirk
78 B6	**Shelley** Suffk
40 F2	**Shellingford** Oxon
60 F6	**Shellow Bowells** Essex
70 D2	**Shelsley Beauchamp** Worcs
70 C2	**Shelsley Walsh** Worcs
74 F2	**Shelton** Beds
92 F5	**Shelton** Norfk
102 C4	**Shelton** Notts
99 J5	**Shelton Under Harley** Staffs
83 G4	**Shelve** Shrops
69 K6	**Shelwick** Herefs
45 L2	**Shenfield** Essex
72 D6	**Shenington** Oxon
59 K7	**Shenley** Herts
74 B7	**Shenley Brook End** M Keyn
74 B7	**Shenley Church End** M Keyn
69 H6	**Shenmore** Herefs
145 H3	**Shennanton** D & G
85 K3	**Shenstone** Staffs
84 F8	**Shenstone** Worcs
86 E4	**Shenton** Leics
59 L4	**Shephall** Herts
44 E4	**Shepherd's Bush** Gt Lon
35 H5	**Shepherdswell** Kent
123 J8	**Shepley** Kirk
43 H6	**Shepperton** Surrey
76 B5	**Shepreth** Cambs
101 J8	**Shepshed** Leics
26 B7	**Shepton Beauchamp** Somset
26 F3	**Shepton Mallet** Somset
27 G5	**Shepton Montague** Somset
33 K3	**Shepway** Kent
151 K7	**Sheraton** Dur
26 F7	**Sherborne** Dorset
56 D5	**Sherborne** Gloucs
26 E1	**Sherborne** Somset
29 L1	**Sherborne St John** Hants
72 C3	**Sherbourne** Warwks
151 H6	**Sherburn** Dur
134 E4	**Sherburn** N York
151 H6	**Sherburn Hill** Dur
124 D4	**Sherburn in Elmet** N York
31 H2	**Shere** Surrey
105 L6	**Shereford** Norfk
28 F6	**Sherfield English** Hants
42 B8	**Sherfield on Loddon** Hants
7 H6	**Sherford** Devon
84 D2	**Sheriffhales** Shrops
133 K6	**Sheriff Hutton** N York
106 E4	**Sheringham** Norfk
74 C5	**Sherington** M Keyn
105 H6	**Shernborne** Norfk
27 L4	**Sherrington** Wilts
39 J3	**Sherston** Wilts
101 K4	**Sherwood** C Nott
101 L2	**Sherwood Forest** Notts
175 H6	**Shettleston** C Glas
121 H8	**Shevington** Wigan
6 B5	**Sheviock** Cnwll
123 G5	**Shibden Head** Brad
16 F5	**Shide** IoW
168 B2	**Shidlaw** Nthumb
200 E2	**Shiel Bridge** Highld
210 C4	**Shieldaig** Highld
155 H5	**Shieldhill** D & G
176 B3	**Shieldhill** Falk
165 J2	**Shieldhill House Hotel** S Lans
175 K7	**Shields** N Lans
190 D3	**Shielfoot** Highld
196 C5	**Shielhill** Angus
173 L4	**Shielhill** Inver
84 D2	**Shifnal** Shrops
169 J7	**Shilbottle** Nthumb
141 G3	**Shildon** Dur
174 E6	**Shillford** E Rens
24 F6	**Shillingford** Devon
41 L2	**Shillingford** Oxon
11 K6	**Shillingford Abbot** Devon
11 K7	**Shillingford St George** Devon
14 F1	**Shillingstone** Dorset
75 G7	**Shillington** Beds
56 E6	**Shilton** Oxon
86 E6	**Shilton** Warwks
92 D6	**Shimpling** Norfk
77 J4	**Shimpling** Suffk
77 K4	**Shimpling Street** Suffk
151 H6	**Shincliffe** Dur
151 H4	**Shiney Row** Sundld
42 B6	**Shinfield** Wokham
225 L5	**Shinness** Highld
33 G3	**Shipbourne** Kent
91 L3	**Shipdham** Norfk
38 C8	**Shipham** Somset
7 K3	**Shiphay** Torbay
42 C5	**Shiplake** Oxon
123 H3	**Shipley** Brad
31 J6	**Shipley** W Susx
32 B5	**Shipley Bridge** Surrey
93 H5	**Shipmeadow** Suffk
41 J2	**Shippon** Oxon
72 B6	**Shipston on Stour** Warwks
56 B4	**Shipton** Gloucs
133 H7	**Shipton** N York
83 L5	**Shipton** Shrops
28 E3	**Shipton Bellinger** Hants
13 L4	**Shipton Gorge** Dorset
17 L3	**Shipton Green** W Susx
39 K3	**Shipton Moyne** Gloucs
57 J5	**Shipton-on-Cherwell** Oxon
125 K2	**Shiptonthorpe** E R Yk
56 F4	**Shipton-under-Wychwood** Oxon
42 B2	**Shirburn** Oxon
120 E7	**Shirdley Hill** Lancs
115 K7	**Shirebrook** Derbys
115 G3	**Shiregreen** Sheff
38 D5	**Shirehampton** Bristl
159 H7	**Shiremoor** N Tyne
38 C2	**Shirenewton** Mons
115 K5	**Shireoaks** Notts
101 H2	**Shirland** Derbys
29 H8	**Shirley** C Sotn
100 E4	**Shirley** Derbys
45 G6	**Shirley** Gt Lon
85 K7	**Shirley** Solhll
29 L8	**Shirrell Heath** Hants
172 E2	**Shirvan** Ag & B
23 J4	**Shirwell** Devon
162 B4	**Shiskine** N Ayrs
69 H3	**Shobdon** Herefs
11 K5	**Shobrooke** Devon
102 B7	**Shoby** Leics
98 C3	**Shocklach** Ches
46 F3	**Shoeburyness** Sthend
35 K4	**Sholden** Kent
16 F1	**Sholing** C Sotn
9 G2	**Shop** Cnwll
78 F2	**Shop Street** Suffk
45 G4	**Shoreditch** Gt Lon
25 K6	**Shoreditch** Somset
45 K7	**Shoreham** Kent
19 G5	**Shoreham Airport** W Susx
19 H5	**Shoreham-by-Sea** W Susx
29 L6	**Shorley** Hants
46 B5	**Shorne** Kent
20 A3	**Shortgate** E Susx
4 C6	**Shortlanesend** Cnwll
74 F5	**Shortstown** Beds
16 F5	**Shorwell** IoW
27 G1	**Shoscombe** BaNES
92 F4	**Shotesham** Norfk
46 C2	**Shotgate** Essex
78 F7	**Shotley** Suffk
150 D4	**Shotley Bridge** Dur
78 F7	**Shotley Gate** Suffk
78 F7	**Shotley Street** Suffk
34 D4	**Shottenden** Kent
71 L4	**Shottery** Warwks
72 E5	**Shotteswell** Warwks
79 G5	**Shottisham** Suffk
100 F3	**Shottle** Derbys
100 F3	**Shottlegate** Derbys
151 K6	**Shotton** Dur
111 J7	**Shotton** Flints
151 J6	**Shotton Colliery** Dur
176 B6	**Shotts** N Lans
111 K6	**Shotwick** Ches
214 F4	**Shougle** Moray
90 F2	**Shouldham** Norfk
90 F2	**Shouldham Thorpe** Norfk
70 E3	**Shoulton** Worcs
83 H1	**Shrawardine** Shrops
72 E5	**Shrawley** Worcs
72 B2	**Shrewley** Warwks
83 J2	**Shrewsbury** Shrops
28 B3	**Shrewton** Wilts
18 C5	**Shripney** W Susx
40 E3	**Shrivenham** Oxon
92 B5	**Shropham** Norfk
69 L6	**Shucknall** Herefs
76 E5	**Shudy Camps** Cambs
55 L4	**Shurdington** Gloucs
42 D5	**Shurlock Row** W & M
230 F4	**Shurrery** Highld
230 F4	**Shurrery Lodge** Highld
25 J3	**Shurton** Somset
86 B5	**Shustoke** Warwks
13 G3	**Shute** Devon
72 E6	**Shutford** Oxon
99 K7	**Shut Heath** Staffs
70 F7	**Shuthonger** Gloucs
73 K4	**Shutlanger** Nhants
85 B3	**Shuttington** Warwks
115 J6	**Shuttlewood** Derbys
122 B6	**Shuttleworth** Bury
232 e2	**Siabost** W Isls
232 f1	**Siadar** W Isls
87 K6	**Sibbertoft** Nhants
72 D6	**Sibford Ferris** Oxon
72 D6	**Sibford Gower** Oxon
77 H7	**Sible Hedingham** Essex
60 F7	**Sibley's Green** Essex
104 B3	**Sibsey** Lincs
89 G4	**Sibson** Cambs
86 D4	**Sibson** Leics
231 K5	**Sibster** Highld
102 C4	**Sibthorpe** Notts
116 B6	**Sibthorpe** Notts
79 H1	**Sibton** Suffk
77 K3	**Sicklesmere** Suffk
124 B2	**Sicklinghall** N York
12 E4	**Sidbury** Devon
84 C6	**Sidbury** Shrops
38 B8	**Sidcot** N Som
45 J5	**Sidcup** Gt Lon
113 J7	**Siddington** Ches
56 B7	**Siddington** Gloucs
106 F4	**Sidestrand** Norfk
12 E4	**Sidford** Devon
18 B6	**Sidlesham** W Susx
20 E4	**Sidley** E Susx
12 E5	**Sidmouth** Devon
126 E2	**Sigglesthorne** E R Yk
36 F6	**Sigingstone** V Glam

41 L7	**Silchester** Hants
87 H1	**Sileby** Leics
128 D3	**Silecroft** Cumb
92 D4	**Silfield** Norfk
114 F1	**Silkstone** Barns
114 F1	**Silkstone Common** Barns
151 J4	**Silksworth** Sundld
103 H4	**Silk Willoughby** Lincs
147 K4	**Silloth** Cumb
134 E2	**Silpho** N York
122 F2	**Silsden** Brad
74 F7	**Silsoe** Beds
27 H5	**Silton** Dorset
177 G6	**Silverburn** Mdloth
129 K4	**Silverdale** Lancs
99 J3	**Silverdale** Staffs
61 K4	**Silver End** Essex
216 E2	**Silverford** Abers
73 J5	**Silverstone** Nhants
12 B2	**Silverton** Devon
84 B7	**Silvington** Shrops
157 L7	**Simonburn** Nthumb
24 A4	**Simonsbath** Somset
25 H7	**Simons Burrow** Devon
122 B4	**Simonstone** Lancs
168 C1	**Simprim** Border
74 C7	**Simpson** M Keyn
48 F4	**Simpson Cross** Pembks
179 G7	**Sinclair's Hill** Border
163 L6	**Sinclairston** E Ayrs
132 E3	**Sinderby** N York
113 G4	**Sinderland Green** Traffd
42 C6	**Sindlesham** Wokham
101 G6	**Sinfin** C Derb
34 D6	**Singleton** Kent
120 E3	**Singleton** Lancs
18 B3	**Singleton** W Susx
46 A6	**Singlewell** Kent
205 K3	**Sinnarhard** Abers
134 B3	**Sinnington** N York
70 E3	**Sinton** Worcs
70 E3	**Sinton Green** Worcs
33 K5	**Sissinghurst** Kent
39 G5	**Siston** S Glos
3 H5	**Sithney** Cnwll
34 B3	**Sittingbourne** Kent
84 E5	**Six Ashes** Shrops
117 K4	**Sixhills** Lincs
76 E3	**Six Mile Bottom** Cambs
34 F5	**Sixmile Cottages** Kent
27 M7	**Sixpenny Handley** Dorset
129 K3	**Sizergh Castle** Cumb
234 d6	**Skaill** Ork
164 B6	**Skares** E Ayrs
207 G6	**Skateraw** Abers
178 F4	**Skateraw** E Loth
208 F5	**Skeabost** Highld
140 F6	**Skeeby** N York
87 L3	**Skeffington** Leics
127 J6	**Skeffling** E R Yk
101 J1	**Skegby** Notts
116 C7	**Skegby** Notts
119 H8	**Skegness** Lincs
223 H3	**Skelbo** Highld
223 H3	**Skelbo Street** Highld
134 D7	**Skelbrooke** Donc
104 B5	**Skeldyke** Lincs
116 F6	**Skellingthorpe** Lincs
124 E7	**Skellow** Donc
123 J7	**Skelmanthorpe** Kirk
112 C1	**Skelmersdale** Lancs
173 L5	**Skelmorlie** N Ayrs
229 L4	**Skelpick** Highld
154 E5	**Skelston** D & G
148 D7	**Skelton** Cumb
125 H5	**Skelton** E R Yk
132 E5	**Skelton** N York
142 E4	**Skelton** R & Cl
133 J7	**Skelton** York
137 K6	**Skelwith Bridge** Cumb
118 F7	**Skendleby** Lincs
206 E4	**Skene House** Abers
54 C4	**Skenfrith** Mons
135 G2	**Skerne** E R Yk
229 K3	**Skerray** Highld
228 C5	**Skerricha** Highld
129 K6	**Skerton** Lancs
86 E5	**Sketchley** Leics
51 J6	**Sketty** Swans
51 K6	**Skewen** Neath
133 K5	**Skewsby** N York
230 E3	**Skiall** Highld
126 C4	**Skidby** E R Yk
232 g1	**Skigersta** W Isls
24 F6	**Skilgate** Somset
102 E7	**Skillington** Lincs
147 K4	**Skinburness** Cumb
176 B2	**Skinflats** Falk
208 C5	**Skinidin** Highld
172 F6	**Skipness** Ag & B
156 C5	**Skipper's Bridge** D & G
135 J8	**Skipsea** E R Yk
122 E1	**Skipton** N York
132 E4	**Skipton-on-Swale** N York
125 G3	**Skipwith** N York
126 F3	**Skirlaugh** E R Yk
165 L2	**Skirling** Border
42 C5	**Skirmett** Bucks
134 B7	**Skirpenbeck** E R Yk
149 G7	**Skirwith** Cumb
231 L2	**Skirza** Highld
199 K2	**Skulamus** Highld
208 F6	**Skye** Highld
61 L4	**Skye Green** Essex
204 B1	**Skye of Curr** Highld
122 E5	**Slack** Calder
216 F5	**Slacks of Cairnbanno** Abers
55 K6	**Slad** Gloucs
23 H3	**Slade** Devon
24 C6	**Slade** Devon
45 K5	**Slade Green** Gt Lon
115 K4	**Slade Hooton** Rothm
149 H4	**Slaggyford** Nthumb
130 D8	**Slaidburn** Lancs
123 G7	**Slaithwaite** Kirk
150 B4	**Slaley** Nthumb
176 B4	**Slamannan** Falk
58 F4	**Slapton** Bucks
7 J6	**Slapton** Devon
73 J5	**Slapton** Nhants
31 L5	**Slaugham** W Susx
39 J5	**Slaughterford** Wilts
87 L5	**Slawston** Leics
30 D4	**Sleaford** Hants
103 H4	**Sleaford** Lincs
138 E4	**Sleagill** Cumb
84 B1	**Sleapford** Wrekin
222 E3	**Sleasdairidh** Highld
134 E6	**Sledmere** E R Yk
140 B5	**Sleightholme** Dur
143 H5	**Sleights** N York
231 K3	**Slickly** Highld
162 B5	**Sliddery** N Ayrs
209 G7	**Sligachan** Highld
173 K1	**Sligrachan** Ag & B
55 H7	**Slimbridge** Gloucs
99 J6	**Slindon** Staffs
18 C4	**Slindon** W Susx
31 J5	**Slinfold** W Susx
133 L4	**Slingsby** N York
59 H4	**Slip End** Beds
75 K6	**Slip End** Herts
88 D7	**Slipton** Nhants
100 B8	**Slitting Mill** Staffs
182 B7	**Slockavullin** Ag & B
146 B2	**Slogarie** D & G
11 H7	**Sloncombe** Devon
119 G7	**Sloothby** Lincs
43 G4	**Slough** Slough
25 L7	**Slough Green** Somset
210 D6	**Slumbay** Highld
129 K6	**Slyne** Lancs
167 K3	**Smailholm** Border
107 G7	**Smallburgh** Norfk
19 G3	**Small Dole** W Susx
101 H4	**Smalley** Derbys
32 B5	**Smallfield** Surrey
85 K6	**Small Heath** Birm
34 B8	**Small Hythe** Kent
13 H3	**Smallridge** Devon
92 B7	**Smallworth** Norfk
29 G2	**Smannell** Hants
34 B6	**Smarden** Kent
34 B6	**Smarden Bell** Kent
32 F5	**Smart's Hill** Kent
190 D2	**Smearisary** Highld
12 F1	**Smeatharpe** Devon
34 E6	**Smeeth** Kent
87 K5	**Smeeton Westerby** Leics
227 L2	**Smerral** Highld
84 F5	**Smestow** Staffs
85 H6	**Smethwick** Sandw
101 G8	**Smisby** Derbys
148 D2	**Smithfield** Cumb
76 F6	**Smith's Green** Essex
219 J6	**Smithstown** Highld
213 H5	**Smithton** Highld
228 F3	**Smoo** Highld
61 L4	**Smythe's Green** Essex
154 E5	**Snade** D & G
83 G3	**Snailbeach** Shrops
76 F2	**Snailwell** Cambs
134 E3	**Snainton** N York
124 F6	**Snaith** E R Yk
132 D3	**Snape** N York
79 H3	**Snape** Suffk
79 H3	**Snape Street** Suffk
45 H3	**Snaresbrook** Gt Lon
86 D2	**Snarestone** Leics
117 H5	**Snarford** Lincs
34 D8	**Snargate** Kent
34 D8	**Snave** Kent
143 J5	**Sneaton** N York
117 H5	**Snelland** Lincs
100 D4	**Snelston** Derbys
92 B5	**Snetterton** Norfk
105 G5	**Snettisham** Norfk
158 C2	**Snitter** Nthumb
117 G3	**Snitterby** Lincs
72 B3	**Snitterfield** Warwks
83 L7	**Snitton** Shrops
46 B7	**Snodland** Kent
95 K2	**Snowdon** Gwynd
96 C6	**Snowdonia National Park**
60 C2	**Snow End** Herts
71 K7	**Snowshill** Gloucs
17 J1	**Soake** Hants
29 L7	**Soberton** Hants
29 L8	**Soberton Heath** Hants
141 J5	**Sockburn** Darltn
90 E8	**Soham** Cambs
232 C5	**Solas** W Isls
29 M4	**Soldridge** Hants
34 E5	**Sole Street** Kent
46 A6	**Sole Street** Kent
85 L7	**Solihull** Solhll
69 H4	**Sollers Dilwyn** Herefs
54 E2	**Sollers Hope** Herefs
48 D3	**Solva** Pembks
156 B6	**Solwaybank** D & G
87 L2	**Somerby** Leics
117 H1	**Somerby** Lincs
101 H2	**Somercotes** Derbys
15 M4	**Somerford** Dorset
40 A2	**Somerford Keynes** Gloucs
17 M3	**Somerley** W Susx
93 K4	**Somerleyton** Suffk
100 C5	**Somersal Herbert** Derbys
118 D6	**Somersby** Lincs
89 L7	**Somersham** Cambs
78 C5	**Somersham** Suffk
57 J3	**Somerton** Oxon
26 C5	**Somerton** Somset
77 J4	**Somerton** Suffk
19 G5	**Sompting** W Susx
42 C5	**Sonning** Wokham
42 B4	**Sonning Common** Oxon
15 M3	**Sopley** Hants
39 J3	**Sopworth** Wilts
145 J5	**Sorbie** D & G
231 G3	**Sordale** Highld
189 H4	**Sorisdale** Ag & B
164 B4	**Sorn** E Ayrs
231 K3	**Sortat** Highld
136 F3	**Sosgill** Cumb
117 K5	**Sotby** Lincs
117 J8	**Sots Hole** Lincs
93 K3	**Sotterley** Suffk
111 H7	**Soughton** Flints
58 E3	**Soulbury** Bucks
139 H5	**Soulby** Cumb
57 K2	**Souldern** Oxon
74 E3	**Souldrop** Beds
215 H4	**Sound Muir** Moray
38 F5	**Soundwell** S Glos
7 G4	**Sourton** Devon
128 F3	**Soutergate** Cumb
91 J2	**South Acre** Norfk
35 H6	**South Alkham** Kent
43 J4	**Southall** Gt Lon
7 J7	**South Allington** Devon
185 J8	**South Alloa** Falk
55 L3	**Southam** Gloucs
72 E3	**Southam** Warwks
30 E7	**South Ambersham** W Susx
29 H8	**Southampton** C Sotn
29 J7	**Southampton Airport** Hants
115 K5	**South Anston** Rothm
34 D6	**South Ashford** Kent
16 D3	**South Baddesley** Hants
191 L5	**South Ballachulish** Highld
124 F1	**South Bank** York
26 E5	**South Barrow** Somset
44 F7	**South Beddington** Gt Lon
46 E3	**South Benfleet** Essex
18 C5	**South Bersted** W Susx
45 H6	**Southborough** Gt Lon
33 G5	**Southborough** Kent
15 L4	**Southbourne** Bmouth
17 L2	**Southbourne** W Susx
124 F7	**South Bramwith** Donc
7 G4	**South Brent** Devon
27 G4	**South Brewham** Somset
159 G3	**South Broomhill** Nthumb
92 B3	**Southburgh** Norfk
93 H3	**South Burlingham** Norfk
134 F8	**Southburn** E R Yk
26 F6	**South Cadbury** Somset

116 F6 **South Carlton** Lincs
115 L5 **South Carlton** Notts
125 L4 **South Cave** E R Yk
40 B2 **South Cerney** Gloucs
19 K3 **South Chailey** E Susx
169 H5 **South Charlton** Nthumb
27 G6 **South Cheriton** Somset
140 F2 **South Church** Dur
46 E3 **Southchurch** Sthend
125 K4 **South Cliffe** E R Yk
116 D7 **South Clifton** Notts
118 E4 **South Cockerington** Lincs
36 C4 **South Cornelly** Brdgnd
9 G5 **Southcott** Cnwll
10 E5 **Southcott** Devon
11 H8 **Southcott** Devon
58 D5 **Southcourt** Bucks
93 K7 **South Cove** Suffk
105 K5 **South Creake** Norfk
87 K2 **South Croxton** Leics
126 B2 **South Dalton** E R Yk
19 K4 **South Downs**
125 G4 **South Duffield** N York
19 L5 **Southease** E Susx
118 E4 **South Elkington** Lincs
124 D7 **South Elmsall** Wakefd
161 H7 **Southend** Ag & B
46 E3 Southend Airport Essex
46 E3 **Southend-on-Sea** Sthend
36 D5 **Southerndown** V Glam
147 G4 **Southerness** D & G
219 H7 **South Erradale** Highld
12 D4 **Southerton** Devon
90 E5 **Southery** Norfk
46 E2 **South Fambridge** Essex
126 B6 **South Ferriby** N Linc
126 C5 **South Field** E R Yk
175 L4 **Southfield** Falk
45 L5 **Southfleet** Kent
44 F2 **Southgate** Gt Lon
51 G7 **Southgate** Swans
15 M1 **South Gorley** Hants
151 G2 **South Gosforth** N u Ty
46 B2 **South Green** Essex
33 L2 **South Green** Kent
92 C2 **South Green** Norfk
177 G4 **South Gyle** C Edin
61 H8 **South Hanningfield** Essex
30 C7 **South Harting** W Susx
17 K3 **South Hayling** Hants
58 E7 **South Heath** Bucks
151 J6 **South Hetton** Dur
124 B7 **South Hiendley** Wakefd
5 M2 **South Hill** Cnwll
57 K7 **South Hinksey** Oxon
31 K3 **South Holmwood** Surrey
45 K4 **South Hornchurch** Gt Lon
7 G7 **South Huish** Devon
116 F8 **South Hykeham** Lincs
151 J4 **South Hylton** Sundld
75 H6 **Southill** Beds
29 J2 **Southington** Hants
117 H2 **South Kelsey** Lincs
213 G5 **South Kessock** Highld
126 E7 **South Killingholme** N Linc
132 F3 **South Kilvington** N York

87 H6 **South Kilworth** Leics
124 C7 **South Kirkby** Wakefd
103 K3 **South Kyme** Lincs
56 F5 **South Lawn** Oxon
12 F4 **Southleigh** Devon
57 H6 **South Leigh** Oxon
116 C5 **South Leverton** Notts
71 J5 **South Littleton** Worcs
92 C7 **South Lopham** Norfk
88 D3 **South Luffenham** Rutlnd
19 L4 **South Malling** E Susx
40 D3 **South Marston** Swindn
32 B3 **South Merstham** Surrey
124 D4 **South Milford** N York
7 G7 **South Milton** Devon
59 L7 **South Mimms** Herts
62 A7 **Southminster** Essex
23 L6 **South Molton** Devon
150 F5 **South Moor** Dur
41 H2 **Southmoor** Oxon
41 K3 **South Moreton** Oxon
196 C5 **Southmuir** Angus
18 B5 **South Mundham** W Susx
125 L4 **South Newbald** E R Yk
57 H2 **South Newington** Oxon
28 C4 **South Newton** Wilts
101 H2 **South Normanton** Derbys
45 G6 **South Norwood** Gt Lon
45 L4 **South Ockendon** Thurr
75 J4 **Southoe** Cambs
78 E2 **Southolt** Suffk
118 E6 **South Ormsby** Lincs
88 F3 **Southorpe** C Pete
132 E3 **South Otterington** N York
14 C4 **Southover** Dorset
117 H3 **South Owersby** Lincs
123 G5 **Southowram** Calder
31 L2 **South Park** Surrey
13 L2 **South Perrott** Dorset
26 B7 **South Petherton** Somset
9 J8 **South Petherwin** Cnwll
91 J3 **South Pickenham** Norfk
6 B4 **South Pill** Cnwll
7 H7 **South Pool** Devon
13 M3 **South Poorton** Dorset
120 D6 **Southport** Sefton
176 F3 **South Queensferry** C Edin
24 B5 **South Radworthy** Devon
103 G4 **South Rauceby** Lincs
105 L7 **South Raynham** Norfk
106 F5 **Southrepps** Norfk
118 E5 **South Reston** Lincs
117 J7 **Southrey** Lincs
56 D7 **Southrop** Gloucs
30 A3 **Southrope** Hants
90 F2 **South Runcton** Norfk
116 D8 **South Scarle** Notts
17 J3 **Southsea** C Port
191 H7 **South Shian** Ag & B
151 J2 **South Shields** S Tyne
120 D4 **South Shore** Bpool
140 E2 **Southside** Dur
132 D6 **South Stainley** N York
39 H7 **South Stoke** BaNES
41 L4 **South Stoke** Oxon

18 D4 **South Stoke** W Susx
34 E3 **South Street** Kent
47 J6 **South Street** Kent
176 D7 **South Tarbrax** S Lans
10 F6 **South Tawton** Devon
118 E6 **South Thoresby** Lincs
93 L3 **Southtown** Norfk
148 D6 **Southwaite** Cumb
93 H2 **South Walsham** Norfk
44 F4 **Southwark** Gt Lon
30 B3 **South Warnborough** Hants
31 J6 **Southwater** W Susx
45 L2 **South Weald** Essex
102 B2 **Southwell** Notts
42 B2 **South Weston** Oxon
9 H6 **South Wheatley** Cnwll
17 J2 **Southwick** Hants
88 E5 **Southwick** Nhants
151 J4 **Southwick** Sundld
19 H5 **Southwick** W Susx
27 J1 **Southwick** Wilts
38 E8 **South Widcombe** BaNES
87 H4 **South Wigston** Leics
34 D6 **South Willesborough** Kent
117 K5 **South Willingham** Lincs
151 K7 **South Wingate** Dur
101 G2 **South Wingfield** Derbys
102 F8 **South Witham** Lincs
93 K7 **Southwold** Suffk
61 J7 **South Woodham Ferrers** Essex
105 G7 **South Wootton** Norfk
39 J7 **South Wraxall** Wilts
10 F6 **South Zeal** Devon
122 F6 **Sowerby** Calder
132 F4 **Sowerby** N York
122 F5 **Sowerby Bridge** Calder
122 G6 **Sowood** Calder
6 D3 **Sowton** Devon
12 C4 **Sowton** Devon
122 F6 **Soyland Town** Calder
76 F6 **Spain's End** Essex
103 L7 **Spalding** Lincs
125 H4 **Spaldington** E R Yk
89 G8 **Spaldwick** Cambs
116 D7 **Spalford** Notts
103 H5 **Spanby** Lincs
106 C8 **Sparham** Norfk
129 G3 **Spark Bridge** Cumb
26 E6 **Sparkford** Somset
85 K6 **Sparkhill** Birm
6 E4 **Sparkwell** Devon
114 C5 **Sparrowpit** Derbys
33 H6 **Sparrows Green** E Susx
29 H5 **Sparsholt** Hants
41 G3 **Sparsholt** Oxon
133 L2 **Spaunton** N York
25 K4 **Spaxton** Somset
201 K8 **Spean Bridge** Highld
28 F6 **Spearywell** Hants
58 D7 **Speen** Bucks
41 J6 **Speen** W Berk
135 J5 **Speeton** N York
112 C5 **Speke** Lpool
32 F5 **Speldhurst** Kent
60 D4 **Spellbrook** Herts
42 B6 **Spencers Wood** Wokham
99 J1 **Spen Green** Ches
131 L2 **Spennithorne** N York
151 G2 **Spennymoor** Dur
70 F4 **Spetchley** Worcs
15 G3 **Spetisbury** Dorset

93 H7 **Spexhall** Suffk
215 H2 **Spey Bay** Moray
204 C1 **Speybridge** Highld
215 G6 **Speyview** Moray
118 E7 **Spilsby** Lincs
115 J5 **Spinkhill** Derbys
222 F4 **Spinningdale** Highld
115 L5 **Spital Hill** Donc
178 B3 **Spittal** E Loth
231 H5 **Spittal** Highld
179 L7 **Spittal** Nthumb
49 G3 **Spittal** Pembks
195 M4 **Spittalfield** P & K
205 G7 **Spittal of Glenmuick** Abers
195 M4 **Spittal of Glenshee** P & K
167 J3 **Spittal-on-Rule** Border
92 F1 **Spixworth** Norfk
10 E4 **Splatt** Devon
19 L2 **Splayne's Green** E Susx
37 K5 **Splottlands** Cardif
124 B1 **Spofforth** N York
101 K5 **Spondon** C Derb
92 D4 **Spooner Row** Norfk
91 J2 **Sporle** Norfk
178 E4 **Spott** E Loth
178 D7 **Spottiswoode** Border
73 K1 **Spratton** Nhants
30 D3 **Spreakley** Surrey
11 G5 **Spreyton** Devon
6 D5 **Spriddlestone** Devon
117 G5 **Spridlington** Lincs
175 G5 **Springburn** C Glas
148 B2 **Springfield** D & G
61 H6 **Springfield** Essex
186 E5 **Springfield** Fife
154 E7 **Springholm** D & G
163 J2 **Springside** N Ayrs
116 E4 **Springthorpe** Lincs
151 H4 **Springwell** Sundld
126 F4 **Sproatley** E R Yk
113 G7 **Sproston Green** Ches
115 K2 **Sprotbrough** Donc
78 D5 **Sproughton** Suffk
168 A3 **Sprouston** Border
92 F2 **Sprowston** Norfk
102 D7 **Sproxton** Leics
133 J3 **Sproxton** N York
98 D2 **Spurstow** Ches
14 A4 **Spyway** Dorset
84 D4 **Stableford** Shrops
114 F4 **Stacey Bank** Sheff
130 F6 **Stackhouse** N York
49 G7 **Stackpole** Pembks
6 D5 **Staddiscombe** C Plym
57 L7 **Stadhampton** Oxon
233 b7 **Stadhlaigearraidh** W Isls
148 F6 **Staffield** Cumb
218 D7 **Staffin** Highld
99 L7 **Stafford** Staffs
74 E5 **Stagsden** Beds
136 E2 **Stainburn** Cumb
123 K2 **Stainburn** N York
102 E7 **Stainby** Lincs
123 L7 **Staincross** Barns
140 E3 **Staindrop** Dur
43 G6 **Staines** Surrey
124 F7 **Stainforth** Donc
130 F6 **Stainforth** N York
120 D4 **Staining** Lancs
123 G6 **Stainland** Calder
143 J5 **Stainsacre** N York
129 L3 **Stainton** Cumb
138 C2 **Stainton** Cumb
115 K3 **Stainton** Donc
140 D4 **Stainton** Dur
141 L4 **Stainton** Middsb

117 H6 **Stainton by**
Langworth Lincs
143 K7 **Staintondale** N York
117 K3 **Stainton le Vale** Lincs
128 F5 **Stainton with**
Adgarley Cumb
163 K5 **Stair** E Ayrs
144 E4 **Stairhaven** D & G
143 G4 **Staithes** N York
159 G5 **Stakeford** Nthumb
17 K2 **Stakes** Hants
27 G7 **Stalbridge** Dorset
27 G7 **Stalbridge Weston**
Dorset
107 H7 **Stalham** Norfk
34 C4 **Stalisfield Green** Kent
26 E7 **Stallen** Dorset
126 F7 **Stallingborough**
NE Lin
120 E2 **Stalmine** Lancs
113 L2 **Stalybridge** Tamesd
77 G6 **Stambourne** Essex
77 G6 **Stambourne Green**
Essex
88 E3 **Stamford** Lincs
169 J5 **Stamford** Nthumb
112 C7 **Stamford Bridge**
Ches
133 L7 **Stamford Bridge**
E R Yk
158 D7 **Stamfordham**
Nthumb
45 G3 **Stamford Hill** Gt Lon
58 F3 **Stanbridge** Beds
122 F3 **Stanbury** Brad
175 K5 **Stand** N Lans
176 C4 **Standburn** Falk
85 G3 **Standeford** Staffs
33 L5 **Standen** Kent
27 J2 **Standerwick** Somset
30 D4 **Standford** Hants
147 J7 **Standingstone** Cumb
121 H7 **Standish** Wigan
57 H7 **Standlake** Oxon
29 H6 **Standon** Hants
60 C4 **Standon** Herts
99 J5 **Standon** Staffs
176 B6 **Stane** N Lans
105 M7 **Stanfield** Norfk
75 H6 **Stanford** Beds
34 F6 **Stanford** Kent
70 C4 **Stanford Bishop**
Herefs
70 C2 **Stanford Bridge**
Worcs
41 L6 **Stanford Dingley**
W Berk
41 G2 **Stanford in the Vale**
Oxon
46 B4 **Stanford le Hope**
Thurr
87 H7 **Stanford on Avon**
Nhants
101 K7 **Stanford on Soar**
Notts
70 C2 **Stanford on Teme**
Worcs
115 J6 **Stanfree** Derbys
142 E4 **Stanghow** R & Cl
89 H4 **Stanground** C Pete
105 J5 **Stanhoe** Norfk
165 L4 **Stanhope** Border
150 C6 **Stanhope** Dur
34 D6 **Stanhope** Kent
88 D6 **Stanion** Nhants
101 H4 **Stanley** Derbys
150 F4 **Stanley** Dur
186 B2 **Stanley** P & K
99 L3 **Stanley** Staffs
150 E7 **Stanley Crook** Dur
55 M3 **Stanley Pontlarge**
Gloucs

19 K4 **Stanmer** Br & H
44 D2 **Stanmore** Gt Lon
29 J5 **Stanmore** Hants
157 J7 **Stannersburn**
Nthumb
77 K3 **Stanningfield** Suffk
158 F6 **Stannington** Nthumb
114 F4 **Stannington** Sheff
158 F5 **Stannington Station**
Nthumb
69 G3 **Stansbatch** Herefs
77 H4 **Stansfield** Suffk
77 J5 **Stanstead** Suffk
60 C5 **Stanstead Abbotts**
Herts
77 J5 **Stanstead Street**
Suffk
45 L7 **Stansted** Kent
60 E4 **Stansted Airport**
Essex
60 E3 **Stansted**
Mountfitchet Essex
71 J7 **Stanton** Gloucs
158 E4 **Stanton** Nthumb
100 C4 **Stanton** Staffs
91 L8 **Stanton** Suffk
101 G6 **Stanton by Bridge**
Derbys
101 J5 **Stanton by Dale**
Derbys
38 E7 **Stanton Drew** BaNES
40 D3 **Stanton Fitzwarren**
Swindn
57 H6 **Stanton Harcourt**
Oxon
114 E8 **Stanton in Peak**
Derbys
83 K7 **Stanton Lacy** Shrops
114 E8 **Stanton Lees** Derbys
83 L5 **Stanton Long** Shrops
101 M6 **Stanton on the**
Wolds Notts
39 G7 **Stanton Prior** BaNES
40 C7 **Stanton St Bernard**
Wilts
57 L6 **Stanton St John**
Oxon
39 K4 **Stanton St Quintin**
Wilts
77 L2 **Stanton Street** Suffk
86 F2 **Stanton under**
Bardon Leics
98 E7 **Stanton upon Hine**
Heath Shrops
38 E7 **Stanton Wick** BaNES
61 M3 **Stanway** Essex
56 B2 **Stanway** Gloucs
43 H5 **Stanwell** Surrey
74 E1 **Stanwick** Nhants
148 D4 **Stanwix** Cumb
233 b8 **Staoinebrig** W Isls
143 G7 **Stape** N York
99 G3 **Stapeley** Ches
100 E7 **Stapenhill** Staffs
35 H4 **Staple** Kent
25 H3 **Staple** Somset
25 G2 **Staple Cross** Devon
20 F2 **Staple Cross** E Susx
32 B7 **Staplefield** W Susx
25 K7 **Staple Fitzpaine**
Somset
76 C4 **Stapleford** Cambs
60 A5 **Stapleford** Herts
102 D8 **Stapleford** Leics
102 E2 **Stapleford** Lincs
101 J5 **Stapleford** Notts
28 B4 **Stapleford** Wilts
45 K2 **Stapleford Abbotts**
Essex
25 K6 **Staplegrove** Somset
25 K6 **Staplehay** Somset
33 K5 **Staplehurst** Kent

34 E3 **Staplestreet** Kent
69 G2 **Stapleton** Herefs
86 E4 **Stapleton** Leics
141 G5 **Stapleton** N York
83 J3 **Stapleton** Shrops
26 C7 **Stapleton** Somset
25 J8 **Stapley** Somset
75 G3 **Staploe** Beds
70 C6 **Staplow** Herefs
186 E6 **Star** Fife
65 H7 **Star** Pembks
38 C8 **Star** Somset
132 E7 **Starbeck** N York
131 H5 **Starbotton** N York
12 C6 **Starcross** Devon
72 D1 **Stareton** Warwks
60 D2 **Starlings Green** Essex
92 F6 **Starston** Norfk
140 D4 **Startforth** Dur
39 L4 **Startley** Wilts
35 J4 **Statenborough** Kent
26 A5 **Stathe** Somset
102 C6 **Stathern** Leics
75 G2 **Staughton Green**
Cambs
54 D5 **Staunton** Gloucs
55 H3 **Staunton** Gloucs
69 G3 **Staunton Green**
Herefs
69 G3 **Staunton on Arrow**
Herefs
69 G5 **Staunton on Wye**
Herefs
129 H3 **Staveley** Cumb
138 C7 **Staveley** Cumb
115 H6 **Staveley** Derbys
132 E6 **Staveley** N York
7 J3 **Staverton** Devon
55 K4 **Staverton** Gloucs
73 G3 **Staverton** Nhants
39 J7 **Staverton** Wilts
26 A4 **Stawell** Somset
25 G6 **Stawley** Somset
231 L5 **Staxigoe** Highld
134 F4 **Staxton** N York
120 E2 **Staynall** Lancs
131 K5 **Stean** N York
73 G6 **Steane** Nhants
133 J5 **Stearsby** N York
25 L3 **Steart** Somset
61 G3 **Stebbing** Essex
61 H4 **Stebbing Green** Essex
61 G3 **Stebbing Park** Essex
30 E6 **Stedham** W Susx
185 L8 **Steelend** Fife
156 F4 **Steele Road** Border
69 K3 **Steen's Bridge** Herefs
30 C6 **Steep** Hants
122 F5 **Steep Lane** Calder
61 M7 **Steeple** Essex
27 K1 **Steeple Ashton** Wilts
57 J3 **Steeple Aston** Oxon
76 F6 **Steeple Bumpstead**
Essex
58 B3 **Steeple Claydon**
Bucks
89 G7 **Steeple Gidding**
Cambs
28 B4 **Steeple Langford**
Wilts
75 K6 **Steeple Morden**
Cambs
122 F2 **Steeton** Brad
208 D3 **Stein** Highld
34 F5 **Stelling Minnis** Kent
26 B7 **Stembridge** Somset
4 F4 **Stenalees** Cnwll
154 D4 **Stenhouse** D & G
176 B2 **Stenhousemuir** Falk
218 D7 **Stenscholl** Highld
101 G6 **Stenson Fields**
Derbys

178 D4 **Stenton** E Loth
232 f2 **Steornabhagh** W Isls
49 K6 **Stepaside** Pembks
45 G4 **Stepney** Gt Lon
74 E7 **Steppingley** Beds
175 H5 **Stepps** N Lans
79 H3 **Sternfield** Suffk
40 B8 **Stert** Wilts
76 F3 **Stetchworth** Cambs
59 L3 **Stevenage** Herts
163 H2 **Stevenston** N Ayrs
29 K2 **Steventon** Hants
41 J3 **Steventon** Oxon
76 E6 **Steventon End** Essex
74 E4 **Stevington** Beds
74 E6 **Stewartby** Beds
175 H7 **Stewartfield** S Lans
163 K1 **Stewarton** E Ayrs
58 D3 **Stewkley** Bucks
25 L7 **Stewley** Somset
19 G4 **Steyning** W Susx
48 F6 **Steynton** Pembks
9 G3 **Stibb** Cnwll
106 B6 **Stibbard** Norfk
10 C2 **Stibb Cross** Devon
40 E7 **Stibb Green** Wilts
88 F4 **Stibbington** Cambs
167 L2 **Stichill** Border
4 F5 **Sticker** Cnwll
104 B1 **Stickford** Lincs
10 F6 **Sticklepath** Devon
104 B2 **Stickney** Lincs
106 A4 **Stiffkey** Norfk
233 b7 **Stilligarry** W Isls
124 F3 **Stillingfleet** N York
133 J6 **Stillington** N York
141 J3 **Stillington** S on T
89 H5 **Stilton** Cambs
55 G7 **Stinchcombe** Gloucs
14 D4 **Stinsford** Dorset
83 G4 **Stiperstones** Shrops
217 L6 **Stirling** Abers
185 G8 **Stirling** Stirlg
75 H2 **Stirtloe** Cambs
131 H8 **Stirton** N York
61 J3 **Stisted** Essex
3 J4 **Stithians** Cnwll
86 D7 **Stivichall** Covtry
117 K7 **Stixwould** Lincs
112 B6 **Stoak** Ches
166 B2 **Stobo** Border
15 H5 **Stoborough** Dorset
167 G7 **Stobs Castle** Border
158 F3 **Stobswood** Nthumb
61 H7 **Stock** Essex
38 C7 **Stock** N Som
29 G4 **Stockbridge** Hants
164 F3 **Stockbriggs** S Lans
46 D7 **Stockbury** Kent
41 H6 **Stockcross** W Berk
88 B4 **Stockerston** Leics
71 H3 **Stock Green** Worcs
54 E7 **Stocking** Herefs
86 D5 **Stockingford** Warwks
60 D3 **Stocking Pelham**
Herts
13 G2 **Stockland** Devon
25 K3 **Stockland Bristol**
Somset
11 K4 **Stockleigh English**
Devon
11 K4 **Stockleigh Pomeroy**
Devon
39 M6 **Stockley** Wilts
26 B7 **Stocklinch** Somset
113 K4 **Stockport** Stockp
114 E2 **Stocksbridge** Sheff
150 D3 **Stocksfield** Nthumb
69 K3 **Stockton** Herefs
93 H5 **Stockton** Norfk
84 C4 **Stockton** Shrops
72 E2 **Stockton** Warwks

27 M4	**Stockton** Wilts
84 D1	**Stockton** Wrekin
112 E4	**Stockton Heath** Warrtn
141 K4	**Stockton-on-Tees** S on T
70 C2	**Stockton on Teme** Worcs
133 K7	**Stockton on the Forest** York
38 F6	**Stockwood** Bristl
14 B2	**Stockwood** Dorset
71 H3	**Stock Wood** Worcs
35 G3	**Stodmarsh** Kent
106 C5	**Stody** Norfk
224 C3	**Stoer** Highld
26 E8	**Stoford** Somset
28 B4	**Stoford** Wilts
25 H4	**Stogumber** Somset
25 J3	**Stogursey** Somset
86 D7	**Stoke** Covtry
22 C6	**Stoke** Devon
17 K3	**Stoke** Hants
29 H2	**Stoke** Hants
46 D5	**Stoke** Medway
13 L3	**Stoke Abbott** Dorset
88 B5	**Stoke Albany** Nhants
78 D1	**Stoke Ash** Suffk
101 M4	**Stoke Bardolph** Notts
70 B2	**Stoke Bliss** Worcs
73 L4	**Stoke Bruerne** Nhants
77 G5	**Stoke by Clare** Suffk
78 B7	**Stoke-by-Nayland** Suffk
12 B3	**Stoke Canon** Devon
29 J4	**Stoke Charity** Hants
6 A2	**Stoke Climsland** Cnwll
70 B4	**Stoke Cross** Herefs
43 J8	**Stoke D'Abernon** Surrey
88 E6	**Stoke Doyle** Nhants
88 C4	**Stoke Dry** Rutlnd
69 L6	**Stoke Edith** Herefs
28 B6	**Stoke Farthing** Wilts
91 G4	**Stoke Ferry** Norfk
7 K6	**Stoke Fleming** Devon
15 G5	**Stokeford** Dorset
7 J4	**Stoke Gabriel** Devon
38 F4	**Stoke Gifford** S Glos
86 E4	**Stoke Golding** Leics
74 B5	**Stoke Goldington** M Keyn
116 C4	**Stokeham** Notts
58 E3	**Stoke Hammond** Bucks
92 F3	**Stoke Holy Cross** Norfk
7 L2	**Stokeinteignhead** Devon
70 B5	**Stoke Lacy** Herefs
57 K3	**Stoke Lyne** Oxon
58 D6	**Stoke Mandeville** Bucks
42 C2	**Stokenchurch** Bucks
45 G3	**Stoke Newington** Gt Lon
7 J7	**Stokenham** Devon
99 K3	**Stoke-on-Trent** C Stke
55 K3	**Stoke Orchard** Gloucs
42 F4	**Stoke Poges** Bucks
69 K3	**Stoke Prior** Herefs
71 G2	**Stoke Prior** Worcs
23 K4	**Stoke Rivers** Devon
102 F6	**Stoke Rochford** Lincs
42 B4	**Stoke Row** Oxon
25 M6	**Stoke St Gregory** Somset
25 K6	**Stoke St Mary** Somset

26 F3	**Stoke St Michael** Somset
83 L6	**Stoke St Milborough** Shrops
83 H6	**Stokesay Castle** Shrops
93 J2	**Stokesby** Norfk
142 B5	**Stokesley** N York
26 C7	**Stoke sub Hamdon** Somset
58 B7	**Stoke Talmage** Oxon
27 H5	**Stoke Trister** Somset
98 F6	**Stoke upon Tern** Shrops
99 K4	**Stoke-upon-Trent** C Stke
14 E2	**Stoke Wake** Dorset
25 K3	**Stolford** Somset
60 F7	**Stondon Massey** Essex
58 C5	**Stone** Bucks
39 G2	**Stone** Gloucs
21 J1	**Stone** Kent
115 K4	**Stone** Rothm
99 K5	**Stone** Staffs
84 F7	**Stone** Worcs
26 B2	**Stone Allerton** Somset
26 F2	**Ston Easton** Somset
38 B7	**Stonebridge** N Som
86 B6	**Stonebridge** Warwks
101 H2	**Stonebroom** Derbys
35 J4	**Stone Cross** Kent
33 J6	**Stonecrouch** Kent
126 D4	**Stonefield** C KuH
172 E4	**Stonefield Castle Hotel** Ag & B
33 H7	**Stonegate** E Susx
133 K4	**Stonegrave** N York
207 G7	**Stonehaven** Abers
28 C3	**Stonehenge** Wilts
6 C5	**Stonehouse** C Plym
112 D7	**Stonehouse** Ches
146 E2	**Stonehouse** D & G
55 J6	**Stonehouse** Gloucs
175 K8	**Stonehouse** S Lans
86 D8	**Stoneleigh** Warwks
102 D7	**Stonesby** Leics
57 H4	**Stonesfield** Oxon
62 E3	**Stones Green** Essex
33 G3	**Stone Street** Kent
93 H6	**Stone Street** Suffk
215 G2	**Stonewells** Moray
233 B8	**Stoneybridge** W Isls
176 D5	**Stoneyburn** W Loth
87 H3	**Stoneygate** C Leic
144 C4	**Stoneykirk** D & G
114 E6	**Stoney Middleton** Derbys
86 F4	**Stoney Stanton** Leics
27 G5	**Stoney Stoke** Somset
26 F4	**Stoney Stratton** Somset
83 H2	**Stoney Stretton** Shrops
207 G3	**Stoneywood** C Aber
175 L2	**Stoneywood** Falk
78 D3	**Stonham Aspal** Suffk
85 J3	**Stonnall** Staffs
42 B3	**Stonor** Oxon
87 K4	**Stonton Wyville** Leics
115 J7	**Stony Houghton** Derbys
73 L6	**Stony Stratford** M Keyn
23 K5	**Stoodleigh** Devon
24 E7	**Stoodleigh** Devon
18 D2	**Stopham** W Susx
59 J3	**Stopsley** Luton
232 f2	**Stornoway** W Isls
232 g2	**Stornoway Airport** W Isls

18 E3	**Storrington** W Susx
125 H2	**Storwood** E R Yk
214 F1	**Stotfield** Moray
75 J7	**Stotfold** Beds
84 C6	**Stottesdon** Shrops
87 J3	**Stoughton** Leics
31 G2	**Stoughton** Surrey
17 L1	**Stoughton** W Susx
200 B6	**Stoul** Highld
70 F4	**Stoulton** Worcs
84 F6	**Stourbridge** Dudley
15 G1	**Stourpaine** Dorset
70 E1	**Stourport-on-Severn** Worcs
27 H6	**Stour Provost** Dorset
27 J7	**Stour Row** Dorset
84 F6	**Stourton** Staffs
72 C5	**Stourton** Warwks
27 H5	**Stourton** Wilts
27 G7	**Stourton Caundle** Dorset
235 c7	**Stove** Shet
93 J6	**Stoven** Suffk
167 G1	**Stow** Border
116 E5	**Stow** Lincs
90 F3	**Stow Bardolph** Norfk
91 L4	**Stow Bedon** Norfk
90 E3	**Stowbridge** Norfk
76 D3	**Stow-cum-Quy** Cambs
82 B5	**Stowe** Shrops
100 A6	**Stowe by Chartley** Staffs
27 G6	**Stowell** Somset
38 E7	**Stowey** BaNES
10 C5	**Stowford** Devon
10 C5	**Stowford** Devon
23 K3	**Stowford** Devon
77 L2	**Stowlangtoft** Suffk
75 G1	**Stow Longa** Cambs
61 K7	**Stow Maries** Essex
78 C3	**Stowmarket** Suffk
56 D3	**Stow-on-the-Wold** Gloucs
34 F6	**Stowting** Kent
34 F6	**Stowting Common** Kent
78 C3	**Stowupland** Suffk
204 B3	**Straanruie** Highld
197 G4	**Stracathro Hospital** Angus
206 D6	**Strachan** Abers
182 F6	**Strachur** Ag & B
92 F8	**Stradbroke** Suffk
77 H4	**Stradishall** Suffk
90 F3	**Stradsett** Norfk
102 E3	**Stragglethorpe** Lincs
177 H5	**Straiton** Mdloth
153 H2	**Straiton** S Ayrs
207 G2	**Straloch** Abers
195 G4	**Straloch** P & K
100 B5	**Stramshall** Staffs
237 C5	**Strang** IoM
113 J2	**Strangeways** Salfd
54 E3	**Strangford** Herefs
144 C3	**Stranraer** D & G
42 A7	**Stratfield Mortimer** W Berk
42 B7	**Stratfield Saye** Hants
42 B7	**Stratfield Turgis** Hants
45 H3	**Stratford** Gt Lon
79 H3	**Stratford St Andrew** Suffk
78 C7	**Stratford St Mary** Suffk
28 C6	**Stratford Tony** Wilts
72 B4	**Stratford-upon-Avon** Warwks
219 J5	**Strath** Highld
224 H3	**Strathan** Highld
229 J3	**Strathan** Highld

164 D1	**Strathaven** S Lans
175 G3	**Strathblane** Stirlg
220 F2	**Strathcanaird** Highld
210 E6	**Strathcarron** Highld
181 K2	**Strathcoil** Ag & B
205 H3	**Strathdon** Abers
187 G4	**Strathkinness** Fife
176 C4	**Strathloanhead** W Loth
202 F6	**Strathmashie House** Highld
186 C5	**Strathmiglo** Fife
212 D3	**Strathpeffer** Highld
194 E5	**Strathtay** P & K
162 D3	**Strathwhillan** N Ayrs
230 B3	**Strathy** Highld
230 B3	**Strathy Inn** Highld
184 C4	**Strathyre** Stirlg
9 G4	**Stratton** Cnwll
14 C4	**Stratton** Dorset
56 A7	**Stratton** Gloucs
57 L3	**Stratton Audley** Oxon
26 F2	**Stratton-on-the-Fosse** Somset
40 D3	**Stratton St Margaret** Swindn
92 E5	**Stratton St Michael** Norfk
106 F7	**Stratton Strawless** Norfk
187 J5	**Stravithie** Fife
19 K3	**Streat** E Susx
44 F5	**Streatham** Gt Lon
59 H3	**Streatley** Beds
41 L4	**Streatley** W Berk
12 F5	**Street** Devon
26 C4	**Street** Somset
86 F6	**Street Ashton** Warwks
97 M5	**Street Dinas** Shrops
34 F4	**Street End** Kent
18 A5	**Street End** W Susx
85 K2	**Streethay** Staffs
141 H7	**Streetlam** N York
76 E5	**Streetly End** Cambs
26 F4	**Street on the Fosse** Somset
186 C1	**Strelitz** P & K
101 K4	**Strelley** Notts
133 K7	**Strensall** York
25 L3	**Stretcholt** Somset
7 J6	**Strete** Devon
113 H3	**Stretford** Traffd
76 C6	**Strethall** Essex
90 D8	**Stretham** Cambs
18 B4	**Strettington** W Susx
101 H1	**Stretton** Derbys
88 D1	**Stretton** Rutlnd
84 F2	**Stretton** Staffs
100 E7	**Stretton** Staffs
112 F5	**Stretton** Warrtn
70 B5	**Stretton Grandison** Herefs
86 E8	**Stretton-on-Dunsmore** Warwks
72 B6	**Stretton on Fosse** Warwks
69 J6	**Stretton Sugwas** Herefs
86 F7	**Stretton under Fosse** Warwks
83 L4	**Stretton Westwood** Shrops
217 H4	**Strichen** Abers
25 J3	**Stringston** Somset
74 C3	**Strixton** Nhants
38 E2	**Stroat** Gloucs
210 D2	**Stromeferry** Highld
234 b6	**Stromness** Ork
183 L5	**Stronachlachar** Stirlg
173 H3	**Stronafian** Ag & B
224 F5	**Stronchrubie** Highld

173 L3 **Strone** Ag & B
192 B1 **Strone** Highld
201 J8 **Stronenaba** Highld
183 G2 **Stronmilchan** Ag & B
234 d5 Stronsay Airport Ork
191 G4 **Strontian** Highld
46 B6 **Strood** Medway
55 J6 **Stroud** Gloucs
30 B6 **Stroud** Hants
55 J6 **Stroud Green** Gloucs
102 E6 **Stroxton** Lincs
208 E6 **Struan** Highld
194 C4 **Struan** P & K
93 H3 **Strumpshaw** Norfk
175 K7 **Strutherhill** S Lans
186 F5 **Struthers** Fife
212 B6 **Struy** Highld
217 H5 **Stuartfield** Abers
17 G2 **Stubbington** Hants
122 B6 **Stubbins** Lancs
102 E3 **Stubton** Lincs
28 D8 **Stuckton** Hants
59 G5 **Studham** Beds
148 A4 **Studholme** Cumb
15 J6 **Studland** Dorset
71 J2 **Studley** Warwks
39 L6 **Studley** Wilts
132 D5 **Studley Roger** N York
132 D5 **Studley Royal** N York
90 D7 **Stuntney** Cambs
77 G5 **Sturmer** Essex
27 H8 **Sturminster Common** Dorset
15 H3 **Sturminster Marshall** Dorset
27 H8 **Sturminster Newton** Dorset
35 G3 **Sturry** Kent
116 F4 **Sturton** N Linc
116 E5 **Sturton by Stow** Lincs
116 C5 **Sturton le Steeple** Notts
92 D7 **Stuston** Suffk
124 D3 **Stutton** N York
78 D7 **Stutton** Suffk
113 J5 **Styal** Ches
215 H3 **Stynie** Moray
115 L4 **Styrrup** Notts
183 K6 **Succoth** Ag & B
70 C4 **Suckley** Worcs
88 D6 **Sudborough** Nhants
79 J4 **Sudbourne** Suffk
102 F4 **Sudbrook** Lincs
38 D3 **Sudbrook** Mons
117 G6 **Sudbrooke** Lincs
100 D6 **Sudbury** Derbys
44 D3 **Sudbury** Gt Lon
77 K6 **Sudbury** Suffk
70 F2 **Suddington** Worcs
134 F2 **Suffield** N York
106 F6 **Suffield** Norfk
99 H6 **Sugnall** Staffs
69 J6 **Sugwas Pool** Herefs
199 J3 **Suisnish** Highld
237 d3 **Sulby** IoM
73 G5 **Sulgrave** Nhants
73 H5 **Sulgrave Manor** Nhants
41 M5 **Sulham** W Berk
41 M6 **Sulhamstead** W Berk
235 c4 **Sullom** Shet
235 c4 **Sullom Voe** Shet
37 J6 **Sully** V Glam
235 c8 Sumburgh Airport Shet
132 C6 **Summerbridge** N York
4 D5 **Summercourt** Cnwll
105 J5 **Summerfield** Norfk
140 F4 **Summerhouse** Darltn
18 B4 **Summersdale** W Susx
122 B7 **Summerseat** Bury
57 K6 **Summertown** Oxon
43 J6 **Sunbury** Surrey
154 E5 **Sundaywell** D & G
170 E5 **Sunderland** Ag & B
147 L7 **Sunderland** Cumb
129 J7 **Sunderland** Lancs
151 J4 **Sunderland** Sundld
151 G7 **Sunderland Bridge** Dur
166 E4 **Sundhope** Border
32 E3 **Sundridge** Kent
42 F6 **Sunningdale** W & M
42 F6 **Sunninghill** W & M
57 J7 **Sunningwell** Oxon
150 E7 **Sunniside** Dur
150 F3 **Sunniside** Gatesd
101 G6 **Sunnyhill** C Derb
121 K6 **Sunnyhurst** Bl w D
185 G7 **Sunnylaw** Stirlg
57 J6 **Sunnymead** Oxon
44 D6 **Surbiton** Gt Lon
103 L6 **Surfleet** Lincs
93 G3 **Surlingham** Norfk
61 L4 **Surrex** Essex
106 E5 **Sustead** Norfk
116 D2 **Susworth** Lincs
9 J3 **Sutcombe** Devon
9 J3 **Sutcombemill** Devon
118 E6 **Sutterby** Lincs
103 M5 **Sutterton** Lincs
75 J5 **Sutton** Beds
89 G4 **Sutton** C Pete
90 C7 **Sutton** Cambs
7 G7 **Sutton** Devon
20 A5 **Sutton** E Susx
44 E7 **Sutton** Gt Lon
35 J5 **Sutton** Kent
124 D5 **Sutton** N York
107 H7 **Sutton** Norfk
102 C5 **Sutton** Notts
84 D6 **Sutton** Shrops
99 H7 **Sutton** Staffs
79 G5 **Sutton** Suffk
18 D3 **Sutton** W Susx
45 K6 **Sutton at Hone** Kent
87 L5 **Sutton Bassett** Nhants
39 L5 **Sutton Benger** Wilts
101 K7 **Sutton Bonington** Notts
104 D7 **Sutton Bridge** Lincs
86 E4 **Sutton Cheney** Leics
85 K4 **Sutton Coldfield** Birm
41 J2 **Sutton Courtenay** Oxon
116 B5 **Sutton cum Lound** Notts
132 D5 **Sutton Grange** N York
31 G1 **Sutton Green** Surrey
132 D4 **Sutton Howgrave** N York
101 J2 **Sutton in Ashfield** Notts
122 F2 **Sutton-in-Craven** N York
84 C3 **Sutton Maddock** Shrops
26 A4 **Sutton Mallet** Somset
27 M5 **Sutton Mandeville** Wilts
26 F6 **Sutton Montis** Somset
126 E4 **Sutton-on-Hull** C KuH
119 G5 **Sutton on Sea** Lincs
133 J6 **Sutton-on-the-Forest** N York
100 E5 **Sutton on the Hill** Derbys
116 D7 **Sutton on Trent** Notts
89 L2 **Sutton St Edmund** Lincs
104 C8 **Sutton St James** Lincs
69 K5 **Sutton St Nicholas** Herefs
29 J4 **Sutton Scotney** Hants
72 C6 **Sutton-under-Brailes** Warwks
133 G3 **Sutton-under-Whitestonecliffe** N York
125 G2 **Sutton upon Derwent** E R Yk
33 L4 **Sutton Valence** Kent
27 K3 **Sutton Veny** Wilts
27 K7 **Sutton Waldron** Dorset
112 D5 **Sutton Weaver** Ches
38 E8 **Sutton Wick** BaNES
41 J2 **Sutton Wick** Oxon
118 E6 **Swaby** Lincs
100 F8 **Swadlincote** Derbys
91 J2 **Swaffham** Norfk
76 D3 **Swaffham Bulbeck** Cambs
76 E2 **Swaffham Prior** Cambs
107 G6 **Swafield** Norfk
141 L6 **Swainby** N York
92 F4 **Swainsthorpe** Norfk
39 H6 **Swainswick** BaNES
72 E6 **Swalcliffe** Oxon
47 J6 **Swalecliffe** Kent
117 K2 **Swallow** Lincs
116 F7 **Swallow Beck** Lincs
27 L6 **Swallowcliffe** Wilts
42 B7 **Swallowfield** Wokham
15 J6 **Swanage** Dorset
58 D3 **Swanbourne** Bucks
113 G6 **Swan Green** Ches
126 B5 **Swanland** E R Yk
45 K6 **Swanley** Kent
45 K6 **Swanley Village** Kent
29 L7 **Swanmore** Hants
86 E1 **Swannington** Leics
106 D8 **Swannington** Norfk
116 F7 **Swanpool Garden Suburb** Lincs
45 L5 **Swanscombe** Kent
51 J6 **Swansea** Swans
51 H7 Swansea Airport Swans
106 F7 **Swanton Abbot** Norfk
92 B1 **Swanton Morley** Norfk
106 B6 **Swanton Novers** Norfk
101 H2 **Swanwick** Derbys
17 G1 **Swanwick** Hants
103 H4 **Swarby** Lincs
92 E3 **Swardeston** Norfk
101 G6 **Swarkestone** Derbys
158 E2 **Swarland** Nthumb
29 K4 **Swarraton** Hants
129 G4 **Swarthmoor** Cumb
103 J5 **Swaton** Lincs
75 L2 **Swavesey** Cambs
16 C3 **Sway** Hants
103 G7 **Swayfield** Lincs
29 H7 **Swaything** S Sotn
11 K5 **Sweetham** Devon
32 E7 **Sweethaws** E Susx
8 F5 **Sweets** Cnwll
5 H4 **Sweetshouse** Cnwll
79 H2 **Swefling** Suffk
86 D2 **Swepstone** Leics
57 G2 **Swerford** Oxon
113 J7 **Swettenham** Ches
78 E4 **Swilland** Suffk
124 B4 **Swillington** Leeds
23 K5 **Swimbridge** Devon
23 J5 **Swimbridge Newland** Devon
56 F5 **Swinbrook** Oxon
132 C2 **Swincliffe** N York
116 E8 **Swinderby** Lincs
55 L3 **Swindon** Gloucs
84 F5 **Swindon** Staffs
40 D4 **Swindon** Swindn
126 E4 **Swine** E R Yk
125 H6 **Swinefleet** E R Yk
74 F2 **Swineshead** Beds
103 L4 **Swineshead** Lincs
227 M2 **Swiney** Highld
87 H7 **Swinford** Leics
35 G6 **Swingfield Minnis** Kent
35 H6 **Swingfield Street** Kent
77 L5 **Swingleton Green** Suffk
169 J4 **Swinhoe** Nthumb
131 K2 **Swinithwaite** N York
100 C3 **Swinscoe** Staffs
137 H3 **Swinside** Cumb
103 G7 **Swinstead** Lincs
179 H8 **Swinton** Border
132 C4 **Swinton** N York
134 B5 **Swinton** N York
115 J2 **Swinton** Rothm
113 H2 **Swinton** Salfd
87 G2 **Swithland** Leics
212 E2 **Swordale** Highld
200 B6 **Swordland** Highld
229 M3 **Swordly** Highld
99 J5 **Swynnerton** Staffs
13 M5 **Swyre** Dorset
81 L3 **Sychtyn** Powys
55 L5 **Syde** Gloucs
45 G5 **Sydenham** Gt Lon
58 B7 **Sydenham** Oxon
6 B2 **Sydenham Damerel** Devon
105 K6 **Syderstone** Norfk
14 C3 **Sydling St Nicholas** Dorset
41 J8 **Sydmonton** Hants
102 C3 **Syerston** Notts
95 K3 Sygun Copper Mine Gwynd
124 F6 **Sykehouse** Donc
235 d4 **Symbister** Shet
163 J3 **Symington** S Ayrs
165 J3 **Symington** S Lans
13 K4 **Symondsbury** Dorset
54 E5 **Symonds Yat** Herefs
229 L6 **Syre** Highld
56 B4 **Syreford** Gloucs
73 J6 **Syresham** Nhants
87 J2 **Syston** Leics
102 F4 **Syston** Lincs
70 E2 **Sytchampton** Worcs
74 B2 **Sywell** Nhants

T

57 J4 **Tackley** Oxon
92 D4 **Tacolneston** Norfk
124 D2 **Tadcaster** N York
114 C7 **Taddington** Derbys
56 C2 **Taddington** Gloucs
41 L7 **Tadley** Hants
75 K5 **Tadlow** Cambs
72 E6 **Tadmarton** Oxon
44 E8 **Tadworth** Surrey
37 H4 **Taff's Well** Rhondd
36 B3 **Taibach** Neath
223 G5 **Tain** Highld
231 J3 **Tain** Highld
232 e4 **Tairbeart** W Isls

60 F4 **Takeley** Essex
60 E4 **Takeley Street** Essex
12 D3 **Talaton** Devon
48 E5 **Talbenny** Pembks
12 E3 **Taleford** Devon
81 K4 **Talerddig** Powys
65 L4 **Talgarreg** Cerdgn
68 D7 **Talgarth** Powys
208 E7 **Talisker** Highld
99 J2 **Talke** Staffs
148 F4 **Talkin** Cumb
219 L7 **Talladale** Highld
165 M5 **Talla Linnfoots** Border
153 J3 **Tallaminnock** S Ayrs
98 C4 **Tallarn Green** Wrexhm
147 K7 **Tallentire** Cumb
66 E7 **Talley** Carmth
88 F2 **Tallington** Lincs
229 J3 **Talmine** Highld
50 D1 **Talog** Carmth
66 D4 **Talsarn** Cerdgn
95 K5 **Talsarnau** Gwynd
4 E3 **Talskiddy** Cnwll
109 G6 **Talwrn** IoA
80 E5 **Tal-y-bont** Cerdgn
109 L7 **Tal-y-Bont** Conwy
95 K7 **Tal-y-bont** Gwynd
109 J7 **Tal-y-bont** Gwynd
53 H4 **Talybont-on-Usk** Powys
109 M7 **Tal-y-Cafn** Conwy
54 B5 **Tal-y-coed** Mons
95 H1 **Talysarn** Gwynd
6 C4 **Tamerton Foliot** C Plym
86 B3 **Tamworth** Staffs
32 C3 **Tandridge** Surrey
150 F4 **Tanfield** Dur
150 F4 **Tanfield Lea** Dur
28 F2 **Tangley** Hants
18 B4 **Tangmere** W Susx
233 b9 **Tangusdale** W Isls
234 c6 **Tankerness** Ork
115 G2 **Tankersley** Barns
47 J6 **Tankerton** Kent
231 K6 **Tannach** Highld
206 E8 **Tannachie** Abers
196 D5 **Tannadice** Angus
85 J8 **Tanner's Green** Worcs
78 F2 **Tannington** Suffk
175 J6 **Tannochside** N Lans
100 F1 **Tansley** Derbys
88 F5 **Tansor** Nhants
150 F4 **Tantobie** Dur
142 B5 **Tanton** N York
71 K1 **Tanworth in Arden** Warwks
65 J5 **Tan-y-groes** Cerdgn
232 d5 **Taobh Tuath** W Isls
42 E4 **Taplow** Bucks
172 B7 **Tarbert** Ag & B
172 E5 **Tarbert** Ag & B
232 e4 **Tarbert** W Isls
183 K6 **Tarbet** Ag & B
200 B6 **Tarbet** Highld
228 B7 **Tarbet** Highld
163 K4 **Tarbolton** S Ayrs
176 D7 **Tarbrax** S Lans
71 H2 **Tardebigge** Worcs
196 D1 **Tarfside** Angus
205 K4 **Tarland** Abers
120 F6 **Tarleton** Lancs
55 L7 **Tarlton** Gloucs
26 B2 **Tarnock** Somset
112 D8 **Tarporley** Ches
25 H5 **Tarr** Somset
15 H2 **Tarrant Crawford** Dorset
27 L8 **Tarrant Gunville** Dorset

15 H1 **Tarrant Hinton** Dorset
15 H2 **Tarrant Keyneston** Dorset
15 H1 **Tarrant Launceston** Dorset
15 H2 **Tarrant Monkton** Dorset
15 H2 **Tarrant Rawston** Dorset
15 H2 **Tarrant Rushton** Dorset
19 L5 **Tarring Neville** E Susx
70 B6 **Tarrington** Herefs
199 J4 **Tarskavaig** Highld
217 G7 **Tarves** Abers
194 F4 **Tarvie** P & K
112 C7 **Tarvin** Ches
92 E4 **Tasburgh** Norfk
100 D7 **Tatenhill** Staffs
118 D5 **Tathwell** Lincs
32 D2 **Tatsfield** Surrey
98 C2 **Tattenhall** Ches
105 K6 **Tatterford** Norfk
105 K6 **Tattersett** Norfk
103 K2 **Tattershall** Lincs
103 L1 **Tattershall Thorpe** Lincs
78 D6 **Tattingstone** Suffk
78 D6 **Tattingstone White Horse** Suffk
13 J2 **Tatworth** Somset
215 J4 **Tauchers** Moray
25 K6 **Taunton** Somset
92 E2 **Taverham** Norfk
49 K5 **Tavernspite** Pembks
6 C2 **Tavistock** Devon
10 F5 **Taw Green** Devon
23 J5 **Tawstock** Devon
114 A5 **Taxal** Derbys
182 F3 **Taychreggan Hotel** Ag & B
194 C4 **Tay Forest Park** P & K
161 H1 **Tayinloan** Ag & B
55 G4 **Taynton** Gloucs
56 E5 **Taynton** Oxon
182 E2 **Taynuilt** Ag & B
187 G2 **Tayport** Fife
172 C2 **Tayvallich** Ag & B
117 J4 **Tealby** Lincs
151 G3 **Team Valley** Gatesd
199 K4 **Teangue** Highld
212 F2 **Teanord** Highld
138 E6 **Tebay** Cumb
59 G3 **Tebworth** Beds
11 J6 **Tedburn St Mary** Devon
55 L2 **Teddington** Gloucs
44 D6 **Teddington** Gt Lon
70 C3 **Tedstone Delamere** Herefs
70 C3 **Tedstone Wafer** Herefs
73 K1 **Teeton** Nhants
27 M5 **Teffont Evias** Wilts
27 M5 **Teffont Magna** Wilts
65 H7 **Tegryn** Pembks
88 C1 **Teigh** Rutlnd
7 K2 **Teigngrace** Devon
12 B7 **Teignmouth** Devon
166 F7 **Teindside** Border
84 C2 **Telford** Wrekin
27 J1 **Tellisford** Somset
19 L5 **Telscombe** E Susx
193 L5 **Tempar** P & K
155 J5 **Templand** D & G
5 J2 **Temple** Cnwll
177 J6 **Temple** Mdloth
66 C4 **Temple Bar** Cerdgn
38 F8 **Temple Cloud** BaNES
27 G6 **Templecombe** Somset

35 H5 **Temple Ewell** Kent
71 K4 **Temple Grafton** Warwks
56 D2 **Temple Guiting** Gloucs
124 F5 **Temple Hirst** N York
115 H7 **Temple Normanton** Derbys
197 K1 **Temple of Fiddes** Abers
212 E7 **Temple Pier** Highld
138 E2 **Temple Sowerby** Cumb
11 K3 **Templeton** Devon
49 J5 **Templeton** Pembks
150 E5 **Templetown** Dur
75 H4 **Tempsford** Beds
69 L2 **Tenbury Wells** Worcs
49 J7 **Tenby** Pembks
62 D3 **Tendring** Essex
62 D3 **Tendring Green** Essex
62 D3 **Tendring Heath** Essex
90 E4 **Ten Mile Bank** Norfk
34 B7 **Tenterden** Kent
61 J5 **Terling** Essex
98 F6 **Ternhill** Shrops
155 G6 **Terregles** D & G
133 K5 **Terrington** N York
104 E7 **Terrington St Clement** Norfk
90 D2 **Terrington St John** Norfk
33 J3 **Teston** Kent
29 G8 **Testwood** Hants
39 K2 **Tetbury** Gloucs
98 B6 **Tetchill** Shrops
9 J5 **Tetcott** Devon
118 D6 **Tetford** Lincs
118 D2 **Tetney** Lincs
58 B7 **Tetsworth** Oxon
84 F4 **Tettenhall** Wolves
101 J1 **Teversal** Notts
76 C3 **Teversham** Cambs
156 D2 **Teviothead** Border
59 L5 **Tewin** Herts
55 K2 **Tewkesbury** Gloucs
34 C3 **Teynham** Kent
123 H3 **Thackley** Brad
18 F3 **Thakeham** W Susx
58 B6 **Thame** Oxon
44 D6 **Thames Ditton** Surrey
45 J4 **Thamesmead** Gt Lon
34 F4 **Thanington** Kent
165 J2 **Thankerton** S Lans
92 E5 **Tharston** Norfk
41 K6 **Thatcham** W Berk
60 F2 **Thaxted** Essex
132 D3 **Theakston** N York
125 K6 **Thealby** N Linc
26 C3 **Theale** Somset
41 M6 **Theale** W Berk
126 D3 **Thearne** E R Yk
56 B7 **The Beeches** Gloucs
79 J2 **Theberton** Suffk
209 H7 **The Braes** Highld
178 E4 **The Brunt** E Loth
237 d4 **The Bungalow** IoM
55 K5 **The Butts** Gloucs
42 C2 **The City** Bucks
28 E5 **The Common** Wilts
83 J6 **The Corner** Shrops
87 J6 **Theddingworth** Leics
118 F4 **Theddlethorpe All Saints** Lincs
119 G4 **Theddlethorpe St Helen** Lincs
174 C7 **The Den** N Ayrs
5 G5 **The Eden Project** Cnwll
34 B5 **The Forstal** Kent
34 D6 **The Forstal** Kent
128 E3 **The Green** Cumb

61 J4 **The Green** Essex
143 G6 **The Green** N York
27 K5 **The Green** Wilts
151 M7 **The Headland** Hartpl
128 E3 **The Hill** Cumb
58 E6 **The Lee** Bucks
237 d2 **The Lhen** IoM
92 B7 **Thelnetham** Suffk
215 G2 **The Lochs** Moray
92 E7 **Thelveton** Norfk
112 F4 **Thelwall** Warrtn
106 C7 **Themelthorpe** Norfk
33 K7 **The Moor** Kent
51 J7 **The Mumbles** Swans
175 H4 **The Murray** S Lans
85 L1 **The National Memorial Arboretum** Staffs
206 D5 **The Neuk** Abers
73 G6 **Thenford** Nhants
55 K4 **The Reddings** Gloucs
75 L6 **Therfield** Herts
185 G3 **The Ross** P & K
21 H1 **The Stocks** Kent
39 L8 **The Strand** Wilts
91 K6 **Thetford** Norfk
91 J5 **Thetford Forest Park**
60 D7 **Theydon Bois** Essex
39 J7 **Thickwood** Wilts
118 C7 **Thimbleby** Lincs
141 K7 **Thimbleby** N York
111 J5 **Thingwall** Wirral
133 G4 **Thirkleby** N York
133 G3 **Thirlby** N York
178 C8 **Thirlestane** Border
137 J4 **Thirlspot** Cumb
132 C3 **Thirn** N York
132 F3 **Thirsk** N York
120 E3 **Thistleton** Lancs
102 E8 **Thistleton** Rutlnd
90 F7 **Thistley Green** Suffk
134 C7 **Thixendale** N York
158 B6 **Thockrington** Nthumb
90 B3 **Tholomas Drove** Cambs
133 G6 **Tholthorpe** N York
216 B6 **Thomastown** Abers
91 K4 **Thompson** Norfk
46 B6 **Thong** Kent
131 J3 **Thoralby** N York
117 K3 **Thoresway** Lincs
117 K3 **Thorganby** Lincs
125 G3 **Thorganby** N York
142 E7 **Thorgill** N York
93 J8 **Thorington** Suffk
78 B7 **Thorington Street** Suffk
131 H8 **Thorlby** N York
60 D7 **Thorley** Herts
16 D5 **Thorley Street** IoW
133 G5 **Thormanby** N York
141 K4 **Thornaby-on-Tees** S on T
106 C5 **Thornage** Norfk
73 L7 **Thornborough** Bucks
132 D4 **Thornborough** N York
123 J4 **Thornbury** Brad
9 K3 **Thornbury** Devon
70 B3 **Thornbury** Herefs
38 F3 **Thornbury** S Glos
87 J7 **Thornby** Nhants
100 A2 **Thorncliff** Staffs
13 J2 **Thorncombe** Dorset
78 D1 **Thorndon** Suffk
10 D6 **Thorndon Cross** Devon
125 G7 **Thorne** Donc
26 D7 **Thorne** Somset
124 B3 **Thorner** Leeds
25 H7 **Thorne St Margaret** Somset

89 K3 **Thorney** C Pete
116 E6 **Thorney** Notts
26 B6 **Thorney** Somset
16 A3 **Thorney Hill** Hants
25 L6 **Thornfalcon** Somset
26 E8 **Thornford** Dorset
149 K2 **Thorngrafton** Nthumb
126 F5 **Thorngumbald** E R Yk
105 H4 **Thornham** Norfk
78 D1 **Thornham Magna** Suffk
92 D8 **Thornham Parva** Suffk
88 F4 **Thornhaugh** C Pete
29 J8 **Thornhill** C Sotn
154 F3 **Thornhill** D & G
114 D5 **Thornhill** Derbys
123 K6 **Thornhill** Kirk
184 E7 **Thornhill** Stirlg
135 H6 **Thornholme** E R Yk
15 G2 **Thornicombe** Dorset
168 D3 **Thornington** Nthumb
150 E7 **Thornley** Dur
151 J6 **Thornley** Dur
174 F6 **Thornliebank** E Rens
77 G4 **Thorns** Suffk
114 A4 **Thornsett** Derbys
137 H3 **Thornthwaite** Cumb
132 B7 **Thornthwaite** N York
196 C6 **Thornton** Angus
123 G4 **Thornton** Brad
73 L7 **Thornton** Bucks
125 H2 **Thornton** E R Yk
186 E7 **Thornton** Fife
120 D3 **Thornton** Lancs
86 F3 **Thornton** Leics
118 C7 **Thornton** Lincs
141 L4 **Thornton** Middsb
179 K8 **Thornton** Nthumb
126 D6 **Thornton Curtis** N Linc
175 G7 **Thorntonhall** S Lans
44 F6 **Thornton Heath** Gt Lon
111 J5 **Thornton Hough** Wirral
122 D2 **Thornton-in-Craven** N York
130 D5 **Thornton in Lonsdale** N York
132 F2 **Thornton-le-Beans** N York
133 L6 **Thornton-le-Clay** N York
134 C3 **Thornton le Dale** N York
117 H3 **Thornton le Moor** Lincs
132 F2 **Thornton-le-Moor** N York
112 C6 **Thornton-le-Moors** Ches
132 F3 **Thornton-le-Street** N York
178 F4 **Thorntonloch** E Loth
131 H2 **Thornton Rust** N York
132 B3 **Thornton Steward** N York
132 C3 **Thornton Watlass** N York
178 D8 **Thornydykes** Border
137 L3 **Thornythwaite** Cumb
102 C4 **Thoroton** Notts
124 C2 **Thorp Arch** Leeds
100 D3 **Thorpe** Derbys
126 B2 **Thorpe** E R Yk
131 J6 **Thorpe** N York
102 C3 **Thorpe** Notts
43 G6 **Thorpe** Surrey
92 E7 **Thorpe Abbotts** Norfk

102 C7 **Thorpe Arnold** Leics
124 D7 **Thorpe Audlin** Wakefd
134 D5 **Thorpe Bassett** N York
46 E3 **Thorpe Bay** Sthend
88 C4 **Thorpe by Water** Rutlnd
86 C2 **Thorpe Constantine** Staffs
93 G2 **Thorpe End** Norfk
62 E4 **Thorpe Green** Essex
77 L4 **Thorpe Green** Suffk
115 G3 **Thorpe Hesley** Rothm
124 F7 **Thorpe in Balne** Donc
87 L5 **Thorpe Langton** Leics
43 G6 **Thorpe Lea** Surrey
62 E4 **Thorpe-le-Soken** Essex
125 K2 **Thorpe le Street** E R Yk
88 B7 **Thorpe Malsor** Nhants
73 G5 **Thorpe Mandeville** Nhants
106 F5 **Thorpe Market** Norfk
92 E1 **Thorpe Marriot** Norfk
77 L4 **Thorpe Morieux** Suffk
79 K3 **Thorpeness** Suffk
116 E7 **Thorpe on the Hill** Lincs
43 G6 **Thorpe Park** Surrey
92 F2 **Thorpe St Andrew** Norfk
104 D1 **Thorpe St Peter** Lincs
115 G3 **Thorpe Salvin** Rothm
87 K2 **Thorpe Satchville** Leics
141 J3 **Thorpe Thewles** S on T
103 J2 **Thorpe Tilney** Lincs
133 G7 **Thorpe Underwood** N York
88 E7 **Thorpe Waterville** Nhants
124 E4 **Thorpe Willoughby** N York
62 C4 **Thorrington** Essex
11 L4 **Thorverton** Devon
92 D7 **Thrandeston** Suffk
88 E7 **Thrapston** Nhants
98 C4 **Threapwood** Ches
100 B4 **Threapwood** Staffs
163 J7 **Threave** S Ayrs
146 C3 **Threave Castle** D & G
32 B5 **Three Bridges** W Susx
33 L5 **Three Chimneys** Kent
68 D6 **Three Cocks** Powys
51 H6 **Three Crosses** Swans
20 D2 **Three Cups Corner** E Susx
103 H5 **Threekingham** Lincs
33 H6 **Three Leg Cross** E Susx
15 K2 **Three Legged Cross** Dorset
42 B6 **Three Mile Cross** Wokham
176 E3 **Three Miletown** W Loth
21 G3 **Three Oaks** E Susx
167 H2 **Threepwood** Border
137 J3 **Threlkeld** Cumb
60 D6 **Threshers Bush** Essex
131 J6 **Threshfield** N York
93 K2 **Thrigby** Norfk
86 E1 **Thringstone** Leics
132 D2 **Thrintoft** N York
76 B5 **Thriplow** Cambs
60 B3 **Throcking** Herts
150 E2 **Throckley** N u Ty
71 H4 **Throckmorton** Worcs

15 L4 **Throop** Bmouth
158 C2 **Thropton** Nthumb
176 B1 **Throsk** Stirlg
154 F1 **Throughgate** D & G
11 G6 **Throwleigh** Devon
34 C4 **Throwley Forstal** Kent
101 J6 **Thrumpton** Notts
231 L6 **Thrumster** Highld
127 H8 **Thrunscoe** NE Lin
55 K7 **Thrupp** Gloucs
87 J1 **Thrussington** Leics
28 F3 **Thruxton** Hants
69 J7 **Thruxton** Herefs
115 J3 **Thrybergh** Rothm
101 H6 **Thulston** Derbys
46 C3 **Thundersley** Essex
87 H2 **Thurcaston** Leics
115 J4 **Thurcroft** Rothm
106 E5 **Thurgarton** Norfk
102 B3 **Thurgarton** Notts
114 F2 **Thurgoland** Barns
87 G4 **Thurlaston** Leics
72 F1 **Thurlaston** Warwks
25 K7 **Thurlbear** Somset
89 G1 **Thurlby** Lincs
102 E1 **Thurlby** Lincs
119 G6 **Thurlby** Lincs
74 F3 **Thurleigh** Beds
7 G7 **Thurlestone** Devon
76 F4 **Thurlow** Suffk
25 L5 **Thurloxton** Somset
114 E2 **Thurlstone** Barns
93 J4 **Thurlton** Norfk
87 H2 **Thurmaston** Leics
87 J3 **Thurnby** Leics
93 J1 **Thurne** Norfk
33 K2 **Thurnham** Kent
88 F6 **Thurning** Nhants
106 C6 **Thurning** Norfk
115 J1 **Thurnscoe** Barns
148 B5 **Thursby** Cumb
106 B5 **Thursford** Norfk
30 E4 **Thursley** Surrey
231 G2 **Thurso** Highld
111 H5 **Thurstaston** Wirral
77 L2 **Thurston** Suffk
148 B4 **Thurstonfield** Cumb
123 H7 **Thurstonland** Kirk
93 G4 **Thurton** Norfk
100 E5 **Thurvaston** Derbys
92 B3 **Thuxton** Norfk
139 K7 **Thwaite** N York
78 D2 **Thwaite** Suffk
129 H2 **Thwaite Head** Cumb
93 G4 **Thwaite St Mary** Norfk
135 G5 **Thwing** E R Yk
185 L3 **Tibbermore** P & K
154 E3 **Tibbers** D & G
55 H4 **Tibberton** Gloucs
70 F3 **Tibberton** Worcs
99 G7 **Tibberton** Wrekin
166 C5 **Tibbie Shiels Inn** Border
92 D5 **Tibenham** Norfk
101 H1 **Tibshelf** Derbys
134 E7 **Tibthorpe** E R Yk
33 H7 **Ticehurst** E Susx
29 L5 **Tichborne** Hants
88 E2 **Tickencote** Rutlnd
38 C6 **Tickenham** N Som
115 J2 **Tickhill** Donc
83 J5 **Ticklerton** Shrops
101 G7 **Ticknall** Derbys
126 E3 **Tickton** E R Yk
40 F8 **Tidcombe** Wilts
57 M6 **Tiddington** Oxon
72 B4 **Tiddington** Warwks
33 G7 **Tidebrook** E Susx
6 A4 **Tideford** Cnwll
38 E2 **Tidenham** Gloucs

114 D6 **Tideswell** Derbys
41 M5 **Tidmarsh** W Berk
72 C6 **Tidmington** Warwks
28 E2 **Tidworth** Wilts
48 F5 **Tiers Cross** Pembks
73 K4 **Tiffield** Nhants
196 E4 **Tigerton** Angus
233 b6 **Tigh a Ghearraidh** W Isls
233 b6 **Tigharry** W Isls
173 G4 **Tighnabruaich** Ag & B
7 H4 **Tigley** Devon
74 F2 **Tilbrook** Cambs
45 M5 **Tilbury** Thurr
86 C7 **Tile Hill** Covtry
42 A5 **Tilehurst** Readg
30 E3 **Tilford** Surrey
31 L4 **Tilgate** W Susx
26 E4 **Tilham Street** Somset
185 J7 **Tillicoultry** Clacks
164 F1 **Tillietudlem** S Lans
62 B7 **Tillingham** Essex
69 J5 **Tillington** Herefs
30 F6 **Tillington** W Susx
69 J5 **Tillington Common** Herefs
206 D4 **Tillybirloch** Abers
205 K5 **Tillycairn** Abers
206 C3 **Tillyfourie** Abers
207 G2 **Tillygreig** Abers
186 B6 **Tillyrie** P & K
35 J4 **Tilmanstone** Kent
104 F8 **Tilney All Saints** Norfk
104 E8 **Tilney High End** Norfk
90 D2 **Tilney St Lawrence** Norfk
28 B2 **Tilshead** Wilts
98 D5 **Tilstock** Shrops
98 C3 **Tilston** Ches
98 E1 **Tilstone Fearnall** Ches
59 G3 **Tilsworth** Beds
87 L3 **Tilton on the Hill** Leics
39 J2 **Tiltups End** Gloucs
103 J2 **Timberland** Lincs
113 K8 **Timbersbrook** Ches
24 E3 **Timberscombe** Somset
132 B8 **Timble** N York
156 B7 **Timpanheck** D & G
113 H4 **Timperley** Traffd
38 F8 **Timsbury** BaNES
29 G6 **Timsbury** Hants
232 d2 **Timsgarry** W Isls
232 d2 **Timsgearraidh** W Isls
77 J2 **Timworth** Suffk
77 J2 **Timworth Green** Suffk
14 E4 **Tincleton** Dorset
149 G3 **Tindale** Cumb
140 F2 **Tindale Crescent** Dur
58 A2 **Tingewick** Bucks
123 K5 **Tingley** Leeds
59 G3 **Tingrith** Beds
235 c6 **Tingwall Airport** Shet
9 K7 **Tinhay** Devon
115 H4 **Tinsley** Sheff
32 B5 **Tinsley Green** W Susx
8 E7 **Tintagel** Cnwll
8 D6 **Tintagel Castle** Cnwll
54 D7 **Tintern Abbey** Mons
54 D7 **Tintern Parva** Mons
26 D7 **Tintinhull** Somset
114 A3 **Tintwistle** Derbys
155 H5 **Tinwald** D & G
88 E3 **Tinwell** Rutlnd
85 G5 **Tipton** Sandw
12 E5 **Tipton St John** Devon
61 L5 **Tiptree** Essex

61 L5 **Tiptree Heath** Essex
67 J6 **Tirabad** Powys
188 C7 **Tiree Airport** Ag & B
172 C6 **Tiretigan** Ag & B
55 J3 **Tirley** Gloucs
53 H7 **Tirphil** Caerph
138 D2 **Tirril** Cumb
27 L5 **Tisbury** Wilts
100 D3 **Tissington** Derbys
22 C6 **Titchberry** Devon
17 G2 **Titchfield** Hants
88 E7 **Titchmarsh** Nhants
105 J4 **Titchwell** Norfk
102 B5 **Tithby** Notts
69 G3 **Titley** Herefs
32 D3 **Titsey** Surrey
99 K5 **Tittensor** Staffs
105 L7 **Tittleshall** Norfk
70 E1 **Titton** Worcs
98 D1 **Tiverton** Ches
24 E8 **Tiverton** Devon
92 E6 **Tivetshall St Margaret** Norfk
92 E6 **Tivetshall St Mary** Norfk
24 E3 **Tivington** Somset
99 L7 **Tixall** Staffs
88 E4 **Tixover** Rutlnd
235 C8 **Toab** Shet
189 L5 **Tobermory** Ag & B
181 L5 **Toberonochy** Ag & B
233 b7 **Tobha Mor** W Isls
216 D7 **Tocher** Abers
215 L2 **Tochieneal** Moray
40 B4 **Tockenham** Wilts
121 K6 **Tockholes** Bl w D
38 E3 **Tockington** S Glos
133 G8 **Tockwith** N York
27 J7 **Todber** Dorset
158 E3 **Todburn** Nthumb
59 G3 **Toddington** Beds
56 B2 **Toddington** Gloucs
72 B7 **Todenham** Gloucs
196 C8 **Todhills** Angus
148 C2 **Todhills** Cumb
122 D5 **Todmorden** Calder
115 J5 **Todwick** Rothm
75 L4 **Toft** Cambs
88 F1 **Toft** Lincs
235 C8 **Toft** Shet
140 E2 **Toft Hill** Dur
93 J4 **Toft Monks** Norfk
117 H4 **Toft next Newton** Lincs
105 L6 **Toftrees** Norfk
159 G2 **Togston** Nthumb
199 J3 **Tokavaig** Highld
42 B5 **Tokers Green** Oxon
232 g2 **Tolastadh** W Isls
25 H5 **Tolland** Somset
27 L7 **Tollard Royal** Wilts
124 E8 **Toll Bar** Donc
14 B3 **Toller Fratrum** Dorset
14 B3 **Toller Porcorum** Dorset
133 H6 **Tollerton** N York
101 L5 **Tollerton** Notts
13 M3 **Toller Whelme** Dorset
62 A6 **Tollesbury** Essex
61 L5 **Tolleshunt D'Arcy** Essex
61 L5 **Tolleshunt Knights** Essex
61 L5 **Tolleshunt Major** Essex
14 B3 **Tolpuddle** Dorset
232 g2 **Tolsta** W Isls
44 D6 **Tolworth** Gt Lon
213 J8 **Tomatin** Highld
201 K3 **Tomchrasky** Highld
201 H5 **Tomdoun** Highld
211 L8 **Tomich** Highld

212 E5 **Tomich** Highld
222 F7 **Tomich** Highld
226 A7 **Tomich** Highld
204 E2 **Tomintoul** Moray
212 D6 **Tomnacross** Highld
204 F1 **Tomnavoulin** Moray
33 G4 **Tonbridge** Kent
36 D4 **Tondu** Brdgnd
25 H6 **Tonedale** Somset
123 J4 **Tong** Brad
34 C4 **Tong** Kent
84 E3 **Tong** Shrops
101 H7 **Tonge** Leics
30 E2 **Tongham** Surrey
146 C4 **Tong Norton** Shrops
84 E2 **Tong Norton** Shrops
123 J4 **Tong Street** Brad
229 J4 **Tongue** Highld
37 H4 **Tongwynlais** Cardif
52 B7 **Tonna** Neath
60 B5 **Tonwell** Herts
36 F3 **Tonypandy** Rhondd
36 F3 **Tonyrefail** Rhondd
57 K7 **Toot Baldon** Oxon
60 E7 **Toot Hill** Essex
40 C4 **Toothill** Swindn
44 F5 **Tooting** Gt Lon
44 F5 **Tooting Bec** Gt Lon
132 F4 **Topcliffe** N York
92 F5 **Topcroft** Norfk
92 F5 **Topcroft Street** Norfk
77 G6 **Toppesfield** Essex
92 K4 **Toprow** Norfk
12 C5 **Topsham** Devon
162 A4 **Torbeg** N Ayrs
223 G2 **Torboll** Highld
213 G6 **Torbreck** Highld
7 J3 **Torbryan** Devon
192 B2 **Torcastle** Highld
7 J7 **Torcross** Devon
212 F4 **Tore** Highld
172 D5 **Torinturk** Ag & B
116 D5 **Torksey** Lincs
39 H5 **Tormarton** S Glos
161 M3 **Tormore** N Ayrs
213 J4 **Tornagrain** Highld
206 C4 **Tornaveen** Abers
212 E8 **Torness** Highld
140 F2 **Toronto** Dur
181 L1 **Torosay Castle** Ag & B
147 L6 **Torpenhow** Cumb
176 C4 **Torphichen** W Loth
206 C5 **Torphins** Abers
6 C5 **Torpoint** Cnwll
7 L3 **Torquay** Torbay
177 L8 **Torquhan** Border
209 J3 **Torran** Highld
175 H4 **Torrance** E Duns
163 J1 **Torranyard** N Ayrs
210 D3 **Torridon** Highld
210 D3 **Torridon House** Highld
199 H3 **Torrin** Highld
161 K3 **Torrisdale** Ag & B
229 K3 **Torrisdale** Highld
227 G5 **Torrish** Highld
129 K6 **Torrisholme** Lancs
226 A7 **Torrobull** Highld
207 H4 **Torry** C Aber
176 D2 **Torryburn** Fife
236 b4 **Torteval** Guern
155 H6 **Torthorwald** D & G
18 D5 **Tortington** W Susx
84 E8 **Torton** Worcs
39 G2 **Tortworth** S Glos
209 H5 **Torvaig** Highld
137 J7 **Torver** Cumb
175 L2 **Torwood** Falk
167 G2 **Torwoodlee** Border
116 A4 **Torworth** Notts
209 L6 **Toscaig** Highld
75 J3 **Toseland** Cambs

130 E7 **Tosside** Lancs
77 L2 **Tostock** Suffk
208 C4 **Totaig** Highld
208 F5 **Tote** Highld
209 H3 **Tote** Highld
16 D5 **Totland** IoW
114 F5 **Totley** Sheff
7 J4 **Totnes** Devon
101 J5 **Toton** Notts
188 F5 **Totronald** Ag & B
208 F2 **Totscore** Highld
45 G3 **Tottenham** Gt Lon
90 F2 **Tottenhill** Norfk
44 E2 **Totteridge** Gt Lon
59 G4 **Totternhoe** Beds
122 B7 **Tottington** Bury
29 G8 **Totton** Hants
25 J5 **Toulton** Somset
223 J5 **Toulvaddie** Highld
33 K3 **Tovil** Kent
173 K5 **Toward** Ag & B
173 J5 **Toward Quay** Ag & B
73 K5 **Towcester** Nhants
2 E4 **Towednack** Cnwll
58 B6 **Towersey** Oxon
205 K3 **Towie** Abers
150 E6 **Tow Law** Dur
90 B4 **Town End** Cambs
128 F2 **Town End** Cumb
174 D3 **Townend** W Duns
114 D2 **Townhead** Barns
155 H4 **Townhead** D & G
146 C3 **Townhead of Greenlaw** D & G
176 F1 **Townhill** Fife
19 L3 **Town Littleworth** E Susx
41 K8 **Towns End** Hants
3 G5 **Townshend** Cnwll
91 H6 **Town Street** Suffk
168 B4 **Town Yetholm** Border
133 K7 **Towthorpe** York
124 D3 **Towton** N York
110 D5 **Towyn** Conwy
111 K4 **Toxteth** Lpool
118 E8 **Toynton All Saints** Lincs
32 E3 **Toy's Hill** Kent
163 K5 **Trabboch** E Ayrs
163 L5 **Trabbochburn** E Ayrs
213 K3 **Tradespark** Highld
65 J4 **Traethsaith** Cerdgn
52 E3 **Trallong** Powys
101 G2 **Tramway Museum** Derbys
177 L4 **Tranent** E Loth
111 J4 **Tranmere** Wirral
230 C5 **Trantelbeg** Highld
230 C5 **Trantlemore** Highld
51 J2 **Trapp** Carmth
178 D4 **Traprain** E Loth
166 E3 **Traquair** Border
23 K6 **Traveller's Rest** Devon
122 D3 **Trawden** Lancs
96 A5 **Trawsfynydd** Gwynd
36 F3 **Trealaw** Rhondd
120 F4 **Treales** Lancs
108 C5 **Trearddur Bay** IoA
208 F4 **Treasaine** Highld
8 D7 **Trebarwith** Cnwll
4 E1 **Trebetherick** Cnwll
24 F4 **Treborough** Somset
5 M1 **Trebullett** Cnwll
6 A1 **Treburley** Cnwll
52 D3 **Trecastle** Powys
64 D7 **Trecwn** Pembks
52 F7 **Trecynon** Rhondd
53 H6 **Tredegar** Blae G
55 K3 **Tredington** Gloucs

72 C5 **Tredington** Warwks
38 B2 **Tredunnock** Mons
2 D6 **Treen** Cnwll
115 H4 **Treeton** Rothm
64 C6 **Trefasser** Pembks
53 H2 **Trefecca** Powys
81 L5 **Trefeglwys** Powys
49 G3 **Treffgarne** Pembks
48 E3 **Treffgarne Owen** Pembks
37 G3 **Trefforest** Rhondd
66 D3 **Trefilan** Cerdgn
64 B3 **Trefin** Pembks
110 E7 **Trefnant** Denbgs
97 K6 **Trefonen** Shrops
94 F4 **Trefor** Gwynd
8 E7 **Trefrew** Cnwll
109 L8 **Trefriw** Conwy
9 H7 **Tregadillett** Cnwll
54 B6 **Tregare** Mons
66 F7 **Tregaron** Cerdgn
109 H7 **Tregarth** Gwynd
9 H7 **Tregeare** Cnwll
97 J5 **Tregeiriog** Wrexhm
108 D3 **Tregele** IoA
3 K6 **Tregidden** Cnwll
48 D2 **Treglemais** Pembks
9 G5 **Tregole** Cnwll
4 E3 **Tregonetha** Cnwll
4 E6 **Tregony** Cnwll
68 E6 **Tregoyd** Powys
65 L5 **Tre-groes** Cerdgn
82 C4 **Tregynon** Powys
37 G3 **Trehafod** Rhondd
6 B4 **Trehan** Cnwll
37 H2 **Treharris** Myr Td
52 E7 **Treherbert** Rhondd
6 A1 **Trekenner** Cnwll
8 F8 **Treknow** Cnwll
110 F5 **Trelawnyd** Flints
65 J7 **Trelech** Carmth
48 C2 **Treleddyd-fawr** Pembks
37 H2 **Trelewis** Myr Td
8 C8 **Trelights** Cnwll
5 G1 **Trelill** Cnwll
4 C7 **Trelissick Garden** Cnwll
54 D6 **Trelleck** Mons
110 F5 **Trelogan** Flints
4 E3 **Trelow** Cnwll
95 K4 **Tremadog** Gwynd
8 F7 **Tremail** Cnwll
65 H5 **Tremain** Cerdgn
9 G6 **Tremaine** Cnwll
5 K3 **Tremar** Cnwll
6 B4 **Trematon** Cnwll
110 F6 **Tremeirchion** Denbgs
4 D3 **Trenance** Cnwll
4 D6 **Trenance** Cnwll
9 G5 **Trencreek** Cnwll
3 H5 **Trenear** Cnwll
9 G5 **Treneglos** Cnwll
26 E7 **Trent** Dorset
99 K4 **Trentham** C Stke
23 K2 **Trentishoe** Devon
36 E5 **Treoes** V Glam
37 G2 **Treorchy** Rhondd
5 G1 **Trequite** Cnwll
36 F5 **Trerhyngyll** V Glam
5 M4 **Trerulefoot** Cnwll
2 a1 **Tresco Heliport** IoS
4 D6 **Trescowe** Cnwll
4 C4 **Tresean** Cnwll
39 H3 **Tresham** Gloucs
4 D6 **Tresillian** Cnwll
9 G5 **Treskinnick Cross** Cnwll
9 G7 **Tresmeer** Cnwll
8 F6 **Tresparrett** Cnwll
194 C4 **Tressait** P & K
235 c5 **Tresta** Shet

235 e3 **Tresta** Shet
116 C5 **Treswell** Notts
80 E5 **Tre Taliesin** Cerdgn
8 F6 **Trethevey** Cnwll
2 C6 **Trethewey** Cnwll
5 G5 **Trethurgy** Cnwll
54 D4 **Tretire** Herefs
53 J4 **Tretower** Powys
97 K2 **Treuddyn** Flints
9 G8 **Trevague** Cnwll
8 E6 **Trevalga** Cnwll
98 B2 **Trevalyn** Wrexhm
4 D3 **Trevarrian** Cnwll
4 C4 **Treveal** Cnwll
8 E8 **Treveighan** Cnwll
3 J2 **Trevellas Downs** Cnwll
5 K3 **Trevelmond** Cnwll
3 K5 **Treverva** Cnwll
2 C6 **Trevescan** Cnwll
4 E5 **Treviscoe** Cnwll
4 D2 **Trevone** Cnwll
97 L4 **Trevor** Wrexhm
8 E7 **Trewalder** Cnwll
9 J8 **Trewarlett** Cnwll
8 E7 **Trewarmett** Cnwll
9 G7 **Treween** Cnwll
9 H7 **Trewen** Cnwll
9 G8 **Trewint** Cnwll
4 D7 **Trewithian** Cnwll
4 F5 **Trewoon** Cnwll
30 D7 **Treyford** W Susx
122 F6 **Triangle** Calder
151 J7 **Trimdon** Dur
151 J7 **Trimdon Colliery** Dur
151 J7 **Trimdon Grange** Dur
107 G5 **Trimingham** Norfk
78 F6 **Trimley** Suffk
50 F5 **Trimsaran** Carmth
23 H3 **Trimstone** Devon
194 B4 **Trinafour** P & K
58 F5 **Tring** Herts
196 F4 **Trinity** Angus
236 d6 **Trinity** Jersey
185 K4 **Trinity Gask** P & K
25 J4 **Triscombe** Somset
191 L2 **Trislaig** Highld
4 D5 **Trispen** Cnwll
158 F4 **Tritlington** Nthumb
194 F7 **Trochry** P & K
65 K5 **Troedyraur** Cerdgn
53 G7 **Troedyrhiw** Myr Td
3 H4 **Troon** Cnwll
163 H3 **Troon** S Ayrs
123 L3 **Tropical World Roundhay Park** Leeds
184 B5 **Trossachs** Stirlg
184 B6 **Trossachs Pier** Stirlg
91 K8 **Troston** Suffk
70 F4 **Trotshill** Worcs
33 H2 **Trottiscliffe** Kent
30 D6 **Trotton** W Susx
157 L4 **Troughend** Nthumb
137 L6 **Troutbeck** Cumb
137 L7 **Troutbeck Bridge** Cumb
115 H5 **Troway** Derbys
39 J8 **Trowbridge** Wilts
101 J4 **Trowell** Notts
92 F3 **Trowse Newton** Norfk
27 H3 **Trudoxhill** Somset
25 K6 **Trull** Somset
208 C3 **Trumpan** Highld
70 B6 **Trumpet** Herefs
76 C4 **Trumpington** Cambs
107 G5 **Trunch** Norfk
4 C6 **Truro** Cnwll
4 C6 **Truro Cathedral** Cnwll
11 K7 **Trusham** Devon
100 E5 **Trusley** Derbys
119 G5 **Trusthorpe** Lincs

84 F5 **Trysull** Staffs
57 H7 **Tubney** Oxon
7 J5 **Tuckenhay** Devon
84 F6 **Tuckhill** Shrops
3 H3 **Tuckingmill** Cnwll
27 L5 **Tuckingmill** Wilts
15 L4 **Tuckton** Bmouth
77 G1 **Tuddenham** Suffk
78 E5 **Tuddenham** Suffk
33 G4 **Tudeley** Kent
151 G7 **Tudhoe** Dur
94 D5 **Tudweiliog** Gwynd
55 J5 **Tuffley** Gloucs
29 J3 **Tufton** Hants
49 H2 **Tufton** Pembks
87 L4 **Tugby** Leics
83 L6 **Tugford** Shrops
169 J4 **Tughall** Nthumb
185 H7 **Tullibody** Clacks
212 F8 **Tullich** Highld
223 J6 **Tullich** Highld
194 F5 **Tulliemet** P & K
216 F7 **Tulloch** Abers
184 C4 **Tulloch** Stirlg
182 D7 **Tullochgorm** Ag & B
192 F1 **Tulloch Station** Highld
185 L1 **Tullybeagles Lodge** P & K
195 J5 **Tullymurdoch** P & K
206 B2 **Tullynessle** Abers
44 F5 **Tulse Hill** Gt Lon
51 G3 **Tumble** Carmth
103 L1 **Tumby** Lincs
103 L2 **Tumby Woodside** Lincs
194 B5 **Tummel Bridge** P & K
33 G5 **Tunbridge Wells** Kent
155 L6 **Tundergarth** D & G
39 G8 **Tunley** BaNES
99 K3 **Tunstall** C Stke
127 H4 **Tunstall** E R Yk
34 B3 **Tunstall** Kent
130 B5 **Tunstall** Lancs
140 F7 **Tunstall** N York
93 J2 **Tunstall** Norfk
99 H6 **Tunstall** Staffs
79 H4 **Tunstall** Suffk
151 J4 **Tunstall** Sundld
114 C6 **Tunstead** Derbys
107 G2 **Tunstead** Norfk
114 B5 **Tunstead Milton** Derbys
30 A4 **Tunworth** Hants
42 B8 **Turgis Green** Hants
56 C4 **Turkdean** Gloucs
87 K5 **Tur Langton** Leics
39 J7 **Turleigh** Wilts
69 G7 **Turnastone** Herefs
152 E2 **Turnberry** S Ayrs
100 F3 **Turnditch** Derbys
32 C6 **Turner's Hill** W Susx
14 F4 **Turners Puddle** Dorset
177 G4 **Turnhouse** C Edin
14 F2 **Turnworth** Dorset
216 D4 **Turriff** Abers
121 L7 **Turton Bottoms** Bl w D
89 L4 **Turves** Cambs
74 D4 **Turvey** Beds
42 C3 **Turville** Bucks
73 H6 **Turweston** Bucks
166 D5 **Tushielaw Inn** Border
98 D3 **Tushingham cum Grindley** Ches
100 E6 **Tutbury** Staffs
38 D2 **Tutshill** Gloucs
106 F6 **Tuttington** Norfk
116 C7 **Tuxford** Notts
234 B2 **Twatt** Ork
235 c5 **Twatt** Shet

175 J3 **Twechar** E Duns
179 K7 **Tweedmouth** Nthumb
166 L4 **Tweedsmuir** Border
3 K3 **Twelveheads** Cnwll
113 H7 **Twemlow Green** Ches
103 J7 **Twenty** Lincs
39 G7 **Twerton** BaNES
44 D5 **Twickenham** Gt Lon
55 J4 **Twigworth** Gloucs
19 H2 **Twineham** W Susx
77 J6 **Twinstead** Essex
24 C5 **Twitchen** Devon
114 F8 **Two Dales** Derbys
86 B4 **Two Gates** Staffs
86 D3 **Twycross** Leics
86 C3 **Twycross Zoo** Leics
58 A3 **Twyford** Bucks
29 J6 **Twyford** Hants
87 K2 **Twyford** Leics
106 B7 **Twyford** Norfk
42 C5 **Twyford** Wokham
146 B4 **Twynholm** D & G
70 F7 **Twyning** Gloucs
70 F6 **Twyning Green** Gloucs
51 L2 **Twynllanan** Carmth
88 D7 **Twywell** Nhants
69 H6 **Tyberton** Herefs
51 H4 **Tycroes** Carmth
97 H8 **Tycrwyn** Powys
104 D8 **Tydd Gote** Lincs
90 B1 **Tydd St Giles** Cambs
104 C8 **Tydd St Mary** Lincs
76 E7 **Tye Green** Essex
113 G2 **Tyldesley** Wigan
34 F3 **Tyler Hill** Kent
36 F1 **Tylorstown** Rhondd
96 F4 **Ty-nant** Conwy
183 K2 **Tyndrum** Stirlg
97 K4 **Ty'n-dwr** Denbgs
151 J2 **Tynemouth** N Tyne
178 D3 **Tyninghame** E Loth
154 E4 **Tynron** D & G
38 D6 **Tyntesfield** N Som
66 F1 **Tynygraig** Cerdgn
109 L7 **Ty'n-y-Groes** Conwy
37 G4 **Tyn-y-nant** Rhondd
74 C5 **Tyringham** M Keyn
36 D5 **Tythegston** Brdgnd
113 K6 **Tytherington** Ches
38 F3 **Tytherington** S Glos
27 K3 **Tytherington** Wilts
13 H2 **Tytherleigh** Devon
39 L5 **Tytherton Lucas** Wilts
5 H5 **Tywardreath** Cnwll
80 D4 **Tywyn** Gwynd

U

79 G1 **Ubbeston Green** Suffk
38 D8 **Ubley** BaNES
141 G6 **Uckerby** N York
19 M2 **Uckfield** E Susx
70 F6 **Uckinghall** Worcs
55 K3 **Uckington** Gloucs
83 L2 **Uckington** Shrops
175 J6 **Uddingston** S Lans
165 G3 **Uddington** S Lans
21 H2 **Udimore** E Susx
207 G1 **Udny Green** Abers
207 G1 **Udny Station** Abers
25 G8 **Uffculme** Devon
88 F3 **Uffington** Lincs
40 F3 **Uffington** Oxon
83 K2 **Uffington** Shrops
89 G3 **Ufford** C Pete
79 G4 **Ufford** Suffk
72 E3 **Ufton** Warwks

41 M6 **Ufton Nervet** W Berk
161 K4 **Ugadale** Ag & B
7 G5 **Ugborough** Devon
93 J7 **Uggeshall** Suffk
143 H5 **Ugglebarnby** N York
114 E4 **Ughill** Sheff
60 E3 **Ugley** Essex
60 E3 **Ugley Green** Essex
143 G5 **Ugthorpe** N York
188 F5 **Uig** Ag & B
208 A4 **Uig** Highld
208 F2 **Uig** Highld
232 d2 **Uig** W Isls
209 G5 **Uigshader** Highld
180 E4 **Uisken** Ag & B
231 K7 **Ulbster** Highld
137 L3 **Ulcat Row** Cumb
118 F6 **Ulceby** Lincs
126 D7 **Ulceby** N Linc
126 E7 **Ulceby Skitter** N Linc
33 L4 **Ulcombe** Kent
147 M7 **Uldale** Cumb
55 H7 **Uley** Gloucs
159 G4 **Ulgham** Nthumb
220 E3 **Ullapool** Highld
71 K2 **Ullenhall** Warwks
124 D3 **Ulleskelf** N York
87 G6 **Ullesthorpe** Leics
115 J4 **Ulley** Rothm
69 L4 **Ullingswick** Herefs
208 E6 **Ullinish Lodge Hotel** Highld
136 E3 **Ullock** Cumb
138 B3 **Ullswater** Cumb
128 E2 **Ulpha** Cumb
135 J7 **Ulrome** E R Yk
235 d3 **Ulsta** Shet
129 G4 **Ulverston** Cumb
15 J6 **Ulwell** Dorset
209 J4 **Umachan** Highld
23 J6 **Umberleigh** Devon
224 F2 **Unapool** Highld
129 K2 **Underbarrow** Cumb
156 E5 **Under Burnmouth** Border
123 J4 **Undercliffe** Brad
83 K2 **Underdale** Shrops
32 K2 **Under River** Kent
101 J3 **Underwood** Notts
38 C3 **Undy** Mons
237 c5 **Union Mills** IoM
115 G6 **Unstone** Derbys
28 C1 **Upavon** Wilts
14 C2 **Up Cerne** Dorset
46 D6 **Upchurch** Kent
24 B5 **Upcott** Devon
24 E6 **Upcott** Somset
12 B2 **Up Exe** Devon
106 D8 **Upgate** Norfk
14 B2 **Uphall** Dorset
176 E4 **Uphall** W Loth
11 K3 **Upham** Devon
29 K7 **Upham** Hants
69 H2 **Uphampton** Herefs
70 E2 **Uphampton** Worcs
37 L8 **Uphill** N Som
112 D1 **Up Holland** Lancs
174 E4 **Uplawmoor** E Rens
55 H3 **Upleadon** Gloucs
142 D4 **Upleatham** R & Cl
13 L4 **Uploders** Dorset
24 F7 **Uplowman** Devon
13 H4 **Uplyme** Devon
30 D8 **Up Marden** W Susx
45 K3 **Upminster** Gt Lon
26 E7 **Up Mudford** Somset
30 B2 **Up Nately** Hants
12 F2 **Upottery** Devon
83 J6 **Upper Affcot** Shrops
222 E4 **Upper Ardchronie** Highld
84 D7 **Upper Arley** Worcs

41 L5 **Upper Basildon**
W Berk
19 G4 **Upper Beeding**
W Susx
88 E5 **Upper Benefield**
Nhants
71 H2 **Upper Bentley** Worcs
230 C4 **Upper Bighouse**
Highld
72 F4 **Upper Boddington**
Nhants
72 C6 **Upper Brailes** Warwks
199 L2 **Upper Breakish**
Highld
70 E4 **Upper Broadheath**
Worcs
102 B7 **Upper Broughton**
Notts
41 K6 **Upper Bucklebury**
W Berk
28 D7 **Upper Burgate** Hants
148 D4 **Upperby** Cumb
75 H5 **Upper Caldecote**
Beds
67 L6 **Upper Chapel** Powys
27 L5 **Upper Chicksgrove**
Wilts
28 F2 **Upper Chute** Wilts
45 G3 **Upper Clapton** Gt Lon
29 G3 **Upper Clatford** Hants
55 M5 **Upper Coberley**
Gloucs
83 K3 **Upper Cound** Shrops
123 J8 **Upper Cumberworth**
Kirk
215 H2 **Upper Dallachy**
Moray
35 K4 **Upper Deal** Kent
74 F2 **Upper Dean** Beds
114 E1 **Upper Denby** Kirk
20 B4 **Upper Dicker** E Susx
230 E3 **Upper Dounreay**
Highld
62 F2 **Upper Dovercourt**
Essex
184 E6 **Upper Drumbane**
Stirlg
133 G6 **Upper Dunsforth**
N York
30 F3 **Upper Eashing**
Surrey
213 J2 **Upper Eathie** Highld
70 B5 **Upper Egleton** Herefs
100 B2 **Upper Elkstone** Staffs
100 C4 **Upper Ellastone**
Staffs
30 B4 **Upper Farringdon**
Hants
55 H6 **Upper Framilode**
Gloucs
30 C3 **Upper Froyle** Hants
208 E4 **Upperglen** Highld
26 C3 **Upper Godney**
Somset
75 G7 **Upper Gravenhurst**
Beds
76 E7 **Upper Green** Essex
41 G7 **Upper Green** W Berk
54 E3 **Upper Grove**
Common Herefs
30 D2 **Upper Hale** Surrey
43 H6 **Upper Halliford**
Surrey
88 C3 **Upper Hambleton**
Rutlnd
34 F3 **Upper Harbledown**
Kent
32 E6 **Upper Hartfield**
E Susx
55 L4 **Upper Hatherley**
Gloucs
123 H6 **Upper Heaton** Kirk

133 L7 **Upper Helmsley**
N York
68 J4 **Upper Hergest** Herefs
73 J3 **Upper Heyford**
Nhants
57 J3 **Upper Heyford** Oxon
69 J4 **Upper Hill** Herefs
123 J6 **Upper Hopton** Kirk
100 A1 **Upper Hulme** Staffs
40 D2 **Upper Inglesham**
Swindn
51 H6 **Upper Killay** Swans
183 G2 **Upper Kinchrackine**
Ag & B
40 F4 **Upper Lambourn**
W Berk
85 H3 **Upper Landywood**
Staffs
38 C7 **Upper Langford**
N Som
115 K7 **Upper Langwith**
Derbys
187 G6 **Upper Largo** Fife
100 A5 **Upper Leigh** Staffs
85 J2 **Upper Longdon** Staffs
75 H7 **Upper & Lower**
Stondon Beds
231 J7 **Upper Lybster** Highld
54 E5 **Upper Lydbrook**
Gloucs
69 H2 **Upper Lye** Herefs
113 M1 **Uppermill** Oldham
84 E8 **Upper Milton** Worcs
40 A3 **Upper Minety** Wilts
215 H4 **Upper Mulben** Moray
83 L5 **Upper Netchwood**
Shrops
100 B5 **Upper Nobut** Staffs
18 C3 **Upper Norwood**
W Susx
133 H8 **Upper Poppleton**
York
71 L5 **Upper Quinton**
Warwks
28 F6 **Upper Ratley** Hants
56 D4 **Upper Rissington**
Gloucs
70 B2 **Upper Rochford**
Worcs
145 L3 **Upper Ruscoe** D & G
70 C2 **Upper Sapey** Herefs
39 L4 **Upper Seagry** Wilts
74 E5 **Upper Shelton** Beds
106 D4 **Upper Sheringham**
Norfk
173 L5 **Upper Skelmorlie**
N Ayrs
56 D4 **Upper Slaughter**
Gloucs
54 F6 **Upper Soudley**
Gloucs
35 H6 **Upper Standen** Kent
154 E5 **Upper Stepford** D & G
92 F3 **Upper Stoke** Norfk
73 J3 **Upper Stowe** Nhants
28 D7 **Upper Street** Hants
93 H1 **Upper Street** Norfk
107 G8 **Upper Street** Norfk
77 H4 **Upper Street** Suffk
78 D4 **Upper Street** Suffk
59 H3 **Upper Sundon** Beds
56 D3 **Upper Swell** Gloucs
92 E4 **Upper Tasburgh**
Norfk
100 A5 **Upper Tean** Staffs
123 H8 **Upperthong** Kirk
30 F6 **Upperton** W Susx
100 E1 **Upper Town** Derbys
69 L5 **Upper Town** Herefs
231 L1 **Uppertown** Highld
38 D7 **Upper Town** N Som
77 K2 **Upper Town** Suffk

51 G3 **Upper Tumble**
Carmth
72 D5 **Upper Tysoe** Warwks
187 J1 **Upper Victoria** Angus
72 F5 **Upper Wardington**
Oxon
19 L3 **Upper Wellingham**
E Susx
92 F7 **Upper Weybread**
Suffk
29 L4 **Upper Wield** Hants
58 C5 **Upper Winchendon**
Bucks
28 C4 **Upper Woodford**
Wilts
39 J5 **Upper Wraxall** Wilts
88 C4 **Uppingham** Rutlnd
83 L2 **Uppington** Shrops
133 G3 **Upsall** N York
168 C1 **Upsettlington** Border
60 C7 **Upshire** Essex
29 H5 **Up Somborne** Hants
35 G3 **Upstreet** Kent
14 C3 **Up Sydling** Dorset
58 C5 **Upton** Bucks
89 G4 **Upton** C Pete
89 H7 **Upton** Cambs
112 B7 **Upton** Ches
5 L2 **Upton** Cnwll
7 G7 **Upton** Devon
12 E2 **Upton** Devon
14 E5 **Upton** Dorset
15 J4 **Upton** Dorset
29 G1 **Upton** Hants
29 G7 **Upton** Hants
86 D4 **Upton** Leics
116 E4 **Upton** Lincs
93 H2 **Upton** Norfk
102 B2 **Upton** Notts
116 C6 **Upton** Notts
41 K3 **Upton** Oxon
43 G5 **Upton** Slough
24 F5 **Upton** Somset
26 C6 **Upton** Somset
124 D7 **Upton** Wakefd
111 J4 **Upton** Wirral
54 F3 **Upton Bishop** Herefs
39 G6 **Upton Cheyney**
S Glos
84 B5 **Upton Cressett**
Shrops
5 L2 **Upton Cross** Cnwll
30 B2 **Upton Grey** Hants
11 J4 **Upton Hellions** Devon
27 L4 **Upton Lovell** Wilts
83 K2 **Upton Magna** Shrops
27 G4 **Upton Noble** Somset
11 L5 **Upton Pyne** Devon
55 K5 **Upton St Leonards**
Gloucs
27 K2 **Upton Scudamore**
Wilts
71 G4 **Upton Snodsbury**
Worcs
70 F6 **Upton upon Severn**
Worcs
71 G2 **Upton Warren** Worcs
18 C3 **Upwaltham** W Susx
90 C3 **Upwell** Norfk
89 J6 **Upwood** Cambs
40 B8 **Urchfont** Wilts
113 H3 **Urmston** Traffd
215 G2 **Urquhart** Moray
142 C6 **Urra** N York
212 D4 **Urray** Highld
197 H5 **Usan** Angus
151 G6 **Ushaw Moor** Dur
54 B7 **Usk** Mons
117 H3 **Usselby** Lincs
151 H4 **Usworth** Sundld
112 D8 **Utkinton** Ches
122 F3 **Utley** Brad

11 J5 **Uton** Devon
118 D3 **Utterby** Lincs
100 C5 **Uttoxeter** Staffs
43 H4 **Uxbridge** Gt Lon
235 d2 **Uyeasound** Shet
49 G5 **Uzmaston** Pembks

V

236 d2 **Vale** Guern
80 F7 **Vale of Rheidol**
Railway Cerdgn
108 C5 **Valley** IoA
209 H2 **Valtos** Highld
232 d2 **Valtos** W Isls
46 B3 **Vange** Essex
235 d2 **Vatsetter** Shet
208 D5 **Vatten** Highld
53 G6 **Vaynor** Myr Td
235 c6 **Veensgarth** Shet
68 D7 **Velindre** Powys
9 K5 **Venngreen** Devon
12 D4 **Venn Ottery** Devon
17 G6 **Ventnor** IoW
6 E4 **Venton** Devon
29 C1 **Vernham Dean** Hants
41 G8 **Vernham Street**
Hants
15 K2 **Verwood** Dorset
4 E7 **Veryan** Cnwll
128 E5 **Vickerstown** Cumb
4 F4 **Victoria** Cnwll
235 d4 **Vidlin** Shet
215 G2 **Viewfield** Moray
175 J6 **Viewpark** N Lans
45 M7 **Vigo** Kent
236 d3 **Village de Putron**
Guern
20 C3 **Vines Cross** E Susx
43 H6 **Virginia Water** Surrey
9 K6 **Virginstow** Devon
27 G2 **Vobster** Somset
235 c4 **Voe** Shet
69 G7 **Vowchurch** Herefs

W

140 E3 **Wackerfield** Dur
92 E5 **Wacton** Norfk
70 F5 **Wadborough** Worcs
58 C5 **Waddesdon** Bucks
7 K4 **Waddeton** Devon
117 G3 **Waddingham** Lincs
121 L2 **Waddington** Lancs
116 F8 **Waddington** Lincs
4 F2 **Wadebridge** Cnwll
13 H1 **Wadeford** Somset
88 E6 **Wadenhoe** Nhants
60 B4 **Wadesmill** Herts
33 H6 **Wadhurst** E Susx
114 F7 **Wadshelf** Derbys
115 K3 **Wadworth** Donc
104 D2 **Wainfleet All Saints**
Lincs
104 D2 **Wainfleet St Mary**
Lincs
9 G5 **Wainhouse Corner**
Cnwll
46 C6 **Wainscott** Medway
122 F5 **Wainstalls** Calder
139 H5 **Waitby** Cumb
118 C7 **Waithe** Lincs
123 L6 **Wakefield** Wakefd
88 D4 **Wakerley** Nhants
61 G3 **Wakes Colne** Essex
93 K8 **Walberswick** Suffk
18 C4 **Walberton** W Susx
146 D2 **Walbutt** D & G

26 D3 **Walcombe** Somset
103 H5 **Walcot** Lincs
83 L2 **Walcot** Shrops
40 D4 **Walcot** Swindn
87 H6 **Walcote** Leics
92 D7 **Walcot Green** Norfk
103 J2 **Walcott** Lincs
107 H6 **Walcott** Norfk
124 E6 **Walden Stubbs** N York
46 C7 **Walderslade** Medway
17 L1 **Walderton** W Susx
13 L4 **Walditch** Dorset
151 G5 **Waldridge** Dur
79 G5 **Waldringfield** Suffk
20 B2 **Waldron** E Susx
115 J5 **Wales** Rothm
26 E6 **Wales** Somset
117 J3 **Walesby** Lincs
116 B7 **Walesby** Notts
54 E4 **Walford** Herefs
83 H8 **Walford** Herefs
98 C8 **Walford Heath** Shrops
99 G3 **Walgherton** Ches
74 B1 **Walgrave** Nhants
113 G2 **Walkden** Salfd
151 H3 **Walker** N u Ty
166 E3 **Walkerburn** Border
116 C3 **Walkeringham** Notts
116 C3 **Walkerith** Lincs
59 M3 **Walkern** Herts
69 K5 **Walker's Green** Herefs
186 D6 **Walkerton** Fife
16 B4 **Walkford** Dorset
6 D2 **Walkhampton** Devon
126 B3 **Walkington** E R Yk
115 G4 **Walkley** Sheff
122 C5 **Walk Mill** Lancs
71 J2 **Walkwood** Worcs
150 A2 **Wall** Nthumb
85 K3 **Wall** Staffs
153 G2 **Wallacetown** S Ayrs
163 J5 **Wallacetown** S Ayrs
19 L4 **Wallands Park** E Susx
111 J3 **Wallasey** Wirral
41 L3 **Wallingford** Oxon
44 F6 **Wallington** Gt Lon
17 H2 **Wallington** Hants
75 K7 **Wallington** Herts
15 K4 **Wallisdown** Poole
235 b5 **Walls** Shet
151 H2 **Wallsend** N Tyne
177 H4 **Wallyford** E Loth
35 K5 **Walmer** Kent
121 G5 **Walmer Bridge** Lancs
85 K5 **Walmley** Birm
93 H8 **Walpole** Suffk
104 E8 **Walpole Cross Keys** Norfk
90 D2 **Walpole Highway** Norfk
104 D8 **Walpole St Andrew** Norfk
90 C1 **Walpole St Peter** Norfk
85 H4 **Walsall** Wsall
122 D6 **Walsden** Calder
78 B1 **Walsham le Willows** Suffk
132 F8 **Walshford** N York
90 C2 **Walsoken** Norfk
165 K1 **Walston** S Lans
59 K3 **Walsworth** Herts
42 D2 **Walter's Ash** Bucks
34 E5 **Waltham** Kent
118 C2 **Waltham** NE Lin
60 C7 **Waltham Abbey** Essex
29 K7 **Waltham Chase** Hants
60 B7 **Waltham Cross** Herts

102 D7 **Waltham on the Wolds** Leics
42 D5 **Waltham St Lawrence** W & M
45 G3 **Walthamstow** Gt Lon
148 F3 **Walton** Cumb
115 G7 **Walton** Derbys
124 C2 **Walton** Leeds
87 H6 **Walton** Leics
74 C7 **Walton** M Keyn
68 F3 **Walton** Powys
26 C4 **Walton** Somset
79 G7 **Walton** Suffk
17 M2 **Walton** W Susx
123 L6 **Walton** Wakefd
98 E8 **Walton** Wrekin
55 K2 **Walton Cardiff** Gloucs
49 H3 **Walton East** Pembks
38 B5 **Walton-in-Gordano** N Som
121 H5 **Walton-le-Dale** Lancs
43 J6 **Walton-on-Thames** Surrey
99 L7 **Walton-on-the-Hill** Staffs
31 L1 **Walton on the Hill** Surrey
62 F4 **Walton on the Naze** Essex
101 L8 **Walton on the Wolds** Leics
100 E8 **Walton-on-Trent** Derbys
38 B6 **Walton Park** N Som
48 E5 **Walton West** Pembks
141 G4 **Walworth** Darltn
45 G4 **Walworth** Gt Lon
48 E5 **Walwyn's Castle** Pembks
13 H2 **Wambrook** Somset
30 F2 **Wanborough** Surrey
40 E4 **Wanborough** Swindn
44 E5 **Wandsworth** Gt Lon
93 K7 **Wangford** Suffk
87 H2 **Wanlip** Leics
165 G6 **Wanlockhead** D & G
20 C5 **Wannock** E Susx
88 F4 **Wansford** C Pete
135 G7 **Wansford** E R Yk
33 K4 **Wanshurst Green** Kent
45 H3 **Wanstead** Gt Lon
27 G3 **Wanstrow** Somset
55 G7 **Wanswell** Gloucs
41 H3 **Wantage** Oxon
72 E2 **Wappenbury** Warwks
73 J5 **Wappenham** Nhants
20 C3 **Warbleton** E Susx
41 L2 **Warborough** Oxon
89 K7 **Warboys** Cambs
120 D3 **Warbreck** Bpool
9 G6 **Warbstow** Cnwll
113 G4 **Warburton** Traffd
139 H4 **Warcop** Cumb
150 A2 **Warden** Nthumb
72 F5 **Wardington** Oxon
98 E2 **Wardle** Ches
122 D6 **Wardle** Rochdl
151 H3 **Wardley** Gatesd
88 B4 **Wardley** Rutlnd
114 D6 **Wardlow** Derbys
90 C6 **Wardy Hill** Cambs
60 B5 **Ware** Herts
15 H5 **Wareham** Dorset
34 D7 **Warehorne** Kent
169 H4 **Warenford** Nthumb
60 C5 **Waresley** Herts
75 J4 **Waresley** Cambs
42 E6 **Warfield** Br For
7 K6 **Warfleet** Devon
42 C5 **Wargrave** Wokham

105 M4 **Warham All Saints** Norfk
105 M4 **Warham St Mary** Norfk
157 L6 **Wark** Nthumb
168 C2 **Wark** Nthumb
23 K6 **Warkleigh** Devon
88 C7 **Warkton** Nhants
72 F6 **Warkworth** Nhants
159 G2 **Warkworth** Nthumb
132 E2 **Warlaby** N York
5 J3 **Warleggan** Cnwll
122 F5 **Warley Town** Calder
32 C2 **Warlingham** Surrey
147 L2 **Warmfield** Wakefd
124 B6 **Warmingham** Ches
99 G1 **Warmington** Nhants
88 F5 **Warmington** Nhants
72 E5 **Warmington** Warwks
27 K3 **Warminster** Wilts
38 F5 **Warmley** S Glos
115 K2 **Warmsworth** Donc
14 E5 **Warmwell** Dorset
29 L6 **Warnford** Hants
31 J5 **Warnham** W Susx
18 D4 **Warningcamp** W Susx
31 L6 **Warninglid** W Susx
113 K7 **Warren** Ches
48 F7 **Warren** Pembks
165 J2 **Warrenhill** S Lans
42 D4 **Warren Row** W & M
34 C4 **Warren Street** Kent
74 C4 **Warrington** M Keyn
112 E4 **Warrington** Warrtn
177 H4 **Warriston** C Edin
16 F2 **Warsash** Hants
100 C2 **Warslow** Staffs
125 K1 **Warter** E R Yk
132 C4 **Warthermaske** N York
133 K7 **Warthill** N York
20 D4 **Wartling** E Susx
102 B7 **Wartnaby** Leics
120 E5 **Warton** Lancs
129 K5 **Warton** Lancs
86 C3 **Warton** Warwks
148 E4 **Warwick** Cumb
72 C2 **Warwick** Warwks
72 C2 **Warwick Castle** Warwks
234 c4 **Wasbister** Ork
137 G5 **Wasdale Head** Cumb
5 G2 **Washaway** Cnwll
7 J5 **Washbourne** Devon
78 D6 **Washbrook** Suffk
11 L2 **Washfield** Devon
140 D6 **Washfold** N York
25 G3 **Washford** Somset
11 J3 **Washford Pyne** Devon
117 G7 **Washingborough** Lincs
151 H4 **Washington** Sundld
18 F3 **Washington** W Susx
72 C3 **Wasperton** Warwks
133 H4 **Wass** N York
25 G3 **Watchet** Somset
40 E3 **Watchfield** Oxon
138 D7 **Watchgate** Cumb
11 H8 **Water** Devon
76 C2 **Waterbeach** Cambs
18 B4 **Waterbeach** W Susx
155 M6 **Waterbeck** D & G
14 C5 **Watercombe** Dorset
125 J3 **Water End** E R Yk
100 B3 **Waterfall** Staffs
175 G7 **Waterfoot** E Rens
60 A5 **Waterford** Herts
8 F8 **Watergate** Cnwll
164 B6 **Waterhead** E Ayrs
177 H7 **Waterheads** Border
100 B3 **Waterhouses** Staffs

33 H3 **Wateringbury** Kent
199 K2 **Waterloo** Highld
175 L7 **Waterloo** N Lans
195 G8 **Waterloo** P & K
49 G6 **Waterloo** Pembks
111 K2 **Waterloo** Sefton
17 J1 **Waterlooville** Hants
138 C3 **Watermillock** Cumb
89 G4 **Water Newton** Cambs
85 L5 **Water Orton** Warwks
57 L6 **Waterperry** Oxon
25 G6 **Waterrow** Somset
18 D3 **Watersfield** W Susx
121 K5 **Waterside** E Ayrs
163 K7 **Waterside** E Ayrs
163 L2 **Waterside** E Ayrs
175 J4 **Waterside** E Duns
208 B5 **Waterstein** Highld
57 M6 **Waterstock** Oxon
48 F6 **Waterston** Pembks
73 J7 **Water Stratford** Bucks
98 F8 **Waters Upton** Wrekin
43 J2 **Watford** Herts
73 H2 **Watford** Nhants
132 B6 **Wath** N York
132 E4 **Wath** N York
115 H2 **Wath upon Dearne** Rothm
90 E2 **Watlington** Norfk
42 B2 **Watlington** Oxon
231 J5 **Watten** Highld
92 B8 **Wattisfield** Suffk
78 B4 **Wattisham** Suffk
13 L4 **Watton** Dorset
126 C1 **Watton** E R Yk
91 K4 **Watton** Norfk
60 A4 **Watton-at-Stone** Herts
175 K4 **Wattston** N Lans
37 J3 **Wattsville** Caerph
206 C6 **Waulkmill** Abers
51 H6 **Waunarlwydd** Swans
80 E6 **Waunfawr** Cerdgn
95 J2 **Waunfawr** Gwynd
74 C6 **Wavendon** M Keyn
147 L5 **Waverbridge** Cumb
112 C8 **Waverton** Ches
147 L5 **Waverton** Cumb
126 D3 **Wawne** E R Yk
107 J7 **Waxham** Norfk
13 K2 **Wayford** Somset
13 L3 **Waytown** Dorset
11 K3 **Way Village** Devon
25 H4 **Weacombe** Somset
56 F7 **Weald** Oxon
44 D3 **Wealdstone** Gt Lon
123 K2 **Weardley** Leeds
26 B2 **Weare** Somset
23 G6 **Weare Giffard** Devon
149 L6 **Wearhead** Dur
26 B5 **Wearne** Somset
105 K7 **Weasenham All Saints** Norfk
105 K7 **Weasenham St Peter** Norfk
113 J2 **Weaste** Salfd
112 E6 **Weaverham** Ches
134 E5 **Weaverthorpe** N York
71 H2 **Webheath** Worcs
216 F7 **Wedderlairs** Abers
86 D5 **Weddington** Warwks
40 B8 **Wedhampton** Wilts
26 C2 **Wedmore** Somset
85 H4 **Wednesbury** Sandw
85 G4 **Wednesfield** Wolves
58 D4 **Weedon** Bucks
73 J3 **Weedon** Nhants
73 H5 **Weedon Lois** Nhants
85 K3 **Weeford** Staffs
29 J5 **Weeke** Hants

88 C7 **Weekley** Nhants
9 H5 **Week St Mary** Cnwll
126 D3 **Weel** E R Yk
62 D4 **Weeley** Essex
62 D4 **Weeley Heath** Essex
194 D6 **Weem** P & K
71 J4 **Weethley** Warwks
91 H5 **Weeting** Norfk
127 H6 **Weeton** E R Yk
120 E4 **Weeton** Lancs
123 K2 **Weeton** N York
123 K3 **Weetwood** Leeds
122 C5 **Weir** Lancs
6 C3 **Weir Quay** Devon
235 c5 **Weisdale** Shet
92 C2 **Welborne** Norfk
102 F2 **Welbourn** Lincs
133 L6 **Welburn** N York
141 J6 **Welbury** N York
102 F5 **Welby** Lincs
22 C7 **Welcombe** Devon
87 J7 **Welford** Nhants
41 H5 **Welford** W Berk
71 K4 **Welford-on-Avon** Warwks
87 L5 **Welham** Leics
116 B5 **Welham** Notts
59 L6 **Welham Green** Herts
30 C3 **Well** Hants
118 F6 **Well** Lincs
132 D3 **Well** N York
70 E6 **Welland** Worcs
196 D8 **Wellbank** Angus
72 C4 **Wellesbourne** Warwks
59 K3 **Well Head** Herts
45 J5 **Welling** Gt Lon
74 C2 **Wellingborough** Nhants
105 L7 **Wellingham** Norfk
103 G2 **Wellingore** Lincs
136 F6 **Wellington** Cumb
69 K5 **Wellington** Herefs
25 H7 **Wellington** Somset
84 B2 **Wellington** Wrekin
70 C6 **Wellington Heath** Herefs
39 H8 **Wellow** BaNES
16 E5 **Wellow** IoW
116 A7 **Wellow** Notts
26 D3 **Wells** Somset
105 L4 **Wells-next-the-sea** Norfk
61 G4 **Wellstye Green** Essex
185 K3 **Welltree** P & K
176 E2 **Wellwood** Fife
90 D5 **Welney** Norfk
98 C5 **Welshampton** Shrops
98 A6 **Welsh Frankton** Shrops
54 D4 **Welsh Newton** Herefs
82 E3 **Welshpool** Powys
36 F5 **Welsh St Donats** V Glam
148 C6 **Welton** Cumb
126 B5 **Welton** E R Yk
117 G3 **Welton** Lincs
73 H2 **Welton** Nhants
119 G7 **Welton le Marsh** Lincs
118 C4 **Welton le Wold** Lincs
127 H6 **Welwick** E R Yk
59 L5 **Welwyn** Herts
59 L5 **Welwyn Garden City** Herts
98 D6 **Wem** Shrops
25 L4 **Wembdon** Somset
44 D3 **Wembley** Gt Lon
6 D6 **Wembury** Devon
10 F3 **Wembworthy** Devon
173 L4 **Wemyss Bay** Inver
76 D7 **Wendens Ambo** Essex
57 K4 **Wendlebury** Oxon
91 L2 **Wendling** Norfk

58 E6 **Wendover** Bucks
3 H5 **Wendron** Cnwll
75 K5 **Wendy** Cambs
93 J7 **Wenhaston** Suffk
89 J7 **Wennington** Cambs
45 K4 **Wennington** Gt Lon
130 C5 **Wennington** Lancs
100 E1 **Wensley** Derbys
131 K2 **Wensley** N York
124 D6 **Wentbridge** Wakefd
83 H5 **Wentnor** Shrops
90 C7 **Wentworth** Cambs
115 G2 **Wentworth** Rothm
37 H6 **Wenvoe** V Glam
69 H4 **Weobley** Herefs
69 H4 **Weobley Marsh** Herefs
18 E4 **Wepham** W Susx
90 F3 **Wereham** Norfk
89 H3 **Werrington** C Pete
9 J7 **Werrington** Cnwll
112 B6 **Wervin** Ches
120 F4 **Wesham** Lancs
101 G2 **Wessington** Derbys
91 H1 **West Acre** Norfk
7 G6 **West Alvington** Devon
24 D6 **West Anstey** Devon
118 C6 **West Ashby** Lincs
17 M2 **West Ashling** W Susx
27 K1 **West Ashton** Wilts
140 F3 **West Auckland** Dur
134 F3 **West Ayton** N York
25 J5 **West Bagborough** Somset
112 D5 **West Bank** Halton
117 K5 **West Barkwith** Lincs
143 G5 **West Barnby** N York
178 E3 **West Barns** E Loth
105 L5 **West Barsham** Norfk
13 L4 **West Bay** Dorset
106 D5 **West Beckham** Norfk
43 H5 **West Bedfont** Surrey
35 G3 **Westbere** Kent
62 A3 **West Bergholt** Essex
14 A5 **West Bexington** Dorset
91 G1 **West Bilney** Norfk
19 J4 **West Blatchington** Br & H
151 J3 **West Boldon** S Tyne
102 D4 **Westborough** Lincs
15 K4 **Westbourne** Bmouth
17 L2 **Westbourne** W Susx
123 H4 **West Bowling** Brad
34 E6 **West Brabourne** Kent
91 K2 **West Bradenham** Norfk
121 L2 **West Bradford** Lancs
26 E4 **West Bradley** Somset
123 K7 **West Bretton** Wakefd
101 L5 **West Bridgford** Notts
85 H5 **West Bromwich** Sandw
35 J2 **Westbrook** Kent
41 H6 **Westbrook** W Berk
166 E6 **West Buccleuch Hotel** Border
23 K5 **West Buckland** Devon
25 J7 **West Buckland** Somset
131 J3 **West Burton** N York
73 J7 **Westbury** Bucks
83 G2 **Westbury** Shrops
27 K2 **Westbury** Wilts
27 K2 **Westbury Leigh** Wilts
55 G5 **Westbury on Severn** Gloucs
38 E5 **Westbury-on-Trym** Bristl
26 D2 **Westbury-sub-Mendip** Somset

116 D1 **West Butterwick** N Linc
120 E4 **Westby** Lancs
43 H7 **West Byfleet** Surrey
144 D8 **West Cairngaan** D & G
93 K2 **West Caister** Norfk
176 D5 **West Calder** W Loth
26 E6 **West Camel** Somset
14 E5 **West Chaldon** Dorset
41 G3 **West Challow** Oxon
7 H7 **West Charleton** Devon
159 G3 **West Chevington** Nthumb
18 E3 **West Chiltington** W Susx
26 C8 **West Chinnock** Somset
31 H2 **West Clandon** Surrey
35 J3 **West Cliffe** Kent
46 E3 **Westcliff-on-Sea** Sthend
26 D8 **West Coker** Somset
27 G4 **Westcombe** Somset
26 E3 **West Compton** Somset
14 B4 **West Compton Abbas** Dorset
56 E4 **Westcote** Gloucs
57 H3 **Westcote Barton** Oxon
58 B5 **Westcott** Bucks
12 C2 **Westcott** Devon
31 J2 **Westcott** Surrey
125 G3 **West Cottingwith** N York
40 E7 **Westcourt** Wilts
124 F6 **West Cowick** E R Yk
51 H7 **West Cross** Swans
148 B5 **West Curthwaite** Cumb
20 B5 **Westdean** E Susx
18 B3 **West Dean** W Susx
28 E6 **West Dean** Wilts
89 G2 **West Deeping** Lincs
111 L3 **West Derby** Lpool
90 F4 **West Dereham** Norfk
23 H3 **West Down** Devon
8 E7 **Westdowns** Cnwll
43 H4 **West Drayton** Gt Lon
116 B6 **West Drayton** Notts
231 J2 **West Dunnet** Highld
126 C5 **West Ella** E R Yk
74 E4 **West End** Beds
29 J8 **West End** Hants
38 C6 **West End** N Som
93 K2 **West End** Norfk
42 F7 **West End** Surrey
27 M6 **West End** Wilts
42 A7 **West End Green** Hants
231 G5 **Westerdale** Highld
142 E6 **Westerdale** N York
212 F7 **Wester Drumashie** Highld
78 E5 **Westerfield** Suffk
18 C5 **Westergate** W Susx
32 D3 **Westerham** Kent
150 F2 **Westerhope** N u Ty
7 K4 **Westerland** Devon
39 G4 **Westerleigh** S Glos
176 D4 **Wester Ochiltree** W Loth
187 J6 **Wester Pitkierie** Fife
220 C5 **Wester Ross** Highld
197 G5 **Westerton** Angus
235 c6 **Westerwick** Shet
33 J3 **West Farleigh** Kent
73 G4 **West Farndon** Nhants
97 M7 **West Felton** Shrops
26 F2 **Westfield** BaNES

136 D2 **Westfield** Cumb
21 G3 **Westfield** E Susx
230 F3 **Westfield** Highld
175 J4 **Westfield** N Lans
92 B2 **Westfield** Norfk
176 C4 **Westfield** W Loth
195 J6 **Westfields of Rattray** P & K
19 M4 **West Firle** E Susx
150 A7 **Westgate** Dur
125 J8 **Westgate** N Linc
35 J2 **Westgate on Sea** Kent
40 E7 **West Grafton** Wilts
30 C1 **West Green** Hants
28 E6 **West Grimstead** Wilts
31 K6 **West Grinstead** W Susx
124 E5 **West Haddlesey** N York
73 J1 **West Haddon** Nhants
41 K3 **West Hagbourne** Oxon
84 F7 **West Hagley** Worcs
93 J7 **Westhall** Suffk
101 H4 **West Hallam** Derbys
125 L6 **West Halton** N Linc
14 C6 **Westham** Dorset
20 D5 **Westham** E Susx
45 H4 **West Ham** Gt Lon
26 B3 **Westham** Somset
18 B4 **Westhampnett** W Susx
115 H6 **West Handley** Derbys
41 H2 **West Hanney** Oxon
61 H7 **West Hanningfield** Essex
28 C5 **West Harnham** Wilts
38 E8 **West Harptree** BaNES
30 C7 **West Harting** W Susx
25 L7 **West Hatch** Somset
27 L5 **West Hatch** Wilts
187 J1 **West Haven** Angus
26 C3 **Westhay** Somset
85 J7 **West Heath** Birm
227 H5 **West Helmsdale** Highld
41 H3 **West Hendred** Oxon
134 E4 **West Heslerton** N York
38 B7 **West Hewish** N Som
69 L5 **Westhide** Herefs
206 F4 **Westhill** Abers
12 D4 **West Hill** Devon
32 C6 **West Hoathly** W Susx
15 G5 **West Holme** Dorset
69 J4 **Westhope** Herefs
83 J6 **Westhope** Shrops
45 M3 **West Horndon** Essex
103 L6 **Westhorpe** Lincs
78 C2 **Westhorpe** Suffk
26 E3 **West Horrington** Somset
31 H2 **West Horsley** Surrey
35 H6 **West Hougham** Kent
112 F1 **Westhoughton** Bolton
130 D5 **Westhouse** N York
101 H2 **Westhouses** Derbys
15 K4 **West Howe** Bmouth
31 K2 **Westhumble** Surrey
185 M3 **West Huntingtower** P & K
25 L3 **West Huntspill** Somset
34 F7 **West Hythe** Kent
41 J4 **West Ilsley** W Berk
17 L3 **West Itchenor** W Susx
40 C6 **West Kennett** Wilts
173 L8 **West Kilbride** N Ayrs
45 L7 **West Kingsdown** Kent

39	J5	West Kington Wilts
111	H4	West Kirby Wirral
134	D4	West Knapton N York
		West Knighton Dorset
27	K5	West Knoyle Wilts
6	F5	Westlake Devon
26	B7	West Lambrook Somset
35	J5	West Langdon Kent
191	L5	West Laroch Highld
30	E7	West Lavington W Susx
28	A2	West Lavington Wilts
140	E5	West Layton N York
101	K7	West Leake Notts
7	H4	West Leigh Devon
11	G4	West Leigh Devon
23	G5	Westleigh Devon
25	G7	Westleigh Devon
25	H5	West Leigh Somset
79	J2	Westleton Suffk
91	J1	West Lexham Norfk
77	J2	Westley Suffk
76	E3	Westley Waterless Cambs
133	K6	West Lilling N York
58	C6	Westlington Bucks
176	F7	West Linton Border
148	D3	Westlinton Cumb
39	H5	West Littleton S Glos
41	H3	West Lockinge Oxon
14	F6	West Lulworth Dorset
134	E5	West Lutton N York
26	E5	West Lydford Somset
25	L5	West Lyng Somset
104	F7	West Lynn Norfk
33	H2	West Malling Kent
70	D5	West Malvern Worcs
30	C8	West Marden W Susx
116	B6	West Markham Notts
35	H3	Westmarsh Kent
127	G8	West Marsh NE Lin
122	D1	West Marton N York
27	K7	West Melbury Dorset
29	M6	West Meon Hants
62	B5	West Mersea Essex
19	K3	Westmeston E Susx
84	E7	West Midlands Safari Park Worcs
60	B3	Westmill Herts
13	L3	West Milton Dorset
44	F4	Westminster Gt Lon
46	E5	West Minster Kent
43	J6	West Molesey Surrey
25	K5	West Monkton Somset
15	K2	West Moors Dorset
15	G4	West Morden Dorset
167	J2	West Morriston Border
26	E7	West Mudford Somset
196	B5	Westmuir Angus
133	L4	West Ness N York
147	K6	Westnewton Cumb
126	F3	West Newton E R Yk
105	H6	West Newton Norfk
25	L5	West Newton Somset
44	F5	West Norwood Gt Lon
151	J2	Westoe S Tyne
7	J2	West Ogwell Devon
39	G6	Weston BaNES
99	G3	Weston Ches
12	E3	Weston Devon
12	F5	Weston Devon
30	B6	Weston Hants
59	L3	Weston Herts
103	M7	Weston Lincs
123	H2	Weston N York
73	H5	Weston Nhants
116	C7	Weston Notts
83	L5	Weston Shrops
97	L6	Weston Shrops
41	H5	Weston W Berk
69	L6	Weston Beggard Herefs
39	J3	Westonbirt Gloucs
87	L5	Weston by Welland Nhants
29	J4	Weston Colley Hants
76	E4	Weston Colville Cambs
30	B3	Weston Corbett Hants
99	L4	Weston Coyney C Stke
73	L3	Weston Favell Nhants
76	F4	Weston Green Cambs
84	D2	Weston Heath Shrops
59	G2	Westoning Beds
38	C5	Weston-in-Gordano N Som
99	H7	Weston Jones Staffs
92	D1	Weston Longville Norfk
98	B7	Weston Lullingfields Shrops
57	K4	Weston-on-the-Green Oxon
30	B3	Weston Patrick Hants
97	L5	Weston Rhyn Shrops
71	K6	Weston Subedge Gloucs
37	L7	Weston-Super-Mare N Som
58	D6	Weston Turville Bucks
84	E2	Weston-under-Lizard Staffs
54	F4	Weston under Penyard Herefs
98	E6	Weston-under-Redcastle Shrops
72	D1	Weston under Wetherley Warwks
100	F4	Weston Underwood Derbys
74	C4	Weston Underwood M Keyn
101	H6	Weston-upon-Trent Derbys
25	M4	Westonzoyland Somset
27	J7	West Orchard Dorset
40	C6	West Overton Wilts
134	B6	Westow N York
15	K3	West Parley Dorset
33	H3	West Peckham Kent
151	G4	West Pelton Dur
26	D4	West Pennard Somset
4	B4	West Pentire Cnwll
75	G2	West Perry Cambs
24	D3	West Porlock Somset
26	B7	Westport Somset
14	D2	West Pulham Dorset
9	K2	West Putford Devon
25	H3	West Quantoxhead Somset
176	B3	Westquarter Falk
11	K4	West Raddon Devon
151	H5	West Rainton Dur
117	H4	West Rasen Lincs
234	c3	Westray Airport Ork
105	L7	West Raynham Norfk
41	K4	Westridge Green W Berk
176	B5	Westrigg W Loth
40	D2	Westrop Swindn
141	K6	West Rounton N York
90	F7	West Row Suffk
105	K6	West Rudham Norfk
106	E4	West Runton Norfk
178	D7	Westruther Border
90	B4	Westry Cambs
11	J4	West Sandford Devon
235	d3	West Sandwick Shet
131	K3	West Scrafton N York
14	D4	West Stafford Dorset
116	C3	West Stockwith Notts
17	M2	West Stoke W Susx
27	H6	West Stour Dorset
35	H3	West Stourmouth Kent
77	J1	West Stow Suffk
40	C7	West Stowell Wilts
78	B1	West Street Suffk
132	D4	West Tanfield N York
5	J3	West Taphouse Cnwll
172	E5	West Tarbert Ag & B
18	F5	West Tarring W Susx
158	F3	West Thirston Nthumb
17	L3	West Thorney W Susx
101	L7	West Thorpe Notts
45	L4	West Thurrock Thurr
46	A4	West Tilbury Thurr
29	M5	West Tisted Hants
117	J5	West Torrington Lincs
17	K3	West Town Hants
38	C6	West Town N Som
28	F5	West Tytherley Hants
90	C2	West Walton Norfk
90	C2	West Walton Highway Norfk
148	B6	Westward Cumb
23	G5	Westward Ho! Devon
34	D5	Westwell Kent
56	E6	Westwell Oxon
34	C5	Westwell Leacon Kent
28	F7	West Wellow Hants
6	D6	West Wembury Devon
186	E7	West Wemyss Fife
76	B2	Westwick Cambs
76	E5	West Wickham Cambs
45	G6	West Wickham Gt Lon
49	H6	West Williamston Pembks
90	F1	West Winch Norfk
28	E5	West Winterslow Wilts
17	L3	West Wittering W Susx
131	K2	West Witton N York
12	C3	Westwood Devon
35	K2	Westwood Kent
39	J8	Westwood Wilts
157	M5	West Woodburn Nthumb
41	M7	West Woodhay W Berk
116	C2	Westwoodside N Linc
30	C4	West Worldham Hants
18	F5	West Worthing W Susx
76	E4	West Wratting Cambs
9	H2	West Youlstone Cnwll
148	E4	Wetheral Cumb
124	B7	Wetherby Leeds
78	B3	Wetherden Suffk
78	D2	Wetheringsett Suffk
61	H2	Wethersfield Essex
78	D2	Wetherup Street Suffk
99	L3	Wetley Rocks Staffs
98	F1	Wettenhall Ches
100	C2	Wetton Staffs
134	E7	Wetwang E R Yk
99	H5	Wetwood Staffs
40	F8	Wexcombe Wilts
92	F7	Weybread Suffk
92	F7	Weybread Street Suffk
43	H7	Weybridge Surrey
13	H3	Weycroft Devon
231	H3	Weydale Highld
28	F3	Weyhill Hants
14	D6	Weymouth Dorset
74	B7	Whaddon Bucks
75	L5	Whaddon Cambs
55	J5	Whaddon Gloucs
28	D6	Whaddon Wilts
39	K7	Whaddon Wilts
115	K7	Whaley Derbys
114	A5	Whaley Bridge Derbys
115	K7	Whaley Thorns Derbys
231	K0	Whaligoe Highld
121	L4	Whalley Lancs
158	E6	Whalton Nthumb
104	A7	Whaplode Lincs
89	K2	Whaplode Drove Lincs
72	E4	Wharf Warwks
130	E5	Wharfe N York
120	F4	Wharles Lancs
74	D5	Wharley End Beds
114	F3	Wharncliffe Side Sheff
134	D7	Wharram-le-Street N York
69	K4	Wharton Herefs
140	E6	Whashton N York
129	L4	Whasset Cumb
72	C5	Whatcote Warwks
86	B4	Whateley Warwks
78	B5	Whatfield Suffk
13	J2	Whatley Somset
27	G3	Whatley Somset
20	F3	Whatlington E Susx
34	F5	Whatsole Street Kent
101	G2	Whatstandwell Derbys
102	C5	Whatton Notts
145	J5	Whauphill D & G
93	K5	Wheatacre Norfk
59	K5	Wheathampstead Herts
84	B6	Wheathill Shrops
30	C4	Wheatley Hants
57	L6	Wheatley Oxon
151	J6	Wheatley Hill Dur
115	L1	Wheatley Hills Donc
84	F2	Wheaton Aston Staffs
24	E4	Wheddon Cross Somset
99	H2	Wheelock Ches
121	J6	Wheelton Lancs
125	G2	Wheldrake York
56	D7	Whelford Gloucs
59	G6	Whelpley Hill Bucks
60	A4	Whempstead Herts
133	K5	Whenby N York
77	J3	Whepstead Suffk
78	E6	Wherstead Suffk
29	H3	Wherwell Hants
114	C6	Wheston Derbys
33	H4	Whetsted Kent
87	G4	Whetstone Leics
128	D3	Whicham Cumb
72	C7	Whichford Warwks
150	F3	Whickham Gatesd
11	G6	Whiddon Down Devon
196	D7	Whigstreet Angus
73	J2	Whilton Nhants
12	D3	Whimple Devon

107 H6 **Whimpwell Green** Norfk
92 B2 **Whinburgh** Norfk
146 C4 **Whinnie Liggate** D & G
217 K7 **Whinnyfold** Abers
17 G4 **Whippingham** IoW
59 G4 **Whipsnade** Beds
59 G4 **Whipsnade Wild Animal Park** Beds
12 B4 **Whipton** Devon
116 E7 **Whisby** Lincs
88 B2 **Whissendine** Rutlnd
105 L7 **Whissonsett** Norfk
183 J8 **Whistlefield** Ag & B
183 G8 **Whistlefield Inn** Ag & B
42 C5 **Whistley Green** Wokham
112 C3 **Whiston** Knows
74 B3 **Whiston** Nhants
115 H4 **Whiston** Rothm
84 F2 **Whiston** Staffs
100 B3 **Whiston** Staffs
128 D3 **Whitbeck** Cumb
70 D3 **Whitbourne** Herefs
151 J3 **Whitburn** S Tyne
176 C5 **Whitburn** W Loth
143 J5 **Whitby** N York
178 F6 **Whitchester** Border
38 F6 **Whitchurch** BaNES
58 D4 **Whitchurch** Bucks
37 J4 **Whitchurch** Cardif
6 D2 **Whitchurch** Devon
29 J2 **Whitchurch** Hants
54 D4 **Whitchurch** Herefs
41 M5 **Whitchurch** Oxon
48 D3 **Whitchurch** Pembks
98 D4 **Whitchurch** Shrops
13 K4 **Whitchurch Canonicorum** Dorset
41 M5 **Whitchurch Hill** Oxon
14 D5 **Whitcombe** Dorset
83 H5 **Whitcot** Shrops
82 F6 **Whitcott Keysett** Shrops
86 B5 **Whiteacre Heath** Warwks
25 H7 **White Ball** Somset
202 D3 **Whitebridge** Highld
54 D6 **Whitebrook** Mons
207 H2 **Whitecairns** Abers
45 G4 **Whitechapel** Gt Lon
121 H3 **White Chapel** Lancs
54 E6 **Whitecliffe** Gloucs
61 L3 **White Colne** Essex
177 K4 **Whitecraig** E Loth
144 E4 **Whitecrook** D & G
3 H6 **White Cross** Cnwll
176 C3 **Whitecross** Falk
70 E7 **White End** Worcs
222 F4 **Whiteface** Highld
161 L2 **Whitefarland** N Ayrs
163 H7 **Whitefaulds** S Ayrs
113 J1 **Whitefield** Bury
25 G5 **Whitefield** Somset
206 D1 **Whiteford** Abers
112 F7 **Whitegate** Ches
234 d5 **Whitehall** Ork
136 D4 **Whitehaven** Cumb
30 C5 **Whitehill and Bordon** Hants
216 C2 **Whitehills** Abers
206 C3 **Whitehouse** Abers
172 D6 **Whitehouse** Ag & B
178 D3 **Whitekirk** E Loth
14 D3 **White Lackington** Dorset
26 B7 **Whitelackington** Somset
71 G4 **White Ladies Aston** Worcs

58 D6 **Whiteleaf** Bucks
17 G6 **Whiteley Bank** IoW
214 B4 **Whitemire** Moray
101 K4 **Whitemoor** C Nott
4 F4 **Whitemoor** Cnwll
235 c6 **Whiteness** Shet
61 J4 **White Notley** Essex
28 E6 **Whiteparish** Wilts
118 E6 **White Pit** Lincs
206 F2 **Whiterashes** Abers
60 E5 **White Roding** Essex
231 L5 **Whiterow** Highld
214 C3 **Whiterow** Moray
55 J6 **Whiteshill** Gloucs
20 B3 **Whitesmith** E Susx
13 H1 **Whitestaunton** Somset
69 L6 **White Stone** Herefs
11 K6 **Whitestone Cross** Devon
42 D5 **White Waltham** W & M
121 K2 **Whitewell** Lancs
35 J5 **Whitfield** Kent
73 H6 **Whitfield** Nhants
149 K4 **Whitfield** Nthumb
38 F3 **Whitfield** S Glos
13 G4 **Whitford** Devon
111 G5 **Whitford** Flints
125 J6 **Whitgift** E R Yk
99 K6 **Whitgreave** Staffs
145 J6 **Whithorn** D & G
162 D4 **Whiting Bay** N Ayrs
124 B4 **Whitkirk** Leeds
49 L4 **Whitland** Carmth
167 G6 **Whitlaw** Border
163 J5 **Whitletts** S Ayrs
124 E6 **Whitley** N York
42 B6 **Whitley** Readg
115 G3 **Whitley** Sheff
39 K6 **Whitley** Wilts
159 J7 **Whitley Bay** N Tyne
150 B4 **Whitley Chapel** Nthumb
123 J6 **Whitley Lower** Kirk
55 H6 **Whitminster** Gloucs
99 J4 **Whitmore** Staffs
25 G7 **Whitnage** Devon
72 D2 **Whitnash** Warwks
68 F5 **Whitney-on-Wye** Herefs
147 M4 **Whitriggels** Cumb
28 C7 **Whitsbury** Hants
179 H7 **Whitsome** Border
38 B4 **Whitson** Newpt
47 J6 **Whitstable** Kent
9 H5 **Whitstone** Cnwll
168 F6 **Whittingham** Nthumb
83 H5 **Whittingslow** Shrops
115 G6 **Whittington** Derbys
56 A4 **Whittington** Gloucs
130 B4 **Whittington** Lancs
91 G4 **Whittington** Norfk
97 L6 **Whittington** Shrops
84 F6 **Whittington** Staffs
85 L2 **Whittington** Staffs
86 C4 **Whittington** Warwks
70 F4 **Whittington** Worcs
73 K5 **Whittlebury** Nhants
121 H6 **Whittle-le-Woods** Lancs
89 J4 **Whittlesey** Cambs
76 C5 **Whittlesford** Cambs
125 L5 **Whitton** N Linc
158 D3 **Whitton** Nthumb
68 F2 **Whitton** Powys
141 J3 **Whitton** S on T
83 L8 **Whitton** Shrops
150 D4 **Whittonstall** Nthumb
41 J8 **Whitway** Hants
115 K6 **Whitwell** Derbys

59 K4 **Whitwell** Herts
17 G6 **Whitwell** IoW
141 M7 **Whitwell** N York
88 D2 **Whitwell** Rutlnd
133 L6 **Whitwell-on-the-Hill** N York
106 D7 **Whitwell Street** Norfk
86 E1 **Whitwick** Leics
122 D6 **Whitworth** Lancs
98 D5 **Whixall** Shrops
133 G7 **Whixley** N York
140 E4 **Whorlton** Dur
141 L6 **Whorlton** N York
69 L3 **Whyle** Herefs
32 C2 **Whyteleafe** Surrey
123 H4 **Wibsey** Brad
86 F6 **Wibtoft** Warwks
70 D2 **Wichenford** Worcs
34 M4 **Wichling** Kent
15 L4 **Wick** Bmouth
231 L5 **Wick** Highld
39 G5 **Wick** S Glos
36 E6 **Wick** V Glam
18 D5 **Wick** W Susx
71 G5 **Wick** Worcs
231 L5 **Wick Airport** Highld
76 E1 **Wicken** Cambs
73 L6 **Wicken** Nhants
60 D2 **Wicken Bonhunt** Essex
117 H5 **Wickenby** Lincs
115 J3 **Wickersley** Rothm
77 L6 **Wicker Street Green** Suffk
46 C2 **Wickford** Essex
17 H1 **Wickham** Hants
41 H6 **Wickham** W Berk
61 K5 **Wickham Bishops** Essex
35 G3 **Wickhambreaux** Kent
77 H4 **Wickhambrook** Suffk
71 J6 **Wickhamford** Worcs
78 D2 **Wickham Green** Suffk
79 G4 **Wickham Market** Suffk
93 J3 **Wickhampton** Norfk
77 J7 **Wickham St Paul** Essex
78 C2 **Wickham Skeith** Suffk
78 C1 **Wickham Street** Suffk
92 C3 **Wicklewood** Norfk
106 E5 **Wickmere** Norfk
38 A7 **Wick St Lawrence** N Som
39 G3 **Wickwar** S Glos
60 E2 **Widdington** Essex
159 G3 **Widdrington** Nthumb
159 G4 **Widdrington Station** Nthumb
7 G1 **Widecombe in the Moor** Devon
5 L4 **Widegates** Cnwll
9 G4 **Widemouth Bay** Cnwll
159 G7 **Wide Open** N Tyne
61 H6 **Widford** Essex
60 C5 **Widford** Herts
42 E7 **Widmer End** Bucks
101 M6 **Widmerpool** Notts
45 H6 **Widmore** Gt Lon
112 D5 **Widnes** Halton
13 G3 **Widworthy** Devon
112 E1 **Wigan** Wigan
26 C7 **Wigborough** Somset
12 E4 **Wiggaton** Devon
90 E2 **Wiggenhall St Germans** Norfk
90 E2 **Wiggenhall St Mary Magdalen** Norfk

90 E2 **Wiggenhall St Mary the Virgin** Norfk
58 F6 **Wigginton** Herts
57 H2 **Wigginton** Oxon
86 B3 **Wigginton** Staffs
133 J7 **Wigginton** York
130 F7 **Wigglesworth** N York
148 B4 **Wiggonby** Cumb
124 D2 **Wighill** N York
105 M4 **Wighton** Norfk
84 F4 **Wightwick** Wolves
29 G7 **Wigley** Hants
69 H2 **Wigmore** Herefs
46 D6 **Wigmore** Medway
116 E7 **Wigsley** Notts
88 F6 **Wigsthorpe** Nhants
87 H4 **Wigston** Leics
86 F5 **Wigston Parva** Leics
115 L5 **Wigthorpe** Notts
103 L5 **Wigtoft** Lincs
148 A5 **Wigton** Cumb
145 J4 **Wigtown** D & G
123 L3 **Wike** Leeds
88 B5 **Wilbarston** Nhants
125 H1 **Wilberfoss** E R Yk
90 C7 **Wilburton** Cambs
74 C2 **Wilby** Nhants
92 B5 **Wilby** Norfk
78 F1 **Wilby** Suffk
40 C7 **Wilcot** Wilts
98 B8 **Wilcott** Shrops
113 M7 **Wildboarclough** Ches
75 G4 **Wilden** Beds
84 E8 **Wilden** Worcs
175 L7 **Wildmanbridge** S Lans
85 G7 **Wildmoor** Worcs
116 D3 **Wildsworth** Lincs
98 F4 **Wilkesley** Ches
223 K4 **Wilkhaven** Highld
176 F5 **Wilkieston** W Loth
12 D1 **Willand** Devon
99 G3 **Willaston** Ches
111 K6 **Willaston** Ches
74 C6 **Willen** M Keyn
86 D7 **Willenhall** Covtry
85 H4 **Willenhall** Wsall
126 C4 **Willerby** E R Yk
134 F4 **Willerby** N York
71 K6 **Willersey** Gloucs
68 F5 **Willersley** Herefs
34 D6 **Willesborough** Kent
34 D6 **Willesborough Lees** Kent
44 E3 **Willesden** Gt Lon
39 J3 **Willesley** Wilts
25 H5 **Willett** Somset
84 C4 **Willey** Shrops
86 F6 **Willey** Warwks
30 F7 **Wiley Green** Surrey
72 F5 **Williamscot** Oxon
59 L2 **Willian** Herts
60 F6 **Willingale** Essex
20 C5 **Willingdon** E Susx
76 B1 **Willingham** Cambs
116 E5 **Willingham by Stow** Lincs
76 F4 **Willingham Green** Cambs
75 G4 **Willington** Beds
100 F6 **Willington** Derbys
150 F7 **Willington** Dur
33 K3 **Willington** Kent
72 C6 **Willington** Warwks
151 H2 **Willington Quay** N Tyne
125 H4 **Willitoft** E R Yk
25 H4 **Williton** Somset
119 G6 **Willoughby** Lincs
73 G2 **Willoughby** Warwks
101 M7 **Willoughby-on-the-Wolds** Notts

87 H5 **Willoughby Waterleys** Leics
116 F3 **Willoughton** Lincs
61 H4 **Willows Green** Essex
26 B6 **Willtown** Somset
71 L3 **Wilmcote** Warwks
13 G3 **Wilmington** Devon
20 B5 **Wilmington** E Susx
45 K5 **Wilmington** Kent
113 J5 **Wilmslow** Ches
121 K4 **Wilpshire** Lancs
123 G3 **Wilsden** Brad
103 G4 **Wilsford** Lincs
28 C4 **Wilsford** Wilts
40 C8 **Wilsford** Wilts
123 G8 **Wilshaw** Kirk
132 B6 **Wilsill** N York
101 H7 **Wilson** Leics
176 C7 **Wilsontown** S Lans
74 F5 **Wilstead** Beds
88 F2 **Wilsthorpe** Lincs
58 E5 **Wilstone** Herts
54 E3 **Wilton** Herefs
134 D3 **Wilton** N York
142 C4 **Wilton** R & Cl
28 C5 **Wilton** Wilts
40 E7 **Wilton** Wilts
167 G6 **Wilton Dean** Border
76 E6 **Wimbish** Essex
76 E7 **Wimbish Green** Essex
44 E6 **Wimbledon** Gt Lon
90 B5 **Wimblington** Cambs
113 G8 **Wimboldsley** Ches
15 J3 **Wimborne Minster** Dorset
28 B8 **Wimborne St Giles** Dorset
90 E3 **Wimbotsham** Norfk
75 L4 **Wimpole** Cambs
72 B5 **Wimpstone** Warwks
27 G5 **Wincanton** Somset
176 E4 **Winchburgh** W Loth
56 A3 **Winchcombe** Gloucs
21 H3 **Winchelsea** E Susx
29 J5 **Winchester** Hants
33 J5 **Winchet Hill** Kent
30 C1 **Winchfield** Hants
42 F2 **Winchmore Hill** Bucks
44 F2 **Winchmore Hill** Gt Lon
113 L7 **Wincle** Ches
115 G3 **Wincobank** Sheff
137 L7 **Windermere** Cumb
72 D6 **Winderton** Warwks
212 E5 **Windhill** Highld
42 F7 **Windlesham** Surrey
4 D2 **Windmill** Cnwll
20 D4 **Windmill Hill** E Susx
25 L7 **Windmill Hill** Somset
56 D5 **Windrush** Gloucs
216 B3 **Windsole** Abers
42 F5 **Windsor** W & M
42 F5 **Windsor Castle** W & M
55 J7 **Windsoredge** Gloucs
77 K4 **Windsor Green** Suffk
72 C1 **Windy Arbour** Warwks
186 E7 **Windygates** Fife
31 L7 **Wineham** W Susx
127 G5 **Winestead** E R Yk
92 D6 **Winfarthing** Norfk
17 G5 **Winford** IoW
38 D7 **Winford** N Som
68 F5 **Winforton** Herefs
14 F5 **Winfrith Newburgh** Dorset
58 E4 **Wing** Bucks
88 C2 **Wing** Rutlnd
151 J7 **Wingate** Dur
115 G7 **Wingerworth** Derbys
59 G3 **Wingfield** Beds
92 F7 **Wingfield** Suffk
27 J1 **Wingfield** Wilts
35 H3 **Wingham** Kent
35 G5 **Wingmore** Kent
58 E4 **Wingrave** Bucks
102 B2 **Winkburn** Notts
42 E6 **Winkfield** Br For
42 E6 **Winkfield Row** Br For
100 B3 **Winkhill** Staffs
10 F4 **Winkleigh** Devon
132 C5 **Winksley** N York
150 F3 **Winlaton** Gatesd
231 K5 **Winless** Highld
120 F2 **Winmarleigh** Lancs
29 J5 **Winnall** Hants
42 C6 **Winnersh** Wokham
112 F6 **Winnington** Ches
38 B8 **Winscombe** N Som
112 F7 **Winsford** Ches
24 E4 **Winsford** Somset
23 H4 **Winsham** Devon
13 J2 **Winsham** Somset
100 F7 **Winshill** Staffs
51 K6 **Winshwen** Swans
149 G7 **Winskill** Cumb
30 A2 **Winslade** Hants
39 J7 **Winsley** Wilts
58 C3 **Winslow** Bucks
56 C6 **Winson** Gloucs
28 F8 **Winsor** Hants
129 J2 **Winster** Cumb
100 E1 **Winster** Derbys
140 E4 **Winston** Dur
78 E3 **Winston** Suffk
55 L6 **Winstone** Gloucs
10 D3 **Winswell** Devon
14 D5 **Winterborne Came** Dorset
14 F2 **Winterborne Clenston** Dorset
14 F2 **Winterborne Houghton** Dorset
15 G3 **Winterborne Kingston** Dorset
14 D5 **Winterborne Monkton** Dorset
14 F2 **Winterborne Stickland** Dorset
14 F3 **Winterborne Whitechurch** Dorset
15 G3 **Winterborne Zelston** Dorset
38 F4 **Winterbourne** S Glos
41 J4 **Winterbourne** W Berk
14 C4 **Winterbourne Abbas** Dorset
40 C5 **Winterbourne Bassett** Wilts
28 D4 **Winterbourne Dauntsey** Wilts
28 D5 **Winterbourne Earls** Wilts
28 D4 **Winterbourne Gunner** Wilts
40 C6 **Winterbourne Monkton** Wilts
14 C4 **Winterbourne Steepleton** Dorset
28 B3 **Winterbourne Stoke** Wilts
131 H7 **Winterburn** N York
125 L6 **Winteringham** N Linc
99 H2 **Winterley** Ches
28 E5 **Winterslow** Wilts
125 L6 **Winterton** N Linc
107 K8 **Winterton-on-Sea** Norfk
102 D2 **Winthorpe** Notts
15 K4 **Winton** Bmouth
139 H5 **Winton** Cumb
134 D5 **Wintringham** N York
89 G7 **Winwick** Cambs
87 J8 **Winwick** Nhants
112 E3 **Winwick** Warrtn
100 F2 **Wirksworth** Derbys
111 J4 **Wirral**
98 D4 **Wirswall** Ches
90 C2 **Wisbech** Cambs
90 B2 **Wisbech St Mary** Cambs
31 H6 **Wisborough Green** W Susx
49 K6 **Wiseman's Bridge** Pembks
116 B4 **Wiseton** Notts
175 L7 **Wishaw** N Lans
85 L5 **Wishaw** Warwks
43 H8 **Wisley Gardens** Surrey
117 K6 **Wispington** Lincs
93 H7 **Wissett** Suffk
62 A2 **Wissington** Suffk
83 H6 **Wistanstow** Shrops
98 F6 **Wistanswick** Shrops
99 G2 **Wistaston** Ches
49 H4 **Wiston** Pembks
165 J3 **Wiston** S Lans
18 F3 **Wiston** W Susx
89 K7 **Wistow** Cambs
124 F4 **Wistow** N York
121 L3 **Wiswell** Lancs
90 C7 **Witcham** Cambs
15 J2 **Witchampton** Dorset
90 C7 **Witchford** Cambs
26 C6 **Witcombe** Somset
61 K5 **Witham** Essex
27 H3 **Witham Friary** Somset
88 F1 **Witham on the Hill** Lincs
118 C5 **Withcall** Lincs
19 J4 **Withdean** Br & H
33 H7 **Witherenden Hill** E Susx
11 J3 **Witheridge** Devon
86 D4 **Witherley** Leics
118 F5 **Withern** Lincs
127 H5 **Withernsea** E R Yk
126 F3 **Withernwick** E R Yk
92 F7 **Withersdale Street** Suffk
76 F5 **Withersfield** Suffk
129 J3 **Witherslack** Cumb
129 J3 **Witherslack Hall** Cumb
4 F3 **Withiel** Cnwll
24 F5 **Withiel Florey** Somset
56 B5 **Withington** Gloucs
69 L5 **Withington** Herefs
113 J3 **Withington** Manch
83 L2 **Withington** Shrops
100 B5 **Withington** Staffs
11 K3 **Withleigh** Devon
85 H8 **Withybed Green** Worcs
86 E6 **Withybrook** Warwks
24 F3 **Withycombe** Somset
32 E6 **Withyham** E Susx
24 D4 **Withypool** Somset
38 E6 **Withywood** Bristl
30 F4 **Witley** Surrey
78 E4 **Witnesham** Suffk
57 G6 **Witney** Oxon
88 F3 **Wittering** C Pete
21 H1 **Wittersham** Kent
85 J5 **Witton** Birm
93 G2 **Witton** Norfk
107 H6 **Witton** Norfk
151 G5 **Witton Gilbert** Dur
140 E2 **Witton le Wear** Dur
140 F2 **Witton Park** Dur
25 G5 **Wiveliscombe** Somset
30 A4 **Wivelrod** Hants
19 K2 **Wivelsfield** E Susx
19 K2 **Wivelsfield Green** E Susx
62 C4 **Wivenhoe** Essex
106 C4 **Wiveton** Norfk
62 E3 **Wix** Essex
71 K4 **Wixford** Warwks
77 G6 **Wixoe** Suffk
58 F2 **Woburn** Beds
58 F2 **Woburn Abbey** Beds
74 D7 **Woburn Sands** M Keyn
43 G8 **Woking** Surrey
42 D6 **Wokingham** Wokham
32 C3 **Woldingham** Surrey
135 G5 **Wold Newton** E R Yk
118 C3 **Wold Newton** NE Lin
165 K3 **Wolfclyde** S Lans
105 G4 **Wolferton** Norfk
186 B2 **Wolfhill** P & K
49 G3 **Wolf's Castle** Pembks
48 F3 **Wolfsdale** Pembks
84 F6 **Wollaston** Dudley
74 C2 **Wollaston** Nhants
83 G2 **Wollaston** Shrops
101 K4 **Wollaton** C Nott
98 F6 **Wollerton** Shrops
85 G6 **Wollescote** Dudley
100 A7 **Wolseley Bridge** Staffs
150 D7 **Wolsingham** Dur
99 J3 **Wolstanton** Staffs
86 E7 **Wolston** Warwks
57 J6 **Wolvercote** Oxon
85 G4 **Wolverhampton** Wolves
84 E5 **Wolverhampton Business Airport** Staffs
84 E7 **Wolverley** Worcs
41 K8 **Wolverton** Hants
74 B6 **Wolverton** M Keyn
72 B3 **Wolverton** Warwks
27 H5 **Wolverton** Wilts
54 C7 **Wolvesnewton** Mons
86 E6 **Wolvey** Warwks
86 E5 **Wolvey Heath** Warwks
141 K3 **Wolviston** S on T
133 K3 **Wombleton** N York
84 F5 **Wombourne** Staffs
115 H2 **Wombwell** Barns
35 G5 **Womenswold** Kent
124 E6 **Womersley** N York
31 G3 **Wonersh** Surrey
12 B4 **Wonford** Devon
29 J4 **Wonston** Hants
42 E3 **Wooburn** Bucks
42 E3 **Wooburn Green** Bucks
115 J5 **Woodall** Rothm
93 G1 **Woodbastwick** Norfk
71 J4 **Wood Bevington** Warwks
101 M3 **Woodborough** Notts
40 C7 **Woodborough** Wilts
12 F4 **Woodbridge** Devon
78 F5 **Woodbridge** Suffk
12 C5 **Woodbury** Devon
12 C5 **Woodbury Salterton** Devon
55 J7 **Woodchester** Gloucs
34 C7 **Woodchurch** Kent
24 E5 **Woodcombe** Somset
44 F7 **Woodcote** Gt Lon
41 M4 **Woodcote** Oxon
84 D1 **Woodcote** Wrekin
38 D2 **Woodcroft** Gloucs
106 C6 **Wood Dalling** Norfk
76 F3 **Woodditton** Cambs
57 K5 **Woodeaton** Oxon
43 J4 **Wood End** Gt Lon

60 B3 **Wood End** Herts
190 F4 **Woodend** Highld
73 H5 **Woodend** Nhants
176 C4 **Woodend** W Loth
17 M2 **Woodend** W Susx
71 K1 **Wood End** Warwks
118 C8 **Wood Enderby** Lincs
60 E3 **Woodend Green** Essex
28 D7 **Woodfalls** Wilts
9 G3 **Woodford** Cnwll
39 G2 **Woodford** Gloucs
45 H2 **Woodford** Gt Lon
88 D7 **Woodford** Nhants
113 K5 **Woodford** Stockp
45 H2 **Woodford Bridge** Gt Lon
73 G4 **Woodford Halse** Nhants
45 H2 **Woodford Wells** Gt Lon
85 H6 **Woodgate** Birm
25 H7 **Woodgate** Devon
18 C5 **Woodgate** W Susx
71 H2 **Woodgate** Worcs
44 F2 **Wood Green** Gt Lon
28 D7 **Woodgreen** Hants
131 J2 **Woodhall** N York
117 K8 **Woodhall Spa** Lincs
58 B4 **Woodham** Bucks
43 H7 **Woodham** Surrey
61 J7 **Woodham Ferrers** Essex
61 K6 **Woodham Mortimer** Essex
61 K6 **Woodham Walter** Essex
85 G3 **Wood Hayes** Wolves
216 E6 **Woodhead** Abers
26 A6 **Woodhill** Somset
159 H4 **Woodhorn** Nthumb
123 K4 **Woodhouse** Leeds
87 G1 **Woodhouse** Leics
115 H4 **Woodhouse** Sheff
124 B6 **Woodhouse** Wakefd
87 G2 **Woodhouse Eaves** Leics
177 H5 **Woodhouselee** Mdloth
156 D6 **Woodhouselees** D & G
100 D8 **Woodhouses** Staffs
89 K7 **Woodhurst** Cambs
19 K5 **Woodingdean** Br & H
123 K5 **Woodkirk** Leeds
207 G2 **Woodland** Abers
6 F5 **Woodland** Devon
7 J3 **Woodland** Devon
140 D2 **Woodland** Dur
34 F6 **Woodland** Kent
152 E3 **Woodland** S Ayrs
206 E6 **Woodlands** Abers
124 E8 **Woodlands** Donc
15 K2 **Woodlands** Dorset
16 C1 **Woodlands** Hants
132 E8 **Woodlands** N York
25 J4 **Woodlands** Somset
42 E5 **Woodlands Park** W & M
7 H6 **Woodleigh** Devon
42 C5 **Woodley** Wokham
39 H2 **Woodmancote** Gloucs
55 L3 **Woodmancote** Gloucs
56 A6 **Woodmancote** Gloucs
17 L2 **Woodmancote** W Susx
19 H3 **Woodmancote** W Susx
29 K3 **Woodmancott** Hants

126 C3 **Woodmansey** E R Yk
30 E6 **Woodmansgreen** W Susx
32 B2 **Woodmansterne** Surrey
12 C5 **Woodmanton** Devon
35 J4 **Woodnesborough** Kent
88 F5 **Woodnewton** Nhants
106 B6 **Wood Norton** Norfk
121 G4 **Woodplumpton** Lancs
92 B3 **Woodrising** Norfk
20 D2 **Wood's Corner** E Susx
99 H7 **Woodseaves** Staffs
115 K5 **Woodsetts** Rothm
14 E4 **Woodsford** Dorset
33 H6 **Wood's Green** E Susx
42 F6 **Woodside** Br For
187 G5 **Woodside** Fife
45 G6 **Woodside** Gt Lon
195 K8 **Woodside** P & K
57 H5 **Woodstock** Oxon
89 H4 **Woodston** C Pete
107 H7 **Wood Street** Norfk
30 F2 **Wood Street** Surrey
93 G5 **Woodton** Norfk
22 F6 **Woodtown** Devon
89 J7 **Wood Walton** Cambs
69 K2 **Woofferton** Shrops
26 D3 **Wookey** Somset
26 D2 **Wookey Hole** Somset
14 F5 **Wool** Dorset
23 G3 **Woolacombe** Devon
35 H5 **Woolage Green** Kent
54 E7 **Woolaston** Gloucs
54 E7 **Woolaston Common** Gloucs
25 M3 **Woolavington** Somset
30 E6 **Woolbeding** W Susx
12 E5 **Woolbrook** Devon
24 F5 **Woolcotts** Somset
168 E4 **Wooler** Nthumb
11 J3 **Woolfardisworthy** Devon
22 E7 **Woolfardisworthy** Devon
176 D6 **Woolfords** S Lans
41 L6 **Woolhampton** W Berk
69 L7 **Woolhope** Herefs
14 E2 **Woolland** Dorset
39 H6 **Woolley** BaNES
89 G8 **Woolley** Cambs
123 L7 **Woolley** Wakefd
71 G2 **Woolmere Green** Worcs
59 L4 **Woolmer Green** Herts
13 K2 **Woolminstone** Somset
77 L3 **Woolpit** Suffk
83 J4 **Woolstaston** Shrops
102 D5 **Woolsthorpe** Lincs
102 F7 **Woolsthorpe-by-Colsterworth** Lincs
16 E1 **Woolston** C Sotn
83 H6 **Woolston** Shrops
97 L7 **Woolston** Shrops
25 H4 **Woolston** Somset
26 F5 **Woolston** Somset
112 F4 **Woolston** Warrtn
55 L3 **Woolstone** Gloucs
74 C6 **Woolstone** M Keyn
40 F3 **Woolstone** Oxon
7 H3 **Woolston Green** Devon
112 B4 **Woolton** Lpool
41 H7 **Woolton Hill** Hants
78 E6 **Woolverstone** Suffk
27 H7 **Woolverton** Somset
45 H4 **Woolwich** Gt Lon

69 G4 **Woonton** Herefs
99 G4 **Woore** Shrops
92 F8 **Wootten Green** Suffk
74 E5 **Wootton** Beds
35 G5 **Wootton** Kent
126 D7 **Wootton** N Linc
73 L3 **Wootton** Nhants
57 H4 **Wootton** Oxon
57 J7 **Wootton** Oxon
100 C4 **Wootton** Staffs
40 B4 **Wootton Bassett** Wilts
17 G4 **Wootton Bridge** IoW
24 E3 **Wootton Courtenay** Somset
13 J4 **Wootton Fitzpaine** Dorset
40 D7 **Wootton Rivers** Wilts
29 L2 **Wootton St Lawrence** Hants
71 L2 **Wootton Wawen** Warwks
70 F4 **Worcester** Worcs
44 E6 **Worcester Park** Gt Lon
84 F6 **Wordsley** Dudley
84 D4 **Worfield** Shrops
136 D2 **Workington** Cumb
115 L5 **Worksop** Notts
126 C7 **Worlaby** N Linc
29 M8 **Worlds End** Hants
41 J5 **World's End** W Berk
19 J2 **Worlds End** W Susx
38 A7 **Worle** N Som
98 F2 **Worleston** Ches
93 J5 **Worlingham** Suffk
11 H3 **Worlington** Devon
91 G8 **Worlington** Suffk
78 F2 **Worlingworth** Suffk
132 D6 **Wormald Green** N York
54 B2 **Wormbridge** Herefs
90 F2 **Wormegay** Norfk
54 C3 **Wormelow Tump** Herefs
114 C6 **Wormhill** Derbys
61 M2 **Wormingford** Essex
57 M6 **Worminghall** Bucks
71 J7 **Wormington** Gloucs
186 F3 **Wormit** Fife
72 F4 **Wormleighton** Warwks
60 B6 **Wormley** Herts
30 F4 **Wormley** Surrey
34 B3 **Wormshill** Kent
69 H5 **Wormsley** Herefs
30 F2 **Worplesdon** Surrey
114 F3 **Worrall** Sheff
115 G2 **Worsbrough** Barns
115 G2 **Worsbrough Bridge** Barns
115 G2 **Worsbrough Dale** Barns
113 H2 **Worsley** Salfd
107 G7 **Worstead** Norfk
122 C4 **Worsthorne** Lancs
6 E5 **Worston** Devon
122 B3 **Worston** Lancs
35 J4 **Worth** Kent
92 C7 **Wortham** Suffk
83 G3 **Worthen** Shrops
98 B4 **Worthenbury** Wrexhm
106 B8 **Worthing** Norfk
18 F5 **Worthing** W Susx
101 H7 **Worthington** Leics
15 H6 **Worth Matravers** Dorset
114 F2 **Wortley** Barns
123 K4 **Wortley** Leeds
131 H2 **Worton** N York
39 L8 **Worton** Wilts

92 F6 **Wortwell** Norfk
39 H2 **Wotton-under-Edge** Gloucs
58 B5 **Wotton Underwood** Bucks
74 C6 **Woughton on the Green** M Keyn
46 B1 **Wouldham** Kent
84 D5 **Woundale** Shrops
62 E2 **Wrabness** Essex
23 H4 **Wrafton** Devon
117 J6 **Wragby** Lincs
124 C6 **Wragby** Wakefd
7 G4 **Wrangaton** Devon
104 C3 **Wrangle** Lincs
25 H7 **Wrangway** Somset
25 L6 **Wrantage** Somset
126 C8 **Wrawby** N Linc
38 C6 **Wraxall** N Som
26 E4 **Wraxall** Somset
130 B6 **Wray** Lancs
43 G5 **Wraysbury** W & M
130 C5 **Wrayton** Lancs
120 C4 **Wrea Green** Lancs
148 D5 **Wreay** Cumb
30 C4 **Wrecclesham** Surrey
151 G3 **Wrekenton** Gatesd
134 B3 **Wrelton** N York
98 E3 **Wrenbury** Ches
92 E4 **Wreningham** Norfk
93 K6 **Wrentham** Suffk
83 H3 **Wrentnall** Shrops
125 G4 **Wressle** E R Yk
126 B8 **Wressle** N Linc
75 J5 **Wrestlingworth** Beds
91 G4 **Wretton** Norfk
97 M3 **Wrexham** Wrexhm
84 E7 **Wribbenhall** Worcs
99 H3 **Wrinehill** Staffs
38 C7 **Wrington** N Som
27 G1 **Writhlington** BaNES
61 G6 **Writtle** Essex
84 B2 **Wrockwardine** Wrekin
116 B2 **Wroot** N Linc
123 H3 **Wrose** Brad
33 G2 **Wrotham** Kent
40 C4 **Wroughton** Swindn
17 G6 **Wroxall** IoW
72 B1 **Wroxall** Warwks
83 L2 **Wroxeter** Shrops
107 G8 **Wroxham** Norfk
72 E6 **Wroxton** Oxon
100 D4 **Wyaston** Derbys
104 B4 **Wyberton East** Lincs
75 H3 **Wyboston** Beds
99 G3 **Wybunbury** Ches
71 G2 **Wychbold** Worcs
85 L1 **Wychnor** Staffs
56 D4 **Wyck Rissington** Gloucs
140 E3 **Wycliffe** Dur
122 D3 **Wycoller** Lancs
102 C7 **Wycomb** Leics
42 E3 **Wycombe Marsh** Bucks
60 B2 **Wyddial** Herts
34 E5 **Wye** Kent
123 H5 **Wyke** Brad
27 H6 **Wyke** Dorset
26 F4 **Wyke Champflower** Somset
134 E3 **Wykeham** N York
86 D7 **Wyken** Covtry
84 D7 **Wyken** Shrops
14 C6 **Wyke Regis** Dorset
98 B7 **Wykey** Shrops
150 E3 **Wylam** Nthumb
85 K5 **Wylde Green** Birm
28 A4 **Wylye** Wilts
101 L7 **Wymeswold** Leics

74 D2 **Wymington** Beds
102 D8 **Wymondham** Leics
92 D3 **Wymondham** Norfk
14 B3 **Wynford Eagle**
　　 Dorset
71 G5 **Wyre Piddle** Worcs
101 L6 **Wysall** Notts
85 J7 **Wythall** Worcs
57 J6 **Wytham** Oxon
113 J4 **Wythenshawe** Manch
89 K8 **Wyton** Cambs
126 E4 **Wyton** E R Yk
78 C2 **Wyverstone** Suffk
78 B2 **Wyverstone Street**
　　 Suffk

Y

116 E1 **Yaddlethorpe** N Linc
141 H7 **Yafforth** N York
7 K4 **Yalberton** Torbay
33 J3 **Yalding** Kent
138 D2 **Yanwath** Cumb
56 B5 **Yanworth** Gloucs
125 J1 **Yapham** E R Yk
18 D5 **Yapton** W Susx
38 B8 **Yarborough** N Som
118 E3 **Yarburgh** Lincs
13 G2 **Yarcombe** Devon
24 B6 **Yard** Devon
85 K6 **Yardley** Birm
73 L5 **Yardley Gobion**
　　 Nhants
74 C3 **Yardley Hastings**
　　 Nhants
85 K7 **Yardley Wood** Birm
69 L6 **Yarkhill** Herefs
26 D3 **Yarley** Somset
26 F5 **Yarlington** Somset
141 K5 **Yarm** S on T
16 D4 **Yarmouth** IoW
27 K1 **Yarnbrook** Wilts
99 K6 **Yarnfield** Staffs
23 J6 **Yarnscombe** Devon
57 J5 **Yarnton** Oxon
69 J2 **Yarpole** Herefs
166 E4 **Yarrow** Border
166 E4 **Yarrow Feus** Border
166 F4 **Yarrowford** Border
88 F4 **Yarwell** Nhants
39 G4 **Yate** S Glos
42 D7 **Yateley** Hants
40 B6 **Yatesbury** Wilts
41 K5 **Yattendon** W Berk
54 F3 **Yatton** Herefs
69 H2 **Yatton** Herefs
38 B7 **Yatton** N Som

39 K5 **Yatton Keynell** Wilts
17 H5 **Yaverland** IoW
92 B2 **Yaxham** Norfk
89 H5 **Yaxley** Cambs
92 D8 **Yaxley** Suffk
69 H5 **Yazor** Herefs
43 J4 **Yeading** Gt Lon
123 J3 **Yeadon** Leeds
129 K5 **Yealand Conyers**
　　 Lancs
129 K4 **Yealand Redmayne**
　　 Lancs
6 E5 **Yealmpton** Devon
133 J5 **Yearsley** N York
98 B8 **Yeaton** Shrops
100 D4 **Yeaveley** Derbys
168 D4 **Yeavering** Nthumb
134 D4 **Yedingham** N York
57 G6 **Yelford** Oxon
75 J3 **Yelling** Cambs
87 H7 **Yelvertoft** Nhants
6 D3 **Yelverton** Devon
93 G3 **Yelverton** Norfk
27 G7 **Yenston** Somset
11 H5 **Yeoford** Devon
9 J7 **Yeolmbridge** Cnwll
26 D7 **Yeovil** Somset
26 D7 **Yeovil Marsh** Somset
26 D6 **Yeovilton** Somset
26 D6 **Yeovilton Fleet Air**
　　 Arm Museum Somset
234 b5 **Yesnaby** Ork
14 B1 **Yetminster** Dorset
12 D5 **Yettington** Devon
185 L6 **Yetts o'Muckhart**
　　 Clacks
85 H4 **Yew Tree** Sandw
109 G7 **Y Felinheli** Gwynd
65 G5 **Y Ferwig** Cerdgn
95 G5 **Y Ffor** Gwynd
97 G2 **Y Gyffylliog** Denbgs
74 E2 **Yielden** Beds
176 B7 **Yieldshields** S Lans
43 H4 **Yiewsley** Gt Lon
96 F4 **Y Maerdy** Conwy
37 G2 **Ynysboeth** Rhondd
37 J2 **Ynysddu** Caerph
36 F3 **Ynyshir** Rhondd
51 K5 **Ynystawe** Swans
37 G2 **Ynysybwl** Rhondd
83 H2 **Yockleton** Shrops
125 J5 **Yokefleet** E R Yk
174 F5 **Yoker** C Glas
124 F1 **York** York
34 E3 **Yorkletts** Kent
54 F6 **Yorkley** Gloucs
124 F1 **York Minster** York
131 G4 **Yorkshire Dales**
　　 National Park

42 E7 **York Town** Surrey
114 E8 **Youlgreave** Derbys
134 B7 **Youlthorpe** E R Yk
133 G6 **Youlton** N York
61 H4 **Young's End** Essex
100 C8 **Yoxall** Staffs
79 H2 **Yoxford** Suffk
94 D6 **Y Rhiw** Gwynd
96 C3 **Ysbyty Ifan** Conwy
67 G1 **Ysbyty Ystwyth**
　　 Cerdgn
111 G7 **Ysceifiog** Flints
52 B6 **Ystalyfera** Neath
36 F2 **Ystrad** Rhondd
66 C4 **Ystrad Aeron** Cerdgn
52 E5 **Ystradfellte** Powys
52 C6 **Ystradgynlais** Powys
66 F2 **Ystrad Meurig**
　　 Cerdgn
37 H2 **Ystrad Mynach**
　　 Caerph
36 F5 **Ystradowen** V Glam
217 G7 **Ythanbank** Abers
216 C6 **Ythanwells** Abers
217 G7 **Ythsie** Abers

Z

11 G4 **Zeal Monachorum**
　　 Devon
27 H5 **Zeals** Wilts
2 E4 **Zennor** Cnwll
101 J7 **Zouch** Notts

Speed camera locations

Speed camera locations provided in association with RoadPilot Ltd

RoadPilot is the developer of one of the largest and most accurate databases of speed camera locations in the UK and Europe*. It has provided the speed camera information in this atlas. RoadPilot is the UK's pioneer and market leader in GPS (Global Positioning System) road safety technologies.

MicroGo (pictured right) is RoadPilot's latest in-car speed camera location system. It improves road safety by alerting you to the

location of accident black spots, fixed and mobile camera sites. RoadPilot's MicroGo does not jam police lasers and is therefore completely legal. RoadPilot's database of fixed camera locations has been compiled with the full co-operation of regional police forces and the Safety Camera Partnerships.

For more information on RoadPilot's GPS road safety products, please visit **www.roadpilot.com** or telephone 0870 240 1701

RoadPilot

SPEED READING

ALARM MODE

GPS Antenna
MicroGo is directional, it only alerts you to cameras on your side of the road

Visual Countdown
To camera location

Your Speed
The speed you are travelling when approaching camera

Camera Types Located
Gatso, Specs, Truvelo, TSS/DS5, Trafipax, mobile camera sites, accident black spots, congestion charges, tolls

Voice Warnings
Only if you are exceeding the speed limit at the camera

Plug and Go
Easy to move from vehicle to vehicle

64 Colour Options
To match vehicle's illumination

Speed Limit at Camera
Screen turns red as additional visual alert

Single Button Operation
For easy access to speed display, camera warning, rescue me location, trip computer, compass heading, congestion charge, max speed alarm, date and time

*European database included